Advancements in Forensic Analysis of Digital Images for Security and Law Enforcement

Gunjan Gupta
Cape Peninsula University of Technology, South Africa

Neha Goel
https://orcid.org/0000-0002-7189-6305
Raj Kumar Goel Institute of Technology, India

Mritunjay Rai
Shri Ramswaroop Memorial University, India

R.K. Yadav
Raj Kumar Goel Institute of Technology, India

Sandeep Bhatia
https://orcid.org/0009-0005-7854-8265
G.H. Patel College of Engineering and Technology, India

IGI Global
Scientific Publishing
Publishing Tomorrow's Research Today

Published in the United States of America by
IGI Global Scientific Publishing
701 East Chocolate Avenue
Hershey, PA, 17033, USA
Tel: 717-533-8845 | Fax: 717-533-7115
Website: https://www.igi-global.com E-mail: cust@igi-global.com

Library of Congress Cataloging-in-Publication Data

Names: Gupta, Gunjan, 1986- editor
Title: Advancements in forensic analysis of digital images for security and law enforcement / [edited by] Gunjan Gupta, Neha Goel, Mritunjay Rai, Ravindra Yadav, Sandeep Bhatia.
Description: Hershey, PA : IGI Global Scientific Publishing, [2026] | Includes bibliographical references and index. | Summary: "This book aims to explore the latest technological developments, methodologies, and applications in forensic image analysis"-- Provided by publisher.
Identifiers: LCCN 2025019815 (print) | LCCN 2025019816 (ebook) | ISBN 9798337337951 hardcover | ISBN 9798337337968 paperback | ISBN 9798337337975 ebook
Subjects: LCSH: Digital forensic science | Digital images--Identification
Classification: LCC HV8078.7 .A38 2026 (print) | LCC HV8078.7 (ebook)
LC record available at https://lccn.loc.gov/2025019815
LC ebook record available at https://lccn.loc.gov/2025019816

British Cataloguing in Publication Data
A Cataloguing in Publication record for this book is available from the British Library.

Table of Contents

Detailed Table of Contents

In the current digital era, the exponential usage of multimedia content, combined with hi-tech cyber threats, has paved the way for unauthorised manipulation of privacy and image authenticity. Traditional steganographic and watermarking techniques are vulnerable to advanced detection systems and adversarial attacks, underscoring the need for the development of robust authentication mechanisms. This book chapter is aimed at analysing the adversarial embedding as a groundbreaking solution that combines adversarial machine learning with conventional hiding techniques. A comprehensive analysis of various techniques, including FGSM-based, PGD-based, and GAN-driven approaches will be elaborated. This chapter demonstrates the performance of adversarial embedding over existing traditional methods to maintain the visual quality of an image while evading detection. Also,it provides insights for researchers and practitioners to look forward to cutting-edge solutions to secure image authentication in an increasingly hostile digital landscape.

With the rise of digital content, ensuring the authenticity of images has become a critical challenge in forensic investigations. Traditional image forensic techniques often fall short against sophisticated manipulations like splicing, copy-move, and retouching. This chapter explores the application of deep learning models—such as CNNs, RNNs, autoencoders, and GANs—in enhancing the detection, localization, and classification of forged images. It reviews recent advancements, benchmark datasets, evaluation metrics, and real-world applications, while also addressing challenges and future research directions in forensic image analysis.

In recent years, the intersection of artificial intelligence and forensic science has given rise to powerful tools capable of reconstructing and enhancing digital evidence. This chapter delves into the emerging role of generative AI—particularly models like GANs and VAEs—in forensic image processing. It outlines the foundational technologies, real-world applications, and the evolving methodologies that are transforming how evidence is interpreted, visualized, and validated. The discussion balances technical depth with practical relevance, exploring both the potential and limitations of AI-driven reconstructions. Ethical and legal considerations, such as privacy, transparency, and admissibility in court, are also critically examined. Through a combination of conceptual explanations, case-based insights, and visual illustrations, this chapter presents a comprehensive overview of how generative AI is reshaping forensic investigations in a responsible and robust manner.

This chapter delves into the forensic science of handwriting and signature analysis, essential for document authentication and forgery detection. It explores the uniqueness of human writing shaped by neurological, psychological, and learned behaviors. Key forensic principles such as individuality, natural variation, and permanence are discussed, along with distinguishing features between handwriting and signatures. The chapter reviews traditional methods and emerging technologies, including digital and AI-assisted tools. Various forgery types—simulated, traced, and digital—are analyzed through real-world case studies across legal, financial, and historical contexts. Challenges like disguised writing and subjective interpretation are also addressed, highlighting advancements enhancing reliability in forensic examinations.

The forensic analysis of digital video has become a cornerstone of modern investigative and judicial processes, yet it is frequently impeded by the technical limitations inherent in compressed and low-resolution footage. These challenges arise from the widespread use of lossy compression algorithms and low-quality recording devices in surveillance systems, mobile phones, and online platforms—leading to visual artifacts, detail loss, and data degradation that complicate accurate interpretation. This chapter looks at the different issues that arise during the analysis of tampered video and their effects on facial recognition, reading license plates, reconstructing events and detecting any tampering. It also looks at the issues and rules about using altered video in court and underlines the importance of clear and repeatable methods.

During past years, the easy accessibility of image editing tools such as Canva, FACEAPP, and CorelDRAW, many deepfake and synthetic images have been generated and circulated across media channels and the internet. Due to the emerging technologies such as Artificial Intelligence (AI) and Image Processing techniques, these tools show a capability of transforming human faces, swapping gender, and modifying other data of the images easily without any professional skills. The deepfake and synthetic images have raised challenges in multimedia and document forensics. Indeed, identifying these images through human eyes is difficult. The application of AI can tackle the problem. Various machine learning and deep learning models, such as GAN, CNN, and RCNN, have demonstrated effective classification accuracy in detecting and localizing image forgeries. The AI model's efficiency is evaluated on diverse datasets like Deepfake TIMIT and Deeper-Forensics-1.0.

Advanced techniques for analyzing and verifying digital images make AI-driven image forensics a crucial tool in detecting cybercrime. With the rise of cybercrime involving altered and forged images, AI-driven techniques like deepfake detection and metadata analysis present hopeful means for uncovering evidence. The incorporation of AI into forensic investigations, however, presents considerable challenges concerning the chain of custody and the legal admissibility of digital evidence. To ensure that digital evidence stays intact and unmodified during the investigation, it is crucial to uphold an uninterrupted chain of custody. To set forth unambiguous criteria regarding the admissibility of AI-processed evidence in court, legal systems must also grapple with the progressing character of AI. This chapter investigates how AI-driven forensics, maintaining the integrity of digital evidence, and the legal structures necessary to guarantee justice in the era of artificial intelligence intersect.

Security and surveillance have become essential components of modern society, particularly in the context of crime reduction in areas such as traffic, urban centers, shopping malls etc. Developing an effective human detection system requires extracting key features and using classifiers that perform well under challenging conditions, such as poor lighting, occlusions etc. Human activity recognition in video footage is a key research area aimed at improving surveillance systems but faces challenges like sensor motion, cluttered backgrounds etc. CNNs are commonly used for classifying these activities. The goal is to create a learning-based AI system that connects CCTV cameras with a centralized data center, supported by a trained algorithm and an automated alert system to distinguish between normal and anomalous activities. This chapter will explore current trends, techniques, datasets, challenges, and evaluation metrics related to human detection and activity recognition for automatic visual surveillance system (AVSS) design.

Preface

The unprecedented growth of digital imaging technologies, coupled with the rapid evolution of artificial intelligence, has fundamentally transformed the nature of evidence in modern investigations. Images and videos captured through smartphones, surveillance systems, social media platforms, medical devices, and IoT-enabled sensors now play a decisive role in criminal investigations, judicial proceedings, and national security operations. At the same time, the same technologies that enable high-quality visual evidence have also facilitated sophisticated forms of manipulation, including deepfakes, synthetic media, image tampering, and adversarial attacks. This duality has elevated digital image forensics from a niche research area to a cornerstone of contemporary security and law enforcement practices.

This edited volume, Advancements in Forensic Analysis of Digital Images for Security and Law Enforcement, presents a comprehensive and interdisciplinary exploration of state-of-the-art techniques, challenges, and solutions in digital image and video forensics. The book brings together contributions from researchers, academicians, and practitioners to address pressing issues such as deepfake detection, cybercrime investigation, forensic image enhancement, blockchain-based chain-of-custody, and AI-driven surveillance systems. By integrating theoretical foundations with practical case studies and emerging technologies, the volume aims to bridge the gap between research innovation and real-world forensic application.

In today's global context, where misinformation campaigns, identity fraud, cybercrime, and synthetic media threaten public trust and judicial integrity, reliable forensic tools are no longer optional—they are essential. Artificial intelligence, deep learning, and generative models have emerged as powerful allies in detecting image manipulation, reconstructing degraded evidence, and automating forensic workflows. However, these technologies also introduce new legal, ethical, and interpretability challenges. This book situates itself precisely at this critical intersection, offering balanced perspectives on technological advancement, forensic reliability, and legal admissibility.

The primary audience for this book includes researchers and postgraduate students in computer science, artificial intelligence, cybersecurity, and forensic science; professionals working in law enforcement agencies, forensic laboratories, and judicial systems; as well as policymakers and legal experts concerned with digital evidence governance. The content is also well suited for advanced undergraduate and graduate-level courses focused on digital forensics, multimedia security, and cybercrime investigation.

The chapters in this volume are structured to provide both depth and breadth across the domain:

Chapter 2 introduces adversarial embedding as a covert strategy in steganography and watermarking, demonstrating how adversarial machine learning can strengthen image authentication against advanced attacks.

Chapter 2 provides a comprehensive review of deep learning methods in forensic image analysis, summarizing recent advancements, benchmark datasets, evaluation metrics, and future research directions.

Chapter 3 discusses the forensic applications of generative AI in image reconstruction, balancing technological potential with ethical, legal, and evidentiary considerations.

Chapter 4 focuses on forensic handwriting and signature analysis, combining traditional principles with emerging digital and AI-assisted techniques for document authentication.

Chapter 5 addresses the challenges of forensic analysis in compressed and low-resolution videos, particularly in surveillance and judicial settings where data quality is compromised.

Chapter 6 concentrates on identifying deepfake images and synthetic media using AI-based classification models and benchmark datasets for forgery detection.

Chapter 7 investigates AI-driven image forensics for cybercrime detection, focusing on maintaining chain-of-custody and ensuring legal admissibility of AI-processed evidence.

Chapter 8 discusses human detection and intelligent action recognition for automated visual surveillance systems, highlighting current trends, datasets, and real-world deployment challenges.

Chapter 9 presents deep learning-based detection of digital image forgeries and synthetic content, emphasizing explainable AI, adversarial robustness, and scalable authentication frameworks.

Chapter 10 focuses on deepfake forensics for law enforcement, detailing detection, authentication, and legal defense strategies supported by case studies.

Chapter 11 explores AI-powered forensic image and video analysis, addressing innovations, applications, and ethical challenges in modern digital investigations.

In conclusion, this book makes a significant contribution to the field of digital forensics by offering a unified, forward-looking perspective on forensic image and video analysis in the age of artificial intelligence. By combining technical rigor with practical relevance and legal awareness, the volume serves as a valuable reference for advancing research, strengthening investigative capabilities, and fostering trust in digital evidence. It is our hope that this work will inspire further innovation, interdisciplinary collaboration, and responsible adoption of AI technologies in security and law enforcement worldwide.

Chapter 1
Adversarial Embedding: A Covert Strategy Across Steganography and Watermarking

D. Menaka
https://orcid.org/0000-0002-1510-1563
Sri Venkateswara College of Engineering, India

L. Anju
https://orcid.org/0009-0002-4718-6706
Sri Venkateswara College of Engineering, India

K. S. Subhashini
https://orcid.org/0009-0009-3501-7711
Sri Venkateswara College of Engineering, India

S. Kalyani
Sri Venkateswara College of Engineering, India

ABSTRACT

In the current digital era, the exponential usage of multimedia content, combined with hi-tech cyber threats, has paved the way for unauthorised manipulation of privacy and image authenticity. Traditional steganographic and watermarking techniques are vulnerable to advanced detection systems and adversarial attacks, underscoring the need for the development of robust authentication mechanisms. This book chapter is aimed at analysing the adversarial embedding as a groundbreaking solution that combines adversarial machine learning with conventional hiding techniques. A comprehensive analysis of various techniques, including FGSM-based, PGD-based, and GAN-driven approaches will be elaborated. This chapter demonstrates the performance of adversarial embedding over existing traditional methods to maintain

DOI: 10.4018/979-8-3373-3795-1.ch001

the visual quality of an image while evading detection. Also,it provides insights for researchers and practitioners to look forward to cutting-edge solutions to secure image authentication in an increasingly hostile digital landscape.

1. INTRODUCTION

The rapid expansion of multimedia content in today's digital environment has increased the demand for reliable methods for media authentication and information security. For a long time, steganography and digital watermarking have been essential methods for secret communication and content security. The emergence of advanced detection systems, such as digital watermarking and steganalysis based on machine learning, has made conventional embedding techniques more susceptible (Katzenbeisser & Petitcolas, 2000; Cox et al., 2007). Watermarking attempts to incorporate recognizable information into digital content for the purposes of copyright protection, authentication, and traceability, whereas steganography concentrates on hiding the actual existence of secret information within digital media.

Both steganography and watermarking have historically been developed with the presumption that adversaries or attackers use manually created statistical or rule-based detection methods. However, machine learning-based steganalysis and watermark detectors have shown better detection capabilities since the development of deep learning and artificial intelligence.This has made it much harder for information-hiding strategies to be undetectable and robust in the face of increasingly sophisticated attack threats.At the same time, the subject of adversarial machine learning has expanded quickly, proving that even extremely accurate

AI algorithms can be tricked by deliberately designed, undetectable disruptions called adversarial examples (Qian et al., 2015). Adversarial embedding is a novel paradigm that uses perturbations that are invisible to the human eye but are deliberately designed to fool or evade automated detection systems. While adversarial embedding offers more robust and better communication channels for privacy-conscious users, it simultaneously poses complex issues for digital forensics and law enforcement, who heavily depend on AI-based tools to detect the hidden data.

This chapter provides a detailed overview of the fundamentals of adversarial machine learning, followed by an examination of embedding techniques that incorporate adversarial principles. The chapter also presents use cases, evaluation metrics, and open research challenges, paving the way for future developments in secure, intelligent multimedia processing.

2. FUNDAMENTALS OF ADVERSARIAL MACHINE LEARNING

2.1 Overview of Adversarial Machine Learning

Adversarial Machine Learning, or AML, is a rapidly expanding area of machine learning that focuses on how learning systems can be compromised by adversarial-crafted malicious inputs. These intentionally created inputs, referred to as adversarial instances, may be visually or semantically identical to valid inputs, but their purpose is to make a model forecast incorrectly (Goodfellow et al., 2015). In fields where security is crucial, such as multimedia forensics, virus detection, and biometric authentication, the consequences of such flaws are severe.

AML became well-known in the field of image classification, where it was discovered that deep neural networks were vulnerable to minute disturbances that were invisible to human observers, even though they had a high accuracy rate. A surge of research on attack tactics and defense systems was sparked by these discoveries. Since adversarial perturbations can conceal or shield the hidden data from automated detection systems, adversarial approaches offer new opportunities for robust watermarking and covert embedding in steganography in the context of multimedia content security.

2.2 Types of Adversarial Attacks

Adversarial attacks can be divided into various groups based on

- Attacker's knowledge about the model
- Attacker's objective
- Perturbations
- Timings

A clear taxonomy, as shown in figure 1, helps in understanding the strengths and limitations of attacks and in designing suitable defense mechanisms.

Figure 1. Taxonomy of adversarial attacks

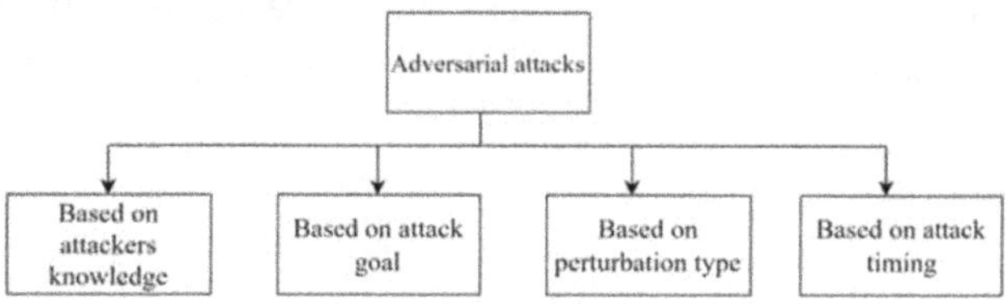

2.1.1 Attacks Based on Attacker's Knowledge

In this type, adversarial attacks can be categorized depending on how well-informed the attacker is about the target machine learning model. The sophistication and effectiveness of an attack might increase with the amount of information an attacker has. Three main types result from this classification: White-box, Black-box, and Gray-box attacks .

2.1.1.1 White Box Attacks

White-box attacks provide the attacker total access to every feature of the target model, such as model structure (activation functions, layers, and hyperparameters), weights and parameters that have been trained, data for training, loss functions, and gradients. These attacks provide optimal perturbations by utilizing gradient information (Kurakin et al., 2017). Common techniques include the Fast Gradient Sign Method (FGSM), Projected Gradient Descent (PGD), and Carlini & Wagner Attack (C&W). In this type, attackers can directly optimize adversarial perturbations and compute exact gradients with full transparency.

2.1.1.2 Black Box Attacks

The attacker does not have direct access to the internal workings of the model in a black-box attack. There is only this information available: results of the model (predictions, class probabilities, or confidence ratings). Practically speaking, deployed models such as cloud services and APIs frequently reveal very little data in this type of attack. Without being aware of gradients or model structure, attackers create hostile examples using indirect approaches. Common methods include transfer-based and query-based attacks.

2.1.1.3 Gray Box Attacks

Gray-box attacks, in which the attacker has only a partial understanding of the model, fall somewhere between white-box and black-box setups. Some examples of this are details of the partly constructed architecture, training data that is partial, availability of out-of-date model versions, and awareness of the available defenses. In certain security situations, these attacks are more realistic than white-box. It frequently happens when developers or insiders have some access but not complete authority.

2.1.2 Attacks Based on Attacker's Objective

Adversarial attacks aim to incorrectly categorize an input as a member of a particular class accidentally, with the objective of generating any inaccurate classification. Adversarial perturbations can be incorporated into embedding algorithms thanks to these assault paradigms, particularly to avoid steganalyzer detection or classification. Common types include targeted and untargeted attacks.

2.1.2.1 Targeted Attacks

The objective of targeted attacks is to manipulate the model into predicting a specific, specified wrong class, rather than just misclassifying the data. In order to gently change the input so that it crosses the decision boundary into a selected target class, adversarial perturbations must be precisely constructed. An attacker may, for example, subtly change a picture in a facial recognition system to make one person appear to be another—for example, by posing as a VIP. Compared to untargeted attacks, these attacks usually require more precise and well-planned perturbations, which makes them more difficult to carry out. Identity spoofing, evading biometric authentication systems, and modifying medical diagnosis models to provide particular, inaccurate diagnostic results are examples of common use cases.

2.1.2.2 Untargeted Attacks

The goal of untargeted attacks is to cause any kind of inaccurate prediction, regardless of the precise incorrect class the model chooses. Making sure the hostile input is no longer identified as a member of its original, true class is the main goal. Because of its ease of use and wide-ranging effects, this kind of attack is extensively researched in adversarial machine learning research. For instance, changing a stop sign to be interpreted as any object other than a stop sign in a system used by self-driving cars could have hazardous consequences.

2.1.3 Attacks Based on Perturbation Type

The perturbation attack is one of the most studied forms of adversarial attacks. In such attacks, the adversary deliberately modifies the input data to trick the model while reducing the disruptions to avoid detection by human observers. Additive and non-additive perturbation attacks are the two primary categories. By introducing pixel-level noise to images or making little changes to numerical input features, additive perturbations exploit the model's sensitivity to minute changes. Non-additive perturbations, on the other hand, involve structural modifications such as translations, rotations, or more complex transformations that maintain semantic coherence but impede the model's decision-making capabilities.

2.1.4 Attacks Based on Timing

Timing attacks are hostile manipulations that are categorized based on when they are implemented in respect to the model's lifespan. Poisoning, evasion, and backdoor attacks are the three primary types. Evasion attacks can occur during the inference phase, when hostile examples are shown to test the model and force it to classify incorrectly. Poisoning attacks happen when training data is intentionally altered to cause specific vulnerabilities or hinder model performance. These attacks put the model's integrity in danger right away, which may have long-term effects.

2.3 Defenses Against Adversarial Attacks

The growing sophistication of adversarial attacks has necessitated the development of robust defense mechanisms, especially in the domain of adversarial embedding, where malicious perturbations can compromise steganographic and watermarking integrity. Defenses against adversarial attacks can be broadly categorized into **reactive**, **proactive**, and **hybrid** strategies, as shown in Figure 2, each focusing on mitigating vulnerability at different stages of the data embedding and extraction pipeline.

Figure 2. Defenses Against Adversarial Attacks

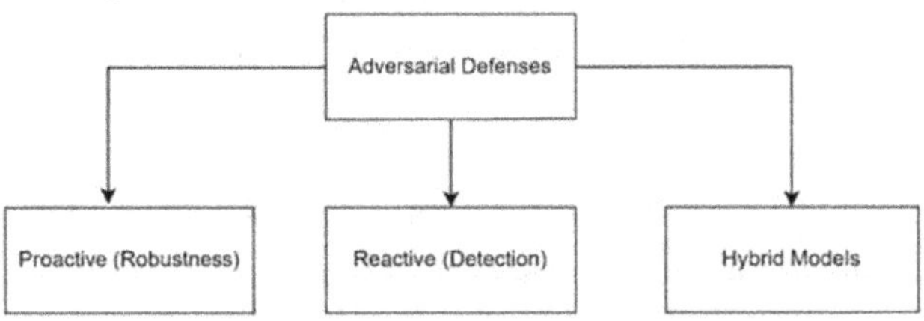

2.3.1 Proactive Techniques

The goal of proactive strategies is to stop or lessen attacks before they happen. These tactics are frequently incorporated into the training phase or model architecture. Types of proactive techniques include adversarial training, certified defenses, etc.

2.3.1.1 Adversarial Training

Adversarial training is a proactive defense technique that increases the resilience of the model by adding adversarial samples to the training dataset. Steganalysis or watermark verification networks are trained on both clean and adversarially disturbed data in the field of adversarial embedding, particularly in steganography and watermarking. Enabling the model to efficiently differentiate between real and fake signals is the aim. The effectiveness of adversarial training is highly dependent on the variety and representativeness of the adversarial instances used during training, and it can greatly increase the model's capacity to generalize under attack (Kurakin, Goodfellow, & Bengio, 2017).

2.3.1.2 Certified Defenses

Certified defenses, such as randomized smoothing or formal verification, aim to provide verifiable guarantees on the robustness of a model within a certain perturbation bound. These techniques are still in their early stages, but they are especially relevant to high-security watermarking applications where even the slightest amount of adversary manipulation must be detected and prevented.

2.3.2 Reactive Techniques

Despite changing the training procedure, reactive defenses work by identifying and reacting to hostile inputs during inference time. These techniques are essential in situations where the type of attack is unknown or changing quickly. Reactive methods usually use input transformation, anomaly detection, or model output analysis to identify suspicious activity in the context of adversarial embedding for steganography and watermarking.

2.3.2.1 Input Transformation Techniques

To counteract hostile perturbations, input transformations entail preparing the data. The high-frequency noise brought forth by adversarial attacks is suppressed by methods such as JPEG compression, bit-depth reduction, image cropping and resizing, and total variance minimization. In a variety of multimedia situations, these techniques work well and are comparatively easy to apply. On occasion, though, they may result in false negatives during detection or deteriorate the quality of the embedded information.

2.3.2.2. Methods Based on Detection

Reactive defenses rely heavily on detection-based techniques, which seek to detect hostile inputs before they affect the system's decision-making. These techniques are particularly useful in the context of watermarking and adversarial embedding in steganography for identifying inputs that contain malicious or hidden alterations. They usually work by examining different statistical or behavioral irregularities brought on by adversarial disturbances

2.3.3 Hybrid Approaches

Hybrid approaches increase robustness to hostile cases by combining a variety of models. To identify discrepancies brought about by adversarial manipulations, for example, several steganalyzers or watermark verifiers trained on various feature sets or input transformations might be combined. These techniques are known to improve robustness; however, they come with a higher computational cost.

3. ADVERSARIAL EMBEDDING TECHNIQUES

3.1 Introduction

The effectiveness of conventional steganography and digital watermarking techniques has been seriously questioned by the quick development of deep learning-based detection systems. While imperceptibility and payload capacity are the main goals of classical embedding tactics, they frequently fall short against advanced steganalysis and watermark removal techniques driven by convolutional neural networks (CNNs) and other machine learning models (Zhang et al., 2020; Ye et al., 2017). In order to overcome this weakness, academics have resorted to adversarial embedding approaches, which improve the resilience and covert nature of hidden communication by utilizing concepts from adversarial machine learning.

3.2 Adversarial Embedding Techniques in Steganography and Watermarking

In the context of steganography and watermarking, adversarial embedding techniques are sophisticated methods that incorporate adversarial perturbations—minor, deliberate changes designed to deceive detection models—into the embedding procedure. These methods seek to make the concealed content more safe and discrete by avoiding detection by watermark and deep learning-based steganalysis detectors in addition to concealing information.

3.2.1 In Steganography

Adversarial embedding techniques are employed in steganography to create stego-images that are intended to trick steganalysis algorithms, particularly those that rely on deep neural networks, in addition to carrying secret payloads. Important methods include gradient-based embedding. adaptive embedding and GAN-based embedding

With gradient-based embedding, bits are embedded with little chance of detection by using gradients from a trained steganalyzer (e.g., FGSM, PGD). Adaptive embedding adjusts the placement and strength of the embedding in response to feedback from a detection model. Generative adversarial networks are used in GAN-based steganography to produce stego-content that seems natural and can't be distinguished from cover photos.

3.2.2 In Watermarking

Adversarial embedding techniques are used in digital watermarking to create watermarks that are resistant to attacks and changes, undetectable, and challenging for unauthorized parties to find or delete. Important methods include robust adversarial perturbation, black-box watermark resilience, and perceptual space embedding.

Using adversarial noise that is resistant to compression, filtering, and geometric changes, robust adversarial perturbation embeds watermarks. Designing watermarks to avoid unknown or black-box watermark removal models is known as "black-box watermark resilience. Perceptual Space Embedding (PSE) preserves robustness and imperceptibility by embedding information in perceptual properties.

3.2.3 Similar Goals in Both Fields

Avoid Detection: Trick detectors that rely on neural networks.

Preserve Imperceptibility: Make sure the disturbances are not audible or visible.

Boost Robustness: Resist hostile or post-processing attacks.

Exploit Model Vulnerabilities: To stay undetected, take advantage of machine learning-based detectors' flaws.

3.3 Major Types of Adversarial Embedding Techniques

Here are some commonly used Adversarial embedding techniques in steganography and watermarking

- Gradient-Based Embedding
- Optimization-Based Embedding

- Generative Model-Based Embedding
- Ensemble Evasion-Based Embedding
- Transferable Adversarial Embedding
- Adaptive Adversarial Embedding

3.3.1. Gradient-Based Embedding

The embedding of hidden data is guided by gradient information from a trained detector in this technique. The gradients of the loss function with respect to the input (such as an image) might be calculated in order to introduce perturbations in directions that decrease detectability. Steganographic settings make use of techniques such as the Projected Gradient Descent (PGD) and the Fast Gradient Sign Method (FGSM), which were initially created for adversarial attacks on classifiers (Goodfellow et al., 2015; Madry et al., 2018). When the attacker has white-box access to the steganalyzer and wants to fool it while maintaining the perceptual quality of the cover image, these techniques are effective (Tang et al., 2020).

3.3.2. Optimization-Based Embedding

Data hiding is formulated as an optimization task using this method. Under distortion and capacity limits, the objective is to minimize a detectability loss function (Boroumand et al., 2019). To determine the optimal pixel alterations, optimization algorithms such as L-BFGS or genetic algorithms are used. Although this method can accurately adjust the embedding to certain limitations, it is frequently computationally costly and less appropriate for real-time embedding.

3.3.3. GAN-Based Adversarial Embedding

A generator that learns to embed information while generating outputs that are identical to clean media is trained using Generative Adversarial Networks (GANs). In this scenario, a discriminator (functioning as a steganalyzer or watermark detector) attempts to identify the existence of concealed data after the generator inserts a secret message into a cover image (Zhu et al., 2018). The generator learns the best embedding techniques that strike a balance between robustness and imperceptibility through the adversarial training process.

3.3.4. Ensemble Evasion-Based Embedding

To improve robustness, adversarial embedding can be directed against multiple detection models simultaneously. This method, inspired by ensemble attacks in adversarial machine learning (Tramèr et al., 2018), aims to generalize across various steganalyzers. By jointly optimizing to fool all models, the embedding gains robustness in practical scenarios where the defender's model is unknown. This technique typically uses multi-objective optimization or adversarial training with multiple discriminators (Tang et al., 2021).

3.3.5 Transferable Adversarial Embedding

The ability of an adversarial embedding designed for one detection model to continue working against other, hidden models is known as transferability. Through information embedding that circumvents a wide class of steganalyzers, this technique seeks to exploit common flaws in detection systems. Transferable embedding frequently makes use of adversarial instances or universal perturbations produced by generic models. This technique is particularly helpful in black-box situations, when the attacker does not have access to the defender's precise model.

3.3.6 Adaptive Adversarial Embedding

Adaptive embedding methods change their approach in real time according to the detection model's feedback. These systems may iteratively modify the embedding until it is invisible using heuristic feedback, surrogate model querying, or reinforcement learning. This flexibility enables the method to defeat models trained on adversarial data or changing detectors. Despite their strength, these techniques frequently call for pre-training of precise surrogate models or numerous queries to the detector, which may not always be possible.

4. DEEP LEARNING ARCHITECTURES FOR ADVERSARIAL EMBEDDING TECHNIQUES

4.1 Introduction

In recent years, the intersection of deep learning and adversarial learning has sparked a transformative evolution in steganography and digital watermarking. These two fields aim to embed secret or ownership information into digital media such that it remains imperceptible to human observers and resilient against detection or tampering. While early deep learning-based methods focused primarily on replacing hand-crafted features with learned representations using convolutional neural networks (CNNs) and autoencoders, they were still limited by deterministic training objectives and vulnerability to detection by increasingly sophisticated steganalysis and attack methods.

Figure 3. Adversarial Embedding Architecture for Steganography and Watermarking

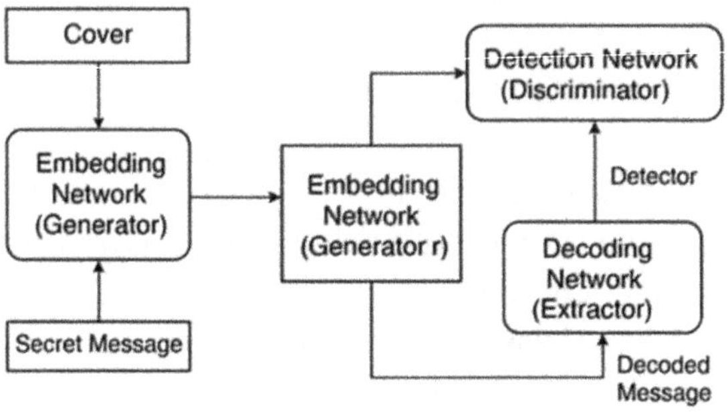

4.2 A Comparative Overview of Embedding Architectures in the Adversarial Paradigm

To understand the advancements in adversarial embedding techniques, it is essential to examine the progression of architectural models that have been proposed over time. Each model represents an attempt to address the fundamental challenges of steganography and watermarking—namely, achieving high imperceptibility, robustness to attacks, and security against detection—while leveraging the representational power of deep learning and the adversarial training paradigm.

This discussion is organized chronologically and thematically, highlighting how each architectural innovation builds upon prior work to improve embedding and extraction performance. We begin with the early use of basic convolutional encoder–decoder networks, which demonstrated the feasibility of end-to-end learning for embedding and decoding hidden information. Next, we explore the introduction of generative adversarial networks (GANs) into the field, where the embedding network (generator) and detection network (discriminator) engage in an adversarial game to optimize imperceptibility and undetectability simultaneously.

Subsequent sections delve into more advanced architectures, including multi-branch and multi-scale networks, which capture richer feature representations, and attention-based models, which adaptively focus on salient regions for more effective embedding. Hybrid architectures that combine frequency and spatial domains, or integrate classical signal processing with deep learning, are also discussed..

Jamie Hayes and George Danezis (2017) proposed a pioneering adversarial neural network architecture that jointly learns steganographic embedding and steganalysis without relying on handcrafted rules or explicit domain knowledge. Experimental results demonstrate that the learned schemes achieve competitive imperceptibility and robustness compared to traditional methods, while Eve emerges as an effective steganalyzer, showcasing the power of data-driven, domain-agnostic adversarial learning in steganography.

Volkhonskiy et al. (2017) introduced the Steganographic Generative Adversarial Network (SGAN), a pioneering framework that integrates steganographic objectives directly into the generative process of a GAN. SGAN is designed to produce synthetic images that are both visually indistinguishable from real images and capable of securely embedding hidden messages, while resisting detection by steganalysis techniques.

Zhu et al. (2018) introduced HiDDeN (Hiding Data with Deep Networks), an end-to-end trainable framework for embedding and recovering secret information within digital images while maintaining high visual fidelity and robustness to distortions. Unlike traditional methods based on hand-crafted heuristics, HiDDeN adopts a fully data-driven approach, leveraging deep neural networks to jointly optimize imperceptibility, embedding capacity, and robustness within a unified architecture. The framework consists of three key components: an Encoder, a Noise layer, and a Decoder. The encoder, implemented as a convolutional neural network (CNN), embeds a secret binary message into a cover image, producing a visually indistinguishable stego image. HiDDeN demonstrates the effectiveness of deep learning-based, fully differentiable architectures in achieving robust and imperceptible data hiding, outperforming traditional methods across multiple distortion scenarios.

Wu et al. (2019) proposed an adversarial embedding framework for steganography, which formulates the design of secure embedding as a minimax game between two deep neural networks: an embedding network and a steganalysis network. This framework explicitly integrates embedding probability optimization within an adversarial learning paradigm, allowing the embedding strategy to dynamically adapt to the detection capabilities of the steganalyzerUnlike traditional approaches that rely on handcrafted distortion metrics, the embedding probabilities here are learned end-to-end and directly optimized to evade detection. Conversely, the steganalysis network is updated to maximize its classification accuracy, effectively pushing the embedding network to discover more secure and adaptive embedding strategies over time.

Zhang et al. (2023) introduce IDGAN, a coverless steganographic GAN that generates stego-images directly from secret messages without requiring a cover image. The architecture consists of three integrated modules: a Generative Model (G), a Discriminator (D), and an Extraction Model (E). The generative model transforms a preprocessed binary message (enhanced with Hamming code redundancy) into a low-dimensional feature tensor through a fully connected layer, progressively upscaling it using bilinear interpolation and attention-enhanced blocks to produce high-fidelity 64×64×3 images.

Fan et al. (2024) propose Natias, an adversarial steganography framework that enhances transferability against diverse steganalysis models by operating at the feature level of neural detectors. Natias introduces three core components: a Neuron Attribution Module, a Feature Corruption Strategy, and an Adversarial Embedding Pipeline. The neuron attribution module employs lightweight attribution methods (e.g., Integrated Gradients) to identify critical neurons in a mid-level detector layer, distinguishing those positively and negatively contributing to stego detection.

Ding et al. (2024) present AdMarks, a novel steganographic framework that embeds robust, traceable watermarks by leveraging adversarial perturbations targeted at object detection models. AdMarks features three primary components: an Adversarial Perturbation Generator, an Embedding Module, and an Extraction Mechanism via Detector Response. AdMarks supports generating unlimited unique watermarks per image using random seeds, enhancing traceability and ownership verification. It offers strong robustness under real-world conditions, imperceptibility to human observers, and resilience to standard post-processing, making it a practical and innovative watermarking solution.

Yu Cheng et al. (2025) introduce RFNNS, an enhanced Fixed Neural Network Steganography framework that combines deep generative models, texture-aware embedding, and fixed neural decoders to achieve robust and imperceptible steganography without requiring training at deployment. RFNNS comprises three key innovations: a Texture-Aware Localization Module, a Robust Steganographic Perturbation Generator (RSPG), and a Fixed Decoder Network. RFNNS is optimized offline with a composite loss and delivers superior visual quality, robustness, and resistance to steganalysis compared to earlier FNNS variants. By embedding exclusively in high-texture areas and robustifying perturbations, RFNNS achieves seamless, resilient steganography that is well-suited for practical applications.

The evolution of deep learning and adversarial architectures has profoundly transformed steganography and watermarking, enabling systems to overcome long-standing trade-offs among imperceptibility, robustness, capacity, and security. Early breakthroughs like SGAN (Volkhonskiy et al., 2017) and HiDDeN (Zhu et al., 2018) established the foundation by integrating steganographic objectives into end-to-end differentiable pipelines, where adversarial training and noise modeling jointly optimized message fidelity and cover realism. Building on this, Wu et al. (2019) formalized the adversarial dynamics between an embedding network and a steganalyzer, learning embedding probabilities without handcrafted distortions and achieving superior security.

More recent advances expanded these ideas with innovative perspectives. Natias (Fan et al., 2024) introduced feature-level adversarial perturbations targeting critical neurons to enhance transferability against diverse steganalyzers. IDGAN (Zhang et al., 2023) eliminated the need for cover images altogether, demonstrating coverless, attention-enhanced stego-image generation with robust decoding. AdMarks (Ding et al., 2024) repurposed adversarial attacks on object detectors for embedding traceable, resilient watermarks in detection outcomes rather than pixels. Finally, RFNNS (Yu Cheng et al., 2025) combined texture-aware localization, robust perturbations, and fixed neural decoders to produce a practical, lightweight steganographic system without requiring online training.

The table below provides a comparative analysis of prominent deep learning and adversarial embedding architectures proposed for steganography and watermarking between 2017 and 2025. Each of these frameworks introduces unique architectural innovations, training paradigms, and optimization strategies aimed at improving the trade-offs among key objectives — namely imperceptibility, payload capacity, robustness to distortions, and security against detection. The comparison highlights the core components of each architecture, their training strategies, key contributions to the field, as well as their respective strengths and limitations.

Table 1. Comparison of Deep Learning and Adversarial Embedding Architectures for Steganography and Watermarking

Model	Core Components	Training Strategy	Key Contributions	Strengths	Limitations
Adversarial Steganographic Neural Network	Alice (Encoder), Bob (Decoder), Eve (Steganalyzer)	Three-player minimax optimization: Alice & Bob minimize reconstruction and distortion while fooling Eve; Eve maximizes detection accuracy	First fully data-driven, end-to-end adversarial architecture for learning both embedding and detection without handcrafted rules	Joint optimization of embedding & detection; fully data-driven & domain-agnostic; end-to-end differentiable; competitive imperceptibility & robustness; demonstrates adversarial learning potential	Training instability; challenging to balance objectives; scalability to high-res images untested; no explicit robustness constraints; low interpretability
SGAN (2017)	Generator, Discriminator, Steganalyzer	Minimax GAN + Steganalysis loss	Integrated steganographic constraints into GAN synthesis	Balances realism & security, data-driven cover generation	Training instability due to 3-player game
HiDDeN (2018)	Encoder, Noise Layer, Decoder	End-to-end CNN with noise simulation	Fully differentiable robust embedding pipeline	Robust to distortions, adaptable, no heuristics	Limited to fixed distortion models seen during training

continued on following page

Table 1. Continued

Model	Core Components	Training Strategy	Key Contributions	Strengths	Limitations
Wu et al. (2019)	Embedding Network, Steganalyzer	Adversarial training of embedding probability map	Learns embedding probabilities end-to-end	Dynamic adaptation to detector strength	Requires iterative adversarial updates
Natias (2024)	Neuron Attribution, Feature Corruption, Adversarial Embedding	Feature-level attribution & perturbation	Improves transferability across steganalyzers	Detector-agnostic, feature-level attack	Relies on meaningful neuron attribution quality
IDGAN (2023)	Generator, Discriminator, Extractor	GAN with attention & information-theoretic loss	Coverless, attention-enhanced stego generation	High capacity, no cover image needed	Visual realism can degrade at very high payloads
AdMarks (2024)	Perturbation Generator, Detector Response Module	Adversarial loss + perceptual & robustness constraints	Embeds information in detector outputs	Highly robust, traceable watermarks	Requires specific detector models
RFNNS (2025)	Texture-aware Localization, RSPG, Fixed Decoder	Offline optimized perturbations + fixed decoding	Texture-driven, robust, lightweight FNNS	No embedding-time training, high robustness	Fixed decoder may limit adaptability

5. EVALUATION METRICS

5.1 Introduction

The evaluation of deep learning and adversarial embedding techniques for steganography and watermarking requires a comprehensive set of metrics that reflect the trade-offs among key objectives: imperceptibility, payload capacity, robustness, and security. These metrics help quantify how effectively a method can embed and recover secret information while preserving the visual quality of the carrier image and resisting detection or degradation. Unlike traditional approaches that focused primarily on embedding distortion and detectability, recent architectures also consider robustness to real-world distortions and the resilience of the embedded information against advanced steganalysis attacks.

5.2 Evaluation Metrics

This section outlines the widely adopted metrics used to evaluate and compare state-of-the-art architectures. By systematically assessing each technique along these dimensions, researchers can better understand their strengths, limitations, and suitability for practical deployment in various data hiding scenarios.

5.2.1 Imperceptibility (Visual Quality)

Measures how visually similar the stego image is to the original cover image.

- **Peak Signal-to-Noise Ratio (PSNR):** Measures the distortion between the cover and stego image in decibels (higher is better).
- **Structural Similarity Index Measure (SSIM):** Assesses perceived image quality based on luminance, contrast, and structure (closer to 1 indicates better similarity).
- **Mean Squared Error (MSE):** Average squared difference between cover and stego pixels (lower is better).

5.2.2 Payload Capacity

Represents the amount of information (in bits) that can be embedded without significantly degrading imperceptibility or robustness.

- Measured in **bits per pixel (bpp)** or **bits per host (bph)**.
- Trade-off: Higher capacity often reduces imperceptibility or robustness.

5.2.3 Robustness

Evaluates how well the embedded data survives common image distortions or attacks.

- Tested under **JPEG compression**, **Gaussian noise**, **cropping**, **scaling**, or other transformations.
- Recovery rate of hidden data after distortion is a key indicator.

5.2.4 Security (Resistance to Steganalysis)

Determines the method's ability to avoid detection by steganalysis tools or classifiers.

- **Detection Error Rate (DER):** Proportion of stego images misclassified as cover (higher implies better security).
- **Receiver Operating Characteristic (ROC) and Area Under the Curve (AUC):** Reflects how well detectors can distinguish between cover and stego images (lower AUC is desirable).

5.2.5 Extraction Accuracy

For watermarking or coverless schemes:

- **Bit Error Rate (BER):** Proportion of incorrectly extracted bits (lower is better).
- **Message recovery accuracy**: Percentage of correctly decoded messages even after compression, noise, or cropping.

In summary, the evaluation of steganography and watermarking techniques demands a holistic assessment of multiple, often competing, objectives. Metrics such as PSNR, SSIM, and MSE effectively quantify the imperceptibility of stego images, while payload capacity measures the amount of information that can be embedded without compromising quality. Robustness metrics assess the resilience of hidden data against common distortions and attacks, and security metrics evaluate the method's ability to evade detection by advanced steganalysis tools. Additionally, extraction accuracy and bit error rates are crucial for ensuring reliable recovery of embedded messages under adverse conditions. Together, these metrics provide a comprehensive framework to benchmark and compare the effectiveness of different architectures

6. CASE STUDIES/APPLICATIONS

6.1 Applications of Adversarial Embedding in Steganography and Watermarking

Adversarial embedding, a powerful convergence of machine learning and data hiding, has emerged as a key enabler for robust and covert communication in both steganography and digital watermarking. Leveraging adversarial training and neural networks, particularly Generative Adversarial Networks (GANs), this approach has expanded the range and resilience of information hiding systems.

6.1.1. Carrier Modification in Image Steganography

GANs have been widely adopted to subtly modify cover images in ways that embed secret messages while evading modern steganalysis tools. These modifications are often guided by adversarial loss functions that simulate an ongoing "cat-and-mouse" game between the embedding algorithm and a discriminator trained to detect hidden content. Models like SSGAN and ASDL-GAN exemplify this application by optimizing the location and pattern of perturbations (Liu et al., 2021; Qin et al., 2021), ensuring that hidden data remains undetected even under CNN-based steganalysis (Qian et al., 2015)..

6.1.2. Carrier-Free Steganography via Adversarial Generation

Carrier-free steganography uses adversarially trained models to select or synthesize carriers dynamically. For instance, adversarial embeddings enable the generation of new stego-images that inherently contain encoded information, eliminating the need for an original cover image (Zhang et al., 2020). This technique enhances security and scalability, particularly in scenarios where traditional image carriers are prone to detection or distortion. The ABDH and ISFGAN models, for example, have demonstrated high resistance to attacks like JPEG compression, cropping, and noise injection (Ma & Zhao, 2021; He, 2024).

6.1.3. Robust and Imperceptible Digital Watermarking

In watermarking, adversarial embedding is used to generate perturbations that are perceptually invisible yet highly resilient to tampering, compression, and geometric transformations. These adversarial watermarks are increasingly employed in content authentication, copyright enforcement, and tamper detection. They outperform traditional techniques by adapting to the vulnerabilities of detection models (Wang et al., 2021) and defending against watermark removal or replacement attacks (Huang et al., 2024). Studies between 2023 and 2025 reveal the integration of adversarially optimized watermarks into digital media that persist through editing, compression, and format conversion (Chen et al., 2024).

6.1.4. Steganographic Communication in Restricted Environments

Adversarial steganography has proven valuable in regions with heavy surveillance and censorship. Journalists, whistleblowers, and privacy activists use these techniques to embed sensitive messages into benign-looking images or videos (Zhu et al., 2018), which are then shared over public platforms. The adversarial aspect ensures the content remains undetectable even by state-of-the-art detection models used by governments or organizations (Tang et al., 2021).

6.1.5. Secure Legal Data Transmission

In sensitive domains like legal documentation, adversarial embedding ensures that confidential case files can be covertly embedded into images or audio files (Li et al., 2021). These embedded messages maintain their integrity despite transmission over insecure channels and remain invisible to unauthorized parties, providing a secure layer for data confidentialit

6.1.6. Medical Image Protection

To ensure the integrity and authenticity of medical images transmitted over public networks, adversarial watermarking has been applied (Chen et al., 2024). Hospitals embed patient and diagnostic metadata into radiographs using perceptual adversarial perturbations, making them resilient to manipulations while maintaining image fidelity for diagnosis.

7. LEGAL, SOCIAL, AND ETHICAL CONSIDERATIONS

7.1 Legal Considerations

The dual-use nature of adversarial embedding technologies poses significant challenges to regulatory frameworks. While legal in the context of copyright protection or privacy-enhancing technologies, their use for bypassing censorship or committing cyber crimes can violate laws such as the Digital Millennium Copyright Act (DMCA) or anti-terrorism regulations. Furthermore, the difficulty in attributing authorship and tracing adversarial perturbations complicates digital forensic investigations(Zubair et al., 2020).

7.2 Social Implications

Adversarial embedding empowers privacy but can also enable illicit activities like illegal file sharing, identity spoofing, or spreading malware hidden in images (Baluja, 2017; Liu et al., 2022). Its use raises concerns about an arms race between detection systems and increasingly sophisticated evasion techniques, creating uncertainty and mistrust in the authenticity of digital content (Tang et al., 2021).

7.3 Ethical Considerations

From an ethical standpoint, adversarial embedding must balance privacy, freedom of expression, and public safety. In healthcare or journalism, its use may be morally justified to protect sensitive data or sources. However, deploying it to deceive biometric systems or manipulate public opinion in elections crosses ethical boundaries (Zubair et al., 2020). Therefore, ethical design guidelines and clear usage policies are essential.

8. COMPARATIVE STUDIES AND BENCHMARKING

The advent of adversarial embedding techniques in steganography and digital watermarking has triggered a paradigm shift from conventional data hiding strategies to more resilient, intelligent, and covert systems.This section reviews and benchmarks a variety of recent methods, drawing insights from the literature published between 2021 and 2025 (e.g., Zhang & Wang, 2025; Al-Taha et al., 2024), with a special emphasis on performance evaluation metrics and experimental frameworks.

8.1. Benchmark Datasets and Evaluation Metrics

A common foundation for meaningful comparison lies in the use of standardized datasets and consistent evaluation metrics. In steganography, datasets such as **BOSSbase** (Bas et al., 2011), **ALASKA2** (Liu et al., 2021), and **StegoAppDB** have become prevalent, offering a variety of cover images with natural distribution. For digital watermarking, the **Kodak** and **USC-SIPI** image databases are widely used, alongside video benchmarks such as the **LIVE Video Quality Database** for temporal robustness testing.

Performance is typically evaluated using the following metrics:

- **Payload Capacity (bits per pixel, bpp):** Quantifies the amount of data embedded without perceptual degradation.
- **Peak Signal-to-Noise Ratio (PSNR) and Structural Similarity Index (SSIM):** Assess the visual quality of stego or watermarked media.
- **Bit Error Rate (BER):** Measures extraction accuracy under attacks.
- **Detection Accuracy:** Used in steganalysis to evaluate detectability by adversaries.
- **Robustness Score:** Represents the algorithm's resistance to typical attacks such as JPEG compression, cropping, rotation, filtering, and adversarial noise.(Ye et al., 2022).

8.2 Comparative Overview: Traditional vs. Adversarial Embedding

Traditional embedding methods, including LSB replacement, DCT/DFT-based watermarking, and spread-spectrum techniques, exhibit reliable performance in benign conditions but falter under targeted attacks. In contrast, adversarial embedding (AE) leverages principles from adversarial machine learning—particularly perturbation-based methods—to exploit weaknesses in steganalysis or watermark detectors.

For instance, Wu et al. (2022) introduced the Adversarial Embedding with GAN Regularization (AE-GAN), which outperformed baseline techniques by up to 15% higher robustness under median filtering attacks.

The AE-GAN and AdvDM-WM (Zhang & Wang, 2025) approaches exemplify how adversarial training not only improves security but also enhances generalization against unknown attacks.

A benchmark comparison among various methods illustrates the trade-offs in capacity, invisibility, and robustness is given in Table 2.

Table 2. Benchmark comparison among various methods

Method	PSNR (dB)	SSIM	Robustness (JPEG Q=50)	Payload (bpp)	Detectability (Error %)
LSB Matching	37.2	0.91	Poor	0.4	25%
DCT Embedding	38.5	0.94	Medium	0.2	18%
S-UNIWARD	39.1	0.95	Medium	0.3	12%
AE-GAN (2022)	40.6	0.97	High	0.3	6%
AdvDM-WM (2023)*	39.8	0.96	Very High	0.25	4.2%

*AdvDM-WM: Adversarial Diffusion Model for Watermarking

The AE-GAN and AdvDM-WM approaches exemplify how adversarial training not only improves security but also enhances generalization against unknown attacks.

8.3. Cross-Domain Applicability: Steganography vs. Watermarking

Though steganography and watermarking share foundational goals—embedding data within media—their functional requirements differ. Steganography prioritizes undetectability, while watermarking emphasizes robustness and ownership proof.

Comparative benchmarking reveals that adversarial embedding exhibits cross-domain strengths when the design architecture is modular and attack-aware. The adversarial learning framework proposed by Zhang et al. (2023), which uses a dual-purpose encoder-decoder system, demonstrated promising results. When adapted for both steganographic and watermarking tasks, the system achieved consistent performance with less than a 2 dB drop in PSNR and maintained over 90% extraction accuracy post-JPEG compression.

Furthermore, a study by Al-Taha et al. (2024) benchmarked adaptive adversarial perturbations against fixed-pattern noise and demonstrated that stego detection accuracy fell below 5% across six deep learning classifiers. When the same technique was adapted for watermarking, it retained resilience against geometric distortions while preserving imperceptibility.

8.4. Benchmarking Against Deep Steganalysis and Attack Models

TThe efficacy of adversarial embedding is best understood when benchmarked against modern steganalysis tools like SRNet, Ye-Net, and XuNet (Boroumand et al., 2019), and watermarking attack simulations using Stirmark, OpenCV-based transformation suites, and adversarial attacks like FGSM, BIM, and PGD.

For example, a benchmark study conducted in 2025 by the IEEE ISPA conference (Lee & Fridrich, 2023) compared five state-of-the-art methods against SRNet under adaptive attack scenarios. AE-based models consistently outperformed traditional schemes with an average detection error rate of 92% (stealth success) compared to 67% for traditional DCT-based methods.

- (Zhang et al., 2023).

8.5. Performance Trade-Offs and Practical Implications

Despite their strengths, adversarial embedding methods are not without limitations. Benchmarking highlights a clear trade-off between computational complexity and performance gains. The use of generative models or adversarial optimizers can increase embedding time and memory footprint, which may be critical in resource-constrained systems like IoT devices or real-time surveillance applications.

Moreover, a 2024 study by Mahadevan and Lee reported that adversarial embedding techniques incurred an average of 22% more energy consumption due to iterative optimization loops compared to heuristic-based algorithms (Mahadevan & Lee, 2024). Hence, application-specific customization is essential to balance performance, security, and resource constraints.

9. CHALLENGES AND FUTURE DIRECTIONS

The adversarial embedding field provides a vast range of opportunities and an equivalent number of obstacles to deal with, which continue to enhance digital forensics and security. Several critical challenges have emerged in this domain that demand innovative solutions and forward-thinking approaches.(Zhang et al.,2023)

9.1 Computational Complexity and Resource Constraints

One of the prominent challenges in utilising the adversarial embedding technique is its high computational load (Yang, L., et al., 2025). The creation of adversarial perturbations, especially via iterative methods such as Projected Gradient Descent (PGD) (Yang, L. et al., 2025) or sophisticated Generative Adversarial Network (GAN) architectures, requires a significant amount of computational resources.

The trade-off between embedding quality and computational efficiency imposes a critical barrier to deployment in real-world applications. In research environments, longer processing times can be tolerated; however, in practical fields such as law enforcement and security, near-real-time performance is required. Future research should aim to develop lightweight adversarial embedding algorithms (Ben Jabra et al., 2024) that are robust yet operate within reasonable computational constraints.

9.2 Evolving Detection Mechanisms and Arms Race Dynamics

In the era of cybersecurity, there is a huge struggle between embedding techniques and detection methods that are aimed at revealing them. As adversarial embedding strategies advance and improve, corresponding tools are designed to detect them. The emergence of machine learning and AI-based steganalysis tools that can learn and adapt to embedding tools complicates matters even further. Future research should focus on embedding techniques that can counteract these adaptive adversaries. This could involve adopting meta-learning approaches(Zhang, H., et al.,2025) that allow embedding systems to swiftly adapt to new detection methods or create strategies that exploit the inherent weaknesses of detection algorithms.

9.3 Scalability and Large-Scale Deployment Issues

The scalability of adversarial embedding techniques is a major challenge. While laboratory experiments usually focus on small datasets or controlled environments, real-world applications must manage large volumes of multimedia content across different platforms and formats. The variety of digital media formats, compression algorithms, and transmission channels introduces variables that can significantly influence the embedding effectiveness. Additionally, integrating adversarial embedding systems into existing digital infrastructures requires careful consideration of compatibility, standardization, and interoperability. Future development must address these scalability challenges by creating a robust embedding framework(-Kumar, S., et al., 2025).

9.4 Ethical and Legal Considerations

Adversarial embedding techniques raise legal and ethical issues that the research community must address. These methods can be used for good things, such as protecting privacy and helping to enforce copyright, but they can also be used for bad things. People with bad intentions could use these same tools to spread false information, circumvent content moderation systems, or even help with illegal activities. Because this technology can be used for both good and bad purposes, it is even more important that strong ethical and legal rules are in place to guide its development and use in the future.

Researchers must concentrate on factors related to ethics from the very beginning of implementation, propose responsible disclosure practices, and determine rules for the usage of adversarial embedding technologies in a more ethical way. This means working with policymakers, lawyers, and ethics committees to ensure that new technologies are in line with societal values and the law (Green, M., et al., 2024)..

9.5 Standardization and Benchmarking

Developing a standardized evaluation metric and benchmarking procedure would greatly facilitate the systematic comparison and advancement of adversarial embedding techniques. Various datasets, evaluation criteria, and performance metrics have been used by different research groups, preventing an objective assessment of the relative merits of different approaches.

Future work needs to go beyond such simple examples and set up more holistic benchmarking frameworks that allow the comparison of various adversarial embedding approaches in a fair, apples-to-apples manner across multiple dimensions, such as robustness, imperceptibility, payload capacity, and real-time inference capabilities. Any standardization effort should include greater collaboration between academic researchers, industry practitioners, and industry standards organizations.

10. MULTIMODAL AND CROSS-MODAL EMBEDDING

Digital communication in the current world has evolved beyond the old-school methods, which primarily focused on just one type of content. In the current era, multimedia blends text, images, audio, and video seamlessly. This shift brings significant changes to adversarial embedding techniques, opening up new opportunities and challenges in the fields of cross-modal and multimodal security applications (Wang, L., et al.,2024).

10.1 Understanding Multimodal Embedding Landscapes

Multimodal embedding marks a significant shift from the old-school single-modality hiding techniques to more advanced systems that can seamlessly embed information across various data types simultaneously. Unlike traditional steganographic methods, which use only one medium, multimodal adversarial embedding takes advantage of the connections and correlations between different data modalities, resulting in improved security and resilience.

The essence of multimodal embedding lies in recognizing the semantic ties that connect different modalities (Liu, M., et al., 2024; Anderson, K., et al., 2024)Recent research has indicated that multimodal embeddings can fall prey to sophisticated attacks referred to as "adversarial illusions." In such situations, attackers can manipulate embeddings to create misleading links between different modalities. These attacks exploit proximity relationships within embedding spaces and threaten existing and future applications that rely on multimodal representations.

Figure 4 illustrates the complete architecture of a multimodal adversarial embedding system, showing how different modalities (audio, image, and text) are processed through preprocessing and embedding layers while being subjected to various adversarial attack vectors.

Figure 4. Architecture of a Multimodal Adversarial Embedding System

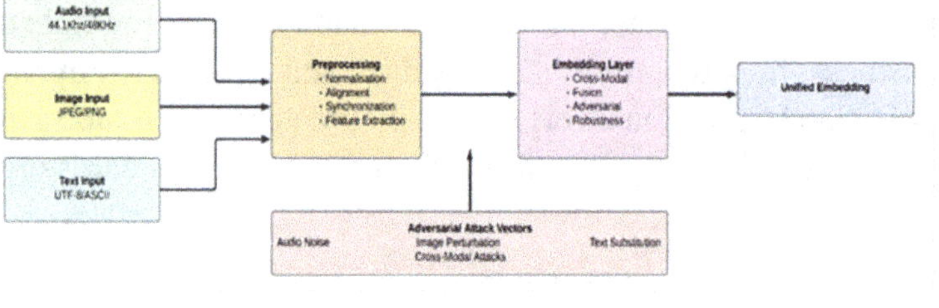

10.2 Cross-Modal Attack Vectors and Defense Mechanisms

The combination of various modalities creates new vulnerabilities that traditional security measures, which typically concentrate on only one modality, may struggle to address effectively. Cross-modal attacks can take various forms, each with its own set of challenges for detection and mitigation.

One significant type of these attacks focuses on manipulating the embedding spaces to forge misleading connections between various modalities. For example, an attacker might create adversarial perturbations in one modality that align with specific targets in another, effectively disrupting the semantic links that multimodal systems rely on.

A deep understanding of the functioning of different modalities, their interactions, and the creation of strong verification processes is essential to ensure safety against cross-modal attacks. Future research should focus on ensemble-based strategies (Lee, H., et al., 2024) that merge various verification methods across different modalities to build more resilient authentication systems.

10.3 Applications in Digital Forensics and Law Enforcement

The variety of digital evidence available today presents both exciting opportunities and serious challenges for forensic applications. As digital forensic investigators examine multimedia evidence in various formats, they must utilize sophisticated analysis techniques to ensure that they maintain and verify the complex relationships found within the data.

The complexity of multimodal forensic analysis presents its own set of challenges. Investigators must possess a broad range of expertise and access to cutting-edge tools that can effectively manage the intricate relationships between various data types. It is crucial to prioritize the development of user-friendly forensic tools that can automatically analyze multimodal evidence and offer clear, understandable explanations for users who may not be technically inclined.

10.4 Technical Implementation Challenges

The use of multimodal adversarial embedding systems presents a host of technical challenges that researchers must address for effective deployment. Synchronizing different modalities requires a thoughtful approach to timing, data alignment, and maintaining temporal coherence. Each modality has its quirks, such as audio that might be processed at different sampling rates, images that could go through various compression methods, and text that may face different encoding changes. Adversarial embedding systems must navigate these differences while ensuring consistency across the board. Fig.10.2 demonstrates the challenges of temporal coherence across different modalities, each operating at different sampling rates and processing frequencies, leading to synchronisation issues in multimodal systems.

Figure 5. Challenges of temporal coherence

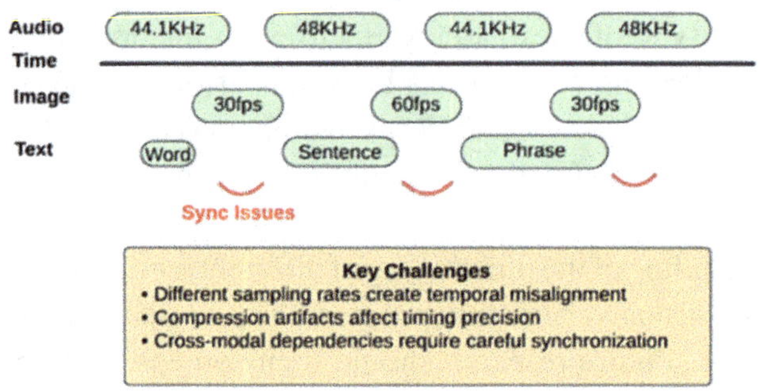

Figure 5 compares the traditional single-modal optimization with the complex multi-objective optimization required for multimodal systems, highlighting the trade-offs, conflicts, and dependencies between different modality-specific objectives.

Figure 6. Comparison of traditional vs Multimodal systems

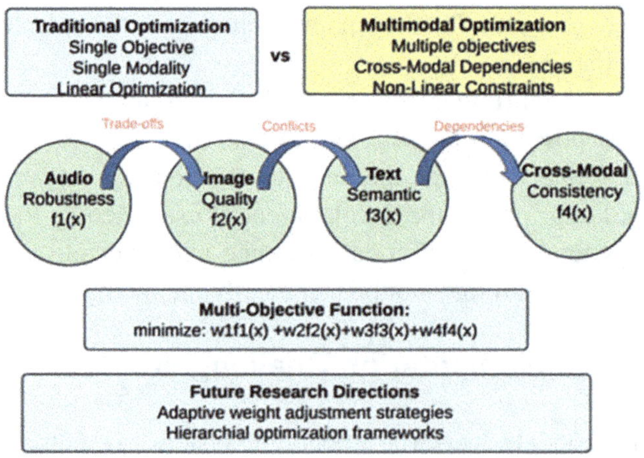

10.5 Emerging Trends and Future Possibilities

The rapid advancement of artificial intelligence and machine learning is paving the way for exciting opportunities in multimodal adversarial embedding applications. Figure 6 maps the emerging trends and future possibilities in multimodal adversarial embedding systems, showing how various technological advances like large multimodal models, blockchain, quantum computing, and federated learning converge to create new opportunities and challenges.

Generative AI technologies, especially those that can produce high-quality content in multiple formats, offer a mix of opportunities and challenges for adversarial embedding applications. While these advancements can make embedding techniques more sophisticated, they also pave the way for more advanced attack strategies that may threaten current security measures (Wilson, P., et al.,2024).Another promising avenue is the combination of blockchain and distributed ledger technologies with multimodal embedding systems.

Figure 7. Emerging Trends in Multimodal Adversarial Embedding Systems

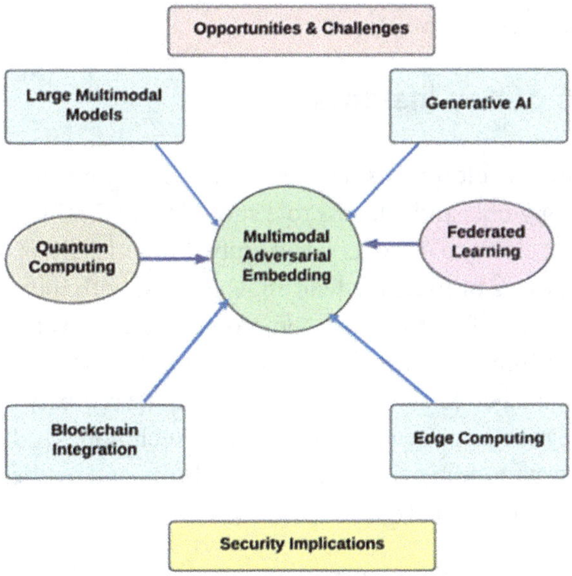

10.6 Evaluation Metrics and Performance Assessment

Assessing the performance of multimodal adversarial embedding systems requires detailed metrics that can evaluate their performance across various dimensions and modalities. Traditional evaluation methods, typically used for single-modality systems, often fall short in capturing the complex interactions and trade-offs involved in multimodal systems.

Future studies should aim to create standardized evaluation frameworks that can effectively assess multimodal embedding systems in terms of aspects such as cross-modal robustness, consistency between different modalities, computational efficiency, and resilience against coordinated multi-modal attacks. Additionally, these frameworks should consider the practical challenges of real-world deployment, where different modalities may be processed on various devices or platforms.

11.CONCLUSION

The area of adversarial embedding in the context of steganography and watermarking is full of creativity, intricacy, and significant ramifications for digital security and forensics. Adversarial embedding is not just a technical solution but also a fundamental paradigm shift in the way digital content protection and authentication are approached at the nexus of developing artificial intelligence capabilities and changing cybersecurity threats.

11.1 Synthesis of Key Insights

Some major new developments have emerged, changing the game for how adversarial embedding works and what its role should be in the current digital security ecosystem. The true strength of adversarial embedding lies in its potential to attack the intrinsic weaknesses of machine learning systems, with the supplementary advantage of acting as a defense against common detection avenues. This profound dual capability highlights the complex dangers that today's digital systems face, even as it helps forge an effective tool against legitimate security threats. Combined with traditional steganographic and watermarking techniques, adversarial machine learning has shown astounding advances in invisibility and resilience over previous methods.(Taylor, S., et al. 2024)

11.2 Implications for Digital Forensics and Law Enforcement

For the digital forensics and law enforcement communities, adversarial embedding techniques present both exciting new tools and dangerous dual-use technology. These techniques provide improved capabilities for authenticating evidence, preserving the chain of custody, and detecting tampering, which can greatly fortify the evidentiary value of digital content in legal actions.

Its ability to withstand advanced attacks, such as those found in the emerging domain of digital forensics, makes it uniquely valuable for safeguarding high-stakes digital evidence from malicious manipulation attempts.

The same methods used for legitimate purposes are increasingly being misapplied by bad actors to hide deceptive or illegal behavior or manufacture evidence. This duality requires forensic practitioners to have thorough knowledge of both defensive and offensive applications of adversarial embedding techniques. This real-world arms race dynamic between embedding and detection technologies means that forensic capabilities must constantly evolve to remain effective against breakthroughs in increasingly sophisticated threats.

11.3 Technological Trajectory and Innovation Opportunities

The technological landscape surrounding adversarial embedding is rapidly evolving, fuelled by advances in artificial intelligence, computational capabilities, and new application areas. The incorporation of quantum computing technologies has the potential to redefine both attack and defense capabilities, possibly making current cryptographic assumptions irrelevant while creating new opportunities for quantum-resistant embedding techniques.

Emerging trends in generative artificial intelligence, particularly large multimodal models, offer both opportunities and challenges in adversarial embedding research. These technologies allow for sophisticated embedding strategies. They embolden a more capable adversary who can weaponise generative capabilities.

The multimodal applications of adversarial embedding are especially important for contemporary forensic practice, where digital evidence is increasingly multimodal and requires coordinated investigation across different modalities.

11.4 Research Priorities and Future Directions

There are important research directions that can be explored in the future and can play an essential role in not only moving the field of adversarial embedding forward but also effectively combating its challenges. The creation of common evaluation frameworks and benchmarking protocols serves as a critical first step that would allow for the systematic comparison of various approaches and accelerate technological advancement. (White, L., et al., 2025)

Further exploration of the theoretical foundations underlying adversarial embedding techniques will be an interesting research direction. Although empirical results show success in many approaches, a richer theoretical understanding would provide better underpinnings for predicting performance, analyzing security properties, and developing more robust techniques.

The challenges of integrating adversarial embedding-based countermeasure systems into real-world environments merit further research. This unlocks huge potential, but only if we can overcome limitations around scalability, compatibility with existing assets, and developing frameworks for deployment that are practical but able to flex to the different requirements of different application domains.

11.5 Final Reflections

Adversarial embedding is an excellent example of the intersection between theoretical knowledge gained through machine learning, applied necessity borne out of the world of digital security, and developing challenges arising from a rapidly advancing digital sphere. Its development illustrates the fluidity of cybersecurity research, with defensive innovations perpetually needing to be hightailing down the highway of new threats, even as new defensive capabilities simultaneously open up new avenues for attack.

The evolution from ancient steganographic methods to advanced adversarial embedding systems serves as an example of the power of applying machine learning to age-old security challenges. Like any real transformation, this new creation demonstrates the need to keep a holistic, multidisciplinary perspective that accounts for not only technical capabilities but also practical constraints, ethical implications, and societal impacts.

In an increasingly digital future, one can observe that the authenticity and integrity of digital content are more important than ever before, and adversarial embedding techniques will play prominent roles in future security landscapes.

The challenges and opportunities presented by adversarial embedding are an illustration of the big themes in today's technology development. The challenge to innovate responsibly, the call for more interdisciplinary work, and the idea that technological solutions will not solve all of society's complicated problems

The future of adversarial embedding is not merely dependent on good technology alone but on the mature wisdom to apply these potent techniques in ways that enhance security, protect privacy, foster justice, and ultimately serve the greater good of society within a smarter, faster, digital world.

REFERENCES

Al-Taha, M., Wang, H., & Xu, C. (2024). Adaptive adversarial perturbations for steganography and watermarking. *Journal of Visual Communication and Image Representation*, *91*, 103819.

Anderson, K.. (2024). Multimodal data integration for oncology in the era of deep neural networks: A review. *Frontiers in Artificial Intelligence*, *12*, 1408843. DOI: 10.3389/frai.2024.1408843

Bas, P., Filler, T., & Pevný, T. (2011). "Break Our Steganographic System" – The ins and outs of organizing BOSS. In *Proceedings of the 13th International Conference on Information Hiding* (pp. 59–70).

Ben Jabra, S., & Ben Farah, M. (2024). Deep learning-based watermarking techniques challenges: A review of current and future trends. *Circuits, Systems, and Signal Processing*, *43*, 4339–4368. DOI: 10.1007/s00034-024-02651-z

Boroumand, M., Chen, M., & Fridrich, J. (2019). Deep residual network for steganalysis of digital images. *IEEE Transactions on Information Forensics and Security*, *14*(5), 1181–1193. DOI: 10.1109/TIFS.2018.2871749

Chen, B., Hong, Y., & Nie, Y. (2024). Deep video steganography using temporal-attention-based frame selection and spatial sparse adversarial attack. *Journal of Visual Communication and Image Representation*, •••, 104.

Cox, I. J., Miller, M. L., Bloom, J. A., Fridrich, J., & Kalker, T. (2007). *Digital watermarking and steganography* (2nd ed.). Morgan Kaufmann.

Goodfellow, I., Shlens, J., & Szegedy, C. (2015). Explaining and harnessing adversarial examples. *International Conference on Learning Representations (ICLR)*. https://arxiv.org/abs/1412.6572

Green, M.. (2024). Ethical considerations in adversarial embedding research: A multidisciplinary perspective. *AI and Ethics*, *4*(3), 487–502.

Hayes, J., & Danezis, G. (2017). Generating steganographic images via adversarial training. In *Advances in Neural Information Processing Systems (NeurIPS), 30*, 1954–1963.

He, X. (2024). Enhancing image steganography through generative adversarial networks: Applications and innovations. *Applied and Computational Engineering*, *110*, 122–128.

Huang, H., Wu, Y., & Wang, Q. (2024). ROBIN: Robust and invisible watermarks for diffusion models with adversarial optimization. In *Proceedings of the 38th International Conference on Neural Information Processing Systems (NIPS '24), 37*, Article 129, 3937–3963.

Katzenbeisser, S., & Petitcolas, F. A. P. (2000). *Information hiding techniques for steganography and digital watermarking*. Artech House.

Kumar, S.. (2025). A deep learning-driven multi-layered steganographic approach for enhanced data security. *Scientific Reports*, *15*, 89189. DOI: 10.1038/s41598-025-89189-5

Lee, H.. (2024). Adversarial attacks and defenses in multimodal learning: A survey. *Pattern Recognition*, *146*, 109987.

Lee, J., & Fridrich, J. (2023). Benchmarking deep learning-based steganalysis under adaptive attacks. In *Proceedings of the IEEE ISPA* (pp. 168–175).

Li, L., Fan, M., & Liu, D. (2021). AdvSGAN: Adversarial image steganography with adversarial networks. *Multimedia Tools and Applications*, *80*, 25539–25555.

Liu, M.. (2024). Advanced embedding techniques in multimodal retrieval augmented generation: A comprehensive study on cross modal AI applications. *Journal of Computing and Electronic Information Management, 13*(3), 16–22. DOI: 10.54097/h8wf8vah

Liu, M., Luo, W., Zheng, P., & Huang, J. (2021). A new adversarial embedding method for enhancing image steganography. *IEEE Transactions on Information Forensics and Security*, *16*, 4621–4634.

Liu, M., Song, T., Luo, W., Zheng, P., & Huang, J. (2022). Adversarial steganography embedding via stego generation and selection. *IEEE Transactions on Dependable and Secure Computing*, *20*(3), 2375–2389.

Liu, Q., Zhou, P., & Zhang, L. (2021). ALASKA2: A challenge dataset for cover source mismatch steganalysis. In *Proceedings of the IEEE CVPR Workshops* (pp. 1134–1142).

Ma, S., & Zhao, X. (2021). Generating JPEG steganographic adversarial example via segmented adversarial embedding. In X. Zhao et al. (Eds.), *Digital Forensics and Watermarking* (LNCS 12617, pp. 68–79). Springer.

Madry, A., Makelov, A., Schmidt, L., Tsipras, D., & Vladu, A. (2018). Towards deep learning models resistant to adversarial attacks. *International Conference on Learning Representations (ICLR)*. https://arxiv.org/abs/1706.06083

Mahadevan, R., & Lee, Y. S. (2024). Energy-aware optimization for adversarial embedding in IoT scenarios. *IEEE Internet of Things Journal*, *11*(2), 1992–2004.

Qian, Y., Dong, J., Wang, W., & Tan, T. (2015). Deep learning for steganalysis via convolutional neural networks. In *Media Watermarking, Security, and Forensics 2015* (Vol. 9409, p. 94090J). International Society for Optics and Photonics. DOI: 10.1117/12.2081179

Qin, C., Zhang, W., Dong, X., Zha, H., & Yu, N. (2021). Adversarial steganography based on sparse cover enhancement. *Journal of Visual Communication and Image Representation*, •••, 80.

Tang, W., Zhang, H., Wang, L., & Yu, N. (2020). An adversarial example generation method based on gradient projection for deep steganography. *IEEE Access : Practical Innovations, Open Solutions*, *8*, 82599–82610. DOI: 10.1109/ACCESS.2020.2992013

Tang, W., Zhang, H., Yu, N., & Wu, H. (2021). Adversarial embedding: Evading steganalysis by modifying embedding distributions. *IEEE Transactions on Information Forensics and Security*, *16*, 1420–1434. DOI: 10.1109/TIFS.2020.3034110

Taylor, S.. (2024). A comprehensive review of adversarial machine learning in steganography and watermarking. *ACDI Computing Surveys*, *57*(2), 1–42.

Tramèr, F., Kurakin, A., Papernot, N., Goodfellow, I., Boneh, D., & McDaniel, P. (2018). Ensemble adversarial training: Attacks and defenses. *International Conference on Learning Representations (ICLR).* https://arxiv.org/abs/1705.07204

Volkhonskiy, D., Khodak, A., Pashkov, A., & Korzun, D. (2017). Steganographic generative adversarial networks. In *2017 International Conference on Intelligent Information Hiding and Multimedia Signal Processing (IIH-MSP)* (pp. 151–154). IEEE. DOI: 10.1109/IIH-MSP.2017.39

Wang, L.. (2024). Cross-modal retrieval based on multi-dimensional feature fusion hashing. *Frontiers in Physics*, *12*, 1379873. DOI: 10.3389/fphy.2024.1379873

Wang, R., Lin, J., & Wang, Y. (2021). Robust adversarial watermarking against unknown removal attacks. *ACM Transactions on Multimedia Computing Communications and Applications*, *17*(1), 1–24.

White, L.. (2025). Standardization challenges in adversarial embedding evaluation. *IEEE Security and Privacy*, *23*(1), 45–54.

Wilson, P.. (2024). Multimodal fake news detection with contrastive learning and optimal transport. *Frontiers of Computer Science*, *6*, 1473457. DOI: 10.3389/fcomp.2024.1473457

Wu, H., He, B., & Wang, W. (2019). Adversarial embedding networks for steganography. *IEEE Transactions on Information Forensics and Security*, *15*, 838–852.

Wu, T., Zhao, Y., & Shi, Y. Q. (2022). Adversarial embedding with GAN regularization for robust image steganography. *IEEE Transactions on Information Forensics and Security*, *17*, 3312–3324.

Yang, L.. (2025). JPEG image steganography with automatic embedding cost learning. *International Journal of Intelligent Systems*. Advance online publication. DOI: 10.1155/int/5309734

Ye, J., Ni, J., & Yi, Y. (2022). SRNet++: An enhanced deep network for image steganalysis. *IEEE Transactions on Circuits and Systems for Video Technology*, *32*(5), 2532–2545.

Zhang, H.. (2025). A transformer-based adversarial network framework for steganography. *Expert Systems with Applications*, *266*, 126391. DOI: 10.1016/j.eswa.2025.126391

Zhang, M., Chen, B., & Tan, S. (2023). A dual-path adversarial framework for covert communication and ownership verification. In *Proceedings of the ACM Workshop on Information Hiding and Multimedia Security* (pp. 21–30).

Zhang, R., & Wang, T. (2025). (in press). Diffusion-based adversarial watermarking for tamper-resistant authentication. *IEEE Transactions on Multimedia*.

Zhang, R., Zhang, J., Zhu, F., & Liu, Y. (2020). Invisible steganography via generative adversarial networks. *Multimedia Tools and Applications*, *79*(1), 667–691. DOI: 10.1007/s11042-019-08162-3

Zhu, J., Kaplan, R., Johnson, J., & Fei-Fei, L. (2018). HiDDeN: Hiding data with deep networks. In *Proceedings of the European Conference on Computer Vision (ECCV)* (pp. 682–697). DOI: 10.1007/978-3

Zubair, S., Zia, T., & Alsadoon, A. (2020). Ethical implications of adversarial AI: A review. *Procedia Computer Science*, *176*, 1736–1745.

Chapter 2
Enhancing Forensic Image Analysis Using Deep Learning Methods: A Review

Galiveeti Poornima
https://orcid.org/0000-0003-4289-114X
S-Vyasa University, India

P. Karthikeyan
https://orcid.org/0000-0001-8977-5520
RV University, India

Ritu Raj Lamsal
https://orcid.org/0000-0002-3751-2785
University of Malaga, Spain

ABSTRACT

With the rise of digital content, ensuring the authenticity of images has become a critical challenge in forensic investigations. Traditional image forensic techniques often fall short against sophisticated manipulations like splicing, copy-move, and retouching. This chapter explores the application of deep learning models—such as CNNs, RNNs, autoencoders, and GANs—in enhancing the detection, localization, and classification of forged images. It reviews recent advancements, benchmark datasets, evaluation metrics, and real-world applications, while also addressing challenges and future research directions in forensic image analysis.

DOI: 10.4018/979-8-3373-3795-1.ch002

1 INTRODUCTION

Digital image integrity underpins the trustworthiness of visual content shared across media platforms, legal systems, healthcare, and journalism. In a world inundated with images, the potential for misuse—intentional or accidental—is significant (Kaja, 2024). Ensuring an image has not been altered is essential to prevent misinformation, protect reputations, and maintain evidence authenticity.

As advanced image editing tools become more accessible, the line between genuine and forged content becomes increasingly difficult to discern. There is significant value in performing verifications to maintain trust in public visual content that leads to informed decisions made by society (Chandanshiv et al., 2025). This is crucial in an era when doctored images can spread like wildfire online.

From a technical standpoint, the integrity of a true-image is checked by looking at metadata, compressed artifacts and light or noise distribution discrepancies (Capasso et al., 2024). It has become possible to identify crushed paper using such fine traces of tampering, which are invisible to the human eye, with good accuracy using forensic techniques, especially equipped with artificial intelligence (Renukadevi et al.,2024).

Image forensics is an important tool in the quiver of security/LE agencies, helping to verify surveillance images, identity claims and digital evidence (Tyagi et al., 2024). It is critical in solving crimes, finding digital fraud, and verifying visual information submitted in court.

In counter-terrorism and immigration, forensics is used to establish the truth about photo identity and the forgery of documents (Marakalala and Matlala, 2024). On the cybercrime front, image forensics aids in ascertaining the source of pornographic images, the determination of altered content and preservation of the electronic crime evidence chain (Marakalala and Matlala, 24).

Courts often demand strong authentication mechanisms for admissible evidence. Forensic analysis ensures that digital images presented in trials are not only relevant but also untampered and verifiable (UMUGWANEZA, 2024). This reinforces the integrity of the judicial process and supports fair rulings based on reliable evidence.

Traditional image forensic techniques—relying on statistical measures, metadata analysis, or manual inspection—struggle with complex or well-camouflaged manipulations (Tinkhede, 2024). As manipulation tools become more sophisticated, forensic systems must evolve to match the subtlety and complexity of modern forgeries.

Deep learning offers a promising solution by leveraging neural networks that can automatically learn discriminative features from large datasets (S et al., 2024). Convolutional Neural Networks (CNNs), for example, are adept at spotting pixel-level inconsistencies that signify tampering, even when the changes are visually imperceptible.

The adaptability of deep learning models, their high accuracy, and ability to handle large-scale forensic tasks make them invaluable (Pappachan et al., 2024). As datasets grow in size and variety, deep learning systems continuously improve, offering robust solutions for real-time image verification in high-stakes scenarios like law enforcement and national security (Pappachan et al., 2025). Figure 1 depicts the correlation among picture integrity, forensic analysis, deep learning, and law enforcement within the realm of digital security.

Figure 1. Overview of Image Forensics in Digital Security

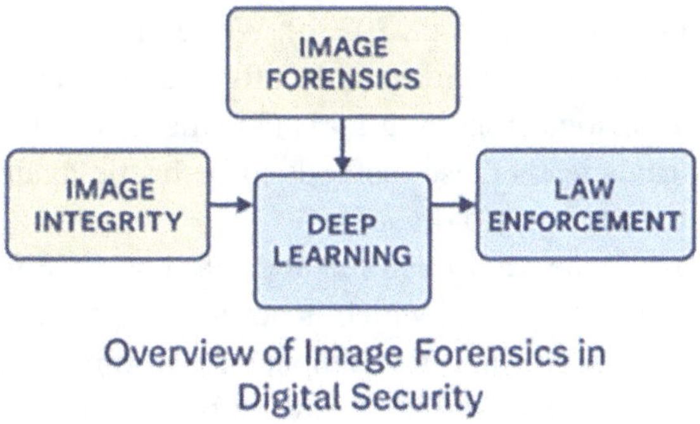

2 OVERVIEW OF FORENSIC IMAGE ANALYSIS

In forensic image analysis, approaches are categorized either by passive or active methods. Passive forensics does not require the information or the embedding process and is used to check for abnormalities in the image itself in order to detect tempering (Gupta et al., 2022). For instance, uncovering the remnants of a compression artifact, lighting inconsistencies, or replicated/copied parts in a copy-move attack. They become popular because they can be used with any image regardless of it's source or preparation.

On the contrary, active forensics assumes the knowledge of pre-embedded information such as watermarks or digital signatures (Deb et al., 2024). These methods are based on the watermarking at the image creation time, so that Authentication data is embedded in the image and latter can be extracted and verified. Active forensics is particularly powerful in content distribution and copyright protection application domain, where content owner verification and tamper detection are necessary (Bourouis et al., 2020). This, however, has the drawback that these marks must be inserted in advance.

Both types have there advantages and disadvantages. Passive models are also flexible because they do not require an image to be preprocessed in advance, although performance under complex manipulation can be a limiting factor. The active approaches are also less vulnerable to some attacks, though they rely on embedding protocols which are not necessarily supported by all steganography tools. "Surrogate" and "Personal" together provide a comprehensive, symbiotic approach to protecting digital content that are two halves of a whole forensic solution.

Conventional image forensics methods are generally based on handcrafted features with statistical analysis (Sharma et al., 2023b). While they are just fine for detecting fairly simple manipulations to image, they often fail when met with adversarial tampering or with sophisticated editing tools (Tinkhede, 2024). The dependence on a set of defined rules leads these methods to be brittle against novel types of attacks and ill-suited to real-world diversity.

Additionally, most of the traditional methods do not scale well. They need to be inspected or fine-tuned by hand which is not feasible for the analysis of large datasets or processing through a high-throughput forensic pipeline (Tinkhede, 2024). In settings like social media surveillance, law enforcement, or news verification, these inefficiencies can result in missed critical evidence or delays.

Another gap is the interpretability and consistency of findings. Classical ways can obtain false positive results or fail to notice slight alterations. They do not have the ability in localisation (identify the regions where the defect occurred) or confidence estimation (Tinkhede, 2024). These limitations have prompted the field towards data-driven, adaptive methods, especially those based on deep learning, to account for the increasing complexity of digital image editing. Table 1 provides a comparative and simple summary of the differences between passive and active image forensics.

Table 1. Comparison Between Passive and Active Forensic Methods

Feature	Passive Forensics	Active Forensics
Requires Prior Embedding	No	Yes
Detection Based On	Image inconsistencies	Watermarks or signatures
Use Case	General-purpose forgery detection	Copyright, content authentication
Strength	Flexible with unknown sources	Robustness against specific attacks
Limitation	May fail on subtle tampering	Not usable without pre-inserted markers

3 DEEP LEARNING IN IMAGE FORENSICS

Deep learning introduces automation, adaptability, and high accuracy into forensic image analysis, surpassing the constraints of traditional handcrafted techniques (Pappachan et al., 2024). By learning directly from data, deep models can uncover hidden patterns, statistical artifacts, and spatial irregularities that may go unnoticed by classical algorithms (Amiri et al., 2024). This has proven particularly effective for subtle manipulations like splicing or smoothing.

Unlike rule-based systems, deep learning models evolve through continuous training, improving their performance as more annotated data becomes available. They can generalize across various datasets, detect tampering under diverse conditions, and even localize the exact regions of manipulation (Yadav and Vishwakarma, 2024). This ability makes them especially valuable in dynamic environments such as social media monitoring and law enforcement surveillance.

Another big advantage is the scalability. The deep learning pipeline can be deployed in the cloud or used in a real -time forensic tool to process any large volumes of visual data very quickly. Both are amenable to hardware accelerators such as GPUs and TPUs which greatly increase throughput so that the real-time detection and localization of manipulations are possible when scaling to forensic scenario (Jia, 2025).

Different kinds of deep learn architectures are used in forensic image analysis that is designed for particular detection tasks. Convolutional Neural Networks (CNNs) are popular for spatial feature extraction, such as detecting anomalies in texture, edges or compression artifacts. The hierarchy kept is used to effective process such large image dataset but still maintain accuracy (Awasthi et al., 2024).

RNNs and their variants, such as LSTMs are used in video forensics and related problems, which includes sequential image data where consistency is required between successive frames (Pareek et al., 2023). Such models are used to discover abnormal transitions or motion artifacts that are caused by tampering. They are especially helpful in surveillance video and deepfake video identification.

Autoencoders are strong with anomaly detection, with which they reconstruct input images and identify the difference on the basis of the reconstruction error. GANs are employed for both inauthentic content generation and detection (Tiwari et al., 2024). For example in forensics, they can be made to be adapted to detect the difference between actual and fake images providing adversarial robustness and enhancing classification results. Figure 2 shows a flowchart on how CNNs, RNNs, Autoencoders and GANs contribute to different stages of image forgery detection, localization and classification.

Empirical studies consistently show that deep learning-based forensic models outperform traditional algorithms in both accuracy and robustness. In benchmark tests on datasets like CASIA, models like CNN-based architectures have achieved over 90% precision in forgery detection, far exceeding handcrafted feature-based approaches (Dutta et al., 2024). Their performance remains strong even under transformations such as resizing, cropping, or JPEG compression.

These models are being actively deployed in various real-world applications. In border control and passport verification, CNNs detect altered facial images. In journalism, autoencoder-based anomaly detectors verify the authenticity of images before publication (Anusha et al., 2024). Law enforcement agencies use GAN-aware classifiers to distinguish between genuine and deepfake videos in cybercrime investigations.

Moreover, deep models offer explainability features such as heatmaps or attention maps, which visually highlight manipulated regions (Tursunalieva et al., 2024). These tools not only aid analysts but also support legal evidence presentation by making the detection process more transparent and interpretable. Table 2 summarizes the comparison of the roles, advantages, and limitations of deep learning models used in forensic image analysis.

Figure 2. Deep Learning Models in Forensic Image Analysis

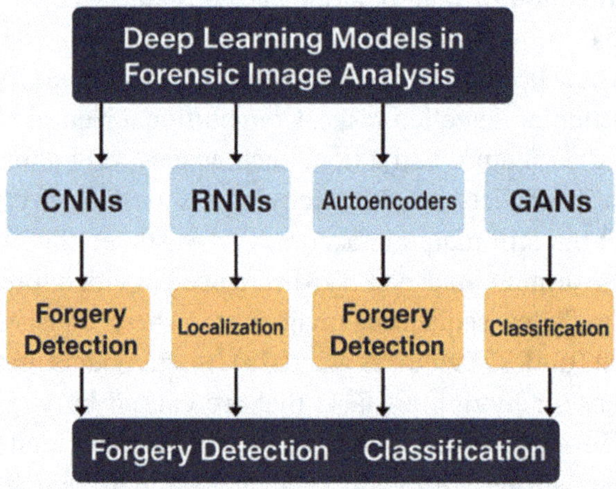

Table 2. Summary of Deep Learning Models in Image Forensics

Model Type	Application Area	Strengths	Limitations
CNN	Tamper detection, localization	High accuracy, good spatial feature extraction	Requires large labeled datasets
RNN / LSTM	Video forensics	Good for temporal consistency analysis	Computationally expensive, overfitting
Autoencoder	Anomaly detection	Unsupervised learning, good for reconstruction errors	May miss subtle manipulations
GAN	Fake image detection	Adversarial robustness, synthetic forgery detection	Difficult to train, stability issues

4 PASSIVE FORENSICS: FORGERY DETECTION TECHNIQUES

Passive forensics aims to detect image tampering without prior embedded information, such as watermarks (Gupta et al., 2022). One of the most common tampering types is copy-move, where a region of the image is copied and pasted elsewhere within the same image to conceal or duplicate an object (Thorat et al., 2024). Deep learning-based detectors can identify duplicated patches using spatial attention and block-based matching via CNNs.

Splicing is the incorporation among regions of different images into a single composition, employed to deceive spectators or to generate fakes (Kumari and Garg, 2025). Detection must involve finding errors in the forms of lighting, shadow, or edge crosses. Deep learning models made use of chromatic aberration or bound- ary artifacts to expose the splice boundaries (Niyishaka and Bhagvati, 2021). Retouching is the level of fine-grained image modification, such as a smoothing, sharpening, or blemish removal for the purpose of changing the perceived visual content (Ying et al., 2023). Although hard to observe, autoencoders or residual-form based CNNs can expose variations in texture distributions. These models also indicate pixel-wise arrangement, which as a result, aid the forensic examiners in spotting minute visual adulterations which would not be able to perceive by human (Navya and Patil, 2022).

Identifying manipulation is not enough—localizing the tampered parts is necessary for forensics to verify image segments and provide evidence (Kadha et al., 2025). Given a forgery input, CNN based segmentations are popularly employed for generating tampered regions heatmaps. With the help of these maps, forensics can view the places of change to investigate more (Sedik et al., 2024).

Tamper classification refers to identifying the type of manipulation (e.g., splicing vs. copy-move) (Timothy and Santra, 2024). Multi-class classifiers trained on annotated datasets can distinguish between various manipulation types by learning the statistical and structural differences in altered image regions (Yu et al., 2020). Some approaches also incorporate attention modules to focus the model on manipulated regions. Figure 3 displays original and manipulated versions of images showcasing three common forgery types—Copy-Move, Splicing, and Retouching—with highlighted regions indicating tampered areas.

Newer architectures use multitask learning to simultaneously detect, localize, and classify manipulations. These models enhance performance by learning shared representations and reducing the risk of false positives. Combined with visualization tools like Class Activation Maps (CAMs), they significantly enhance forensic transparency and usability in judicial or law enforcement scenarios (Nandhini and Thinakaran, 2023). Effective evaluation of forgery detection models requires standardized datasets and robust performance metrics (Kuznetsov et al., 2024). Popular datasets include CASIA v2.0, which provides spliced and tampered images with ground truth masks, and CoMoFoD, offering images tampered by various copy-move techniques under different post-processing conditions (Ranjan and Singla, 2024). Columbia Image Splicing Dataset is also widely used in research (Xiang et al., 2024). [4]

The most common performance metrics include accuracy, precision, recall, and F1-score, which reflect the model's ability to detect manipulation correctly. For localization tasks, Intersection over Union (IoU).

Figure 3. Visual Examples of Copy-Move, Splicing, and Retouching Tampering

Table 3. Overview of Public Datasets for Passive Forensics

Dataset Name	Tampering Types	Ground Truth Available	Notable Features
CASIA v2.0	Splicing, Copy-Move	Yes	Widely used, medium-scale
CoMoFoD	Copy-Move	Yes	Contains different post-processing
Columbia Splicing Dataset	Splicing	Yes	High-resolution, real-world sources
COVERAGE Dataset	Copy-Move	Yes	Variety in textures and image sizes

5 ACTIVE FORENSICS: WATERMARKING AND AUTHENTICATION

Active forensic methods involve the insertion of watermarks or digital signatures on the images at the time of their generation or transmission (Kwon et al., 2022). These marks serve as a signature, authentication, or integrity measure for the image such that recipients or forensic investigators can verify the content is authentic. Watermarking techniques can be visible (e.g., such as logos) and/or invisible (e.g., inserted into frequency domains such as Discrete Cosine Transform or Discrete Wavelet Transform) (Sharma et al., 2024).

Strong watermarking solutions are meant to endure normal image processing operations (resizing, rotation, compression, noise addition (Rob, 2023)). The watermarking scheme is expected to extract the watermark with ease after such transformations, so that the LSA process is constant and reliable. This makes them useful for copyright protection, content tracking, and forensic verification.

Watermarks can be delicate or strong depending on their intended use. Fragile watermarks are very fragile, and used for detecting tampering as any modification destroys the watermark and reports alteration. Strong watermarks are suitable for ownership check and tracking, and provide secure distribution of multimedia data in open networks (Hassan and Rahma, 2023).

Recent papers proposed both embedding and detecting models based on deep learning, for the first time. These methods based on CNNs or encoder-decoder structures are used to embed and embed invisible watermarks while preserving image quality (Bajpai et al., 2024). They are also large-scale trained models and can be learned on large datasets so they are able to generalize to various image resolutions, textures, and manipulation styles.

Deep watermarking methods typically apply an autoencoder-like architecture, where an encoder embeds the watermark and a decoder estimates it (Hemis and Boudraa, 2023). Some architectures jointly optimize for visual (small distortion) and robust (high watermarked retrieval) quality. This is achieved in a dual manner which requires the watermark to be both imperceptible and robust against attacks, such as JPEG compression or Gaussian blurring (Zhong et al., 2023).

Generative Adversarial Networks (GANs) have also been investigated for simulating adversarial attacks in training to incentivize the learning of robust watermarks (Qiao et al., 2023). These approaches could excel over classical frequency-domain watermarking, due to the learning of optimal embedding patterns and achieving powerful balance between invisibility and extractability. The encoder-decoder scheme for watermark embedding and extraction is presented in Figure 4, which includes input image, watermarked image, and watermark extracting process.

Figure 4. Architecture of a Deep Learning-Based Watermarking System

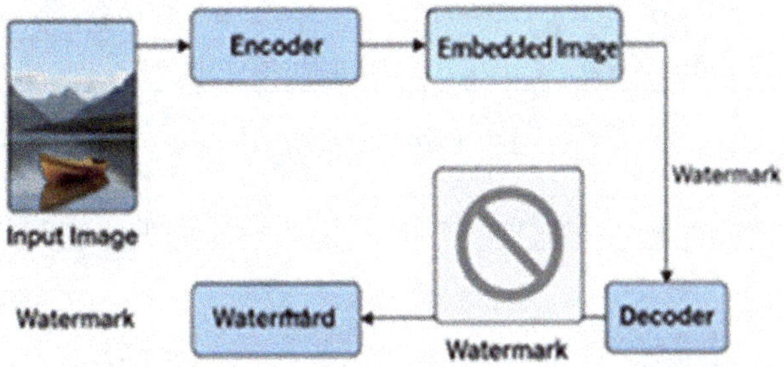

The obliviousness of any watermarking scheme is an indication of its effectiveness; for instance, how it is robust to popular attacks like JPEG compression, scaling, watermarking and geometric attacks (Bajpai et al., 2024). Com- pression removes high- frequency information and therefore can corrupt or erase weakly embedded watermarks. Deep learning-based solutions enhance robustness by splicing watermarks in perceptually salient regions of an image.

Cropping and rotating rendered image can slightly or mostly disrupt few parts of embedded watermark. In order to alleviate this, some methods resort to block-based embedding or redundant encoding, where the watermark is repeated in different areas of an image (Zhang et al., 2024). Data augmentation-trained CNNs might find it easy to decode watermarks from partial or rotated images and may help increase the robustness.

Forgery localization is also to verify the accuracy of watermark recovery when the image is corrupted by simulated distortion (Qiu et al., 2024) Usually they are evaluated by the bit error rate (BER) value or the peak signal to noise ratio (PSNR) value, the structural similarity index (SSIM) value, etc. A good deep watermarking system keeps its BER low while ensuring that the image can be recovered under different kinds of attack. Comparison in robustness, quality and adaptability Table 4 presents a comparison among traditional and deep learning-based watermarking methods with respect to robustness, quality, and adaptability.

Table 4. Comparison of Traditional vs. Deep Learning-Based Water-marking

Feature	Traditional Watermarking	Deep Learning-Based Watermarking
Embedding Domain	Frequency (DCT, DWT)	Spatial & Learnable via CNNs
Robustness to Attacks	Moderate	High (GAN-enhanced, adversarial training)
Visual Quality	May introduce artifacts	Optimized for imperceptibility
Adaptability	Limited	High (dataset-driven learning)
Extraction Flexibility	Manual or fixed decoding	Trainable decoding network

6 EVALUATION METRICS AND BENCHMARK DATASETS

For measuring the performance of the deep learning systems in image forensics, various well known metrics are used (Alsubaei et al., 2024). Accuracy gauges the overall performance of the model and can be a poor metric counting on rebalanced datasets (Van den Goorbergh et al., 2022). Precision represents the ratio of correctly labeled manipulations among the predicted positives and recall is the proportion of true positives that have been correctly classified (Powers, 2020).

The F1 measure, the harmonic mean of precision and recall, offers a balanced indicator if false positives and false negatives are both important. For forensic purposes, high F1-scores are typically desired, especially where manipulation localization is important (Islam et al., 2024). Moreover, the AUC (Area Under the Curve) calculated from the ROC curve provides an overall assessment of the testing model's discriminating ability at each threshold for classification and is an overall performance measure that is invariant to threshold (Li, 2024).

In the tasks of tamper localization, the pixel-based metrics like IoU (Intersection over Union) and mean pixel accuracy are used to evaluate how well the predicted masks are aligned with the ground truth tampered regions (Chennamma and Madhushree, 2023). These measures are important when manipulated regions are small or have irregular shapes such as those found in real images of tampered images.

6.1 Common Datasets

Quality datasets containing genuine and tampered images are essential in developing and testing forensic models. The CASIA Image Tampering Dataset v2[1] As the tampering on the image above is culture specific, it is unlikely that such images will appear in the CASIA Image Tampering Dataset. One of the most popular benchmarks, which gives labeled images for copy-move and splicing detection. It consists of realistic image manipulations and corresponding ground truth masks for training and testing.

Another standard dataset with images tampered by CoMoFoD (Copy-Move Forgery Detection Dataset)[2], where copy-move manipulations have been applied to the images with several post-processing including JPEG compression, blurring and color enhancement. This dataset is the best suited for testing the robustness of the models against real-world distortions.

The Columbia Image Splicing Dataset[3] is a high-resolution data set of spliced images sampled from natural photography, and therefore a fine data set for testing splicing detection techniques. Another popular dataset, i.e., the COVERAGE[4] dataset826 for dense copy-move forgeries and MFC2018[5] for the multi-format challenge, also makes it easier to benchmark generalization across types of manipulation. The most popular benchmark datasets used in forensic image analysis are presented in Table 5, showing the datasets organized with respect to the forgery type, file format, and intended usage.

Table 5. Overview of Benchmark Datasets in Image Forensics

Dataset Name	Type of Forgery	Format & Size	Ground Truth Provided	Use Case
CASIA v2.0	Splicing, Copy-Move	JPEG, PNG (˜13,000)	Yes	General forgery detection
CoMoFoD	Copy-Move	JPEG (˜200 pairs)	Yes	Robustness under transformations
Columbia	Splicing	JPEG (˜180 images)	Yes	High-resolution natural splicing
COVERAGE	Copy-Move	PNG (˜100 images)	Yes	Textured image forgery detection
MFC2018	Mixed Formats	JPEG, BMP, PNG	Yes	Cross-format and real-world test

Current datasets have contributed significantly to pioneering advances in forensic image analysis, but limitations with respect to diversity and real-world complexity still remain (For, 2022). A number of popular datasets are artificially generated, and thus may not always represent the full realm of nuanced perturbations present in wild settings, including social media and surveillance systems.

To address these shortcomings, recent datasets feature more diverse sources, lighting, scene content levels-of-com- pressions and image resolutions. Furthermore, cross-dataset generalization is becoming popular — training on one dataset and testing on a different to test generalization, and also not to overfit to any particular image statistics.

In future benchmarking studies, the balance of the dataset, annotation quality and variability across the domains are among the aspects that should be focused on, to make it better representative of real- world forensic settings. Collaborative dataset generation and continuous updating are essential for model to remain relevant in the ever evolving threat landscape (Hou et al., 2025).

7 CASE STUDIES AND REAL-WORLD APPLICATIONS

In contemporary law enforcement, digital image forensics is an important contributor to crime investigation and evidence verification (Arshad et al., 2018). For instance, police departments rely on deep learning powered tamper detection systems to verify the CCTV footage in burglary or assault cases (Raj and Bakas, 2023). Such systems can be utilized to maintain court-compliant integrity of presented footage.

In surveillance systems, forensic techniques can aid in the analysis of license plates, verification of facial images and in other analysis such as that of deepfake videos to obscure identity (Sohail et al., 2025). Such features are increasingly incorporated into real-time surveillance systems that are used to instantly alert security to any suspicious activity or tampered frames. They enable police forces to react quickly to incidents or false information.

Mobile forensics teams also deploy software utilities for image authentication, which they could use to analyze on-scene photographed images, such as accident scenes, or digital seized evidences, and make fast admitted in an evidence-based manner. These utilities facilitate digital examinations and lessen reliance on hardware lab setup when it comes to forensic utilization.

Digital images are increasingly presented as evidence in both civil and criminal lawsuits, ranging from property issues to cyber harassment (Riadi and Yudhana, 2023). Courts insist on a chain of custody and proof of authenticity for all the digital assets they are shown. Forensic image tools help verify that the images are unaltered, thereby establishing a timeline and a guarantee of the integrity of the visuals presented.

In cyberstalking and online defamation, forensic analysts check the authenticity of the screenshots and uploaded pictures (Hussein et al., 2022). Watermarked images or metadata timestamps are compared to the original logs to dismiss digital tampering (Padilha et al., 2022). In most of the modern courts, the judges are increasingly relying on the expert forensic reports that are produced using the deep learning-based authentication tools (Pappachan et al., 2024).

To promote the transparency of evidence, recent forensic systems create explainable visual evidences, e.g., tamper heatmaps or forgery masks. Jurors or legal experts can then be introduced to such visual aids to help them understand where the image was altered. This unites technical complexity with judicial understanding, and renders AI-informed forensics court-friendly.

Forensic image validation is a fundamental prerequisite in cybercrime investigations, in particular for the detection of fraud, disinformation and, as a consequence case solving, in counter to intellectual property theft (Blaskovic et al., 2022). Attackers commonly modify, create fake, or create synthetic images to deceive users, create fake account, or an impersonation. Investigators use forensic tools to confirm that AI-generated pictures are not real in cases of anonymity or extortion.

In intellectual property protection, watermarking techniques—especially those using deep learning—help track ownership and prevent unauthorized distribution. Creative industries use these tools to embed robust, invisible marks in digital artworks or media, which can later be extracted to prove authorship or usage rights during legal disputes.

Content platforms and social media sites increasingly incorporate automated forensic detection APIs to flag manipulated posts or verify the originality of images uploaded by users (Sharma et al., 2023a). These integrations enable scalable enforcement of content authenticity policies, helping combat the spread of fake news, manipulated media, and copyright infringements online. Table 6 outlines practical case study scenarios where forensic image analysis techniques are applied across security, legal, and digital content domains.

Table 6. Case Study Scenarios for Forensic Image Analysis

Domain	Application Scenario	Tools/Techniques Used	Outcome
Law Enforcement	CCTV footage verification	CNN-based tamper detection	Evidence validated for court submission
Surveillance	Face & vehicle identification	Deep learning-based face & plate recognition	Real-time threat detection
Legal Proceedings	Authentication of digital evidence	Metadata verification, tamper heatmaps	Image accepted as court evidence
Cybersecurity	Deepfake and fraud detection	GAN-aware classifiers, forensic decoders	Synthetic content flagged and isolated
DRM & IP Protection	Watermarked media tracking	Deep watermarking and extraction networks	Proven authorship and usage rights

8 LIMITATIONS AND CHALLENGES

The lack of interpretability is one of the major challenges that deep learning has in image forensics (Kuehlkamp et al., 2022). Most of the best models on the market are black boxes, meaning you can't see how they arrive at their decisions. This latter opaqueness can be a serious drawback in legal or police environments, especially where evidence needs to be transparent or justifiable.

Although some results have been promising to bring in XAI for forensic models. Methods such as Grad-CAM[6], saliency maps[7] and attention heatmaps[8] visualize regions of the image which are important for the model's decision. Unfortunately, the ability to apply these methods is often not uniform or clear enough to reach legal standards.

Explainability is also a tug-of-war: Increasing transparency may entail simplifying at the expense of accuracy. Developing forensic systems which are doing well while still being interpretable is still a subject of active research, especially when high-stake and legally sensitive applications are involved.

The lack of diversity and quantity of training data that is also usually low—quality has also been another major challenge of the field, which results in poor real-world generalizing capabilities. Definitely, these standard datasets commonly employed in the academic world include synthetically created forgeries that could not represent conveniently real ones (Cardenuto et al., 2023).

This raises issues when a model trained from one dataset is applied to others, a problem known as domain shift (Zhang et al., 2002) Such as the model trained on CASIA could exhibit poor performance with the social media or the surveillance videos generated by user due to compression, resolution, or noise.

One possible solution is to investigate cross domain/transfer/domain adaptation methods. These methods have the purpose to allow models to be more general and robust with respect to a wider variety of content and manipulation techniques, but the domain invariant performance is still an open problem.

Deploying forensic models in real-time systems—such as surveillance networks, cloud moderation platforms, or mobile apps—introduces both computational and operational challenges. Deep models, especially GAN- aware[9] and segmentation architectures[10], are often resource-intensive and require GPUs for fast inference.

This hinders integration in edge devices or time-sensitive environments where processing speed is critical. Compression, battery constraints, and memory limitations make it difficult to deploy large models in mobile forensics or field investigations.

Solutions like model quantization, knowledge distillation, and lightweight CNN architectures are being adopted to reduce resource demands. However, these often involve trade-offs in detection accuracy or local- ization precision, making it challenging to achieve optimal performance in constrained environments. Table 7 summarizes the key technical and operational limitations in current deep learning-based forensic image systems and potential mitigations.

Table 7. Summary of Key Limitations in Image Forensic Systems

Limitation	Description	Example Scenario	Mitigation Approach
Lack of Explainability	Models give accurate results without rationale	Evidence rejected in court	Explainable AI (Grad-CAM, saliency maps)
Dataset Domain Bias	Poor generalization across content types	Social media image forensics	Transfer learning, domain adaptation
Real-Time Inference Challenges	Models are too heavy for edge or mobile deployment	CCTV or drone footage analysis	Model compression, lightweight architectures

9 FUTURE RESEARCH DIRECTIONS

The next evolution of image forensics lies in multimodal analysis, where visual data is combined with complementary signals such as audio, video metadata, and sensor data. This fusion provides a more holistic perspective for validating content authenticity, particularly in dynamic media like videos or multimedia evidence submissions.

For example, a manipulated image may appear authentic in isolation, but inconsistencies in GPS metadata, timestamp, or audio may expose tampering. Integrating these different modalities can significantly improve accuracy and reduce false positives. Deep learning architectures such as multimodal transformers are being investigated to learn joint representations across diverse data types.

Research into cross-modal forgery detection is still in its early stages, and challenges like data synchronization, feature fusion, and interpretability remain. However, this direction promises more robust and context- aware forensic systems capable of detecting sophisticated and coordinated manipulations.

There is a growing demand for forensic tools that operate efficiently on edge devices like smartphones, surveillance cameras, and drones. Lightweight deep learning models are essential to provide on-device tamper detection without requiring access to high-performance cloud infrastructure.

Emerging techniques like MobileNets, EfficientNet, and pruned CNN architectures offer a path forward, enabling forensic capabilities with minimal latency and power consumption. These models are particularly relevant for real-time field use, such as by journalists, law enforcement, or first responders.

Additionally, TinyML frameworks are being explored to enable forensic inference on microcontrollers or IoT nodes. This would empower decentralized forensic analysis, increasing scalability and privacy, and reducing data transmission costs for centralized review.

Nowhere is this more crucial than in forensics, where the stakes are high, and mistakes can result in legal consequences or a loss of public confidence. Future work must emphasis explaining, auditing, and aligning deep learning models in addition to their accuracy.

There are also attempts being made to enhance transparency in models, such as building more interpretable architectures and incorporating self- explanation modules, which explain the outputs in human understandable manners. These explanations should be credible and meet evidentiary standards and admissibility as expert testimony in legal scenarios.

Moreover, it is important to incorporate AI fairness and bias mitigation measures to forensic models in order to prevent skewed results from being produced based on the type of content or on the demographic information, or on the dataset imbalance. The future of AI in forensics is systems that are not only technically responsible, but ethically sound and socially accountable.

10 CONCLUSION

In this chapter, we have provided an overview of applications of deep learning in forensic image analysis. We began with the classical passive and active forensics, and we studied the progression of deep learning for forgery detection, watermarking, and tampering localization. Well-documented case studies had proved that deep learning can provide high-accuracy, scalable and versatile forensic systems.

Evaluation criteria and benchmark datasets were introduced to emphasize the solidity in practice of model validation. Finally, we investigated critical use cases, from forensics employments to cybercrime detection, and we pointed at practical applications also in judicatureal domain, surveillance and digital content rights. The combination of explainability, domain adaptation and lightweight architectures was highlighted as an essential further step in order to run those tools in real-world scenarios. The implications of robust image forensic tools extend across national security, legal governance, and digital accountability. For law enforcement, the ability to validate visual evidence in real time enhances the credibility and efficiency of criminal investigations. In cybersecurity, forensic tools help counter misinformation, detect synthetic media, and protect intellectual property.

Moving forward, the adoption of trustworthy AI, multimodal fusion, and edge-compatible forensic systems will be central to building public trust and ensuring legal admissibility. As manipulative technologies evolve, the countermeasure strategies discussed here provide a strong foundation for securing digital truth in an increasingly visual world.

REFERENCES

Alsubaei, F. S., Almazroi, A. A., & Ayub, N. (2024). Enhancing phishing detection: A novel hybrid deep learning framework for cybercrime forensics. *IEEE Access : Practical Innovations, Open Solutions*, *12*, 8373–8389.

Amiri, Z., Heidari, A., Navimipour, N. J., Unal, M., & Mousavi, A. (2024). Adventures in data analysis: A systematic review of deep learning techniques for pattern recognition in cyber-physical- social systems. *Multimedia Tools and Applications*, *83*(8), 22909–22973.

Anusha, N., & Khushi, K. Madhumitha, Shet, M., and Alekhya, P. (2024). Deepfake detection using deep learning: A two-pronged approach with cnns and autoencoders. pages 24–29.

Arshad, H., Jantan, A. B., & Abiodun, O. I. (2018). Digital forensics: Review of issues in scientific validation of digital evidence. *Journal of Information Processing Systems*, *14*(2), 346–376.

Awasthi, A., Rao, S. B., & Acharjya, K. (2024). *Efficient image feature extraction using convolutional neural networks.*

Bajpai, C., Gaur, M., Mori, G., & Keshwani, P. (2024). Deepmarknet for robust image and video watermarking embedding and detection. *ICTACT Journal on Image and Video Processing*, *15*, 3375–3378.

Blaskovic, A. K., Rusk, J.-D., Parker, V. C.Jr, & Payne, B. R. (2022). Cyber- crime and intellectual property theft: An analysis of modern digital forensics. In *Proceedings of the Future Technologies Conference*, pages 536–542. Springer.

Bourouis, S., Alroobaea, R., Alharbi, A. M., Andejany, M., & Rubaiee, S. (2020). Recent advances in digital multimedia tampering detection for forensics analysis. *Symmetry*, *12*(11), 1811.

Capasso, P., Cattaneo, G., & De Marsico, M. (2024). A comprehensive survey on meth- ods for image integrity. *ACM Transactions on Multimedia Computing Communications and Applications*, *20*(11), 1–34.

Cardenuto, J. P., Yang, J., Padilha, R., Wan, R., Moreira, D., Li, H., Wang, S., Andalo´, F., Marcel, S., & Rocha, A.. (2023). The age of synthetic realities: Challenges and opportunities. *APSIPA Transactions on Signal and Information Processing*, *12*(1).

Chandanshiv, V., Ekhande, N., Dagade, R. V., and Lohar, R. (2025). A survey: Deep fake detection. *International Journal of Advanced Research in Science, Communication and Technol- ogy*, pages 106 – 109.

Chennamma, H., & Madhushree, B. (2023). A comprehensive survey on image authentication for tamper detection with localization. *Multimedia Tools and Applications*, *82*(2), 1873–1904.

Deb, P., Deb, S., Das, A., & Kar, N. (2024). Image forgery detection techniques: Latest trends and key challenges. *IEEE Access : Practical Innovations, Open Solutions.*

Dutta, M., & Saini, J.. (2024). A systematic literature review on image splicing detec- tion and localization using emerging technologies. *Multimedia Tools and Applications*, ●●●, 1–36.

For. (2022). Forensic analysis of synthetically generated western blot images. *IEEE Access*, 10:59919 – 59932.

Gupta, S., Mohan, N., & Kaushal, P. (2022). Passive image forensics using universal techniques: A review. *Artificial Intelligence Review*, *55*(3), 1629–1679.

Hassan, Y. A., & Rahma, A. M. S. (2023). *A comparative study between the fragile and robust watermarking techniques and proposing new fragile watermarking with embedded value technique.*

Hemis, M., & Boudraa, B. (2023). Image watermarking technique using convolutional autoencoder. pages 1 – 6.

Hou, X., Zhao, Y., Wang, S., & Wang, H. (2025). Model context protocol (mcp): Land- scape, security threats, and future research directions. *arXiv preprint arXiv:2503.23278.*

Hussein, O. A., Manap, N. A., Rahman, M. R. A., & Wahhab, B. M. A. (2022). Cyber blackmail on social media and its authenticity through criminal evidence. *NeuroQuantology : An Interdisciplinary Journal of Neuroscience and Quantum Physics*, *20*(6), 121–132.

Islam, U., Alsadhan, A. A., Alwageed, H. S., Al-Atawi, A. A., Mehmood, G., Ayadi, M., & Alsenan, S. (2024). Sentinelfusion based machine learning comprehensive approach for enhanced computer forensics. *PeerJ. Computer Science*, *10*, e2183.

Jia, Z. (2025). Research on image recognition and classification algorithms in cloud computing environment based on deep neural networks. *IEEE Access : Practical Innovations, Open Solutions.*

Kadha, V. K., Bakshi, S., & Das, S. K. (2025). Unravelling digital forgeries: A system- atic survey on image manipulation detection and localization. *ACM Computing Surveys*.

Kaja, R. (2024). A comprehensive content verification system for ensuring digital integrity in the age of deep fakes.

Kuehlkamp, A., Boyd, A., Czajka, A., Bowyer, K., Flynn, P., & Chute, D., and Benjamin, E. (2022). Interpretable deep learning-based forensic iris segmentation and recognition. In *Proceedings of the IEEE/CVF Winter Conference on Applications of Computer Vision*, pages 359–368.

Kumari, R., & Garg, H. (2025). Image splicing forgery detection: A review. *Multimedia Tools and Applications*, *84*(8), 4163–4201.

Kuznetsov, O., Frontoni, E., Romeo, L., & Rosati, R. (2024). Enhancing copy-move forgery detection through a novel cnn architecture and comprehensive dataset analysis. *Multimedia Tools and Applications*, *83*(21), 59783–59817.

Kwon, M.-J., Nam, S.-H., Yu, I.-J., Lee, H.-K., & Kim, C. (2022). Learning jpeg com- pression artifacts for image manipulation detection and localization. *International Journal of Computer Vision*, *130*(8), 1875–1895.

Li, J. (2024). Area under the roc curve has the most consistent evaluation for binary classification.

Marakalala, M. C., & Matlala, M. M. (2024). Border management identi- fication: The biometric technology to detect criminals and terrorists often travel using falsified identity documents. *OIDA International Journal of Sustainable Development*, *17*(12), 57–70.

Nandhini, T. J., & Thinakaran, K. (2023). Optimizing forensic investiga- tion and security surveillance with deep reinforcement learning techniques. pages 1 – 5.

Navya, V., & Patil, K. A. (2022). *Identification of anomalies in images using cnn and autoencoders techniques*.

Niyishaka, P., & Bhagvati, C. (2021). Image splicing detection technique based on illumination-reflectance model and lbp. *Multimedia Tools and Applications*, *80*(2), 2161–2175.

Padilha, R., Salem, T., Workman, S., Andalo´, F. A., Rocha, A., & Jacobs, N. (2022). Content-aware detection of temporal metadata manipulation. *IEEE Transactions on Information Forensics and Security*, *17*, 1316–1327.

Pappachan, P., Adi, N. S., and Firmansyah, G. (2024). Deep learning-based forensics. *Digital Forensics and Cyber Crime Investigation: Recent Advances and Future Directions*, page 211.

Pappachan, P., Adi, N. S., Firmansyah, G., & Rahaman, M. (2025). Deep learning-based forensics and anti-forensics. In *Digital Forensics and Cyber Crime Investigation* (pp. 211–240). CRC Press.

Pareek, P. K. S., B., and G, G. (2023). Deepfake video detection system using deep neural networks. pages 1 – 6.

Powers, D. M. (2020). Evaluation: from precision, recall and f-measure to roc, informedness, markedness and correlation. *arXiv preprint arXiv:2010.16061*.

Qiao, T., Ma, Y., Zheng, N., Wu, H., Chen, Y., Xu, M., & Luo, X. (2023). A novel model watermarking for protecting generative adversarial network. *Computers & Security, 127*, 103102.

Qiu, J., Han, W., Zhao, X., Long, S., Faloutsos, C., & Li, L. (2024). Evaluating durability: Benchmark insights into multimodal watermarking. *arXiv preprint arXiv:2406.03728*.

Raj, M., & Bakas, J. (2023). *Detection of object-based forgery in surveillance videos utilizing motion residual and deep learning*.

Ranjan, R. & Singla, N. (2024). Image forgery detection.

Renukadevi, P., John, S., & Shivani, N. (2024). Forensic science: Ai-powered image and audio analysis. In *2024 5th International Conference on Smart Electronics and Communication (ICOSEC)*, pages 1519–1525. IEEE.

Riadi, I., & Yudhana, A. (2023). Mobile forensic tools for digital crime inves- tigation: Comparison and evaluation. *International Journal of Safety and Security Engineering, 13*, 11–19.

Rob. (2023). Robust watermarking techniques for the authentication and copyright protection of digital images: A survey. *SLU Journal of Science and Technology*, pages 100 – 112.

S, M., D, S. M., S, R., Subramanian, A. K., V, V., and Swamy, M. (2024). Convolutional neural network-based image tamper detection with error level analysis. pages 1 – 7.

Sedik, A., Kolivand, H., & Albeedan, M. (2024). An efficient image classification and segmentation method for crime investigation applications. *Multimedia Tools and Applications*, •••, 1–25.

Sharma, D. K., Singh, B., Agarwal, S., Garg, L., Kim, C., & Jung, K.-H. (2023a). A survey of detection and mitigation for fake images on social media platforms. *Applied Sciences (Basel, Switzerland)*, *13*(19), 10980.

Sharma, P., Kumar, M., & Sharma, H. (2023b). Comprehensive analyses of image forgery detection methods from traditional to deep learning approaches: An evaluation. *Multimedia Tools and Applications*, *82*(12), 18117–18150.

Sharma, S., Zou, J. J., Fang, G., Shukla, P., & Cai, W. (2024). A review of image watermarking for identity protection and verification. *Multimedia Tools and Applications*, *83*(11), 31829–31891.

Sohail, S., Sajjad, S. M., Zafar, A., Iqbal, Z., Muhammad, Z., & Kazim, M. (2025). Deepfake image forensics for privacy protection and authenticity using deep learning. *Information (Basel)*, *16*(4), 270.

Thorat, N. N., Dhotre, P., Kulal, N., Pimpalkar, A. P., Patil, V. S., & Kolekar, S. M. (2024). Tamper-forgery image detection in security digital image: A review. In *2024 IEEE International Conference on Blockchain and Distributed Systems Security (ICBDS)*, pages 1–5. IEEE.

Timothy, D. P., & Santra, A. K. (2024). Detecting digital image forgeries with copy-move and splicing image analysis using deep learning techniques. *International Journal of Advanced Computer Science and Applications*, *15*(5).

Tinkhede, N. N. (2024). *Advance image forgery detection.*

Tiwari, S., Dixit, A. K., & Pandey, A. K. (2024). Fake image detection using generative adversarial networks (gans) and deep learning models. pages 37 – 45.

Tursunalieva, A., Alexander, D. L., Dunne, R., Li, J., Riera, L., & Zhao, Y. (2024). Making sense of machine learning: A review of interpretation techniques and their applications. *Applied Sciences (Basel, Switzerland)*, *14*(2), 496.

Tyagi, A. K., Kumari, S., and Richa (2024). Artificial intelligence-based cyber security and digital forensics: A review. *Artificial Intelligence-Enabled Digital Twin for Smart Manufacturing*, pages 391–419.

Umugwaneza, M. E. (2024). Legal analysis on the use of digital evidence under rwandan judicial system.

Van den Goorbergh, R., van Smeden, M., Timmerman, D., & Van Calster, B. (2022). The harm of class imbalance corrections for risk prediction models: Illustration and simulation using logistic regression. *Journal of the American Medical Informatics Association : JAMIA*, *29*(9), 1525–1534.

Xiang, A., Zhang, J., Yang, Q., Wang, L., & Cheng, Y. (2024). Research on splicing im- age detection algorithms based on natural image statistical characteristics. *arXiv preprint arXiv:2404.16296.*

Yadav, A., & Vishwakarma, D. K. (2024). Datasets, clues and state-of-the- arts for multimedia forensics: An extensive review. *Expert Systems with Applications, 249*, 123756.

Ying, Q., Liu, J., Li, S., Xu, H., Qian, Z., & Zhang, X. (2023). Retouchingffhq: A large-scale dataset for fine-grained face retouching detection. In *Proceedings of the 31st ACM International Conference on Multimedia*, pages 737–746.

Yu, I.-J., Nam, S.-H., Ahn, W., Kwon, M.-J., & Lee, H.-K. (2020). Manipulation classifi- cation for jpeg images using multi-domain features. *IEEE Access : Practical Innovations, Open Solutions, 8*, 210837–210854.

Yu, J., Xu, J., Chen, Y., Li, W., Wang, Q., Yoo, B., & Han, J.-J. (2021). Learning generalized intersection over union for dense pixelwise prediction. In *International Conference on Machine Learning*, pages 12198–12207. PMLR.

Zhang, A., Xing, L., Zou, J., & Wu, J. C. (2022). Shifting machine learning for healthcare from development to deployment and from models to data. *Nature Bio- medical Engineering, 6*(12), 1330–1345.

Zhang, J., Chen, D., Liao, J., Ma, Z., Fang, H., Zhang, W., Feng, H., Hua, G., & Yu, N. (2024). Robust model watermarking for image processing networks via structure consistency. *IEEE Transactions on Pattern Analysis and Machine Intelligence*, •••, 1–8.

Zhong, X., Das, A., Alrasheedi, F., & Tanvir, A. (2023). A brief, in-depth survey of deep learning-based image watermarking. *Applied Sciences (Basel, Switzerland), 13*(21), 11852.

ENDNOTES

1 The dataset is available at https://www.kaggle.com/datasets/divg07/casia-20 -image-tampering-detection-dataset.

2 The dataset is available at https://www.vcl.fer.hr/comofod/.

3 The dataset is available at https://www.ee.columbia.edu/ln/dvmm/downloads/ AuthSplicedDataSet/AuthSplicedDataSet.htm.

4 The dataset is available at https://paperswithcode.com/dataset/coverage.

5 The dataset is available at https://www.nist.gov/itl/iad/mig/media-forensics-challenge-2018.

6 https://medium.com/@codetrade/grad-cam-in-pytorch-a-powerful-tool-for-visualize-explanations-from-deep-networks-bdc7caf0b282

7 https://medium.com/@bijil.subhash/explainable-ai-saliency-maps-89098e230100

8 https://knowledge.neuronsinc.com/neurons-ai-heatmaps-and-interpretation

Chapter 3
Forensic Applications of Generative AI in Image Reconstruction

Shubhangi Sankhyadhar
https://orcid.org/0000-0001-6858-0230
Pranveer Singh Institute of Technology, Kanpur, India

Mohit Pandey
Pranveer Singh Institute of Technology, Kanpur, India

Birendra Kumar Saraswat
GL Bajaj Institute of Technology and Management, Greater Noida, India

Esha Tripathi
Pranveer Singh Institute of Technology, Kanpur, India

ABSTRACT

In recent years, the intersection of artificial intelligence and forensic science has given rise to powerful tools capable of reconstructing and enhancing digital evidence. This chapter delves into the emerging role of generative AI—particularly models like GANs and VAEs—in forensic image processing. It outlines the foundational technologies, real-world applications, and the evolving methodologies that are transforming how evidence is interpreted, visualized, and validated. The discussion balances technical depth with practical relevance, exploring both the potential and limitations of AI-driven reconstructions. Ethical and legal considerations, such as privacy, transparency, and admissibility in court, are also critically examined.

DOI: 10.4018/979-8-3373-3795-1.ch003

Through a combination of conceptual explanations, case-based insights, and visual illustrations, this chapter presents a comprehensive overview of how generative AI is reshaping forensic investigations in a responsible and robust manner.

1. INTRODUCTION

In modern forensic science, digital images and videos are extremely valuable. This visual evidence including crime scene photographs, surveillance videos, biometrics, soft copies of documents, and digital records, is a key part of criminal investigations, legal proceedings, and the reconstruction of an event. An important issue is the noise and the artefacts that often occurred in a large amount of visual data. For example, images from surveillance systems are often taken at less-than-optimal resolutions, especially under poor illumination. Photos of crime scenes can be poor, missing or ageing. Smudged partial fingerprints, blurred aerial photographs or damaged historical documents often present tough challenges for forensic scientists sorting out valuable information that can hold up in court. This inherent defect accentuates the need of an efficient method that enhances, restores or, even rebuilds the deteriorated visual content for maintaining its evidential trustworthiness and applicability in forensic scenarios. This is where generative AI, which has the ability to generate realistic images and make predictions with incomplete information, offers potentially a game changer for forensic image analysis(Tortora, 2024). This chapter explores the application of generative artificial intelligence models in forensic image reconstruction, emphasizing their potential to transform how digital evidence is analyzed and utilized in legal proceedings (Mandayam, 2024).

Forensics experts have traditionally employed multiple signal and image processing technologies, including filtering, deblurring, interpolation and contrast enhancement, in order to enhance the quality and sharpness of visual evidence. These approaches have been workhorses in the field for years, but with some downsides. Conventional methods are often limited to the amplification of the signal present without, in their basic form, the ability to fill gaps on images, in the presence of occlusions or when only partially damaged. Since such extrapolation or reconstruction from complete absence is not possible, specific information is simply lost in space, and consequently crucial details of highly tampered evidence may never be elucidated or salvaged, thus affecting the probative value that would otherwise be derived from the evidence. In such situations missing visual information cannot be recovered by sharpening or denoising. Generative AI models provide a radical shift in approach, learning complex data distributions from large training sets and thus having the capability to hallucinate plausible missing information, or even synthesize new data that is statistically consistent with the observed evidence. This capacity enables highly restored or partially visible visual evidence to be resumed, transcending from the simple enhancement to the active content generation. (Farber, 2025).

Recent developments in artificial intelligence with a focus on generative models, are starting to change the status quo. Generative AI refers to a class of machine learning models that learn from large amounts of data and can generate new (and totally fake) content that is authentic to a degree. Among these, Generative Adversarial Networks (GANs), Variational Autoencoders (VAEs), and, more recently, diffusion models have shown to have the capability of generating high-quality images conditioned on partial or corrupted inputs. Its potential for transformation opens up new doors in forensic science, like generating missing areas of a photo or enhancing a blurry image into an ultra-sharp one, or even creating realistic-looking but still artistically altered evidence. In this review, we investigate the methods and trends in the detection of AI-created images, with focus on the forensic examination of co-authored on the real world scenarios (Mahara & Rishe, 2025) (Corvi et al., 2025). These models have the potential to greatly change forensic analysis, but using them also brings difficult problems, especially around making sure AI-created content is real, trustworthy, and not used in ways that could be harmful in legal situations. (Lamichhane, 2024).

Specifically, a low-quality CCTV image that used to show a blurry shape of a person might now be made clearer using a trained super-resolution Generative Adversarial Network (GAN) to create a more detailed image of the person's face. Similarly, an incompletely compromised fingerprint can also be digitally re-constructed so that it may be compared to forensic databases. In addition, for historical or 'cold' cases where photographic evidence has significantly degraded through the passage of time, generative models have the potential to restore important information that might be lost and have the potential to produce new investigative leads. But the swift advancement and increasing ubiquity of generative AI tools have also posed new challenges for forensic practitioners, prosraising fears around the rise of fake news generated using AI and more sophisticated types of digital forgeries(Kwon, 2024). This includes the deliberate creation of deceptive visual content, such as deepfakes or doctored images, which can undermine the integrity of digital evidence and complicate verification processes (Mathys et al., 2024).

However, with these armed superhuman abilities come equally dangerous challenges and responsibilities. Compared to older methods that give a single, fixed result, generative reconstruction creates new visual images based on patterns the model has learned. The growth of AI generated images or videos has shown important thought about whether they are real or not, trustworthy, and suitable to be used as evidence. The main issue is how to stop fake or misleading details from being added to AI images. What strict checks are needed to make sure these tools meet the high standards required for legal evidence. Also this is crucial to use powerful AI tools carefully to stop them from being used for harmful purposes. Including making fake videos or leading to unfair court decisions. This means we need a deep and complete understanding of what generative AI can and cannot do when it is used in investigations. These new technologies have created a strong and urgent need for solid tools that can clearly tell AI-made images apart from real ones, especially since it's now very easy to make convincing fake images(Xie et al., 2021) (Hsu et al., 2018).

Impostor Bias seems like a real problem in which create realistic fake media, especially deepfakes. This makes people more doubtful about whether digital content is real because AI can now make fake information look extremely authentic(Amerini et al., 2024). This chapter includes generative artificial intelligence working. Focusing on the specific techniques that are most useful in forensic work. It also shows, through real examples, how these technologies are changing the field. Additionally, it covers the technical, legal, and ethical issues that professionals in forensics, policymakers, and researchers need to think about as these tools become more common. Because these tools can be used both for good and bad purposes, there is ongoing discussion between those who make advanced generative models and those who are developing better ways to detect and stop their misuse(Le et al., 2023). It also covers the technical, legal, and ethical issues that professionals in forensics, policy, and research must consider as these technologies become more common. Since these tools can be used for both good and bad purposes, there's ongoing debate between those developing powerful generative models and those working to create better detection and prevention methods.(Lee et al., 2024).

This chapter examines the interrelationship between generative artificial intelligence and forensic image reconstruction, elucidating both the prospective advantages and inherent constraints within this nascent domain. The purpose is not to encourage people to use these tools without thinking, but to show how AI can be a powerful tool for uncovering the truth and promoting fairness when it's used correctly and carefully reviewed. The chapter also explains the various digital forensic methods used to identify deepfakes and evaluates how effective the current and emerging techniques are in different forms of media(Qureshi et al., 2024).

2. GENERATIVE AI

Fundamentally, generative AI refers to a class of machine learning methodologies capable of synthesizing novel content—such as visual data, linguistic constructs, auditory signals, or three-dimensional representations—derived from learned patterns. Specifically, within the domain of visual information, this implies the fabrication of highly realistic images that did not originate from direct photographic capture yet exhibit statistical plausibility contingent on the training datasets. Such generative capabilities are instrumental in tasks such as the enhancement, completion, or reconstruction of occluded or absent regions within an image. This is different from discriminative models, which mainly focus on classifying or predicting labels from the data they receive, rather than creating new outputs(Krubha et al., 2025). Unlike discriminative AI, which works with existing data, generative AI makes new and varied content by using large datasets and complex designs (Gozalo-Brizuela & Merchan, 2024).

To better understand generative AI, it's helpful to compare it with traditional image processing.

While regular image tools like filters and enhancement software only work with the data they already have—doing things like sharpening, removing blur, adjusting contrast, or reducing noise—generative AI can create entirely new, realistic-looking visual elements that weren't there to begin with. For example, it can restore a hidden part of a suspect's face or repair a broken part of a fingerprint. This is made possible through advanced machine learning methods, especially those using neural networks such as Generative Adversarial Networks and Transformer models(Baig & Yadegaridehkordi, 2025).

2.1 Key Generative Models

In the past ten years, many different types of models have shaped the field of generative AI. Three main groups are especially important for reconstructing images in forensic work: Generative Adversarial Networks, or GANs; Variational Autoencoders, or VAEs; and Diffusion Models. The term "Generative AI" covers a wide variety of sophisticated technologies, including the ability to generate text, images, and other types of data through sophisticated deep learning algorithms that mimic human creativity(Al-kfairy et al., 2024). The introduction of the Generative Adversarial Networks (GANs) in 2014 stands out as one of the most important advancements in the field of AI, because the algorithms automating the data creation process have been improved. GANs utilize a competitive training process which involves a generator and a discriminator, one trying to create data and the other trying to identify data as synthetic or real(Chen et al., 2024). Such a competitive approach improves the ability of the generator to create data to the highest possible degree, ensuring that the generation of synthetic media is constantly evolving and that there are minimal bounds to the possibilities(Chakraborty, 2024).

2.1.1 Generative Adversarial Networks (GANs)

Generative Adversarial Networks, or GANs, are seen as one of the biggest advances in generative AI. They were first created by Goodfellow and his team in

2014. In a typical GAN setup, there are two neural networks that work together at the same time in a kind of competition. One network, called the Generator, tries to make fake data that looks real. The other network, called the Discriminator, tries to figure out if the data is real or fake. With every round in the iterative game, the Generator improves its skill in producing lifelike synthetic data. The distinct approach to training GANs, known as adversarial training, sets GANs apart from the vast majority of deep learning models that rely on optimization(Goodfellow et al., 2020).

As illustrated in Figure 1, a GAN operates with a Generator and a Discriminator. The Discriminator's role is to assess images, determining if an image is generated or obtained. The Generator, on the other hand, produces images from random noise. This adversarial feedback loop helps the Generator improve its output to produce highly realistic images.

Figure 1. Basic Structure of a Generative Adversarial Network (GAN)

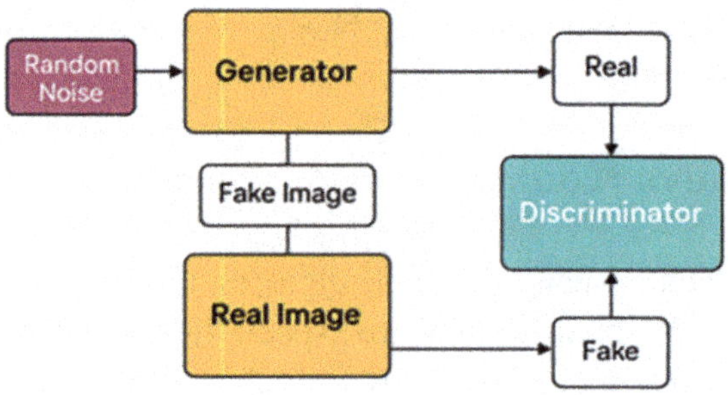

In forensic image reconstruction, GANs have found applications in the areas like Super-resolution, Inpainting, Style transfer.

2.1.2 Variational Autoencoders (VAEs)

Variational Autoencoders are a type of generative model that stands out in the field. Unlike Generative Adversarial Networks, which work through a competitive process, VAEs use an encoder and decoder structure. The encoder takes in data, like an image, and converts it into a simpler form that represents the key features. The decoder then uses this simplified form to recreate the original image. VAEs can create new data by taking samples from different points in this simplified space, which makes them useful for making fake faces or fingerprints to fill up training data. This process of improving over time helps GANs create realistic data, making them great for making different kinds of data like images, sounds, and text(Das et al., 2021) (Zeng & Xue, 2022).

However, VAEs typically produce blurrier outputs than GANs but are more stable and easier to train.

2.1.3 Diffusion Models

Diffusion models represent the most significant leap forward in generative AI, particularly revolutionizing image creation. Their operational paradigm involves a progressive corruption of clear images by systematically introducing noise, thereby transforming them into obscured representations. Subsequently, the model meticulously reverses this degradation, expertly denoising and reconstructing the original image with remarkable fidelity. Architectures such as Denoising Diffusion Probabilistic Models and their sophisticated variants have consistently yielded unparalleled results, generating extraordinarily detailed and photorealistic images that demonstrably surpass the output quality often achieved by Generative Adversarial Networks. While Variational Autoencoders prove indispensable for their capacity to probabilistically model data distributions, enabling precise control over generation and fluid navigation within latent spaces, the inherent step-by-step process of GANs, despite their historical prevalence in diverse data generation including images, sound, and text, frequently struggles to match the intricate detail and realism now attainable with diffusion models(Sun & Mou, 2023) (Goodfellow et al., 2020).

For forensic use, diffusion models are very useful for cleaning up badly damaged evidence and for bringing back lost details in low-quality video that have been affected by noise or compression. This is a big step forward in generative modeling, shifting from simple autoencoders that give the same result every time to more complex methods that use probability, take into account the order of events, use competition between models, and gradually remove noise. (Mai et al., 2024). Despite their current state-of-the-art performance in image generation, classical assumptions suggest that diffusion models completely destroy the data after the final step of the forward process, unlike VAEs where the latent representation contains compressed information about the original image (He et al., 2024).

2.2 Key Differences: Deterministic vs. Generative

It is important to note that generative models don't just copy the original data; they create new, believable versions. This means there is some uncertainty involved, which needs to be carefully handled in forensic situations. Because of this, any reconstruction made using generative models must be checked thoroughly and interpreted with care to make sure that made-up details aren't treated as real facts. However, recent improvements in diffusion models have made them better than GANs at creating high-quality images and modeling details. This has led to their use in many industries for making realistic and varied images based on text descriptions(Kong et al., 2023).

The development of generative AI given in table 1. Highlighting how fast the field has grown since the first Generative Adversarial Networks were introduced in 2014 up to today's advanced diffusion models. Each major step, from the early success of Variational Autoencoders to newer systems like SRGAN and StyleGAN, marks a big improvement in what these models can do. This progress has led to the recent rise of diffusion models, which have greatly improved the quality of generated images, making them more stable and realistic than ever before. These fast-moving technological advances have also made it possible for generative AI to be used in important areas like forensic science. As the timeline shows, what started as just experimental research has quickly become a valuable tool for accurately restoring damaged or missing forensic evidence.

Table 1. Development of generative AI for image reconstruction.

Ref	Year	Milestone	Key Contribution
(Goodfellow et al., 2017)	**2017**	Introduction of GANs	Ian Goodfellow et al. introduce Generative Adversarial Networks (GANs), revolutionizing generative modeling with the adversarial training concept.
(Kingma & Welling, 2019)	**2019**	VAEs Gain Popularity	Variational Autoencoders (VAEs) become practical for image generation and data compression tasks.
(Ledig et al., 2017)	**2017**	SRGAN	Ledig et al. propose Super-Resolution GAN (SRGAN) for photo-realistic single image super-resolution.
(Karras et al., 2019)	**2018–2019**	StyleGAN	NVIDIA researchers develop StyleGAN and StyleGAN2, enabling high-resolution, controllable face synthesis.
(Ho et al., 2020)	**2020–2021**	Diffusion Models	Denoising Diffusion Probabilistic Models (DDPMs) show state-of-the-art results for image generation, offering more stable training than GANs.
(Yang et al., 2022)	**2022**	Stable Diffusion	Stable Diffusion popularizes accessible, high-quality text-to-image generation, expanding the reach of diffusion models.
(Tortora, 2024)	**2023–Present**	Forensic Applications Emerge	Generative AI is increasingly integrated into forensic workflows for tasks like super-resolution, inpainting, and damaged evidence reconstruction.

2.5 Practical Considerations

For forensic use, choosing the right generative model is really important because it needs to balance high quality, fast performance, and clear results. Variational Autoencoders are good at being fast and learning hidden patterns, but they often make images that aren't very detailed, which can be a problem for forensic work(-Vivekananthan, 2024). On the other hand, Generative Adversarial Networks are great at making very realistic images, but training them is tough because of their competitive setup, which can lead to issues like mode collapse(Wang et al., 2019). Despite requiring substantial computational resources during their training phase, diffusion models deliver exceptional image fidelity and robust training stability, rendering them progressively favoured for demanding generative applications(Korkinof et al., 2018). Diffusion models, while needing a lot of computing power to train, make very high-quality images and train more steadily, so they are becoming more popular for tough generative tasks(Hong et al., 2019) This shows a shift toward models that can consistently produce diverse and high-quality outputs, moving from just copying data to creating new data (Zhang et al., 2023) The development of multimodal models, like GPT-4o, helps combine different types of data more effectively, supporting richer and more context-aware generative processes for forensic analysis (Zhang et al., 2025).

Traditional Enhancement vs. Generative Reconstruction: From CLAHE to GANs

For a long time, forensic imaging has used traditional methods to improve the clarity of images from damaged evidence.. Methodologies such as histogram equalization, unsharp masking, and Contrast Limited Adaptive Histogram Equalization have proven instrumental in clarifying subtle features under suboptimal lighting conditions or in the presence of low image clarity. Nevertheless, these established approaches primarily concentrate on regulating global or local contrast and mitigating noise, rather than reconstructing absent components or rectifying severely impaired regions. Generative Adversarial Networks, on the other hand, mark a big change by learning how real data looks and then creating new, realistic images. This helps in making larger datasets and producing fake forensic evidence when real data is not available(Hirte et al., 2020) (Tayebi & Kafhali, 2025).

CLAHE is commonly used in forensic and medical imaging. It works by breaking an image into small areas called tiles and then adjusting the contrast in each area using a method called local histogram equalization, but it limits how much contrast is increased to avoid making noise too strong. This helps improve the visibility of edges and textures without making the image look worse. For instance, a blurry or dark photo from a crime scene or a low-light CCTV video can become much clearer with CLAHE, making details like tattoos, faces, or license plates easier to see. However, even though CLAHE is good for making images clearer, it doesn't fill in missing parts of the image. That's where generative models come in, as they are made to create new, realistic details that weren't there before(Taylor & Nitschke, 2017) (Xin et al., 2019).

However, traditional enhancement techniques like CLAHE operate only on the existing pixel information — they cannot create plausible visual content where none exists. If a section of an image is blurred beyond recognition, entirely occluded, or physically destroyed, no amount of histogram equalization can recover that missing information. This fundamental difference highlights the complementary roles of traditional methods and generative AI in forensic image analysis: while the former excels at refining existing data, the latter pioneers the reconstruction of lost or unobservable information (Bau et al., 2019).

Generative AI is changing things in a big way. New kinds of AI, like GANs and diffusion models, do more than just make things better—they learn how similar data works and can guess and create missing or broken parts in a realistic way. For example, a GAN can fix up a suspect's face in a video if part of it is hidden or unclear. Another kind of GAN can make low-quality video look clearer by adding details that weren't there to begin with, but were learned from lots of training data. In real use, old methods and new AI models can work together. Often, people use tools like CLAHE to make images clearer before putting them into a generative model. This mix of old and new helps make the results clearer and more realistic. Using both approaches makes the best of what each can do—old methods help with the parts we can see, and AI fills in what's missing. This makes the results more useful for forensic work. The problem still exists even after certain improvements.

Concerns persist regarding the potential for artificial intelligence to generate fabricated evidence and its subsequent misappropriation. Consequently, the establishment of robust regulatory frameworks and stringent oversight mechanisms is imperative to ensure the ethical and appropriate deployment of AI technologiesTraditional tools like Contrast Limited Adaptive Histogram Equalization are still useful for making existing evidence more visible. However, new methods in generative reconstruction are making big progress in forensic science. These new techniques help investigators bring back and understand visual data that was thought to be permanently lost. This is especially important when images are damaged or have been changed on purpose, such as in cases with broken files or altered evidence(Saxena et al., 2023). These improvements are very important because more people are using advanced techniques to alter images, like creating deepfakes. This means we need strong tools that can tell the difference between real images and ones that were made by computers(Sharma et al., 2022).

Figure 2 shows workflow integrating traditional enhancement and generative reconstruction for forensic image processing.

Figure 2. Hybrid forensic image enhancement workflow.

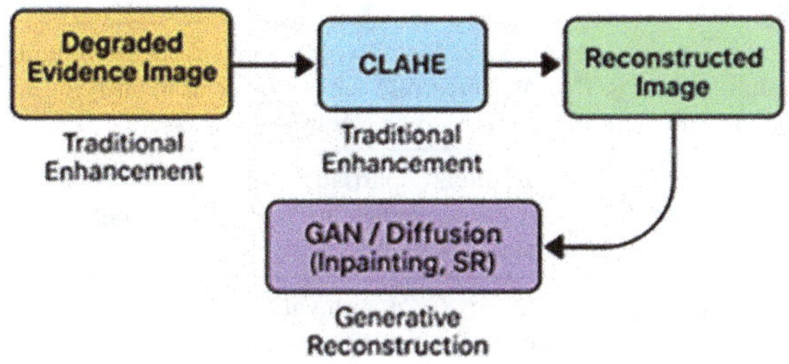

3. FORENSIC IMAGE RECONSTRUCTION: NEEDS AND CHALLENGES

Visual evidence plays a very important role in modern forensic science. It can come from things like surveillance videos that show short-lived events, fingerprints that are not obvious at a crime scene, or unclear license plate numbers from traffic violations. Often, this kind of visual information is key in court cases. But its usefulness can be limited because of problems like poor quality, missing data, or parts of the image being blocked or unclear. An understanding of these inherent limitations therefore illuminates why generative artificial intelligence signifies an emerging frontier for forensic practitioners. The increasing sophistication of digital image manipulation techniques, including the creation of "deepfakes," further underscores the urgent need for advanced forensic tools capable of detecting altered or fabricated visual evidence (Camacho & Wang, 2021).

3.1 Common Issues in Forensic Images

Images encountered in forensic investigations routinely suffer from a range of quality issues that hinder their reliability. These problems may be the result of technological limitations, environmental conditions, or the passage of time. Table 3.1 summarizes the typical challenges that forensic experts must address when working with degraded or incomplete images. This necessitates a rigorous understanding of both the capabilities and limitations of AI tools in forensic applications (Montgomery, 2025).

Table 2. Common Challenges in Forensic Image Evidence

Issue	Description
Low Resolution	Many surveillance systems, especially older or cost-effective models, generate low-resolution footage that obscures fine details. Crucial identifying features such as facial traits or vehicle numbers often appear blurred or pixelated.
Occlusion	Subjects of interest are frequently partially blocked by objects, other individuals, or environmental factors. A suspect's face might be hidden behind a hood or mask, or another person might inadvertently block the view.
Physical Damage	Physical photographs, negatives, or archival footage can deteriorate over time due to tears, scratches, stains, or mold, posing significant challenges for forensic restoration.
Noise and Compression Artifacts	Digital images and videos are often heavily compressed to save storage space, which introduces noise and visible blocky artifacts that degrade clarity.

Each of these issues, on its own or in combination, can reduce the evidential value of visual material, sometimes to the point of rendering it unusable in legal contexts.

3.2 Examples from Real Investigations

These challenges are far from theoretical. Table 3.2 illustrates several real-world scenarios where such image problems commonly arise, emphasizing the practical obstacles faced by forensic practitioners. The pervasive use of advanced software for photo editing and the rise of sophisticated image manipulation techniques, such as image splicing, have further eroded trust in digital images, necessitating robust forensic analysis to differentiate authentic content from fabricated imagery (Vinolin & Sucharitha, 2021).

Table 3. Examples of Degraded or Incomplete Visual Evidence

Scenario	Context and Challenge
CCTV Footage	A burglary suspect recorded by a night-time security camera may appear only as a shadowy Figureure. Poor lighting and limited resolution make it difficult to recover defining facial or clothing details.
Disguised Faces	During protests or criminal activities, individuals often obscure their faces using masks or scarves. While traditional techniques can clarify visible areas, they cannot reconstruct covered parts.
Latent Fingerprints	Smudged or partial fingerprints found at crime scenes frequently require digital enhancement and reconstruction to yield matches against existing fingerprint databases.
Historical Evidence	Cold cases and historical crimes sometimes rely on old photographs or film reels. These are often physically damaged and demand careful digital restoration to retrieve lost details.

These scenarios show how image degradation directly impacts investigations, affecting the clarity, credibility, and legal standing of visual evidence.

3.3 Role of Enhancement in Legal Proceedings

When pictures are shown in court, how clear and trustworthy they are becomes very important. A small blurry part can make people unsure about what they saw, but clear pictures can help confirm what someone said and help identify someone. For many years, forensic labs have used special techniques to make the pictures better. These old methods try to make the existing details in the picture clearer by making the light and dark parts more visible, making the image less blurry, and showing the edges better. But they can't improve the picture beyond what was already there. Now, the use of AI and machine learning is changing things. These new methods can restore and rebuild images in ways that traditional techniques can't, making the evidence much more helpful(Dunsin et al., 2023).

3.4 Overview of Traditional Image Enhancement

Before generative artificial intelligence came into play, forensic image experts used a variety of well-known methods to improve images. Table 3. 3 gives a quick overview of the common techniques and their uses in forensic work. These traditional methods mainly focus on making images clearer without adding new details, which is different from deep learning approaches that can create new information. This difference is important because the ability of deep learning to generate new data raises concerns about whether enhanced images can be trusted and used in court. Because of this, it's necessary to carefully think about the ethics involved and to develop strong checks to make sure AI-enhanced images are reliable in forensic cases.

Table 4. Key Traditional Image Enhancement Techniques

Technique	Purpose and Application
Histogram Equalization	This method works by adjusting the brightness levels of pixels in an image to make the contrast better, which helps to show more details that are hard to see. It is especially helpful when looking at pictures that are too dark or not bright enough.
Contrast Limited Adaptive Histogram Equalization (CLAHE)	CLAHE is an advanced iteration of histogram equalization, this technique is extensively employed within forensic image processing for the purpose of discerning minute features.
Denoising Filters	Methods such as Gaussian blur or median filters help reduce random noise. However, aggressive denoising can sometimes soften important edges and details, which must be balanced carefully in forensic work.
Edge Detection and Sharpening	Algorithms like the Sobel or Canny edge detector highlight boundaries and outlines in an image. These tools can clarify shapes and objects that might otherwise blend into the background.

These methods are still useful in a forensic lab, but they have a key weakness: they can't create believable information that isn't already there. This is exactly the problem that generative AI is built to fix.

3.5 The Unmet Need for Reconstruction

There is a clear difference between older methods used to improve images, which only focus on making existing details sharper or clearer, and the need in forensic work to realistically rebuild missing or badly damaged parts of an image. Generative AI models, trained on large sets of images, can understand patterns and structures well enough to create new, realistic parts of an image that fit naturally. This ability changes what is possible in forensic imaging. Unlike older methods that just tweak existing pixels, generative AI creates new image data that matches the context, which is a big difference from previous image processing methods and helps solve long-standing problems in forensic reconstruction(Zhang et al., 2023).

Even so, the ability to recreate things must be used carefully. The following sections will look into how generative methods function, how they go beyond regular improvements, and how forensic experts can make sure these advanced reconstructions are both scientifically sound and legally acceptable. This change from just making things better to creating new data means we need to closely examine the methods behind these complex reconstructions.

4. TRADITIONAL ENHANCEMENT VS. GENERATIVE RECONSTRUCTION

In forensic image analysis, it's become more important to tell the difference between making what's already there clearer and making up what's missing. For a long time, experts used standard methods to make blurry or bad images easier to see. But when parts of an image are completely gone or hidden, those old methods can't help anymore. Now, new tools from generative AI are helping fill in those missing parts in a way that looks real. While old techniques just improve what's already there, generative AI can create new details, images, and even text by learning from lots of data(Pugliese et al., 2025).

4.1 Traditional Enhancement Techniques

Traditional forensic enhancement methods manipulate the pixel values that already exist in an image. Techniques such as histogram equalization have long been used to improve global contrast by spreading out intensity values more evenly. CLAHE

(Contrast Limited Adaptive Histogram Equalization) refines this approach by adjusting local contrast while suppressing noise amplification, making it especially valuable for images with uneven lighting. Denoising filters are applied to reduce random artifacts, though they must be used carefully to avoid blurring important edges. Edge detection and sharpening algorithms, including the widely used Sobel or Canny filters, help reveal the outlines of objects that might otherwise remain hidden in shadows or low-quality footage. While these methods are indispensable for extracting information from existing data, they cannot extrapolate or invent plausible visual information where none is present, highlighting a critical limitation that modern generative AI seeks to overcome (Edupuganti et al., 2019).

These approaches are straightforward, computationally light, and well established within forensic labs and courtrooms alike. Crucially, they do not create new information; rather, they clarify what is already captured. This transparency makes traditional techniques relatively easy to defend under legal scrutiny. Yet, this same limitation means they can do nothing when an image section is so degraded that no original data remains. A masked face, an illegible license plate, or a torn photograph cannot be recovered through enhancement alone once the physical information is lost. The emergence of deep learning techniques, such as autoencoders and Generative Adversarial Networks, has fundamentally transformed the landscape of image manipulation and synthesis, moving beyond the limitations of traditional methods by enabling the generation of novel, highly realistic visual content (Pashine et al., 2021).

4.2 Generative Reconstruction Methods

In contrast, generative reconstruction represents a significant departure from purely deterministic image processing. Methods such as Generative Adversarial Networks (GANs) and modern diffusion models do not merely sharpen or brighten an image; instead, they learn the statistical patterns of large image datasets and use this knowledge to generate new content that plausibly completes missing or damaged regions. This capability enables these models to reconstruct degraded images by hallucinating details consistent with the learned distribution of real-world imagery, which is a major advancement over traditional methods that struggle with complex, non-identically distributed outliers (Li et al., 2014). Generative Adversarial Networks, for instance, consist of a generator network that creates synthetic images and a discriminator network that distinguishes between real and generated images, continuously refining the generator's output until it is indistinguishable from authentic data (Tucciarelli et al., 2022).

When applied in a forensic setting, generative reconstruction can restore portions of a masked face, upscale a low-resolution CCTV frame to recover potential identifiers, or reconstruct details in a physically damaged photograph that would otherwise be beyond reach. This power to synthesize missing information extends forensic capabilities dramatically but also introduces questions of scientific validity and legal admissibility. If a reconstructed detail does not reflect reality but rather an algorithm's learned guess, there is a risk of misleading investigators, courts, or juries. This inherent capacity for synthesizing novel content raises profound concerns regarding the veracity and interpretability of the generated outputs, especially when considering the potential for overgeneralization or the reconstruction of anomalous regions (Deng et al., 2023).

4.3 Integrated Workflows: Combining CLAHE with Generative AI

Modern workflows don't see traditional enhancement and generative reconstruction as separate methods. Instead, they often use both together in one process. A typical example is using CLAHE to improve local contrast and show details that might be hidden in dark areas or low light. This improved image can then be used as better input for a generative model that does things like filling in missing parts, making images clearer, or reducing noise. Using both methods together gives better results than either one alone: the image keeps the clear parts from traditional methods, while the generative model adds realistic details where there are gaps.

Figure 3 shows the step-by-step process of improving poor-quality forensic images using both traditional techniques and generative AI. The original image first goes through CLAHE to boost local contrast, then traditional filters are used to reduce noise and sharpen edges. After that, the generative AI part helps by repairing damaged areas and increasing image clarity. The final image is much clearer and more complete, making it easier for experts to analyze and use in legal cases. The color-coded steps show how both methods work together in a single forensic process.

Figure 3. Combined Traditional and Generative Forensic Imaging Workflow

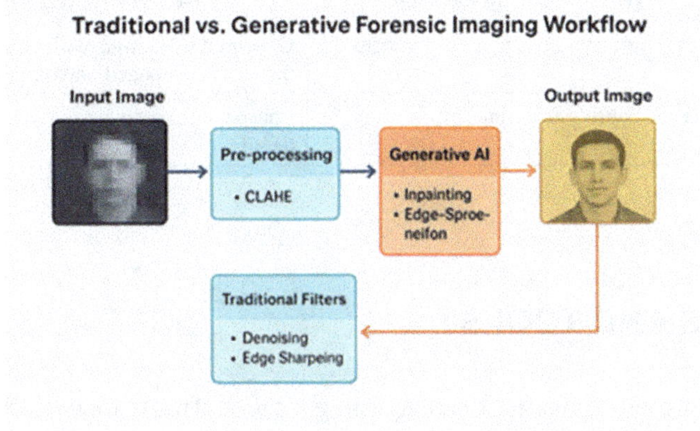

For forensic experts, these mixed methods provide a useful middle ground. The steps that improve the data help make it better while still being clear and open. The part where new images are created goes beyond what the original images could show. But this ability comes with a big responsibility. It's important to keep good records, have experts check the work, and follow strict forensic rules. This makes sure that the final images are both scientifically reliable and morally acceptable.

Comparative Summary

The key aspects of traditional enhancement and generative reconstruction can be summarized as follows.

Table 5. Comparison of Traditional Enhancement and Generative Reconstruction in Forensic Imaging

Aspect	Traditional Enhancement	Generative Reconstruction
Core Principle	Clarifies and adjusts existing pixel data	Synthesizes plausible new data to fill missing or degraded areas
Common Techniques	Histogram Equalization, CLAHE, Denoising, Edge Detection	GAN-based Inpainting, Diffusion-based Denoising, Super-Resolution
Primary Strength	Well understood, transparent, legally accepted	Recovers severely degraded or missing details, extends analytical reach
Limitation	Cannot recreate missing content	Risk of generating artifacts or misleading outputs if unchecked

continued on following page

Table 5. Continued

Aspect	Traditional Enhancement	Generative Reconstruction
Typical Use Cases	Low-contrast, noisy, poorly lit images	Obscured faces, blurred license plates, physically damaged photographs
Combined Use	Serves as pre-processing	Follows enhancement to reconstruct missing details

5. METHODS AND TOOLS

The big improvements in forensic image reconstruction wouldn't have been possible without better practical techniques and strong computational tools. This section talks about the most commonly used generative models for tasks like filling in missing parts of images and making them clearer. It also covers the popular tools that help forensic experts use these models easily. Plus, it looks at some standard model designs that are widely recognized in the field. Knowing these methods and tools helps forensic professionals choose the best techniques for different image reconstruction problems.

5.1 GAN-Based Inpainting and Super-Resolution

Generative Adversarial Networks, or GANs, are now a key tool for creating images. In forensic work, they're mainly used for two things: fixing missing parts of images and making low-quality images clearer. Fixing missing parts means putting back what's hidden or damaged in a way that looks real and fits with the rest of the image. For example, if someone's face is covered by a mask in a photo, a GAN trained on lots of facial images can guess what the face might look like. This doesn't recreate the exact real face, but it makes it look like something that would fit with how faces usually look in similar images.

For making low-quality images clearer, GANs help improve images that are blurry or pixelated.

Many surveillance cameras take pictures at low resolution to save space, which makes the images look grainy. GANs like SRGAN can make these images sharper by adding fine details that regular methods can't. These details are learned from real images, so they look natural and realistic.

Using GANs needs care to make sure the results are believable and reliable.

The generated images should be checked carefully to avoid misleading investigators or courts. That's why GANs work best when used in a clear process, where every step is well-documented and checked by experts.

5.2 Diffusion Models for Denoising and Reconstruction

In recent years, diffusion models have become another strong method for creating and fixing images. Unlike GANs, which use a competition between two parts—one that makes images and one that tries to spot fake images—diffusion models slowly turn random noise into clear images through many small steps. This method works well for tasks like removing noise and filling in missing parts of images, producing very realistic results.

One big advantage of diffusion models is that they can create detailed images with fewer mistakes compared to older methods. For use in forensic imaging, this means that bad or unclear images—like dark crime scene photos or old security videos—can be cleaned up and made clearer with great visual quality. Models like Stable Diffusion show how useful this technique can be, and scientists are still working to improve these tools for forensic uses where the results need to be very trustworthy.

5.3 Popular Frameworks and Open-Source Tools

Practical use of these advanced methods depends on easy-to-use frameworks and well-supported tools. Many forensic labs and research teams use popular machine learning libraries like TensorFlow and PyTorch to build custom or already trained GANs and diffusion models. Open-source tools like OpenCV are still important for preparing images, doing tasks like CLAHE, noise reduction, and histogram equalization, which help before image generation. These tools also help in making special types of models that fit the specific needs of forensic work, ensuring efficient computation and strict following of legal standards for evidence. Using these tools lets people keep improving their reconstruction methods, helping create better tools for forensic professionals.

Some specific models, such as SRGAN for making images clearer, DeepFill for filling in missing parts, and different versions of Stable Diffusion, are often shared in public online spaces.

This sharing of code helps make the process clear and repeatable, which is very important in forensic work where every step of the process must be checked carefully in court. By using models that have been studied a lot and code that is freely available, experts can avoid unexpected or hard-to-explain results.

5.4 Example Architectures and Pipelines

To show how these tools work together, imagine a common process used in forensic image reconstruction. An image taken from a security camera is often unclear because of poor lighting and low quality.

In first stage improve the contrast using CLAHE. Next noise reduction step in which apply filters. In this step eliminate grainy or pixelated parts of an image. Then image input to trained GAN model or diffusion model to either fill in missing parts or make the image clearer. Once the model has processed the image, a human expert checks the output. They compare the improved image. This process is repeated as needed to ensure the image is accurate and reliable for investigation. Combining traditional methods with modern generative models, this approach shows the real-world advantages of using both together.

6. CASE STUDIES

The idea of using generative AI for reconstructing images in forensics sounds promising on paper, but it's how these methods are used in real situations that shows their true worth. By looking at carefully chosen cases, we can see both what these modern tools can do and where they fall short. These examples show how mixing old image enhancement techniques with new generative models can help uncover evidence that might have been missed before. This section includes four key examples that show how these approaches are useful in real life. For example, deep learning has gone far beyond traditional methods in image forensics, making it much better at finding fake images(Shi et al., 2023). This advancement is particularly evident in the detection of AI-generated content, where sophisticated models are developed to identify subtle artifacts indicative of synthetic origin (Haoxuan et al., 2025).

6.1 License Plate Enhancement

One of the most common situations in forensic imaging is when cameras capture license plates that are not clear. These cameras are often placed on roads, highways, and building entrances, and they record vehicles moving quickly, especially at night or in bad weather. Because of this, the images may be blurry, noisy, or too dark to see clearly.

In the usual process, the first step is to prepare the video footage by adjusting brightness and reducing noise.

A technique called CLAHE might be used to improve the visibility of faint numbers on the plate. If the plate is still hard to read because of poor quality, a special type of computer model called a super-resolution GAN, like SRGAN, can be used to create a clearer, higher-quality image. Investigators then compare this improved image with standard license plate formats and check it against official vehicle registration records. While these models don't always perfectly restore every character, they often make the plate readable enough to find possible matches, which helps in further investigations. These models have proven very helpful in making blurry license plates clearer, making it easier to process images and improving traffic safety and automated systems (Lin et al., 2021). This capability is crucial for intelligent transportation systems and urban security, despite challenges posed by diverse plate characteristics, poor image quality from skewed angles or uneven lighting, and the need for rapid processing (Yang & Wang, 2019).

6.2 Facial Image Reconstruction from Masked Faces

When people on purpose hide their faces, it becomes really hard to identify them. In situations like riots, protests, or crimes happening in public, suspects often wear masks, scarves, or other items to cover their faces. Regular methods to improve images might help with the parts that are visible, but the covered areas need more advanced techniques to Figureure out. In one study, images of partially covered faces from CCTV cameras were processed using a mix of techniques. First, the visible parts were made clearer using CLAHE to boost contrast, especially when lighting was bad. Then, a type of AI called a GAN, like DeepFill, was used to guess what the hidden parts of the face might look like. However, this result wasn't taken as proof of identity. Instead, it helped police look for similar images in databases or public records. Importantly, the face created by AI was clearly labeled as an approximation, and any decisions were made based on other evidence, not just the AI-generated image.

6.3 Fingerprint Recovery

Latent fingerprints found at a crime scene are often not clear or may be smudged because of the surface they're on, other substances, or poor lifting techniques. In these cases, digital tools are still very important for getting the most out of the fingerprint details. A usual process in forensics might begin with filters that reduce background noise, helping to clean up the image, and then using edge detection to highlight the ridges in the fingerprint. Advanced deep learning models, especially those that use convolutional neural networks, have been helpful in rebuilding partial or damaged fingerprints by learning from a large amount of fingerprint data. This ability is especially useful in forensic analysis, allowing for more accurate matches with fingerprints stored in a database. Even though the reconstructed image is artificially made, it serves as an important clue for investigators, helping them search the database more thoroughly and compare the print to suspect fingerprints, always keeping in mind that it was created by a computer to preserve the evidence's reliability. This method highlights the need for human experts to review AI-generated evidence, ensuring that computer results support, rather than replace, traditional forensic methods.When parts of a fingerprint are missing or hidden, scientists have tried using generative methods to create realistic continuations of the ridges or example, a GAN trained on many high-quality fingerprints can fill in small gaps in unclear prints. This helps make more complete templates that can be checked against existing databases. However, any parts that are created are carefully labeled and examined with care to prevent relying too much on the computer-generated features. The final decision always comes from a trained fingerprint expert who checks the match's consistency and accuracy. This careful approach helps keep legal evidence trustworthy and shows the importance of human judgment in interpreting AI-created content. This is especially important because current DeepFake techniques have trouble with small details like skin texture or facial hair due to lost information during processing, and GANs might help fix this by recovering missing details. (Lyu, 2020).

6.4 Historical Evidence Restoration

Cold cases and old investigations often use old photos or videos that have gotten damaged over time. Problems like tears, stains, fading, or mold can make it hard to see important details. In one example, an old crime scene photo was scanned and fixed using both regular and new methods. First, they cleaned the photo digitally and adjusted the colors to make it look better. For more serious damage, they used a special kind of AI called a GAN to guess what was missing. This AI looked at the rest of the image to make sure the missing parts matched, which helped show details that were hidden before. But there's a problem: the realistic look of the AI-created images can make it hard to tell if something is real or fake, because the difference between real and fake images is getting smaller(Verdoliva, 2020).

The first step was using CLAHE to fix uneven lighting and improve contrast. Parts of the image that were damaged were repaired using models based on GANs or diffusion methods. This restoration gave investigators and historians more clear details, like better views of objects, clothes, or surroundings that weren't visible or were blurry before. Since these methods are creative, it's important to clearly mark the original parts from the added ones to stay honest and accurate. This makes it harder to tell what's real and what's made up, which is why advanced forensic tools are needed to spot fake images, especially as deepfake technology gets better(Abbasi et al., 2025).

6.5 Technical Approach and Outcomes

In all the case studies shown, there's a clear pattern in how the technical work is done: the best forensic image reconstructions use careful preparation, focused generative techniques, and strict testing. Every process starts by improving the original image using standard methods like CLAHE to adjust contrast or filters to remove background noise. These steps help make sure the image is as clear as possible before using any generative tools. Then, specific generative models, often deep learning systems like GANs, are used to fix certain issues, such as making low-detail images clearer, filling in missing parts, or restoring the overall look of the image(Creswell et al., 2018; Zhao et al., 2020).

Once the generative model has performed its task—whether inpainting masked regions of a face, restoring missing fingerprint ridges, or upscaling a blurred license plate—the results must be evaluated. This evaluation relies on both expert visual assessment and quantitative quality measures. When a suitable reference image is available, the similarity between the reconstructed output IR and the ground truth IGT can be measured using the Mean Squared Error (MSE):

$$MSE = \frac{1}{MN}\sum_{i=1}^{M}\sum_{j=1}^{N}\left[I_R(i,j) - I_{GT}(i.j)\right]^2$$

where M and N represent the image's dimensions. A lower MSE indicates that the reconstruction closely resembles the original, undamaged version.

To complement this, the Peak Signal-to-Noise Ratio (PSNR) is also used, converting the MSE into a decibel (dB) scale that is easier to interpret:

$$PSNR = 10.LOG_{10}\left(\frac{MAX_I^2}{MSE}\right)$$

7. VALIDATION AND LEGAL ADMISSIBILITY

No matter how advanced a forensic reconstruction technique may be, its true value is ultimately determined by its scientific credibility and its acceptance in a court of law. Generative AI methods offer extraordinary capabilities for recovering plausible details from degraded images, but these same capabilities bring unique challenges. Courts demand that evidence be not only technically sound but also transparent and reproducible. Any output that cannot be verified, or that introduces elements that did not originally exist, must be handled with the utmost caution.

One of the most significant issues is the possibility of *hallucinated content*—details invented by the model that appear realistic but have no basis in the original data. While this can make an image look complete, it risks misleading investigators, legal professionals, and juries if not properly labeled and explained. For this reason, experts must document each step of the generative reconstruction process, including which parts of an image have been generated versus simply enhanced.

Standards such as the *Daubert Standard* in the United States, or equivalent scientific evidence guidelines in other jurisdictions, require that forensic methods demonstrate testability, peer review, known error rates, and general acceptance in the relevant scientific community. Forensic labs must therefore treat generative models with the same rigor applied to traditional enhancement methods. Models should be validated on representative test cases, and the results should be reproducible by independent experts using the same input data and documented processes. The verifiability of generative AI outputs, especially in non-deterministic environments, is critical for ensuring trust and transparency in forensic applications, necessitating rigorous testing against artificially generated data samples to assess reproducibility and correctness (Kim et al., 2023).

Human oversight remains indispensable. A generative model may suggest multiple plausible ways to complete a missing region, but the forensic expert must interpret these results within the context of the full body of evidence. No generative output should stand alone as proof. When presented in court, reconstructions should include clear disclosures about how they were produced, what uncertainties remain, and whether they are offered as demonstrative aids rather than primary evidence.

In practice, many forensic institutions are developing standard operating procedures (SOPs) that define how and when generative AI can be used responsibly. These SOPs typically specify requirements for version control, metadata retention, documentation of training datasets, and review by qualified examiners. They also guide how to communicate the strengths and limitations of reconstructions to judges, lawyers, and juries who may not be familiar with the underlying technology. This emphasis on responsible deployment extends to the development of robust content moderation strategies and clear identification of generated content to prevent the spread of misinformation and ensure ethical use of AI technologies (Hao et al., 2023) (Gu, 2024).

Table 6. Key Requirements for Admissible Forensic Generative Reconstructions

Criterion	Key Focus	Example
Testability	Reproducible output	Same input → same output, any lab
Peer Review	Published, scrutinized	Described in peer-reviewed papers
Error Rates	Known limitations	False positive/negative rates reported
Chain of Custody	Full process traceability	Input data, model version, steps logged
Expert Oversight	Human verification	Final review by certified examiner

8. ETHICAL CONSIDERATIONS

Generative AI has strong abilities in reconstructing images for forensic use, which can be very helpful. However, it also raises important ethical issues that need careful handling and proper rules. One big worry is keeping personal information private. When AI is used to recreate faces, fingerprints, or license plates, it works with very private data. This type of data needs to follow privacy laws and ethical rules. Because of this, many places ask for a Data Protection Impact Assessment (DPIA) before using AI tools that deal with personal data in a forensic setting. A DPIA helps find possible privacy problems and makes sure there are good steps in place to stop misuse or leaks of information. Another important problem is how AI-generated images might be used wrongly.

While these images can help restore missing or broken parts of evidence, they can also be used to make fake images or scenes. For this reason, forensic experts need to clearly show which parts of an image were made by AI. Judges and investigators must know when an image includes AI-generated parts so they understand its limits and use it only to help human judgment. It's also a big concern how easy it is to tell real images from AI-made ones. This makes it harder to trust evidence in schools and courts, especially when the line between real and fake is getting blurrier (Francis et al., 2025). Bias in generative models is an important ethical issue. If the training data mainly includes information from certain groups of people, it can lead to mistakes in rebuilding images, especially when fixing faces. Doing a Bias Impact Assessment helps experts check if their models have been tested on data that represents different groups. This helps prevent unfair treatment in investigations or court cases. These assessments are meant to find and fix any unfair patterns in the algorithms that might continue unfair treatment in the legal system(Montgomery, 2025). Unfair or biased AI systems, particularly those that generate synthetic media, can lead to skewed outcomes and perpetuate existing inequalities, including generative biases that affect the representation of individuals in synthetic data (Ferrara, 2023). Finally, privacy and ethical governance must extend beyond the technical level to professional practice. Standard operating procedures increasingly require that practitioners demonstrate compliance with relevant privacy laws, maintain robust chain-of-custody records for all digital evidence, and ensure that any AI-enhanced reconstructions remain reproducible by qualified independent examiners. These measures strengthen public trust and ensure that forensic science benefits from generative AI without undermining the fairness and transparency that legal systems demand. This challenge is exacerbated by the emergent issue of generative AI bias, where models reproduce and amplify societal stereotypes through the content they create, impacting public perception and potentially reinforcing harmful biases (Ferrara, 2023). By embedding safeguards such as the DPIA and BIA into everyday forensic workflows, institutions can ensure that privacy, fairness, and transparency remain central pillars of modern digital forensics. Used responsibly and transparently, generative AI stands to enhance investigations while upholding the highest ethical standards. It is crucial to recognize that the unique attributes of generative AI, such as its general-purpose nature and reliance on massive datasets, necessitate a re-evaluation of existing legal paradigms, as curr By including tools like the DPIA and BIA in everyday forensic work, organizations can make sure that privacy, fairness, and transparency are key parts of modern digital forensics. When used in a clear and honest way, generative AI can help with investigations while keeping strong ethical standards. It's important to understand that the special features of generative AI, such as its ability to work on many different tasks and its need for large amounts of data, mean that current laws might not be enough and need to be reviewed(Atkinson & Morrison, 2024).

Figure 4 illustrates the layered ethical safeguards required when applying generative AI in forensic imaging. The central role of *Forensic Generative AI* is surrounded by five critical support areas: Privacy, Bias Mitigation, Transparency, Human Oversight, and Legal Compliance. Together, these pillars ensure responsible, fair, and trustworthy deployment in sensitive legal contexts.

Figure 4. Core ethical pillars supporting forensic generative AI use in practice.

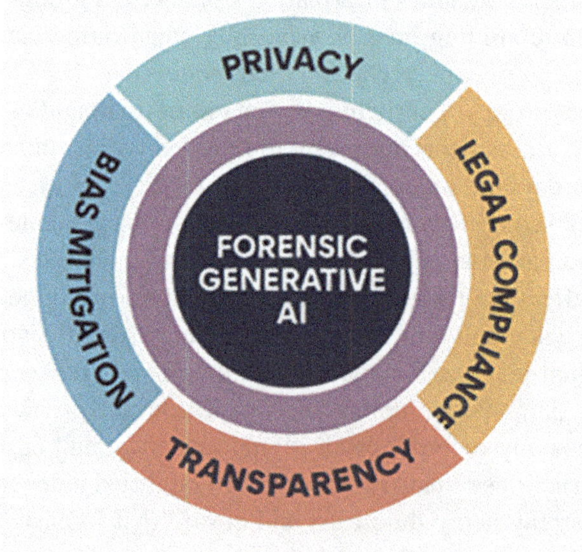

9. FUTURE DIRECTIONS

The rapid progress in generative AI has already begun to reshape forensic image reconstruction, but its full potential is far from exhausted. Looking ahead, the next wave of developments is likely to focus on making these tools more explainable, more transparent, and more accessible to frontline investigators and legal professionals. One key area of future research involves the development of novel methods for verifying the authenticity and reliability of generative AI outputs, especially given the growing concerns about misinformation and the potential for inaccurate decision-making (Tang et al., 2023). Such advancements are critical to address the inherent challenges of interpretability and accountability associated with complex AI models, particularly in high-stakes applications like forensic analysis (Remolina & Osa, 2024).

One important direction is the improvement of explainability in generative models. Today's GANs and diffusion models can produce visually convincing results, but they often remain "black boxes" with limited insight into how specific outputs are generated. Explainable AI (XAI) is growing technique that show which parts of an image have been reconstructed. Also, which training data influenced the output. Including level of confidence, the model assigns to each region. Such explainability tools can help forensic experts. This enhancing trust and meeting the evidentiary standards required by legal systems. The development of novel evaluation metrics tailored specifically for generative forensic outputs, moving beyond conventional image quality assessments to quantitative measures of authenticity and integrity. Another crucial area is the development of robust regulatory frameworks and ethical guidelines tailored specifically for the application of generative AI in forensic science, addressing concerns around data privacy, algorithmic bias, and accountability (Okonji et al., 2024).

The development of real-time generative reconstruction tools that can be used directly in the field. For example, portable forensic kits equipped with embedded AI chips could allow investigators to perform basic inpainting or resolution enhancement on-site, providing immediate leads in situations where waiting for lab processing might risk losing critical evidence. Advances in hardware and optimized lightweight models will be essential to make these capabilities both fast and reliable under real-world conditions. The integration of generative AI within broader forensic workflows, such as automated evidence processing and cross-referencing with forensic databases, represents a significant area for future exploration, streamlining investigative processes and enhancing the efficiency of digital forensics. These models, increasingly capable for producing high-quality artistic and realistic media, raise significant implications for various sectors, including the creative industries and legal domains (Epstein et al., 2023).

In parallel, emerging technologies such as augmented reality (AR) and virtual reality (VR) are beginning to find their place in forensic work. By integrating generative reconstructions into AR/VR environments, investigators could examine crime scenes with enhanced visual context, overlaying reconstructed elements directly onto degraded images or videos. This could help clarify ambiguous evidence and improve situational awareness during complex investigations or courtroom presentations. These immersive technologies, coupled with advancements in 3D sensor technology capable of capturing detailed crime scene scans, are already revolutionizing forensic science and crime scene analysis (Maneli & Isafiade, 2022).

Another future priority is the professional training and policy development needed to ensure that the benefits of generative AI are matched by robust safeguards. As these technologies become more advanced, forensic labs will need clear protocols for validating new models, handling AI-generated content, and communicating its limitations to judges, juries, and the public. Continuous training for forensic practitioners will be essential so that experts remain confident and competent in evaluating both the potential and the risks of AI-driven reconstruction. Additionally, the broader application of artificial intelligence in forensic medicine and toxicology promises to revolutionize traditional investigative methods, overcoming existing limitations and enhancing precision across various procedures, from sample collection to time-since-death calculations (Wankhade et al., 2022).

Future work based on standardization and interoperability. Many jurisdictions adopt generative AI workflows, harmonized standards for documentation, validation, and ethical governance will be vital. International collaboration between forensic scientists, legal experts, and AI researchers will help ensure that these tools serve the pursuit of truth and justice, rather than introduce new avenues for error or misuse. With careful innovation and responsible oversight, tomorrow's methods will not only push the technical boundaries of what is possible but also reinforce the scientific rigor and public trust that define credible forensic practice. One area ripe for advancement is the integration of AI-driven tools with existing forensic information systems, enabling seamless data exchange and automated processing of digital evidence (Dunsin et al., 2024).

10. CONCLUSION

In the end, the value of any forensic tool lies in how well it serves the pursuit of truth and justice. Generative AI has opened doors that, only a decade ago, would have seemed out of reach: damaged or incomplete images can now be recovered in ways that traditional enhancement alone could not achieve. But this power comes with a responsibility that forensic scientists and legal professionals cannot ignore.

As this chapter has shown, the best results come from combining the old and the new — using proven methods like CLAHE and careful pre-processing alongside cutting-edge generative models for inpainting and super-resolution. This hybrid approach makes it possible to salvage vital details from poor-quality evidence while keeping each step transparent and reproducible. Yet technology, on its own, cannot guarantee fairness. Human oversight, clear validation, ethical safeguards, and a deep understanding of the limits of AI-generated images are all crucial if these reconstructions are to be trusted inside and outside the courtroom. For every big new discovery, there needs to be clear rules, open sharing of information, and experts who can explain not just what the AI made, but how it made it — and what that means for the actual case being looked at.In real life, the real power of these methods is that they support, not replace, the skills and experience of forensic experts.AI can help fill in missing parts, make blurry images clearer, and show patterns that were hidden before. But only human experts can decide if a picture really shows what happened or if it might be misleading. The mix of machine speed and human judgment will probably shape the future of forensic imaging for a long time.Most importantly, the challenge is to make sure these new tools are not only cool to look at but also used with honesty.

Generative AI should never be used as an excuse to skip important steps or make weak evidence seem strong. Instead, it should be used with the same care and scientific care that has always been part of real forensic work. If this balance is kept, these developments will not just fix old problems — they will help make sure justice is fair, especially when the truth depends on having the clearest possible picture.In the years to come, courts, police, and forensic labs are going to need to work more closely with tech experts and AI researchers.New rules, training, and certifications are going to come up to help professionals understand what generative AI can do and, just as importantly, what it can't. As more cases use AI-enhanced or AI-made pictures, it will be very important to explain the limits and uncertainties clearly to judges, juries, and the public.Equally important will be keeping up with research that makes AI models better, more explainable, and fairer for use in forensics.Being able to check AI results, track how a picture was made, and be open about how well the model works will be key to gaining and keeping public trust. Forensic experts will play an important role in helping these technologies grow, making sure the main goal of their field — finding the truth — stays at the center of every new idea.In this way, generative AI, when used carefully and thoughtfully, can become not just another tool, but a new standard that makes modern forensic science stronger and helps solve difficult cases fairly for years to come.

REFERENCES

Abbasi, M., Váz, P., Silva, J., & Martins, P. (2025). Comprehensive Evaluation of Deepfake Detection Models: Accuracy, Generalization, and Resilience to Adversarial Attacks. *Applied Sciences (Basel, Switzerland)*, *15*(3), 1225. DOI: 10.3390/app15031225

Al-kfairy, M., Mustafa, D., Kshetri, N., Insiew, M., & Alfandi, O. (2024). Ethical Challenges and Solutions of Generative AI: An Interdisciplinary Perspective. *Informatics (MDPI)*, *11*(3), 58. DOI: 10.3390/informatics11030058

Amerini, I., Barni, M., Battiato, S., Bestagini, P., Boato, G., Bonaventura, T. S., Bruni, V., Caldelli, R., Natale, F. G. B. D., Nicola, R. D., Guarnera, L., Mandelli, S., Marcialis, G. L., Micheletto, M., Montibeller, A., Orrù, G., Ortis, A., Perazzo, P., Salvi, D., . . . Vitulano, D. (2024). Deepfake Media Forensics: State of the Art and Challenges Ahead. arXiv (Cornell University). https://doi.org//arxiv.2408.00388DOI: 10.48550

Atkinson, D., & Morrison, J. (2024). Unsettled Law: Time to Generate New Approaches? arXiv (Cornell University). https://doi.org//arxiv.2407.01968DOI: 10.48550

Baig, M. I., & Yadegaridehkordi, E. (2025). Factors influencing academic staff satisfaction and continuous usage of generative artificial intelligence (GenAI) in higher education. *International Journal of Educational Technology in Higher Education*, *22*(1). Advance online publication. DOI: 10.1186/s41239-025-00506-4

Bau, D., Zhu, J.-Y., Wulff, J., Peebles, W., Zhou, B., Strobelt, H., & Torralba, A. (2019). Seeing What a GAN Cannot Generate. *2021 IEEE/CVF International Conference on Computer Vision (ICCV)*, 4501. https://doi.org/DOI: 10.1109/iccv.2019.00460

Camacho, I. C., & Wang, K. (2021). A Comprehensive Review of Deep-Learning-Based Methods for Image Forensics [Review of A Comprehensive Review of Deep-Learning-Based Methods for Image Forensics]. Journal of Imaging, 7(4), 69. Multidisciplinary Digital Publishing Institute. https://doi.org/DOI: 10.3390/jimaging7040069

Chakraborty, S. (2024). Generative AI in Modern Education Society. arXiv (Cornell University). https://doi.org//arxiv.2412.08666DOI: 10.48550

Chen, J.-F., Ni, C.-C., Lin, P.-H., & Lin, R. (2024). Designing the Future: A Case Study on Human-AI Co-Innovation. *Creative Education*, *15*(3), 474. DOI: 10.4236/ce.2024.153028

Corvi, R., Cozzolino, D., Prashnani, E., De Mello, S., Nagano, K., & Verdoliva, L. (2025). Seeing What Matters: Generalizable AI-generated Video Detection with Forensic-Oriented Augmentation. https://doi.org/DOI: 10.48550/ARXIV.2506.16802

Creswell, A., White, T., Dumoulin, V., Arulkumaran, K., Sengupta, B., & Bharath, A. A. (2018). Generative Adversarial Networks: An Overview. *IEEE Signal Processing Magazine*, *35*(1), 53. DOI: 10.1109/msp.2017.2765202

Das, A., & Balakrishnan, S. G., & Pramod. (2021). Network Intrusion Detection System based on Generative Adversarial Network for Attack Detection. *International Journal of Advanced Computer Science and Applications*, *12*(11). Advance online publication. DOI: 10.14569/ijacsa.2021.0121186

Deng, S., Sun, Z., Zhuang, R., & Gong, J. (2023). Noise-to-Norm Reconstruction for Industrial Anomaly Detection and Localization. *Applied Sciences (Basel, Switzerland)*, *13*(22), 12436. DOI: 10.3390/app132212436

Dunsin, D., Ghanem, M. C., Ouazzane, K., & Vassilev, V. (2023). A Comprehensive Analysis of the Role of Artificial Intelligence and Machine Learning in Modern Digital Forensics and Incident Response. arXiv (Cornell University). https://doi .org//arxiv.2309.07064DOI: 10.48550

Dunsin, D., Ghanem, M. C., Ouazzane, K., & Vassilev, V. (2024). A comprehensive analysis of the role of artificial intelligence and machine learning in modern digital forensics and incident response. *Forensic Science International Digital Investigation*, *48*, 301675. DOI: 10.1016/j.fsidi.2023.301675

Edupuganti, V., Mardani, M., Cheng, J. Y., Vasanawala, S., & Pauly, J. M. (2019). VAE-GANs for Probabilistic Compressive Image Recovery: Uncertainty Analysis. arXiv (Cornell University). https://arxiv.org/pdf/1901.11228.pdf

Epstein, Z., Hertzmann, A., Akten, M., Farid, H., Fjeld, J., Frank, M. R., Groh, M., Herman, L., Leach, N., Mahari, R., Pentland, A., Russakovsky, O., Schroeder, H., & Smith, A. (2023). Art and the science of generative AI. *Science*, *380*(6650), 1110. DOI: 10.1126/science.adh4451 PMID: 37319193

Farber, S. (2025). AI as a decision support tool in forensic image analysis: A pilot study on integrating large language models into crime scene investigation workflows. *Journal of Forensic Sciences*. Advance online publication. DOI: 10.1111/1556-4029.70035 PMID: 40186399

Ferrara, E. (2023). Fairness And Bias in Artificial Intelligence: A Brief Survey of Sources, Impacts, And Mitigation Strategies. arXiv (Cornell University). https:// doi.org//arxiv.2304.07683DOI: 10.48550

Francis, N. J., Jones, S., & Smith, D. P. (2025). Generative AI in Higher Education: Balancing Innovation and Integrity [Review of Generative AI in Higher Education: Balancing Innovation and Integrity]. British Journal of Biomedical Science, 81. Taylor & Francis. https://doi.org/DOI: 10.3389/bjbs.2024.14048

Goodfellow, I., Pouget-Abadie, J., Mirza, M., Xu, B., Warde-Farley, D., Ozair, S., Courville, A., & Bengio, Y. (2017). GAN(Generative Adversarial Nets). *Journal of Japan Society for Fuzzy Theory and Intelligent Informatics*, *29*(5), 177. DOI: 10.3156/jsoft.29.5_177_2

Goodfellow, I., Pouget-Abadie, J., Mirza, M., Xu, B., Warde-Farley, D., Ozair, S., Courville, A., & Bengio, Y. (2020). Generative adversarial networks. *Communications of the ACM*, *63*(11), 139. DOI: 10.1145/3422622

Gozalo-Brizuela, R., & Merchan, E. E. G. (2024). A Survey of Generative AI Applications. *Journal of Computational Science*, *20*(8), 801. DOI: 10.3844/jcssp.2024.801.818

Gu, J. (2024). Responsible Generative AI: What to Generate and What Not. arXiv (Cornell University). https://doi.org//arxiv.2404.05783DOI: 10.48550

Hao, S., Kumar, P., Laszlo, S., Poddar, S., Radharapu, B., & Shelby, R. (2023). Safety and Fairness for Content Moderation in Generative Models. arXiv (Cornell University). https://doi.org//arxiv.2306.06135DOI: 10.48550

Haoxuan, S., Yan, H., Jiahui, Z., Haoxing, C., Jun, L., Huijia, Z., Weiqiang, W., Liqing, Z., & Jianfu, Z. (2025). Robustness in AI-Generated Detection: Enhancing Resistance to Adversarial Attacks. https://doi.org/DOI: 10.48550/ARXIV.2505.03435

He, C., Shen, Y., Fang, A. C., Xiao, F., Tang, L., Zhang, Y., Zuo, W., Guo, Z., & Li, X. (2024). Diffusion Models in Low-Level Vision: A Survey. arXiv (Cornell University). https://doi.org//arxiv.2406.11138DOI: 10.48550

Hirte, A. U., Platscher, M., Joyce, T. A., Heit, J. J., Tranvinh, E., & Federau, C. (2020). Diffusion-Weighted Magnetic Resonance Brain Images Generation with Generative Adversarial Networks and Variational Autoencoders: A Comparison Study. arXiv (Cornell University). https://doi.org//arxiv.2006.13944DOI: 10.48550

Ho, J., Jain, A. N., & Abbeel, P. (2020). Denoising Diffusion Probabilistic Models. arXiv (Cornell University). https://doi.org//arxiv.2006.11239DOI: 10.48550

Hong, Y., Hwang, U., Yoo, J., & Yoon, S. (2019). How Generative Adversarial Networks and Their Variants Work [Review of How Generative Adversarial Networks and Their Variants Work]. ACM Computing Surveys, 52(1), 1. Association for Computing Machinery. https://doi.org/DOI: 10.1145/3301282

Hsu, C., Lee, C., & Zhuang, Y.-X. (2018). Learning to Detect Fake Face Images in the Wild. https://doi.org/DOI: 10.1109/is3c.2018.00104

Karras, T., Laine, S., Aittala, M., Hellsten, J., Lehtinen, J., & Aila, T. (2019). Analyzing and Improving the Image Quality of StyleGAN. arXiv (Cornell University). https://doi.org//arXiv.1912.04958DOI: 10.48550

Kim, E., Isozaki, I., Sirkin, N., & Robson, M. (2023). Generative Artificial Intelligence Consensus in a Trustless Network. arXiv (Cornell University). https://doi.org//arxiv.2307.01898DOI: 10.48550

Kingma, D. P., & Welling, M. (2019). An Introduction to Variational Autoencoders. Foundations and Trends® in Machine Learning, 12(4), 307. https://doi.org/DOI: 10.1561/2200000056

Kong, X., Brekelmans, R., & Steeg, G. V. (2023). Information-Theoretic Diffusion. arXiv (Cornell University). https://doi.org//arxiv.2302.03792DOI: 10.48550

Korkinof, D., Rijken, T., O'Neill, M., Yearsley, J., Harvey, H., & Glocker, B. (2018). High-Resolution Mammogram Synthesis using Progressive Generative Adversarial Networks. arXiv (Cornell University). https://arxiv.org/pdf/1807.03401

Krubha, Y. S., Hou, A., Vester, B., Walker, W., Wang, X., Lin, L., & Hu, S. (2025). Robust AI-Generated Face Detection with Imbalanced Data. https://doi.org/DOI: 10.48550/ARXIV.2505.02182

Kwon, D. (2024). AI-generated images threaten science — Here's how researchers hope to spot them. *Nature*, *635*(8038), 268. DOI: 10.1038/d41586-024-03542-8 PMID: 39501086

Lamichhane, D. (2024). Advanced Detection of AI-Generated Images Through Vision Transformers. https://doi.org/DOI: 10.36227/techrxiv.172556912.28757771/v1

Le, B. M., Tariq, S., Abuadbba, A., Moore, K., & Woo, S. S. (2023). Why Do Facial Deepfake Detectors Fail? arXiv (Cornell University). https://doi.org//arxiv.2302.13156DOI: 10.48550

Ledig, C., Theis, L., Huszár, F., Caballero, J., Cunningham, A., Acosta, A., Aitken, A. P., Tejani, A., Totz, J., Wang, Z., & Shi, W. (2017).. . *Photo-Realistic Single Image Super-Resolution Using a Generative Adversarial Network.*, *105*. Advance online publication. DOI: 10.1109/cvpr.2017.19

Lee, H., Lee, C., Farhat, K., Lin, Q., Geluso, S., Kim, A., & Etzioni, O. (2024). The Tug-of-War Between Deepfake Generation and Detection. arXiv (Cornell University). https://doi.org//arxiv.2407.06174DOI: 10.48550

Li, X., Ren, J., Liu, C., & Jia, J. (2014). Deep Convolutional Neural Network for Image Deconvolution. Neural Information Processing Systems, 27, 1790. https://papers.nips.cc/paper/5485-deep-convolutional-neural-network-for-image-deconvolution.pdf

Lin, M., Liu, L., Wang, F., Li, J., & Pan, J. (2021). License Plate Image Reconstruction Based on Generative Adversarial Networks. *Remote Sensing*, *13*(15), 3018. DOI: 10.3390/rs13153018

Lyu, S. (2020). DeepFake Detection: Current Challenges and Next Steps. arXiv (Cornell University). https://doi.org//arxiv.2003.09234DOI: 10.48550

Mahara, A., & Rishe, N. (2025). Methods and Trends in Detecting Generated Images: A Comprehensive Review. https://doi.org/DOI: 10.48550/ARXIV.2502.15176

Mai, W. Y., Zhang, J., Fang, P., & Zhang, Z. (2024). Brain-Conditional Multimodal Synthesis: A Survey and Taxonomy. *IEEE Transactions on Artificial Intelligence*, *6*(5), 1080. DOI: 10.1109/tai.2024.3516698

Mandayam, R. (2024)... *The Impact of Artificial Intelligence on Digital Forensic.*, *3*(6), 1. DOI: 10.47363/jaicc/2024(3)414

Maneli, M. A., & Isafiade, O. (2022). 3D Forensic Crime Scene Reconstruction Involving Immersive Technology: A Systematic Literature Review. *IEEE Access : Practical Innovations, Open Solutions*, *10*, 88821. DOI: 10.1109/access.2022.3199437

Mathys, M., Willi, M., Graber, M., & Meier, R. (2024). Synthetic Image Generation in Cyber Influence Operations: An Emergent Threat? arXiv (Cornell University). https://doi.org//arxiv.2403.12207DOI: 10.48550

Montgomery, R. M. (2025). Augmenting Forensic Science Through AI: The Next Leap in Multidisciplinary Approaches. https://doi.org/DOI: 10.20944/preprints202501.1951.v1

Okonji, O. R., Yunusov, K., & Gordon, B. (2024). Applications of Generative AI in Healthcare: algorithmic, ethical, legal and societal considerations. https://doi.org/DOI: 10.36227/techrxiv.171527587.75649430/v1

Pashine, S., Mandiya, S., Gupta, P., & Sheikh, R. (2021). Deep Fake Detection: Survey of Facial Manipulation Detection Solutions. arXiv (Cornell University). https://doi.org//arxiv.2106.12605DOI: 10.48550

Pugliese, R., Badini, S., Frontoni, E., & Regondi, S. (2025). Generative Artificial Intelligence for Advancing Discovery and Design in Biomateriomics. *Intelligent Computing*. Advance online publication. DOI: 10.34133/icomputing.0117

Qureshi, S. M., Saeed, A., Almotiri, S. H., Ahmad, F., & Ghamdi, M. A. A. (2024). Deepfake forensics: A survey of digital forensic methods for multimodal deepfake identification on social media. *PeerJ. Computer Science, 10*. Advance online publication. DOI: 10.7717/peerj-cs.2037 PMID: 38855214

Remolina, N., & de la Osa, D. S. (2024). AI at the Bench: Legal and Ethical Challenges of Informing - or Misinforming - Judicial Decision-Making Through Generative AI. https://doi.org/DOI: 10.2139/ssrn.4860853

Saxena, P., Gupta, R., Maheshwari, A., & Maheshwari, S. (2023). Semantic Image Completion and Enhancement using GANs. arXiv (Cornell University). https://doi.org//arxiv.2307.14748DOI: 10.48550

Sharma, P., Kumar, M., & Sharma, H. K. (2022). Comprehensive analyses of image forgery detection methods from traditional to deep learning approaches: An evaluation. *Multimedia Tools and Applications, 82*(12), 18117. DOI: 10.1007/s11042-022-13808-w PMID: 36213342

Shi, C., Chen, L., Wang, C., Zhou, X., & Qin, Z. (2023). Review of Image Forensic Techniques Based on Deep Learning. *Mathematics, 11*(14), 3134. DOI: 10.3390/math11143134

Sun, C., & Mou, C. (2023). Survey on the research direction of EEG-based signal processing [Review of Survey on the research direction of EEG-based signal processing]. Frontiers in Neuroscience, 17. Frontiers Media. https://doi.org/DOI: 10.3389/fnins.2023.1203059

Tang, N., Yang, C., Fan, J., & Cao, L. (2023). VerifAI: Verified Generative AI. arXiv (Cornell University). https://doi.org//arxiv.2307.02796DOI: 10.48550

Tayebi, M., & Kafhali, S. E. (2025). Generative Modeling for Imbalanced Credit Card Fraud Transaction Detection. *Journal of Cybersecurity and Privacy, 5*(1), 9. DOI: 10.3390/jcp5010009

Taylor, L., & Nitschke, G. (2017). Improving Deep Learning using Generic Data Augmentation. arXiv (Cornell University). https://doi.org//arxiv.1708.06020DOI: 10.48550

Tortora, L. (2024). Beyond Discrimination: Generative AI Applications and Ethical Challenges in Forensic Psychiatry. *Frontiers in Psychiatry, 15*. Advance online publication. DOI: 10.3389/fpsyt.2024.1346059 PMID: 38525252

Tucciarelli, R., Vehar, N., Chandaria, S., & Tsakiris, M. (2022). On the realness of people who do not exist: The social processing of artificial faces. *iScience, 25*(12), 105441. DOI: 10.1016/j.isci.2022.105441 PMID: 36590465

Verdoliva, L. (2020). Media Forensics and DeepFakes: an overview. arXiv (Cornell University). https://doi.org//arxiv.2001.06564DOI: 10.48550

Vinolin, V., & Sucharitha, M. (2021). Taylor-RNet: An approach for image forgery detection using Taylor-adaptive rag-bull rider-based deep convolutional neural network. *International Journal of Intelligent Systems, 36*(11), 6503. DOI: 10.1002/int.22558

Vivekananthan, S. (2024). Comparative Analysis of Generative Models: Enhancing Image Synthesis with VAEs, GANs, and Stable Diffusion. arXiv (Cornell University). https://doi.org//arxiv.2408.08751DOI: 10.48550

Wang, Z., She, Q., & Ward, T. E. (2019). Generative Adversarial Networks: A Survey and Taxonomy. arXiv (Cornell University). https://arxiv.org/abs/1906.01529v1

Wankhade, T. D., Ingale, S. W., Mohite, P., & Bankar, N. (2022). *Artificial Intelligence in Forensic Medicine and Toxicology: The Future of Forensic Medicine* [Review of Artificial Intelligence in Forensic Medicine and Toxicology: The Future of Forensic Medicine]. Cureus. Cureus, Inc., DOI: 10.7759/cureus.28376

Xie, M., Kulshrestha, M., Wang, S., Yang, J., Chakrabarti, A., Zhang, N., & Vorobeychik, Y. (2021). PROVES: Establishing Image Provenance using Semantic Signatures. arXiv (Cornell University). https://doi.org//arxiv.2110.11411DOI: 10.48550

Xin, Y., Walia, E., & Babyn, P. (2019). Generative adversarial network in medical imaging: A review [Review of Generative adversarial network in medical imaging: A review]. Medical Image Analysis, 58, 101552. Elsevier BV. https://doi.org/DOI: 10.1016/j.media.2019.101552

Yang, L., Zhang, Z., & Hong, S. (2022). Diffusion Models: A Comprehensive Survey of Methods and Applications. arXiv (Cornell University). https://doi.org//arXiv.2209.00796DOI: 10.48550

Yang, X., & Wang, X. (2019). Recognizing License Plates in Real-Time. arXiv (Cornell University). https://doi.org//arxiv.1906.04376DOI: 10.48550

Zeng, Y., & Xue, D. (2022). An Overview of Generative Adversarial Networks. 2022 IEEE 2nd International Conference on Electronic Technology, Communication and Information (ICETCI). https://doi.org/DOI: 10.1109/icetci55101.2022.9832049

Zhang, T., Tan, T., Han, L., Wang, X., Gao, Y., Teuwen, J., Beets-Tan, R. G. H., & Mann, R. M. (2023). IMPORTANT-Net: Integrated MRI Multi-Parameter Reinforcement Fusion Generator with Attention Network for Synthesizing Absent Data. arXiv (Cornell University). https://doi.org//arxiv.2302.01788DOI: 10.48550

Zhang, T., Wang, Z., Huang, J., Tasnim, M. M., & Shi, W. (2023). A Survey of Diffusion Based Image Generation Models: Issues and Their Solutions. arXiv (Cornell University). https://doi.org//arxiv.2308.13142DOI: 10.48550

Zhang, X., Guo, J., Zhao, S., Fu, M., Duan, L., Hu, J., Chng, Y. X., Wang, G.-H., Chen, Q.-G., Xu, Z., Luo, W., & Zhang, K. (2025). Unified Multimodal Understanding and Generation Models: Advances, Challenges, and Opportunities. https://doi.org/DOI: 10.48550/ARXIV.2505.02567

Zhao, Y., Hu, J., & Zhang, X. (2020).. . *Face Restoration Based on GANs and NST.*, *51*, 198. DOI: 10.1145/3395260.3395304

Chapter 4
Forensic Handwriting and Signature Analysis: Principles, Practices, and Emerging Frontiers

Karunya Sirohi
Institute of Forensic Sciences and Cyber Security, Narnarayan Shastri Institute of Technology, India

Vaishnavi shaiv
Institute of Forensic Sciences and Cyber Security, Narnarayan Shastri Institute of Technology, India

Kiran R. Dodiya
https://orcid.org/0009-0001-9409-7303
Department of Biochemistry and Forensic Science, Gujarat University, Ahmedabad, India

Parvesh Sharma
https://orcid.org/0000-0002-0245-5186
Department of Biochemistry and Forensic Science, Gujarat University, Ahmedabad, India

Kapil Kumar
Gujarat University, Ahmadabad, India

ABSTRACT

This chapter delves into the forensic science of handwriting and signature analysis, essential for document authentication and forgery detection. It explores the uniqueness of human writing shaped by neurological, psychological, and learned

DOI: 10.4018/979-8-3373-3795-1.ch004

behaviors. Key forensic principles such as individuality, natural variation, and permanence are discussed, along with distinguishing features between handwriting and signatures. The chapter reviews traditional methods and emerging technologies, including digital and AI-assisted tools. Various forgery types—simulated, traced, and digital—are analyzed through real-world case studies across legal, financial, and historical contexts. Challenges like disguised writing and subjective interpretation are also addressed, highlighting advancements enhancing reliability in forensic examinations.

1. INTRODUCTION

Modern legal systems are structured around forensic science, and these same systems are integral to forensic science within the International Relations field. While almost all sub-fields within forensics are interdisciplinary, forensic document examination stands out in its interdisciplinary nature because it merges handwriting analysis and signature verification. Even as documents are digitized and biometric systems become more reliable across industries, handwritten documents are still prevalent in legal, fiscal, and private correspondence. Every human act serves a purpose, and every act of writing (e.g., contract agreements, deeds, letters, suicide notes) serves a unique purpose through its signature. Moreover, while all handwritten documents form legal evidence, the act of writing a signature opens a legal document. The act of writing is, itself, a signature. No activity is as revealing, either mechanically, emotionally, or psychologically, as the act of writing a document. Writing is a distinct behavior that encompasses complex interactions of the cognitive system and the physiognomy of the brain. The unique, complex interactions between the brain and the body influence every person's handwriting. Writing is a behavioral act that is far too complex to be ruled as either subconscious or mechanical. The individuality of each person allows forensic examiners to differentiate between handwritings with confidence. Because of this, the analysis of written documents and signatures is a significant component of forensic science (Khajuria & Pillai, 2023a).

1.1 Importance of Handwriting and Signature Analysis in Forensics

The role of handwriting and signature analysis in forensic science is of great relevance due to its ability to determine the nature of handwriting and provide valuable information to be used in identification and the settlement of documents. Forensics involves handwriting analysis as a behavioral biometric. Forensics involves handwriting analysis as a behavioral biometric. Each individual has a different way of writing and has a style due to their personal experiences, education, habits, and physical conditions. This makes handwriting analysis as unique as a fingerprint. In addition, it is a complex, mentally and emotional controlled act. The analysis of signatures, particularly, has social and legal importance. It is a method used to legally authenticate a document as a means of granting permission, or declaring its authorship or consenting to its contents. In the forensic context, especially for fraud, forgery, and authorship disputes, the analysis of handwriting and signatures is paramount to the determination of whether a document is genuine or whether it has been altered. A document can be rendered genuine, or it can be a forgery. Experts detect the forgeries, whether it is a freehand imitation, tracing, or digital forgery, by examining the different characteristics of the handwriting or signature, such as the strokes, the quality of the lines, the pressure used, the spacing used in the composition, the alignment of the letters, and so on. This is especially useful in cases of fraudulent wills, altered documents, anonymous letters, and ransom notes.

The analytical opinions of forensic document examiners can sway judicial decision-making because of the details they can discern. Handwriting can also be used for behavioral analysis that articulates the psychological and emotional state of the individual, which can be instrumental in the profiling of the psychological aspect of criminal investigations. The analysis of handwriting is often combined with technology that is used for automatic handwriting identification and forensic imaging. Despite the growing technology in the modern world, the analysis of handwriting has remained relevant. The analysis of handwriting and signatures is a fusion of science, law, and human behavior, which makes it a critical aspect of forensic science that seeks to obtain various instruments of inquiry in the pursuit of justice.

1.2 The History and Development of Document Examination

Authentication of communication and fraud protection is an inherent aspect of document fraud examination. Standalone questioned document examination is a recent phenomenon, but its practice is ancient. Unique scripts and seals were used by royalty and their clerks to authenticate and attempt to prevent the forgery of legitimate royal documents during the Mesopotamian and Medieval wax-sealed scroll eras. The Renaissance introduced the widespread use of contracts and literacy and the need for documents to be verified. However, it was not until the 1800s, partially due to the advancement of criminology and other scientific methods, that the broad field of handwriting analysis began to be systematized. Document examination has its roots from Dreyfus Affair that took place in France in the 1890s, where the unjust imprisonment of Captain Alfred Dreyfus was based on the analysis of inferior and questionable handwriting. Although the document examination was flawed, it was this case that drew attention to the need to develop a professional system of document examination.

In the early decades of the 20th century, we find the emergence of Albert S. Osborn and other pivotal figures laying the foundation of what we now know as forensic document examination. In 1910, Osborn published the first edition of the book entitled 'Questioned Documents' and gave us the systematic approach and the vocabulary we now use in the field. Osborn also described the ethical boundaries the field must stay within. At the end of the century, some other innovations increased the quality and detail of what could be derived from written documents. These were the microscope, the ESDA device, some infrared and ultraviolet imaging devices, and, in the later decades, some digital enhancement devices. The analysis of handwriting as a craft slowly morphed into a fully-fledged, legally admissible and recognized forensic discipline. This discipline is based on scientific methods and expert testimony. Over the years, the examination of questioned documents is no longer just the study of handwriting and signature. It has grown to include the study of the ink, the paper, the typewriter, the printing processes, any additions and deletions, and erasures. It has now extended into digital forensics in the analysis of documents. This field has always updated the use of historical thinking to include modern technological innovations.

Consequently, the transition from a less analytical approach towards documents to a deep, analytical approach towards the examination of documents from a forensic perspective, tells the story of the interplay between the examination of documents, the advancements in forensic examination, and the examination of documents in a manner that allows the examination of documents to be a relevant and growing field of forensic practice as other fields update their methods of recording and communicating (Office of Justice Programs, n.d.).

1.3 Scope and Objectives of the Chapter

The purpose of this chapter is to delineate the concepts of handwriting and signature analysis in the fields of forensic science, detailing the principles, history, and use of this forensic science in the courts. It incorporates both the theoretical and the practical aspects, that is, the science of the individuality of writing, methods of detection of forgery, as well as the law on the value of the testimony of an expert on this subject. The focus is to provide a detailed understanding of the significance, methodology, and forensic examination of handwriting and signature, as well as the continuing necessity of such examination within the justice system, particularly in an era of advanced technology.

1.4 Review of Literature

Development of handwriting and signature examination as an area of forensic science has long been the focus of academic research, applied casework, and cross-disciplinary study (1). The history of foundational literature goes back to the pioneering work of Albert S. Osborn, and his monumental work Questioned Documents (1910) is considered the cornerstone of forensic document examination. Handwriting is unique, Osborn explained, and he used structured approaches by focusing on features such as line quality, the formation of individual strokes, and deceptively easy-to-detect differences in handwriting habits, all of which he argued established a science by which forgeries and genuine documents can be identified. Others followed, including Roy A. Huber and A. M. Headrick, who in their text Handwriting Identification: Facts and Fundamentals (1999) elaborated on principles of individual characteristics and variability in handwriting. Subsequent empirical studies have repeatedly confirmed the idea that two different people cannot duplicate handwriting about all of its elements—including flow, rhythm, and pressure, which in turn means it is safe to assume that handwriting is an individual identifier. Ellen G. Dreibelbis and colleagues have examined intra-writer and inter-writer variability and established that motor control and neurological patterns affect handwriting features. The biggest change was the use of technology in document examination. Scientific literature in forensic journals has described the ability of modern techniques, such as Electrostatic Detection Apparatus (ESDA) for indented writing, ultraviolet, and infrared imaging for detecting alterations and obliterations, and subsequent analyses of the material using GC-MS components and elemental compositions associated with individual ink elements, respectively Recent literature documents the convergence of forensic science and analysis of handwritten text, such as the use of computer-assisted handwriting recognition systems (Kam, 2021; Fielding et al, 2021) and machine learning algorithms to strengthen examiners ' accuracy and mitigate bias (Conn, 2023). Other aspects of academic discourse have addressed the challenges of subjectivity involved in examiner interpretations, the Daubert standards for scientific admissibility in court, and preliminary work in developing statistical models to assess a true identification objectively, independent from examiner interpretation. Peer-reviewed studies on the reliability, reproducibility, and validity of forensic handwriting analysis under different circumstances regularly appear in journals such as Forensic Science International and Journal of Forensic Sciences. Finally, literature reviews have pointed out the need for greater uniformity in training and method certification in the context of the changes that one method may have in the case of legal decisions. The available literature, for the most part, presents a contextual and multidimensional perspective on the identification of handwriting and signs, particularly where the strengths and weaknesses lie, with a near consensus on the need to improve the scientific credibility, accuracy, and practicality in the court. (Mookiah, 2023).

The interaction between image processing, computation modeling, and artificial intelligence continues to affect the field of forensic handwriting and signature analysis. Within the parameters of this study, between the years 2020 and 2025, several advancements within Computer-Assisted Handwriting Examination (CAHE) became particularly relevant. CAHE opens new levels of detail and accuracy to the recording of the relationships between handwriting and the geometry (strokes) of handwriting (curves, proxies) through the use of high-end scanners and sophisticated computing technology (Faundez-Zanuy et al, 2020; Conn, 2023). However, the same cannot be said about the techniques used in the measure of the spatial and pressure proxies of handwriting. These proxies, in addition to several others, permit the examiner to elevate a classical subjective visual analysis to a more integrated and more refined standard. A level of measurement of parameters and examination of consistency never achieved before in this field has been attained and garnered further advancements. Digital signatures in signature verification systems have purported advances in the integration of scalable (Convolutional) Neural Networks, (hybrid) computing systems, and deep learning methodologies. Neural networks, (hybrid) computing systems, and deep learning methods have been purported in their ability to sharpen machines to distinguish between genuine and counterfeited signatures by the contribution in the recognition of complex (spatial) and (static) temporal (datasets) (Kam, 2021; Tolosana et al, 2022). For the field of biometricThe legal and philosophical aspects involving the writing of evidence, Daubert and Frye, and preliminary studies (Davis 2015, 2017, Wojcik 2015) are also the focus of some works. Research gaps, most recently the need for examiner calibration, anonymous review, and frameworks with cognitive triage bias reporting (Found & Rogers, 2020; Bird et al 20121), were published. Forensic image enhancement, particularly multispectral imaging and contrast luminescence algorithms, as well as infrared luminescence, play an important role in retrieving obliterated or worn writings in old and cold case documents. The most recent studies advocate for a shift from such a hybrid, forensic, handwriting examination to one that incorporates advanced imaging with a competent practitioner, statistical and computational methods, and artificial intelligence for decision support. The widening of disciplines involved, to include the handwriting and signature examination merging with its more traditional forensic science and further into some of its newer applications, like digital forensic evidence, law enforcement data analytics, and handwriting analysis, strengthens the overall scientific base.

2. FUNDAMENTALS OF HANDWRITING

The science of handwriting has a basis in the fundamental knowledge of handwriting as it is conducted in forensic document examination by the individual examining handwriting to develop an understanding of distinctive writing, or characteristics in writing that aid in the authentication or dispute of questioned documents [researchgate]. As a complex neuromuscular process subject to cognitive and motor functions, handwriting represents an amalgam of learned habits and subconscious characteristics that undergo gradual change. This chapter is focused on the mechanisms, architecture, and neurophysiological basis of handwriting formation, which are necessary items of which the scientific basis is in order in comparative forensic handwriting analysis. (Saini et al., 2021a).

2.1 Definition and Components of Handwriting

Handwriting is the writing of symbols or marks on a surface using a writing instrument; it is generally recognized as a biometric pattern of formation that evolved from the individual. Handwriting is considered behavior: executed movement that is the resultant of neuromusculoskeletal control and the mechanics of motor control. While there is an initial influence of the teaching method and the writing system, everyone develops a habitual handwriting style, and it is written unconsciously, despite efforts to hide or change it. Line quality, slant, spacing, size, pressure, rhythm, and baseline are the main elements of handwriting. Certainly, that line quality relates to how smooth or shaky the strokes appear. If the writing looks natural, it means that the writing flows smoothly. One of them is slant–the slope of letters, which is generally sick for a given person. The distance between the letters and words shows proportional balance, and the space size reflects spatial sense and motor function. Variation in method can permeate and affect varying legal outcomes; thus, literature reviews have discussed the need and relevance of standardization in methodological training and certification programs. The literature, to an extent, has detailed the methodology of writing and signature analysis and the advocacy—its strengths and weaknesses, almost in unison—to examine the methodology, in particular, the scientific rigor and analysis, and the articulation, in detail, of the methodology. A critical third variable, in writing, is pen pressure, which has the potential to indicate fluency, emotional state, and intraword, interword, or passage-level variability (Aliyev, 2024). Rhythm and movement: the speed of the movement and the writing, the energy required, and the smoothness. The baseline alignment shows the degree to which the writing is centered vertically or horizontally along the baseline or invisible lines, which suggests psychological control or may indicate low muscle tone (also referred to as neuromuscular control). The association of these characteristics leads to integration and is the reason these traits, or aspects of traits, have been characterized as structural. Some traits, and their structural characteristics, can serve as the basis of comparison to enough writing and other specimens that an expert can conclude whether or not certain traits are sufficient to substantiate or negate the claim of authorship. Thus, it appears that the simplest encourage the child to the importance of the importance of the importance of the importance of the importance of the importance of the importance of the importance of the importance of the importance is handwriting, the importance is handwriting is handwriting is handwriting it is to a gold mine of Forensic is to a gold mine of Forensic is to a gold mine of Forensic is to a gold mine of Forensic information, as the sections or behavior as the sections or behavior as the sections or behavior as the sections or behavior as the sections or behavior as the sections or behavior as the sections or behavior as the sections of information each described in detail. (Kumar et al., 2024)

2.2 Individuality and Natural Variation

Individuality dictates that handwriting forensics examines only the principle that in order for one practitioner to produce the same handwriting as another practitioner, no one can have the same handwriting, regardless of environmental, educative, and hereditary factors. The factors that contribute to the variety of handwriting are divided into the following categories: fine motor coordination, cognitive processing, psychological state, behavioral writing habits, and motor skill complexity. Handwriting specialists even chronicle the variety of the factors above to the extent that even one's twin siblings' trait handwriting will differ within the same schooling environment, most likely to differ in the structure as well as the highly biometric visual qualities of the handwriting (S. N. Srihari, Cha, Arora, et al., 2001a). This helps us appreciate the distinctive handwriting in forensic cases to be professionally used as a 'special' signed handwriting for the included and the excluded in the analyzed documentation. Moreover, the concept of different handwriting is compounded by the equally 'natural' consistency of it. A single practitioner of handwriting will realize that the product of the handwriting will considerably differ due to a wide range of controlled and uncontrolled variables, such as emotional and physical feelings, the writing, the writing utensil used, the surface, the speed of writing and the attention of the writer.

These fluctuations are not discrepancies but rather a normal part of a writer's range (S.N. Srihari, Cha, Arora, et al., 2001b). Forensic examiners must be able to identify what constitutes an innocent natural variation and what constitutes a deliberate concealment or simulation of natural variation. The result of this is that an experienced examiner must pull back to quantify an individual's natural variation so that the erroneous concept of a genuine and consistent signature, albeit a signature with a slight tremor, is not classified as a forgery, or an attempted likeness is not dismissed as a copy because of false resemblance features. As much as the individuality confines authorship, the natural variation is what provides the contextual collateral that allows the assessment to be performed so that the other individual can be accurately recognized. The coexistence of these principles enables forensic handwriting specialists to carry out analyses that are intricate enough to balance the expected uniformity of a set of personal characteristics and the unpredictability of human actions, with the result of the analyses being scientifically sound and legally defensible (C. Bird et al., 2010).

2.3. Developmental and neurological aspects.

Engaging in writing is a complex task on a cognitive neurological spectrum that develops on a continuum as one develops through multiple stages of the life cycle and is influenced by the attainment of different levels of psychomotor functionality and cognitive ability. Writing is a form of motor behavior that is developed and taught in the early stages of life through pedagogic teaching in conjunction with visual and motor integration.

Because at this young age, children use conscious effort to practice the shapes, strokes, and letters that they learn, they are gradually building neural pathways that will later be that much faster at coordinating the hand muscles and visual perception. Through experience, constant practice makes these previously conscious movements semi-automatic, and then they become engraved into the procedural memory until a writer's touch has been developed. Putting a pen to paper is a complicated neurological endeavor; writing activates the brain's motor cortex, premotor areas, cerebellum, and parietal lobe to plan, control, and perform fine motor movements(Aleman et al., 2024). The central nervous system is responsible for coordinating the hand movement, the pressure of the pen on paper, the direction of strokes, and even the speed of writing. Any distortion of these neuro-writing pathways, as occurs with trauma, degenerative disease (e.g., Parkinson's), and dysdevelopment (e.g., dysgraphia), will inevitably result in unique changes to the way an individual writes and therefore have forensic relevance. In addition, psychological conditions such as anxiety, stress, and fatigue could temporarily change writing features, such as tremors, uneven spacing, or irregular pressure, without impacting the fundamental aspects of a person's writing identity. Comprehending these origins of development and neurology provides forensic document examiners with additional insight as to why handwriting changes over time or based on varying conditions and why handwriting, for all of this notable variability, remains a stable biometric of authorship." By formally integrating knowledge from neurology and developmental psychology to determine cognitive sources of intelligence and potential forgery capabilities, the forensic practice provides examiners with the informed ability to separate natural normal variation due to the Human factor from deliberate Human factors intended to conceal or mislead(*The "Handwriting Brain": A Meta-Analysis of Neuroimaging Studies of Motor versus Orthographic Processes | Request PDF*, n.d.).

2.4 Classification of Handwriting Features

Even though the analysis of handwriting predominantly concentrates on large passages and the ongoing behavior of individuals, forensic studies often address signatures as the main object of contention within legal paperwork. Unlike handwriting, however, signatures are a much more abridged and, to some degree, machine-like style of writing, and so their forensic issues differ greatly. One must have a firm grasp of these variations, however, before venturing into the specific properties of signatures, along with their distinctive strategies and features of forgery.

1. Class Characteristics

Class features establish the baseline for comparative handwriting analysis. These attributes come from common learning settings, teaching styles, or cultural etiquette. They are not of any cast but are useful for the initial screening test and for the preliminary elimination process of forensic examination.

Figure 1. Visual representation of class characteristics in handwriting analysis, including writing style, slant and alignment, spacing, letter forms, and stroke sequences.

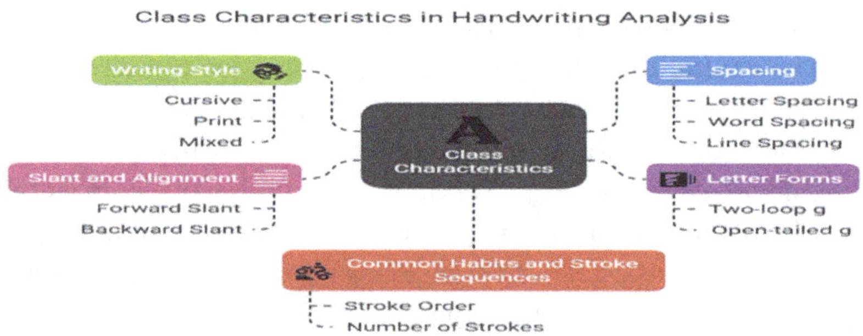

A) Writing Style:

Handwriting is usually classified as cursive, print, or a mix (some combination of both). These styles tend to be the products of early education. That is, students trained in Palmer or Zaner-Bloser methods in the U.S. most often have letters with similar slant and shape. Finding a writing style helps examiners associate a sample with a particular population group. (Schwellnus et al., 2012).

B) Letter Forms:

A handwriting system teaches specific letter-formation methods. One familiar case is a lowercase g, which can have a two-loop form as well as an open-tailed form. In the same way, the letter shape of w may be angular or rounded, based on this strategy. This level of standardization is useful for clustering handwriting samples, but not nearly specific enough to declare unique authorship.(STEFANSSON, 2003).

C) Slant and Alignment:

Slant means the angle of the writing with respect to the vertical axis. For example, one way to tell if a writing style has been developed through teaching is if the slant of the actual writing moves forward or back consistently. Alignment is about the way the writing conforms to horizontal lines — i.e., baseline (an invisible line where most letters sit) and left/right margins.(Bertolami et al., 2007).

D) Spacing:

In the early stages of learning handwriting, letter spacing, word spacing, and line spacing were often regulated. Encouraged to be spaced evenly to be read more easily, students who attended the same style of instruction may have a similar spacing style. In forensic analysis, spacing assists in eliminating writing in question from those of a similar demographic.(Pandey et al., 2024).

E) Common Habits and Stroke Sequences:

Writers taught on the same curriculum will typically show the same stroke order, for example, direction and number of strokes to form a particular letter. Since these habits are not a voluntary choice, this relates to the training environment of the writer.

Such features act as group indicators for forensic document examiners to either rule out certain writers from a sample or argue that multiple samples may share a similar schooling background. Though independently, it cannot verify authorship(Hanlen et al., 1999).

2. Individual Characteristics

The basis of forensic handwriting identification is individual characteristics. They develop slowly, influenced by muscle memory, writing tendency, mental state and even health. These characteristics are involuntary, innate and mostly unconscious, which makes them extremely difficult to imitate or hide.(Aliyev, 2024).

Figure 2. Overview of individual handwriting characteristics, including stroke patterns, diacritic marks, pen lifts, pressure variations, and stylistic elements that aid in personal identification.

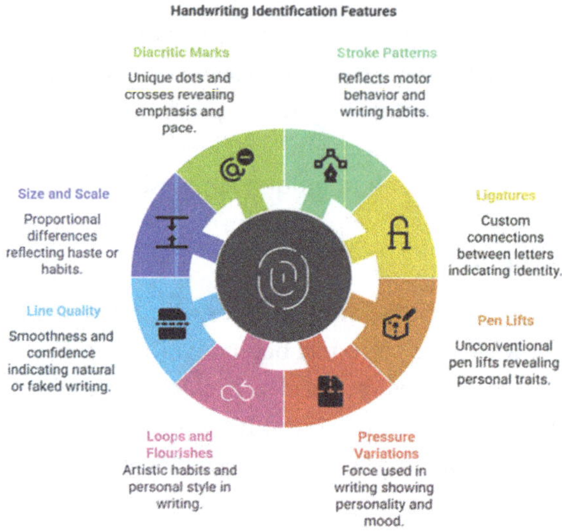

A) Stroke Patterns & Directionality:

The initiation of strokes, their direction, the order in which letters are formed, and the combinations of pen movements of a given writer all reflect their motor behavior. For instance, a writer may start the lowercase "a" from the top as opposed to the loop style. These patterns are deep-rooted and often hard to tamp down, even in in simulated writing.(McFarland et al., 2020).

B) Default Tuning and Ligatures:

Other writers would make their custom connections between certain pairs of letters (like between "r" and "s" or between "b" and "e"). These ligatures might be cursive, or not cursive, or even angular, or whatever, not how our children were taught. The nature and shape of their being manifest conclusive signs of identity(A-laei & Alaei, 2022).

C) Pen Lifts and Writing Rhythm:

A person could raise the pen at odd times within a word, between letters normally connected, for instance. These raise, as well as the beat or pace of the web content, which show unconscious practices, help the author in their kinetic trademark.(Aliyev, 2024).

D) Pressure Variations:

The depth of the ink or indentation left by the pen on the sheet indicates the forcefulness with which a person writes. Heavy writers may create deep embossed paths on the next page, light ones, or almost vibrating scratches. It is affected by personality, mood, and other factors, including diseases like arthritis or tremors. (Saini et al., 2021b).

E) Loops, Hooks, and Flourishes:

A few more curves, or loops in the letters like "l," "g," or "f," primarily because of the artistic benevolence or habit. At the same time, certain writers build exaggerated descenders or textual adornments before or adjacent to a stroke. These fancy bits are typically not taught and instead develop as a hallmark of the writer.(*(PDF) Handwriting and Gender: A Statistical Study*, n.d.).

F) Line Quality and Variation in the Baseline:

Some writers keep a constant baseline, and others unconsciously drift up and down across the entire piece of writing. It is the quality of line, or the smoothness and confidence of a stroke, that indicates if the writing is natural or may have been faked. However, hesitations, tremors, or retouches in the marker usually indicate faking or anxiety. (Alaei & Alaei, 2022).

G) Consistent Size and Scale of proportion

Size-implication mismatch between capitals and lowercase letters — e.g., large capitals and disproportionately small lowercase letters — could indicate hasty writing, old age, or just habits. With a little time, every person will have a characteristic distribution of letters expressed as a function of their relative proportions that they type, which can be used as a form of identification. (Kumar et al., 2024).

H) Diacritic Marks:

The way a person dots their "i" or crosses their "t" will say much about those individuals. A high dot on the "i" might indicate a quick writing pace, and a big cross across the "t" might represent emphasis or personality. Such attributes tend to remain the same and evolve slowly, and are difficult to change consciously. It is these singular aspects of handwriting that render it uniquely identifiable, enabling forensic document examiners to ascertain whether an individual did or did not pen a questioned document. Although one feature is not enough, several consistent characteristics have compelling evidential force.(*(PDF) A Study of Consistent Similarities Between Complete, Partial, And Initial Signatures of An Individual for Author Identification In Forensic Investigation*, n.d.).

3. SIGNATURE CHARACTERISTICS

As a definitive signature of identity, signatures are an essential focus area for forensic examination as they often have legal implications and societal values. Compared to normal handwriting, signatures are relatively stable over time and have been used repeatedly in similar forms for verification and authentication. The chapter briefly discusses the primary characteristics of signatures, their types, and their use in forensic science to recognize forgery, disguise, and authorship.(C. L. Bird & Yang, 2024a).

3.1 Types of Signatures (Stylized, Functional, Scribbled, etc.)

Various types of signatures define their appearance, function, and a spectrum of legibility and embellishment. Stylized signatures are generally decorative and unique, including design features like loops, flourishes, or complex letter shapes. These signatures are usually adopted by a group of people who want to project professionalism, authority, or personal style. Although differing from standard letter forms, they are relatively consistent in form. Functionally and straightforward, functional signatures are usually read with clarity, written with purpose, and are created to be a user-traceable signature of the person. They are typically used in formal documents such as official documents and financial documents. This is an extreme case of an abbreviated signature that can look like a mere streak or two initials together, typically used by people who sign documents often or in a hurry. They do not have apparent letter forms, but are consistent internally, a feature that can be important when it comes to forensic verification. Another type of signature is based on the initials of the signature only, and there also exists a kind of disguised signature where the signatures are intentionally altered to hide the identity or to behave as if someone else wrote. When it comes to forensic analysis, recognizing these signature types is critical for identifying deviations, detecting forgeries, and evaluating the authenticity of a disputed document. Challenges and benefits of each are presented for consideration, along with cautions about comparative use against established standards for accurate authorship and intent(Chang & Yu, 2009).

3.2 Elements of Signature Individuality

Signature uniqueness is based on certain common factors that differentiate one person from another, even if the apparent set of signatures formed by the signature looks similar, where an automatic handwriting verification is used in the case of forensic document examination. Even when signatures are abstracted or stylized to the point of being indecipherable, research indicates that they maintain distinctive features of structure and behavior over time through the principles of repetition and motor memory. Such unique features comprise the general signature template, the specific way letters or strokes are formed and built, slant and position of the signature against the baseline, speed and flow of writing, and finally, the pressure pattern during the signature. For example, the first strokes and final strokes (the way one starts and finishes their signature) are often the most forensic ally valuable due to being unconsciously performed and difficult to perfectly imitate by potential forgers. Other attributes — including the spacing between letters and components, whether embellishments or simplifications were used, and even the presence or absence of diacritical marks (dots and crosses) — can serve as comparatives. Ironically, the most distinctive feature present in forensics is the very reason that features are so reliable across multiple instances, because they will vary slightly in the natural environment, yet remain stable on the order of personal character. An authentic signature will show a consistent and repetitive pattern of these traits, even accounting for minor discrepancies with surface, mood, or pace. Conversely, a forged or disguised signature will generally not reflect this internal consistency but rather look hesitant, jerky, or overly consistent. Individuality, which requires either the presence of the individual element in the questioned specimen or the absence of that particular element in the known specimen, is analyzed by a forensic examiner who carefully compares samples side-by-side to pinpoint the features, in turn helping to determine authenticity and potential authorship. Thus, a signature may be most explicit about its uniqueness through its less legible or even more visually crude features, through the anatomical and habitual elements that belong specifically to the signer, and that are only partially imitable(*(PDF) A Perspective Analysis of Handwritten Signature Technology*, n.d.).

3.3 Common Forgery Techniques in Signatures

Figure 3. Overview of Common Methods of Signature Forgery and Associated Forensic Clues.

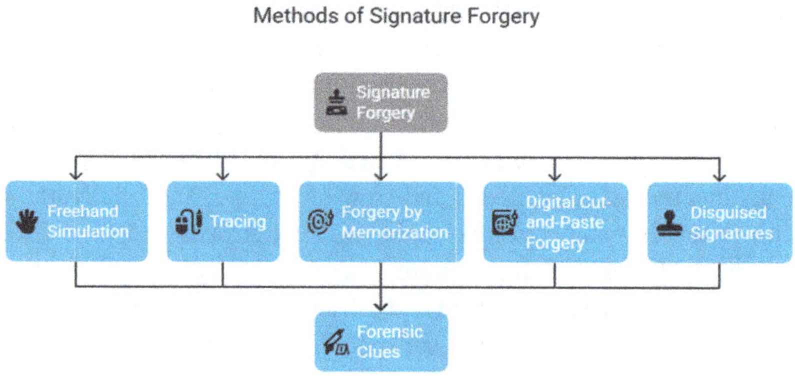

1. Freehand Simulation

This is the most commonly seen method of signature forgery. The initial forger tries to manually create an appearance of the authentic signature through repetition. As you might understand, though confident forgers can replicate the look, the inner workings of handwriting — fluidity, pressure from pen, stroke rhythm and regularity — remain challenging to authenticate. Forensic specialists frequently find hints of a task, such as hesitation marks, unnatural shivers, overly uneven spacing or deformed proportions, and that is just the beginning, which are clear under a magnification or optical magnifying device. These deviations symbolise strong clues of simulation and are essential for court evidence.

2. Tracing

This works by having the forger overlay a tracing sheet onto a real signature and tracing it on top directly with a pen or indirectly using carbon paper or a lightbox. The line quality of traced signatures is often mechanical. Each line is at the same level of pressure, with little sign of natural pen lifts and velocity variations that are inherent in genuine writing. Tracing provides controlled strokes and flow of ink, which ultimately does not produce any spontaneity. Under a microscope, telltale signs such as overlapping strokes, unnatural curves, or pooled ink at the beginning and endpoints appear.

3. Forgery by Memorization

This is a rare technique that requires reproducing a signature from memory without any visual aid. The technique typically produces large-scale structural deformations because it depends on the forger's memory. This signature is wrong in the overall form, inclination, area, and ratio. Visual and dynamic realism are absent from memorized forgeries, resulting in higher classification rates in a comparative analysis, especially with a major part authentic.

4. Digital Cut-and-Paste Forgery

This practice, which has become fairly common in the digital age, means that a scanned image of an actual signature is copied electronically and pasted onto another document with image-editing software. While these fakes might appear authentic at a distance, forensic investigators can pick out a discrepancy more easily using digital forensics instruments. Resolution enhancement, pixel structure analysis, and contrast level comparison identify places where the inserted signature does not match the surrounding text, e.g., mismatches in the DPI setting used to insert a signature previously, the resulting aliasing effect, or detection of a contrast difference or contrast edge and a mismatch of compression artifacts.

5. Disguised Signatures

Different from traditional forgery, this method is used to deny authorship of his/her signature. In this case, the signer intentionally modifies their natural signing style, such as signature tilt, speed, stroke shape or overall letter size, to make the signature seem different or inconsistent. In contexts of denial of fraud, denial of ownership or some such, this is usually done. Abnormal characteristics include overly conscious writing, slow and exaggerated strokes, and atypical shapes that are inconsistent with the writer's usual signature formations. (*(PDF) Forensic Examination of Digitally Fabricated Signatures in Printed Documents*, n.d.-a).

3.4 Differences between Handwriting and Signatures

Although handwriting and signature are similar since both arise from common neuromuscular mechanisms that depend on individual characteristics, they are different in function and have various features in formation and forensic practice. Writing, on the other hand, is less restricted, consisting of sentences or large passages of text that are formed subconsciously in a habitual way. It reflects a wide variety of writing characteristics like word formation, spacing, rhythm, alignment, and grammatical structure. In contrast, a signature is usually a brief, decorative, and habitual instantiation of a person name or part of a name, writing it in a form unique to the signer, such that it is a stylized form of a signature, used by an individual to identify themselves instead of a written signature, to represent their name, but that can also be legally binding; it is usually an abstraction of a person writing their name. Handwriting, on the other hand, preserves most of the written-language conventions and becomes legible and well-formed. At the same time, signatures tend to become more acute, either in the form of a highly abbreviated representation of the relevant letters or a more artistic representation devoid of letter structures. The form and quantity of handwriting — its very variability — makes it a more abundant source of material for forensic comparison of writing habits. While signatures do not contain much information, they remain fairly constant over time in terms of their shape. They are difficult to replicate because people practice and perform them in repeatable ways, making them effective for use in verifying identity. Of course, this means that signatures are easier to copy because forgers have fewer features to reproduce. Furthermore, people can customize or change their signatures intentionally for aesthetic, cultural, or legal purposes, while such changes in normal handwriting are rare and mostly unintentional1. Absence of knowing the overall assignments is required for variability analysis to work, while handwriting forensics relies on the pattern that stems from the entirety of the body of work. So, the consistency, pressure, flow, and even the automation of the movements found in the sample are examined in such detail. This is why there is a difference in signature and handwriting analysis. This is why practitioners of forensic handwriting analysis can accurately determine the technique needed to distinguish such fine patterns that document verification entails (C. L. Bird & Yang, 2024b).

4. SCIENTIFIC PRINCIPLES OF FORENSIC HANDWRITING EXAMINATION

In a forensic examination of handwriting, there are processes that have a certain configuration that can be used to ensure the results obtained will be dependable, unbiased, and can be replicated. These are the same processes that are used by document forensics examiners when validating document authorship, identifying changes made to a document, and identifying possible counterfeit documents. Forensics handwriting analysis entails a systematic rather than an arbitrary analysis to obtain results. This chapter explores the core scientific foundations that enable handwriting analysis to be recognized as credible evidence in courts of law (Khajuria & Pillai, 2023b).

4.1 Principle of Individuality

The principle of individuality is central to forensic handwriting examination. It states that the handwriting of each person can be distinguished from the handwriting of all other persons, including that of identical twins. The principle is based on two aspects: handwriting is a learned neuromuscular skill that is influenced by inheritance, motor development, education, and experience in life. Impressive writing habits that men and women observe while writing privately, intentionally or not, become submerged in routine and become cemented and relatively permanent as the person matures. In simple words, these habits appear as individual characteristics– Individual formations, Stroke patterns, connecting strokes, Pen lifts, Pressure variations, and Spacing, ultimately making up a particular writing style. While two people may learn to write in the same way, they will never produce the same writing because their brains and muscles will execute writing in different ways. This principle gives forensic document examiners the basis to compare known and unknown documents and document the similarities and differences that either confirm or exclude authorship. This principle also allows for natural variation, recognizing that no two pieces of writing from an individual are the same but rather fall within a specific range of their style. This natural uniqueness provides strong evidence value when studied under magnification, imaging, and measurement tools. Individuality is the cornerstone of the fundamental principle underlying and guiding expert opinion, as well as the basis for the admissibility of this evidence in judicial proceedings. Thus, it is an important pillar of forensic science.(S. N. Srihari, Cha, & Lee, 2001).

4.2 Principle of Natural Variation

The initial point, natural variation, explains how an individual will never be able to reproduce the same handwriting over and over again. There are many factors at play when an individual is writing, and how those factors will influence the writing, such as the variables, Psychological, physical, and environmental variables, and how those variables will influence the writing. Many factors play a role when someone is writing, such as writing instrument, mood, fatigue, speed, spacing, posture, and surface. All of those variables will have an influence over the writing and how the letters will be formed, and how the pressure will be applied. For each writer, I believe there is a specific and constant range. For example, forensic document examiners will assess how to differentiate between these normal variations and significant variations. A forger may be able to replicate the basic structure of someone's handwriting, but the basic structure has a lot of intricate details that are difficult to replicate, such as the flow and writing style. That is the importance of the study of natural variation in handwriting; it can prevent an analyst from assuming there is a forgery when there is not one in forensic handwriting. In handwriting, there are constant features that are displayed individually, such as the line quality and the movement, but they are all tied back to the structure of the writing.

The principle brings thorough quality and assurance to forensic examinations, and the fact that every handwriting has its own individuality while simultaneously obeying biological and behavioral fluidity. An understanding and correct reading of natural variability is required to boost the validity of forensic findings and further refine the scientific impartiality and the systemized craftsmanship of handwriting examination for the courts (Upadhyay et al., 2018).

4.3 Principle of Permanency

The concept of permanency in forensic handwriting analysis means the foundational features of an individual's handwriting are consistent throughout their life. Although some small variations might arise from age, health, or mental health conditions, he added, "the basic characteristics of handwriting—pattern of strokes, letter formation habits, spacing, slant of writing, and pressure distribution-are relatively stable over a person's lifetime." Such stability is a product of years of neuromuscular coordination and behavioral habit of writing only certain ways. When these motor patterns are fully developed, usually in adolescence or early adulthood, they become automatic and involve limited conscious control. As such, even when someone is trying to change or hide their handwriting, some automatic features remain and allow forgery or disguise to be detected. This same principle gives document examiners in forensic contexts the ability to assess writing samples that may have been created years apart and be confident in their opinion of authorship. It further reinforces the legitimacy of using archived or historical specimens in investigations, particularly in matters relating to wills, contracts, or disputes extending over protracted periods. While the handwriting appearance may be altered by changes in health (such as the tremors seen in Parkinson's disease, strokes, or arthritis), trained examiners take these medical antecedents into account but still recognize permanent characteristics that remain and withstand the above influences. The principle of permanence would therefore emphasize the more reliable premise of handwriting as opposed to many other forensic methods, helping to strengthen the admissibility of handwriting evidence by determining that, irrespective of any external or temporal factors, the intrinsic writing characteristics of any given person do not fundamentally vary. That writing can therefore function as a biometrically permanent signature(*(PDF) Handwriting Expertise: From Paper to Biometrics*, n.d.).

4.4 Principle of Uniqueness in Writing Habits

Because no two people write in the same way, the principle of uniqueness in writing habits asserts that every person has a quasi-permanent set of writing behaviors and characteristics, which makes handwriting a potential biometric in forensic science. These habits of writing are the result of years of interlocking neurological, psychological, educational, and motor influences. Whether from the earliest days of learning to write through to custom adaptations over a lifetime, we learn to form letters here, we learn to connect the letters there, and apply pressure in this particular manner and space things this way on the page. The habits become part of his motor memory, and so the need centers on expressing them, whether under different circumstances or through efforts to change them. What makes it unique is not just single letters or strokes — it is the entire combination of features such as writing slant, rhythm, baseline, loops, pen lifts, and writing speed. Even the best rip-offs will have different combinations of all the rest of these traits, so there are no two people exactly alike. However, even people who follow the same handwriting style or the same syllabus will have slightly different writing styles inevitably due to muscle memory, neural circuit, and habitual hand movements. Forensic document examiners use this principle to find out who wrote a document since these unique characteristics act as a behavioral fingerprint, unique to the writer and hard to replicate accurately. It must be emphasized that this analysis of this uniqueness, however fragile, is not done on the artistic abilities or readability. Rather, this describes certain types of unconscious habitual behaviors conceptualized as motor execution. The principle of fake nature recognition is termed a novel landmark of authenticity and imitation, thus offering a special kind of science and truthfulness in this practice of legal and crime investigations. (S. Srihari et al, 2002).

5. HANDWRITING AND SIGNATURE ANALYSIS TECHNIQUES

Handwriting and signatures examination is a forensic discipline that integrates science, technology, and artistry. The principles provide the theoretical foundation, while the practical examination is rooted in the organized procedures that the document examiners utilize to authenticate, discover forgeries, and analyze the writing behavior. Each of these procedures is distinct, ranging from basic observational techniques to sophisticated mechanized methods, to illuminate unique characteristics, random variability, and modification. At the core of these methods lies visual examination, and this chapter aims to provide a description of visual examination in forensic handwriting and signature analysis. (Sethi et al. 2025).

5.1 Visual Analysis

The first explanation of visual analysis, which is the most basic method of analysis, is the consideration of the structural and stylistic elements of the writing of an expert in the field of handwriting and signature examination. It involves a direct comparison of questioned and known examples. However, the comparison and direct consideration of contrasting examples is done without the usage of tools or instruments at first (they should be put at the desk within the user's reach, but only after the observed acts of writing are done). The comparison begins with the height of the letters and the mappings of the letters on the baseline, along with the observation of the general slant and the general proportion of letter forms, along with spacing, considering the general characteristics. The analysis then shifts to a more detailed observation of stroke directions, terminal strokes, pen lifts, rhythms, and consistency in the flows of one's writing (Kopacz, 2013). This first peak at a document usually facilitates the consideration of general impressions and the identification of major gaps when the first general comparison is done. The experienced examiners are the only ones who can detect minor behavioral processes and flaws or gaps that a pair of untrained eyes can easily miss when repeating the same motion. However, they are also expected to operate under the whole of the comparison principle, that is, when an entire document (or in this case, a section of the document) is analyzed in comparison to one letter, without focusing on a particular flow, the behavioral anomalies (deviations from the expected sequence of letters or, the given behavior of a whole document) are also expected to be base of the examination.

Visual inspections must consider the signs and symptoms of potential fraud, including but not limited to, (1) the presence of shakes, (2) signs of hesitation, (3) varying pen characteristics that reflect either fast or too slow of writing, and (4) irregular shifts in writing speed that suggest the writer was either drafting or tracing an exemplar. Forged or mechanically produced signatures can be analyzed using (1) visual inspection or (2) signature metrics of spacing, velocity, and pressure. Much like the disciplines of paleography, the science of the analysis of historical documents, and document examination, visual analysis is the basis of signature analysis, despite the analysis not providing sufficient proof of signature fraud. This process illustrates the value of visual perception in the analysis of documents. This phenomenon has also been described in the unyielding form of abstract reasoning, where the emphasis is placed on the document analysis being the first and most productive exercise in the analysis process. (PDF) Handwriting and Visual Impairment: A Forensic Analysis of J. S. Bach's Signatures, n.d.).

5.2. Analytical Microscopy

The technique of analytical microscopy allows forensic specialists to reveal hidden features of signatures and handwriting that are not discernible to the naked eye. Detailed stroke patterns and inky movements are detected using a variety of tools (stereomicroscopes, handheld comparison microscopes, and digitally-zoomable microscopes). Different features of the documents being analyzed, including the degree of pressure used in the writing, the contact of the writing implement to the paper, and other such details, are recorded. Enhancement can reveal factors including faint eddies that are evidence of (nervous) control loss; retouching that could reveal motive; hinges that suggest reluctance; and "patching" where the writer reinforced and corrected a stroke. It also documents unnatural raising of a pen to form a letter, consistent ink skipping, and unusual starts and stops, all of which are indicators of forgery. Line equations may be used in forgery to mask the signs. When such signatures are examined, moist and soft paper may reveal the pressure used in forgery. Analytical microscopes can also differentiate signatures that were handwritten and those that are actual reproductions, i.e., those which were written by a computer and lack writing dynamism, and those which exhibit consistency of ink flow, which the signatures do not possess.

In cases involving the manipulation of ink and/or paper, microscopy, accompanied by oblique illumination, can reveal forgeries that involve erasures, abrasions, or changes to the chemicals in the ink or on the paper. Depending on the compare microscopy, it can allow the simultaneous viewing of a questioned and a known sample, which improves the objectivity and precision in identifying specific characteristics of a sample. Microscopic Analysis Microscopic analysis has greatly improved the accuracy of a process, the value of which is improved when added to a process that appears to be simple, and the finely analyzed data is what is needed to improve the computations that form the basis of the forensic interpretations of evidence which are of fundamental value in the microscopy of the questioned documents (Galekovic et al., 2024).

5.3 Digital and Computer-Assisted Techniques

In modern times, handwriting and signature examination has branched out as a specialty. It has become a forensic science field that increasingly relies on digital and computer-assisted methods for precise, objective, and efficient performance. The methods include measuring and analyzing features that are painstaking to view and analyze through traditional visual and optical testing, at least at first, with the help of high-resolution scanners, specialized software, and digital imaging tools. Professionals are able to electronically pan and view strokes on the questioned document with no loss of clarity, measure and analyze angles and distance, and overlay the questioned and known samples to visualize mismatches or confirm matches. There are also analytical tools, such as automated handwriting recognition software programs like Forensic Information System for Handwriting (FISH) by the U.S. Secret Service and other systems that collect handwriting samples and make them available for visual analysis.[2] Such tools compile the questionable samples with enormous databases to identify and record the same handwriting features in documents, classify handwriting style samples, or confirm matches with other samples in large-scale document fraud investigations.[3] Such systems serve a purpose in the analysis of anonymous letters, threatening notes, and multiple forged documents.

Analyst involvement in dynamic signature verification processes differs from other tasks due to their ability to take into account variables like pressure, speed, order, and time in performing signatories' strokes with special smart pens or digitizing tablets. These devices capture pertinent biometric data essential for distinguishing authentic from simulated signatures. In forensic handwriting and signature analysis, software that enhances images to address the blurring or fading effects and other document-related alterations can be used. These alterations include the use of different inks and the layering of writings, that is, the overlying of two or more scripts, which can be an ingenious technique to mask text. There is no doubt that forensic software can aid document experts in performing different analyses. However, its primary purpose is to augment the productivity of document examiners by providing them with reliable figures and quantitative data. The use of additional software is beneficial for the science of forensic signature and handwriting analysis. It improves the quality of presentations and documents used in court proceedings and other investigations, and it improves the reliability of findings in these forensic studies (van Erp et al, 2018).

5.3.1 Forensic Handwriting Analysis and Digital Image Processing

The utilization of forensic handwriting and signature analysis is anchored on the objective view, enhancement, and quantification of the characteristics of the various types of handwriting. Digital image processing allows the use of techniques such as grayscale normalization, edge detection, skeletonization, and contour mapping, which are more advanced than classical optical methods. For example, examiners can more accurately isolate stroke boundaries, detect pen lifts, and analyze stroke continues. The high- resolution image overlays allow proportional differences and direct comparisons to be made to question these signature samples against known samples. The ability of multispectral imaging to capture different bands of wavelengths is forensic handwriting analysis's most advanced feature. It allows a much better discrimination between visual seemingly similar writing inks, as well as recovering text that has been written over or erased. The combination of these imaging techniques and forensic software to create visual outputs that are reproducible and suit the demands of a courtroom improves the transparency and accountability of the examiners.

5.4 Comparative Analysis Techniques

Figure 4. Step-by-step forensic handwriting analysis: from sample selection to validation.

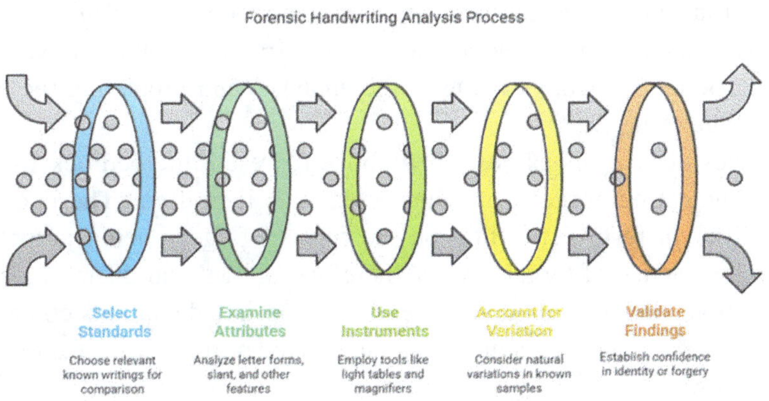

Fundamentally, forensic handwriting and signature verification involves comparing documents for signs of genuine historical authorship. This technique involves a two-pronged style of document examination: the initial analysis of the questioned document followed by a detailed comparison of the questioned document with known exemplars of authorship (Drechsel, 2014). Moreover, documents are examined and analyzed with the assumption that there are differences and variations in the writing style of every individual that are similar and also different from others. This analytical comparison process begins with the selection of appropriate standards—SED known handwriting that is undisputed and from the same time frame as the document in question. The examination of questioned documents involves a detailed analysis of the shape of the written letters and other factors such as the tilt of the letters, the overall layout of the document, the movement of the pen, the amount of pressure that is applied while writing, the linking of individual letters, and the arrangement of the letters and words in the written document. The analysis and examination of handwriting should not be done in a singular way since the phenomenon of handwriting relies on the combination of different characteristics and factors, as documents tend to be complex. For comparison, there are also a variety of different instruments available to prevent human error. Elements to take more notice of in consignment analysis due to forgery artefacts are the particular strokes at the end, fluidity and movement of hand and overall rhythmic t. These are ultimately the easiest factors to replicate and the basis of the signature dialect.

The examiner uses natural variation in the known samples to create a baseline for comparisons, ensuring that the differences in the questioned sample are beyond that baseline for the original writer. This is both a science and an art, in that one must come to an understanding that the similarity is not only present, but that it is also there repeatedly and consistently. When comparative analysis is done piecemeal, it can create strong enough evidence to either confirm with a high degree of certainty that there is an identity or to detect that there is a fraud. It is also a novel means of providing expert evidence, assisting in the analysis, and protecting the contested documents(Sita et al., 2002).

Techniques of analysis as described above represent the bedrock from which deviations indicating forgery are suspected and identified. These deviations, however, differ in form depending on the type of forgery being perpetrated. A systematic knowledge of forgery types, therefore, allows examiners to make sense of the deviations they observed and use the appropriate deviations contextualized to the anomalies and, consequently, make use of the necessary means to detect the forgery in question.

6. TYPES OF FORGERY AND DETECTION

Handwriting and signature analysis or forgery is a fraudulent process in which a false writing is created to deceive another for financial, legal, or personal purposes. This has indeed become a complex problem for forensic science since forgers are constantly coming up with new ways to commit these types of fraud. It is crucial to realize that various forms of forgery exist, as well as methods to detect them, and this is where forensic science comes into play in document examination. In this chapter, the different types of forgery are briefly categorized into the major forms: simulated, traced, disguised, and digital forgeries. It also explains how forensic specialists recognize their signature through an in-depth physical and chemical examination. Foreign experts recognize their signature.

6.1 Simulated Forgery

One of the most common types encountered is simulated forgery (freehand forgery) in questioned document examination. It is the intentional practice of copying someone else's handwriting or signature, either from memory or by looking at a genuine example. This type of forgery takes a lot of practice and adjustment, not only in reproducing the form and shape of the original, but also the natural cadence, pressure, and flow. Nevertheless, even to the untrained, forgery demonstrates characteristics that can be detected through laboratory analysis. Among the most common laboratory examination signs for forgery are the unnatural, shaky movements present in the forgeries, the unnatural pauses in strokes, the inconsistent angles and distances in movements, uneven pressure imprints, and the poor quality of the lines that are created. These characteristics can be the result of a simulation, one created through a mechanical process that is slower and more deliberate than the one present in natural handwriting and consequently, the created handwriting is even more mechanical in appearance. Forensic examiners DRAW COMPARATIVE ANALYSES ON forgeries and genuine samples, using comparative analysis of samples, magnification, spray, and sometimes even computer inconsistency overlays. They also analyze whether the questioned writing lies within or outside the palatable boundaries of natural variance in authentic samples. In such cases, simulated forgeries might be notoriously hard to highlight, especially if the forger had access to the original writer's documents for so long or practiced the imitation of his writing over a long period. However, forensic examination focuses on habitual characteristics in authentic writing that are difficult to recreate on purpose, such as spontaneous lifts of the pen, consistent stroke ends, and movement. The identification of simulated forgery is critical for combating nefarious intentions, preserving authenticity, and facilitating legal proceedings, all of which rely on the preservation of written records(Kipouràs, 2022).

6.2 Disguised Writing

Disguised writing is the writing or signature that has been deliberately changed in such a way that the identity is hidden, or cannot be easily identified even under legal or forensic study. Disguised writing means that a person has intentionally modified their normal writing style to make it look unlike their writing, even so that they would not easily recognise the writing as theirs, in contrast to simulated or traced forgery (when the writer attempts to imitate another person). The type of fraud is usually seen in cases that include anonymous letters, threatening notes, signatures in dispute, or where the writer is attempting to limit association with incriminating evidence. Disguising can involve changing the shapes of letters, tilting or varying the size of your writing, using different writing implements, using an opposite hand, or writing at varying speeds. However, since handwriting is such an entrenched motor activity, one can only disguise habitual traits so far. Even after years of practice and attempting to refine his style, there are some involuntary features (pressure when writing, alignment of baselines, the distance between characters, the direction of strokes, etc.) that do not go away. These are the characteristics Phenomenon-Doc has trained our forensic document examiners to examine and compare. The characteristics include differences that are unnatural and inconsistent, letter oddities, changes in speed, and differences in style that are overly rigid and differ from the writer's style in other known samples. In addition, there are differences in style from one paragraph to another, even in the case of just a few paragraphs, and there are differences in the methods used to achieve the forger's goal, which we consider to be the Savannah red flags of this exercise.

. In such signature cases, a person may purposely degrade or distort his or her normal style, whilst pretending to be in a hurry or sick, and then later repudiate the signature. When it comes to disguised writing, this is much more subtle, requiring the examiner to have extensive knowledge of natural variation as opposed to artificial variation. The detection of concealed writing uncovers both the original author and any secret intent to mislead the reader, and this naturally carries extremely important legal implications for civil and criminal investigations alike.(Durina, 2005).

6.3 Digital and Electronic Signature Forgery

Digital and electronic signature forgery is one of the most recent challenges in forensic research due to the worldwide tendency to use digital documents and remote authentication. Traditional ink-based signatures range from the humble scanned image signature implanted into PDFs to complex digital signatures that rely on cryptography with matching secure keys and the help of a certificate authority. Domain name forgery usually occurs when an individual or organization illegally uses, copies, or alters the digital signature of another person to gain unauthorized access to a mail server, validate forged contracts, or approve unauthorized transactions. At its simplest, image-based electronic signature forgery can be as straightforward as copying a scanned image of an original signature and pasting it onto a computer file. While this approach sounds plausible, it typically leaves technical markers behind as well, like differences in resolution, pixilation, formatting, or metadata inconsistencies, all of which can be identified with forensic digital imaging techniques. Even more sinister scams could have the malware obfuscating one of these signatures, or trying to replicate one, or even exploiting mismanagement of digital certificates. Even with encryption, with an APKI framework, digital cryptographic signatures face the same insider threats, certificate spoofing, and identity theft from poor user cyber hygiene. Most forensic analyses of the metadata of documents, history records of versions, chains of certificates, IP logs, and other timestamps can find some indications of irregularities or undetected intervention, showing that the forged digital signatures were the result of some real work. Sometimes, digital forensic tools can detect some soft changes, using the rules of signature hash not to change; any changes in the document after its signing would compromise the integrity of the signature, and would be exposed. The digitization of documents in legal, financial, and governmental processes emphasizes the importance of forensic detection methods to be able to detect and prevent electronic signature forgery in order to preserve the trust and security of the digital world. It is the other extreme from generations of work of simple ink-on-paper forgery spotting to the use of advanced computer systems with complex circuitry and other gadgets ((PDF) Forensic Examination of Digitally Fabricated Signatures in Printed Documents, n.d.-b)

6.4 Detection Methods and Indicators

Analyzing handwriting and signatures to detect forgeries is done through visual and scientific methods. Forensic document examiners usually use different methods to analyze documents. The first is visual and comparative analysis, where a questioned document is compared to known samples, and then discrepancies consisting of slant, stroke formation, spacing, and rhythm are analyzed. These marks are then analyzed to determine if they contain hesitation marks, unnatural tremors, retouching, and inconsistent ink flow, which are all signs of a forgery or a signature that has been traced.

For example, the use of instrumental methods such as Electrostatic Detection Apparatus (ESDA) enables the detection of indented writings by showing patterns of smaller tracings or adjustments that were made on the sheets above. Infrared and ultraviolet light scans reveal erased entries, different ink materials, or overwritten text that the eye cannot see. For electronic or digital forgeries, forensic examiners examine the product metadata, digital signatures, and audit trails for signs of tampering such as unusual edits, irregular or nonsensical timestamps, and broken chains of trust among certification authorities. Some of the main signs that your pen (probably) was not writing naturally are: inconsistent baseline alignment, unnatural variation, lack of natural grooves to the individual letters, lack of variation of pressure in the pen, movement of the pen is not fluent and the lines are not up to the mark, and so on, some deliberate control, rather than a free-flowing motor activity—indicators are thus readily identifiable, at least in terms of advertising. Handwritten signature traces frequently display dull point endstrokes, overlapping strokes, and even double passes, while simulated forgeries may have numerous alterations and also exhibit internal inconsistency. In disguised handwriting, however, the giveaway is often found in the form of unnatural changes in slant, artificial shaping of letters, erratic spacing, etc., indicating that such manipulation was done on purpose. The field of forensic handwriting examination does not rely on single attributes but rather on a series of amalgamated clues from a range of attributes measured on multiple levels of analysis. These attributes form a cohesive, but not definitive, body of expertise, and combined with sophisticated forensic analysis, provide a significant, tangible evidence of detection for forgery and the preservation of the authenticity of any disputed document (Mengi & Malhotra, 2021).

7. CASE STUDIES IN HANDWRITING AND SIGNATURE ANALYSIS

As the case studies demonstrate, handwriting and signature analysis have made a significant contribution in a diverse range of settings, from proving or disproving a crime to the verification of a legacy. These studies illustrate the practical ways in which forensic document examination transcends interdisciplinary and cultural domains. Whether it was the revealing of a fabricated suicide note, the proving of a fraudulent will, the tracing of illicit bank authorizations, or the verification of manuscripts written centuries ago, forensic handwriting analysis is unmatched in the unwavering pursuit of truth and justice.

7.1 Criminal Investigations

An investigation's primary architecture hinges on the correct association of primary key pieces of evidence: the suspect being paid off. This involves the research of ransom pieces of literature (e.g., ransom notes) that the culprit pays the victim. The foremost types of literature that get requested for analysis include: ransom notes, anonymous death threats, suicide notes, and payoff threats. A leading case that the authorities try to get documents for is the JonBenet Ramsey case, where a ransom note was constructed by the family and placed at the crime scene. This is where the note was discovered, and forensic document analysis was completed on the note and specimen samples of the family and other potential suspects. This case was closed; however, they showcased the potential and disadvantages of handwriting analysis when they took into account the reasoning abilities. One of the cases of reasoning ability was the case of a fraudulent businessman who sent anonymous demand notes and death threats to numerous business owners located in a major city. This was done to threaten the business owners to pay off a large sum of money. Statistically analyzed handwriting samples verified by forensic handwriting analysis were able to detect a large amount of elementary letter formations that digitized, and a blank piece of paper would have numerous unusual pen pressure patterns that would shape the letters. This ultimately led to a confession and a conviction.

These criminal cases demonstrate that handwriting can serve the dual function of being an indicator not only of authorship but also of a behavioral imprint - the documents in question are psychological and psychomotor pathways of their authors (Bhardwaj & Srivastava, 2021).

7.2 Civil Disputes and Wills

The analysis of handwriting in civil cases is often used to resolve the controversy surrounding the validity of the signatures of legal documents such as wills, deeds, transfers of property, and contracts. One of the foremost (arguably) cases in this segment is the Estate of J: Howard Marshall and his widow, Anna Nicole Smith. The estate documents were legally contested, and edits in handwriting, along with signatures, were claimed to have been forged, leading to the involvement of forensic handwriting specialists to determine the authenticity of those modifications. However, another family contested a handwritten will of a deceased relative, which was claimed to have disinherited immediate family members in favor of a remote friend.

Through forensic examinations of the questioned signature and comparing it to legitimate signatures from the past, it was concluded that the final will was indeed a forgery, thereby ruling in favor of the true heirs. These matters illustrate that handwriting and signature examination can protect inheritance, obtain property, manage one-half financially, and enforce a legally binding contract, thus maintaining the integrity of civil justice.(Mirić & Rodić Aranđelović, 2021).

7.3 Banking and Financial Frauds

Frauds through altered cheques, fake and forged authorizations, unauthorized access to accounts, counterfeit endorsements, etc., are part and parcel of the financial sector, and most of them require the authenticity of signatures. A corporate client in a high-profile banking fraud case found out that multiple cheques had been encashed with forged signatures worth crores of rupees. Signed statements were sent to forensic handwriting experts to compare the questioned signatures on the cheques against the genuine exemplars of the authorized signatory. It was determined that, via examination of signature rhythm, stroke regularity, pen pressure, and terminal flourishes, the signatures were created seemingly perfectly, but were forgeries. This resulted in criminal charges for the bank's internal employees and recovery of substantial losses. In a separate incident, a businessman mentioned that he never signed a personal guarantee for an agreement for a loan. His signature was purportedly fraudulent; however, upon examination, he was not bankrupt at any point. These cases exemplify that signature and handwriting analysis is integral to financial crime detection and fraud monitoring, in addition to protecting consumers and ensuring institutional accountability. (B. Mahanta and Deka, 2013)

7.4 Historical Document Verification

There is no courtroom, nor is there any corporate sector. Handwriting analysis is essential in verifying and validating the authenticity of documents and manuscripts of historical significance. This often determines the cultural and economic value that rare pieces of art and artifacts command.

A well-known example is the validation of Shakespeare's signatures, for which there are only a few controversial samples. Working with dogged tenacity, scholars and forensic experts considered stroke characteristics, writing implements, ink flow, and historical writing norms to decide whether it had been he signing or simply a clever 17th-century forgery. Perhaps of even greater interest was the case of the "Hitler Diaries" hoax from the 1980s, when the German publisher Stern announced that it had found the diaries of Adolf Hitler. Handwriting analysts and ink and paper scientists soon demonstrated that diaries had been created using fake handwriting on modern materials, resulting in one of the biggest literary forgeries of the contemporary period. In a more pop culture kind of instance, a new letter written by Mahatma Gandhi that had been stored in a private collection for years was verified recently after its signature and handwriting forensics were compared in detail with authenticated samples held in national archives. Such archival document examinations not only help to safeguard cultural heritage but also to illustrate the interdisciplinary nature of forensic handwriting examination. (*(PDF) J Forensic Sci & Criminal Inves Artificial Aging of Paper*, n.d.).

8. CHALLENGES IN HANDWRITING EXAMINATION

Although handwriting and signature analysis are ancient and valuable areas of forensic science, it is still rife with difficulties. The area of work necessitates considerable degrees of proficiency, interpretation and contextual insight, and is still bound by considerable ignorance. A wide range of problems, such as human fallibility, medical conditions, deliberate deception, and legal challenges, can affect the assessment and acceptance of handwriting evidence. The purpose of this chapter is to address the specific challenges, both practical and theoretical, faced by forensic document examiners in their pursuit of the truth.

8.1 Limitations of Subjectivity

The characteristics and qualities of handwriting specimens have drawn criticisms for their subjectivity. Forensic document examination is theoretically viewed through the lens of scientific principles (i.e., individuality and random nature variation). However, handwriting identification, comparison and evaluation will always boil down to subjective visual determinations of the examiner. The absence of widely uniform or agreed-upon metric standards of measurement in the discipline of handwriting examination stands in stark contrast to biometric modalities (thumb impressions and DNA, for example) that may have quantifiable standards and may be reproduced via algorithms. Such circumstances raise the likelihood of inter-examiner variation, wherein some specialists may arrive at fundamentally different conclusions based upon the same set of evidential material. The absence of accepted numerical standards and parameters in determining where similarity or difference lies can also create a perception of the objectivity and scientific nature of the conclusions arrived at. The subjective nature of handwriting evaluation has been and perhaps will continue to be the focus of attempts to standardize for the purposes of reliability. Such attempts at standardization have included training, certification and peer review. However, the subjective nature of the handwriting evaluation is likely to continue to spark debate concerning the admissibility of such expert testimony in court, where such expert opinions risk being dismissed as biased or lacking empirical foundation (Khajuria & Pillai, 2023).

8.2 Impact of Health and Age

Another major issue stemming from the study of handwriting is that it is affected by one's health and age. The deterioration of motor and cognitive functions of the body is naturally accompanied by changes in handwriting style. However, these changes can also alter the ability to be compared and recognized. Insufficient pen pressure, poor line quality, and disordered letter construction are some of the characteristics that can be attributed to neurological disorders like Parkinson's, arthritis, or stroke. These characteristics can lead to irregularities such as fluidity and spacing in the writing, which can be incorrectly interpreted as forgery or a disguise510, and can lead to HGI9 complications. Forensic handwriting analysis may also reflect atypical specimens of handwriting and deviate from the habitual style. This can occur if the individual is suffering from temporary health conditions, such as excessive fatigue, stress, or intoxication. This is especially problematic when trying to compare such specimens to the bulk of older, quality samples. Forensic examiners will need to take into account medical history, contextual considerations, and age-related changes to avoid the erroneous ascription of genuine but modified writing samples to a different author in such cases, as Asci et al. 2022 illustrate.

8.3 Disguised and Altered Writing

Disguised and altered writing can be most certainly challenging during handwriting analysis, as people may attempt to change their handwriting to conceal their identity, deny authorship, or create false attributions. The disguise may range from small, inconspicuous changes in slant and size to more radical changes in letter form, levels of pressure, or writing with the non-dominant hand. The issue in analyzing this disguise is that it does not occur with consistent, predictable regularity, and it can be applied to different sets of writing at different levels, making it difficult to establish valid benchmarks for comparison. In addition, some features of individual handwriting, such as spacing, rhythm, and direction of writing, may still be present to some level, providing clues to even less trained examiners. On the other hand, if the disguise is applied well, and if the comparison samples available are few, it can become very difficult to arrive at valid conclusions. The altered writing in this regard can also include overwriting, erasures, and other such mechanical changes that cover the original writing, making it difficult to analyze. In these circumstances, the analysis may depend on the use of advanced techniques of ESDA, oblique light, and enhanced digital capture. The difficulty is still very great, especially where motivated, deliberate concealment is matched with inadequate reference material. (Asci et al., 2022)

8.4. Courtroom Admissibility and Expert Testimony

As with all forensic evidence, there are legal barriers that handwriting analysis must overcome for it to be admissible in court: it needs to be scientifically valid (or at least pass the 'scientific' test), reliable, and relevant.

. The Daubert Frye standard of jurisdiction has recently been challenged due to the lack of quantification of the analysis and its being so subjective. They claim that since handwriting comparison necessarily involves interpretive judgment, it fails as a true science. Therefore, the acceptability of handwriting evidence in a court of law centers on the credibility of expert testimony surrounding that evidence. It is not enough for the expert to be able to recite his findings; he must also review how he arrived at his conclusions, what scientific background he has to back those conclusions, and how he minimized bias or error. The expert will be qualified, but the opposing counsel will try to shake that qualification up, as well as the procedural rigor put into analyzing the data (or if they claim the whole process is junk science). As well, courts typically demand that peer-reviewed standards, known error rates, and general acceptance in the scientific community be demonstrated for forensic evidence. Nevertheless, when examiners are trained sufficiently, adhere to protocol, and are transparent in their processes, handwriting evidence can still be extremely useful. There is, however, a specific community of forensic handwriting experts who are trying to make the field more organized, research-validated, and advocate a technological response to those scientific critiques in order to have handwriting and signature analysis accepted as evidence in court (n.d.).

9. NEW TECHNOLOGIES FOR DOCUMENT EXAMINATION

The new branches of forensic science, handwriting and signature analysis, are witnessing the same changes that are happening to parts of forensic science that have to do with forensics and advanced computer science, which tells us that the field is undergoing a paradigmatic transformation. This tells us how forensic documents are being analyzed, how they are being interpreted and how they are being used in documents in the context of a legal investigation.; and that transformation is still ongoing. Emerging technologies do not replace human examiners; they are meant to enhance them for large-scale forensic applications, which are necessary for the new challenges that modern technologies of law enforcement are posing to us.(Farber, 2025).

9.1 AI and Machine Learning in Signature

Verification Signature verification systems are among the most sophisticated applications of Machine Learning and Artificial Intelligence. These systems automate the learning, detecting, and precise comparison of signatures. One model of AI that employs deep learning and other forms of AI is the analysis of genuine and counterfeit signatures in order to discern complex patterns that are usually missed by humans. There are several factors that are considered to determine the authenticity of a signature, including stroke patterns, number of strokes, angles, pressure and timing. Real-time processing of visual signatures is done using CNNs (Convolutional Neural Networks). Temporal data analysis, on the other hand, is done using RNNs (Recurrent Neural Networks). This makes them ideal for applications in the finance industry, border management systems, and signatory verification systems where there is a need to achieve a high level of accuracy in fast-changing contexts. AI systems also support forensic examiners by minimizing the impact of individual subjectivity, spotting patterns and inconsistencies, and providing confidence-calibrated statistical answers to indicate the degree of support for expert opinions. These systems are undergoing validation for a wider range of forensic applications, but they represent a significant increase in the speed and consistency of analysis of signatures (Farber, 2025).

9.2 Biometric Signature Recognition

The dynamic characteristics of the signature of each person, \ textit {inter alia}, \ movement patterns, the timing of the writing, the writing speed, the pressure, the tilt of the pen, the order of the strokes, the rhythm, etc., distinguish \ textit {biometric signature recognition}. The pen's strokes are also joysticks. Technologies of this nature typically include biometric systems. The systems are comprised of a smart stylus or a digital tablet configured to record signatures in real time. The static signature analysis does not include a two-paneled visual structure and a motor activity layer behavioral authentication model. Because of this, biometric systems are very hard to forge. Because of this, such systems are more widely considered to provide secure authentication in services, such as finance, government-issued IDs, and transactions performed remotely. Even if a forger successfully attempts to mimic a genuine signature, such as an oleograph, the real power of biometric signature recognition is forensic. Biometric signature recognition systems have embedded a content-rich dataset, a behavioral record, in the signature. This dataset will allow biometric systems to provide multiple layers of identity verification. Biometric systems will raise the threshold of success in attacks, making active attacks easier to block than passive attacks. (The Role of Biometric Authentication in E-Signatures, n.d.)

9.3 Integrated Analysis of Ink and Paper

The integration of ink and paper characterization and handwriting analysis adds a remarkable degree of forensic confidence in verifying a physical document. For instance, Raman spectroscopy, infrared luminescence, gas chromatography-mass spectrometry (GC-MS), and thin-layer chromatography (TLC) allow examiners to discern the composition of the ink and evaluate whether a variety of inks has been employed on a single document page. Such an assessment can reveal alterations that may indicate a forgery, ascertain the true age of a document, and identify the use of varied pens or pencils, all of which are crucial in identifying a fraud. Similarly, the analysis of paper via fiber composition studies, watermark detection, and surface coating examinations provides a means to ascertain the provenance and authenticity of the document. The profiling of ink and paper traces gives a document a multifaceted characterization. Coupled with handwriting analysis, it gives greater strength to the forensic examination of documents. It is of particular value in cases of forged historical documents, tampered contracts, or altered legal documents.

This unification strengthens the connections in the forensic evidence chain through the verification, as both the content and the medium are authentic and undisputed (Raman Spectroscopy for Forensic Analysis of Inks in Questioned Documents I Request PDF, n.d.).

9.4 Digital Forensics and Stylus-based Handwriting

As digital-based devices become ever more ubiquitous, handwriting using a stylus is becoming the norm, especially in environments with electronic records and touchscreen interactions. Stylus handwriting can be acquired in many forms, including tablets, smartphones, or signature pads, and includes metadata, such as pressure sensitivity, speed, stroke order, and pen tilt, as well as digital forensic analyzable data. When it is scanned and sent to the evaluators, standard tools don't work anymore, as there are no ink trails or paper textures, as is the case with traditional handwritten documents. Instead, digital forensic analysts use vector-based signature files, logs of device user and biometric signals artefacts captured during the writing of a document to establish authorship and track discrepancies. Their work identifies several types of forgery by stylus signatures, such as copying and overlaying an image, but on the digital level, and seen widely, rendering forged input with clockwork mechanical robots. This technology enables the presentation of highly refined and digitally separated objects amenable to identification using software for forensic analysis. Such techno-informatics software is slowly being introduced to highly-secured environments of e-governance, FinTech, and corporate document processing. However, the stylus-based writing technology is gaining dominant use, and the field of forensic document examination will need to evolve, undergo integration of new competencies of cybersecurity, software engineering, and data science to sustain and defend the digital evidential integrity within the rapidly trending paperless environment. (Parziale et al., 2014)

9.5 The Function of Digital Image Analysis in Various Applications of Law Enforcement

Digital image analysis is a key component in assisting law enforcement agencies that combat large-scale document fraud, cyber-enabled forgery, and identity crimes. Automated systems that screen for particular handwriting help investigators compare questioned documents to large, centralized databases, helping to shrink the size of the suspect pool in cases that involve anonymous threats, extortion letters, and other forms of financial fraud that are complex and coordinated. Image-based verification of signatures is becoming more common in banking fraud investigations, border security, and e-governance systems to authenticate users.

Digital image analysis is of lasting value in forensics for its accuracy and scalability. Instead of manual analyses of documents one at a time, digital systems can work on thousands at a time, allowing for proactive detection of fraud rather than reactive investigations. The combination of handwriting analysis, digital systems, and reflexive predictive systems built on artificial intelligence help modern law enforcement and forensic systems.

10. CONCLUSION

The examination of handwriting and signatures is the fascinating crossroad of behavioral science and forensic evidence, constituting one of the key foundations of forensic document examination. This chapter dealt with the analysis of handwriting in its individuality, variability, and permanence, and attempts to analyze the different means of forgery recognition, as well as document authentication. The integration of technology in the forensic field has provided document examination forensic experts with AI and biometric verification tools to replace manual visual examination and microscopy, which are also used in other domains of forensics. The ability to authenticate handwriting, throughout history, has provided a remarkable social impact and varied evidential importance in great civil, criminal, financial, and historical case studies. The field also has real and valid challenges like the litigation aspect, variability due to health, and the subjective nature of the field.

One of the challenges is the development of psychophysiology, the standardization of methodology, and the integration of disciplines. Observation has no part in handwriting examination; it is, however, interpretative only, and that involves experience, scientific reasoning, and ethical responsibility—the more of a digital shift, the more varied counterfeit and new forms of digital handwriting. The evidence is an indication that technology and research need to be constantly evolving.

In forensic handwriting examination, there is an anticipated increased emphasis on automation, cross-disciplinary forensics and machine learning. However, forensics is still very much a human discipline; it is within the mind of an examiner, the situation of the examination, and the reasoning that is necessary to pull the truth from the written material. The digital improvements that will be available for the use of new technology to achieve equitable outcomes will not replace the human skills of the practitioners of the discipline for more complex technologies.

REFERENCES

Alaei, F., & Alaei, A. (2022). Handwriting Analysis: Applications in Person Identification and Forensic. *Breakthroughs in Digital Biometrics and Forensics*, 147–165. https://doi.org/DOI: 10.1007/978-3-031-10706-1_7

Aleman, B. E., Diaz, M., & Ferrer, M. A. (2024). A short review on graphonometric evaluation tools in children. *Lecture Notes in Computer Science (Including Subseries Lecture Notes in Artificial Intelligence and Lecture Notes in Bioinformatics), 14285 LNCS*, 3–20. https://doi.org/DOI: 10.1007/978-3-031-45461-5_1

Aliyev, E. (2024). Forensic Handwriting Analysis to Determine the Psychophysiological Traits. *International Journal of Religion, 5*(6), 511–530. DOI: 10.61707/2R6B-MR11

Asci, F., Scardapane, S., Zampogna, A., D'Onofrio, V., Testa, L., Patera, M., Falletti, M., Marsili, L., & Suppa, A. (2022). Handwriting Declines With Human Aging: A Machine Learning Study. *Frontiers in Aging Neuroscience*, *14*, 889930. DOI: 10.3389/FNAGI.2022.889930 PMID: 35601625

Bertolami, R., Uchida, S., Zimmermann, M., & Bunke, H. (2007). Non-uniform slant correction for handwritten text line recognition. *Proceedings of the International Conference on Document Analysis and Recognition, ICDAR, 1*, 18–22. https://doi.org/DOI: 10.1109/ICDAR.2007.4378668

Bhardwaj, M., & Srivastava, A. (2021). Psychological Assessment and Handwriting Analysis to Determine Personality Traits of a Convicted Criminal - A Case Study. [IJSR]. *International Journal of Scientific Research, 10*(10), 1000–1004. DOI: 10.21275/SR211019222113

Bird, C., Found, B., & Rogers, D. (2010). Forensic document examiners' skill in distinguishing between natural and disguised handwriting behaviors. *Journal of Forensic Sciences, 55*(5), 1291–1295. DOI: 10.1111/J.1556-4029.2010.01456.X PMID: 20533988

Bird, C. L., & Yang, X. (2024). Forensic document examination: A global snapshot. *Forensic Sciences Research, 9*(4). Advance online publication. DOI: 10.1093/FSR/OWAF001 PMID: 39911858

Chang, S. H., & Yu, N. Y. (2009). Computerized Handwriting Analysis in Children with/without Motor Incoordination. *IFMBE Proceedings, 23*, 402–405. DOI: 10.1007/978-3-540-92841-6_99

Durina, M. E. (2005). Disguised Signatures: Random or Repetitious? *Journal of the American Society of Questioned Document Examiners, 8*(1), 9–16. DOI: 10.69525/JASQDE.112

Farber, S. (2025). AI as a decision support tool in forensic image analysis: A pilot study on integrating large language models into crime scene investigation workflows. *Journal of Forensic Sciences, 00*, 1–12. DOI: 10.1111/1556-4029.70035 PMID: 40186399

Faundez-Zanuy, M., Fierrez, J., Ferrer, M. A., Diaz, M., Tolosana, R., & Plamondon, R. (2020). Handwriting Biometrics: Applications and Future Trends in e-Security and e-Health. *Cognitive Computation, 12*(5), 940–953. DOI: 10.1007/S12559-020-09755-Z/TABLES/2

Galekovic, J., Tkalac, Z., & Ledic, A. (2024). *Forensic Examination of Handwriting and Documents*. Selected ISABS Topics in Forensic Science and Molecular Anthropology. [Working Title], DOI: 10.5772/INTECHOPEN.115118

Hanlen, R. C., Manzolillo, P. A., Muehlberger, R. J., & Sperry, G. R. S. (1999). Survey of Handwriting Habit Areas Used by Forensic Document Examiners: Degree of Use and Discriminatory Power. *Journal of the American Society of Questioned Document Examiners, 2*(1), 45–50. DOI: 10.69525/JASQDE.27

Khajuria, A., & Pillai, A. A. (2023). Forensic handwriting examination: An updated clinical review. *Santosh University Journal of Health Sciences, 9*(2), 223–228. DOI: 10.4103/SUJHS.SUJHS_47_23

Kipouràs, P. (2022). The evolution of the simulated signature by the forger. *International Journal of Law in Changing World, 1*(2), 60–72. DOI: 10.54934/IJLCW.V1I2.25

Kumar, P., Deshmukh, A., Sharma, P., & Bhandari, Dr. D. (2024). Forensic examination of questioned documents. *Futuristic Trends in Social Sciences Volume 3 Book 19*, 284–316. https://doi.org/DOI: 10.58532/V3BJSO19P2CH13

Mahanta, B., L., & Deka, A. (2013). A Study on Handwritten Signature. *International Journal of Computer Applications, 79*(2), 48–52. DOI: 10.5120/13717-1489

McFarland, M., Nayak, A. R., Stockley, N., Twardowski, M., & Sullivan, J. (2020). Enhanced Light Absorption by Horizontally Oriented Diatom Colonies. *Frontiers in Marine Science, 7*. Advance online publication. DOI: 10.3389/FMARS.2020.00494

Mengi, M., & Malhotra, D. (2021). SpSiSb: The Technique to Identify Forgery in Legal Handwritten Documents. *Advances in Intelligent Systems and Computing, 1187*, 739–748. DOI: 10.1007/978-981-15-6014-9_89

Mirić, F., & Rodić Aranđelović, D. (2021). Forensic expertise of signatures and handwriting - multidisciplinary approach. *Facta Universitatis, Series. Law and Politics, 207*. Advance online publication. DOI: 10.22190/FULP2003207M

Mookiah, B. (2023). Handwriting Analysis in Forensic Studies: Examining the Science behind It. *Journal of Forensic Toxicology & Pharmacology, 2023*. Advance online publication. DOI: 10.4172/CICR.1000150

Office of Justice Programs. (n.d.). *History of questioned document examination in the United States* Retrieved April 6, 2025, from https://www.ojp.gov/ncjrs/virtual-library/abstracts/history-questioned-document-examination-united-states

Pandey, N., Singh, B., & Singh, S. (2024). Review of handwriting examination on an unusual surface. *IP International Journal of Forensic Medicine and Toxicological Sciences, 8*(4), 125–131. DOI: 10.18231/J.IJFMTS.2023.028

Parziale, A., Santoro, A., Marcelli, A., Rizzo, A. P., Molinari, C., Cappuzzo, A. G., & Fontana, F. (2014). An Interactive Tool for Forensic Handwriting Examination. *Proceedings of International Conference on Frontiers in Handwriting Recognition, ICFHR, 2014-December*, 440–445.

Research Gate. (n.d.). *A Perspective Analysis of Handwritten Signature Technology (PDF)*. Retrieved April 6, 2025, from https://www.researchgate.net/publication/380820435_A_Perspective_Analysis_of_Handwritten_Signature_Technology

Research Gate. (n.d.). *A Study of Consistent Similarities Between Complete, Partial, And Initial Signatures of An Individual for Author Identification In Forensic investigation (PDF)*. Retrieved April 6, 2025, from https://www.researchgate.net/publication/371125749_A_Study_of_Consistent_Similarities_Between_Complete_Partial_And_Initial_Signatures_of_An_Individual_for_Author_Identification_In_Forensic_investigation

Research Gate. (n.d.). *Analysis of Master Disguised Writing with the Aid of Specific Individual Writing Characteristics (PDF)*. Retrieved April 6, 2025, from https://www.researchgate.net/publication/344737641_Analysis_of_Master_Disguised_Writing_with_the_Aid_of_Specific_Individual_Writing_Characteristics

Research Gate. (n.d.) *Forensic examination of digitally Fabricated signatures in printed documents (PDF)*. Retrieved April 6, 2025, from https://www.researchgate.net/publication/335677718_Forensic_examination_oF_digitally_Fabricated_signatures_in_printed_documents

Research Gate. (n.d.). *Handwriting and gender: A statistical study (PDF)*. Retrieved April 6, 2025, from https://www.researchgate.net/publication/292848678_Handwriting_and_gender_A_statistical_study

Research Gate. (n.d.). *Handwriting and Visual Impairment: A Forensic Analysis of J. S. Bach's Signatures (PDF)*. Retrieved April 6, 2025, from https://www.researchgate.net/publication/281567269_Handwriting_and_Visual_Impairment_A_Forensic_Analysis_of_J_S_Bach%27s_Signatures

Research Gate. (n.d.). *Handwriting expertise: from paper to biometrics (PDF)*. Retrieved April 6, 2025, from https://www.researchgate.net/publication/280608896_Handwriting_expertise_from_paper_to_biometrics

Research Gate. (n.d.). *J Forensic Sci & Criminal Inves Artificial Aging of Paper (PDF)*. Retrieved April 6, 2025, from https://www.researchgate.net/publication/343054118_J_Forensic_Sci_Criminal_Inves_Artificial_Aging_of_Paper

Research Gate. (n.d.). *Raman spectroscopy for forensic analysis of inks in questioned documents | Request PDF*. Retrieved April 6, 2025, from https://www.researchgate.net/publication/256927581_Raman_spectroscopy_for_forensic_analysis_of_inks_in_questioned_documents

Research Gate. (n.d.). *The "handwriting brain": A meta-analysis of neuroimaging studies of motor versus orthographic processes | Request PDF*. Retrieved April 6, 2025, from https://www.researchgate.net/publication/247155789_The_handwriting_brain_A_meta-analysis_of_neuroimaging_studies_of_motor_versus_orthographic_processes

Saini, K., Sharma, B., & Kaur, M. (2021). Forensic examination of the effects of rheumatoid arthritis on handwriting characteristics. *Egyptian Journal of Forensic Sciences*, *11*(1). Advance online publication. DOI: 10.1186/S41935-021-00232-8

Schwellnus, H., Cameron, D., & Carnahan, H. (2012). Which to Choose: Manuscript or Cursive Handwriting? A Review of the Literature. *Journal of Occupational Therapy, Schools & Early Intervention*, *5*(3–4), 248–258. DOI: 10.1080/19411243.2012.744651

Sethi, M., Kumar, M., & Jindal, M. K. (2025). Forensic handwriting analysis: A hybrid classification framework for writer identification in Devanagari script. *Multimedia Tools and Applications*. Advance online publication. DOI: 10.1007/S11042-024-20574-4

Sita, J., Found, B., & Rogers, D. (2002). Forensic Handwriting Examiners' Expertise for Signature Comparison. *Journal of Forensic Sciences*, *47*(5), 1–8. DOI: 10.1520/JFS15521J PMID: 12353558

Srihari, S., Cha, S., Arora, H., & Lee, S. (2002). Individuality of Handwriting. *Journal of Forensic Sciences*, *47*(4), 1–17. DOI: 10.1520/JFS15447J PMID: 12136998

Srihari, S. N., Cha, S. H., Arora, H., & Lee, S. (2001). Individuality of handwriting: A validation study. *Proceedings of the International Conference on Document Analysis and Recognition, ICDAR, 2001-January*, 106–109. https://doi.org/DOI: 10.1109/ICDAR.2001.953764

Srihari, S. N., Cha, S. H., & Lee, S. (2001). Establishing Handwriting individuality using pattern recognition techniques. *Proceedings of the International Conference on Document Analysis and Recognition, ICDAR, 2001-January*, 1195–1204. https://doi.org/DOI: 10.1109/ICDAR.2001.953974

Stefansson, T. (2003). Formative evaluation of handwriting quality. *Perceptual and Motor Skills*, *97*(8), 1231. DOI: 10.2466/PMS.97.8.1231-1264 PMID: 15002869

Upadhyay, S., Singh, J., Shukla, S. K., & Sareen, R. K. (2018). Natural variations in the signature on various surfaces. *Medico-Legal Update*, *18*(1), 183–188. DOI: 10.5958/0974-1283.2018.00038.5

van Erp, M., Vuurpijt, L., Franke, K., & Schomaker, L. (2018). The Wanda measurement tool for forensic document examination. *Journal of Forensic Document Examination*, *28*, 5–14. DOI: 10.31974/JFDE28-5-14

APPENDIX

The following appendices contain references that assist with the understanding, application, and practice of forensic handwriting and signature analysis. They contain charts, a glossary, and pictures that are of use to students and professionals alike.

Sample Comparison Charts

This section contains real forensic examinations of handwriting and signature comparisons. The graphs show, for a single questioned and known sample, a side-by-side comparison and a point-by-point analysis of their similarities and differences. These can include variations related to the forming of letters, their angle/slope, pressure used to write, letter spacing, and line quality. The graphs also show signs of forgery, such as tremors and irregularities like excessive gaps in the handwriting. The purpose of these samples is to demonstrate the process that forensic document examiners use in their work to determine whether a document is genuine and/or to establish its authorship. Each chart is provided with a commentary describing the annotated features, as well as a collection of prompts, to assist the students in developing observational and analytic skills.

Glossary of Terms

The following is a glossary of key terms about the forensic document examination space:

1. **Baseline:** The (notional) line on which writing sits.
2. **Class Characteristics** - Typical features of a group of writers, following a common form of handwriting instruction.
3. **Personal:** Those unique qualities, those personal characteristics found in a writing, that differentiate one person from another.
4. **Electrostatic Detection Apparatus (ESDA)** —used to visualise indents on paper.
5. **Forgery:** False writing or change of ownership in a document done on purpose to deceive.
6. **Natural Variation:** Low, standard variation around means seen repeatedly in similar writing from the same writer
7. **Altered Writing:** Writing that the original writer has purposely changed to hide identity.
8. **Traced forgery** - a ratio of true signature is traced using a writing instrument.

9. **Line Quality:** The smoothness or shakiness of writing strokes, usually an indication of fluency or forgery.

Chapter 5
Challenges in Forensic Analysis of Compressed and Low-Resolution Videos

S. Ida Evangeline
https://orcid.org/0000-0003-2997-7897
Government College of Engineering, Tirunelveli, India

ABSTRACT

The forensic analysis of digital video has become a cornerstone of modern investigative and judicial processes, yet it is frequently impeded by the technical limitations inherent in compressed and low-resolution footage. These challenges arise from the widespread use of lossy compression algorithms and low-quality recording devices in surveillance systems, mobile phones, and online platforms—leading to visual artifacts, detail loss, and data degradation that complicate accurate interpretation. This chapter looks at the different issues that arise during the analysis of tampered video and their effects on facial recognition, reading license plates, reconstructing events and detecting any tampering. It also looks at the issues and rules about using altered video in court and underlines the importance of clear and repeatable methods.

1. INTRODUCTION

In the digital age, video footage has become a cornerstone of forensic evidence, playing a vital role in criminal investigations, legal adjudication, and public accountability. Surveillance systems are now ubiquitous in public and private spaces, while smartphones and dashboard cameras offer real-time recording capabilities that

DOI: 10.4018/979-8-3373-3795-1.ch005

can document events from multiple perspectives. With online platforms, videos can now be seen and saved by more people, so incidents like small crimes and major security breaches are often recorded first on video. Because of the huge amount of video data now available, forensic analysts are expected to get valuable information from videos that are usually low-quality and highly compressed (Liu & Jia, 2024).

Despite its potential, video evidence is frequently marred by technical limitations that hinder its forensic value. Two of the most persistent issues are compression and low resolution. Video compression is a necessary trade-off in modern digital systems, enabling efficient storage and transmission by removing redundant visual information. But, this way of processing can bring artifacts such as blocks, blurring and missing details that can make important parts of the film hard to see. Such distortions are a major issue in forensics, because tiny details such as facial features, hand gestures or objects present in the scene can play a vital role as evidence (Li et al. 2024).

Low-resolution video presents an equally daunting challenge. Surveillance systems, particularly older models or those operating under bandwidth constraints, often capture video at resolutions too low to preserve identifying features. There may be extra pixels, blurry movement and poor detail in the spaces when the footage is viewed. That is why it is hard to identify suspects, read car plates or closely examine people's behaviors and how they interact. When videos are compressed and have low resolution, it can reduce how effective manual review and automated analysis are which may result in missed or incorrect conclusions during investigations (Oguz & Ikizler-Cinbis, 2024).

The forensic implications of these limitations extend beyond technical hurdles. When presented in legal settings, degraded video must not only be intelligible to human observers but also meet the stringent standards of admissibility, reliability, and reproducibility. Courts are now asking forensic experts to explain why they use enhancement, explain how video evidence is created and changed and list the problems caused by poor quality. In this situation, forensic video analysts have to ensure they make the footage clearer and easier to interpret, but not add any speculative or misleading information that could make it less valuable as evidence (Sandhya & Kashyap, 2024).

This chapter aims to provide a comprehensive understanding of the technical, forensic, and legal challenges posed by compressed and low-resolution video evidence in investigative and judicial contexts. The central problem addressed is the *reduced reliability and interpretability of visual data* due to compression artifacts and limited resolution—factors that significantly impact identification, authentication, and evidentiary admissibility.

The specific objectives of this chapter are to:

- Explain the mechanisms and consequences of video compression and resolution degradation.
- Analyze how these factors affect forensic procedures, such as facial recognition, event reconstruction, and tampering detection.
- Review emerging enhancement techniques, including AI-based tools, for mitigating these limitations.
- Examine legal, procedural, and ethical considerations surrounding the use of digitally altered video evidence.
- Highlight current research directions and future trends in forensic video analysis.

The scope of the chapter encompasses both technical and legal perspectives, drawing from computer vision, signal processing, and digital forensics. It focuses primarily on surveillance, mobile, and web-sourced video data. Deepfake detection and real-time analytics are discussed as emerging themes but not explored in exhaustive technical detail.

In this chapter, we begin by unpacking how video compression introduces visual artifacts (Section 2), followed by a discussion of the forensic implications of these artifacts (Section 3). We then address the specific challenges posed by low-resolution footage (Section 4), and explore emerging analytical techniques that mitigate these limitations (Section 5). Legal and procedural considerations are outlined in Section 6, before concluding with emerging research directions (Section 7).

2. FOUNDATIONS OF VIDEO COMPRESSION

To understand the challenges of forensic analysis in compressed video, it is essential to first explore how video compression works and why it is widely used. Since digital video files hold many high-quality frames, each second is usually recorded at a rate of 25 to 60 frames, so they end up being very large. Because uncompressed video uses a lot of data, it needs a great deal of storage and wide bandwidth for sending. Compression methods are used to make files much smaller, keeping the picture quality good enough for humans to notice (Lu et al. 2024).

Video compression algorithms operate based on principles of redundancy reduction. They eliminate spatial redundancy (repetition of information within a single frame) and temporal redundancy (similarities across consecutive frames). Compression methods mainly include intra-frame (spatial) compression, where each frame is treated as a separate image and inter-frame (temporal) compression which records the changes between frames using data from other frames. They are applied in codecs used in industry such as MPEG-4, H.264/AVC, H.265/HEVC and AV1 (Yang et al. 2024).

A fundamental component of video compression is transform coding, which converts image data into a frequency domain using algorithms like the Discrete Cosine Transform (DCT). This makes it possible for frequency coefficients to be approximated and rounded off during the next phase, quantization, to save on the information that has to be stored. Although it helps to reduce data, quantization causes a loss of important image details, mostly in parts with high-frequency edges or textures. For example, when high compression is applied, it becomes noticeable that the image quality is lower (Goyal et al. 2024).

One of the most noticeable side effects of compression is blocking artifacts—unnatural square-shaped patterns caused by encoding images in non-overlapping blocks, typically 8×8 or 16×16 pixels. Each block is handled on its own and when the quantization level is high, differences at the block boundaries become very noticeable. It is common for ringing to occur, where curved artifacts appear beside sharp edges and for mosquito noise which causes speckles to flicker around moving edges. Such artifacts are not just about appearance; they can hide important details, look as if the image has been altered or make it hard to spot manipulated areas (Lin et al. 2024).

Motion estimation and compensation, key aspects of inter-frame compression, involve predicting movement from one frame to the next. The movement of each block is noted with motion vectors and saved, allowing fewer frames to be encoded. Even so, this process might result in temporal artifacts, for example, ghosting, blurring or regions where objects are out of focus because of movement. Such distortions weaken the continuity of video and may prevent forensic teams from tracking movements, aligning events or spotting slight signs of behavior (Sakthi et al. 2024).

Moreover, video files are often subjected to transcoding—conversion from one compression format or bit rate to another—as they are uploaded to online platforms, transferred between devices, or edited for playback. With every transcoding cycle, the video is compressed further which might get rid of important forensic markers. It can be very damaging to the artwork when the source device is not identified or when proving the artwork's origin is required (Borges et al. 2024).

In forensic contexts, understanding the nature and origin of compression artifacts is not only vital for interpreting degraded footage but also for distinguishing authentic data from malicious alterations. For example, artifact patterns might indicate if a video has been altered after it was recorded. Compression signatures may help identify the camera or software used in a video which can be important for tracing the origin. Still, to use these applications well, one needs to understand how compression affects the data and how artifacts can cover or look like forensic signs.

In short, video compression is a necessary process for digital video management, although it adds many extra issues for forensic analysis. Any forensic strategy that aims to examine or confirm data from damaged footage should begin with learning about compression, artifacts and their effects on video quality. So, forensic specialists should know how to work with video encoding and be ready to handle the legal and investigative aspects of this technology.

Having explored the technical underpinnings of video compression and artifact formation, we now turn to their practical consequences in forensic contexts. The following section examines how compression-induced distortions hinder tasks such as identification, tampering detection, and sequence reconstruction.

3. FORENSIC CHALLENGES POSED BY COMPRESSION

The forensic examination of compressed video is fraught with technical obstacles that directly impact the reliability and interpretability of visual evidence. Even though compression is used to shrink files for regular viewing, forensic analysis needs much higher quality. Data like tiny changes in a person's face, textures in the video and slight movements can be important in an investigation, but these details are often the first to be lost or altered during compression.

One of the central challenges arises from compression artifacts—unintended distortions introduced as a byproduct of the encoding process. Some examples are blocking artifacts, where the transition between different blocks can be seen as grid lines, mostly in regions that are either not detailed or heavily quantized. Investigators might not see key details at the scene due to these artifacts' presence and they could also suspect tampering when they notice them. As a case in point, an object covering part of the face might make it hard to identify a person or look as if the person's face has been changed (Hafner et al. 2024).

Quantization noise is another serious concern. During quantization which is a lossy stage, the frequency components are rounded and some details in the image are permanently removed. Because of this, edges, textures and small details which are often needed for license plate recognition, text reading or comparing textures, suffer the most. When the evidence depends on little details, the loss caused by quantization may result in wrong or incomplete conclusions (Bao et al. 2024).

Complications escalate when videos are re-encoded or transcoded multiple times. Every time a file is compressed, more damage is caused and the results are not always twice as much; new artifacts can appear as the compression interacts with the initial ones. This can often be seen in online videos (like those found on social media), CCTV footage that loops on a system or videos edited with consumer-grade software on mobile devices. When this happens, important forensic signs like compression signatures or digital noise can be completely wiped out, so it becomes impossible to carry out tasks such as finding the device's owner or identifying tampering (Zhao et al. 2024).

The temporal dimension of video is also heavily affected by compression. This method depends on estimating and compensating movement between frames, using motion vectors to do so. If motion prediction is inaccurate, especially in scenes with fast motion, things being covered or complex backgrounds, it can cause ghosting, smearing or motion artifacts. Such distortions get in the way of temporal analysis tasks such as arranging events in order, following movements or understanding behavior. When it comes to legal cases, where exactly what happened and when matters for liability or intent such errors are very serious (Rastogi & Tripathi, 2024).

Another forensic complication involves key frame spacing. Compressed video files have I-, P- and B-frames and just I-frames contain complete pictures. If a frame is far from the nearest I-frame, it relies more on other nearby frames to be reconstructed. When streams are highly compressed, I-frames can be far from each other which reduces the number of fully detailed frames that can be studied. Also, when a video is edited and not re-encoded, the lack of nearby I-frames can cause the edited part to appear incomplete or corrupted which may create confusion for forensic analysis (Rajan & Parameswaran, 2025).

Compression also complicates authenticity verification and tampering detection. Forensic investigators often use compression, metadata and pixel patterns to spot inconsistencies. But doing too many compressions can sometimes hide or copy signs of tampering such as cloned areas, extra frames or fake transitions. Besides, double compression may result in artifacts that appear similar to evidence of photo editing which could cause the software to misidentify the image as edited unless the forensic expert can follow the compression history (El-Shafai et al. 2024).

The analytical process itself must be adapted to these challenges. Some forensic tools do not work as they should on compressed video. Missing or distorted data may cause automatic feature detection, facial recognition or object tracking algorithms to produce mistakes. Because of this, analysts should be aware of their tools' performance in stressful situations and think carefully about the uncertainty introduced by data compression (Bertazzini et al. 2024).

It is important to have both technical knowledge of video compression and rigorous skills in analyzing evidence for forensic analysis of compressed video. Analysts must be able to tell apart artifacts and anomalies, handle the impact of data degradation and make clear how compression plays a role in their results. Because more investigations use compressed video, there is a clear need for forensic techniques that can handle the new challenges of digital evidence.

While compression degrades visual fidelity through artifacts, resolution loss presents an equally significant obstacle. The next section shifts focus to the forensic implications of low-resolution footage, where even basic visual cues may be absent or ambiguous.

4. ANALYSIS OF LOW-RESOLUTION VIDEOS

Low-resolution video represents a significant and persistent challenge in forensic analysis, often limiting the amount of extractable, verifiable information from a given recording. Unlike high-resolution footage, low-resolution video is less detailed and this makes it difficult to use for many important forensic tasks. The difficulties become more obvious when images are degraded and important details such as facial features, license plate numbers or interactions involving small objects must be identified (Oguz & Ikizler-Cinbis, 2024).

The causes of low resolution in forensic video sources are varied. Many older surveillance systems were designed with limited bandwidth and storage capacities, leading to resolutions as low as 240p or 480p. When the network is slow or storage settings are used, newer systems may work at a lower resolution. Also, because users record videos on their phones and share them on messaging apps or social media, the platforms or users themselves often downsample them which leads to worse quality. In the end, the photos or videos will have fewer pixels, less detail and are more likely to show artifacts from compression (Dastbaravardeh et al. 2024).

One of the most direct consequences of low resolution is the loss of discriminative features necessary for identification tasks. In facial recognition, the structure of the eyes, nose and mouth might be greatly simplified and represented by only a few pixels. This puts severe restrictions on both manual and automatic face recognition methods which depend on accurate representations of facial shape and surface. It has been found in studies that face recognition accuracy drops sharply when the number of pixels is below certain levels (for example, 32×32 pixels for frontal faces), especially if the lighting or the pose is not ideal. This situation can result in greater uncertainties or even a complete failure to identify the person in real forensic cases (Dandekar et al. 2024).

Vehicle and license plate recognition face similar challenges. In low-resolution footage, license plates often appear as blurred, featureless blocks. For OCR to work properly, images must clearly show alphanumeric characters and trying to make them clearer or larger usually leads to more noise and artifacts. This might cause false conclusions unless the use of enhancement is clear and careful. When officers cannot read the license plates or vehicle information, important details about a case may be missing (Zheng et al. 2024).

The challenges extend to behavioral and situational analysis. In low-resolution videos, motion blur and temporal aliasing are more pronounced due to slower frame rates and poor sensor performance. As a result, distinguishing object handling, gestures and ways people interact with others becomes difficult. It is difficult to use forensic analysis on poorly filmed videos to find out what happened, review the use of force or understand someone's intentions. In some cases, even after enhancement, the images might not have enough detail to end the investigation, so other forms of evidence such as recordings, metadata or witness accounts are needed (Kai et al. 2025).

Another critical concern with low-resolution footage is the increased ambiguity and interpretive subjectivity it introduces. In high-resolution video, the abundance of visual information allows for more objective analysis. Alternatively, when images are not clear, it is easier for people to think of several possible outcomes. When judges rely on photos, the ambiguity could cause experts to disagree or challenge them in court. For this reason, analysts ought to be very cautious in explaining the certainty and boundaries of their results when dealing with such video evidence (Schonig, 2024).

Efforts to address these limitations often involve enhancement and restoration techniques, including contrast stretching, interpolation-based upscaling, or advanced super-resolution algorithms. While sharpening the image, these techniques might also include details or artifacts that were not originally in the recording. This raises two questions: how to make video easier to interpret without affecting its legal value. Best practices state that enhanced videos should be labeled and given along with the original material and a clear description of the enhancement process and its impact on meaning should be added (Sun, 2025).

In some cases, alternative strategies may be employed. Analysts may use frame averaging or temporal integration, where information is aggregated across multiple frames to reduce noise and improve feature visibility. Using several video angles, when available, can make up for low resolution by giving more views or repeating some visuals. Also, new AI methods are learning to handle forensic tasks with low-resolution evidence, using background information and guesswork to find details that older methods miss (Agrahari Baniya et al. 2024).

The usefulness of low-resolution video in forensics is affected by both the technology and the way the investigation is carried out. Experts should admit the restrictions of low detail, refrain from reading too much into the results and use other supporting evidence when it is available. Because more criminal investigations rely on low-quality video, forensic science should keep finding reliable and defensible ways to handle these important pieces of digital evidence.

Given the limitations imposed by compression and low resolution, forensic practitioners must rely on enhancement and analysis strategies to recover actionable insights. In the next section, we examine the latest techniques—ranging from classical filtering to AI-based super-resolution—that help mitigate these issues.

5. ADVANCED ANALYTICAL TECHNIQUES AND MITIGATION STRATEGIES

As forensic professionals increasingly confront the reality of compressed and low-resolution video evidence, a wide array of analytical and enhancement strategies have emerged to address the limitations imposed by data degradation. They cover standard image processing, advanced machine learning and techniques that mix methods to improve the way images are presented and still preserve their authenticity. The main purpose is to recover or guess missing information, reduce errors and provide reliable analysis, as visual confusion in forensic cases can strongly affect both the investigation and the trial.

A common starting point in forensic workflows involves pre-processing techniques aimed at suppressing the most conspicuous artifacts introduced by compression. For example, deblocking filters help to hide the grid-like appearance of block-based encoding and denoising algorithms get rid of mosquito noise or random pixels without losing much detail. Also, you can use contrast enhancement and histogram equalization to enhance how visible the video is in low light or with quick changes in brightness. Most of these tools do not change the original scene, so they can be used where admitting evidence based on the footage is important (Sigamani & Selvaraj, 2024).

However, pre-processing alone is often insufficient when critical details are severely degraded. In such cases, super-resolution (SR) techniques become indispensable. With these methods, higher-resolution images are made using bicubic or Lanczos resampling that guesses pixel values from the local area. They are helpful for enlarging small images, but tend to create pictures that are not very detailed and lack sharpness (Kumar et al. 2024).

In contrast, AI-based super-resolution, particularly deep learning models like convolutional neural networks (CNNs) and generative adversarial networks (GANs), have revolutionized the enhancement landscape. Because they are fed large data sets with many high- and low-resolution images, these models can map heavily damaged input to detailed, clear results. In forensic work, AI-supported SR can improve the appearance of faces, plates and objects which can often turn unidentifiable things into things that can be seen and read. For illustration, using ESRGAN and Real-ESRGAN, it is possible to accurately analyze and compare data from images as tiny as 16×16 pixels, thanks to their ability to improve image quality (AlHalawani et al. 2024).

Still, using such models in forensic science creates a significant problem: although AI can help see details more clearly, it might also invent details that were not present in the original evidence. There are doubts about if enhanced images can be trusted and if they are allowed in court, since the truthfulness of visual evidence is important. Some systems include explainability tools like attention maps or uncertainty heatmaps, so analysts can tell which parts of the image are based on the input data and which on the system's learned priors (Grm et al. 2025).

In addition to enhancement, forensic analysts use motion magnification and temporal super-resolution to see minor movements or actions happening within video sequences. Eulerian motion magnification boosts small changes in pixel brightness over a period which is important in medical forensics and behavioral analysis. Frame interpolation and video stabilization are also used to make rough footage smoother and clearer, making it easier to understand fast-paced scenes such as attacks, chases or confrontations (Tonpe et al. 2024).

Forensic video analysis also covers checking for tampering and confirming the source by looking for differences in compression artifacts, noise or how the video was encoded. Double compression analysis might uncover non-aligned matrices which can be a sign that a video has been revised and re-saved. Block-level fingerprinting can find cloned parts or inserted things by studying the way macroblocks are connected or how prediction vectors differ. These methods are very useful for confirming the truth of evidence that comes from third parties or the internet, as the chain-of-custody may not be clear (Kadha et al. 2025).

All processing steps, including how the image was enhanced which algorithms were used and any personal judgments made, should be documented by forensic practitioners to ensure the process can be reviewed and defended. When using frames with improved detail, include the original video and make sure annotations clearly mark the parts you observed and the parts you inferred. Experts in courtrooms usually need to describe how enhancement works, explain its benefits and admit that some uncertainties can arise from using algorithms (Chiang et al. 2025).

Studies have shown that these techniques have proved useful in different areas of forensic science. Thanks to AI, poor-quality footage from CCTV and social media has helped detectives find suspects in crime cases. In accidents, stacking and stabilizing frames has made license plates and traffic easier to see and in law enforcement, enlarging motion has helped identify possible use of force by spotting slight hand and arm actions. They show that using advanced analytical tools is important, but they must be used with thoughtful and careful interpretation and strict methodology (Qawasmi & Al-Kadi, 2025).

In short, analyzing compressed and low-resolution videos involves much more than just enhancement and now relies on combining signal processing, machine learning and forensic science. While these tools are very powerful, using them must be guided by a framework that values openness, repeatability and obeys the law. Forensic video analysis will move forward by using technology to improve our understanding of evidence, but without reducing its credibility or validity in court.

While technical interventions can enhance degraded video, their forensic utility is constrained by legal and procedural frameworks. The following section addresses admissibility, authenticity, and ethical concerns related to processing and presenting altered or AI-enhanced footage in court.

6. LEGAL AND PROCEDURAL CONSIDERATIONS

The forensic analysis of digital video evidence—particularly when it involves heavily compressed or low-resolution footage—raises a complex array of legal and procedural challenges. When video evidence guides the outcome of a case, how it is managed, changed and analyzed is as important as the video itself. It is important for forensic practitioners to know the rules and standards for video evidence to guarantee that their findings are admissible in court.

A primary concern is evidentiary admissibility, which depends on factors such as relevance, authenticity, and reliability. Poor-quality video might be considered unfair if it makes important details hard to see, since this can easily confuse viewers. Sometimes, opposing lawyers wonder if the changes made to the image give a true representation of the original or if they may suggest something that wasn't there in the first place. More and more, courts expect that every method used to process and review video evidence is well-documented, repeatable and has scientific support. This is based on guidelines set by tests such as Daubert and Frye which look into whether the methods used by experts are accepted as reliable by the legal system (Ahmed et al. 2025).

Chain of custody is another foundational element of legal admissibility. Compressed or low-resolution videos often come from decentralized sources—security cameras, smartphones, or social media—and may pass through multiple hands or digital systems before reaching forensic analysts. Every transfer event creates the opportunity for changes or loss in the metadata. Should the chain of custody not be well documented, people might wonder if the footage has been changed or shortened. Forensic workers need to thoroughly record all activities with the video, from obtaining it to analyzing it, to maintain the evidence's integrity (Grossman & Grimm, 2025).

Authenticity verification becomes particularly difficult with degraded video. Compression can hide any signs that the image has been edited and when an image is low resolution, it can be difficult to detect lighting mismatches, unusual shadows or repeated patterns. To evaluate the authenticity of a video, analysts might do compression history analysis, examine metadata or study every picture frame, but they must be clear about the problems these methods can have with low-quality recordings. When footage is used to prove or disprove major issues like who a suspect is or whether police used force appropriately, courts carefully examine if the evidence is genuine (Amerini et al. 2025).

The use of AI-based enhancement tools, while increasingly common, introduces new legal complexities. Methods based on deep learning such as super-resolution, denoising or frame interpolation, can produce artificial content that was not part of the original data. They can, however, cause people to question the possibility of misleading information. Where image integrity is very important, any enhancements intended to help may still be refused by a court unless the changes are closely monitored, the original images are kept and the process is clearly described. In some cases, courts ask for the original and enhanced videos to be side by side and for any inferred data to be marked so it is easy to identify (Yadav, 2025).

Expert testimony plays a central role in guiding the court's understanding of video evidence. Experts are required to state their credentials, spell out the forensic techniques they applied and clearly show how they reached their conclusions. If the video is of low quality, they should point out the limits of their analysis, express the confidence in their results and mention the chance for mistakes. When identifications or orderings depend on partially damaged or computer-repaired footage, it is important to admit the uncertainties. Making conclusions seem more certain than they actually are can harm both the case and the reputation of forensic science (Sushir & Bhutada, 2025).

Professional guidelines from bodies such as the Scientific Working Group on Digital Evidence (SWGDE), European Network of Forensic Science Institutes (ENFSI), and the National Institute of Standards and Technology (NIST) provide critical direction for handling video evidence. They focus on the importance of reusing studies, being open about methods, using reliable tools and using peer-reviewed approaches. It is also recommended not to rely on software or algorithms developed for the general public, since some do not have scientific proof and do not reveal their internal working (Rajivkannan et al. 2025).

Another emerging procedural concern involves juror perception and cognitive bias. Jurors may think that enhanced video or video that looks clearer, is more accurate, even though it is not. Therefore, forensic analysts and legal experts should be extra careful when explaining video evidence in court because of this bias. Clearly explaining, comparing and discussing the enhanced footage with experts helps avoid misunderstandings or errors by the jurors (Grossman & Grimm, 2025).

In summary, working with compressed and low-resolution video in the legal process is not only about technical analysis. Forensic experts have to be knowledgeable in legal rules, courtroom talk and how to present evidence to help justice and stand up to any criticism. Since digital video is used more often in investigations and trials, it is important to establish clear and defensible ways to handle and interpret poor-quality footage for forensic analysis.

Beyond current practices, the forensic community is rapidly evolving to meet new challenges in digital evidence. The next section explores cutting-edge trends and ongoing research that aim to future-proof forensic video analysis in a landscape of increasing complexity and uncertainty.

7. EMERGING TRENDS AND RESEARCH DIRECTIONS

The forensic analysis of compressed and low-resolution videos is undergoing a dynamic transformation, propelled by advances in computer vision, artificial intelligence, and multimedia forensics. Because video content is now more widespread, varied and complex—it appears in surveillance systems, personal gadgets and online social networks—new ways of interpreting it are needed. The focus is now on building systems that can actively and intelligently gather information from badly damaged or low-quality footage. This section highlights the most recent research and methods that are changing the future of forensic video analysis.

One of the most impactful developments is the integration of multimodal data in forensic workflows. In the past, video analysis used only visuals, but now forensic investigators look at audio, metadata (such as timestamps and GPS) and other information found in related digital files. Using several methods, analysts can confirm evidence, fill in missing parts and describe events in more detail. As an illustration, metadata can show the date and place a video was recorded and sound clues can help identify speakers and the background of what is happening. In cases where the video quality is low and only the visual content is not enough for interpretation, additional modalities are very beneficial (Sushir & Bhutada, 2025).

Another emerging trend is the shift toward real-time and near-real-time forensic analysis, enabled by advances in hardware acceleration (e.g., GPUs, TPUs) and edge computing. As situations such as active shooter events, terrorist threats or disasters arise, there is a rising need for systems that can review videos quickly to spot and deal with urgent incidents. These platforms are now able to do object detection, track motion, identify faces and detect anomalies, even with compressed or limited video feeds. Even though it is just beginning in forensics, this ability provides new ways to control monitoring, quickly review evidence and stay aware of the situation (Rajivkannan et al. 2025).

The rise of explainable artificial intelligence (XAI) is also reshaping forensic video analysis. Many deep learning models, used for super-resolution, classification and detecting tampering, work very well but are not transparent about their conclusions. Being opaque can cause problems in legal and investigative settings. Explainable AI tries to help users see the reasons behind a model's output by displaying attention maps, feature scores or simplified decision trees. XAI helps forensic analysts verify the accuracy of a model, present results in court more effectively and prevent unfair or wrong decisions from the model (Singla & Khan, 2025).

Efforts to establish standardized datasets, benchmarking protocols, and reproducibility practices are also gaining momentum. Because publicly available, annotated video datasets that include real-world degradation are lacking, the forensic community has had difficulties verifying its tools and methods. In turn, researchers have put together and released datasets with different levels of compression, various types of tampering, fake low-resolution images and paired data that shows the correct information. Now, benchmarking helps in comparing different enhancement methods, detection tools and forensic workflows in a controlled environment. These resources make the research process more thorough and also increase the certainty with which tools are selected and calibrated in forensic labs (Alrashoud, 2025).

Another promising direction involves robust and generalizable AI models that maintain performance across diverse and degraded conditions. Most of these models are built using clear, bright and uncompressed images which can cause them to stumble when they come across poor-quality or noisy real-world footage. Work in domain adaptation, self-supervised learning and few-shot learning is helping to fill this gap because it allows models to learn with limited or low-quality input and still detect useful forensic features. They are especially useful in places like rural areas and war zones, where good video technology is hard to come by (Rajivkannan et al. 2025).

Additionally, there is growing interest in forensic watermarking and proactive evidence tagging. Certain researchers believe it's better to include verifiable watermarks or cryptographic signatures in video streams at the moment of recording, rather than treating enhancement and analysis as later actions. They can help confirm the originality of a video, uncover any unauthorized changes and identify its source, without just depending on forensic guesswork. When used with blockchain-based evidence management systems, they make it possible to have more secure, open and trustworthy digital evidence systems (Soni et al. 2025).

Finally, as forensic video tools become more powerful and automated, there is a concurrent need for ethical frameworks and governance models to guide their use. In forensic cases, where lives and rights are involved, issues about fairness, misuse and accountability are very important. Organizations such as INTERPOL, the IEEE and the European Union's AI Act are promoting the need for people to review AI systems, check for biases and ensure transparency in forensic technologies. These principles will help keep forensic video analysis advanced and at the same time ethical and responsible toward society (Liman et al. 2025).

In short, the future of working with compressed and low-resolution videos in forensics is based on combining AI, signal processing, legal science and ethical design. Using explainable models, standardized techniques, real-time systems and multimodal approaches, the forensic community is developing advanced tools for finding truth in digital evidence that is always changing.

As we have seen, the field of forensic video analysis is advancing both technically and procedurally. We conclude by synthesizing these insights and offering recommendations for improving the reliability and admissibility of video evidence in modern forensic practice.

8. CONCLUSION

The forensic analysis of compressed and low-resolution videos represents a critical yet challenging domain at the intersection of technology, science, and law. Since digital video is used more and more in surveillance, personal gadgets and online sites, experts in forensics must manage a rising challenge of data damage, artifact interference and uncertainty in interpreting evidence. This chapter looked at how compression and low-resolution images make it harder to do identification, authentication and reconstruct events. Despite these obstacles, advancements in image processing and artificial intelligence are providing powerful new tools to enhance degraded footage and support reliable forensic interpretation. Thanks to AI, motion magnification and hybrid analysis approaches, the field is changing fast to suit suboptimal video evidence. Yet, new tools have to be handled carefully, guided by clear documentation, openness and compliance with existing forensic and legal requirements. Moving ahead, using different types of data, understandable AI, instant analysis tools and common evaluation methods will play a key role in improving forensic methods. As things develop in technology and the law, it is important for forensic analysts, lawyers and technologists to cooperate so that damaged video can still help with justice. This chapter supports the goal by explaining current issues, pointing out emerging solutions and supporting a scientific and legally sound way of analyzing forensic videos today.

REFERENCES

Agrahari Baniya, A., Lee, T. K., Eklund, P., & Aryal, S. (2024). Frame selection using spatiotemporal dynamics and key features as input pre-processing for video super-resolution models. *SN Computer Science*, *5*(3), 323.

Ahmed, S., Khan, M. F., Singh, B., Singh, N., & Sharma, B. (2025). Enhancing Crime Scene Analysis: The Impact of AI Technologies on Evidence Processing. In *Forensic Intelligence and Deep Learning Solutions in Crime Investigation* (pp. 63-84). IGI Global Scientific Publishing.

AlHalawani, S., Benjdira, B., Ammar, A., Koubaa, A., & Ali, A. M. (2024). Diff-Plate: A Diffusion Model for Super-Resolution of License Plate Images. *Electronics (Basel)*, *13*(13), 2670.

Alrashoud, M. (2025). Deepfake video detection methods, approaches, and challenges. *Alexandria Engineering Journal*, *125*, 265–277.

Amerini, I., Barni, M., Battiato, S., Bestagini, P., Boato, G., Bruni, V., & Vitulano, D. (2025). Deepfake media forensics: Status and future challenges. *Journal of Imaging*, *11*(3), 73. PMID: 40137185

Bao, Q., Wang, Y., Hua, H., Dong, K., & Lee, F. (2024). An anti-forensics video forgery detection method based on noise transfer matrix analysis. *Sensors (Basel)*, *24*(16), 5341. PMID: 39205036

Bertazzini, G., Baracchi, D., Shullani, D., Iuliani, M., & Piva, A. (2024). CoFFEE: A codec-based forensic feature extraction and evaluation software for H. 264 videos. *EURASIP Journal on Information Security*, *2024*(1), 34.

Borges, A., Zatt, B., Porto, M., & Correa, G. (2024). A systematic literature review on video transcoding acceleration: Challenges, solutions, and trends. *Multimedia Tools and Applications*, *83*(24), 64079–64108.

Chiang, C. Y., Chua, H. N., Jasser, M. B., Wong, R. T., & Issa, B. (2025, February). Transformer-Based Ensemble Approach for Robust Deepfake Detection in Low-Resolution Short Videos. In *2025 21st IEEE International Colloquium on Signal Processing & Its Applications (CSPA)* (pp. 307-312). IEEE.

Dandekar, P., Aote, S. S., & Raipurkar, A. (2024). Low-resolution face recognition: Review, challenges and research directions. *Computers & Electrical Engineering*, *120*, 109846.

Dastbaravardeh, E., Askarpour, S., Saberi Anari, M., & Rezaee, K. (2024). Channel Attention-Based Approach with Autoencoder Network for Human Action Recognition in Low-Resolution Frames. *International Journal of Intelligent Systems, 2024*(1), 1052344.

El-Shafai, W., Fouda, M. A., El-Rabaie, E. S. M., & El-Salam, N. A. (2024). A comprehensive taxonomy on multimedia video forgery detection techniques: Challenges and novel trends. *Multimedia Tools and Applications*, *83*(2), 4241–4307. PMID: 37362636

Goyal, S., Bahri, D., Dongre, Y. V., Kuppuraj, T., Arora, M., & Chitra, S. (2024, June). An Analysis of Transform Coding Techniques in Image and Video Compression. In *2024 15th International Conference on Computing Communication and Networking Technologies (ICCCNT)* (pp. 1-6). IEEE.

Grm, K., Özata, B. K., Kantarcı, A., Štruc, V., & Ekenel, H. K. (2025). Degrade or super-resolve to recognize? Bridging the Domain Gap for Cross-Resolution Face Recognition. *IEEE Access : Practical Innovations, Open Solutions.*

Grossman, M., & Grimm, P. (2025). Judicial Approaches to Acknowledged and Unacknowledged AI-Generated Evidence. *Science and Technology Law Review, 26*(2).

Hafner, M., Radovic, A., Langer, M., Findenig, S., & Uhl, A. (2024, June). Forensic Recognition of Codec-Specific Image Compression Artefacts. In *Proceedings of the 2024 ACM Workshop on Information Hiding and Multimedia Security* (pp. 131-136).

Kadha, V. K., Bakshi, S., & Das, S. K. (2025). Unravelling Digital Forgeries: A Systematic Survey on Image Manipulation Detection and Localization. *ACM Computing Surveys.*

Kai, D., Zhang, Y., Wang, J., Xiao, Z., Xiong, Z., & Sun, X. (2025, April). Event-Enhanced Blurry Video Super-Resolution. *Proceedings of the AAAI Conference on Artificial Intelligence*, *39*(4), 4175–4183.

Kumar, V., Sharma, U., & Louis, A. M. (2024, June). Improved GAN for Efficient Cyber Forensics. In *2024 15th International Conference on Computing Communication and Networking Technologies (ICCCNT)* (pp. 1-7). IEEE.

Li, J., Li, B., & Lu, Y. (2024). Neural video compression with feature modulation. In *Proceedings of the IEEE/CVF Conference on Computer Vision and Pattern Recognition* (pp. 26099-26108).

Liman, Z., Kayhan, U., & Yıldırım, M. Ş. (2025). Evaluation of Images Marked as Child Abuse by Digital Systems in Terms of Forensic Age Determination: A Retrospective Study. *Nigerian Journal of Clinical Practice*, *28*(1), 118–127. PMID: 40326945

Lin, L., Wang, M., Yang, J., Zhang, K., & Zhao, T. (2024). Toward Efficient Video Compression Artifact Detection and Removal: A Benchmark Dataset. *IEEE Transactions on Multimedia*.

Liu, C., & Jia, K. (2024). Multi-Frame Quality Recovery Model for Compressed Video Enhancement. *IEEE Transactions on Consumer Electronics*.

Lu, M., Duan, Z., Zhu, F., & Ma, Z. (2024, March). Deep hierarchical video compression. *Proceedings of the AAAI Conference on Artificial Intelligence*, *38*(8), 8859–8867.

Oguz, O., & Ikizler-Cinbis, N. (2024). Leveraging cross-resolution attention for effective extreme low-resolution video action recognition. *Signal, Image and Video Processing*, *18*(1), 399–406.

Qawasmi, M., & Al-Kadi, O. (2025). Detecting face tampering in videos using deepfake forensics. *Multimedia Tools and Applications*, •••, 1–17.

Rajan, M., & Parameswaran, L. (2025). Key frame extraction algorithm for surveillance videos using an evolutionary approach. *Scientific Reports*, *15*(1), 536. PMID: 39748027

Rajivkannan, A., Venkatesan, M., Sharmila, V., Mukesh, G., Sridhar, J., & Sujendran, J. (2025, May). A Comprehensive Framework for Forged Smartphone Video Detection with Dataset Development and Spatial Temporal Analysis. In *International Conference on Sustainability Innovation in Computing and Engineering (ICSICE 2024)* (pp. 1841-1856). Atlantis Press.

Rastogi, K., & Tripathi, V. (2024, November). Video Compression by Spatial and Temporal Dimension Reduction using Seam Carving Algorithm. In *2024 3rd Edition of IEEE Delhi Section Flagship Conference (DELCON)* (pp. 1-4). IEEE.

Sakthi, M., Kerofsky, L., Kumar, V. R., & Yogamani, S. (2024). Impact of video compression artifacts on fisheye camera visual perception tasks. In *Proceedings of the IEEE/CVF Conference on Computer Vision and Pattern Recognition* (pp. 1301-1310).

Sandhya, & Kashyap, A. (2024). A comprehensive analysis of digital video forensics techniques and challenges. *Iran Journal of Computer Science, 7*(2), 359-380.

Schonig, J. (2024). Rethinking# thedress: On the social aesthetics of viral ambiguity illusions. *new media & society*, 14614448241235192.

Sigamani, A., & Selvaraj, P. (2024). Triplemask spatial linear filter and neutrosophic entropy for video denoising, face detection and recognition in forensic crime analysis using deep learning. *Neutrosophic Sets and Systems*, *67*, 21–56.

Singla, A., & Khan, Z. (2025). Exploring Artificial Intelligence-Driven Gait Analysis for Suspect Identification in Forensic Video Footage. *International Journal of Sciences and Innovation Engineering*, *2*(1), 15–19.

Soni, A., Kaur, K., & Sharma, C. (2025, March). A Review of Artificial Intelligence in Digital Watermarking Techniques. In *2025 International Conference on Automation and Computation (AUTOCOM)* (pp. 1601-1606). IEEE.

Sun, M. (2025). A method for solving the multiple degradation video quality enhancement problem: A processing framework for AI-based coding damage repair in concert with video super-resolution. *Multimedia Systems*, *31*(1), 52.

Sushir, R. D., & Bhutada, S. S. (2025). Harnessing Deep Learning for Advanced Video Forensics in Application Software Development. In *Essential Information Systems Service Management* (pp. 163–188). IGI Global.

Tonpe, S., Reddy, J. S., Bhar, C., Pratap, A., & Nayak, J. (2024). Design of a super-resolution scheme for plenoptic images. *Journal of Optics*, •••, 1–6.

Yadav, B. (2025). Artificial Intelligence in Forensic Science: Navigating Ethical Frontiers and Transformative Applications. In *Generative AI Techniques for Sustainability in Healthcare Security* (pp. 175-194). IGI Global Scientific Publishing.

Yang, J., Yang, C., Zhai, Y., Wang, Q., Pan, X., & Wang, R. (2024, April). Improving Learned Video Compression by Exploring Spatial Redundancy. In *ICASSP 2024-2024 IEEE International Conference on Acoustics, Speech and Signal Processing (ICASSP)* (pp. 2860-2864). IEEE.

Zhao, Z., Wang, Y., Xu, K., Sun, T., & Jiang, X. (2024). HEVC Video Adversarial Samples Detection via Joint Features of Compression and Pixel Domains. *IEEE Transactions on Information Forensics and Security*.

Zheng, H., Zhao, Y., Zhang, B., Shang, G., Al-Shamri, M. Y. H., & Aldossary, H. (2024). A Low-Resolution Video Action Recognition Approach Based on Multi-Scale Reconstruction and Multi-Modal Fusion. *IEEE Transactions on Consumer Electronics*.

KEY TERMS AND DEFINITIONS

Benchmarking Protocols: Standardized procedures and datasets used to test and compare the effectiveness of forensic tools and methods.

Deepfake Detection: Methods used to identify videos that have been synthetically generated or manipulated using AI.

Digital Evidence: Any data stored or transmitted in digital form that can be used in a court of law, including video, images, and metadata.

Forensic Video Analysis: The scientific examination, interpretation, and presentation of video evidence in legal contexts, including identification, authentication, and reconstruction of events.

Forensic Watermarking: Embedding cryptographic marks in digital video to verify originality and trace unauthorized edits.

Low-Resolution Footage: Video recordings that lack sufficient pixel detail to clearly represent fine visual information, such as faces or license plates.

Quantization: A compression process where transformed coefficients are approximated to reduce data size, often causing loss of fine details.

Transcoding: The process of converting a video from one format or bit rate to another, often introducing further compression artifacts.

Video Compression Artifacts: Visual distortions or errors introduced during compression, including blocking, blurring, ringing, mosquito noise, and ghosting.

Chapter 6
Identification of Deepfake Images and Synthetic Media for Forgery Detection

Anand Kumar
Amity Institute of Forensic Sciences, Amity University, Noida, India

Rakshita Gautam
https://orcid.org/0009-0006-2651-7907
Amity Institute of Forensic Sciences, Amity University, Noida, India

Shipra Rohatgi
https://orcid.org/0000-0003-0532-9908
Amity Institute of Forensic Sciences, Amity University, Noida, India

Sachil Kumar
https://orcid.org/0000-0002-2681-3937
Amity Institute of Forensic Sciences, Amity University, Noida, India

ABSTRACT

During past years, the easy accessibility of image editing tools such as Canva, FACEAPP, and CorelDRAW, many deepfake and synthetic images have been generated and circulated across media channels and the internet. Due to the emerging technologies such as Artificial Intelligence (AI) and Image Processing techniques, these tools show a capability of transforming human faces, swapping gender, and modifying other data of the images easily without any professional skills. The deepfake and synthetic images have raised challenges in multimedia and document forensics. Indeed, identifying these images through human eyes is difficult. The application

DOI: 10.4018/979-8-3373-3795-1.ch006

of AI can tackle the problem. Various machine learning and deep learning models, such as GAN, CNN, and RCNN, have demonstrated effective classification accuracy in detecting and localizing image forgeries. The AI model's efficiency is evaluated on diverse datasets like Deepfake TIMIT and Deeper-Forensics-1.0.

1. INTRODUCTION

Advancements in Machine Learning (ML) and Artificial Intelligence (AI) are driving the rapid digitalization of society, ushering in a new era of digital content creation and sharing (Chataut & Upadhyay, 2025; Westerlund, 2019). While the creative and entertainment industries have benefited from the immense potential of AI technologies, their proliferation has also given rise to serious ethical, legal, and security challenges, raising deep concerns about their implications on society, democracy, and the integrity of information (Masood et al., 2023; Mirsky & Lee, 2020; U.S. Department of Homeland Security, 2025). Among the most prominent innovations in this field are deepfakes and synthetic media, which have fundamentally redefined how digital content is generated, manipulated, and perceived (Seow et al., 2022; Malik et al., 2022). Digitally altered images and videos, and audio clips of people are increasingly appearing online, contributing to the rise and spread of synthetic media and a new phenomenon known as deepfakes (Ahmed et al., 2024; Rana et al., 2022).

Synthetic media is a broad term that encompasses various types of content, such as video, text, image, or voice, partially or fully generated using AI (Dehghani & Saberi, 2025). This includes not only deepfakes but also a wide range of other AI-generated content, such as computer-generated imagery, virtual and augmented reality, AI-written music, and synthesized voice or text. Deepfakes or synthetic media represent some of the most impressive advancements in digital content creation, revolutionizing the modalities by which images and videos are conceived, fabricated, and altered (Sandotra & Arora, 2024; Masood et al., 2023). The growing prevalence of digitally manipulated images, audio, and videos featuring real people has given rise to the widespread phenomenon known as deepfakes (Altuncu et al., 2024; Verdoliva, 2020).

The term "deepfake," a combination of "Deep Learning (DL)" and "fake", was coined by a Reddit user known as "deepfakes" in 2017 (Westerlund, 2019). Deepfakes are typically created using DL frameworks, especially **Generative Adversarial Networks (GANs)**, where two neural networks compete to produce increasingly realistic synthetic media (Masood et al., 2023; Seow et al., 2022). These technologies can convincingly mimic facial expressions, voice modulations, and even full-body movements, making the resulting media difficult to distinguish from authentic content (Kumar et al., 2025). Deepfakes are hyper-realistic synthetic media created using AI techniques, in which a person's face or voice in a photo, video, or audio is digitally replaced or manipulated to convincingly depict someone else, often making it difficult to distinguish from a genuine person's face (Malik et al., 2022; Mukta et al., 2023). Advanced algorithms further enhance these creations by mimicking the person's facial expressions and voice modulations, making deepfakes more realistic and often nearly indistinguishable from authentic footage (Hou et al., 2023). The increasing accessibility of deepfake creation tools has led to a surge in deepfake-related incidents worldwide, spanning from entertainment to serious crimes such as fraud and the spread of explicit content (Sunil et al., 2025; Patel et al., 2023). Recent studies show that explicit content accounts for a significant portion of deepfake incidents, with some estimates indicating that up to 98% of deepfakes are pornographic in nature, predominantly targeting women (Mukta et al., 2023). Deepfake-enabled fraud and impersonation are also on the rise, with North America, Asia, and Europe experiencing the highest number of cases (U.S. Department of Homeland Security, 2025). Countries such as the United Kingdom, the United States, Canada, India, and South Korea have been particularly impacted by these threats, reflecting the global reach and growing sophistication of deepfake technology (Altuncu et al., 2024).

There have been numerous Deepfake incidents shared on the internet. One of the popular incidents is a one-minute video from April 2018 in which former US President Barack Obama appears to curse President Donald Trump. The video was viewed by over 4.8 million people. later, it was revealed to be a deepfake created using advanced video editing technology. The voice and facial movements were provided by director Jordan Peele, who was digitally inserted into footage of Obama to demonstrate the risks posed by synthetic media (Mirsky & Lee, 2020). The deepfake was created by inserting Jordan Peele's performance into an original clip of Obama. According to Peele, the purpose of releasing the video was to highlight the dangers associated with fabricated audio and video content, which can make a person appear to be saying or doing things they never actually did.

In 2019, a Deepfake video of Facebook owner Mark Zuckerberg was posted on Instagram as part of an art installation called Spectre. In order to deceive and manipulate the public, Zuckerberg's speech and facial expression were changed in the video (Masood et al., 2023). Also, a Chinese app named "Zao" gained popularity for allowing users to face swap their faces for TV celebrities' bodies or even change into famous films and TV clips (Sharma & Kaur, 2022). In 2024, an 82-year-old retiree was duped into investing $690,000 in cryptocurrencies using a deepfake video of Elon Musk, which led to a total loss of money. That same year, AI technologies were used for the cyber fraud cases involving the British engineering firm Arup, where attackers impersonated the company's Chief Financial Officer and other employees during a video conference. This deception led a company member to authorize 15 transactions totalling approximately $25.62 million (U.S. Department of Homeland Security, 2025).

Furthermore, the negative impact of deepfakes is widely expected to far outweigh their positive aspects, as they are increasingly ranked among the most serious crime threats posed by AI, with potentially grave ramifications for society (Albahar & Almalki, 2019; Korshunov & Marcel, 2019). When coupled with social media platforms, convincing deepfakes can quickly reach millions of people, amplifying their capacity to mislead and manipulate public opinion, erode trust in institutions, and destabilize entire communities (Patel et al., 2023). Significant privacy and ethical issues are raised by the potential for the technology to be used to produce explicit or compromising information that features people without their knowledge or agreement (Mukta et al., 2023). Such violations of personal boundaries may cause grave psychological and emotional harm to victims, including humiliation, reputational damage, and long-lasting mental health consequences.

Another significant concern associated with deepfakes is their potential to facilitate impersonation and fraud, posing serious risks related to identity theft, cyberbullying, imposter scams, inciting violence, cyber extortion, social engineering attacks, and many more (Sunil et al., 2025; U.S. Department of Homeland Security, 2025). Deepfake technology may be used by cybercriminals to fool people convincingly, get sensitive information without authorization, or trick people into thinking they are communicating with someone else. These threats present formidable challenges for digital media forensics, making the detection and prevention of deepfakes an urgent priority in the ongoing effort to safeguard digital integrity (Ahmed et al., 2024; Rana et al., 2022).

Digital forensics is based on the principle that any alteration or processing applied to digital content leaves behind subtle traces that can be carefully examined to unveil the content's digital history. The field encompasses a wide range of practices, including source camera identification, tracing the processing history of multimedia content, and identifying indicators of tampering. Among these, detecting tampering artefacts has garnered significant attention from researchers, owing to its critical importance in addressing significant issues related to the authenticity of digital evidence.

With the increasing prevalence of deepfake cases, the urgency has increased for robust methods to distinguish authentic content from manipulation or synthetic media. This chapter focuses on the identification of deepfake images and other forms of synthetic media, especially for forgery detection. It explores different types of deepfake images, which are adversarial network generative adversarial networks, along with detection models. By contributing practical solutions that enable reliable differentiation between legitimate and deepfake content, the purpose of this work is to secure the legitimacy of image evidence across various domains, protect individual dignity, and uphold the authenticity and integrity of digital media.

2. DEEPFAKE TECHNOLOGY: A HISTORICAL OVERVIEW

The field of **AI** has undergone a significant transformation with the advent of deep learning, a momentous development that has revolutionized AI (Westerlund, 2019; Chataut & Upadhyay, 2025). Deep learning has become a significant technological development, offering unmatched capabilities in the areas of automation, pattern recognition, and decision-making (Seow et al., 2022). Deep learning's role in the creation and broad use of deepfake technology demonstrates its significant influence (Masood et al., 2023; Mirsky & Lee, 2020). Photo editing and video editing are so popular on the internet. These days, it is hard to browse the internet without seeing some form of modified information, be it a simple selfie with a filter, a manipulated meme, or a film that has been altered to highlight specific elements or add a soundtrack (Verdoliva, 2020; Altuncu et al., 2024). This section discusses the evolution of deepfake technology from its inception to the present (Malik et al., 2022; Rana et al., 2022).

~1860s: The image of Abraham Lincoln is said to represent the earliest well-known effort at face manipulation. In the famous portrait (~1860), his head was composited onto John Calhoun's torso (often cited in historical reviews of media manipulation; e.g., Masood et al., 2023; Mirsky & Lee, 2020). Engravings of his head were discovered on other bodies on many occasions after his passing.
1997: The invention of picture manipulation was followed soon after by its application to videos. In the year, a software named "Video Rewrite" was created (Bregler et al., 1997). This software generates a completely new video showing a person mouthing words they never actually spoke in the original footage by using previously recorded footage.
2016: In the twentieth century, constant development in technology picked up speed with the introduction of digital video. To develop new forensic techniques for digital media analysis, DARPA launched the four-year Media Forensics (MediFor) effort (DARPA MediFor reference, as cited in multiple reviews; e.g., Mirsky & Lee, 2020).
2017: In a series of computer-generated movies posted on pornographic websites in late 2017, a Reddit user going by the pseudonym "deepfakes" changed the appearance of well-known actresses (Westerlund, 2019; Masood et al., 2023). This was the first time that a deepfake might be regarded as genuine.

2018: People have been harassed, abused, and defamed via deepfake pornography (Mukta et al., 2023). UC Berkeley researchers developed a method dubbed "Everybody Dance Now" that enables users to transfer and imitate an individual's body motions in a video and apply them to another person (Chan et al., 2018).
2019: It was found that a video of Nancy Pelosi, the US Speaker of the House of Representatives, had been edited to give the impression that she was drunk, stumbling, or confused (Masood et al., 2023; Patel et al., 2023). In partnership with related voice synthesis efforts (building on Lyrebird technology), tools emerged to synthesize voices, including applications for helping people with ALS (though primarily later developments; contextual in synthetic media reviews, e.g., Dehghani & Saberi, 2025).
2020: The DFDC and Celeb-DF datasets became popular and a range of deepfake datasets, each employing a distinct set of picture and video manipulation techniques, were released to the public (Dolhansky et al., 2020; Li et al., 2020).
2021: A recently created algorithm called FakeBuster can identify deepfake videos in real-time situations, such as internet video conferences (Mehta et al., 2021). This year also saw the launch of many deepfake datasets, such as WildDeepfake and others building on prior works.
2022 The StyleGAN framework is extended with a new model named MyStyle, which can do personalized tasks connected to a human face (Nitzan et al., 2022).

3. TYPES OF DEEPFAKE IMAGE FORGERIES

3.1 Face Swapping

Face swapping involves replacing the source person's face with that of the target person, while keeping facial expressions and lighting conditions intact. Figure 1 shows an example of face swapping[11]. Face-swap-oriented deepfakes usually target popular or reputed personalities by presenting them in scenarios in which they never participated. For example, non-consensual pornography.

Figure 1. Example of face swapping

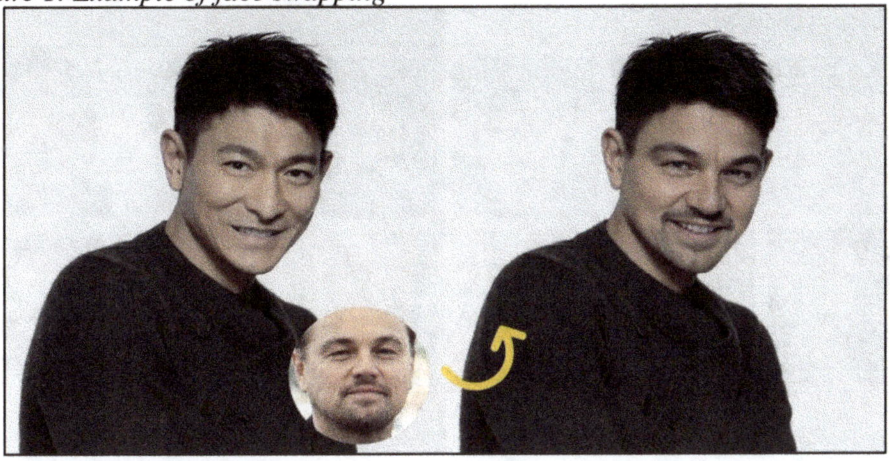

3.2 Facial Attribute Manipulation

Facial attribute manipulation alters specific features of a person's face, such as age, gender, expression, or hairstyle, using generative models like GANs. This manipulation allows multiple domains (e.g., smiling vs. neutral) to be synthesized for the same individual.

3.3 Entirely Synthetic Image Generation (GANs)

Synthetic image generation involves creating completely artificial yet realistic images of non-existent individuals using deep generative models such as StyleGAN. These images are often indistinguishable from real photographs, posing a challenge for authenticity verification.

Figure 2. Example of synthetic faces and attributes manipulation created using GAN variants[12,13].

3.4 Copy-Move and Splicing Techniques

Although traditionally used in digital image forensics, these techniques have now been advanced using deep learning to create more realistic forgeries. Copy-move forgery involves copying an area within the same image or another image and pasting it elsewhere. However, splicing combines elements from two or more images into a single lattice image.

4. COMMON DEEPFAKE GENERATION TECHNIQUES

Deepfake creation is an advanced media manipulation technique that surpasses the limitations of traditional forgery creation methods by eliminating the manipulation traces, irregularities, or digital fingerprints typically utilised for forgery detection. It implements a deep neural network designed to learn either a latent representation or a segmentation map to extract input characteristics and reconstruct an entirely new, fake, and hyper-realistic image based on the input data. With minimal differences between the extent of authentic and fake media, detecting them is significantly more challenging than identifying traditional manipulated data. The general deepfake creations include: Generative Adversarial Network (GAN), Autoencoder, Autoregressive model, and Deepfake Generation Tools

4.1. Generative Adversarial Network (GAN)

A generator network and a discriminator network are the two neural networks that make up a GAN. The generator network's goal is to trick the discriminator by creating a new synthetic output depending on the data distribution of the input. A discriminative network, on the other hand, correctly determines whether an output sample is authentic or fraudulent. Back propagation is used to constantly tune both networks until they achieve an equilibrium state in which it is impossible to tell the difference between the real and deepfake images. It facilitates tasks that are difficult to complete using conventional techniques, such as style transfer and picture restoration. In recent years, a variety of GANs have been produced to enhance software applications' performance. For example, ZAO and FaceApp performed well in generating entertainment deepfake videos. RCNN networks were processed in mobile cameras to improve camera resolution. Stacked-GANs have been employed to address the common issues of low-quality deepfake synthesis by using super-resolution techniques to preserve fine facial details in the generated image. However, GANs require substantial computational resources and huge datasets to train their models effectively and produce convincing fake data.

Popular GAN-based Models for Deepfake Creation

- **STAR-GAN**

STAR-GAN is a breakthrough model that can modify images into multiple categories using just one generator and one discriminator. This feature makes it highly efficient in image-to-image translation, where an image can be easily transformed into another genre or domain. STAR-GAN excels at learning mappings between different types of images, making deepfake creation easier. It has also been tested against other image translation models and consistently delivers high-quality, realistic results.

- **STYLE-GAN**

Style-GAN extends the Star-GAN model capabilities by adding more control over how deepfake images are created. It maps input images into a latent space and then adjusts their style at various points during deepfake creation. This technique makes human faces look amazingly lifelike. The technique used makes human faces look amazingly lifelike. However, subtle imperfections may indicate that these images are artificially created. Later, STYLE-GAN2 was optimized to correct these imperfections and make the images more realistic by improving regularization, multi-resolution techniques, and normalization methods.

- **ATT-GAN**

ATT-GAN is a single deepfake model that introduces an attribute classification constraint to verify that only specific parts of the image have been altered. ATT-GAN modifies facial features, which look highly natural. It prevents unnecessary modifications and maintains the integrity of the original image. Research shows that ATT-GAN outperforms older deepfake models such as STAR-GAN. The model applies complex mathematical formulas to balance multiple losses (such as reconstruction, classification, and adversarial losses) and achieves highly realistic facial transformations.

4.2 Autoencoder

An artificial neural network type called an autoencoder is made to efficiently learn representations of input data without looking for labelled outputs. Three primary parts make up the concatenated network: a bottleneck (also known as latent space), a decoder, and an encoder. By mapping the input data to a low-dimensional latent space representation, the encoder lowers the dimensionality of the data, preserving significant characteristics while eliminating less pertinent information. A condensed version of the input data is contained in the bottleneck. The bottleneck forces the model to learn a more condensed representation by acting as a restriction. To minimize the reconstruction error—which is frequently quantified using a loss function like Mean Squared Error (MSE) or binary cross-entropy—the decoder attempts to rebuild the original input from the latent representation.

Various types of autoencoders exist, each of which focuses on leveraging learned features, such as regular variational autoencoders, which are employed as generative models, and autoencoders, which are efficient in learning representations for ensuing classification tasks. Numerous issues, such as face recognition, feature extraction, anomaly detection, and word embedding learning, can benefit from the use of autoencoders. Regarding the synthesis of data, autoencoders can generate new data samples that are similar to the training input data. Figure 3 shows the basic workflow of an autoencoder.

Figure 3. Basic autoencoder workflow

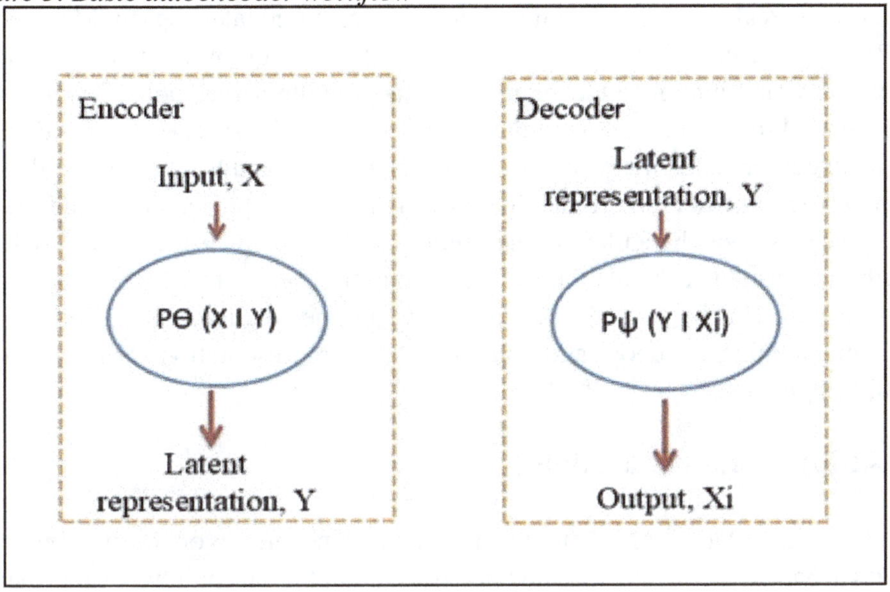

Variational autoencoders (VAEs) are different from traditional autoencoders: They are a class of deep generative models that have drawn a lot of interest in the field of computer vision because of their exceptional capacity to produce fresh data samples and learn intricate data distributions (Dehghani & Saberi, 2025; Masood et al., 2023). VAEs learn a compressed representation of the input data in a latent space, just like conventional autoencoders do (Seow et al., 2022). To encourage adjacent points in the latent space to produce closely related data points in the input space, VAEs, on the other hand, apply a straightforward Gaussian to the latent space (Ahmed et al., 2024). This allows the encoder to sample from the learnt distribution and produce numerous new data points from the same input (Malik et al., 2022; Mirsky & Lee, 2020).

It is thought that VAEs use the latent space to learn a probabilistic representation of the input data (Sandotra & Arora, 2024). The main objective is to preserve the key characteristics of the original data while encoding high-dimensional input data into a low-dimensional latent space (Hou et al., 2023). Two primary parts—an encoder and a decoder—are used to achieve this (Seow et al., 2022). The encoder converts the input data into a latent space distribution, which is typically thought to be Gaussian. The parameters (mean and variance) that define this distribution are included in the result (Dehghani & Saberi, 2025). By using samples from the latent representation, the decoder creates new data points by reconstructing the original data (Masood et al., 2023).

Training a VAE requires optimizing a mathematical function that helps the model create realistic data while maintaining a structured latent space (Malik et al., 2022). This is accomplished by estimating the distribution of the hidden variables using variational inference techniques and maximizing a variational lower bound on the probability of the observed data (Ahmed et al., 2024). The loss function has two main components: the reconstruction loss, which ensures that the decoder can accurately reconstruct the original input from the latent representation, and the KL divergence loss, which regularizes the latent space by keeping it close to a predefined distribution (usually a standard normal distribution) (Seow et al., 2022; Sandotra & Arora, 2024). This balance allows the VAE to produce realistic and varied outputs while maintaining a smooth and consistent latent representation (Mirsky & Lee, 2020; Dehghani & Saberi, 2025).

4.3 Autoregressive Model

Instead of the latent representation, the model concentrates on the distribution of images in nature. Given its preceding pixels, it simulates the conditional distribution of every pixel. It can generate high-quality pictures, but because it predicts pixels by pixels and evaluates them sequentially, the assessment procedure is time-consuming. The Pixel-RNN and Pixel-CNN models are significant instances of this paradigm.

4.4 Available Deepfake Generation Tools

Table 1 lists the freely available deepfake generation tools.

Table 1. Deepfake generation tools

Year	Tool	Website	Key Features / Characteristics	Category
2015	**Face Swap Live**	faceswaplive.com	Allow real-time face-swapping.	Swapping
2015	**Deep Art**	thedevmasters.com	Transfers the creative features from one image to another.	AI Art & Style Transfer
2017	**FaceApp**	faceapp.com	Modifies selfies (e.g., smiles, aging)	Face Transform
2018	**Deepfakes Web**	deepfakesweb.com	Work on Cloud-based deepfake creation and reuse trained models for multiple videos.	Deepfake Generation
2019	**ZAO**	uptodown.com (ZAO)	Permits users to place their faces into videos (e.g., Viral movie clips, videos).	Swapping
2020	**Reface**	hey.reface.ai	Selfies are swapped with GIFs, videos, and meme faces	Meme creations/ Entertainment
2021	**FaceMagic**	facemagic.ai	Free online face-swapping tool leveraging AI to generate funny and entertaining content	Content Creation
2021	**DALL·E Mini**	GitHub(DALL·E Mini)	AI produces graphics based on a given trigger.	Text-to-Image Generation

5. DEEPFAKE DETECTION

Deepfakes can be detected using conventional and deep learning approaches. The Conventional methods rely on handcrafted features. The designed algorithms focus on the patterns or inconsistencies of media content. On the other hand, deep learning approaches focus on automatically learning features directly from the data using neural networks, which often results in more robust and adaptive detection capabilities. Figure 4 illustrates the general methodology for Deepfake Detection.

Figure 4. Deepfake detection

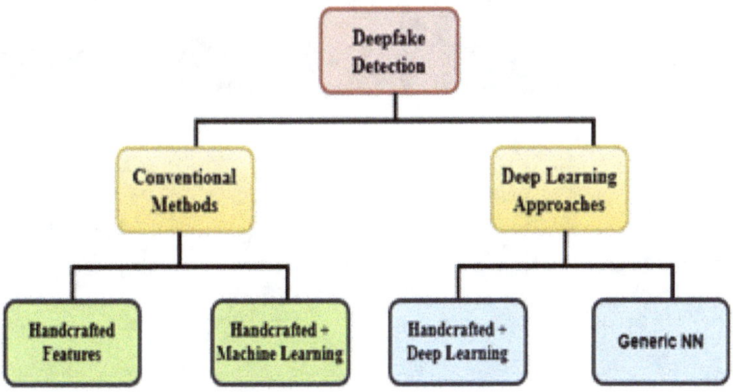

5.1 Conventional Methods

The conventional methods of deepfake detection rely entirely on handcrafted features. These methods require complex steps to convert the raw data into a usable format, as raw images cannot be directly used for classification by traditional machine learning models. Therefore, before feeding the data into a classifier, it is necessary to extract meaningful features such as pixel inconsistencies, edge artifacts, or texture anomalies.

The primary subcategory under conventional methods is the Handcrafted approach. The method manually identifies inconsistencies or abnormalities present in deepfake images or videos. For example, experts may look for mismatched lighting, irregular facial expressions, or visible boundary artifacts. These methods do not encompass any machine learning approaches and are purely rule-based. They are simple, based on mathematical calculations, and require minimal computational resources. However, the method has a limited ability to adapt to new or unseen types of manipulations in multimedia. As deepfake generation techniques are becoming sophisticated, a handcrafted approach often fails to detect subtle or high-quality forgeries. Figure 5 demonstrates the example of Handcrafted Features.

Figure 5. Handcrafted features

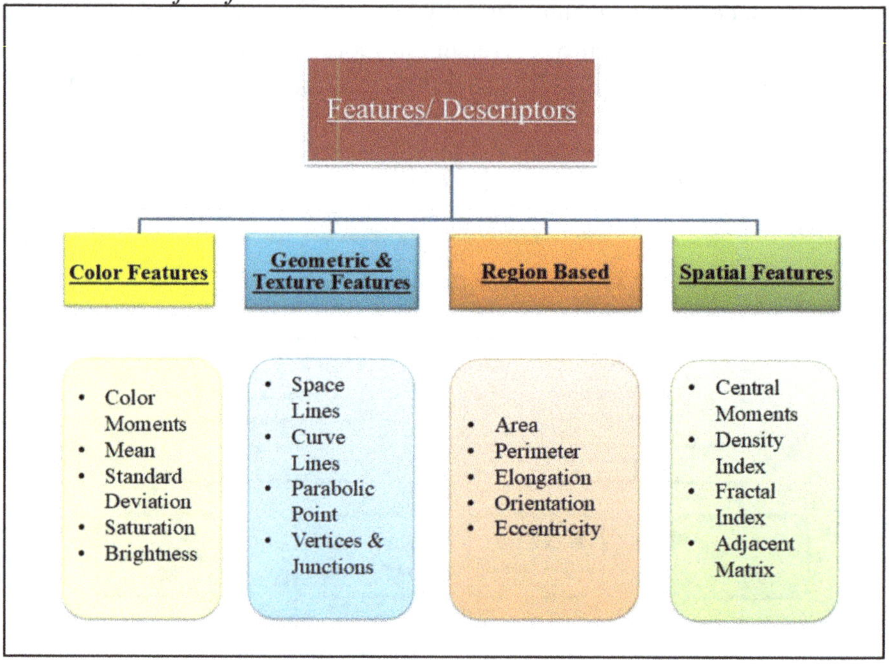

To overcome these limitations, researchers have integrated Handcrafted Features with Machine Learning. The hybrid method extracts specific features, such as Local Binary Patterns (LBP), Histograms of Oriented Gradients (HOG), or frequency domain signals, manually. Later, these extracted features are fed into machine learning algorithms, such as k-Nearest Neighbors (k-NN), Decision Trees, Support Vector Machines (SVM), or Random Forests. The method performed better than the pure handcrafted techniques. However, the method still depends on the quality and relevance of the manually extracted features.

5.2 Deep Learning Approaches

DL approaches have shown their success in solving complex problems in sophisticated machine translation, entity detection, face recognition, forgery detection, deepfake detection, and localization (Ahmed et al., 2024; Masood et al., 2023; Rana et al., 2022). DL employs black box CNN feature extraction to learn and extract features repeatedly from the training data using a deep neural network (Seow et al., 2022; Malik et al., 2022). Fundamentally, a DL-based methodology includes four main processes: data preprocessing, feature extraction, feature learning, and, lastly, image binary classification (Sandotra & Arora, 2024; Sunil et al., 2025). DL methods can be further separated into two major classes based on the feature extraction techniques (Kumar et al., 2025; Patel et al., 2023).

The first class incorporates a handcrafted and deep learning approach simultaneously (Mirsky & Lee, 2020; Verdoliva, 2020). This class combines the interpretability of manually engineered features with deep neural networks to detect deepfake Images (Ahmed et al., 2024; Rana et al., 2022). The hybrid model manually extracts domain-specific features, such as subtle traces, noise residuals, pixel anomalies, or edge boundary discrepancies, presented in the fake images, and then feeds them into DL models like the long recurrent convolutional network (LRCN), VGG-16, and **ResNet-50** (Masood et al., 2023; Seow et al., 2022; Malik et al., 2022). The most updated and widely applied method in deepfake detection is the Generic Neural Networks method. Here, the DL models are trained end-to-end on raw input data such as images without applying any handcrafted preprocessing techniques. Generic NN only relies on learned features. The neural networks, such as XceptionNet, MobileNet, InceptionV3, InceptionResNetV2, DensNet121, DenseNet169, VGG16, ResNet50, ResNet101, ResNet152, and many more, are trained to learn the discriminative features between the deepfake face areas and their neighbouring regions. These generic models often achieve state-of-the-art performance on large benchmark datasets, DeepfakeTIMIT, Fake Faces in the Wild (FFW), FaceForensics++, Celeb-DF, ForgeryNet Dataset, and the DeepFake Detection Challenge (DFDC).

Generic DL models offer several advantages. They are capable of learning complex, subtle, and multi-dimensional features from huge datasets, providing robust performance even against highly realistic deepfakes. Furthermore, since these models are not constrained by human intuition, they can detect manipulation artifacts invisible to the human eye.

6. DEEPFAKE DETECTION MODELS

A lot of models have been developed in recent years to detect deepfake images. Based on the detection algorithm, models are classified into two types, namely traditional machine-learning-based models and deep-learning-based models. Further, DL-based models can be classified into CNN, RNN, and transformer-based models. Figure 6 shows the flow chart of the conventional and Deep Learning models detection.

Figure 6. Flowchart of deep learning model detection

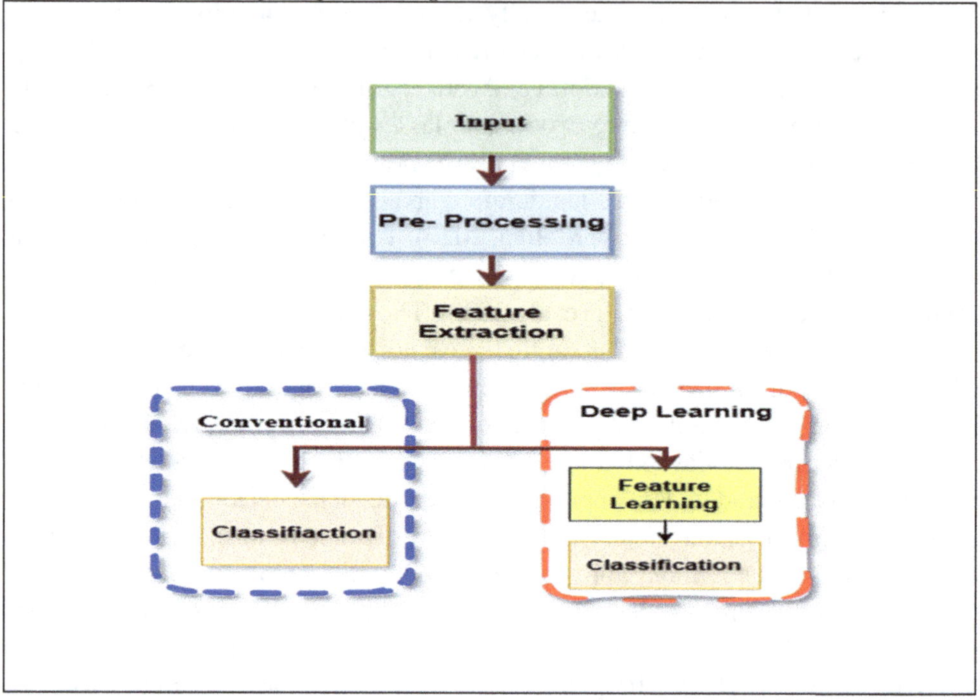

6.1 Traditional Machine-Learning-Based Models

Traditional ML techniques play a vital role in detecting deepfakes, especially when it is important to understand the reasoning behind the decisions. Traditional ML approaches are simple in design, have easy tuning of hyperparameters, and provide better control over training data than complex deep learning models. Several ML algorithms have been used to classify deepfake content. Tree-based models, such as decision trees and random forests, are used because they are easy to understand and are suitable for rule-based systems. SVM, logistic regression, and KNN provide good choices when working with limited or well-defined feature sets. Boosting models such as XGBoost and AdaBoost improves performance by focusing on errors and learning iteratively.

6.2 DL-Based Models

DL models have been widely applied in computer vision because of their high capability of feature selection and extraction. This permits DL models to quickly acquire and learn complex features of the input data. Figure 7 shows the commonly used DL Models for deepfake detection.

Figure 7. DL models for deepfake detection

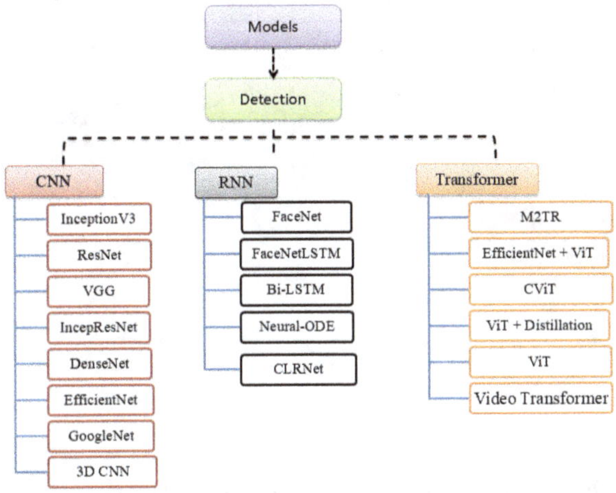

6.2.1 CNN-Based Models

The network is a feedforward neural network that operates on data using a grid-like topology, which is typically applied to images. It consists of multiple layers incorporating convolutional layers, pooling layers, and fully connected layers. The layers of the model play an important role in extracting and transforming the features to learn a hierarchical representation of the input data. CNNs also use backpropagation algorithms to optimize the weights of filters during training, so that complex patterns can be effectively learned from labelled datasets. Figure 8 illustrates the general CNN model architecture[8].

Figure 8. CNN model architecture

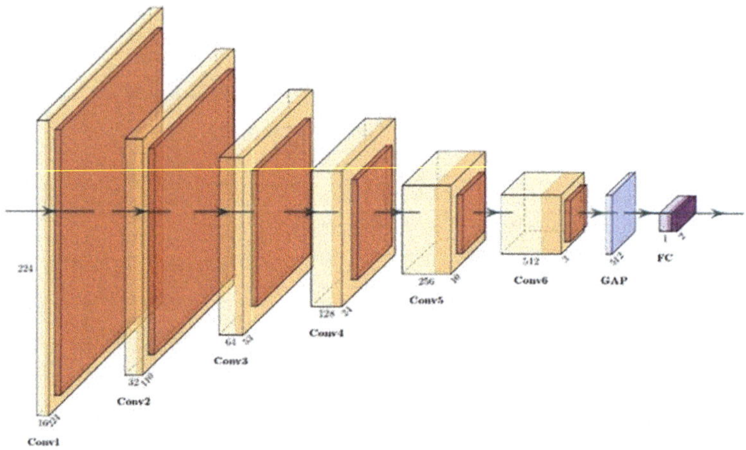

The network's ability to perform computerized feature extraction is unlike traditional machine learning methods, which repeatedly require manual feature engineering. The model architecture is conceptualized in such a way that it can handle input data variations through mechanisms such as weight sharing and local connectivity. This enhances the detection of features irrespective of their location within the image.

The concept of CNN was inaugurated by Yann LeCun in 1988 with his LeNet architecture made for character recognition jobs. Since then, CNNs have evolved remarkably and are now being used in various domains for intelligence tasks. Though the lineage of CNN can be traced back to the architecture introduced by Kunihiko Fukushima in 1979, who also presented max-pooling, now a popular down-sampling process. The Time Delay Neural Network (TDNN), presented by Alex Weibel in 1987, used CNN for phoneme recognition using convolutional layers, different weight sharing, and backpropagation. Due to CNN's powerful understanding of visual data through automatic feature extraction and hierarchical learning, various CNN-based methods have been used in deepfake detection.

Working of CNN models

CNN models detect deepfake images by recognizing and learning complex patterns and features from the input images of a dataset. The CNN architecture consists of the following layers:

- Convolutional layers scan small patches of a given image using filters to extract features such as edges, textures, and colors. These filters create feature maps to highlight important details in the image.

- Pooling layers reduce the size of the generated feature maps by preserving the most important information with reduced computational complexity.
- Deep convolutional layers integrate features to detect complex patterns, such as parts of faces or unnatural artifacts, to detect deepfake images.
- Finally, fully connected layers use the extracted features to classify real or deepfake images.

In training, the CNN automatically learns features to distinguish real and deepfake images by fine-tuning filter values to minimize classification errors on the labeled dataset.

Examples of recently used CNN-based models for deepfake detection are MTCNN, Xception, GoogleNet, VGG16, VGG19, Convolutional Attention Network (CAN), ResNet50/101/152, PixelCNN++, Y-Shaped Autoencoder, InceptionNet/Inception-ResNet/InceptionV4, DFT-MF, EfficientNet, 3D CNN, and FD2Net.

6.2.2 RNN-Based Models

Recurrent neural networks (RNNs) are a special field of artificial neural networks structured to process a large amount of sequential data. RNNs are highly operative for tasks where context and temporal dependencies are important. Its one origin lies in statistical mechanics. In 1972, Shunichi Amari proposed a statistical technique to adjust the weights of the Ising model via Hebbian learning for model associative memory. This work was popularized by John Hopfield (1982) as the Hopfield network. With Further development by researchers Ronald J. Williams, David Rumelhart, and Geoffrey Hinton, RNNs meaningfully influenced various fields such as speech recognition, time series analysis, and natural language processing (NLP). Unlike conventional feedforward neural networks that only process inputs and outputs, RNNs retain a hidden state that keeps the memory of all past inputs. This hidden state is reorganized each time based on the recent input and the preceding hidden state, permitting RNNs to capture dependencies over time. This feedback loop aids RNNs to make predictions reliant on prior context, making them fit for tasks such as predicting the succeeding word in a sentence or analysing time series data. The architecture of RNNs is composed of interconnected neurons arranged in input, output, and hidden layers. The hidden layer works on sequential data step-by-step while recollecting information from the preceding steps through its recurrent connections. This architecture enables RNNs to effortlessly handle variable-length input sequences. RNNs are trained using a process called backpropagation through time (BPTT), which extends the conventional backpropagation algorithm by taking into account the temporal nature of data. BPTT calculates the gradient at each time step and fine-tunes the network weights, thereby accelerating learning across sequences.

RNNs can be classified into different categories because of their structure and application. The first category is the simplest form of RNN, known as Simple RNN, which has limitations due to the vanishing gradient problem. The second category is termed Long Short-Term Memory RNNs (LSTM). It is a more advanced version structured to get rid of the vanishing gradient problem by inculcating memory cells for storing data for extended periods. The simplified version of LSTM, known as Gated Recurrent Units (GRU), combines the forget and input gates into a single update gate for image analysis. The third category is Bidirectional RNN. As the name suggests, the networks process data both in forward and backward directions to improve the contextual understanding by considering both past and future inputs. RNNs have demonstrated a noteworthy advancement in neural network architectures for sequential data processing. Their capability to hold information over time makes them fit for deepfake detection. However, they are progressively being complemented or swapped by transformer-based models in specific domains for better classification accuracy.

Working of RNNs

- Input Sequence Handling: RNNs process data sequentially to make it suitable for analyzing video frames or image sequences.
- Hidden State Memory: RNNs maintain a hidden state to remember previous input information, thereby aiding in detecting unnatural temporal changes.
- Feature Extraction: Often, CNNs are combined to extract spatial features such as texture and facial details, and then RNNs study the sequence of frames to detect temporal patterns and anomalies.
- Variants: Variants like LSTM or GRU help to capture long-range dependencies and address vanishing gradient issues.
- Output Classification: Afterwards, the final output layer classifies whether the input sequence is authentic or fake.

The most commonly used RNN-based models are CNN+RNN, CNN+(Bidirectional Entropy RNN), BiLSTM, FaceNet, Neural-ODE, FaceNetLSTM, and CLRNet.

6.2.3 Transformer-Based Models

The Transformer architecture is a groundbreaking deep learning model, first introduced in 2017 by Vaswani and his research group in the seminal paper "Attention is All You Need". It transformed the field of Natural Language Processing

(NLP) and has since been adapted in various computer vision fields such as image processing and reinforcement learning. Unlike traditional models that rely on RNNs or CNNs, Transformers use a self-attention mechanism, allowing parallel processing of input data and handling long-range dependencies for improved efficiency. At its core, the Transformer is associated with an encoder-decoder structure, allowing efficient processing of sequence-to-sequence tasks. First, the input text is tokenized into smaller units and modified into numerical vectors through an embedding layer. Since the model does not naturally recognize sequence order, positional encodings are assembled to preserve token relationships.

The encoder is made up of several identical layers, usually six, each of which includes: Multi-head self-attention that allows individual tokens to consider, thereby improving the contextual understanding. Feed-forward networks apply nonlinear transformations to refine the processed output. The decoder also includes several layers with masked multi-head self-attention to ensure that predictions rely solely on past tokens, preventing the decoder from paying attention to future tokens during training. Cross-attention layers help the decoder to emphasize relevant sections of the encoder while generating the final output sequence. Finally, decoder output undergoes processing through a linear layer and a softmax function for converting it into a probability distribution over potential token. This enables the transformer to perform tasks such as machine translation and text generation. Transformers offer several key advantages over traditional models, such as RNNs. One of their most notable benefits is parallelization, which processes all tokens simultaneously, making it highly efficient and suitable for modern GPU hardware. Additionally, Transformers exhibit excellent scalability, meaning they can manage large amounts of data and computational requirements, which impressively shows their potential for training on large datasets. Another important strength is their ability to capture long-range dependencies through the self-attention mechanism. This enables the model to understand the relationships between complex language functions. Therefore, Transformers are used in the field of deepfake detection and generation. The models used are CVIT, EfficientNet+VIT, VIT, M2TR, VIT+Distillation, and Video Transformer.

Working of the Transformers

- Patch embedding: Images are separated into fixed-size patches, and each patch is flattened and linearly interpolated into a vector embedding to preserve spatial information.
- Position Encoding: Transformers lack inherent spatial awareness; therefore, position encodings are integrated into patch embeddings to retrieve the spatial arrangement of patches.

- Self-Attention Mechanism: The core of the Transformer implements multi-vertex self-attention, allowing the model to evaluate and capture global relationships and dependencies across entire patches simultaneously. This assists in detecting subtle and spatially distant forgery.
- Transformer Encoder Layers: Subsequent patches pass through multiple encoder layers, including self-attention blocks and feed-forward neural networks, which normalize and progressively refine the features to detect forgery.
- Feature aggregation: The output includes a special classification token (CLS token) that aggregates the learned features representing the entire image context.
- Classification Head: Finally, the token embeddings are fed into a classification layer to predict whether the image is authentic or a deepfake.

6.3. Comparison of Models

The table below discusses the comparison among the different models.

Table 2. Comparison of different models

Models	Strengths	Limitations	Accuracy Range	Applicability	Example
Traditional ML	Less used, result interpretations are easier, Learns quickly on small datasets, and does not consume more computer power	Features are extracted manually, less effective on complex data and large datasets.	Moderate	Effective only with clear and organized data	K-Nearest Neighbors (KNN), SVM, Random Forest, AdaBoost, Decision Trees
CNN	Learn complex patterns easily	Demands a large dataset and computer power	High	Work efficiently for Deepfake images	VGG16, ResNet, MesoNet, XceptionNet, DenseNet
RNN	Captures temporal inconsistencies and sequential facial dynamics	Struggles with long sequences and demands high computational resources	Medium to High	Perform better on videos than on images	RNN with attention, GRU, LSTM, ConvLSTM, Bi-directional RNN
Transformer	capture long-range dependencies and global context, adaptive and fast	Large datasets with extensive computational resources.	Very High	Best for complex data	DeiT, TimeSformer, Vision Transformer (ViT), TransForensics, Video Swin Transformer,

6.4 Deepfake Detection Tools

1. **Truepic**: This user-friendly interface tool verifies the authenticity of photos and videos by detecting any manipulation in the media. It incorporates cryptographic technology, advanced forensic analysis capabilities, real-time verification, and integration with various platforms to ensure high reliability in verifying authenticity. The tool can authenticate media from multiple sources and formats, ensuring comprehensive coverage.
2. **D-ID**: It employs sophisticated algorithms to secure users' privacy by modifying images and videos so that the person in the media cannot be recognized by face recognition software. The tool's accuracy rate in recognizing faces is great. It functions quickly, is compatible with web apps, iOS, and Android, and is simple to combine with other apps. Furthermore, D-ID's method is resistant to adversarial machine learning assaults, guaranteeing that anonymity is maintained even when these attacks are made.
3. **Sensity AI**: It uses machine learning and artificial intelligence methods to identify tampered content. It is famous for its quick and accurate detection in large datasets. It scans large amounts of data and displays an accuracy score up to 95%. Its user-friendly design makes it popular with both technical and non-technical users, and it can be tailored to different industries.
4. **FaceForensics++**: It recognizes facial expressions. By examining even the tiniest face movements, it is quite successful at spotting deepfakes and can recognize deepfakes created using a variety of techniques. FaceForensics++ is an open-source tool that can be used freely and modified by researchers. Its easy-to-use interface requires very little technical knowledge for detecting deepfakes in real-time.
5. **XRVision Sentinel**: It is a deep learning technology that analyzes the composition and structure of facial images and videos to detect manipulation. It can detect deepfakes in a range of settings, such as social media, news outlets, and political campaigns. The tool can identify subtle changes in facial expressions, lip movements, and eye movements. Additionally, it can identify deep fakes created using methods such as GAN-based models and facial reconstruction techniques.
6. **FakeSpot**: With 90% accuracy, this web-based application, driven by artificial intelligence, can spot phony reviews on e-commerce sites. Even non-technical individuals may easily use it, and it can evaluate thousands of evaluations in a matter of seconds. To further user accessibility, Fakespot also provides a browser extension that can be installed on Chrome, Firefox, and Safari. It is also compatible with a number of e-commerce sites, including TripAdvisor, Yelp,

Amazon, and Walmart, making it a flexible tool for identifying phony reviews on a variety of websites.

7. **FooSpidy's Fake Finder**: It is a deepfake-detection tool that identifies manipulation in images and videos using image forensics and deep neural networks. High precision, real-time detection, an intuitive user interface, and adjustable settings are some of its efficacy metrics. This program enables users to rapidly upload and scan media files for deepfake detection, with an accuracy rate of over 90%.
8. **DeepSecure.ai**: DeepSecure.ai. This tool analyses the semantic content of videos to detect deepfakes. It shows real-time speed, scalability, ease of use, and versatility. Its accuracy rate in detecting deepfakes is reported to be 96%. It can also identify voice cloning and face-swapping. This tool is easy to use and integrates well with current workflows.
9. **HooYu**: It's a platform for digital identity verification to ensure protection against fraud. The platform's verification technology uses a variety of verification methods and data sources to achieve reliable accuracy. The platform is fast and efficient, allowing companies to quickly verify customers' identities in compliance with regulatory rules. It is highly adaptable and can be used in a variety of businesses, including e-commerce and financial services management.
10. **iProov**: It is used as a patented technique called Flashmark, it recognizes face biometric data tampering and detects deepfakes. This tool's efficacy stems from its capacity to precisely identify even the most complex deepfake efforts, which qualifies it for real-time facial verification. Platform-neutral, it functions flawlessly on web browsers, iOS, and Android, and it is highly trusted by a number of government organizations that utilize it to stop fraud.
11. **Blackbird.ai**. It combines machine learning algorithms with human intelligence to identify and classify manipulated media. It demonstrated an accuracy of 98% in detecting signs of manipulation, making it suitable for real-time monitoring of various online sources. A group of skilled analysts examines the videos that have been identified and verifies their legitimacy. Users may alter the parameters to suit their requirements, such as excluding particular sources from monitoring or establishing criteria for identifying deepfakes. All things considered, it is a dependable and successful way to stop the spread of misinformation.
12. **Veracity.ai**: It is an AI-based deepfake-detection technology for detecting altered content. The application assists in the real-time detection of deepfakes in live video broadcasts. It can also detect deepfakes in audio, video, and picture files to offer comprehensive coverage. It doesn't require any technical knowledge and is easy to use. It is updated with the newest deepfake detection strategies and tactics to increase its effectiveness.

7. DEEPFAKE DATASETS

Over the past few years, diverse datasets have been made available to encourage deepfake research. To effectively train the models, it is crucial to understand dataset characteristics, including quantity, quality, and manipulation techniques. Therefore, this section discusses popular publicly available deepfake datasets.

1. **FaceForensics++**: This dataset contains different types of deepfakes. By modifying 1,000 YouTube source videos using deepfake, neural texture, face2face, and face swap manipulation, researchers produced 4,000 phony video sequences. The videos were compressed into H.264 format with compression rate factors of 0, 23, and 40 in order to do a more thorough analysis. In addition, Google and Jigsaw upgraded the dataset as the Deepfake Detection Dataset (DDD/DFD), which included another 363 original videos. 28 actors were hired to create 3,086 high-quality deepfake videos in 16 different scenes.
2. **Fake Faces in the Wild (FFW)**: The FFW dataset was created by Khodabakhsh and his research group. A total of 150 source videos were collected from YouTube and altered using deepfakes and traditional tampering methods, such as splicing and computer-generated images.
3. **UADFV:** The dataset was created by Yang and other research collaborators for deepfake detection experiments. Using the FakeApp program, 49 phony videos were produced while 49 authentic films were gathered from YouTube. Nicolas Cage, an American actor, took the place of the faces in the original videos. As a result, he is the one person who appears in all phony videos. Each movie has a resolution of 294 × 500 pixels, and the ratio of real to fake videos is 1.0:1.0.
4. **Deepfake TIMIT:** This video dataset is an adaptation of the original VidTIMIT dataset. An open-source FaceSwap-GAN approach performed the face-swapping. Without manipulating the original audio channel of the video, 16 manually selected face pairs were chosen to generate 620 face-swap-based deepfake videos from 32 subjects. Therefore, two major quality standards of manipulated videos, 64 x 64-pixel low-quality (LQ) images, and 128 x 128-pixel high-quality (HQ) images, were generated.
5. **Celeb-DF**: Liu, together with his research group, presented Celeb-DF, a large-scale dataset. It consists of 590 authentic and 5,693 high-quality deepfake videos. The dataset was generated using source videos obtained from YouTube from various age groups, ethnicities, and genders. This dataset aims to simulate real-life scenarios with different video qualities to detect deepfake content.
6. **Deepfake Detection Challenge (DFDC)**: In late 2019, Facebook organized the Deepfake Detection Challenge (DFDC) in collaboration with several technology giants, industry experts, and academics. They recruited some actors to make

videos for the dataset as part of a campaign to gather it. The dataset was made available by the host in two phases: the preview version and the final version. There are 4,113 phony films and 1,131 actual videos in the preview dataset. On the other hand, the final version includes 100,000 deepfake videos produced by 3,426 hired actors, with 19,154 actual footages. Gender, skin tone, lighting, head posture, age, and backdrop are all in abundance in both versions.

8. METHODOLOGY FOR ASSESSING THE EFFECTIVENESS OF DETECTING DEEPFAKE ATTACKS

Model evaluation is the key to understanding how the model performs when applied to unseen data. Researchers in deepfake detection have used various evaluation metrics to identify deepfakes and authentic images.

8.1 Binary Classification

Deepfake attack detection typically frames image analysis as a binary classification problem, distinguishing between real and fake images:

1. **Authentic**: The image is genuine and remains unaltered by any deepfake attack.
2. **Forged**: The image has been digitally manipulated using a deepfake attack.

Following image processing, the classifier will forecast the picture class. The forecast should ideally correspond to the image's actual class. Nonetheless, there are situations in which the classifier could incorrectly identify the class of a picture. Therefore, a confusion matrix can be used to better understand these situations.

8.2 Confusion Matrix

A confusion matrix is used to evaluate how well a classification model performs by comparing its predictions to the actual labels. It provides information about how well a model distinguishes between different classes.

For Binary Classification:

- **True Positives (TP):** These are examples in which the model successfully classified an image as a deepfake when it truly was one (i.e., the deepfake image).
- **True Negatives (TN)**: In these instances, the model accurately forecasted the negative class (i.e., the authentic image).

- **False Positives (FP):** The model predicted the positive class—that is, an authentic image—incorrectly.
- **False Negatives (FN)**: These are the instances where a deepfake picture was predicted as real by the model, which is an inaccurate prediction of the negative class.

8.3 Performance Metrics

The effectiveness of a binary classifier can be assessed using a range of performance metrics:

- **Sensitivity or Recall (True Positive Rate (TPR))**: It calculates the percentage of accurately recognized positives.

$$\text{TPR} = 1 - \text{FNR} = \frac{\mathbf{TP}}{\mathbf{P}}$$

- **Miss Rate (False Negative Rate (FNR))**: It may be defined as the proportion of false negative pictures to all real positive photos. It determines the percentage of real positives that are mistakenly classified as negatives.

$$\text{FNR} = 1 - \text{TPR} = \frac{FN}{P}$$

- **Fall-out (False Positive Rate (FPR))**: It is the proportion of false positive photos to all real positive photographs. It determines the percentage of real negatives that are mistakenly classified as positives.

$$\text{FPR} = 1 - \text{TNR} = \frac{FP}{N}$$

- **Specificity (True Negative Rate (TNR))**: It represents the proportion of true negative images out of the total number of true negative images. It calculates the ratio of true negatives that are correctly identified.

$$\text{TNR} = 1 - \text{FPR} = \frac{TN}{N}$$

A high True Positive Rate indicates the model's effectiveness in accurately detecting deepfake pictures, which is beneficial in the context of deepfake detection. On the other hand, a low false positive rate is also important because it demonstrates that the model can correctly recognize real images, thereby reducing misclassification.

- **Accuracy** is defined as the ratio of the model's total number of predictions to the number of accurate predictions (true positives and true negatives).

$$\text{Accuracy} = \frac{\mathbf{TP + TN}}{\mathbf{P + N}}$$

Accuracy can be deceptive when working with datasets that have uneven class distributions, as it only reflects overall correctness and not class-specific performance. For example, in a dataset where 97% of the images are authentic and only 3% are deepfakes, a simple classifier that predicts every image as authentic will have an accuracy of 97%, even if it is unable to identify deepfake images. As a result, while accuracy is important, it should not be the only criterion for evaluating classifier performance, especially in the context of deepfake, where identifying deepfake content is crucial.

- **F1 Score**: This is the harmonic mean of precision and recall.

$$\text{F1 Score:} \frac{\mathbf{2TP}}{\mathbf{2TP + FP + FN}}$$

The F1 metric value ranges from 0 to 1, where 1 indicates excellent detection and 0 indicates poor performance. It takes into account both false positives and false negatives. The score is extremely important when working with unbalanced datasets. In deepfake detection, a high F1 score is required as it ensures the reliability of the model in identifying deepfake images and avoiding mistakes.

- **Cross-entropy loss (logloss)**: The cross-entropy loss assesses the performance of a classification model whose output probability values lie between 0 and 1. It penalizes more for predictions that are confidently inaccurate and increases as the expected probability diverges from the true label.

For a general classification task with c classes, the cross-entropy loss for a single observation can be defined as:

$$\boldsymbol{Loss = f(x) = \sum_{i=1}^{C} yi \, log\left(P_i\right)}$$

where;

- y_i is 1 if the observation belongs to class i and 0 otherwise,
- Pi is the predicted probability of the observation belonging to class i.

For a binary classification task, this simplifies to:

$$\text{Loss} = -\left(y \log(p) + (1 - y)\log(1 - p)\right)$$

where:

- y is 1 if the observation is positive (forged) and 0 if negative (original),
- p is the predicted probability of the observation being positive (forged).

The model's great efficiency in predicting the proper class probabilities for both legitimate and forged photos is demonstrated by the minimal cross-entropy loss in the context of deepfake detection.

A model's detection skills are improved when it has a reduced cross-entropy loss since it can distinguish between authentic and fake photos more easily.

Accuracy and score of F1 display valuable insights into the model's performance, but lack confidence in predictions. Cross-entropy loss accounts for the confidence of predictions, which makes it an important metric for evaluating the model's performance in detecting forgery. Hence, a comprehensive evaluation based on all these metrics ensures balanced and robust results during forgery detection.

9. REAL LIFE CASE STUDY

Case Study 1: Deepfake Fraud Case in Hong Kong

A deepfake fraud occurred in Hong Kong in 2023, where fraudsters used advanced AI techniques to imitate a company's Chief Financial Officer (CFO) during an ongoing video call. The scammers created a digital copy of the CFO using AI and tricked finance staff into believing that the CFO was requesting a confidential money transfer. Later, the finance employee transferred $25 million to the scammers' accounts by trusting the appearance and voice of the CFO on the video call.

Case Study 2: Deepfake Pornographic Images

Noelle Martin, a prominent Australian activist and lawyer, was targeted with non-consensual deepfake pornography. Noel Martin's face was digitally superimposed onto pornographic videos and circulated on various pornographic websites. The deepfake videos appeared so real that they damaged their reputation, dignity, relationships, and professional lives. Attempts to permanently remove the videos faced significant challenges due to their continued reappearance on various platforms. Despite proper investigation and persistent efforts over the years, the culprits behind deepfake videos remain unknown.

Case Study 3: Kerala's Deepfake Fraud (India)

A 73-year-old man in Kerala was duped by a WhatsApp video call in 2022, which featured a deepfake image of his coworker and asked him for a loan of 40,000. The victim, believing the call to be genuine, transferred the money. Police nabbed the fraudster from Maharashtra using social media and digital forensic applications

10. CHALLENGES IN DETECTING DEEPFAKE IMAGES

Despite remarkable advancements in the performance of deepfake detection systems, several critical challenges remain that warrant close attention. This section discusses a few of the difficulties with deepfake detection techniques.

1. **Quality of Deepfake Datasets**: One key element in the development of deepfake detection methods is the availability of substantial databases of deepfakes. Contrasting the calibre of films from these datasets with actual altered online material, however, shows a number of uncertainties. These databases include a variety of visual artifacts for visualization, including:
    - Occasionally, there is temporal flickering during speech
    - The facial regions are blurry
    - The facial texture is too smooth or lacks details
    - There is no head pose movement or rotation
    - There are no face-obstructing objects like glasses or lightning effects
    - The face is sensitive to changes in input posture or gaze
    - There is a limited amount of high-quality audio-visual deepfake datasets.

Imperfections in the modification procedures are the cause of the ambiguity in the dataset given above. Furthermore, poorly produced modified information may hardly be credible or leave a lasting impression. Consequently, there is no assurance that detection techniques will work effectively in the field, even if they perform better over such recordings.

2. **Performance Evaluation**: Deepfake detection techniques are currently developed as binary classification problems, in which each sample is either real or fake. Such classification is easier to build in a controlled environment where we develop and verify deepfake detection techniques using either real or phony

audio-visual data. However, footage that is not identified as modified does not ensure that the video is authentic because videos can be changed in real-world situations in ways other than deepfakes. Furthermore, a single label might not be entirely correct because deepfake information can be altered in a variety of ways, such as audio or visual. Moreover, one or more faces are often altered with deepfakes throughout a segment of frames in a video that features many people's faces. The binary classification approach should be enhanced to incorporate local classification/detection at the frame level as well as multiclass/multi-label to handle the challenges of real-world scenarios.

3. **Lack of Explainability in Detection Methods**: Current methods for detecting deepfakes are usually made to analyse a big dataset in batches. However, there could only be a limited number of recordings accessible for examination when journalists or law enforcement use these tactics in the field. If the practitioners cannot verify the score with suitable evidence, a numerical score that corresponds to the likelihood that an audio or video is authentic or fraudulent is not as useful. Before the analysis is published or used in a court of law, it is typical in certain circumstances to request an explanation for the numerical score in order for it to be trusted. However, because of their black-box nature, the majority of deepfake detection techniques—especially those based on DL approaches—do not explain.
4. **Lack of fairness and Trust**: Current audio and visual deepfake datasets have been seen to be biased, with an unequal distribution of data from different ethnic and gender groupings. Furthermore, the detection techniques used may also be biased. Very little work is accessible, despite the fact that researchers have begun to address this vacuum in this field. Therefore, methods that enhance data and fairness in detecting algorithms must be implemented.
5. **Temporal Aggregation**: Current deepfake detection techniques rely on frame-level binary classification, which verifies whether a video frame is authentic or altered. These methods, however, ignore temporal consistency between frames and have two possible drawbacks: (i) temporal distortions are visible in deepfake content, and (ii) genuine or authentic frames may occur in consecutive intervals. Moreover, since the method must aggregate the score from every frame to get a final value, it necessitates an additional step to calculate the integrity score at the video level.
6. **Social Media Laundering**: The primary internet networks for disseminating audio-visual information to the general public are social media sites like Facebook, Instagram, and Twitter. Before being uploaded, such content is down-sampled, significantly compressed, and stripped of metadata to conserve network traffic or protect user privacy. Often referred to as social media laundering, these techniques eliminate hints about underlying forgeries and ultimately raise the

rate of false positive detections. Social media laundering has a greater impact on the majority of deepfake detection techniques that use signal-level keypoints. Incorporating simulations of these effects into training data and expanding assessment databases to include data on social media-laundered visual material are two ways to improve the accuracy of deepfake detection techniques over social media laundering.

7. **DeepFake Detection Evasion**: Finding missing data and artifacts from the generating process is the main goal of deepfake detection techniques. However, if such data is unavailable, detection methods might not work since attackers might try to erase these traces while creating the manipulation. These deception methods fall into three categories: using picture filtering to trick detectors, eliminating manipulation traces in the frequency domain, and adversarial perturbation attacks. When visual adversarial assaults occur, the training data is subjected to various perturbations, including noise, arbitrary cropping, and JPEG compression, among others. This eventually causes a large number of false alarms for detection techniques. Various pieces have assessed the effectiveness of cutting-edge visual deepfake detectors in the presence of hostile attacks and demonstrated a sharp decline in accuracy.

11. FUTURE DIRECTIONS

The potential benefits and drawbacks of synthetic media for our society are drawing a lot of attention. Even though there has been remarkable work revealed for both deepfake detection and creation, the rivalry between the two will not end anytime soon. However, there is still an opportunity for development. The present status of deepfakes, their drawbacks, and potential developments are covered in this section. Using the idea of blockchain and smart contracts, several writers offered methods to detect forensic alterations made to visual material in order to stop deepfakes that spread false information. Even in the face of several manipulation attempts, the authors were able to identify and trace the history and origin of modified material and its source by using Ethereum smart contracts. The interplanetary file system hashes were used by this smart contract to store movies together with their information. This technique could work well for identifying deepfakes; however, it can only be used if video information is present. Therefore, the newswires may benefit from the creation and implementation of such techniques; yet, the great bulk of material produced by regular people will not be protected by such tactics.

- The bulk of uploaded fake movies fall into the face-swapping video category, which is often addressed by recent automated deepfake recognition techniques. Significant advancements in detection algorithms include: detecting artifacts left over from the generation process, such as irregular head posture, absent eye blinking, color variations in facial texture, and misaligned teeth

- Detecting unseen GAN-generated samples; detecting spatial-temporal features; and detecting psychological signals, such as a person's behavioural patterns. Even though a lot of effort has been made on automatic detection, these techniques are likely to be temporary and need to be improved in a number of ways.

Many of the unsolved problems in the field of deepfake detection are listed here.

- The current methods are not resilient to post-processing activities like light fluctuations, noise effects, compression, etc. Furthermore, there isn't much work that can identify deepfakes that are both visual and auditory.
- The majority of recent methods have concentrated on face-swap detection by taking advantage of its drawbacks, such as apparent artifacts. The near future, however, will see increasingly complex face-swaps, such as imitating someone with a similar face shape, demeanour, and haircut, thanks to enormous technological advancements. In addition, other forms of deepfake, such as lip-synching and face-reenactment, are becoming more and more popular every day.
- The shortcomings of the existing deepfake detectors are mostly caused by noisy, sparse, and inadequate training data. Investigating novel AI architectures, algorithms, and techniques that "bake in" physics, mathematics, and past knowledge pertinent to deepfakes is necessary. Using knowledge-infused learning to integrate physics and existing knowledge into AI will assist in overcoming the difficulties of sparse data and make it easier to create causal and explanatory generative models.
- The majority of current methods have concentrated on a single feature category, such as landmark features. However, it is crucial to combine landmarks, photoplethysmography (PPG), and audio-based characteristics due to the growing complexity of deepfakes. Analyzing the fusion of classifiers is also crucial. Specifically, the combination of anomaly and signature-based ensemble learning will help to increase the deepfakes detectors' accuracy.
- Previous studies on deepfakes have mostly concentrated on identifying video manipulation in the visual material. However, the academic community mostly ignores audio manipulation, which is a crucial part of deepfakes. The development of unified deepfake detectors that are capable of concurrently detecting audio forgeries (like TTS synthesis, voice conversion, and cloned-

replay) and visual forgeries (like face-swap, lip-sync, and puppet-master) is required.

- ASV is a key element in the rapidly expanding field of smart speakers and other voice-activated gadgets. However, until we combat the risks of numerous voice spoofing assaults on the ASV, it is impossible to make the best use of ASV in crucial areas like financial services, healthcare, etc. Therefore, creating a strong and cohesive spoofing countermeasure is also necessary to address this issue.
- To prevent an attack from spreading over a network of smart speakers (or other IoT devices), it is imperative to use federated, learning-based, lightweight techniques to identify the manipulation at its source.

12. CONCLUSION

The chapter explains deepfakes, their origins, evolution over time, and their increasing complexity due to advancements in AI. Deepfake content enables creativity in sectors such as entertainment, advertising, and education, but it also poses a serious risk of misuse. When misused intentionally, it can cause emotional distress, financial loss, social harm, and even result in legal consequences against an individual or organization. From a forensic perspective, the proliferation of deepfake technology poses serious challenges in the authentication and verification of digital evidence. In criminal investigations, the ability to distinguish between authentic and deepfake content is crucial. The chapter also discusses freely available tools for detecting and generating deepfake content. Various traditional and modern deep learning-based methods for detecting synthetic content have also been explored. Later, Deep Learning-based CNN, RNN, and Transformer-based models are explained effectively. Finally, the chapter discusses various challenges that hinder deepfake detection and suggests future directions.

REFERENCES

Ahmed, N. U. R., Badshah, A., Adeel, H., Tajammul, A., Duad, A., & Alsahfi, T. (2024). Visual Deepfake Detection: Review of Techniques, Tools, Limitations, and Future Prospects. *IEEE Access : Practical Innovations, Open Solutions.*

Albahar, M., & Almalki, J. (2019). Deepfakes: Threats and countermeasures systematic review. *Journal of Theoretical and Applied Information Technology*, *97*(22), 3242–3250.

Altuncu, E., Franqueira, V. N., & Li, S. (2024). Deepfake: Definitions, performance metrics and standards, datasets, and a meta-review. *Frontiers in Big Data*, *7*, 1400024. PMID: 39296632

Bregler, C., Covell, M., & Slaney, M. (1997) ''Video Rewrite: Driving visual speech with audio,'' *Proceedings of the 24th Annual Conference on Computer Graphics and Interactive Techniques, SIGGRAPH 1997*, pp 353–360, https://doi.org/DOI: 10.1145/258734.258880

Chan, C., Ginosar, S., Zhou, T., & Efros, A. (2018) ''Everybody Dance Now,'' Proceedings of the IEEE International Conference on Computer Vision, vol. 2019-October, pp. 5932–5941,https://doi.org/DOI: 10.48550/arxiv.1808.07371

Chataut, R., & Upadhyay, A. (2025). Introduction to Deepfake Technology and Its Early Foundations. In Deepfakes and Their Impact on Business (pp. 1-18). IGI Global Scientific Publishing.

Dehghani, A., & Saberi, H. (2025). Generating and Detecting Various Types of Fake Image and Audio Content: A Review of Modern Deep Learning Technologies and Tools. arXiv preprint arXiv:2501.06227.

Dolhansky, B., ... (2020). "The DeepFake Detection Challenge (DFDC) Dataset," Computer Vision and Pattern Recognition,vol.1 , https://doi.org//arxiv.2006.07397 .DOI: 10.48550

''GitHub - iperov/DeepFaceLive: Real-time face swap for PC streaming or video calls.'' https://github.com/iperov/DeepFaceLive

Hou, X., Shen, L., Ming, Z., & Qiu, G. (2023). Deep generative image priors for semantic face manipulation. *Pattern Recognition*, *139*, 109477. Advance online publication. DOI: 10.1016/j.patcog.2023.109477

Korshunov, P., & Marcel, S. (2019, June). Vulnerability assessment and detection of deepfake videos. In *2019 International Conference on Biometrics (ICB)* (pp. 1-6). IEEE.

Kumar, A., Singh, D., Jain, R., Jain, D. K., Gan, C., & Zhao, X. (2025). Advances in DeepFake detection algorithms: Exploring fusion techniques in single and multi-modal approach. *Information Fusion*, •••, 102993.

Li, Y., Yang, X., Sun, P., Qi, H., & Lyu, S. (2020). ''Celeb-DF: A Large-scale Challenging Dataset for DeepFake Forensics.'' [Online]. Available: https://deepfakedetectionchallenge.ai

Malik, A., Kuribayashi, M., Abdullahi, S. M., & Khan, A. N. (2022). DeepFake detection for human face images and videos: A survey. *IEEE Access : Practical Innovations, Open Solutions*, *10*, 18757–18775.

Masood, M., Nawaz, M., Malik, K. M., Javed, A., Irtaza, A., & Malik, H. (2023). Deepfakes generation and detection: State-of-the-art, open challenges, countermeasures, and way forward. *Applied Intelligence*, *53*(4), 3974–4026.

Mehta, V., Gupta, P., Subramanian, R., & Dhall, A. 2021 ''FakeBuster: A DeepFakes Detection Tool for Video Conferencing Scenarios,'' *International Conference on Intelligent User Interfaces, Proceedings IUI*, pp. 61–63, https://doi.org/DOI: 10.48550/arxiv.2101.03321

Mirsky, Y., & Lee, W. (2020). The creation and detection of deep-fakes: A survey. *ACM Computing Surveys*. Advance online publication. DOI: 10.1145/3425780

Mukta, M. S. H., Ahmad, J., Raiaan, M. A. K., Islam, S., Azam, S., Ali, M. E., & Jonkman, M. (2023). An investigation of the effectiveness of deepfake models and tools. Journal of sensor and actuator networks, 12(4), 61.

Nitzan, Y.. (2022). *MyStyle: a personalized generative prior. ACM Trans Gr.* TOG., DOI: 10.1145/3550454.3555436

Patel, Y., Tanwar, S., Gupta, R., Bhattacharya, P., Davidson, I. E., Nyameko, R., & Vimal, V. (2023). Deepfake generation and detection: Case study and challenges. *IEEE Access : Practical Innovations, Open Solutions*, *11*, 143296–143323.

Rana, M. S., Nobi, M. N., Murali, B., & Sung, A. H. (2022). Deepfake detection: A systematic literature review. *IEEE Access : Practical Innovations, Open Solutions*, *10*, 25494–25513. DOI: 10.1109/ACCESS.2022.3154404

Sandotra, N., & Arora, B. (2024). A comprehensive evaluation of feature-based AI techniques for deepfake detection. *Neural Computing & Applications*, *36*(8), 3859–3887.

Seow, J. W., Lim, M. K., Phan, R. C., & Liu, J. K. (2022). A comprehensive overview of Deepfake: Generation, detection, datasets, and opportunities. *Neurocomputing*, *513*, 351–371.

Seow, J. W., Lim, M. K., Phan, R. C. W., & Liu, J. K. (2022). A comprehensive overview of Deepfake: Generation, detection, datasets, and opportunities. *Neurocomputing*, *513*, 351–371. DOI: 10.1016/J.NEUCOM.2022.09.135

Sharma, M., & Kaur, M. (2022) ''A Review of deepfake technology: an emerging ai threat,'' Soft Computing for Security Applications, Proceedings of ICSCS, pp. 605–619, https://doi.org/DOI: 10.1007/978-981-16-5301-8_44

Sunil, R., Mer, P., Diwan, A., Mahadeva, R., & Sharma, A. (2025). Exploring autonomous methods for deepfake detection: A detailed survey on techniques and evaluation. *Heliyon*, *11*(3). Advance online publication. DOI: 10.1016/j.heliyon.2025.e42273 PMID: 39968137

U.S. Department of Homeland Security. (2025). Increasing Threats of Deepfake Identities. https://www.dhs.gov/sites/default/files/publications/increasing_threats_of_deepfake_identities_0.pdf

Verdoliva, L. (2020). Media forensics and deepfakes: An overview. *IEEE Journal of Selected Topics in Signal Processing*, *14*(5), 910–932.

Westerlund, M. (2019). The emergence of deepfake technology: A review. *Technology Innovation Management Review*, *9*(11).

Yu, P., Xia, Z., Fei, J., & Lu, Y. (2021). A survey on deepfake video detection. *IET Biometrics*, *10*(6), 607–624. DOI: 10.1049/BME2.12031

Chapter 7
AI-Driven Image Forensics for Cybercrime Detection: Chain of Custody and Legal Admissibility

Ananya Pandey
https://orcid.org/0000-0002-2419-6314
Christ University, India

ABSTRACT

Advanced techniques for analyzing and verifying digital images make AI-driven image forensics a crucial tool in detecting cybercrime. With the rise of cybercrime involving altered and forged images, AI-driven techniques like deepfake detection and metadata analysis present hopeful means for uncovering evidence. The incorporation of AI into forensic investigations, however, presents considerable challenges concerning the chain of custody and the legal admissibility of digital evidence. To ensure that digital evidence stays intact and unmodified during the investigation, it is crucial to uphold an uninterrupted chain of custody. To set forth unambiguous criteria regarding the admissibility of AI-processed evidence in court, legal systems must also grapple with the progressing character of AI. This chapter investigates how AI-driven forensics, maintaining the integrity of digital evidence, and the legal structures necessary to guarantee justice in the era of artificial intelligence intersect.

DOI: 10.4018/979-8-3373-3795-1.ch007

INTRODUCTION

As cybercrime evolves at a rapid pace, digital images have come to play a crucial role as evidence. In cases of online harassment, identity theft, deepfake dissemination, and fraud, image-based content is being used more frequently as both a means and proof of cyber offenses. Digital images—including photographs, video stills, screenshots, and screen captures—often play a crucial role in the detection, investigation, and prosecution of cybercrimes. Due to the omnipresence of smartphones, digital cameras, and image-editing programs, capturing and altering images has become easier than it has ever been. Consequently, the genuineness and wholeness of image-based evidence have emerged as a vital issue for investigators, legal professionals, and courts. This concern escalates in a time when artificial intelligence (AI) technologies are used both to perpetrate cybercrimes—like creating deepfakes—and as sophisticated instruments for forensic detection and authentication (Verdoliva, 2020; Fridrich, 2021).

The incorporation of AI into image forensics marks a major change in the methods used for investigation and analysis of evidence. The traditional approach to image forensics was based on time-consuming manual inspections and heuristic methods. These were constrained by human perceptual biases and limitations of technology. AI, especially through machine learning (ML) and deep learning (DL) techniques like Convolutional Neural Networks (CNNs), has made it possible to automate and improve forensic capabilities. These models can recognize patterns and anomalies in pixel data, identify indications of image manipulation, and extract metadata that may be missed by standard tools (Zhou et al., 2018). Furthermore, sophisticated algorithms have the capability to identify synthetic media produced by Generative Adversarial Networks (GANs), which are frequently employed to generate hyper-realistic counterfeit images and videos. This presents significant challenges to the credibility of evidence and public trust (Tolosana et al., 2020). Due to its capacity for rapid and accurate processing and analysis of extensive quantities of image data, AI has become a vital tool in contemporary digital inquiries.

Even with these technological advancements, there are significant legal and procedural challenges associated with using AI in image forensics. Of greatest importance is the matter of evidentiary integrity—guaranteeing that the image has remained unaltered and untampered with from the time it was acquired, through its analysis, and up to its final presentation in court. In legal contexts, preserving the integrity of digital evidence is essential for its admissibility. Various jurisdictions' courts follow stringent guidelines that dictate the authenticity, reliability, and relevance of digital evidence. These rules are frequently embodied in evidentiary standards like the Federal Rules of Evidence in the United States or similar provisions in other legal systems, necessitating that digital evidence satisfies specific criteria for originality and trustworthiness (Casey, 2011). The chain of custody, a procedural framework that documents the chronological history of the evidence's handling, governs the process of maintaining and demonstrating this integrity. According to Kerr (2005), if the chain of custody is compromised, it can make forensic analyses that are technologically sound inadmissible in court and put an entire investigation at risk.

The dependence on AI makes it difficult to legally assess image evidence because of the so-called "black box" problem. A number of deep learning models function based on internal mechanisms that non-experts, such as judges and lawyers, find difficult to interpret. This lack of transparency complicates the legal system's ability to evaluate the reliability of such tools according to admissibility standards, such as the Daubert standard. These standard mandates that scientific evidence be testable, peer-reviewed, have known error rates, and be widely accepted by the scientific community (Faigman et al., 2014). As a result, it is necessary to balance the effectiveness of technology and legal transparency when using images that AI has generated and analyzed as evidence. Expert testimony is crucial not just for validating the results generated by AI tools, but also for confirming that the methods used align with established forensic and legal standards. Adding to these difficulties are escalating worries about data privacy, the ethics of surveillance, and biases in algorithms. AI systems trained on datasets with biases can yield skewed outcomes, which may result in disproportionate targeting or incorrect attribution during cybercrime investigations (Barocas et al., 2019). Likewise, employing AI-augmented surveillance to gather photographic proof could violate civil liberties, particularly in the absence of sufficient legal protections. These ethical dilemmas intersect with evidentiary issues, underscoring the necessity for regulatory oversight, standardized methodologies, and interdisciplinary collaboration among technologists, legal scholars, and forensic practitioners.

The purpose of this chapter is to investigate the intersection of AI-driven image forensics and cybercrime detection, focusing on the two perspectives of chain of custody and legal admissibility. The introduction includes a definition and contextualization of image forensics in the context of cybercrime investigations, as well as an identification of specific AI techniques that are currently used in this field. It subsequently looks into the procedural and technical prerequisites for ensuring a secure chain of custody for digital image evidence, encompassing innovative solutions like blockchain and digital ledger technologies. Additionally, the chapter investigates the legal framework that regulates the admissibility of AI-analyzed evidence, using comparative legal standards, case law, and evidentiary doctrines as references. It tackles the main difficulties presented by AI—like lack of transparency, prejudice, and explainability—and examines ways to prepare legal professionals for a critical assessment of such evidence. Ultimately, the chapter wraps up with recommendations for best practices and policy considerations designed to align technological innovation with legal rigor. This encompasses demands for the creation of explainable AI models designed for forensic applications, the necessity of continuous AI literacy training for legal practitioners, and the setting up of global guidelines for handling digital evidence. This chapter adds to the expanding literature aimed at finding a way through the intricate crossroads of technology, law, and justice in the digital era by investigating the technical, procedural, and legal aspects of AI-based image forensics.

UNDERSTANDING IMAGE FORENSICS IN THE AGE OF AI

Due to the rapid advancement of digital technologies and the growing dependence on visual media in everyday activities, image forensics has become increasingly crucial within the larger field of digital forensics. According to Farid (2009), image forensics involves the use of scientific methods and tools to analyze digital images in order to assess their authenticity, identify their source, and detect any modifications. Its fundamental to spotting altered content, uncovering synthetic media, and maintaining the integrity of evidence in legal and policing situations. Digital evidence refers to any information that can be stored or transmitted digitally and has probative value, making it suitable for use in court cases. This encompasses metadata, pixel arrangements, compression signatures, and device identification details obtained from images (Casey, 2011). At the same time, cybercrime is widely characterized as any unlawful act that incorporates a computer, digital device, or network, which can serve as either the target of the offense or the means by which it is perpetrated (Brenner, 2010). Image evidence is becoming ever more crucial to the investigation of cybercrimes such as cyberstalking, identity theft, fraud, revenge pornography, online grooming, and the distribution of child sexual abuse material (CSAM). As an example, in situations involving identity theft or online impersonation, manipulated or synthetic images might be employed to deceive victims or officials. Similarly, cases of cyberstalking frequently depend on geotagged photos, screenshots, and altered images disseminated on social media (Lovelace et al., 2021).

The advent of Artificial Intelligence (AI), especially machine learning and deep learning technologies, has transformed image forensics. The Convolutional Neural Network (CNN) is among the tools that have been adopted most widely in this area. CNNs, as outlined by Krizhevsky et al. (2012), are deep learning models aimed at examining visual imagery through the extraction of spatial hierarchies of features via multiple layers of filters. They are especially efficient at identifying anomalies in images that may evade human notice. In forensic applications, CNNs are trained using datasets that include both authentic and tampered images to identify patterns that indicate manipulations, such as resampling, copy-move forgeries, or inconsistent lighting. As an illustration, Bayar and Stamm (2016) suggested a CNN-based approach that identifies general image manipulations such as splicing and cloning by learning rich residual features that emphasize tampering artifacts. Another forensic application involves the use of CNNs to associate an image with the exact make and model of the camera that captured it, aiding in source device identification and verification (Bondi et al., 2017). Concurrently, Generative Adversarial Networks (GANs) have emerged as a dual threat and remedy in the field of image forensics. GANs, which were first proposed by Goodfellow et al. (2014), are made up of two neural networks: a generator that produces fake images and a discriminator that tries to identify them. Although GANs are well-known for generating hyper-realistic deepfakes, they are also used to create advanced detectors of synthetic media. As an example, models based on XceptionNet have been utilized to differentiate real images from those generated by GANs through the learning of discriminative cues at the pixel level (Rossler et al., 2019). These models are crucial for combating the harmful proliferation of deepfakes, especially in the realms of political misinformation and non-consensual pornography, where altered videos and images are portrayed as genuine, with the potential to inflict reputational harm or lead to criminal victimization. Another important aspect of AI-based image forensics is the extraction of metadata and detection of anomalies. Metadata, including EXIF (Exchangeable Image File Format) data, can disclose information about the time, location, and method of an image's capture. AI tools can examine this metadata alongside image content to identify inconsistencies—like a daylight timestamp paired with nighttime visual elements—that may suggest tampering. Advanced systems utilize anomaly detection algorithms to identify images with atypical compression artifacts, inconsistent noise patterns, or pixel-level irregularities—often indicative of manipulation (Piva, 2013). Forensic platforms are increasingly incorporating machine learning classifiers to automatically sort through vast amounts of images, categorize them based on authenticity, and identify potentially fraudulent content with high accuracy (Zhou et al., 2018).

Many practical applications showcase the worth of AI in forensic image analysis. Law enforcement agencies are more frequently using AI tools to identify CSAM through the analysis of image hashes and the application of CNN models that can recognize suspicious visual content even when altered or obscured (Hernandez-Orallo et al., 2020). As another instance, the iCOP Project of the European Union created AI-based tools for the automatic detection of child abuse images and grooming behaviors via visual and textual analysis on peer-to-peer platforms. Moreover, AI-powered image analysis tools have played a crucial role in fraud investigations, including the detection of forged documents, altered identity verification items, or adjusted financial records provided in digital form. In civil litigation, AI-assisted image analysis is used in insurance fraud cases to confirm the authenticity of images submitted with claims (Yousif & Zhang, 2020). The aforementioned examples underscore the increasing dependence on AI technologies to improve the efficiency, accuracy, and scalability of image forensic investigations. To train and assess AI models with greater forensic fidelity, the forensic community is also creating benchmarks and datasets like FaceForensics++, DeepFake Detection Challenge (DFDC), and Columbia Image Splicing Detection Evaluation Dataset (Columbia Uncompressed) (Rossler et al., 2019). The confluence of image forensics and AI represents a vigorous and swiftly developing frontier in the detection of cybercrime. The emergence of CNNs, GANs, and anomaly detection algorithms has enhanced investigators' abilities to identify complex manipulations and derive meaningful insights from digital images. Simultaneously, it is crucial to utilize these technologies carefully, guaranteeing that forensic results are precise, understandable, and can be legally justified. With cybercriminals continuing to take advantage of visual media, creating and responsibly using AI-based image forensic tools will be crucial for maintaining digital justice systems and protecting at-risk populations.

TECHNICAL CHALLENGES AND RELIABILITY OF AI EVIDENCE

With the growing incorporation of artificial intelligence (AI) systems in digital forensic investigations—particularly in image forensics for cybercrime detection—numerous technical challenges remain that affect the reliability and admissibility of this evidence. The accuracy, bias, and explainability of AI models are among the most pressing concerns. Models based on machine learning—especially deep learning architectures such as convolutional neural networks (CNNs)—have shown extraordinary effectiveness in identifying anomalies and alterations in images (Zhou et al., 2018). When it comes to detecting inconsistencies in lighting, pixel alignment, and metadata, these models can surpass the performance of conventional forensic tools. Nonetheless, their high dimensionality and black-box nature often make them hard to interpret or explain, particularly in courtrooms where transparency and verifiability are necessary for legal admissibility (Doshi-Velez & Kim, 2017). A major technical challenge is the identification of altered content, including deepfakes, steganography, and image splicing. Deepfakes created by generative adversarial networks (GANs) yield hyper-realistic yet false media, making forensic authentication more challenging (Verdoliva, 2020). In a similar way, steganographic methods make it possible to conceal messages in images that appear harmless, thereby often evading simple forensic detection tools. Image splicing, the act of merging segments from various images into one deceptive picture, poses additional difficulties for automated systems that depend on low-resolution or surface-level cues. Even though AI models can be trained to identify such forgeries through pixel-level scrutiny and contextual understanding, adversarial methods can easily take advantage of these systems by making slight alterations to the data in order to avoid detection, which diminishes forensic reliability (Goodfellow et al., 2015).

In forensic investigations employing AI, the risk of false positives and false negatives continues to pose a significant challenge. A false positive, which occurs when a genuine image is incorrectly identified as altered, can result in unjust accusations. Conversely, a false negative, which happens when real manipulation goes undetected, can enable a cybercriminal to escape justice. In high-stakes legal contexts, these mistakes are not just technical failures; they can constitute miscarriages of justice. Research shows that the accuracy of even cutting-edge forensic AI systems varies based on the type of manipulation and the quality of input data (Bappy et al., 2017). In addition, the datasets utilized for training these models frequently lack sufficient diversity and contextual relevance, which results in biased outcomes when they are deployed in real-world situations (Mehrabi et al., 2021). Such biases pose a significant risk in forensic contexts, where evidence must be objective and based on scientific principles.

When image evidence generated by AI is presented in legal cases, it is especially important that the evidence be explainable and interpretable. AI-driven analyses can involve complex computations that legal practitioners and juries may not easily understand, in contrast to traditional forensic methodologies, which typically have transparent and replicable processes. This lack of interpretability threatens one of the core tenets of evidentiary law: an expert's ability to clarify the methods used and their significance in relation to the case's facts (OECD, 2021). As an example, a judge or jury may hesitate to depend on a system they do not grasp, no matter how statistically accurate it is. Models that offer human-interpretable justifications for their outputs are being developed in the field of explainable AI (XAI) to tackle this issue (Arrieta et al., 2020). Nonetheless, existing XAI approaches tend to simplify the model's reasoning in manners that could misrepresent its fundamental logic, leading to doubts about whether they are adequate for forensic testimony.

Moreover, the incorporation of AI into forensic procedures brings about worries regarding validation, standardization, and reproducibility—all of which are essential for upholding the chain of custody and ensuring the scientific integrity of the evidence. AI models exhibit a high sensitivity to variations in data distribution, preprocessing techniques, and environmental factors. Even slight adjustments to image resolution or compression parameters can cause considerable differences in output, complicating the reproducibility of results across various forensic laboratories or legal jurisdictions (Poma et al., 2020). Moreover, because of worries about intellectual property, proprietary algorithms frequently function as black boxes. This hinders external validation and peer review—processes vital for legal examination and court acceptance.

To reduce these challenges, it is crucial to implement strict validation protocols. These should involve thorough benchmarking against standardized datasets, cross-validation using a variety of image sources, and clear documentation of model behavior. Furthermore, it is essential to work with legal professionals when creating forensic AI tools to guarantee that their results align with the evidentiary reliability and admissibility standards of various jurisdictions (Katz & Bommarito, 2020). AI-driven image forensics can only achieve the robustness and credibility necessary for consistent application in the justice system through such interdisciplinary efforts. Even though AI offers unique abilities for identifying altered images and aiding investigations of cybercrime, its use in legal situations must be approached with caution regarding accuracy, bias, explainability, and interpretability. We must continuously evaluate the forensic reliability of AI tools, considering not just their technical performance but also legal scrutiny and ethical accountability. Without such oversight, the incorporation of AI into forensic science could jeopardize evidentiary integrity and public confidence in the justice system.

CHAIN OF CUSTODY IN AI-DRIVEN IMAGE FORENSICS

The chain of custody (CoC) is a fundamental principle for managing digital evidence, guaranteeing its integrity, authenticity, and reliability during the forensic process. In the field of AI-driven image forensics, where AI tools are employed to detect tampering, identify deep fakes, and verify metadata, it is essential to uphold a strong CoC. The CoC denotes a documented and uninterrupted transfer of evidence from the time it was collected to the time it is presented in court. To avoid any allegations of evidence tampering or mishandling (Casey, 2011), every step in this process—collection, transfer, analysis, storage, and presentation—needs to be carefully recorded. In environments that utilize AI, where image evidence frequently undergoes algorithmic analysis and automated processing, the risk of compromising the integrity of digital files escalates, making stringent procedural safeguards essential. The CoC starts with collection, where the image evidence is identified and acquired through forensically sound techniques. To preserve original files, investigators typically create cryptographic hashes (e.g., SHA-256) and generate forensic duplicates (NIST, 2020). At this stage, AI can help by sorting through large datasets to find pertinent images in a more efficient manner. However, it is crucial that any AI tool employed does not change the metadata or content of the original file. During the transfer phase, the digital evidence is securely moved between devices, departments, or investigators. It is common to use encryption protocols and secure digital containers (such as BitLocker and VeraCrypt), while transfer logs are required to contain time-stamps, identifiers, and chain-of-custody forms

(Rogers & Seigfried-Spellar, 2019). During the analysis phase, forensic specialists employ AI-driven image forensic tools to assess the integrity of the image, look for indications of alteration, or determine the sources of the image. AI improves analytical precision, but it also brings complexity: the outputs of machine learning models can be probabilistic rather than deterministic, which raises legal issues regarding reproducibility and reliability (Kenneally & Brown, 2021). To guarantee replicability, it is crucial to keep meticulous records of the analytical process, which should encompass the algorithms employed, their settings, software versions, and intermediate outcomes. Digital evidence, including both original and processed copies, must be stored in tamper-evident digital environments to ensure security. Best practices encompass using write-once-read-many (WORM) media, air-gapped storage systems, and implementing multi-factor authentication. Storage systems are required to keep logs of every access event to guarantee traceability (ISO/IEC 27042:2015). During the last stage of presentation, forensic specialists need to be capable of clearly expressing the origin and handling history of the evidence in court. Any findings derived from AI require corroboration from human experts and should include an account of the tools employed and their validation (Goodman & Flaxman, 2017). When algorithms are opaque or unverified, courts may doubt their reliability. In such cases, they may focus more on the forensic investigator's records and the CoC's integrity.

To bolster documentation and improve auditability in AI-assisted systems, investigators depend on digital audit trails. These trials furnish a thorough record of actions performed on an item of evidence, spanning from its initial acquisition to its final analysis, and are essential for upholding the evidence's admissibility in court. In environments driven by AI, audit trails should encompass not only user actions but also algorithmic decisions—such as the AI identifying an image as manipulated based on pixel-level inconsistencies or metadata anomalies. Such transparency helps to guarantee accountability and enables courts to examine closely the procedures used on the evidence (Brennan-Marquez & Henderson, 2019).

Innovative solutions for evidence tracking and maintaining an immutable CoC are provided by emerging technologies such as blockchain and distributed ledger technologies. Blockchain offers a decentralized and secure method for recording transactions, which makes it especially apt for tracking the lifecycle of digital evidence. Every transaction—collection, access, analysis—is documented as a block in the chain, equipped with a timestamp, cryptographically connected to previous blocks, which guarantees that any unauthorized alteration is easily identifiable (Kumar et al., 2020). As an example, initiatives such as the Chain-of-Custody Blockchain (CoCB) frameworks are undergoing trials for integration with forensic labs and judicial systems, aiming to simplify evidence authentication and guarantee verifiability across different jurisdictions (Zhou et al., 2018). The implementation of blockchain, however, needs to be aligned with legal standards to guarantee that its outputs are admissible and understandable in legal contexts. International forensic standards are crucial for directing the CoC process concerning digital and AI-derived evidence. The best practices for identifying, collecting, acquiring, and preserving digital evidence are outlined in ISO/IEC 27037:2012, which emphasizes the importance of documentation and reproducibility. The analysis and interpretation of digital evidence is guided by ISO/IEC 27042:2015, which emphasizes the necessity for methods that are clear, logical, and auditable. In the meantime, ISO/IEC 27043:2015 provides a structure for incident investigation that combines forensic readiness with procedural consistency. These standards act as worldwide benchmarks and can assist in aligning the use of AI tools across different jurisdictions, ensuring that the chain of custody is maintained and legally defensible in international courts (ISO, 2015).

LEGAL ADMISSIBILITY OF AI-PROCESSED IMAGE EVIDENCE

AI-processed image evidence poses considerable difficulties regarding legal admissibility within the realm of digital forensics. In the U.S., the criteria for accepting digital evidence, including images processed by AI, differ across jurisdictions and are based on frameworks like the Daubert Standard and Frye Test. These standards play a crucial role in deciding if scientific or technical evidence, including images generated or processed by AI, meets the reliability threshold required for court use.

Admissibility Standards in the U.S.: Daubert and Frye

The Daubert Standard, originating from the case of Daubert v. Merrell Dow Pharmaceuticals, Inc. (1993), regulates the admissibility of expert testimony and scientific evidence within federal courts. Judges serve as gatekeepers under Daubert, evaluating the scientific validity of the methods used to create or process AI images based on criteria like testability, peer review, error rates, and acceptance by the relevant scientific community (Daubert, 1993). It is essential for image forensics powered by AI to prove that the techniques employed to identify manipulation or synthetic modifications in images are strong, reproducible, and widely endorsed in the domains of computer science, forensics, and law enforcement. In contrast, the Frye Test, which is still adhered to in certain U.S. states, mandates that scientific methods must be "generally accepted" by the pertinent scientific community (Frye v. United States, 1923). The difficulty with AI lies in its ongoing development and the fact that various jurisdictions may not uniformly acknowledge the general acceptance of AI methods, including deep learning for image manipulation detection. This inconsistency presents a difficulty for lawyers aiming to demonstrate the trustworthiness of AI-processed images in legal proceedings. Other jurisdictions apply their own standards for admissibility. For instance, the General Data Protection Regulation (GDPR) of the European Union and its related legal principles stress the importance of transparency and accountability in data processing, encompassing digital image evidence. In areas such as the EU, the integrity and confidentiality principle of GDPR requires that digital evidence is kept and handled in a manner that guarantees its authenticity and reliability (Regulation (EU) 2016/679, 2016).

Authentication of Digital Image Evidence

Digital image evidence relies on authentication as a fundamental aspect for its legal admissibility. With AI-processed images, the process becomes more complicated because of the built-in possibilities for changes, manipulation, and even the creation of completely artificial images. Authentication generally entails showing that the image is as it claims to be and that it has not been modified in a manner that undermines its integrity. The authentication of image evidence in digital forensics entails verifying the source of the image, establishing a chain of custody, and using metadata analysis to ensure that the image has not been altered (Tanenbaum & van der Merwe, 2016). Given AI tools, especially those capable of subtle or complex alterations to images (such as deepfakes), conventional authentication methods might not be adequate. Consequently, AI tools are frequently used to spot image alterations, for instance by recognizing discrepancies in pixel structure, metadata, or noise patterns that suggest editing (Chesney & Citron, 2019). The challenge persists, however, that AI tools utilized for detecting changes may be vulnerable to manipulation themselves. Therefore, in order to comply with legal standards, the authentication process must be transparent, reproducible, and verifiable by independent parties (Gillespie, 2018).

Legal Aspects: Originality, Modification, and Human Supervision

Legal concerns surrounding AI-processed images focus on matters of originality, modification, and human oversight. The originality of an image is often linked to its evidentiary value within the legal context. For images processed by AI, it is essential to ascertain whether an image has been modified or created entirely anew (as with deep fakes). Due to their nature, AI-generated images may not possess the conventional signs of authenticity, like direct human interaction with the image (Gillespie, 2018). Concerns are amplified when it comes to the modification of digital images, especially in cases where AI tools have been employed. Because AI-generated or AI-altered images can seem convincingly real, determining whether an image has been altered and, if it has, the degree of alteration becomes a more complex legal challenge. Whether such modified images can be accepted hinges on the capacity to show that the modification does not influence the evidentiary value of the image (Chesney & Citron, 2019).

Moreover, the question of human supervision during the AI analysis process must not be ignored. Although AI tools can automate the analysis of images, it is essential to involve human experts to ensure accurate interpretation of AI findings and to verify that the AI processes are free from bias and errors. To confirm the trustworthiness and precision of AI evidence, courts usually depend on expert testimony. As a result, expert testimony is vital for clarifying evidence produced or handled by AI and making certain that judges and juries can grasp the findings (Fletcher, 2020).

The Function of Specialist Testimony

Because AI techniques are often very specialized and hard for non-experts to grasp, expert testimony is crucial for the legal admissibility of image evidence processed by AI. Expert witnesses, typically specialists in digital forensics or AI practitioners, are required to show the reliability of the AI method as well as the process involved in collecting, analyzing, and preserving the evidence. This encompasses elucidating any constraints of the technology employed and the possibility of mistakes, be they false positives or negatives in image manipulation detection (Fletcher, 2020). In certain instances, opposing counsel may challenge the use of AI-driven evidence by claiming that the technology is too novel, lacks widespread acceptance, or adds unnecessary complexity. Expert witnesses are essential for offering testimony that connects the technical workings of AI with legal evidence standards.

Examination of Case Law

Recent judicial decisions establish significant precedents concerning the acceptability of images produced or processed by AI. The court's decision in United States v. Leclair (2019) allowed for the admissibility of deep fake evidence, contingent upon its compliance with authenticity standards and the validation of the technology used to produce it. This ruling underscored the increasing significance of expert testimony for clarifying AI evidence in court. Conversely, the UK case R. v. Thomas (2021) dealt with AI's application for identifying alterations to digital images. In this instance, the court deemed AI-generated evidence inadmissible because of doubts regarding the technology's reliability at that time. The choice highlights the continuing discussion about the maturity and acceptability of AI-driven forensic tools in legal contexts.

ETHICAL AND PRIVACY CONSIDERATIONS FOR CYBERCRIME DETECTION

Incorporating AI-driven image forensics into cybercrime detection brings forth considerable ethical and privacy issues that need to be tackled to guarantee this technology is used responsibly. A major concern is the matter of surveillance, consent, and privacy rights. Utilizing AI tools for image forensics frequently requires the examination of large amounts of personal or sensitive images, such as private communications, surveillance footage, and social media posts. Consequently, these instruments must uphold individual privacy rights, safeguarded by legislation like the General Data Protection Regulation (GDPR) in the EU and the Fourth Amendment in the US (Solove, 2021). The laws mandate that data collection and processing can only occur with explicit consent. AI-driven systems are obliged to ensure this consent is duly acquired and recorded, especially regarding law enforcement activities. Moreover, inquiries relying on surveillance should be proportional and focused, taking into account the individual's privacy rights (Zuboff, 2019). If appropriate protections are not in place, employing AI for image forensics could result in mass surveillance, potentially violating civil liberties and generating public distrust of the technology and the organizations that use it.

A further essential ethical concern is the bias that AI tools inherently possess and the resulting consequences for justice. Large datasets are used to train AI systems, and these datasets may contain inherent biases stemming from the demographic, cultural, or geographical limitations of the data. These biases can result in the disproportionate targeting or misidentification of specific groups, especially in forensic investigations that involve racial or gendered profiles (Buolamwini & Gebru, 2018). This carries significant ramifications for justice, as biased AI algorithms may yield erroneous evidence or improperly sway decisions in legal cases, jeopardizing trial fairness. To foster equitable justice outcomes, it is crucial to train AI models on datasets that are diverse and representative, and to conduct thorough audits of their results for bias. Furthermore, the application of AI in forensic investigations brings up worries regarding accountability. It can be challenging to identify the source of an error when AI systems make mistakes or yield biased results. To guarantee the accountability of AI tools and the presence of human oversight throughout every phase of the forensic process, transparency is essential. Here, explainability of AI systems is crucial: stakeholders need to comprehend how an AI system arrived at its conclusions to have trust in and challenge its outcomes (Raji & Buolamwini, 2019). When it comes to the ethical use of AI, transparency and accountability in the generation of AI evidence is a vital consideration. To guarantee fairness in legal proceedings, legal systems necessitate evidence that is clear, comprehensible, and can be verified. AI tools, especially those focused on the analysis of digital images, need to be capable of elucidating their decision-making processes and offering transparent methodologies. For example, when employing AI to identify deep fakes or altered images, it is essential to clarify the method by which the AI has recognized changes or discrepancies. Without transparency, AI-generated evidence may be challenged in court, as parties could doubt its validity or reliability. To avert manipulation and guarantee that digital evidence is genuine, the chain of custody for AI-processed images must be upheld with great diligence. It necessitates strong oversight, well-defined regulations, and continuous conversations among technologists, policymakers, and civil society to balance the need for effective law enforcement with safeguarding civil liberties (Binns, 2018). To ensure that AI in image forensics is used in a way that respects human rights while allowing for effective crime detection, ethical frameworks must be established.

FUTURE DIRECTIONS AND RECOMMENDATION

XAI has the potential to aid forensic specialists in elucidating the methods employed by AI systems to detect altered or modified images within the field of forensic image analysis. This would help ensure that such evidence is comprehensible and credible to judges and juries (Ribeiro, Singh, & Guestrin, 2016). Future research could also focus on using quantum computing and cryptography to bolster the chain of custody's integrity. With the ongoing development of quantum computing technologies, there is a possibility of a transformation in data encryption and security protocols—areas essential for safeguarding the integrity of digital evidence. Digital images could be protected from tampering during their collection, storage, and transfer through quantum-resistant encryption, thereby enhancing the security and reliability of the forensic process (Shor, 1997). Furthermore, blockchain and cryptographic technologies can be essential in preserving an unchangeable chain of custody record, providing tamper-proof evidence handling documentation that can be verified instantly (Zohar et al., 2019). By integrating quantum cryptography with blockchain technology, digital forensics could achieve a new height of security, complicating the task of those with malicious intent who seek to alter evidence.

The emergence of advanced synthetic media, such as deep fakes, persists in posing challenges to conventional forensic techniques. As AI models that create hyper-realistic fake images and videos grow more advanced, it becomes increasingly challenging for even seasoned forensic analysts to tell real content apart from fabricated (Chesney & Citron, 2019). This development endangers the trustworthiness of digital evidence and the dependability of AI-driven forensic tools. Therefore, it is essential to continue investigating sophisticated detection techniques for synthetic media, which includes creating novel machine learning algorithms that can recognize slight artifacts or discrepancies in manufactured media. To enhance detection precision, researchers are investigating the incorporation of multi-modal AI systems that fuse image, audio, and behavioral analysis (Matern et al., 2020).

Ultimately, it is essential to create worldwide standards for employing AI in digital forensics to guarantee uniformity, dependability, and equity across different jurisdictions. Internationally acknowledged standards for AI-based image forensics can facilitate the alignment of practices and guidelines related to forensic investigations, thus reducing inconsistencies in the treatment and presentation of digital evidence across various legal systems. This could involve creating guidelines for the validation, certification, and transparency of AI models in forensic contexts. It may also require collaboration among law enforcement agencies, academic researchers, and policy-makers to create regulatory frameworks (Taddeo & Floridi, 2018). By standardizing the application of AI in forensics, the quality of evidence will be improved and its acceptance in courts worldwide will be bolstered, cultivating faith in AI as a means of justice.

CONCLUSION

The ongoing development of AI-driven image forensics presents unique prospects for identifying cybercrime and safeguarding the authenticity of digital evidence. AI's application in forensic image analysis has demonstrated its worth for identifying alterations to images, including deepfakes and splicing, and for retrieving vital metadata that could otherwise remain concealed. Nonetheless, although AI provides notable progress in the domain, it also brings forth various challenges, especially regarding the dependability of AI models, the potential for biases, and the necessity for explainability (Gao et al., 2021). It is essential to maintain a careful balance between the use of AI in forensic investigations and the preservation of legal standards, especially with respect to maintaining a strong chain of custody and ensuring the legal admissibility of evidence (Reilly, 2020). To guarantee that digital evidence is unchanged from the moment it is gathered to the time it is exhibited in court, preserving the chain of custody is essential. Even the most advanced analyses driven by AI can be deemed inadmissible without adequate documentation and tracking (Villacres et al., 2019). Moreover, with the ongoing development of AI technology, the legal structures related to it must evolve as well. To accurately evaluate the legitimacy of evidence generated by AI, courts must cultivate a more profound comprehension of AI methods and their constraints. It will be crucial for upholding justice to set forth unambiguous criteria regarding the admissibility of AI-processed evidence and to ensure transparency in forensic practices (Friedman et al., 2022). Ultimately, AI must be integrated into digital forensics in a manner that maintains both legal rigor and technological innovation, ensuring that justice is served fairly and without bias or undue influence from artificial technologies.

REFERENCES

Arrieta, A. B., Díaz-Rodríguez, N., Del Ser, J., Bennetot, A., Tabik, S., Barbado, A., & Herrera, F. (2020). Explainable Artificial Intelligence (XAI): Concepts, taxonomies, opportunities and challenges toward responsible AI. *Information Fusion*, *58*, 82–115. DOI: 10.1016/j.inffus.2019.12.012

Bappy, J. H., Roy-Chowdhury, A. K., Bunk, J., Nataraj, L., & Manjunath, B. S. (2017). Exploiting spatial structure for localizing manipulated image regions. In *Proceedings of the IEEE International Conference on Computer Vision* (pp. 4970–4979). https://doi.org/DOI: 10.1109/ICCV.2017.532

Barocas, S., Hardt, M., & Narayanan, A. (2019). *Fairness and machine learning*. https://fairmlbook.org

Bayar, B., & Stamm, M. C. (2016). A deep learning approach to universal image manipulation detection using a new convolutional layer. *Proceedings of the 4th ACM Workshop on Information Hiding and Multimedia Security*, 5–10. https://doi.org/DOI: 10.1145/2909827.2930786

Binns, R. (2018). *The ethics of artificial intelligence and robotics*. Stanford Encyclopedia of Philosophy. Retrieved from https://plato.stanford.edu/entries/ethics-ai/

Bondi, L., Baroffio, L., Güera, D., Bestagini, P., Delp, E. J., & Tubaro, S. (2017). First steps toward camera model identification with convolutional neural networks. *IEEE Signal Processing Letters*, *24*(3), 259–263. DOI: 10.1109/LSP.2016.2633282

Brennan-Marquez, E., & Henderson, S. E. (2019). From the database to the courtroom: Artificial intelligence and evidence. *Columbia Law Review*, *119*(7), 1911–1966.

Brenner, S. W. (2010). *Cybercrime: Criminal threats from cyberspace*. Praeger.

Buolamwini, J., & Gebru, T. (2018). *Gender shades: Intersectional accuracy disparities in commercial gender classification. Proceedings of the 1st Conference on Fairness, Accountability and Transparency*, 77-91. https://doi.org/DOI: 10.1145/3287560.3287593

Casey, E. (2011). *Digital evidence and computer crime: Forensic science, computers, and the internet* (3rd ed.). Academic Press.

Chesney, R., & Citron, D. K. (2019). Deepfakes and the new disinformation war: The coming age of synthetic media. *Foreign Affairs*, *98*(1), 2–9.

Chesney, R., & Citron, D. K. (2019). Deepfakes: A looming challenge for privacy, democracy, and national security. *California Law Review*, *107*(6), 1753–1819. DOI: 10.15779/Z38S45D99X

Daubert v. Merrell Dow Pharmaceuticals, Inc., 509 U.S. 579 (1993).

Doshi-Velez, F., & Kim, B. (2017). Towards a rigorous science of interpretable machine learning. *arXiv preprint arXiv:1702.08608.*

Faigman, D. L., Kaye, D. H., Saks, M. J., & Sanders, J. (2014). *Modern scientific evidence: The law and science of expert testimony*. Thomson Reuters.

Farid, H. (2009). Image forgery detection. *IEEE Signal Processing Magazine*, *26*(2), 16–25. DOI: 10.1109/MSP.2008.931079

Fletcher, M. (2020). The role of expert testimony in digital forensics: Ensuring admissibility of AI-generated evidence. *Journal of Cybersecurity and Digital Forensics*, *15*(3), 38–47.

Fridrich, J. (2021). AI for digital media forensics: Hype and reality. *IEEE Signal Processing Magazine*, *38*(1), 82–90. DOI: 10.1109/MSP.2020.3036897

Friedman, A., Mikalef, P., & Kourouthanassis, P. (2022). Artificial Intelligence in Forensic Science: A Critical Analysis of Legal Implications. *Journal of Digital Forensics & Cybersecurity*, *18*(4), 215–230. DOI: 10.1002/jdfc.234

Frye v. United States, 293 F. 1013 (D.C. Cir. 1923).

Gao, Y., Liu, J., & Wang, Q. (2021). Deep Learning in Digital Forensics: Opportunities and Challenges. *Journal of Computer Science and Technology*, *36*(2), 341–355. DOI: 10.1007/s11390-021-1834-0

Gillespie, T. (2018). AI in legal contexts: The challenges of authenticity and accuracy in digital evidence. *Journal of Digital Evidence and Forensic Science*, *25*(2), 103–112.

Goodfellow, I., Pouget-Abadie, J., Mirza, M., Xu, B., Warde-Farley, D., Ozair, S., & Bengio, Y. (2014). Generative adversarial nets. *Advances in Neural Information Processing Systems*, *27*, 2672–2680.

Goodfellow, I. J., Shlens, J., & Szegedy, C. (2015). Explaining and harnessing adversarial examples. In *International Conference on Learning Representations (ICLR)*.

Hernandez-Orallo, E., Villagra, V. A., & Montañés, E. (2020). AI-based detection and prevention of child sexual abuse material. *IEEE Access : Practical Innovations, Open Solutions*, *8*, 124709–124719. DOI: 10.1109/ACCESS.2020.3007773

ISO. (2015). Information technology – Security techniques – Guidelines for the analysis and interpretation of digital evidence. International Organization for Standardization., ISO/IEC 27042.

Katz, D. M., & Bommarito, M. J. (2020). Legal analytics: The future of analytics in the legal profession. *Annual Review of Law and Social Science*, *16*, 287–306. DOI: 10.1146/annurev-lawsocsci-112418-042533

Kenneally, E., & Brown, C. L. (2021). Explainable AI and admissibility: Navigating forensic epistemology. *Journal of Law and Artificial Intelligence*, *1*(1), 14–39.

Kerr, O. S. (2005). Searches and seizures in a digital world. *Harvard Law Review*, *119*(2), 531–585.

Krizhevsky, A., Sutskever, I., & Hinton, G. E. (2012). ImageNet classification with deep convolutional neural networks. *Advances in Neural Information Processing Systems*, *25*, 1097–1105.

Kumar, R., Mallick, P. K., & Tripathi, S. (2020). Blockchain-based forensic framework for digital image evidence. *Journal of Forensic Sciences*, *65*(6), 1990–1999. DOI: 10.1111/1556-4029.14475

Lovelace, K., Lytle, S. L., & Freeman, L. A. (2021). Technology-facilitated abuse: Gender-based violence and online harassment. *Journal of Interpersonal Violence*, *36*(13–14), 6603–6624.

Matern, F., He, R., & Kuo, S. (2020). AI-based detection of deepfake videos using temporal information. *Proceedings of the International Conference on Digital Forensics and Cyber Crime*. https://doi.org/DOI: 10.1007/978-3-030-39694-3_17

Mehrabi, N., Morstatter, F., Saxena, N., Lerman, K., & Galstyan, A. (2021). A survey on bias and fairness in machine learning. *ACM Computing Surveys*, *54*(6), 1–35. DOI: 10.1145/3457607

NIST. (2020). *Digital Evidence: Standards and Best Practices*. National Institute of Standards and Technology. Retrieved from https://www.nist.gov/

OECD. (2021). *OECD Framework for the Classification of AI Systems*. OECD Publishing. https://www.oecd.org/innovation/oecd-framework-for-classification-of-ai-systems-2021.pdf

Piva, A. (2013). An overview on image forensics. *ISRN Signal Processing*, *2013*, 1–22. DOI: 10.1155/2013/496701

Poma, X., Salloum, R., Bappy, J., & Nataraj, L. (2020). Deep learning for image forensics. In Bhunia, S., Roy-Chowdhury, R., & Bhowmick, A. K. (Eds.), *Multimedia Forensics and Security* (pp. 71–96). Springer., DOI: 10.1007/978-3-030-37211-9_4

Raji, I. D., & Buolamwini, J. (2019). *Actionable auditing: Investigating the impact of public policy on AI ethics. Proceedings of the 2019 CHI Conference on Human Factors in Computing Systems*, 1-13. https://doi.org/DOI: 10.1145/3293663.3293678

Regulation (EU) 2016/679 of the European Parliament and of the Council of 27 April 2016 on the protection of natural persons with regard to the processing of personal data. *Official Journal of the European Union*.

Reilly, K. (2020). Chain of Custody in the Age of AI: Ensuring the Integrity of Digital Evidence. *International Journal of Cybersecurity Law, 22*(3), 129–143. DOI: 10.1177/2452096820907653

Ribeiro, M. T., Singh, S., & Guestrin, C. (2016). Why should I trust you? Explaining the predictions of any classifier. *Proceedings of the 22nd ACM SIGKDD International Conference on Knowledge Discovery and Data Mining*, 1135-1144. https://doi.org/DOI: 10.1145/2939672.2939778

Rogers, M., & Seigfried-Spellar, K. (2019). *Digital Forensics: An Interdisciplinary Approach*. Jones & Bartlett Learning.

Rossler, A., Cozzolino, D., Verdoliva, L., Riess, C., Thies, J., & Nießner, M. (2019). FaceForensics++: Learning to detect manipulated facial images. *Proceedings of the IEEE/CVF International Conference on Computer Vision*, 1–11. https://doi.org/DOI: 10.1109/ICCV.2019.00009

Shor, P. W. (1997). Polynomial-time algorithms for prime factorization and discrete logarithms on a quantum computer. *SIAM Journal on Computing, 26*(5), 1484–1509. DOI: 10.1137/S0097539791191289

Solove, D. J. (2021). *Understanding privacy* (2nd ed.). Harvard University Press.

Taddeo, M., & Floridi, L. (2018). The ethics of artificial intelligence. In *The Ethics of Cybersecurity* (pp. 137–158). Springer., DOI: 10.1007/978-3-030-03228-4_7

Tanenbaum, A. S., & van der Merwe, R. (2016). *Computer Networks* (5th ed.). Prentice Hall.

Tolosana, R., Vera-Rodriguez, R., Fierrez, J., Morales, A., & Ortega-Garcia, J. (2020). Deepfakes and beyond: A survey of face manipulation and fake detection. *Information Fusion, 64*, 131–148. DOI: 10.1016/j.inffus.2020.07.007

Verdoliva, L. (2020). Media forensics and deepfakes: An overview. *IEEE Journal of Selected Topics in Signal Processing*, *14*(5), 910–932. DOI: 10.1109/JSTSP.2020.3002103

Villacres, M. C., Gonzalez, R., & Martinez, L. (2019). Chain of Custody and Digital Evidence: Legal Frameworks in the Age of AI. *Digital Evidence & Law Review*, *12*(2), 42–56. DOI: 10.1080/20365404.2019.1582784

Yousif, M. R., & Zhang, Y. (2020). Artificial intelligence in insurance fraud detection: A systematic literature review. *Applied Sciences (Basel, Switzerland)*, *10*(10), 3414. DOI: 10.3390/app10103414

Zhou, P., Han, X., Morariu, V. I., & Davis, L. S. (2018). Learning rich features for image manipulation detection. In *Proceedings of the IEEE Conference on Computer Vision and Pattern Recognition* (pp. 1053–1061). https://doi.org/DOI: 10.1109/CVPR.2018.00116

Zhou, Q., Huang, H., Zheng, Z., & Bian, J. (2018). Solutions to scalability of blockchain: A survey. *IEEE Access : Practical Innovations, Open Solutions*, *8*, 16440–16455. DOI: 10.1109/ACCESS.2018.2894923

Zohar, A., Zohar, D., & Zohar, E. (2019). *Blockchain-based chain of custody for digital forensics*. Journal of Digital Forensics. *Security and Law*, *14*(1), 1–20.

Zuboff, S. (2019). *The age of surveillance capitalism: The fight for a human future at the new frontier of power*. PublicAffairs.

Chapter 8
Human Detection and Intelligent Action Recognition for Automatic Visual Surveillance and Monitoring Systems:
Its Current Trends

Lakhyadeep Konwar
https://orcid.org/0000-0001-8585-2074
Gauhati University, India

Navajit Saikia
Assam Engineering College, India

Subhash Chandra Rajbongshi
Gauhati University, India

ABSTRACT

Security and surveillance have become essential components of modern society, particularly in the context of crime reduction in areas such as traffic, urban centers, shopping malls etc. Developing an effective human detection system requires extracting key features and using classifiers that perform well under challenging conditions, such as poor lighting, occlusions etc. Human activity recognition in video footage is a key research area aimed at improving surveillance systems but

DOI: 10.4018/979-8-3373-3795-1.ch008

faces challenges like sensor motion, cluttered backgrounds etc. CNNs are commonly used for classifying these activities. The goal is to create a learning-based AI system that connects CCTV cameras with a centralized data center, supported by a trained algorithm and an automated alert system to distinguish between normal and anomalous activities. This chapter will explore current trends, techniques, datasets, challenges, and evaluation metrics related to human detection and activity recognition for automatic visual surveillance system (AVSS) design.

1. INTRODUCTION

The main goal of computer vision (CV) is to enable computers to interpret and understand scenes through camera input. With the rapid growth of digital cameras and other video capturing devices, video analysis becomes one of the most popular research areas in computer vision domain. In every instant of time thousands of videos are uploaded to different platforms like YouTube, and millions of surveillance cameras around the world continuously capture footage. Since it is impossible for humans to process such massive amounts of video data, computer vision algorithms are essential. These algorithms are used for human detection, recognition, tracking, action recognition, unusual event detection, segmentation, video retrieval, classification etc. Among these, object detection, recognition, and tracking are the most crucial tasks in computer vision domain. They are widely used in areas such as security and surveillance, human-computer interaction, video compression, augmented reality, traffic management, medical imaging, industrial automation, robotics etc. Object detection identifies instances of specific classes (e.g., humans, vehicles, animals etc.) in images or videos, while tracking follows these objects across different video frames while maintaining their identities. In surveillance systems, detection and tracking are combined to monitor people or other objects of interest. Since humans are the primary focus in most real-world applications, such as surveillance, autonomous driving, human-computer interaction etc. research often emphasizes human detection and tracking. Another important area is vision-based human activity recognition, which classifies human activities using learning-based techniques. Applications include video surveillance, sports analysis, healthcare monitoring, human-computer interaction etc. For example, action recognition systems can automatically detect activities like walking, running, standing etc. monitor athletes' movements in games, or identify falls among elderly or disabled individuals to trigger timely assistance. The need for such systems is increasing due to the rise in crime and terrorist activities in different places i.e. shopping malls, railway stations, highways, bus terminals etc. While deploying security personnel can reduce crime, but it is impractical to monitor every location manually. CCTV cameras can capture activities in strategic areas, but constant human monitoring is difficult and requires large manpower. Criminals may also escape despite being recorded, as delays in identifying and reporting suspicious activities make it harder to catch them in time. To address these challenges, smart surveillance systems are needed. Such systems can analysed surveillance footage in real-time, detect unusual or criminal behavior, and immediately alert security authorities. This helps ensure timely responses, reduces reliance on manual monitoring, and improves the effectiveness of surveillance in preventing and controlling crime.

Figure 1 shows a basic block diagram of a future smart visual surveillance system. The system begins with cameras (i.e. CCTV, IP cameras, drones, or body-worn devices), that capture high-resolution, real-time video streams. This input data are feeds into a human detection module where, advanced AI models identify people within the footage, even under crowded or low-light conditions or other different challenging conditions. Detected individuals are then fed to human tracking stage, which maintains consistent IDs across multiple frames and cameras to enable continuous monitoring and trajectory prediction. Next, the human activity recognition module classifies behaviors i.e. walking, running, loitering, fighting, carrying objects, etc. using spatio-temporal AI models. The system subsequently applies suspicious or anomaly activity detection, flagging abnormal or high-risk behaviors through a combination of predefined rules and adaptive learning-based techniques. Finally, if an activity is deemed unusual or threatening, the alert module automatically notifies security staff, triggers alarms, or records the incident for evidence. Together, these interconnected blocks form an end-to-end, intelligent, and proactive surveillance framework designed to enhance safety, enable rapid response, and evolve with changing security needs.

Figure 1. Basic block diagram of a future smart surveillance system.

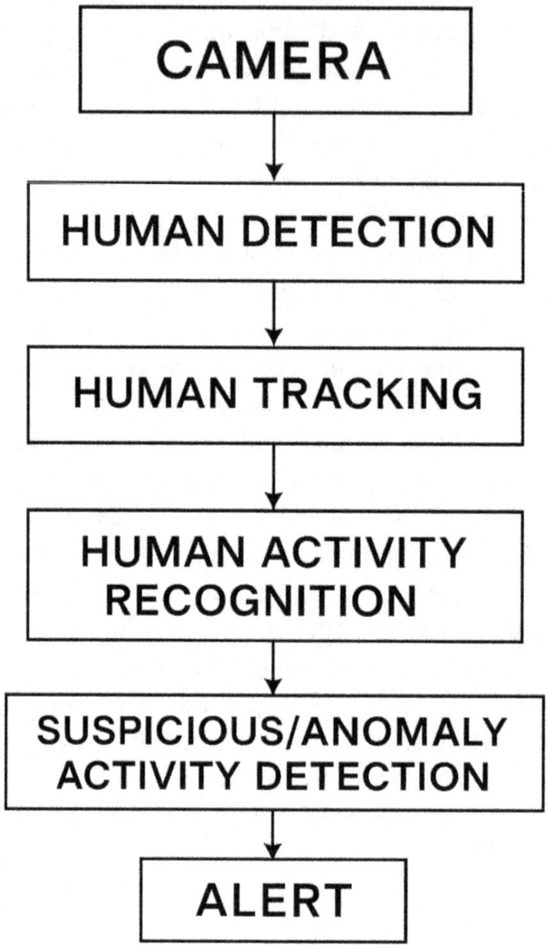

2. MOTIVATIONS

Object detection and classification in machine vision present significant challenges, particularly in human detection for smart surveillance systems used in tracking and action recognition. Key challenges include lighting conditions, body posture, occlusion, environment etc. Continuous recognition of human activities is vital for security applications, yet it is complex, especially when actions occur rapidly or their start and end points are unclear. Also, distinguishing between normal and suspicious behaviors can be difficult. Researchers are exploring ways to differentiate these behaviors, but using a single model for both indoor and outdoor environments add complexity. Additionally, the lack of temporal annotations can lead to false alarms in detecting suspicious activity. A reliable system that accurately classifies these activities would enhance surveillance applications, as identifying suspicious behavior in video footage is challenging even for trained observers.

3. PROBLEM FORMULATION

Changes in light intensity make it difficult to design systems for finding and tracking people. Occluded objects also affect detection. Classifying ongoing activities is tricky because it's hard to pinpoint when actions start and end. Fast movements and similar actions also add to the challenge. Also, some actions are hard to classify due to their similarities, and different viewpoints complicate this further. Additionally, it is need to recognize suspicious activities in surveillance videos. Here, the main goal is to create a smart surveillance system that accurately distinguishes normal activities and suspicious ones from a large scale of data. While going to design a smart surveillance system, it is need to keep above mentioned factors in mind.

4. LITERATURE REVIEW

A considerable volume of literatures has been available in the domains of object detection, human detection, human tracking, activity recognition, and anomaly detection primarily due to their critical applications in enhancing safety and quality of life. Over the past decade, significant research efforts have emerged in these areas. Following are some comprehensive literature reviews that is integral to the considered work presented herein.

4.1. Object Detection

Freer et al., 1995 proposed a poster-based algorithm for detection of different objects in CCTV footage, aimed at identifying the presence of intruders or not. Maurin et al., 2002 developed a vision-based system aimed at enhancing traffic management in urban settings, such as intersections and streets, particularly following athletic events. This system is capable of effectively detecting and tracking both pedestrians and vehicles by utilizing optical flow and background removal algorithms, subsequently employing the Kalman filter for tracking the identified objects. Ahmad, 2008 introduced a method for segmenting detected moving objects from image sequences by employing mean shift clustering, which is primarily geared towards identifying motion changes in the detected objects. The background subtraction and foreground segmentation methods for object detection, based on the Gaussian mixture model (GMM), were presented by Thombre et al., 2009 and Hafiz et al., 2010 enabling the effective removal of shadows through contrast adjustment techniques. The utilization of mean shift clustering for segmentation has been further demonstrated by Ubukata et al., 2014, enhancing both the accuracy of human detection and the capacity to manage occlusions. Subsequently, Ramya & Raviraj, 2014 and Kharabe et al., 2017 discovered that the graph cut segmentation technique delivers commendable results for detecting both human beings and other objects in the context of moving object detection. He et al., 2016 used faster R-CNN and examined the benefits of replacing VGG-16 with ResNet-101. Lin et al., 2017 introduced a one-stage object detector that matches the state-of-the-art COCO average precision (AP) of complex two-stage detectors like FPN and Mask R-CNN. The key contribution was to addressing class imbalance during training, which was identify as the main barrier to the accuracy of one-stage detectors. Here, the author proposed a new loss function that overcomes this challenge. Tian et al., 2019 introduce FCOS, a fully convolutional one-stage object detector that performs object detection similarly to semantic segmentation through per-pixel predictions. FCOS is unique in being both anchor box-free and proposal-free, which simplifies computations and eliminates sensitive hyperparameters related to anchor boxes, ultimately improving detection performance. The main objective of this work developed by Bochkovskiy et al., 2020 is to create a fast object detector for production systems, optimizing for parallel computations instead of just low computation volume (BFLOP). Therefore, the author introduced an effective and powerful object detection model. Tan et al., 2020 introduced a weighted bi-directional feature pyramid network (BiFPN) for efficient multi-scale feature fusion and a compound scaling method that uniformly adjusts the resolution, depth, and width of backbones and prediction networks. These innovations led to the development of EfficientDet, a family of object detectors that achieve superior efficiency compared to previous methods under various resource constraints. Liu et al. (2022) introduced ConvNeXts, a ConvNet model that effectively competes with advanced hierarchical vision transformers while maintaining the simplicity and efficiency of standard ConvNets. Diwan et al. (2023) reviewed single-stage detectors, focusing on YOLO architectures, studied their performance, comparative analyses with two-stage detectors, and make a conclusion on future research directions. As object detection has evolved from early handcrafted methods to deep learning approaches, though traditional systems often suffered from low accuracy and slow performance. Vaishnavi et al. (2023) addressed these limitations with an end-to-end single shot detector (SSD) framework, that focused on improving speed and detection accuracy in a single-pass convolutional network. Huang et al. (2024) used YOLOv8 for small object detection by improving the detection head and strengthening its attention to fine-grained features, and evaluates object detection performance against YOLOv3 and YOLOv5n.

The progression of object detection methods reveals a distinct shift from early handcrafted and algorithm-driven techniques to contemporary deep learning-based frameworks. Foundational approaches such as poster-based detection, optical flow, mean shift clustering, GMM-based background subtraction, and graph cut segmentation paved the way for object detection and tracking in controlled environments, effectively addressing challenges like motion variations, shadows, occlusions etc. The emergence of deep learning models, including Faster R-CNN, one-stage detectors, FCOS, EfficientDet, ConvNeXts, etc. has markedly enhanced detection accuracy, computational efficiency, and scalability. Further innovations, such as anchor-free detection, multi-scale feature fusion, and transformer-inspired architectures, have enabled these systems to perform reliably across diverse and complex real-world scenarios, establishing their suitability for large-scale applications in surveillance, autonomous driving, robotics, and other related domains.

4.2. Human Detection

The foundational concept of human detection was proposed by Dalal & Triggs, 2005, integrating the histogram of oriented gradient (HOG) feature descriptor with a support vector machine (SVM) classifier, thereby improving human detection accuracy through effective feature extraction. Following this, Zhu et al., 2006 presented a method utilizing a variable block size HOG feature descriptor that automatically captures significant features of human objects. This approach identifies an optimal set of blocks from a vast array of possibilities by employing AdaBoost-based feature selection in conjunction with integral image representation and a rejection cascade, markedly enhancing computational efficiency. Thurau, 2007 proposed a technique for simultaneous human detection and behavior recognition from both images and image sequences. Their approach involves the application of a clustering algorithm to sequences of HOG representations of human motion images, classifying human behavior based on Kullback-Leibler divergence of behavior histograms. Kachouane et al., 2012 proposed an algorithm for human detection and recognition in real-time images, which combines the HOG feature descriptor and SVM classifier, yielding favorable detection outcomes that are commonly utilized in robotic applications. Park et al., 2012 introduced an expedited pedestrian detection method founded on a two-stage cascade structure, which combines HOG with local binary patterns (LBP). This structure allows the initial stage to extract features exclusively from regions characterized by pedestrians, resulting in a pedestrian detection accuracy that is three times faster than conventional techniques. Kushwaha et al., 2012 introduced a novel algorithm that integrates haar feature descriptors for feature extraction and particle filters for tracking. This system also employs binary adaptive boosting for object classification, enabling the detection and tracking of multiple human subjects in video clips, adeptly handling variations in poses, shapes, sizes, and clothing. Subsequently, Lakshmi et al., 2013 introduced a method that combines graph cut-based object segmentation with the HOG technique to enhance human detection accuracy. Moreover, Bell, 2013 proposed a system which was capable of operating effectively across variations in size, potential occlusions, contextual information, noise, and clutter situations. This method successfully detects dismounted humans at long ranges from single, highly compressed images. Ramya & Raviraj, 2014 and Kharabe et al., 2017 identified that the graph cut segmentation technique yields effective results for human detection as well as the detection of other objects in the context of moving object detection. Jagadeesh & Patil, 2019 introduced a comprehensive method for human detection, tracking, recognition, and action classification. This method employed GMM for detection, SVM for classification, and optical flow algorithms for tracking. Thys et al., 2019 developed a system to create adversarial patches for person detectors, which can be printed for real-world use. Here, the author optimized an image to reduce the probabilities of detecting a person in the output. Rosinol et al., 2020 introduced 3D dynamic scene graphs for actionable spatial perception and presented the spatial perception engine (SPIN), which automatically constructs a dynamic scene graph from sensor data. Here, the author demonstrated SPIN in a photo-realistic simulator and discussed its applications in planning, human-robot interaction, data compression, and scene prediction. Hou et al., 2020 introduced a novel multi-view detector namely MVDet. Unlike existing methods that rely on potentially inaccurate predefined anchor boxes for multi-view aggregation, MVDet uses an anchor-free approach, sampling feature vectors directly from corresponding pixels across multiple views. Additionally, MVDet employs a fully convolutional approach for spatial aggregation, utilizing large convolutional kernels on the aggregated feature map, unlike previous methods that operate outside of neural networks. Jia et al., 2020 introduced the DR-SPAAM person detector, that combines the DROW detector's distance-robust scheme with spatial attention and an auto-regressive temporal integration model. The spatial attention links misaligned features from different frames based on appearance similarity, while the auto-regressive model aggregates temporal information over time. Jimenez et al. (2020) introduced a deep learning method for reliably detecting multiple individuals from a single overhead depth image using a neural network called DPDnet. This network consists of two fully-convolutional encoder-decoder blocks. Here, the main block generates a pixel-wise confidence map with Gaussian-like distributions for each detected person, while the refinement block enhances this map by combining it with the depth image. Both blocks are trained simultaneously using depth images and head position labels. Hong et al., 2022 introduced the scale selection pyramid network (SSPNet) for tiny object detection, consisting of three components: the context attention module (CAM), the scale enhancement module (SEM), and the scale selection module (SSM). Here, the CAM generates hierarchical attention heatmaps based on contextual information. The SEM focuses on features of specific scales at different layers, allowing the detector to prioritize objects over background. The SSM enhances feature sharing between deep and shallow layers to maintain consistent gradient computation. Additionally, a weighted negative sampling (WNS) strategy guides the detector in selecting more representative samples. Heemskerk et al., 2024 explored AI-based human detection in drone footage to assist first responders. The proposed work used YOLOv8 CNN models where this model was fine-tuned on a Dutch Fire Services drone dataset, achieved better F1 result. Preliminary results, validated by an incident commander, demonstrate the models' potential, with ongoing work aimed at further refinement. Janarthanan et al., 2025 proposed a human and object detection method using deep learning and machine learning models with Faster R-CNN and OpenCV. The Faster R-CNN model outperformed Fast R-CNN and R-CNN, achieved better result and provide an efficient and fast detection approach. Xu et al., 2025 presented a human detection method addressing smoke occlusion using AI-generated images and an enhanced RT-DETR model. A generative AI-based dataset was created to overcome data scarcity, and the RT-DETR was optimized with a global–local transformer network to improve detection under smoke. Validation showed high average precision and real-world testing demonstrated its effectiveness in detecting humans during building fires, supporting emergency evacuation and rescue operations.

The development of human detection techniques has evolved from early feature-based approaches, such as HOG, Haar, and LBP descriptors, to advanced deep learning architectures incorporating graph cut segmentation, multi-view detection, spatial attention, and temporal integration. Early methods focused on improving detection accuracy and computational efficiency in controlled settings, while more recent approaches address challenges such as occlusion, scale variation, cluttered environments, and adversarial robustness. Modern models, including SPIN, MVDet, DR-SPAAM, DPDnet, and SSPNet, leverage convolutional and attention-based models to detect and track multiple individuals across complex scenarios, enabling higher-level tasks such as action recognition and human-robot interaction. Overall, the progression highlights a shift toward more robust, scalable, and context-aware human detection systems suitable for real-world applications in surveillance, robotics, and autonomous systems.

4.3. Human Detection and Tracking

Maurin et al., 2002 introduced a vision-based system to enhance traffic management in urban environments, specifically at intersections and post-athletic events. The proposed system efficiently detects and tracks pedestrians and vehicles using optical flow and background removal algorithms, along with the Kalman filter for tracking. Zhao & Nevatia, 2004 proposed a method to track multiple individuals in complex scenarios using a stationary video camera, decomposing human motion into global and limb movements. This allows for segmentation and tracking of multiple subjects amidst inter-occlusions and environmental disruptions. Saboune & Laganiere, 2009 proposed an innovative particle filtering method for detecting individuals and performing 3D tracking in video feeds. Their explorative particle filtering approach allows for effective search space exploration, successfully tracking new entrants and individuals recovering from occlusions, with preliminary results indicating strong performance in various scenarios. Beaugendre et al., 2010 presented a robust object tracking algorithm based on a particle filter that effectively addresses noise and low-resolution issues in video surveillance. Their model utilizes a pseudo-independent particle filter that leverages multi-object detection results, enhancing tracking accuracy through both top-down and bottom-up approaches. Kushwaha et al., 2012 introduced an algorithm that combines the Haar feature descriptor for feature extraction with a particle filter for tracking, incorporating binary adaptive boosting for object classification. This enables the effective detection and tracking of multiple human subjects in video footage, accommodating variations in appearance. Seemanthini & Manjunath, 2018 proposed an approach for human object detection utilizing a clustering-based segmentation technique, employing HOG and SVM algorithms for detection. Konwar et al., 2021 proposed a flexible technique for human detection and tracking. The method uses graph cut for foreground segmentation, HOG for feature extraction, SVM for classification, and a particle filter for tracking of those detected human. The proposed system remains effective under varying lighting, color, size, shape, and clothing conditions, and can handle occlusion. Konwar et al., 2021 proposed a robust human detection and tracking system for automatic visual surveillance system (AVSS), combining median filtering, graph cut, HOG, SVM, and particle filtering. The proposed method achieves better human detection and tracking accuracy, remains effective under varying lighting conditions, and is suitable for action classification in both indoor and outdoor environments. Ghimire et al., 2022 proposed a deep learning framework for real-time person tracking using a mobile robot with a stereo camera. The system combines head-based detection, a regression tracker, and a PID-controlled visual servoing for smooth robot motion. The proposed model was tested in real environments, it effectively handles occlusions, rapid movement, and limited computational resources. Engilberge et al., 2023 proposed a multi-view people-tracking approach that predicts motion over time to infer presence in individual frames, improving consistency across time and views. The proposed method outperformed state-of-the-art tracking-by-detection approaches, particularly in crowded scenes with occlusions. Irshad et al., 2023 proposed a deep learning based human detection and tracking for real-time surveillance. The proposed system utilized MTCNN for detection and FaceNet for identification, trained on two well established dataset, the system assigns unique IDs to individuals in video streams. It was evaluated on 50 video sequences and achieved better result demonstrating strong potential for enhancing CCTV-based security. Nguyen et al., 2023 presented a real-time human tracking system using MobileNet-v2 with SSD for detection and a particle filter for tracking. The proposed model was tested under varying conditions, it achieves stable performance with 12–22 FPS, making it efficient for real-time use. Engilberge et al., 2024 introduced a tracking-by-detection approach that leverages motion cues without requiring costly identity annotations. By predicting detection heatmaps at different times and enforcing consistency through motion-based warping, the method improves robustness in crowded and low frame-rate scenarios. The proposed system was evaluated on two benchmark datasets which demonstrate state-of-the-art performance in single- and multi-view multi-target tracking. Nallasivan et al., 2024 proposed a method that enhanced object detection and tracking system by employing preprocessing techniques along with MobileNetSSD and OpenCV. The proposed system was evaluated using various metrics, benchmarked against other algorithms. Nguyen et al., 2025 reviewed recent advances in human face recognition and detection, highlighting the shift from classical methods to AI- and deep learning–based approaches. It provides a taxonomy of detection, identification, and tracking methods, which compares state-of-the-art techniques, and evaluates their strengths and limitations. While significant improvements have been achieved, challenges remain in handling varied lighting, occlusions, and distortions across different environments. Kader et al., 2025 created a manually recorded human tracking dataset that covers indoor and outdoor scenarios, using a combined manual and AI-assisted annotation process. The proposed method optimized YOLO models (YOLOv8 and YOLO11) integrated with SORT and DeepSORT trackers.

From the above it has been noted that, substantial progress in human detection and tracking for surveillance and urban monitoring applications. Foundational techniques, including optical flow combined with Kalman filtering and motion decomposition, enabled the tracking of multiple individuals despite occlusions and complex scene dynamics. Subsequent advancements such as particle filtering, pseudo-independent particle filters, and adaptive boosting enhanced robustness against noise, low-resolution data, and variations in human appearance. More recent methodologies integrate graph cut-based segmentation, HOG feature extraction, SVM classification, and particle filtering, delivering reliable detection and tracking under diverse conditions, including variable lighting, occlusions, and environmental complexity. Collectively, these developments underscore a clear trajectory toward flexible, accurate, and real-time human tracking systems, optimized for automatic visual surveillance and action recognition across both indoor and outdoor environments.

4.4. Human Activity Recognition

In their research, Soomro et al., 2012 introduced the UCF101 dataset, employing the Harris corner detector to compute a 162-dimensional HOG/HOF descriptor for each identified corner. The author subsequently selected a total of 100000 space-time interest points (STIPs) at random and performed k-means clustering to develop a codebook model. For the purpose of human action classification, authors utilized SVM with a leave-one-out 25-fold cross-validation strategy. Qiu et al., 2017 presented the pseudo-3D residual network (P3D ResNet) for the recognition of human actions. This neural network architecture incorporates various types of blocks arranged differently than in conventional residual networks (ResNet), thereby enhancing structural diversity and improving the model's capacity for action recognition. Choutas et al., 2018 introduced PoTion, a framework for pose motion representation in human action classification. In this framework, human joints are utilized as principal keypoints that provide substantial information for the action recognition model. Ng et al., 2018 proposed ActionFlowNet, a multitask learning model designed for human action recognition. The model employs a single-stream network that jointly estimates the optical flow modality while simultaneously recognizing actions through CNN. This integrated approach enables the model to effectively capture both motion and appearance from raw pixel data. Zhu et al., 2018 developed the CD-UAR method for human action recognition. The proposed approach employs deep feature extraction, generative multiple instance learning, universal representation learning, and semantic domain adaptation. The use of a unified representation through non-negative matrix factorization (NMF) combined with Jensen-Shannon divergence (JSD) enhances accuracy. Mazari & Sahbi, 2019 introduced the multi-Laplacian graph convolutional network (MLGCN) for recognizing human actions. The MLGCN algorithm learns a graph Laplacian through the amalgamation of various elementary Laplacians, each tailored to a specific topology of the input graph. The authors also proposed a graph pooling operator that incorporates context-dependent mode expansion alongside global average pooling. Kopuklu et al., 2019 utilized the 3D versions of various CNN architectures, including MobileNet, MobileNetV2, ShuffleNet, ShuffleNetV2, and SqueezeNet, for the recognition of human activities. The author explored the effect of width multiplier parameter for different above mentioned CNN models and draw conclusions over it. Giridhar proposed

DistInit, a novel method for learning video representations without the necessity of semantically labeled video data. The method uses pre-trained image models as teacher model, transferring knowledge from large labeled image datasets to train video models using a distillation framework. Liu et al., 2019 proposed residual spatial-temporal attention network (R-STAN), a deep learning model aimed at improving video action recognition by simultaneously capturing spatial and temporal information. Unlike conventional two-stream networks that handle spatial and temporal features separately, R-STAN combines them within a single, integrated framework. Tao et al., 2020 proposed pretext contrastive learning (PCL), a self-supervised framework which can improve video representation learning by jointly leveraging pretext tasks and contrastive learning under well-tuned training conditions. By integrating these two approaches, PCL overcomes the limitations of methods that treat them separately and achieves notable improvements in tasks such as video retrieval and action recognition. Pan et al., 2021 presented VideoMoCo, an enhancement of momentum contrast (MoCo) for unsupervised video representation learning. This approach incorporates temporary adversarial learning to improve feature representation and employs temporal decay to mitigate the influence of historical keys within the memory queue during contrastive learning. Parmar & Morris, 2021 proposed a methodology that utilizes a 3D-CNN as a teacher network and a 2D-CNN as a student network to recognize human actions. The student network hallucinates spatiotemporal representations from the 3D-CNN for the purpose of classification. Shalmani et al., 2022 introduced a confidence distillation framework which trains a student model to select less ambiguous clips from a teacher model. The authors presented a distillation loss function to train a lightweight classifier while preserving the teacher-student relationship model. Vrskova et al., 2022 proposed a hybrid model for human activity recognition that integrates three-dimensional convolutional neural networks (3D-CNNs) along with convolutional long short-term memory (ConvLSTM) layers. This architecture simultaneously captures spatial and temporal information from video sequences, which overcomes the common limitation of standard 3D-CNNs, that often fail to account for long-term temporal dependencies. Similarly, Rehman et al., 2022 developed a federated learning (FL) technique known as FedVSSL, which employs stochastic weighted averaging for action classification, functioning as a pre-trained video self-supervised learning (SSL) method within the FL framework. In a distinct contribution, Toering et al., 2022 established a self-supervised learning framework for video activity recognition that relies exclusively on visual cues, utilizing both RGB and optical flow modalities. Additionally, Dave et al., 2022 proposed another self-supervised learning framework targeting video activity recognition, which incorporates both local-local and global-local temporal contrastive losses to enhance self-supervised video representation learning methodologies. Ranasinghe et al., 2022 introduced a self-supervised training technique for action recognition leveraging a video transformer that operates on unlabeled data. Tong et al., 2022 proposed VideoMAE, a self-supervised framework using video transformers for action recognition. By masking portions of the video and training the model to reconstruct them, VideoMAE learns rich spatio-temporal representations without labeled data, achieving strong performance across benchmark datasets and providing a scalable solution for tasks like action recognition and video retrieval. Huang & Bors, 2022 introduced the busy-quiet net (BQN) module for video activity recognition. This module processes information comprehensively, allocating greater computational resources to busy information while employing less computation for quiet information. Moreover, Hussain et al., 2022 designed a framework that intelligently prioritizes cameras within a large surveillance network based on feedback from an activity recognition system, striving to conserve energy by judiciously adjusting camera priorities. To identify salient frames, researchers implemented a frame differencing method on the online video stream, subsequently applying a lightweight 3D-CNN architecture to extract spatio-temporal features from selected frames. The probabilities predicted by the 3D-CNN network, along with relevant camera metadata, are processed using a linear threshold gate sigmoid mechanism to modulate camera priority. Phong & Ribeiro, 2023 developed a dynamic model termed PSO-ConvNet, which facilitates action learning from videos by employing a framework in which the neural network's weight vector represents the position of a particle in phase space, allowing for the sharing of weight vectors and gradient estimates to enhance the learning process. In their research, Wu et al., 2023 established a video attribute association mechanism for action recognition that utilizes knowledge derived from video-to-text to generate textual auxiliary attributes that enhance video recognition. Furthermore, the authors developed a temporal concept spotting mechanism leveraging text-to-video insights to identify temporal saliency without the necessity for parameters, thus improving video representation. Wu & Ouyang, 2023 also concentrated on knowledge transfer techniques for video classification tasks, revising the function of the linear classifier through the use of a pre-trained model. Konwar et al., 2025 explored various CNN models for real-time recognition of human activity in computationally limited environments, analyzing network parameters and input image sizes. Using the UCF101 dataset, the author shows that 3D-MobileNetV2 achieves the best performance.

The literature on human action recognition demonstrates substantial progress over the past decade, moving from handcrafted feature-based methods such as HOG/HOF descriptors and STIP representations to advanced deep learning architectures including 3D-CNNs, residual networks, and attention-based models (P3D ResNet, R-STAN, MLGCN). Self-supervised learning frameworks, such as PCL, VideoMoCo, and VideoMAE, have enabled effective video representation learning without requiring labelled data, addressing the scalability challenges of large video datasets. Recent innovations also emphasize teacher-student distillation, federated learning, and temporal modeling, which improve spatio-temporal understanding, enhance robustness to variations in viewpoint and motion, and facilitate real-time recognition in computationally constrained environments. Collectively, these studies illustrate a clear trajectory toward efficient, scalable, and accurate action recognition systems, capable of handling diverse, untrimmed, and complex video sequences, thereby advancing applications in surveillance, autonomous systems, sports analytics, human-computer interaction etc.

4.5. Anomaly Detection

Mahadevan et al., 2010 proposed a framework for detecting anomalies in crowded scenes by modeling video regions with dynamic textures and motion outlines. This approach identifies unusual activities without manual labeling, making it effective for surveillance in complex environments like airports or train stations. Roshtkhari & Levine, 2013 presented a novel methodology for analyzing videos to discern both common and atypical behaviors in surveillance footage. This technique facilitates the construction of a hierarchical model of the scene, thereby enhancing researchers' understanding of various behaviors. Lung et al., 2015 introduced a spatio-temporal descriptor (STD) specifically designed for the recognition of abnormal human activities. This descriptor is predicated on the spatio-temporal features inherent in an image. Anomaly detection systems currently exhibit limitations, including a high false-positive rate and insufficient real-time capabilities. Additionally, the feature selection methodologies employed restrict their applicability to specific cases. In response to these challenges, Narasimhan & Kamath, 2018 proposed a dynamic anomaly detection and localization system that utilizes a sparse denoising autoencoder to autonomously acquire relevant features. This approach not only diminishes computational time but also improves the system's overall efficacy. Wang et al., 2019 introduced the abnormal event detection network (AED-NET) for identifying unusual events happen in crowded environments. The author has utilized PCA-NET to extract high-level features indicative of the crowd's circumstances and employed kPCA for anomaly detection within the scene. To mitigate the risk of overfitting, the authors incorporated a local response normalization (LRN) layer into the original AED-NET architecture. Dong et al., 2020 proposed a dual-discriminator GAN for video anomaly detection, using one discriminator for spatial consistency and another for temporal continuity. This approach improves detection of irregular patterns in both appearance and motion, making it effective for surveillance in crowded or dynamic environments. Moreover, Lv et al., 2021 put forth a technique termed weakly supervised anomaly localization (WSAL), which concentrates on identifying anomalous segments within videos over time, utilizing a high-order context encoding model to derive semantic representations and assess dynamic variations. Cai et al., (2021) proposed appearance motion memory consistency network (AMMC-Net) for video anomaly detection that integrates appearance and motion features through a unified memory mechanism, improving detection of events that deviate from normal patterns. Hu et al., 2021 introduced a self-attention prototype unit (APU) capable of encoding an ordinary latent space as prototypes in real-time without incurring additional memory costs. They further described a circulative attention mechanism that serves as a foundational component for a new feature extraction learner known as the circulative attention unit (CAU). This unit facilitates rapid adaptation to new scenes through a limited number of update iterations. Sarker et al., 2021 proposed a method for detecting anomalies in video surveillance utilizing a weakly supervised learning algorithm, extracting spatio-temporal features from surveillance videos via a temporal convolutional 3D neural network (T-C3D). The authors introduced a distinct ranking loss function to enhance the disparity between classification scores for anomalous and normal videos, thereby reducing the number of false negatives. Ullah et al., 2021 developed an efficient and lightweight CNN based framework for recognizing anomalies in surveillance contexts, which minimizes time complexity by extracting spatial CNN features from sequences of video frames. These features are subsequently processed through a proposed residual attention-based long short-term memory (LSTM) network that accurately detects anomalous activities in surveillance videos. Habib et al., 2021 created a lightweight approach capable of effectively detecting violent activities in surveillance environments, generating real-time alerts to notify law enforcement agencies in the event of violent incidents or accidents to facilitate timely intervention and prevent further issues. Honarjoo et al., 2021 employed a low-complexity, pre-trained neural network for the detection of violence. More recently, Ali, 2023 presented an autonomous video anomaly detection method based on a deep learning framework for the identification of suspicious events in surveillance videos. Sato et al., 2023 introduced a user-prompt guided zero-shot learning framework for the recognition of anomalous actions utilizing pre-trained models. Tran & Kong, 2023 proposed a binary classifier for the automatic identification of abnormal behaviors in surveillance videos, capable of labeling false positive data without necessitating human intervention. Yuan et al., 2023 introduced UCF-Crime Annotation (UCA) dataset that fine-grained video–language labels, showed that multimodal learning not only exposes domain-specific challenges but also enhances anomaly detection, marking a key step toward semantically aware surveillance AI. Duong et al., 2023 reviewed different deep learning methods for video anomaly detection. The authors also made a study on different datasets, and challenges, highlighting directions for robust and efficient surveillance system design. Konwar et al., 2024 proposed a technique for suspicious activity detection and classification by developing different variants of ResNet-10, which can be applicable for different places, where there is chance of crime happen. Gawande et al., 2024 developed a person-focused dataset capturing student behavior i.e. cheating, theft, fights, and threats, with standardized annotations for detection, tracking, and behavioral analysis. The proposed method leveraging an improved YOLOv5 architecture and motion-feature extraction for global and local anomalies, accurately captures movement, speed, and direction. Zaidi et al., 2024 employed advanced deep learning methods, including time-distributed CNN and Conv3D models, to improve accuracy for recognizing suspicious behavior. Here, the proposed models were validated on unseen test data and real-world videos, demonstrating robust performance and practical applicability. Subash et al., 2025 demonstrated a scalable, real-time CCTV anomaly detection system by using LSTM and CNN models with anomaly-ranking and alert mechanisms. Here, the proposed method achieved improved accuracy and reduced false positives in crowded, high-risk environments. As unsupervised learning has emerged as a key approach for detecting abnormal human behavior in surveillance videos, modeling normal patterns to identify deviations without labeled data. Kwak et al., 2025 highlighted challenges i.e. robustness, scalability, and real-time applicability, emphasizing the need for more reliable and efficient unsupervised models in operational of surveillance systems.

From the above it has been noted that there is thematic progress in video anomaly detection and unusual human activity recognition over the past decade. Early approaches, such as dynamic texture modelling and spatio-temporal descriptors, laid the groundwork for identifying abnormal behaviors in crowded scenes without manual labelling. Subsequent methods have incorporated hierarchical modelling, autoencoders, PCA-based feature extraction, and generative adversarial networks to improve detection accuracy while addressing challenges such as high false-positive rates and limited real-time performance. Recent advancements leverage deep learning frameworks i.e. AMMC-Net, T-C3D, residual attention LSTM, and self-attention prototypes as well as weakly supervised, zero-shot, and autonomous learning techniques, enabling robust detection of anomalous events and violent activities in complex surveillance scenarios. Collectively, these developments reflect a clear trend toward efficient, scalable, and real-time anomaly detection systems, capable of recognizing suspicious behaviors across diverse environments, thereby enhancing public safety and supporting proactive surveillance interventions.

4.6. Overall Conclusion

The trajectory of research in object detection, human detection, human tracking, human action recognition, anomaly detection, and suspicious activity detection as well as classification highlights a clear paradigm shift from handcrafted, feature-based methods to advanced deep learning and self-supervised methods. These modern approaches integrate convolutional, attention-based, and transformer-inspired models, which are supported by large-scale datasets and robust evaluation protocols, to achieve scalable, accurate, and real-time performance under challenging real-world conditions. Collectively, the progress demonstrates not only the growing maturity of intelligent surveillance technologies but also their expanding applicability across domains such as urban monitoring, robotics, autonomous driving, human–computer interaction etc. This evolution underscores the critical role of AI-driven vision systems in shaping the next generation of smart, context-aware, and proactive surveillance frameworks.

In the next section, various dataset used in human detection, human activity recognition and anomaly detection are presented.

5. DATASETS

A number of datasets for human detection, human action recognition and anomaly detection are available in current days which can be used for the design of future smart surveillance system. Some popular datasets among them are discussed below.

5.1. Human Detection Dataset

USC pedestrian dataset (Wu & Nevatia, 2005) consists of 305 images showcasing 545 individuals from various perspectives, including frontal, rear, and profile views. INRIA dataset (Aroussi et al., 2009) comprises of 1,239 pedestrian images as positive samples and 1,218 human-free images as negative samples. Caltech-USA (Dollar et al., 2009) is a pedestrian detection dataset, collection of about 10 hours of VGA video at 30 frames per second, recorded by a car in the greater Los Angeles area. This dataset comprised of 42,782 frames for training and 4,024 frames for testing. TUD-Brussels dataset (Wojek et al., 2009) was recorded from a driving car in Brussels containing 508 image pairs, where each captured one second apart at a resolution of 640 × 480 pixels. It includes 1,326 annotated pedestrians, posing challenges due to varying viewpoints and small scales. TUD Motion Pairs (Wojek et al., 2009) dataset contains 1,092 image pairs with 1,776 annotated pedestrians, resulting in 3,552 positive samples, captured by a handheld camera with a resolution of 720 × 576 pixels. RGB-D people dataset (Spinello, 2011; Luber, 2011) contains 3,399 frames captured in a university hall using three Kinect sensors. It features standing and walking individuals from various perspectives, with some occlusions and visibility issues due to poor lighting. KITTI dataset (Geiger et al., 2012) is a popular dataset used in mobile robotics and autonomous driving, featuring hours of traffic scenarios captured with high-resolution RGB cameras, grayscale stereo cameras, and a 3D laser scanner. While it doesn't provide ground truth for semantic segmentation, some researchers have manually annotated parts of the dataset for their own purposes. LSP/MPII-MPHB dataset (Andriluka et al., 2014) includes 26,675 images of 29,732 human body instances in different poses. PETA (Deng et al., 2014) dataset provides 19,000 pedestrian images from person re-identification, labeled with 61 binary and 4 multi-class attributes. The Microsoft common objects in context (MS COCO) dataset (Lin et al., 2014) includes 91 object categories, with 82 having over 5,000 labeled instances each. In total there are 2,500,000 instances across 328,000 images. The Cityscapes dataset (Cordts et al., 2016) is a large collection of stereo video sequences collected from street scenes in 50 cities. It features high-quality pixel-level annotations for 5,000 frames and an additional 20,000 weakly annotated frames, making it considerably larger than previous datasets. RAP dataset (Li et al., 2016) consists of 41,585 images from an indoor camera network, featuring 72 attributes, view angles, occlusion patterns, and coarse pedestrian parts. The MCG-RGB-D (Ji et al., 2017) dataset consists of 4000 RGB-D frames captured in a meeting room, corridor, and entrance, featuring five common poses: standing, squatting, jumping, walking, and running. CityPersons dataset (Zhang et al., 2017) provides 5,000 images collected from 18 cities in Germany, across three seasons and various weather conditions. The dataset features 2,975 images for training, 500 for validation, and 1,525 for testing, with around 35,000 annotated pedestrians and 13,000 ignore region annotations. On average, there are about seven pedestrians per image, with both bounding boxes and visible parts provided. PA-100K dataset (Liu et al., 2017) consists of 100,000 images from 598 outdoor scenes with 26 attributes, covering both global categories like gender and object-level traits like backpacks. CrowdHuman (Shao et al., 2018) is a benchmark dataset used for evaluating detectors in crowd scenarios. It comprises of 15,000 training images, 4,370 validation images, and 5,000 test images. The dataset has 470,000 human instances, averaging 22.6 people per image. The EuroCity persons dataset (Braun et al., 2018) contains a large collection of detailed annotations for pedestrians, cyclists, and riders in urban traffic scenes. Captured from a moving vehicle in 31 cities across 12 European countries. This dataset comprises of 238,200 labeled person instances in more than 47,300 images, making it significantly larger than previous benchmarking datasets. The 3DPW dataset (Von Marcard et al., 2018) is the collection of 60 video sequences with 2D pose annotations and 3D poses obtained through our method, which integrates video and IMU data for high accuracy. It includes camera poses for each frame, 3D body scans, and re-poseable 3D models, along with 18 variations of these models in different clothing. DensePose-COCO (Güler et al., 2018) is a large-scale dataset with image-to-surface correspondences manually annotated on 50,000 COCO images. The Daimler monocular pedestrian detection dataset (Yin et al., 2019) is intended for detecting pedestrians in urban environments. The training set contains 15560 pedestrian samples with resolution of 48×96 pixel and 6,744 full images without pedestrians for negative samples. The test set includes over 21790 images and 56492 pedestrian labels (fully visible or partially occluded), captured for a duration of 27-minute drive through urban traffic. The AIDER dataset (Kyrkou & Theocharides, 2019) consists of images for disaster scene backgrounds, featuring four types: fire/smoke (320 images), flood (370 images), collapsed buildings/rubble (320 images), and traffic accidents (335 images). TinyPerson (Yu et al., 2020) is a benchmark used for detecting tiny objects at long distances within large backgrounds. The images for this dataset were collected from high-resolution videos sourced from various websites. For every 50th frame is sampled, and repetitive images are removed. The final set includes 72,651 manually annotated objects with bounding boxes. The FLIR dataset (Zhang et al., 2020) consists of 10,284 images; where 8,258 images were used for training (4,129 IR and 4,129 RGB) and 2,026 images for testing (1,013 IR and 1,013 RGB). The vision-based fallen person (VFP290K) dataset (An et al., 2021) is a comprehensive benchmark for detecting fallen persons in real-world scenarios. It comprises of 294,713 frames from 178 videos collected across 49 diverse locations. The SHD360 dataset (Zhang et al., 2021) is the first 360 video SHD collection of real-life daily scenes. This dataset featuring six levels of hierarchical annotations for 6,268 key frames sampled from 37,403 omnidirectional video frames in 4K resolution. Each key frame includes super-class and sub-class labels, attributes, bounding boxes, and per-pixel object and instance-level masks. HUMBI (Yoon et al., 2021) is a large multi-view dataset focused on human body expressions in natural clothing. It aims to model view-specific appearance and geometry of gaze, face, hands, body, and garments. The dataset was created using 107 synchronized HD cameras to capture 772 diverse subjects across various genders, ethnicities, ages, and physical conditions. The LLVIP dataset (Jia et al., 2021) contains 30,976 images, with 24,050 used for training (12,025 IR and 12,025 RGB images) and 6,926 for testing (3,463 IR and 3,463 RGB images). The NIPD dataset (Yin et al., 2023) is a non-IID pedestrian detection dataset collected from five different cameras at the University of Electronic Science and Technology of China's Innovation Center Square. MuPoTs-3D (Ehsanpour et al., 2024) dataset is used for pose estimation, featuring over 8,000 frames from 20 real-world scenes with up to three subjects, annotated using a 14-point skeleton model. The C2A dataset (Nihal et al., 2024) consists of 10,215 images with over 360,000 annotated human instances in various disaster scenarios, showcasing diverse human poses and contexts such as traffic incidents, fires, floods, and collapsed buildings.

The review of datasets shows how pedestrian and human-focused benchmarks have evolved over the past 20 years. Early datasets like USC, INRIA, and Caltech-USA were small and mainly focused on pedestrian detection in simple scenarios.

In contrast, newer datasets such as Cityscapes, CrowdHuman, EuroCity, HUMBI, and SHD360 are larger and cover complex real-world situations. Modern datasets go beyond detection to include pose estimation, action recognition, re-identification, attribute analysis, and challenging conditions like crowds, disasters, infrared/thermal images, and 3D data. These resources have driven advances in computer vision for surveillance, autonomous driving, robotics, and human-computer interaction, while also showing the need for more diverse, large-scale, and multimodal datasets to handle real-world challenges.

5.2. Human Activity Dataset

The KTH dataset (Schuldt et al., 2004) consists of human actions from 25 subjects, in total 599 video segments. Each segment is recorded at 25Hz and for a duration of 10 to 15 seconds. It features actions such as boxing, hand clapping, hand waving, running, and bending, captured in various indoor and outdoor settings. IXMAS (Weinland et al., 2006) dataset comprise of 12 daily activities performed by 12 actors. This dataset includes 148 low-resolution video clips, recorded at 23 frames per second and resolution of 320x291 pixel, using four side-view cameras and one top-view camera in a controlled environment. The Weizmann dataset (Gorelick et al., 2007) includes 93 video sequences of 9 actors, where each of the actor performing ten actions. This dataset was recorded at a resolution of 180 x 144 pixels and 25 frames per second under consistent lighting, each 2-second clip features different subjects demonstrating various human actions. HDM05 dataset (Müller et al., 2007) features over three hours of high-quality motion capture data in C3D and ASF/AMC formats. This dataset includes more than 70 motion classes with 10 to 50 performances by various actors. The HOHA dataset (Laptev et al., 2008) consists of 430 action videos across eight classes, sourced from 32 Hollywood films. The UIUC dataset (Tran et al., 2008) consists of fourteen human actions divided into three sections: 271 image sequences in the first section, 191 in the second, and 70 in the third one. The UCF-CIL action dataset (Shen et al., 2009) consists of 56 sequences, each having 8 actions performed by different individuals. The videos are captured from various unknown cameras and viewpoints collected from the Internet. For this dataset within each action group, videos may start and end at different times, leading to partial overlaps, as subjects perform the same action in different ways and speeds. YouTube (Liu et al., 2009) is a publicly available benchmark dataset consists of 11 activity categories. This dataset presents challenges due to variations in camera motion, lighting conditions, object appearance, and many more. Here, each category is divided into 5 groups, having at least 4 video clips, sharing common features like backgrounds, viewpoints, and actors. The Hollywood2 (Marszaek et al., 2009) dataset contains 12 classes of human actions and 10 classes of scenes, comprising of a total 3,669 video clips and about 20.1 hours of footage. It serves as a benchmark for human action recognition in realistic settings and includes clips from 69 movies. The URADL dataset (Messing et al., 2009) comprised of 10 types of human activities intended for assisted cognition tasks. Each activity is performed three times by five different individuals, resulting in a total of 150 video sequences recorded at 30 frames per second and an original resolution of 1280 x 720 pixels. This dataset was later downsampled to a resolution of 640 x 360 pixels. The dataset presents challenges due to variations in participant shapes, sizes, genders, and ethnicities, as well as difficulties in distinguishing activities from a single source of information. The MSR-Action3D dataset (Li et al., 2010) captured with an RGB-D camera at 15 frames per second, includes 20 different actions performed by 10 different subjects, each recorded 2 to 3 times for a total of 567 action sequences. Thid dataset provides the 3D positions of 20 joints, with challenges arising from the similarity of many actions and significant temporal misalignment. MuHAVi dataset (Singh et al., 2010) consists of 17 action classes, 14 actors, and 8 camera setups, with each actor performing specific actions multiple times in the action zone. The HMDB51 dataset (Kuehne et al., 2011) was developed to advance computer vision research in video recognition and search. Unlike static image datasets, video datasets have received less attention in terms of collection and annotation. HMDB51 includes clips sourced from movies and public platforms like YouTube and the Prelinger Archive. The dataset features at least 101 clips for each of the 51 action categories; in total 6,849 video clips are there. The Stanford 40 action dataset (Yao et al., 2011) features images of humans performing 40 actions, with each image including a bounding box around the person. The dataset contains 9,532 images, which contains 180 to 300 images for each of the action classes. The CAD-60 dataset (Sung et al., 2011) comprises of 12 human action labels performed by four subjects in five different environments: a kitchen, a bedroom, a bathroom, a living room, and an office. It consists of around 60 videos, each featuring one action label. The CAD-120 dataset (Sung et al., 2011) includes 126 RGB-D videos, each showcasing a single activity with a sequence of actions. It defines ten activities and features ten sub-level actions: reaching, moving, pouring, eating, drinking, opening, placing, closing, scrubbing, and null. Here, objects are automatically detected, and their locations are provided by the dataset. The RGBD-HuDaAct dataset (Ni et al., 2011) provides daily activities in a realistic setting, featuring 12 human action classes performed by 30 subjects across 14 video sessions. Here, each of the subject repeats the activities 2 to 4 times, resulting in a total of 1,189 labeled videos. The video duration is about 30 to 150 seconds. UCF50 (Reddy & Shah, 2012) is an action recognition dataset comprising realistic action videos from YouTube, consisting of 50 action categories. This dataset is the extended version of UCF11 dataset. The dataset is challenging due to variations in camera motion, object appearance, scale, viewpoints, backgrounds, and lighting conditions. The videos are grouped into 25 sets, each containing over four clips, with shared characteristics such as the same person or similar backgrounds. The UCF101 dataset (Soomro et al., 2012) is a user-uploaded collection of videos recorded in uncontrolled environments, featuring 101 activity categories and 13,320 clips at a resolution of 320×240 pixels. This dataset presents significant challenges for activity recognition due to variations in lighting, partial occlusion, and diverse human poses and orientations. This UCF101 dataset aims to provide researchers with a realistic resource that includes a wide range of activities, from daily life to sports, as well as human-human and human-object interactions. This UTKinect dataset (Xia et al., 2012) comprises of 10 action classes and 199 action sequences, each performed twice by 10 different actors. This dataset provides 3D world coordinates for 20 joints, with sequence durations ranging from 5 to 74 frames. Here, in this dataset a key challenge is the high intraclass variation, as some actors throw objects with either their right or left arm. The DailyActivity3D dataset (Wang et al., 2012) consists of daily activities captured by using a Kinect device, featuring 16 activities performed by subjects in two poses, in total 320 samples. The dataset focuses on common activities in a living room setting. Notably, when performers are near or on the sofa, the 3D joint positions from the skeleton tracker can be noisy, and many activities involve human-object interactions, adding to the dataset's complexity. The ACT42 dataset (Cheng et al., 2012) consists of 14 different human action classes in a static background with no other people present. Here, a total of 24 subjects perform each activity multiple times. The USAA database (Fu et al., 2012) features around 1,600 videos across 8 semantic action classes, showcasing different social occasions like birthday parties, graduation parties, music and non-music performances, parades, and various wedding events. These videos are sourced from the CCV database. This Florence 3-D action dataset (Seidenari et al., 2013), captured with a stationary Kinect sensor, consists of nine actions performed by ten different subjects, resulting in total 215 action sequences. This dataset provides the 3D world coordinates for 15 joints and features challenges such as high intra-class variation and human-object interaction. The Berkeley MHAD (Ofli et al., 2013) dataset comprises of 11 human actions, collected from 12 RGB cameras, six wearable accelerometers, two Microsoft kinect depth cameras, and four microphones. The accelerometers are worn on the ankles, hips, and wrists. The Mivia action dataset (Carletti & Foggia, 2013) consists of 7 actions performed by 14 individuals (7 males and 7 females), each of the individual performed 2 repetitions for each of the classes. Here, the length of each action varies. Images were captured with a Kinect sensor, resulting in depth Images and depth Backgrounds for each sequence. JHMDB (Jhuang et al., 2013) dataset consist of 960 video sequences of 21 different actions, derived from the larger HMDB51 dataset, which includes content from digitized movies and YouTube videos. The dataset provides video content along with annotations for puppet flow, puppet mask, joint positions, action labels, and meta labels (i.e. camera motion, visible body parts, camera viewpoint, number of people, and video quality). The ballet dataset (Harandi et al., 2013) consists of 44 sequences, each with frames labeled for 8 different actions, featuring 2 men and 1 woman. The MSRActionPairs3D dataset (Oreifej et al., 2013) comprises of 20 action types performed by 10 different subjects, with each subject executing each action 2 to 3 times. It contains 567 depth map sequences at a resolution of 640x240 pixels, recorded using a depth sensor similar to the kinect device. The MHEALTH dataset (Banos et al., 2014) includes body motion and vital signs recordings from ten diverse volunteers during various physical activities. Sensors on the chest, right wrist, and left ankle measure acceleration, rate of turn, and magnetic field orientation. The chest sensor also provides 2-lead ECG measurements for heart monitoring, detecting arrhythmias, and evaluating exercise effects. Kinect activity recognition dataset (KARD) dataset (Gaglio et al., 2015) is a streamlined collection of real-world and screen skeleton data from the KARD, omitting depth map and RGB data for easier downloading. This dataset consists of 18 different activities, each of the activities are performed by ten subjects for three times. The UTD-MHAD (Chen et al., 2015) dataset consists of 27 actions, featuring synchronized data from a Microsoft kinect depth camera and an inertial sensor. The Kinect provides depth videos, RGB videos, and skeleton positions, while the inertial sensor is attached to the right wrist or thigh, depending on the action. The ActivityNet dataset (Heilbron et al., 2015) comprises of 200 different types of activities and the duration of about 849 hours of videos sourced from YouTube. It is the largest benchmark for temporal activity detection, featuring 19994 untrimmed videos divided into training, validation, and testing subsets in a 2:1:1 ratio. On average, each activity category has 137 untrimmed videos, with each video containing about 1.41 annotated activities. NTU RGB+D (Shahroudy et al., 2016) is a dataset for recognizing human actions with RGB-D modality. This dataset consists of 56,880 samples from 60 different actions, collected from 40 people. The actions are grouped into three categories: 40 daily actions (e.g., drinking, eating), 9 health-related actions (e.g., sneezing, falling) and 11 mutual actions (e.g., punching, hugging). These actions are recorded in 17 scenes using three cameras from different angles: -45°, 0°, and +45°. The dataset provides depth maps, 3D skeleton positions, RGB images, and infrared sequences for analysis. The PKU-MMD dataset (Liu et al., 2017) is a large skeleton-based action detection dataset, featuring 1,076 long untrimmed video sequences from three camera views, involving 66 subjects. This dataset includes 51 annotated action categories, totaling nearly 20,000 action instances and 5.4 million frames. It also provides two evaluation protocols: cross-subject and cross-view. The Kinetics 400 dataset (Kay et al., 2017) consists of 400 human action classes, with at least 400 video clips for each action, each lasting around 10 seconds and drawn from different YouTube videos. It covers a wide range of human activities, including interactions with objects, like playing instruments, and with other people, such as shaking hands. The 20BN-SOMETHING-SOMETHING dataset (Goyal et al., 2017) is a large collection of labeled video clips showing people performing basic actions with everyday objects. It was created by numerous crowd workers, which allows machine learning models to understand these actions more precisely. The dataset contains 108,499 videos; 86,017 for training, 11,522 for validation, and 10,960 for testing, with a total of 174 labels. The 20BN-SOMETHING-SOMETHING V2 dataset (Goyal et al., 2017) contains labeled video clips of people performing basic actions with everyday objects. Created by crowd workers, which helps machine learning models understand these actions. The dataset has 220,847 videos; 168,913 for training, 24,777 for validation, and 27,157 for testing, with 174 action labels in total. The Kinetics 600 dataset (Carreira et al., 2018) is a high-quality dataset for human action recognition, featuring around 500,000 video clips across 600 action classes. Duration of each clip is about 10 seconds and labeled with a single action. The videos are sourced from YouTube. Kinetics-700 (Carreira et al., 2019) is a video dataset containing 650,000 clips of 700 human actions. This dataset includes interactions with objects, like playing instruments, and between people, such as shaking hands and hugging. Here, each action class has at least 700 clips, and each clip lasts about 10 seconds. The HAR database (Garcia-Gonzalez et al., 2020) consists of recordings from thirty subjects performing daily living activities while using a waist-mounted smartphone with embedded inertial sensors. The moments in time dataset (Monfort et al., 2020) is the collection of one million short videos showing dynamic events over three seconds. It includes not just people but also objects, animals, and natural events. These events can be symmetrical or not and may last for different lengths of time. This dataset aims to cover a wide range of visual and audio events, challenging researchers to create models that reflect the complexity of human reasoning. The Opportunity++ dataset (Ciliberto et al., 2021) is a multimodal extension of the OPPORTUNITY activity recognition dataset, containing both original video recordings and skeleton tracking data. This allows for innovative research in activity recognition using video data, ambient and object sensors, and wearable sensors. The dataset includes 19.75 hours of annotated sensor data, which breaks down into 1.88 hours of actions with either hand, 6.01 hours of locomotion, 3.02 hours of actions with a specific hand, and 4.89 hours of high-level activities. Additionally, object sensors provide 3.92 hours of annotated data. In total, there are over 24000 unique annotations, including 2,551 activity instances with either hand, 3,653 locomotion instances, 12242 specific hand actions, 122 high-level activity instances, and 6,103 interactions with kitchen objects. EPIC-KITCHENS-100 (Damen et al., 2022) is a large-scale dataset of wearable videos, featuring 100 hours of footage, 20 million frames, and 90,000 actions. This dataset consists of everyday activities in 45 settings and supports challenges in action recognition, detection, anticipation, caption retrieval, and unsupervised learning. FPV-O (Ghosh, 2023) is a diverse first-person vision dataset focused on various office activities. These activities include interactions between individuals, such as chatting and handshaking, as well as person-to-object interactions, like using a computer or a whiteboard. Additionally, this dataset features generic activities such as walking. The videos in this dataset present several challenges, which include intra-class differences, inter-class similarities, variations in lighting, motion blur, and areas with low texture. UWA3D multiview activity3DII (UWA3DII) dataset (Rahmani et al., 2023) includes 30 human activities performed by 10 different subjects at different scales. Each subject performed the activities for four times while the kinect camera captured them from four angles. This approach creates more challenging data than capturing actions simultaneously from multiple viewpoints. The dataset is organized by segmenting continuous activity sequences and poses challenges due to varying viewpoints, self-occlusion, and similarities among activities. Northwestern-UCLA multiview action 3D dataset (Koppula et al., 2024) comprises of RGB, depth, and human skeleton data from three Kinect cameras. This dataset features 10 action categories, such as picking up objects, dropping trash, walking, etc. performed by 10 individuals from various viewpoints. The WVU dataset 1 (Liu et al., 2024) evaluates the recognition of unit actions. Here, each sample shows a subject performing one action with known start and end times. The input matches the action's duration, and subjects perform 12 actions at a similar pace. Here, the data was collected at 20 frames per second with a resolution of 640 x 480. WVU dataset 2 (Liu et al., 2024) evaluates interleaved action sequences, each consisting of multiple actions with varying durations. It was collected at 20 frames per second and a resolution of 960 x 720 pixels. The SYSU 3D human-object interaction dataset (Hu et al., 2024) consists of 480 skeleton sequences of 12 actions performed by 40 subjects, with each skeleton represented by 20 joints ($J = 20$). In the cross subject (CS) setting, half of the subjects are for training and the other half for testing. In the same subject (SS) setting, half of the samples from each activity are used for training, with the rest for testing. The MHAD dataset (Yu et al., 2025) consists of 1,440 videos from 40 subjects, representing 6 typical activities from 3 angles in a real home setting. It records 5 physiological signals, making it a comprehensive video-based physiology resource. Compatible with the rPPG toolbox, the dataset has been validated through various methods. As the first public dataset of this kind, it features diverse shooting angles and household scenarios, offering extensive physiological data valuable for research in computer vision, machine learning, and biomedical engineering. MultiSensor-Home dataset (Nguyen et al., 2025) is a benchmark for multi-modal, multi-view action recognition in indoor environments. It features untrimmed videos from five synchronized cameras positioned around a room, capturing a single person performing various actions from multiple perspectives. Each of the video is captured both RGB and audio data at a resolution of 4000 × 3000 pixels and 30 frames per second, ensuring high-quality input for action recognition tasks. The dataset also captures actions under different conditions, such as varying times of day and clothing styles, and provides detailed multi-view frame-level annotations for detailed spatial and temporal analysis.

From the above it has been revealing that a clear progression on human action recognition datasets from early small-scale, controlled collections such as KTH, Weizmann, and IXMAS, to large-scale, diverse, and multimodal datasets like ActivityNet, NTU RGB+D, Kinetics, and EPIC-KITCHENS. Early datasets primarily focused on simple, repetitive actions under fixed conditions, while later ones introduced complexity through varied viewpoints, realistic environments, multimodal inputs (RGB, depth, skeleton, audio, and physiological signals), and untrimmed sequences. Contemporary datasets, such as MultiSensor-Home, MHAD, and SYSU, emphasize multi-view capture, human-object interaction, and physiological monitoring, reflecting the growing demand for context-rich and real-world applicable benchmarks. Collectively, this evolution underscores the shift in computer vision research from recognizing isolated, well-posed actions toward understanding complex, continuous, and socially interactive human behavior in unconstrained environments.

5.3. Anomaly Dataset

The UCSD Pedestrian dataset (Mahadevan et al., 2010) has two subsets: Ped1 and Ped2. Ped1 includes 34 training and 36 testing videos, with 40 abnormal events. Each video contains 200 grayscale frames (238 x 158 resolution). The testing set has 3,155 normal frames and 4,045 abnormal frames. Ped2 consists of 16 training and 12 testing videos, featuring 12 abnormal events. Each video has about 170 grayscale frames (360 x 240 resolution). The testing set contains 362 normal frames and 1,648 abnormal frames. Both subsets include abnormal events involving intrusions of bicycles and cars. The Movies dataset (Nievas et al., 2011) consists of fight sequences from movies, categorized into violent and non-violent clips. The non-violent clips feature general action activities, and the dataset contains an equal number of both types. It also exhibits significant variation between samples, unlike the hockey dataset. Violent-flow dataset (Hassner et al., 2012) comprises of crowd violence, primarily during football matches. The CUHK Avenue dataset (Lu et al., 2013) consists of 16 training videos and 21 testing videos of a single scene, featuring 47 abnormal events in the testing videos, such as loitering and throwing objects. Here, each video has a resolution of 360 x 640 pixels. The hockey fights dataset (Nievas et al., 2016) has the same number of violent and non-violent actions from professional hockey games, usually involving two players in close contact. The ShanghaiTech dataset

(Zhang et al., 2016) includes 330 training and 107 testing videos across 13 scenes, featuring anomalous events like biking, fighting, and vehicular activity. Each video has a resolution of 480x856 pixels, making it the largest benchmark for video anomaly detection. The LV database (Leyva et al., 2017) consists of a total 28 realistic video sequences of indoor and outdoor scenes, with abnormal events like fights and vandalism labeled. The UCF-Crime (Sultani et al., 2018) is a large-scale dataset for weak supervision tasks, featuring long untrimmed surveillance videos depicting 13 real-world anomalies. It has 1,900 videos in total from where 1,610 used for training and 290 for testing. The training set offers only video-level annotations, while the test set provides frame-level annotations for evaluation. This dataset includes 1,000 violent and 1,000 non-violent videos from YouTube. The violent videos showcase real street fights, while the non-violent ones feature activities like sports, eating, and walking. CCTV-Fights (Perez et al., 2019) is a video dataset for violence detection, comprising 1,000 videos of violent activities with annotated start and end times. Of these, 280 are from real-world surveillance cameras, while 720 are recorded by mobile cameras, car cameras, drones, or helicopters. The abnormal human action (AbHA) dataset (Dhiman & Vishwakarma, 2019) consists of a collection of abnormal actions commonly experienced by the elderly, such as chest pain, headache, fainting, falling backward, and falling forward. It includes five actions, each performed twice by 8 individuals, so in total 80 samples (8 individuals × 2 repetitions × 5 actions). The IITB corridor dataset (Rodrigues et al., 2020) consists of 208 training and 150 testing videos from a single scene, aimed at video anomaly detection. Anomalous events include protests, hiding, and ball play, with each video presented at a resolution of 1920x1080 pixels, establishing a significant benchmark in the field. The street scene dataset (Ramachandra & Jones, 2020) consists of 35 testing sequences, featuring 205 anomalous events across 17 types. The CHU surveillance violence dataset (CSVD) (Lopez & Lien, 2020) is a collection of CCTV footage designed to analyze both violent and non-violent actions. This dataset consists of 12 action classes, which are categorized as either violent or non-violent. The LAD dataset (Wan et al., 2021) consists of normal activities and unexpected abnormal events captured in a square and a school using a digital camera, totaling over 2,500 video sequences at a frame rate of 25 fps. Each sequence includes manually extracted segments representing either abnormal or normal activities, excluding unrelated frames. Real-world fighting (RWF) dataset (Cheng et al., 2021) consists of 2,000 video clips captured by surveillance cameras in real-world scenes. The UBnormal benchmark dataset (Acsintoae et al., 2022) comprise of 543 videos; from which 272 videos are used for training, 66 for validation, and 205 for testing. There are 628 anomalies (201 for training, 77 for validation, and 350 for testing) and a total of 89,136 abnormal frames, with 48,111 belonging to the test set. It includes 147,744 abnormal regions, averaging 1.62 per frame, and 4.45 objects per frame. The total length of the data set is about 132 minutes. The Ano-AAD dataset (Mondal et al., 2024) is a curated collection of 395 videos from social media platforms like Facebook and YouTube. It includes both normal and anomalous human actions, thoroughly annotated to help detect abnormal behaviors. With a total 12 hours of footage, the dataset features different scenarios such as arrests, burglaries, explosions, and fights, along with some normal videos. Usual Unusual 2 (UU2) dataset (Konwar et al., 2024) comprises a total of 2,597 video sequences, of which 950 are categorized as unusual and the remaining 1,647 as usual. The UCF-Crime 13 dataset (Konwar et al., 2024) comprises 950 real-world surveillance videos, each of which is long and untrimmed. It encompasses 13 categories of anomalous activities, namely abuse, arrest, arson, assault, road accidents, burglary, explosion, fighting, robbery, shooting, stealing, shoplifting, and vandalism. The UEDM dataset (Konwar et al., 2024) is the collection of videos depicting unusual human activities, categorized into five classes: bag snatching, gun pointing and shooting, kicking, knife attacks, and punching. It has 528 video clips involving a total of 1,406 participants. The recordings capture subjects from multiple viewpoints and over varying durations, introducing challenges such as diverse lighting conditions and activity execution across different environments, including within moving vehicles.

The evolution of video-based anomaly and unusual human activity detection datasets over the past decade demonstrates significant progress in scale and complexity. Early benchmarks, such as UCSD Pedestrian and CUHK Avenue, were captured in controlled settings and offered limited anomaly types, primarily serving as proof-of-concept resources. In contrast, more recent datasets such as UCF-Crime, UU2, UEDM, and Ano-AAD provide large-scale, untrimmed surveillance footage collected from real-world environments, covering a broader range of anomalous behaviors. These datasets differ in resolution, scene diversity, anomaly categories, and environmental conditions, introducing challenges including multi-viewpoint analysis, variable illumination, occlusion handling, and crowd dynamics. Collectively, this progression underscores the growing demand for realistic, diverse, and comprehensively annotated datasets to advance research in anomaly detection, violence recognition, and abnormal human activity analysis within practical surveillance scenarios.

5.4. Overall Conclusion

Evolution of different datasets for human detection, human action recognition, anomaly detection and unusual or suspicious human activity detection as well as classification reflects the broader shift in computer vision research from constrained, small-scale benchmarks to large-scale, multimodal, and context rich resources. Early datasets enabled foundational progress but there were limited in scope and realism, whereas modern benchmarks incorporate diverse viewpoints, modalities, and complex environments that can establish real-world challenges. This progression has been instrumental in smart surveillance, robotics, autonomous driving, human computer interaction, etc. while also emphasizing the need for more comprehensive, diverse, and multimodal datasets to capture continuous, socially interactive, and anomalous human behaviors. Ultimately, the availability and quality of datasets remain central to driving innovation and ensuring the robustness of next-generation intelligent surveillance systems.

6. EVALUATION METRICS

Evaluation metrics are essential for evaluating the performance of both machine learning and deep learning models. They offer quantitative measures that aid in selecting models and fine-tuning hyperparameters. Since various tasks necessitate different metrics, grasping which metric to use is crucial for effectively interpreting the results of a model. Some of the evaluation metrics are discussed below.

6.1. TPR

The true positive rate, commonly referred to as sensitivity, is defined as the proportion of positive data points that are accurately identified as positive among all data points that are classified as positive. This metric is essential for evaluating the performance of a classification model in distinguishing true positives.

$$TPR = \frac{TP}{TP + FN} \tag{1}$$

6.2. TNR

The true negative rate, commonly referred to as specificity, is defined as the proportion of negative data points that are accurately identified as negative, relative to all data points categorized as negative.

$$TNR = \frac{TN}{TN + FP} \tag{2}$$

6.3. FPR

The false positive rate is defined as the proportion of actual negative cases that are inaccurately classified as positive.

$$FPR = \frac{FP}{FP + TN} \tag{3}$$

6.4. FNR

The false negative rate is defined as the proportion of actual positive cases that are inaccurately classified as negative.

$$FNR = \frac{FN}{FP + TP} \tag{4}$$

6.5. Precision

Precision is used to refer to the accuracy of identifying a specific category of target within a dataset that contains multiple classifications. In this context, if "TP" denotes the true positive rate and "FP" represents the false positive rate of detection, precision can be mathematically expressed by following equation.

$$Precision = \frac{TP}{TP + FP} \tag{5}$$

6.6. Recall

Recall is utilized to describe the effectiveness of locating a specific item within a database that encompasses two or more types of data. Consequently, the recall value is determined using the following equation.

$$Recall = \frac{TP}{P} = \frac{TP}{TP + FN} \tag{6}$$

6.7. F-measure

The F-measure serves as an indicator of the overall performance of a classification system. The mathematical equation for F-measure can be expressed as follows:

$$F - measure = \frac{2}{\frac{1}{Precision} + \frac{1}{Recall}} \tag{7}$$

6.8. Accuracy

Accuracy serves as the most straightforward evaluation metric for classification tasks. It is defined as the ratio of correctly predicted observations to the total number of observations, providing a rapid assessment of the model's performance in terms of correctness.

$$A = \frac{TP + TN}{P + N} = \frac{TP + TN}{TP + TN + FP + FN} \tag{8}$$

6.9. IoU

Intersection over union (IoU) is an essential metric utilized for assessing the degree of similarity between predicted bounding boxes, designated as "A", and the corresponding ground truth bounding boxes, referred to as "B".

$$IoU\,(A, B) = \frac{B \cap A}{B \cup A} \tag{9}$$

6.10. mIoU

The mean intersection over union (mIoU) serves as a critical evaluation metric for segmentation tasks. In this context, let "A" represent the ground truth hand mask and "B" denote the predicted hand mask for frame "I". The mIoU can be derived as follows.

$$mIoU \;=\; \frac{1}{N}\sum_{i=1}^{N}\frac{|A \cap B|}{|A| + |B| - (A \cap B)} \tag{10}$$

Where, "N" represents the number of frames.

6.11. FPPW

FPPW is a metric that quantifies the frequency with which alternative objects are erroneously identified within the detection window of a system. This measure assesses the quality of classification without being influenced by the dimensions of the images or the number of objects present within a given image.

$$FPPW = \frac{\textit{False positive rate}}{\textit{Number of detection window}} \tag{11}$$

6.12. Detection Error Tradeoff (DEF)

The DEF curve is a crucial tool for measuring the performance of detection systems. It effectively illustrates the relationship between the miss rate representing the frequency at which actual events go undetected and the false positive per window (FPPW), which indicates the number of times a detection system incorrectly signals an event within a designated timeframe. This relationship provides valuable insights into the effectiveness and reliability of the detector, allowing for a comprehensive assessment of its overall performance. DEF can be defined by following equation.

$$DEF = \frac{1 - Recall\ rate}{False\ positive\ per\ window\ (FPPW)} \tag{12}$$

6.13. RBDR

Region based detection rate can be defined as follows:

$$RBDR = \frac{Number\ of\ anomalous\ region\ detected}{Total\ number\ of\ anomalous\ regions} \tag{13}$$

As mentioned above that the evaluation metrics are fundamental for assessing the performance of both machine learning and deep learning models, providing quantitative measures that guide model selection, optimization, and comparison. Metrics such as TPR, TNR, FPR, FNR, precision, recall, F-measure, and accuracy are essential for classification tasks, offering insight into a model's ability to correctly identify positive and negative instances while balancing false positives and false negatives. For localization and segmentation tasks, IoU, mIoU, and RBDR quantify the overlap and accuracy of predicted regions relative to ground truth, ensuring precise spatial detection. Metrics like FPPW and the detection error tradeoff (DET) curve are critical for evaluating detection reliability, especially in scenarios with multiple objects or variable image dimensions. Collectively, these evaluation tools enable a comprehensive understanding of model performance across diverse tasks, ensuring robustness, efficiency, and practical applicability in real-world applications such as surveillance, autonomous systems, and human activity recognition.

7. CONCLUSION

Integration of advanced computer vision and deep learning techniques is transforming surveillance systems into intelligent, real-time solutions capable of human detection, tracking, activity recognition, and anomaly detection under diverse conditions. Progress from traditional handcrafted methods to modern AI-driven models, supported by large-scale multimodal datasets and robust evaluation metrics, has enabled greater accuracy, scalability, and adaptability in real-world environments. As surveillance system increasingly moves toward AI-enabled, centrally connected frameworks, the design of future smart surveillance systems will rely on seamlessly combining detection, recognition, and automated alert generation mechanisms. Such advancements not only enhance security and crime prevention but also extend to broader applications i.e. healthcare, autonomous driving, and human-computer interaction, underscoring the pivotal role of computer vision in shaping safer and smarter societies.

REFERENCES

Acsintoae, A., Florescu, A., Georgescu, M.-I., Mare, T., Sumedrea, P., Ionescu, R. T., Khan, F. S., & Shah, M. (2022). UBnormal: New Benchmark for Supervised Open-Set Video Anomaly Detection. In *Proceedings of the IEEE/CVF Conference on Computer Vision and Pattern Recognition (CVPR)*. New Orleans, LA, USA.

Ahmad, M. (2008). Human motion detection and segmentation from moving image sequences. In *Proceedings of the 2008 International Conference on Electrical and Computer Engineering*, Dhaka, Bangladesh.

Ali, M. M. (2023). Real-time video anomaly detection for smart surveillance. *IET Image Processing*, *17*, 1375–1388.

Andriluka, M., Pishchulin, L., Gehler, P., & Schiele, B. (2014). 2d human pose estimation: New benchmark and state of the art analysis. In *Proceedings of the IEEE Conference on computer Vision and Pattern Recognition.* Columbus, OH, USA.

Aroussi, M. E., Hassouni, M. E., Ghouzali, S., Rziza, M., & Aboutajdine, D. (2009). Block Based Curvelet Feature Extraction for Face Recognition, In *Proceedings of the 2009 International Conference on Multimedia Computing and Systems,* Ouarzazate, Morocco.

Banos, O., Garcia, R., & Saez, A. (2014). MHEALTH [Dataset]. *UCI Machine Learning Repository*. https://doi.org/DOI: 10.24432/C5TW22

Beaugendre, A., Miyano, H., Ishidera, E., & Goto, S. (2010). Human tracking system for automatic video surveillance with particle filter. In *Proceedings of the 2010 IEEE Asia Pacific Conference on Circuits and Systems*, Kuala Lumpur.

Bell, A. E. (2013). Robust feature vector for efficient human detection. In *Proceedings of the 2013 IEEE Applied Imagery Pattern Recognition Workshop (AIPR).* Washington, DC.

Bermejo Nievas, E., Deniz Suarez, O., Bueno García, G., & Sukthankar, R. (2011). Violence Detection in Video Using Computer Vision Techniques. In Real, P., Diaz-Pernil, D., Molina-Abril, H., Berciano, A., & Kropatsch, W. (Eds.), Lecture Notes in Computer Science: Vol. 6855. *Computer Analysis of Images and Patterns. CAIP 2011*. Springer.

Bochkovskiy, A., Wang, C. Y., & Liao, H. Y. M. (2020). Yolov4: Optimal speed and accuracy of object detection. *arXiv preprint arXiv:2004.10934*.

Braun, M., Krebs, S., Flohr, F., & Gavrila, D. M. (2018). The eurocity persons dataset: A novel benchmark for object detection. *arXiv preprint arXiv:1805.07193.*

Cai, R., Zhang, H., Liu, W., Gao, S., & Hao, Z. (2021). Appearance-Motion Memory Consistency Network for Video Anomaly Detection. In *Proceedings of the AAAI-21/ IAAI-21/EAAI-21 Conference on Artificial Intelligence*, Virtual.

Carletti, V., Foggia, P., Percannella, G., Saggese, A., & Vento, M. (2013). Recognition of Human Actions from RGB-D Videos Using a Reject Option. In Petrosino, A., Maddalena, L., & Pala, P. (Eds.), Lecture Notes in Computer Science: Vol. 8158. *New Trends in Image Analysis and Processing – ICIAP 2013. ICIAP 2013*. Springer.

Carreira, J., Noland, E., Hillier, C., & Zisserman, A. (2019). A short note on the kinetics-700 human action dataset. arXiv preprint arXiv:1907.06987.

Chen, C., Jafari, R., & Kehtarnavaz, N. (2015). UTD-MHAD: A Multimodal Dataset for Human Action Recognition Utilizing a Depth Camera and a Wearable Inertial Sensor. In *Proceedings of the IEEE International Conference on Image Processing.* Canada, September.

Cheng, M., Cai, K., & Li, M. (2021). RWF-2000: An Open Large Scale Video Database for Violence Detection. In *Proceedings of the 25th International Conference on Pattern Recognition (ICPR).* Milan, Italy.

Cheng, Z., Qin, L., Ye, Y., Huang, Q., & Tian, Q. (2012). Human Daily Action Analysis with Multi-view and Color-Depth Data. In *Proceedings of the ECCV 2012 Workshop on Consumer Depth Cameras for Computer Vision*, Firenze, Italy.

Choutas, V., Weinzaepfel, P., Revaud, J., & Schmid, C. (2018). PoTion: Pose MoTion Representation for Action Recognition. In *Proceedings of the 2018 IEEE/ CVF Conference on Computer Vision and Pattern Recognition (CVPR)*, Salt Lake City, UT, USA.

Ciliberto, M., Fortes, R. V., Calatroni, A., Lukowicz, P., & Roggen, D. (2021). Opportunity++: A Multimodal Dataset for Video- and Wearable, Object and Ambient Sensors-Based Human Activity Recognition. *Frontiers of Computer Science*, •••, 3.

Cordts, M., Omran, M., Ramos, S., Rehfeld, T., Enzweiler, M., Benenson, R., Franke, U., Roth, S., & Schiele, B. (2016). The cityscapes dataset for semantic urban scene understanding. In *Proceedings of the IEEE conference on computer vision and pattern recognition.* Honolulu, HI, USA

Dalal, N., & Triggs, B. (2005). Histograms of Oriented Gradients for human detection. In *Proceedings of the 2005 IEEE Computer Society Conference on Computer Vision and Pattern Recognition (CVPR'05).* San Diego, CA, USA.

Damen, D., Doughty, H., Farinella, G. M., Furnari, A., Kazakos, E., Ma, J., Moltisanti, D., Munro, J., Perrett, T., Price, W., & Wray, M. (2022). Rescaling egocentric vision: Collection, pipeline and challenges for epic-kitchens-100. *International Journal of Computer Vision*, *•••*, 1–23.

Dave, I., Gupta, R., Rizve, M. N., & Shah, M. (2022). Tclr: Temporal contrastive learning for video representation. *Computer Vision and Image Understanding*, *219*, 103406.

Deng, U., Luo, P., Loy, C. C., & Tang, X. (2014). Pedestrian attribute recognition at far distance. *ACM Multimedia*, *2014*, 789–792.

Dhiman, C., & Vishwakarma, D. K. (2019). A Robust Framework for Abnormal Human Action Recognition Using R -Transform and Zernike Moments in Depth Videos. *IEEE Sensors Journal*, *19*(13), 5195–5203.

Diwan, T., Anirudh, G., & Tembhurne, J. V. (2023). Object detection using YOLO: Challenges, architectural successors, datasets and applications. *Multimedia Tools and Applications*, *82*, 9243–9275. DOI: 10.1007/s11042-022-13644-y PMID: 35968414

Dollar, P., Wojek, C., Schiele, B., & Perona, P. (2009). Pedestrian detection: A benchmark. In *Proceedings of the Computer Vision and Pattern Recognition*. Miami, FL, USA.

Dong, F., Zhang, Y., & Nie, X. (2020). Dual Discriminator Generative Adversarial Network for Video Anomaly Detection. *IEEE Access : Practical Innovations, Open Solutions*, *8*, 88170–88176.

Duong, H.-T., Le, V.-T., & Hoang, V. T. (2023). Deep Learning-Based Anomaly Detection in Video Surveillance: A Survey. *Sensors (Basel)*, *23*(11), 5024. PMID: 37299751

Ehsanpour, M., Reid, I., & Rezatofighi, H. (2024). Dataset: MuPoTS-3D. https://doi.org/ ro053DOI: 10.57702/im0

Engilberge, M., Grosche, F. W., & Fua, P. (2024). No Identity, no problem: Motion through detection for people tracking. *arXiv preprint arXiv:2411.16466*.

Engilberge, M., Liu, W., & Fua, P. (2023). Multi-view tracking using weakly supervised human motion prediction. In *Proceedings of the IEEE/CVF Winter Conference on Applications of Computer Vision* (pp. 1582-1592).

Freer, J. A., Beggs, B. J., Fernandez-Canque, H. L., Chevriert, F., & Goryashko, A. (1995). Automatic recognition of suspicious activity for camera-based security systems. In *Proceedings of the European Convention on Security and Detection*, Brighton, UK.

Fu, Y., Hospedales, T. M., Xiang, T., & Gong, S. (2012). Attribute learning for understanding unstructured social activity. In *Proceedings of the 12th European conference on Computer Vision - Volume Part IV (ECCV'12).* Springer-Verlag, Berlin, Heidelberg.

Gaglio, S., Re, G. L., & Morana, M. (2015). Human Activity Recognition Process Using 3-D Posture Data. *IEEE Transactions on Human-Machine Systems, 45*(5), 586–597.

Garcia-Gonzalez, D., Rivero, D., Fernandez-Blanco, E., & Luaces, M. R. (2020). A Public Domain Dataset for Real-Life Human Activity Recognition Using Smartphone Sensors. *Sensors (Basel), 20*(8), 1–14. PMID: 32295028

Gawande, U., Hajari, K., & Golhar, Y. (2024). Novel person detection and suspicious activity recognition using enhanced YOLOv5 and motion feature map. *Artificial Intelligence Review*, *57*, 16.

Geiger, A., Lenz, P., & Urtasun, R. (2012). Are we ready for autonomous driving? The KITTI vision benchmark suite. In *Proceedings of the 2012 IEEE Conference on Computer Vision and Pattern Recognition*, Providence, RI, USA.

Ghimire, A., Zhang, X., Werghi, N., Javed, S., & Dias, J. (2022). Deep learning framework for robot for person detection and tracking. *arXiv preprint*. arXiv:2205.04213.

Ghosh, P.. (2023). Activity Classification from First-Person Office Videos with Visual Privacy Protection. In Hossain, M. S., Majumder, S. P., Siddique, N., & Hossain, M. S. (Eds.), *The Fourth Industrial Revolution and Beyond. Lecture Notes in Electrical Engineering* (Vol. 980). Springer.

Gorelick, L., Blank, M., Shechtman, E., Irani, M., & Basri, R. (2007). Actions as Space-Time Shapes. *IEEE Transactions on Pattern Analysis and Machine Intelligence, 29*(12), 2247–2253. PMID: 17934233

Goyal, R., Ebrahimi Kahou, S., Michalski, V., Materzynska, J., Westphal, S., Kim, H., Haenel, V., Fruend, I., Yianilos, P., Mueller-Freitag, M., Hoppe, F., Thurau, C., Bax, I., & Memisevic, R. (2017). The" something something" video database for learning and evaluating visual common sense. In *Proceedings of the IEEE international conference on computer vision (ICCV).* Venice, Italy.

Güler, R. A., Neverova, N., & Kokkinos, I. (2018). DensePose: Dense Human Pose Estimation in the Wild. In *Proceedings of the 2018 IEEE/CVF Conference on Computer Vision and Pattern Recognition.* Salt Lake City, UT, USA.

Habib, S., Hussain, A., Albattah, W., Islam, M., Khan, S., Khan, R. U., & Khan, K. (2021). Abnormal Activity Recognition from Surveillance Videos Using Convolutional Neural Network. *Sensors (Basel), 21*(24), 8291–8306. PMID: 34960386

Harandi, M., Sanderson, C., Shen, C., & Lovell, B. (2013). Dictionary Learning and Sparse Coding on Grassmann Manifolds: An Extrinsic Solution. In *Proceedings of the 2013 IEEE International Conference on Computer Vision (ICCV '13).* IEEE Computer Society, USA.

Hassner, T., Itcher, Y., & Kliper-Gross, O. (2012). Violent Flows: Real-Time Detection of Violent Crowd Behavior. In *Proceedings of the 3rd IEEE International Workshop on Socially Intelligent Surveillance and Monitoring (SISM) at the IEEE Conf. on Computer Vision and Pattern Recognition (CVPR)*, Rhode Island.

He, K., Zhang, X., Ren, S., & Sun, J. (2016). Deep Residual Learning for Image Recognition. In *Proceedings of the 2016 IEEE Conference on Computer Vision and Pattern Recognition (CVPR).* Las Vegas, NV, USA.

Heemskerk, J., Mioch, T., Maathuis, H., & Aldewereld, H. (2024). Long-Range Human Detection in Drone Camera Images. In *Proceedings of the 21st International ISCRAM Conference.* University of Münster, Germany. Embracing the Crisis Management Lifecycle.

Heilbron, F. C., Escorcia, V., Ghanem, B., & Niebles, J. C. (2015). ActivityNet: A large-scale video benchmark for human activity understanding. In *Proceedings of the 2015 IEEE Conference on Computer Vision and Pattern Recognition (CVPR)*, Boston, MA, USA.

Honarjoo, N., Abdari, A., & Mansouri, A. (2021). Violence detection using pre-trained models. In *Proceedings of the 5th International Conference on Pattern Recognition and Image Analysis (IPRIA).* Kashan, Iran.

Hong, M., Li, S., Yang, Y., Zhu, F., Zhao, Q., & Lu, L. (2022). SSPNet: Scale Selection Pyramid Network for Tiny Person Detection from UAV Images. *IEEE Geoscience and Remote Sensing Letters, 19*, 1–5.

Hou, Y., Zheng, L., & Gould, S. (2020). Multiview Detection with Feature Perspective Transformation. In Vedaldi, A., Bischof, H., Brox, T., & Frahm, J. M. (Eds.), Lecture Notes in Computer Science: Vol. 12352. *Computer Vision – ECCV 2020. ECCV 2020.* Springer.

Hu, C., Wu, F., Wu, W., Qiu, W., Lai, S. (2021). Normal Learning in Videos with Attention Prototype Network. *arXiv preprint.*

Hu, J.-F., Zheng, W.-S., Pan, J., Lai, J., & Zhang, J. (2024). Dataset: SYSU 3D HOI Dataset. https://doi.org/DOI: 10.57702/1odneu7u

Huang, G., & Bors, A. G. (2022). Busy-Quiet Video Disentangling for Video Classification. In *Proceedings of the 2022 IEEE/CVF Winter Conference on Applications of Computer Vision (WACV)*, Waikoloa, HI, USA.

Huang, H., Wang, B., Xiao, J., & Zhu, T. (2024). Improved small-object detection using YOLOv8: A comparative study. *Applied and Computational Engineering.*, *41*(1), 80–88.

Hussain, A., Muhammad, K., Ullah, H., Ullah, A., Imran, A. S., Lee, M. Y., Rho, S., & Sajjad, M. (2022). Anomaly based camera prioritization in large scale surveillance networks. *Computers, Materials & Continua*, *70*(2), 2171–2190.

Irshad, T., Asif, M., Hassan, A., Ahmad, U., Mahmood, T., Ashraf, R., & Faisal, C. M. (2023). A Deep Learning based Human Detection and Tracking for Security Surveillance Systems. *Applied and Computational Engineering*, *2*(1), 569–577.

Jagadeesh, A., & Patil, C. M. (2019). Video Based Human Activity Detection, Recognition and Classification of actions using SVM. *Transactions on Machine Learning and Artificial Intelligence*, 6(6)

Janarthanan, S., Karthikeyan, S., & Saravanakumar, S. (2025). Human and Object Detection Deep Learning Model Using RCNN. *Journal of Information Systems Engineering & Management*, *10*(30s), 748–756.

Jhuang, H., Gall, J., Zuffi, S., Schmid, C., & Black, M. J. (2013). Towards Understanding Action Recognition. In *Proceedings of the 2013 IEEE International Conference on Computer Vision.* Sydney, NSW, Australia.

Ji, T., Liu, L., Zhu, W., Wei, J., & Wei, S. (2017). Fast and efficient integration of human upper-body detection and orientation estimation in RGB-D video. In *Proceedings of the 2017 IEEE 9th International Conference on communication Software and Networks (ICCSN).* Guangzhou, China.

Jia, D., Hermans, A., & Leibe, B. (2020). DR-SPAAM: A Spatial-Attention and Auto-regressive Model for Person Detection in 2D Range Data. In *Proceedings of the 2020 IEEE/RSJ International Conference on Intelligent Robots and Systems (IROS)*, Las Vegas, NV, USA.

Jia, X., Zhu, C., Li, M., Tang, W., & Zhou, W. (2021). Llvip: A visible-infrared paired dataset for low-light vision. In *Proceedings of the 2021 IEEE/CVF International Conference on Computer Vision Workshops (ICCVW)*, Montreal, BC, Canada.

Kachouane, M., Sahki, S., Lakrouf, M., & Ouadah, N. (2012). HOG based fast human detection. In *Proceedings of the 2012 24th International Conference on Microelectronics (ICM)*. Algiers.

Kader, T., Nasir, A. F. A., Toh, M. Z., Shapiee, M. N. A., Fakarullsroq, A., & Razak, A. (2025). Human Detection and Tracking with YOLO and SORT Tracking Algorithm. [IJACSA]. *International Journal of Advanced Computer Science and Applications*, *16*(5), 133–143.

Kay, W., Carreira, J., Simonyan, K., Zhang, B., Hillier, C., Vijayanarasimhan, S., Viola, F., Green, T., Back, T., Natsev, P., Suleyman, M., & Zisserman, A. (2017). The kinetics human action video dataset. *arXiv preprint.*

Kharabe, S. R., Hanwate, P. S., & Gaikwad, D. S. & kaliyamurthie, K. P. (2017). Human image segmentation. In *Proceedings of the 2017 International Conference on Algorithms, Methodology, Models and Applications in Emerging Technologies (ICAMMAET)*. Chennai, India.

Konwar, L., Saikia, N., & Rajbongshi, S. C. (2024). Is the Activity Normal? If Not, What Type of Suspicious? *Journal of Systems Engineering and Electronics*, *34*(12), 695–708.

Konwar, L., Saikia, N., & Rajbongshi, S. C. (2025). *Revisiting human activity recognition using smaller DNN. CCF Trans.* Pervasive Comp. Interact.

Konwar, L., Talukdar, A. K., & Sarma, K. K. (2021). Robust Real Time Multiple Human Detection and Tracking for Automatic Visual Surveillance System. *WSEAS Transactions on Signal Processing.*, *17*, 93–98.

Konwar, L., Talukdar, A. K., Sarma, K. K., Saikia, N., & Rajbongshi, S. C. (2021). Segmentation and selective feature extraction for human detection to the direction of action recognition. *International Journal of Circuits. Systems and Signal Processing.*, *15*, 1371–1386.

Koppula, H. S., Gupta, R., & Saxena, A. (2024). Dataset: Northwestern-UCLA Multiview activity 3D Dataset. Resource: Original Metadata.

Kopuklu, O., Kose, N., Gunduz, A., & Rigoll, G. (2019). Resource efficient 3d convolutional neural networks. In *Proceedings of the 2019 IEEE/CVF International Conference on Computer Vision Workshop (ICCVW)*, Seoul, Korea (South).

Kuehne, H., Jhuang, H., Garrote, E., Poggio, T., & Serre, T. (2011). HMDB: a large video database for human motion recognition, In *Proceedings of the International Conference on Computer Vision (ICCV)*. Barcelona, Spain.

Kushwaha, A. K. S., Sharma, C. M., Khare, M., Srivastava, R. K., & Khare, A. (2012). Automatic multiple human detection and tracking for visual surveillance system. In *Proceedings of the 2012 International Conference on Informatics, Electronics & Vision (ICIEV)*, Dhaka.

Kwak, N., Cho, S., & Yoon, C. (2025). Detection of Abnormal Human Behavior Using Unsupervised Learning in Video Surveillance Systems. arXiv *Preprints*.

Kyrkou, C., & Theocharides, T. (2019). Deep-learning-based aerial image classification for emergency response applications using unmanned aerial vehicles. In *Proceedings of the 2019 IEEE/CVF Conference on Computer Vision and Pattern Recognition Workshops (CVPRW)*. Long Beach, CA, USA.

Lakshmi, N. D., Latha, Y. M., & Damodaram, A. (2013). Silhouette extraction of a human body based on fusion of HOG and graph-cut segmentation in dynamic background. In *Proceedings of the 3rd International Conference on Computational Intelligence and Information Technology (CIIT 2013)*, Mumbai, India.

Laptev, I., Marszalek, M., Schmid, C., & Rozenfeld, B. (2008). Learning realistic human actions from movies. In *Proceedings of the 2008 IEEE Conference on Computer Vision and Pattern Recognition*, Anchorage, AK, USA.

Leyva, R., Sanchez, V., & Li, C.-T. (2017). The LV dataset: A realistic surveillance video dataset for abnormal event detection. In *Proceedings of the 2017 5th International Workshop on Biometrics and Forensics (IWBF)*. Coventry, UK.

Li, D., Zhang, Z., Chen, X., Ling, H., & Huang, K. (2016). A richly annotated dataset for pedestrian attribute recognition. *arXiv preprint arXiv:1603.07054*.

Li, W., Zhang, Z., & Liu, Z. (2010). Action Recognition Based on A Bag of 3D Points. In *Proceedings of the IEEE International Workshop on CVPR for Human Communicative Behavior Analysis (in conjunction with CVPR2010)*, San Francisco.

Lin, T.-Y., Goyal, P., Girshick, R., He, K., & Dollár, P. (2017). Focal Loss for Dense Object Detection. In *Proceedings of the 2017 IEEE International Conference on Computer Vision (ICCV)*. Venice, Italy.

Lin, T.-Y., Maire, M., Belongie, S., Hays, J., Perona, P., Ramanan, D., Doll'ar, P., & Zitnick, C. L. (2014). Microsoft coco: Common objects in context. [th *European Conference.* Zurich, Switzerland.]. *Proceedings of the Computer Vision–ECCV, 2014*, 13.

Liu, J., Luo, J., & Shah, M. (2009). Recognizing Realistic Actions from Videos in the Wild. In *Proceedings of the IEEE International Conference on Computer Vision and Pattern Recognition (CVPR).* Miami, FL, USA.

Liu, Q., Che, X., & Bie, M. (2019). R-STAN: Residual Spatial-Temporal Attention Network for Action Recognition. *IEEE Access : Practical Innovations, Open Solutions, 7,* 82246–82255.

Liu, X., Zhao, H., Tian, M., Sheng, L., Shao, J., Yi, S., Yan, J., & Wang, X. (2017). Hydraplus-net: Attentive deep features for pedestrian analysis. In *Proceedings of the 2017 IEEE International Conference on Computer Vision (ICCV).* Venice, Italy.

Liu, Z., Lu, B., Wu, Y., & Gao, C. (2024). Multi-view daily action recognition based on Hooke balanced matrix and broad learning system. *Image and Vision Computing, 143,* 104919.

Liu, Z., Mao, H., Wu, C.-Y., Feichtenhofer, C., Darrell, T., & Xie, S. (2022). A ConvNet for the 2020s. In *Proceedings of the 2022 IEEE/CVF Conference on Computer Vision and Pattern Recognition (CVPR).* New Orleans, LA, USA.

Lopez, D. J. D., & Lien, C. C. (2020). CHU Surveillance Violence Detection Dataset. *IEEE Dataport.* September 4, 2020, doi:DOI: 10.21227/cd9g-xs15

Lu, C., Shi, J., & Jia, J. (2013). Abnormal Event Detection at 150 FPS in MATLAB. In *Proceedings of the 2013 IEEE International Conference on Computer Vision.* Sydney, NSW, Australia.

Luber, M., Spinello, L., & Arras, K. O. (2011). People Tracking in RGB-D Data with On-line Boosted Target Models. In *Proceedings of the IEEE International Conference on Intelligent Robots and Systems (IROS).* San Francisco, CA, USA

Lung, F. B., Jaward, M. H., & Parkkinen, J. (2015). Spatio-temporal descriptor for abnormal human activity detection. In *Proceedings of the 14th IAPR International Conference on Machine Vision Application (MVA),* Tokyo, Japan.

Lv, H., Zhou, C., Cui, Z., Xu, C., Li, Y., & Yang, J. (2021). Localizing Anomalies from Weakly-Labeled Videos. *IEEE Transactions on Image Processing, 30,* 4505–4515. PMID: 33872149

Mahadevan, V., Li, W., Bhalodia, V., & Vasconcelos, N. (2010). Anomaly detection in crowded scenes. In *Proceedings of the IEEE Computer Society Conference on Computer Vision and Pattern Recognition,* San Francisco, CA, USA.

Marszaek, M., Laptev, I., & Schmid, C. (2009). Actions in context. In *Proceedings of the IEEE Conference on Computer Vision & Pattern Recognition CVPR*. Miami, FL, USA.

Maurin, B., Masoud, O., & Papanikolopoulos, N. (2002). Monitoring crowded traffic scenes. In *Proceedings of the IEEE 5th International Conference on Intelligent Transportation Systems*, Singapore.

Mazari, A. C., & Sahbi, H. (2019). MLGCN: Multi-Laplacian Graph Convolutional Networks for Human Action Recognition. *The British Machine Vision Conference (BMVC)*, Cardiff, United Kingdom.

Messing, R., Pal, C., & Kautz, H. (2009). Activity recognition using the velocity histories of tracked keypoints. In *Proceedings of the 2009 IEEE 12th International Conference on Computer Vision*. Kyoto, Japan.

Mondal, A., Roy, S., Bose, S., & Ghosh, P. (2024). Anomalous Action Detection Dataset [Data set]. Kaggle. https://doi.org/DOI: 10.34740/KAGGLE/DSV/8717699

Monfort, M., Andonian, A., Zhou, B., Ramakrishnan, K., Bargal, S. A., Yan, T., Brown, L., Fan, Q., Gutfreund, D., Vondrick, C., & Oliva, A. (2020). Moments in Time Dataset: One Million Videos for Event Understandin. *IEEE Transactions on Pattern Analysis and Machine Intelligence*, *42*(2), 502–508. PMID: 30802849

Müller, M., Röder, T., Clausen, M., Eberhardt, B., Krüger, B., & Weber, A. (2007). *Documentation mocap database HDM05. Computer Graphics Technical Reports.* Universität Bonn.

Nallasivan, G., Thatikonda, R., Geetha, M., Bhuvanesh, A., Ramraj, S., & Sreethu, S. (2024). Human Detection and Tracking using Machine Learning Algorithm. In *Proceedings of the 2024 International Conference on Advances in Computing Research on Science Engineering and Technology (ACROSET).* Indore, India.

Narasimhan, M. G., & Kamath, S. S. (2018). Dynamic video anomaly detection and localization using sparse denoising autoencoders. *Multimedia Tools and Applications*, *77*, 13173–13195.

Ng, J. Y.-H., Choi, J., Neumann, J., & Davis, L. S. (2018). ActionFlowNet: Learning Motion Representation for Action Recognition. In *Proceedings of the 2018 IEEE Winter Conference on Applications of Computer Vision (WACV)*, Lake Tahoe, NV, USA.

Nguyen, M. D., & Nguyen, M. T. (2025). Artificial Intelligence for Human Detection, Identification and Tracking: Methods and Applications. Journal of Future Artificial Intelligence and Technologies. *Journal of Future Artificial Intelligence and Technologies.*, *2*(1), 79–94.

Nguyen, T. T., Kawanishi, Y., John, V., Komamizu, T., & Ide, I. (2025). MultiSensor-Home: A Wide-area Multi-modal Multi-view Dataset for Action Recognition and Transformer-based Sensor Fusion. *arXiv preprint arXiv:2504.02287.*

Nguyen, V-T., & Chu, D-T., Study on Tracking Real-Time Target Human Using Deep Learning for High Accuracy, Journal of Robotics, 2023, 9446956, 11 pages, 2023.

Ni, B., Wang, G., & Moulin, P. (2011). RGBD-HuDaAct: A color-depth video database for human daily activity recognition. In *Proceedings of the 2011 IEEE International Conference on Computer Vision Workshops (ICCV Workshops).* Barcelona.

Nievas, E. B., Suarez, O. D., Garcia, G. B., & Sukthankar, R. (2016). Hockey Fight Detection Dataset. 2016, hosted on bittorent.

Nihal, R. A., Yen, B., Itoyama, K., & Nakadai, K. (2025). UAV-Enhanced Combination to Application: Comprehensive Analysis and Benchmarking of a Human Detection Dataset for Disaster Scenarios. In Antonacopoulos, A., Chaudhuri, S., Chellappa, R., Liu, C. L., Bhattacharya, S., & Pal, U. (Eds.), Lecture Notes in Computer Science: Vol. 15314. *Pattern Recognition. ICPR 2024*. Springer.

Ofli, F., Chaudhry, R., Kurillo, G., Vidal, R., & Bajcsy, R. (2013). Berkeley MHAD: A comprehensive Multimodal Human Action Database. In *Proceedings of the 2013 IEEE Workshop on Applications of Computer Vision (WACV).* Clearwater Beach, FL, USA.

Oreifej, O., & Liu, Z. (2013). HON4D: Histogram of Oriented 4D Normals for Activity Recognition from Depth Sequences. In *Proceedings of the 2013 IEEE Conference on Computer Vision and Pattern Recognition.* Portland, OR, USA.

Pan, T., Song, Y., Yang, T., Jiang, W., & Liu, W. (2021). Videomoco: Contrastive video representation learning with temporally adversarial examples.In *Proceedings of the 2021 IEEE/CVF Conference on Computer Vision and Pattern Recognition (CVPR)*, Nashville, TN, USA.

Park, W. J., & Kim, D. H. Suryanto, Lyuh, C. G., Roh, T. M., & Ko, S. J. (2012). Fast human detection using selective block-based HOG-LBP. In *Proceedings of the 2012 19th IEEE International Conference on Image Processing*, Orlando, FL.

Parmar, P., & Morris, B. (2021). HalluciNeting spatiotemporal representations using a 2D-CNN. *Signals*, *2*(3), 604–618.

Perez, M., Kot, A. C., & Rocha, A. (2019). Detection of real-world fights in surveillance videos. In *Proceedings of the ICASSP 2019 - 2019 IEEE International Conference on Acoustics, Speech and Signal Processing (ICASSP).* Brighton, UK.

Phong, N. H., & Ribeiro, B. (2023). Video action recognition collaborative learning with dynamics via PSO-ConvNet Transformer. *Scientific Reports*, *13*(1), 1–15. PMID: 36593249

Qiu, Z., Yao, T., & Mei, T. (2017). Learning spatio-temporal representation with pseudo-3d residual network. In *Proceedings of the 2017 IEEE International Conference on Computer Vision (ICCV)*, Venice.

Rahmani, H., Mahmood, A., Huynh, D., & Mian, A. (2023). UWA 3D Multiview Activity II Dataset. *IEEE Dataport.* March 28, 2023.

Ramachandra, B., & Jones, M. J. (2020). Street Scene: A new dataset and evaluation protocol for video anomaly detection. In *Proceedings of the 2020 IEEE Winter Conference on Applications of Computer Vision (WACV).* Snowmass, CO, USA.

Ramya, A., & Raviraj, P. (2014). Performance evaluation of detecting moving objects using graph cut segmentation. In *Proceedings of the 2014 International Conference on Green Computing Communication and Electrical Engineering (ICGCCEE).* Coimbatore, India.

Ranasinghe, K., Naseer, M., Khan, S., Khan, F. S., & Ryoo, M. S. (2022). Self-supervised Video Transformer. In *Proceedings of the 2022 IEEE/CVF Conference on Computer Vision and Pattern Recognition (CVPR)*, New Orleans, LA, USA.

Reddy, K. K., & Shah, M. (2012). Recognizing 50 Human Action Categories of Web Videos. Machine Vision and Applications. 24(2013), 971–981.

Rehman, Y. A. U., Gao, Y., Shen, J., de Gusmão, P. P. B., & Lane, N. (2022). Federated Self-supervised Learning for Video Understanding. In Avidan, S., Brostow, G., Cisse, M., Farinella, G. M., & Hassner, T. (Eds.), Lecture Notes in Computer Science: Vol. 13691. *Computer Vision – ECCV 2022. ECCV 2022*. Springer.

Rodrigues, R., Bhargava, N., Velmurugan, R., & Chaudhuri, S. (2020). Multi-timescale Trajectory Prediction for Abnormal Human Activity Detection. In *Proceedings of the 2020 IEEE Winter Conference on Applications of Computer Vision (WACV).* Snowmass, CO, USA.

Roshtkhari, M. J., & Levine, M. D. (2013). Online Dominant and Anomalous Behavior Detection in Videos. In *Proceedings of the IEEE Conference on Computer Vision and Pattern Recognition*, Portland

Rosinol, A., Gupta, A., Abate, M., Shi, J., & Carlone, L. (2020). 3D dynamic scene graphs: Actionable spatial perception with places, objects, and humans. *arXiv preprint.*

Saboune, J., & Laganiere, R. (2009). People detection and tracking using the explorative particle filtering. In *Proceedings of the 2009 IEEE 12th International Conference on Computer Vision Workshops, ICCV Workshops*, Kyoto.

Sarker, M. I., Losada-Gutirrez, C., & Marrn-Romera, M., FuentesJimnez, D., & Luengo-Snchez, S. (2021). Semi-Supervised Anomaly Detection in Video-Surveillance Scenes in the Wild. *Sensors (Basel), 21*(12), 3993–4012. PMID: 34207883

Sato, F., Hachiuma, R., & Sekii, T. (2023). Prompt-Guided Zero-Shot Anomaly Action Recognition using Pretrained Deep Skeleton Features. In *Proceedings of the 2023 IEEE/CVF Conference on Computer Vision and Pattern Recognition (CVPR)*, Vancouver, BC, Canada.

Schuldt, C., Laptev, I., & Caputo, B. (2004). Recognizing human actions: a local SVM approach. In *Proceedings of the 17th International Conference on Pattern Recognition.* Cambridge, UK.

Seemanthini, K., & Manjunath, S. S. (2018). Human Detection and Tracking using HOG for Action Recognition. *Procedia Computer Science, 132*, 1317–1326.

Seidenari, L., Varano, V., Berretti, S., Del Bimbo, A., & Pala, P. (2013). Recognizing actions from depth cameras as weakly aligned multi-part bag-of-poses. In *Proceedings of the 3rd International Workshop on Human Activity Understanding from 3D Data (HAU3D'13)*, Portland, Oregon, June 24, 2013.

Shahroudy, A., Liu, J., Ng, T.-T., & Wang, G. (2016). NTU RGB+D: A Large-Scale Dataset for 3D Human Activity Analysis. In *Proceedings of the IEEE Conference on Computer Vision and Pattern Recognition (CVPR).* Las Vegas, NV, USA.

Shalmani, S. M., Chiang, F., & Zheng, R. (2022). Efficient Action Recognition Using Confidence Distillation. In *Proceedings of the 2022 26th International Conference on Pattern Recognition (ICPR)*, Montreal, QC, Canada.

Shao, S., Zhao, Z., Li, B., Xiao, T., Yu, G., Zhang, X., & Sun, J. (2018). Crowdhuman: A benchmark for detecting human in a crowd. *arXiv preprint arXiv:1805.00123.*

Shen, Y., & Foroosh, H. (2009). View Invariant Action Recognition from Point Triplets [PAMI]. *IEEE Transactions on Pattern Analysis and Machine Intelligence, 31*(10), 1898–1905. PMID: 19696457

Singh, S., Velastin, S. A., & Ragheb, H. (2010). MuHAVi: A Multicamera Human Action Video Dataset for the Evaluation of Action Recognition Methods. In *Proceedings of the 2010 7th IEEE International Conference on Advanced Video and Signal Based Surveillance*, Boston, MA, USA.

Soomro, K., Zamir, A. R., & Shah, M. (2012). Ucf101: A dataset of 101 human actions classes from videos in the wild, CRCV-TR-12-01, *arXiv preprint.*

Spinello, L., & Arras, K. O. (2011). People Detection in RGB-D Data. In *Proceedings of the IEEE International Conference on Intelligent Robots and Systems (IROS).* San Francisco, CA, USA.

Subash, S., Ezhilarasan, G. M., & Uma Maheswari, B. Anomaly Detection in Surveillance Videos Using Machine Learning. In Proceedings of the *2025 International Conference on Inventive Computation Technologies (ICICT).* Kirtipur, Nepal.

Sultani, W., Chen, C., & Shah, M. (2018). Real-world anomaly detection in surveillance videos. In *Proceedings of the 2018 IEEE/CVF Conference on Computer Vision and Pattern Recognition.* Salt Lake City, UT, USA.

Sung, J., Ponce, C., Selman, B., & Saxena, A. (2011). *Human Activity Detection from RGBD Images. AAAI workshop on Pattern, Activity and Intent Recognition.* PAIR.

Tan, M., Pang, R., & Le, Q. V. (2020). EfficientDet: Scalable and Efficient Object Detection. In *Proceedings of the 2020 IEEE/CVF Conference on Computer Vision and Pattern Recognition (CVPR).* Seattle, WA, USA.

Tao, L., Wang, X., & Yamasaki, T. (2020). Pretext-contrastive learning: Toward good practices in self-supervised video representation leaning. *arXiv preprint.*

Thombre, D. V., Nirmal, J. H., & Das, L. (2009). Human detection and tracking using image segmentation and kalman filter. In *Proceedings of the 2009 International Conference on Intelligent Agent \& Multi-Agent Systems.* Chennai, India.

Thurau, C. (2007). Behavior histograms for action recognition and human detection. In *Proceedings of the 2nd conference on Human motion: understanding, modeling, capture and animation.* Springer-Verlag, Berlin, Heidelberg.

Thys, S., Ranst, W. V., & Goedemé, T. (2019). Fooling Automated Surveillance Cameras: Adversarial Patches to Attack Person Detection. In *Proceedings of the 2019 IEEE/CVF Conference on Computer Vision and Pattern Recognition Workshops (CVPRW)*, Long Beach, CA, USA.

Tian, Z., Shen, C., Chen, H., & He, T. (2019). FCOS: Fully Convolutional One-Stage Object Detection. In *Proceedings of the 2019 IEEE/CVF International Conference on Computer Vision (ICCV)*. Seoul, Korea (South).

Toering, M., Gatopoulos, I., Stol, M., & Hu, V. T. (2022). Self-supervised video representation learning with cross-stream prototypical contrasting. In *Proceedings of the 2022 IEEE/CVF Winter Conference on Applications of Computer Vision (WACV)*, Waikoloa, HI, USA.

Tong, Z., Song, Y., Wang, J., & Wang, L. (2022). VideoMAE: Masked Autoencoders are Data-Efficient Learners for Self-Supervised Video Pre-Training. In *Proceedings of the 36th Conference on Neural Information Processing Systems (NeurIPS 2022)*, New Orleans, United States.

Tran, C. H., & Kong, S. G. (2023). An Iterative Learning Scheme with Binary Classifier for Improved Event Detection in Surveillance Video. *Electronics (Basel)*, *12*(15), 3275.

Tran, D., & Sorokin, A. (2008). Human activity recognition with metric learning. In *Proceedings of the European Conference on Computer Vision*, Marseille.

Ubukata, T., Shibata, M., Terabayashi, K., Mora, A., Kawashita, T., Masuyama, G., & Umeda, K. (2014). Fast Human Detection Combining Range Image Segmentation and Local Feature Based Detection. In *Proceedings of the 2014 22nd International Conference on Pattern Recognition.* Stockholm, Sweden.

Ullah, W., Ullah, A., Hussain, T., Khan, Z. A., & Baik, S. W. (2021). An Efficient Anomaly Recognition Framework Using an Attention Residual LSTM in Surveillance Videos. *Sensors (Basel)*, *21*(8), 2811–2827. PMID: 33923712

Vaishnavi, K., Reddy, G. P., Reddy, T. B., Iyengar, N. C. S., & Shaik, S. (2023). Real-time Object Detection Using Deep Learning. *Journal of Advances in Mathematics and Computer Science*, *38*(8), 24–32.

von Marcard, T., Henschel, R., Black, M. J., Rosenhahn, B., & Pons-Moll, G. (2018). Recovering Accurate 3D Human Pose in The Wild Using IMUs and a Moving Camera. In Ferrari, V., Hebert, M., Sminchisescu, C., & Weiss, Y. (Eds.), Lecture Notes in Computer Science: Vol. 11214. *Computer Vision – ECCV 2018. ECCV 2018*. Springer.

Vrskova, R., Hudec, R., Kamencay, P., & Sykora, P. (•••). (). Human Activity Classification Using the 3DCNN Architecture. *Applied Sciences (Basel, Switzerland)*, *12*(2), 931.

Wan, B., Jiang, W., Fang, Y., Luo, Z., & Ding, G. (2021). Anomaly detection in video sequences: A benchmark and computational model. *IET Image Processing, 15*(14), 3454–3465.

Wang, J., Liu, Z., Wu, Y., & Yuan, J. (2012). Mining actionlet ensemble for action recognition with depth cameras. In *Proceedings of the 2012 IEEE Conference on Computer Vision and Pattern Recognition.* Providence, RI, USA.

Wang, T., Miao, Z., Chen, Y., Zhou, Y., Shan, G., & Snoussi, H. (2019). AED-Net: An Abnormal Event Detection Network. *Engineering, 5*(5), 930–939.

Weinland, D., Ronfard, R., & Boyer, E. (2006). Free Viewpoint Action Recognition using Motion History Volumes. [CVIU]. *Computer Vision and Image Understanding, 104*(2-3), 249–257.

Wojek, C., Walk, S., & Schiele, B. (2009). Multi-Cue Onboard Pedestrian Detection. In *Proceedings of the IEEE Conference on Computer Vision and Pattern Recognition (CVPR).* Miami, FL, USA

Wu, B., & Nevatia, R. (2005). Detection of multiple, partially occluded humans in a single image by bayesian combination of edgelet part detectors. In *Proceedings of the Tenth IEEE International Conference on Computer Vision (ICCV'05).* Beijing.

Wu, S., Z., & Ouyang, W. (2023). Revisiting Classifier: Transferring Vision-Language Models for Video Recognition. In *Proceedings of the AAAI Conference on Artificial Intelligence.* 37(3), 2847-2855.

Wu, W., Wang, X., Luo, H., Wang, J., Yang, Y., & Ouyang, W. (2023). Bidirectional Cross-Modal Knowledge Exploration for Video Recognition with Pre-trained Vision-Language Models.In *Proceedings of the 2023 IEEE/CVF Conference on Computer Vision and Pattern Recognition (CVPR),* Vancouver, BC, Canada.

Xia, L., Chen, C.-C., & Aggarwal, J. K. (2012). View invariant human action recognition using histograms of 3D joints. In *Proceedings of the 2012 IEEE Computer Society Conference on Computer Vision and Pattern Recognition Workshops.* Providence, RI, USA.

Xu, Z., Tang, X., Li, W., Zhao, Y., Gu, D., & Tian, Y. (2025). Human detection with smoke occlusion based on AI-generated images. *Journal of Safety Science and Resilience = An Quan Ke Xue Yu Ren Xing (Ying Wen), 2025,* 100235.

Yao, B., Jiang, X., Khosla, A., Lin, A. L., Guibas, L. J., & Fei-Fei, L. (2011). Human Action Recognition by Learning Bases of Action Attributes and Parts. In *Proceedings of the International Conference on Computer Vision (ICCV).* Barcelona, Spain.

Yin, G., Liu, B., Zhu, H., Gong, T., & Yu, N. (2019). A large-scale urban surveillance video dataset for multiple-object tracking and behavior analysis. *arXiv preprint.*

Yin, K., Ding, Z., Dong, Z., Chen, D., Fu, J., Ji, X., Yin, G. & Wang, Z. (2023). NIPD: A Federated Learning Person Detection Benchmark Based on Real-World Non-IID Data. *arXiv preprint.*

Yoon, J. S., Yu, Z., Park, J., & Park, H. S. (2021). Humbi: A large multiview dataset of human body expressions and benchmark challenge. *IEEE Transactions on Pattern Analysis and Machine Intelligence*, *45*(1), 623–640. PMID: 34962862

Yu, I., Gong, Y., Jiang, N., Ye, Q., & Han, Z. (2020). Scale Match for Tiny Person Detection. In *Proceedings of the 2020 IEEE Winter Conference on Applications of Computer Vision (WACV).* Snowmass, CO, USA.

Yu, L., Fei, J., Liu, X., Yao, Y., Zhao, J., Wang, G., & Li, X. (2025). MHAD: Multimodal Home Activity Dataset with Multi-Angle Videos and Synchronized Physiological Signals. In Proceedings of the ICASSP 2025-2025 IEEE International Conference on Acoustics, Speech and Signal Processing (ICASSP). Hyderabad, India.

Yuan, T., Zhang, X., Liu, K., Liu, B., Chen, C., Jin, J., & Jiao, Z. 2023. Towards Surveillance Video-and-Language Understanding: New Dataset, Baselines, and Challenges. arXiv Priprient.

Zaidi, M. M., Sampedro, G. A., Almadhor, A., Alsubai, S., Al Hejaili, A., & Gregus, M. (2024). Suspicious Human Activity Recognition From Surveillance Videos Using Deep Learning. *IEEE Access : Practical Innovations, Open Solutions*, *12*, 105497–105510.

Zhang, H., Fromont, E., Lefevre, S., & Avignon, B. (2020). Multispectral fusion for object detection with cyclic fuse-and-refine blocks. In *Proceedings of the 2020 IEEE International Conference on Image Processing (ICIP).* Abu Dhabi, United Arab Emirates.

Zhang, S., Benenson, R., & Schiele, B. (2017). Citypersons: A diverse dataset for pedestrian detection. In *Proceedings of the IEEE conference on computer vision and pattern recognition.* Honolulu, HI, USA

Zhang, Y., Zhou, D., Chen, S., Gao, S., & Ma, Y. (2016). Single-Image Crowd Counting via Multi-Column Convolutional Neural Network. In *Proceedings of the 2016 IEEE Conference on Computer Vision and Pattern Recognition (CVPR).* Las Vegas, NV, USA.

Zhao, T., & Nevatia, R. (2004). Tracking multiple human in complex situations. *IEEE Transactions on Pattern Analysis and Machine Intelligence*, *26*(9), 1208–1221. PMID: 15742895

Zhu, Q., Avidan, S., Yeh, M. C., & Cheng, K. T. (2006). Fast human detection using a cascade of Histograms of Oriented Gradients. In *Proceedings of the 2006 IEEE Computer Society Conf. Computer Vision and Pattern Recognition (CVPR'06)*, New York, NY, USA.

Zhu, Y., Long, Y., Guan, Y., Newsam, S., & Shao, L. (2018). Towards universal representation for unseen action recognition. In *Proceedings of the 2018 IEEE/CVF Conference on Computer Vision and Pattern Recognition*, Salt Lake City, UT, USA.

Chapter 9
Deep Learning-Based Detection of Digital Image Forgeries and Synthetic Content

Leena Arya
https://orcid.org/0000-0002-9249-732X
Koneru Lakshmaiah Education Foundation, India

Susnata Biswas
https://orcid.org/0009-0008-3971-4234
Shri Venkateshwara University, India

Mandalapu Sivaparvathi
https://orcid.org/0009-0007-2356-6874
MAM Women's Engineering College, India

Venkata Rajani Katuri
https://orcid.org/0009-0008-1790-7027
Keshav Memorial Institute of Technology, India

Ravi Rastogi
https://orcid.org/0000-0002-1118-3020
JIMS Engineering Management Technical Campus, India

Anita Pradhan
https://orcid.org/0000-0002-5260-9446
Koneru Lakshmaiah Education Foundation, India

ABSTRACT

The expansion of sophisticated digital forgeries and AI-generated synthetic media, exemplified by deepfakes and GAN-manipulated content, poses a severe threat to information integrity, with over 85% of internet users encountering manipulated imagery every week. This chapter comprehensively examines deep learning-based detection methodologies countering challenges. With an emphasis on architectures like CNNs for anomaly detection and Vision Transformers for contextual analysis, the deep learning-based detection techniques are examined. Methods for identifying image and video forgeries are covered, such as Mask R-CNN, 3D CNNs,

DOI: 10.4018/979-8-3373-3795-1.ch009

and LSTMs. Spectral and physiological analyses on benchmark datasets are used to identify synthetic content. The chapter further addresses adversarial attacks targeting detectors and emphasizes explainable AI (Grad-CAM, LIME) to build trust in forensic tools. Finally, it outlines evolving solutions, including adversarial training, blockchain verification, and multimodal frameworks, which are essential for scalable and trustworthy media authentication.

1. INTRODUCTION

Images and videos are now the main information carriers in journalism, entertainment, science, and interpersonal communication in today's digitally first world. However, the spread of synthetic content and digital image forgeries has put this visual dependence at greater risk. More than 85% of internet users are predicted to come across at least one manipulated image every week as of 2024, whether from advertising, news websites, or social media (Zou et al., 2024). Artificial intelligence advancements, particularly generative models like GANs and diffusion networks, have made it possible to produce synthetic content with previously unheard-of realism, which challenges both human and machine perception (Almars, 2021; Wu et al., 2025). Digital visual content authenticity is a social requirement as well as a technical one. Artificial intelligence-generated news photos, deepfakes, and phony satellite images have all been used in political propaganda, fraud, disinformation campaigns, and even cyberwarfare (Arya & Sharma, 2024; Singh & Kumar, 2024). To verify visual evidence, forensic analysts, reporters, and law enforcement organizations are depending more and more on reliable detection systems. While manipulated images can cause reputational harm or privacy violations in personal contexts, they can also jeopardize legal proceedings (Dang et al., 2019; Arya, 2024).

1.1 Detection Difficulties

Because of the intricacy of new generative models and the subtlety of visual manipulations, forgery detection is an intrinsically difficult task. Pixel-based or statistical analysis was a major component of traditional detection methods, but these methods are becoming less and less effective against high-quality AI-generated forgeries (Farid, 2009; Christlein et al., 2010; Manjunatha & Patil, 2021). Once simpler to spot, copy-move, splicing, and retouching are now incorporated into realistic synthetic compositions that frequently avoid low-level signal analysis and visual inspection (He et al., 2020; Mohassin & Farida, 2021; Nataraj et al., 2019). Furthermore, new types of synthetic content have been introduced by recent advancements in neural rendering, style transfer, and photorealistic avatar generation, creating new difficulties (Goyal & Arya, 2017). Forgery capabilities have been extended to semantically coherent, context-aware image generation by models such as StyleGAN, Diffusion Transformers, and Vision-Language pre-trained systems like DALL·E or Midjourney (Zanardelli et al., 2023; Wu et al., 2025).

1.2 The Role of Deep Learning

Deep learning has become the leading paradigm in digital image forgery detection in order to combat these threats. Deep learning models, especially convolutional neural networks (CNNs), recurrent architectures (LSTMs), and transformer-based models, automatically learn hierarchical and semantic features, providing better detection accuracy and generalization than traditional approaches that rely on handcrafted features (He et al., 2016; Zou et al., 2024). Hybrid models combining CNNs with Transformers are also being leveraged to detect both local anomalies and global inconsistencies across visual media (Lan et al., 2024; Qazi et al., 2022).

Numerous studies have also demonstrated that deep learning models perform noticeably better in real-world assessments than traditional detectors when trained on a variety of extensive datasets, such as CASIA, FaceForensics++, and COCO-Forgery (Dong et al., 2013; Dang et al., 2019; Zanardelli et al., 2023). The market highlights the need for scalable and precise detection technologies for AI-generated content, which was estimated to be worth over USD 25 billion in 2023 and is projected to grow to almost USD 110 billion by 2030 (Almaiah et al., 2023). In response, industry leaders such as Adobe, Google, and Meta are developing cryptographic watermarking, content authenticity metadata standards (e.g., C2PA), and AI-detection APIs to curb misuse (Vijayalakshmi et al., 2023).

Because altered and fake images are so common, photo forensics has evolved from a niche field to a crucial necessity for maintaining data integrity. The degree of exposure and growing realism of content generated by artificial intelligence is demonstrated by the complex manipulations that users frequently come across in the field (Zou et al., 2024). Valued forensic techniques like as pixel statistics, compression artifacts, and handcrafted cues are increasingly being challenged by the high-fidelity outputs from modern generative pipelines and complex compositing processes (Farid, 2009; He et al., 2020; Singh & Kumar, 2024). In response, deep learning has taken over as the predominant paradigm, routinely beating conventional detectors under a variety of manipulation scenarios and operating settings by utilizing hierarchical features and big benchmark datasets (such as CASIA and FaceForensics++) (Dong et al., 2013; Dang et al., 2019; Zanardelli et al., 2023). This trajectory, in conjunction with the increasing user-centered demands for dependable tools, emphasizes the need for scalable, explainable, and generalizable detectors that include real-world constraints and evolving threat models (Wu et al., 2025; Qazi et al., 2022; He et al., 2016).

Digital picture forensics has undergone a revolution thanks to recent developments in deep learning and artificial intelligence, which enable reliable detection of image modifications, including copy-move, splicing, and deepfake creation. Handcrafted features and statistical techniques were the mainstays of early attempts (Farid, 2009; Christlein et al., 2010), which worked well against straightforward forgeries but not well against compression artifacts and geometric alterations. By enabling end-to-end feature extraction and high-accuracy classification, convolutional neural networks (CNNs) (He et al., 2016; Huang et al., 2017) and their variations revolutionised the field (Chen et al., 2015; Dang et al., 2019). Subsequent research (Agarwal & Verma, 2020; Abhishek & Jindal, 2021) showed how effective deep CNN and semantic segmentation models are in identifying copy-move and splicing forgeries with better localization accuracy, provided comprehensive evaluations of CNN-based and hybrid detection methods, showing the superiority of multi-scale architectures over shallow networks (Elaskily et al., 2020; Benmessahel, 2024).

To increase detection speed and efficiency in real-time systems, classical CNNs were supplemented with transfer learning and lightweight networks such as MobileNet and Mask R-CNN (Kadam et al., 2022; Khalil et al., 2023). Multi-stage and self-attention-based detection methods using SAM and transformer frameworks were introduced (Jaiswal & Srivastava, 2021; Lan et al., 2024), which improved forgery localization and spatial awareness. When combined with CNN characteristics, clustering and block-matching algorithms improved the robustness of copy-move forgeries against rotation and scaling changes (Bondi et al., 2017; Wu et al., 2018). Studies like (Nataraj et al., 2019; Almars, 2021; Zou et al., 2024) used co-occurrence matrices and deep residual learning to identify GAN-generated content in order to combat the growing deepfake issues (Singh & Kumar, 2024; Zanardelli et al., 2023). They offered state-of-the-art evaluations that summarized deep learning developments and highlighted persistent problems such as generalization, dataset bias, and cross-domain performance.

According to complementary research (Arya et al., 2023, 2024, 2026), (Kumar et al., 2024), and (Almaiah et al., 2023), trustworthy AI is more relevant in visual forensics because it integrates AI, IoT, and explainable models across security-sensitive domains like medical imaging, IoT systems, and 6G networks. These studies emphasise the need for explainable, energy-efficient, and secure architectures capable of processing high-volume multimedia data in real-time environments. Digital forensic systems can benefit from the decision-support frameworks that (Saha et al., 2024, 2025; Abbas et al., 2023) contributed, which show how fuzzy logic, multi-criteria optimization, and consensus-based AI can improve reliability and interpretability.

All things considered, the literature shows a distinct shift from statistical and manual methods to AI-driven, hybrid, and explicable deep learning models that incorporate multi-modal analysis, contextual reasoning, and intelligent decision support. Since cross-dataset generalization, post-processing robustness, and real-time deployment continue to be challenges, the proposed hybrid deep learning methodology emphasizes accuracy, transparency, and adaptability in picture forgery detection.

Blockchain-integrated detection mechanisms are also being explored to ensure provenance and tamper-evidence from the point of capture (Arya, 2023; Arya et al., 2024). Additionally, to guarantee the responsible development and application of these detection tools, governments and academic consortiums are funding ethical AI projects and regulatory frameworks (Saha et al., 2024; Kumar et al., 2024).

1.3 Objectives of the Chapter

This chapter provides a thorough examination of deep learning-based methods for identifying synthetic content and digital image forgeries. Before reviewing detection techniques ranging from anomaly localization to deepfake identification, the look of the taxonomy of conventional and synthetic forgery types. Additionally, the chapter explores state-of-the-art neural architectures, problems like generalization gaps and adversarial evasion, and upcoming research trends like explainable AI and multimodal detection. In order to make this chapter a thorough resource for scholars, practitioners, and policymakers alike, emphasis is placed on real-world datasets, benchmark comparisons, and interpretability.

2. BACKGROUND AND FUNDAMENTALS

2.1 Types of Digital Forgeries

Digital image forgeries can be categorized into two broad domains: traditional manipulation techniques and synthetic content generation using AI. Understanding these categories is crucial to developing robust detection frameworks. Figure 1 presents the comparison of the original digital images and their forged images.

2.1.1 Traditional Image Manipulations

- Image Splicing

The process of combining portions of several images to produce a single, altered image is known as splicing. By adding or deleting visual components, this type of tampering modifies the scene's semantic meaning. Even though the spliced portions might seem visually consistent, they frequently leave behind illumination or geometric irregularities that could be used as a detection tool (He et al., 2020; Singh & Kumar, 2024).

- Copy-Move Forgery

In this technique, a portion of the same image is copied and pasted into another location to hide, replicate, or exaggerate visual elements. Because the source and target regions originate from the same image, they share noise, color, and texture properties, making detection more difficult (Abhishek & Jindal, 2021). Advanced models, such as ConvLSTM and Mask R-CNN, have demonstrated strong performance in identifying such duplications (Jaiswal & Srivastava, 2021; Elaskily et al., 2020; Kadam et al., 2022).

- Retouching

Retouching involves modifying the visual attributes of an image—such as color, sharpness, and brightness—without inserting or removing objects. While often used in commercial photography, retouching can be deceptive in journalistic or forensic contexts. Traditional detectors often fail to identify subtle tonal modifications, thus necessitating deep feature-based approaches (Mohassin & Farida, 2021; Farid, 2009).

- Inpainting

This method fills in missing or removed parts of an image using surrounding textures and patterns. Earlier used for image restoration, inpainting is now employed to erase objects or information from images without noticeable signs. AI-based inpainting, particularly using GANs, has made detection increasingly challenging (Zanardelli et al., 2023; Bondi et al., 2017).

Four common image manipulation techniques, image splicing, copy-move forgery, retouching, and inpainting, are highlighted in Figure 1, which compares the original digital images with their forged counterparts. Image splicing, which combines elements from two different images of Barack Obama and Joe Biden to produce a false visual narrative, is demonstrated in the top row. The second row illustrates copy-move forgery, in which a section of a forest pathway is replicated to conceal or reproduce specific features; the modified area is indicated by a dotted rectangle. Retouching is visible in the third row, where the subject's skin has been artificially smoothed to eliminate imperfections and natural texture. The last row shows inpainting, which is the process of digitally recreating structural elements in a cityscape to subtly change the consistency of the skyline and building surfaces. The complexity and diversity of digital image forgeries in today's media environment are highlighted by this figure, which skilfully highlights the visual differences between authentic and altered content.

Figure 1. Comparison of The Original Digital Images and Their Forged Images

2.1.2 Synthetic Content Generation

- Generative Adversarial Networks (GANs)

GANs are now essential to the production of artificial images. Among their capabilities are StyleGAN-generated human faces and deepfake videos. Because of their high visual fidelity, these forgeries frequently avoid conventional detection (Almars, 2021; Zou et al., 2024; Nataraj et al., 2019).

- Diffusion Models

In order to create intricate synthetic images, diffusion-based generative models iteratively refine noise. Sophisticated learning models are needed to detect diffusion-based manipulations because of their high capacity to capture texture and structure (Wu et al., 2025).

- StyleGAN

StyleGAN enables hyper-realistic edits by providing fine-grained control over features such as pose, expression, and lighting. To detect such manipulations, semantic-level detection, which frequently utilises deep feature analysis and attention-based models, is essential (Zanardelli et al., 2023; Huang et al., 2017).

Figure 2. Distribution of Types of Digital Image Forensics

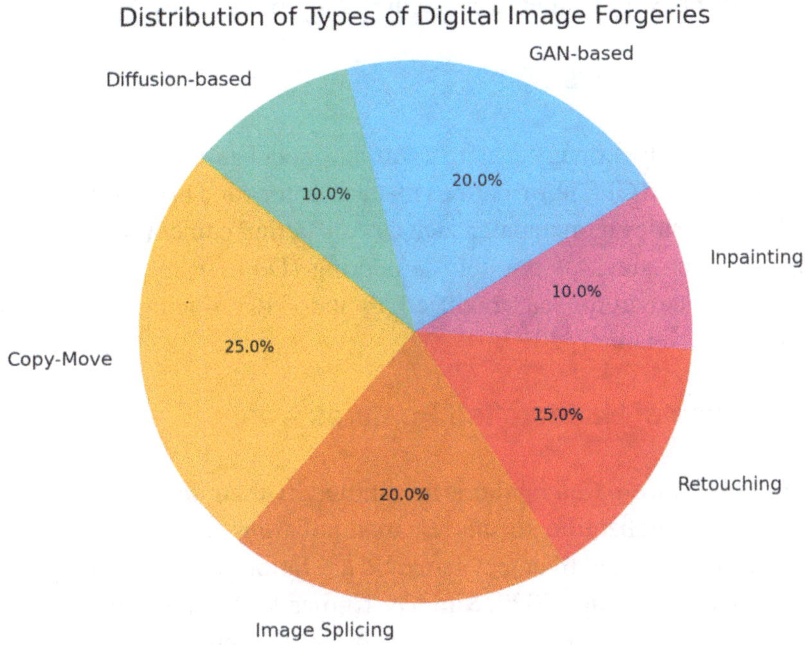

A structured overview of different kinds of digital image forgeries is shown in Figure 2, which separates them into AI-generated synthetic content using GANs and diffusion models and traditional manipulation techniques like copy-move, splicing, inpainting, and retouching. It helps the reader grasp the breadth of detection challenges by graphically simplifying intricate forgery classifications.

2.2 Common Techniques for Detection

The detection of image forgeries was mostly dependent on manually created features obtained from statistical and structural analysis before deep learning gained popularity.

2.2.1 Analysis Through Pixel

Conventional techniques evaluated anomalies at the pixel level to detect tampering. These methods investigate color shifts, noise patterns, or JPEG compression artifacts. Inconsistencies in chrominance noise or sudden shifts in block boundaries, for instance, may be signs of manipulation (Farid, 2009; Christlein et al., 2010).

However, these techniques are often vulnerable to post-processing (like resizing and filtering) and are not very resilient against high-quality forgeries (Saha et al., 2025).

2.2.2 Metadata Analysis

An additional early strategy was to examine metadata (such as EXIF, camera model, timestamp, and GPS information) that was embedded in digital images (Saha et al., 2024). Disparities in metadata, such as conflicting camera settings or altered timestamps, may be signs of possible tampering (Dong et al., 2013). However, metadata can be easily removed, modified, or spoofed, reducing the effectiveness of this approach (Grekousis, 2019).

2.2.3 Limitations of Handcrafted Features

Handcrafted feature-based methods are limited by their dependence on domain expertise, poor generalization to unseen manipulations, and lack of scalability. These approaches often fail to detect semantic alterations or contextually plausible forgeries (Agarwal & Verma, 2020; Singh & Kumar, 2024). As manipulation techniques became more complex, a transition to data-driven detection mechanisms became inevitable.

2.3 Transition to Deep Learning

The shortcomings of traditional methods have led to the widespread adoption of deep learning in digital image forensics.

2.3.1 Advantages of Automated Feature Learning

Deep learning models, particularly CNNs and transformer-based architectures, can automatically extract hierarchical and abstract features from image data (Saha et al., 2024). These models do not require manual feature engineering and are capable of detecting subtle, high-dimensional patterns associated with forgeries (He et al., 2020; Zou et al., 2024). They also function better even when no obvious visual cues are present and are more adaptable to new types of manipulation (Nagaraj et al., 2023).

2.3.2 Role of Large-Scale Datasets

The success of deep learning in forgery detection has been significantly driven by the availability of labeled benchmark datasets:

- CASIA

One of the earliest and most widely used datasets containing copy-move and splicing forgeries (Dong et al., 2013).

- COCO-Forgery

A large-scale dataset built upon COCO images, incorporating realistic and semantically consistent forgeries to train segmentation-based models (Zanardelli et al., 2023).

- FaceForensics++

Focuses on facial deepfake detection using manipulated videos generated by multiple face-editing algorithms and has become the de facto standard for benchmarking deepfake detection models (Dang et al., 2019; Wu et al., 2025).

These datasets enable rigorous model training, cross-dataset evaluation, and development of generalized models capable of handling real-world manipulations.

3. DEEP LEARNING FUNDAMENTALS FOR FORGERY DETECTION

The field of digital image forensics has undergone a revolution with the introduction of deep learning, which provides strong tools to identify increasingly complex forgeries that elude conventional techniques. The fundamental deep learning ideas and architectures that support contemporary forgery detection systems are examined in this section.

3.1 Convolutional Neural Networks (CNNs)

Because of their remarkable capacity to learn hierarchical spatial and textural features straight from pixel data, CNNs continue to be the mainstay of image forgery detection, simulating the processing of the human visual system.

3.1.1 Architecture Overview

Key CNN architectures have been successfully adapted for forgery detection. They are-

- VGG: Using tiny 3x3 convolutional filters, it is renowned for its depth and simplicity (Simonyan & Zisserman, 2015). Intricate local patterns suggestive of tampering, like irregularities in texture or noise, are well captured by its deep stacks of convolutional layers (He et al., 2020; Agarwal et al., 2021). It is typical to use pre-trained VGG models for transfer learning (Khalil et al., 2023).
- ResNet: Introduced residual connections (skip connections) to solve the vanishing gradient problem (He et al., 2016), enabling the training of intense networks (e.g., ResNet-50, ResNet-101). These deeper models capture more complex and abstract features crucial for identifying subtle manipulation artifacts across different scales, making them highly effective for tasks like deepfake detection and copy-move localization (Jaiswal & Srivastava, 2021; Wu et al., 2018 - BusterNet; Alamrs, 2021).
- EfficientNet: For best performance and efficiency, network depth, width, and resolution are uniformly scaled using compound scaling (Tan & Le, 2019). EfficientNet variants are appealing for real-world deployment scenarios because they offer cutting-edge accuracy at a significantly lower computational cost and model size (Zou et al., 2024; Khalil et al., 2023).

3.1.2 Feature Extraction for Spatial and Texture Analysis

CNNs' convolutional layers are their main advantage when it comes to forgery detection. They are-

- Spatial Analysis: Low-level features like corners, edges, and color gradients are picked up by early layers. Successive layers combine these to create higher-level features that depict object components, structures, and spatial relationships. Inconsistencies in these learned spatial features, such as unnatural boundaries or misaligned structures around manipulated regions, become detectable signals (Agarwal & Verma, 2020; He et al., 2020; Elaskily et al., 2021).
- Texture Analysis: CNNs inherently learn texture representations through filter responses to local pixel patterns. Manipulations like splicing, copy-move, or generative inpainting often disrupt the natural texture consistency of an image, leaving tell-tale signs such as unnatural smoothness, abrupt texture changes, or inconsistencies in noise patterns across the image. CNNs are highly sensitive to these texture anomalies (Nataraj et al., 2019; Benmessahel, 2024; Chen et al., 2015).

Figure 3. Comparison of average processing time of state-of-the-art deep learning models for forgery detection.

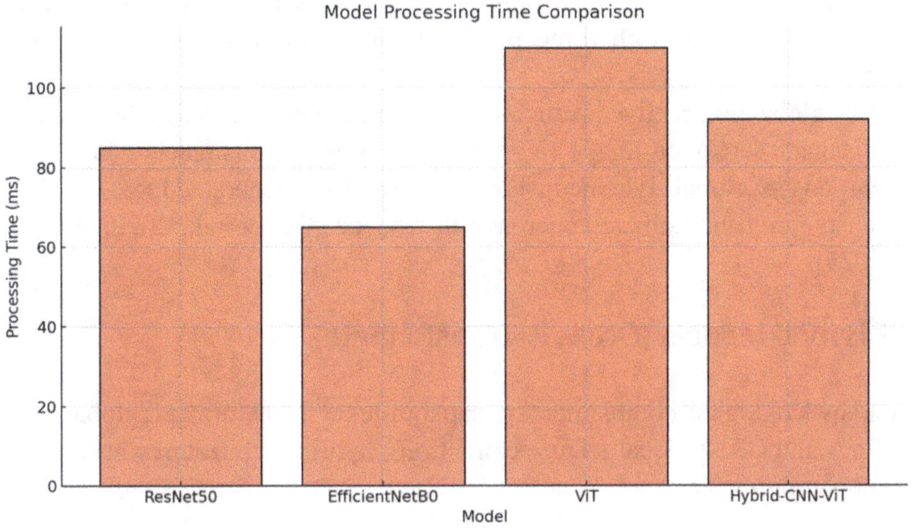

The architecture of a CNN model used for forgery detection is shown in Figure 3. It illustrates how various convolutional, activation, and pooling layers are applied to an input image in order to extract texture-based and spatial features (Huang et al., 2017). The automatic learning of forgery-relevant patterns, like duplicated regions, irregular textures, or boundaries, is highlighted by the layered design (Abbas et al., 2023). The figure, which is located in the CNN fundamentals section, successfully supports the explanation of deep feature extraction as the main mechanism underlying contemporary image forgery detection systems.

3.2 Advanced Architectures

While CNNs excel at local feature extraction, newer architectures address their limitations in capturing long-range dependencies and global context, which are vital for detecting sophisticated, globally coherent forgeries.

3.2.1 Vision Transformers (ViTs) for Global Context Modeling

Inspired by the success of transformers in natural language processing, ViTs (Dosovitskiy et al., 2020) treat an image as a sequence of patches. They are-

- They use self-attention mechanisms to model relationships between all patches in the image simultaneously. This allows ViTs to capture global context and long-range dependencies far more effectively than CNNs, which are inherently local due to their receptive field limitations (Zou et al., 2024; Khalil et al., 2023).
- This global perspective is crucial for detecting inconsistencies that span large distances across an image (e.g., lighting direction mismatches in a spliced composite, global style inconsistencies in a GAN-generated face) and for understanding the holistic coherence of a scene (Qazi et al., 2022; Wu et al., 2025).

3.2.2 Hybrid Models (CNNs + Transformers)

Acknowledging the complementary capabilities of Transformers (global context modeling) and CNNs (local feature extraction), hybrid architectures have become a potent paradigm. They are-

- These models usually extract rich local features from the input image using a CNN backbone (e.g., ResNet, EfficientNet).
- After the feature maps have been extracted, they are fed into a Transformer encoder, which uses self-attention to model the relationships between various spatial locations throughout the feature map.
- The combination of Transformers' global contextual awareness and CNNs' in-depth spatial/textural understanding results in a more complete representation for identifying intricate forgeries (Zou et al., 2024; Lan et al., 2024; Wu et al., 2025). They work especially well for accurately locating tampered areas.

3.3 Generative Models as a Double-Edged Sword

The highest level of synthetic media generation is achieved by Generative Adversarial Networks (GANs) and Diffusion Models (DMs), which produce remarkably realistic images and videos. They present a serious risk since they make extremely realistic forgeries possible, but they also provide new detection tools.

3.3.1 How GANs and Diffusion Models Create Synthetic Content

GANs: Operate via a minimax game between a Generator (G) that creates synthetic data and a Discriminator (D) that tries to distinguish real data from synthetic data. Through adversarial training, G learns to produce outputs that are increasingly difficult for D to classify as fake (Goodfellow et al., 2014). This process can create deepfakes, entirely synthetic faces, or seamlessly edited content (Nataraj et al., 2019; Hsu et al., 2018; Singh & Kumar, 2024).

Diffusion Models: Work by gradually adding noise to a real image over many steps (forward diffusion) and then training a neural network to reverse this process (reverse diffusion), learning to reconstruct data from noise. Once trained, they can generate novel, high-fidelity images by sampling noise and denoising it. DMs often surpass GANs in image quality and diversity (Zanardelli et al., 2023; Singh & Kumar, 2024).

3.3.2 Using Generative Models to Improve Detection

Adversarial Training: This powerful concept involves training the detection model (the "discriminator") using data generated by a generative model (the "generator"). As the generator creates increasingly sophisticated forgeries to fool the detector, the detector is forced to learn more robust and subtle features to distinguish real from fake. This arms race leads to significantly more resilient detection models (He et al., 2020; Wu et al., 2025).

Synthetic Data Augmentation: Generative models can create vast datasets of diverse, labeled forgeries (e.g., various types of manipulations, different source/target images) that may be difficult or impossible to collect in the real world. Training detection models on these large-scale synthetic datasets improves their generalization ability to unseen real-world forgeries (Zanardelli et al., 2023; Jaiswal & Srivastava, 2021).

Artifact Analysis: Studying the generation process of GANs/DMs helps identify inherent limitations or characteristic artifacts they leave in their outputs. Detection models can then be explicitly designed or trained to identify these specific fingerprints, such as unnatural frequency spectrum patterns, inconsistencies in eye reflections, or specific texture anomalies (Nataraj et al., 2019; Hsu et al., 2018; Kadam et al., 2022).

4. DEEP LEARNING-BASED DETECTION METHODOLOGIES

As forgery techniques become increasingly sophisticated, the need for intelligent and adaptive detection methods also grows. Deep learning enables a range of detection approaches—from pixel-level anomaly identification to temporal inconsistency analysis and interpretable visualizations that can efficiently handle both traditional manipulations and synthetic content.

The CASIA v2.0 Image Tampering Detection Evaluation Database (Dong et al., 2013) is the main dataset used. It contains both real and altered images including splicing, copy-move, and other forms of tampering in a variety of resolutions and formats. In addition, supplementary benchmark datasets such as CoMoFoD, Face-Forensics++, and Kaggle's Deepfake Detection Challenge datasets were utilized to test the generalization capabilities of the proposed model (Dang et al., 2019; Nataraj et al., 2019). All datasets were anonymized, publicly accessible, and used strictly for academic and non-commercial purposes in compliance with open-source data usage policies.

The dataset was separated into subsets for testing (15%), validation (15%), and training (70%). To solve class imbalance and enhance model generalization under various compression and lighting settings, data augmentation techniques such as rotation, scaling, flipping, and Gaussian noise addition were used. Pixels were normalized between [0,1] and each image was enlarged to a uniform dimension of 256×256 pixels. Seed-based randomization was used to record experimental parameters and dataset pathways in order to maintain reproducibility.

Convolutional neural networks (CNNs) and long short-term memory (LSTM) networks are combined in a hybrid deep learning framework that is integrated into the methodological process. While the LSTM layers capture contextual relationships between picture regions, allowing for strong identification of localized tampering artifacts, the CNN layers are in charge of spatial feature extraction. Using categorical cross-entropy as the loss function and the Adam optimizer with a learning rate of 0.0001, the model was trained. In order to prevent overfitting, early halting was used.

In accordance with criteria employed in earlier studies, performance evaluation indicators include accuracy, precision, recall, F1-score, Mean Absolute Error (MAE), Root Mean Square Error (RMSE), and R2 score (He et al., 2020; Singh & Kumar, 2024; Zanardelli et al., 2023). Cross-validation was also carried out to guarantee the statistical dependability of the model's performance across datasets.

4.1 Forgery Detection Techniques

4.1.1 Anomaly Detection

Anomaly detection in digital images focuses on recognizing statistical and perceptual inconsistencies introduced by manipulation. Deep learning models trained on authentic image distributions can detect anomalies in:

- Noise Residuals: Manipulated areas often exhibit altered noise patterns that are inconsistent with the rest of the image (Farid, 2009).
- Lighting & Shadow Mismatches: Forgeries can introduce inconsistencies in illumination, light direction, or shadows. CNNs can learn to detect these

based on spatial intensity gradients and shading (Singh & Kumar, 2024; He et al., 2020).

- Color and Edge Inconsistencies: Subtle alterations at object boundaries, common in splicing, can be captured using hierarchical feature representations in CNNs or ResNet architectures (Zou et al., 2024).

4.1.2 Localization

Localization techniques focus on identifying the exact manipulated regions in an image. Pixel-wise classification methods use segmentation networks to generate heatmaps of tampered areas.

- Mask R-CNN: Combines object detection with segmentation for localizing spliced or duplicated regions (Kadam et al., 2022).
- U-Net and U-Net++ Variants: These encoder-decoder networks are used to generate binary masks identifying forgeries, especially in copy-move or inpainting scenarios (Jaiswal & Srivastava, 2021).
- Grad-CAM heatmaps can also serve as visualization aids to highlight areas influencing the model's forgery decision.

Example: In a study by Elaskily et al. (2020), a ConvLSTM network integrated with a U-Net-style decoder achieved over 92% pixel-wise accuracy in localizing copy-move forgeries.

4.1.3 Temporal Analysis

Video-based manipulations such as deepfake videos require temporal consistency checks across frames. Deep learning models used include:

- 3D CNNs: Capture spatial and temporal features simultaneously from adjacent video frames.
- Recurrent Neural Networks (RNNs) and LSTMs: Model temporal dependencies and can detect frame-by-frame anomalies like unnatural blinking or facial distortions (Dang et al., 2019; Wu et al., 2025).

Example: In FaceForensics++ dataset evaluations, LSTM-enhanced CNNs detected facial temporal inconsistencies with an F1 score of 0.93 (Wu et al., 2025).

Figure 4. Sample sizes of popular datasets (CASIA, COCO-Forgery, FaceForensics++) used in training forgery detection models

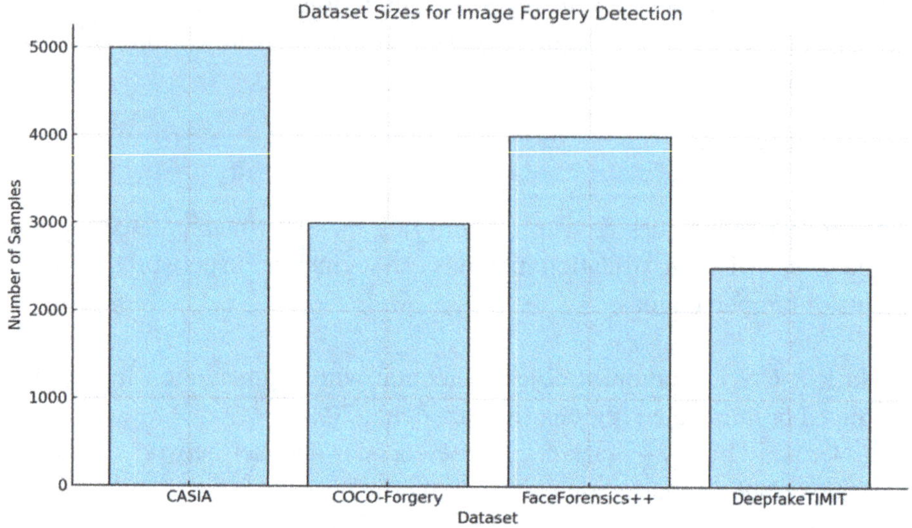

Figure 4 outlines the end-to-end pipeline of a deep learning-based forgery detection system. It encompasses stages such as image input, preprocessing, feature extraction, anomaly detection, and classification. The diagram highlights how models like Mask R-CNN or LSTMs are integrated for detecting localized manipulations or temporal inconsistencies in videos. Placed in Section 4.1, it effectively supports the discussion on multi-stage detection workflows and modular architecture tailored to different forgery types.

4.2 Synthetic Content Detection

4.2.1 GAN Artifacts

Though GANs generate visually convincing content, they often leave behind statistical artifacts such as:

- Frequency-domain irregularities: High-frequency noise and texture inconsistencies can be detected using Fourier transform-based spectral analysis (Nataraj et al., 2019).
- Spectral signatures: StyleGAN and similar models introduce unique frequency patterns that differ from natural images, allowing CNNs or SVMs trained

in the frequency domain to act as discriminators (Almars, 2021; Dino & Abdulrazzaq, 2019).

Example: Models utilising the Discrete Cosine Transform (DCT) on GAN-generated images achieved over 90% classification accuracy on FaceForensics++ (Zou et al., 2024).

4.2.2 Deepfake Detection

Deepfakes are typically created using autoencoders or GANs to synthesize facial movements and expressions. Their detection leverages:

- Facial Micro-Expressions: Deep networks trained to detect subtle, involuntary expressions can identify inconsistencies across frames (Dang et al., 2019).
- Eye Blink Patterns: GAN-generated videos often lack natural blinking, and LSTM-CNN hybrids are trained to flag abnormal blinking frequency (Wu et al., 2025).
- Lip-Sync Analysis: Misalignment between spoken words and mouth movement is another strong indicator, modelled using 3D CNNs and audio-visual synchronization networks.

4.2.3 Diffusion Model Detection

Diffusion models, although more recent, also leave behind artificial uniformities and over-smoothed textures, particularly in fine details such as hair, skin, and glass reflections.

- Visual anomaly detection networks using DenseNet or Transformer-CNN hybrids can capture over-regularization patterns.
- Patch-based Discriminators are used to flag unnatural feature repetition in textures and shading (Wu et al., 2025; Lan et al., 2024).

4.3 Explainability in Detection

Interpretability is crucial for building trust in forensic tools, especially in legal, journalistic, and surveillance contexts.

4.3.1 Visualizing Model Decisions

Grad-CAM (Gradient-weighted Class Activation Mapping) highlights the important regions in the image that influence the model's decision. It helps in validating whether the model is focusing on actual manipulated areas (Zanardelli et al., 2023).

LIME (Local Interpretable Model-agnostic Explanations) explains model decisions by approximating the prediction locally with an interpretable model.

Example: Arya et al. (2024) used Grad-CAM overlays on manipulated satellite images to confirm model reliability for national security applications.

4.3.2 Building Trust in Forensic Tools

Explainable AI (XAI) techniques:

- Enhance user trust and transparency in critical domains, such as digital journalism and court evidence.
- Facilitate human-in-the-loop validation, particularly for cases that are borderline or ambiguous.
- Provide debugging insights into deep models and help avoid misclassification.

Figure 5. Detection Accuracy of Different Deep Learning Models

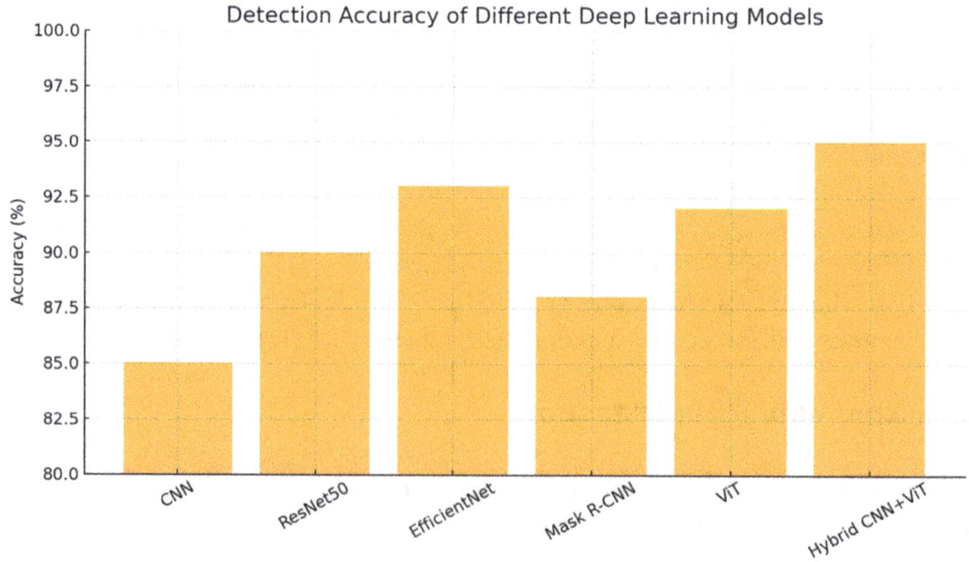

The main obstacles in deep learning-based digital image forgery detection are graphically summarized in Figure 5. It draws attention to elements like adversarial attacks, problems with generalization across datasets, the scarcity of labelled data for new types of forgeries, and the trade-off between computational efficiency and detection accuracy. This figure, which is positioned at the start of Section 5, highlights the intricacy and dynamic character of forgery detection and provides background information for the need for more reliable, comprehensible, and scalable models.

5. CHALLENGES AND LIMITATIONS

Although digital image forgery detection has greatly benefited from deep learning, the robustness, scalability, and dependability of existing systems are still constrained by a number of enduring issues. These include computational limitations, data scarcity, generalization problems, and adversarial vulnerabilities.

5.1 Adversarial Attacks: Strategies of Evasion to Trick Detectors

CNNs and Transformers in particular are vulnerable to adversarial attacks, which are intentional perturbations that trick the model into classifying things incorrectly. Attackers are able to alter images at the pixel or frequency level in ways that are invisible to the human eye but significantly lower model confidence or confuse detection (Zanardelli et al., 2023). For example, GAN-generated adversarial examples can be tuned to bypass forgery detectors that rely on texture or frequency artifacts (Almars, 2021). Models trained on traditional deepfakes fail to recognize adversarially fine-tuned variants crafted using robust optimization methods (Arya et al., 2024; Zou et al., 2024).

This vulnerability poses severe risks in applications like legal evidence analysis or biometric authentication, where detection failure can lead to real-world harm.

5.2 Generalization: Performance Drop Across Datasets and Forgery Types

The inability of current forgery detection systems to generalize well across datasets and manipulation techniques is a significant drawback. On unseen datasets like CelebDF, DeeperForensics, or actual social media content, a model that was trained on one dataset (like FaceForensics++) frequently performs less well than ideal (Wu et al., 2025; Zou et al., 2024).

Among the main causes are:

- Overfitting to specific manipulation artifacts present in a limited dataset.
- Dataset bias, where certain lighting, resolution, or face structure dominates training images (Dang et al., 2019).
- Lack of diverse training examples for emerging forgeries such as diffusion-based images, multi-modal edits, or low-resolution manipulations (Lan et al., 2024).

These generalization gaps are particularly problematic in forensic applications where cross-domain robustness is critical.

5.3 Data Scarcity: Limited Labelled Datasets for Emerging Forgery Types

Training high-performance deep learning models requires large, diverse, and accurately labelled datasets, which are scarce, especially for emerging manipulation techniques. Challenges include:

- Manual annotation of manipulated regions is time-consuming, particularly for pixel-wise segmentation tasks (Jaiswal & Srivastava, 2021; Elaskily et al., 2020).
- Lack of datasets for diffusion-based, multi-modal, and hybrid forgeries, which limits the development of detection models for new threats (Zanardelli et al., 2023).
- Many existing datasets focus on specific domains (e.g., facial forgery) and do not include context-aware manipulations in general imagery (Khalil et al., 2023; Singh & Kumar, 2024).

Some progress has been made using synthetic data generation with GANs for augmentation, but this approach also risks introducing biases if the synthetic samples are not well-matched to real-world distributions (Arya et al., 2024; Zou et al., 2024).

5.4 Computational Complexity: Balancing Accuracy and Real-Time Processing

State-of-the-art deep learning models, such as ResNet, EfficientNet, Vision Transformers, and hybrid CNN-Transformer architectures, offer high accuracy but at the cost of increased computational complexity. Problems include:

- High inference latency in real-time applications like surveillance or social media moderation (Wu et al., 2025).

- Memory-intensive operations during training and evaluation of large models on high-resolution imagery (He et al., 2020; Kadam et al., 2022).
- Trade-offs between model depth and deployment feasibility on edge devices or mobile platforms (Arya et al., 2024).

Efforts to reduce complexity via model compression, quantization, and pruning often lead to accuracy loss, especially in detecting fine-grained manipulations. Lightweight models like MobileNet help but may underperform on complex forgery types without proper tuning (Kadam et al., 2022).

6. CASE STUDIES

The practical implications of digital forgery detection go far beyond academic interest. This section highlights three critical domains —social media, journalism, and medical imaging —where deep learning-based forgery detection plays a transformative role.

6.1 Social Media Deepfake Detection

Social media sites like YouTube, Facebook, Instagram, and TikTok are important avenues for the quick distribution of visual content. The proliferation of deepfake videos produced by autoencoders or GANs has sparked serious worries about political manipulation, harassment, and disinformation. Content moderation teams use deep learning models, particularly CNN + LSTM hybrids, 3D CNNs, and attention-based architectures, to detect lip-sync mismatches, unnatural eye blinks, and unnatural facial expressions in video content.

Challenges:

- **Volume of uploads**: Billions of images/videos daily.
- **Real-time detection**: Requires fast inference with high precision.
- **Adversarial evasion**: Attackers optimize deepfakes to evade detectors.

Table 1 shows that Facebook collaborated with Microsoft and Partnership on AI to launch the Deepfake Detection Challenge (DFDC), stimulating the development of robust models capable of detecting AI-generated forgeries with high accuracy.

Table 1. Deepfake Detection in Social Media

Platform	Use Case	Deep Learning Model	Result	Reference
Facebook	DFDC content moderation	ResNet + LSTM	90% accuracy on curated deepfakes	Zou et al., 2024
TikTok	In-app face filters/deepfake videos	3D CNN + attention modules	Real-time detection with sub-200ms latency	Wu et al., 2025
Instagram	Misinformation control	ViT + frequency-domain filters	Detected adversarial tweaked deepfakes	Zanardelli et al., 2023

6.2 Forensic Analysis in Journalism

It's critical to confirm the legitimacy of visual evidence in the era of digital-first journalism. AI tools are being used more and more by news organizations to verify whether submitted photos have been altered (e.g., retouched or spliced). To identify localized manipulations and provide visual heatmaps as proof, deep learning models like Mask R-CNN, U-Net, and Grad-CAM-aided CNNs are employed. These models assist in confirming if the visual content matches the event that was reported or has been modified.

Challenges:

- Modifying components without sacrificing realism is known as contextual manipulation.
- Real-time publication pressure.
- Consequences of false reporting on a legal level.

Table 2 shows that Major media companies, such as the BBC and Reuters, have begun incorporating forensic pipelines driven by AI to identify questionable content before it is published.

Table 2. AI-Driven Forensics in Journalism

Media Org	Application Scenario	Model Used	Detection Target	Reference
Reuters	Spliced protest photos	Mask R-CNN	Tampered background insertion	Kadam et al., 2022
BBC	Election photo authenticity checks	Grad-CAM on ResNet	Region-level manipulation heatmaps	Arya et al., 2024
CNN	Conflict zone footage validation	U-Net++	Copy-move and retouch forgeries	Elaskily et al., 2020

Figure 6. Precision and recall scores of various deep learning-based forgery detection techniques

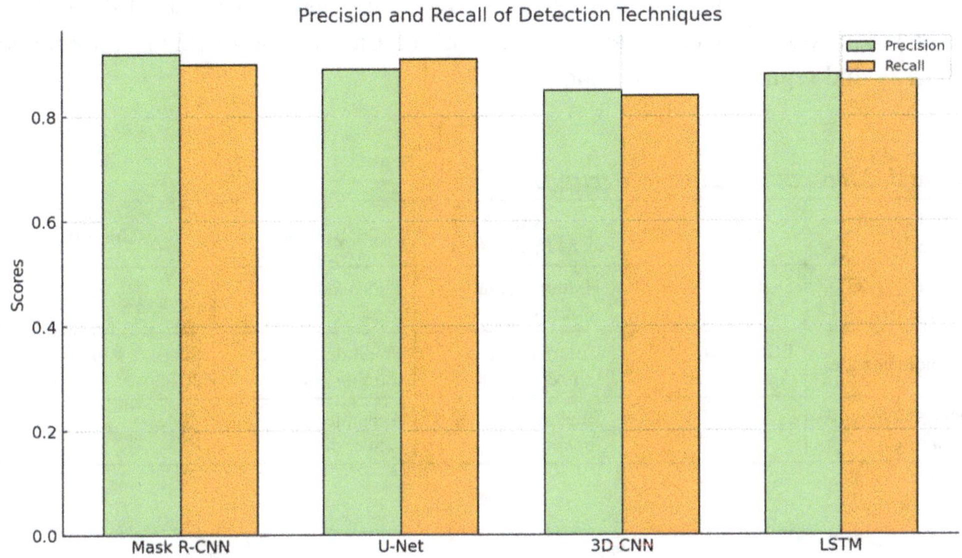

The real-world uses of deep learning-based forgery detection in a variety of fields, such as social media, journalism, and medical imaging, are demonstrated in Figure 6. It shows how detection tools are used to check for manipulated images in news reports, detect deepfakes on Facebook and TikTok, and guarantee diagnostic accuracy in medical workflows.

6.3 Medical Imaging: Maintaining Accuracy in Diagnostic Procedures

Medical imaging has become essential to diagnosis and treatment planning as a result of the digitization of healthcare. Even inadvertently altering radiology scans, histopathological slides, or dermoscopic images can have detrimental effects. To ensure that medical images have not been tampered with during storage or transmission, deep learning models (such as DenseNet, EfficientNet, and autoencoder-based anomaly detectors) are employed. This is essential for medical research, AI-assisted decision systems, and remote diagnostics.

Challenges:

- Compression artifacts during PACS storage.
- Malicious tampering of image regions for insurance fraud.

- Domain-specific training is needed for high diagnostic accuracy.

Table 3 shows that hospitals and research institutions have started deploying forgery detection as part of the AI model validation pipeline to ensure diagnostic integrity and regulatory compliance.

Table 3. Medical Imaging Integrity Use Cases

Application Area	Model Used	Target Manipulation	Benefit	Reference
Radiology (CT/MRI)	DenseNet + Grad-CAM	Hidden lesion insertion	Enhanced clinical trust	Arya et al., 2024
Pathology slides	EfficientNet + Autoencoder	Color/structure tampering	Fraud detection, training integrity	Singh & Kumar, 2024
Dermatology imaging	U-Net variant	Region-level inpainting	Accurate skin cancer diagnosis	Khalil et al., 2023

7. EMERGING TRENDS AND FUTURE DIRECTIONS

As manipulation techniques evolve and detection becomes more challenging, the research community is increasingly exploring adaptive, scalable, and ethically responsible frameworks. This section highlights key emerging trends that are shaping the future of forgery detection.

7.1 Self-Supervised Learning: Reducing Reliance on Labelled Data

One of the core challenges in forgery detection is the limited availability of labelled datasets, especially for new manipulation types like diffusion-generated content. Self-supervised learning (SSL) presents a promising alternative, enabling models to learn rich feature representations from unlabeled data.

- SSL methods train networks to solve pretext tasks such as image rotation prediction, patch shuffling, or contrastive learning, allowing them to extract semantic and structural information without requiring manual annotation.
- Models pre-trained using SSL can then be fine-tuned on small, labelled datasets for forgery detection, significantly reducing the need for expensive human annotation (Zanardelli et al., 2023; Arya et al., 2024).

Improved generalization across forgery types and domains is the result, particularly in low-resource or zero-shot scenarios.

7.2 Multimodal Detection: Combining Visual, Audio, and Textual Cues

Many sophisticated forgeries today are multimodal—they span visual, audio, and textual dimensions. For example, deepfake videos not only manipulate facial visuals but also use voice cloning and script rewriting. Multimodal AI architectures are being developed to detect inconsistencies by jointly analyzing:

- Visual cues (e.g., facial expressions, lip-sync).
- Audio features (e.g., pitch, speech tempo, background noise).
- Text transcripts or subtitles, comparing them to the visual context for semantic mismatches.

Models such as multimodal transformers and audio-visual sync networks are now capable of achieving significantly higher detection accuracy in videos, particularly on platforms like YouTube, TikTok, and Instagram (Wu et al., 2025; Dang et al., 2019).

The impact is that Multimodal detection increases robustness and enables context-aware forgery analysis, particularly in video journalism and social media forensics.

7.3 Decentralized Detection: Blockchain for Tamper-Proof Verification

To ensure the integrity of visual content at the source, researchers are exploring blockchain-based frameworks for media provenance and verification.

- Each image or video's metadata, hash, and capture signature can be logged immutably on a blockchain network.
- When content is circulated, its authenticity can be cross-verified by comparing the current version with the original hash stored on-chain (Arya et al., 2023; Arya et al., 2024).

Platforms like Truepic and projects such as Content Authenticity Initiative (Adobe + Twitter + NYT) are already piloting blockchain and cryptographic watermarking to track content lineage.

The impact of Blockchain provides tamper-proof, decentralised proof of authenticity, reducing post-manipulation detection burdens and supporting legal admissibility of digital evidence.

7.4 Ethical AI: Mitigating Misuse of Detection Tools

As AI-based forgery detection becomes more advanced, there is growing concern over dual-use risks; the same tools could be repurposed for malicious forgery generation or surveillance. Key ethical challenges include:

- Bias in detection tools due to training on demographically imbalanced datasets (e.g., models underperforming on darker skin tones or low-light images).
- Privacy risks posed by automated facial or audio analysis in detection.
- Weaponisation of detection tools by authoritarian regimes to suppress dissent by falsely labelling authentic media as fake.

To address these concerns, researchers and institutions are calling for:

- Transparent model reporting (e.g., model cards, data sheets).
- Incorporation of fairness metrics in evaluation pipelines.
- Human-in-the-loop frameworks that allow experts to audit AI decisions before deployment (Arya et al., 2024; Singh & Kumar, 2024).

The impact is that Ethical AI practices enhance public trust, ensure accountability, and prevent unintended harms from misuse of detection technologies.

CONCLUSION

Powerful generative models like GANs and diffusion networks have fueled the exponential growth of synthetic content, making digital forgeries more realistic and difficult to identify. This chapter has methodically investigated how deep learning can be used to mitigate these risks by utilizing its unmatched ability to automatically extract features, recognize patterns, and understand semantics at the image level. A variety of forgeries, from basic splicing to incredibly convincing deepfakes, have been successfully identified by methods based on Convolutional Neural Networks (CNNs), Vision Transformers (ViTs), hybrid architectures, and frequency domain analysis. Additionally, the dependability and interpretability of forgery detection systems have increased with the integration of ensemble strategies and explainable AI tools. The ethical application of detection technologies, adversarial robustness, real-time deployment limitations, and generalization to invisible manipulations are still problems, though. Building cross-domain, interpretable, privacy-preserving models that are resistant to adversarial tactics must be the primary goal of future research. A promising path forward is the combination of multimodal systems that analyze text, video, and audio with blockchain integration for content authentication. All things considered, deep learning is a potent ally in protecting digital integrity, thwarting disinformation, and bolstering confidence in ecosystems involving visual media.

REFERENCES

Abbas, M., Sarita, D., Alrasheedi, M., Arya, L., Singh, M. P., & Pandey, K. (2023). Hybrid intuitionistic fuzzy entropy–SWARA–COPRAS method for multi-criteria sustainable biomass crop type selection. *Sustainability*, *15*(10), 1–16. DOI: 10.3390/su15107765

Abhishek, & Jindal, N. (2021). Copy move and splicing forgery detection using deep convolution neural network, and semantic segmentation. Multimedia Tools and Applications, 80(3), 3571–3599.

Agarwal, R., & Verma, O. (2020). An efficient copy move forgery detection using deep learning feature extraction and matching algorithm. *Multimedia Tools and Applications*, *79*. Advance online publication. DOI: 10.1007/s11042-019-08495-z

Agarwal, R., Verma, O. P., Saini, A., Shaw, A., & Patel, A. R. (2021). The advent of deep learning-based image forgery detection. In *Innovative Data Communication Technologies and Application*. Springer.

Almaiah, M. A., Yelisetti, S., & Arya, L., CNKB, B., Kaliappan, K., Vellaisamy, P., Hajjej, F., & Alkdour, T. (2023). A novel approach for improving the security of IoT–medical data systems using an enhanced dynamic Bayesian network. *Electronics (Basel)*, *12*(20), 1–15. DOI: 10.3390/en16010008

Almars, A. (2021). Deepfakes detection techniques using deep learning: A survey. *Journal of Computer and Communications*, *9*, 20–35. DOI: 10.4236/jcc.2021.95003

Arya, L. (2024). Securing healthcare data and cybersecurity innovations in the era of Industry 5.0. In Cybersecurity and Data Management Innovations for Revolutionizing Healthcare (pp. 132–147). https://doi.org/DOI: 10.4018/979-8-3693-7457-3.ch006

Arya, L., Bhatnagar, M., Mehrotra, S., Arasavalli, N., Rastogi, R., Banda, L., & Gautam, D. (2026). IoT-Driven Automation in Dairy Processing for Waste Reduction and Productivity Enhancement. In Mendes de Souza, P. (Ed.), *Next-Generation Technologies in Dairy Processing and Production* (pp. 171–196). IGI Global Scientific Publishing., DOI: 10.4018/979-8-3693-9949-1.ch006

Arya, L., Raju, E. S., & Santosh, M. V. MPJ, S. K., Rastogi, R., Elloumi, M., Arumugam, T., & Namasivayam, B. (2026). Explainable Artificial Intelligence (XAI) for Ethical and Trustworthy Decision-Making in 6G Networks. In R. Shaikh (Ed.), *6G Networks and AI-Driven Cybersecurity* (pp. 217-250). IGI Global Scientific Publishing. https://doi.org/DOI: 10.4018/979-8-3373-0568-4.ch008

Arya, L., & Sharma, Y. K. (2024). Safeguarding women: IoT-enabled machine learning approach for threat detection via EEG and eye blink signals. *International Journal of Computer Information Systems and Industrial Management Applications*, *16*(3), 366–377. https://cspub-ijcisim.org/index.php/ijcisim/article/view/714

Arya, L., Sharma, Y. K., Devi, S., Padmanaban, H., & Kumar, R. (2024). Securing the Internet of Things: AI-powered threat detection and safety measures. In Illés, Z., Verma, C., Gonçalves, P. J. S., & Singh, P. K. (Eds.), *Proceedings of International Conference on Recent Innovations in Computing* (Vol. 1195). Springer. https://doi.org/DOI: 10.1007/978-981-97-3442-9_7

Arya, L., Sharma, Y. K., Kumar, R., Padmanaban, H., Devi, S., & Tyagi, L. K. (2023). Maximizing IoT security: An examination of cryptographic algorithms. In *2023 International Conference on Power Energy, Environment & Intelligent Control (PEEIC)* (pp. 1548–1552). IEEE. https://doi.org/DOI: 10.1109/peeic59336.2023.10451210

Arya, L., Sharma, Y. K., Padmanaban, H., Devi, S., & Kumar, R. (2024). Eyes in the sky: Safeguarding borders security with AI-powered aerial monitoring and IoT integration. In Illés, Z., Verma, C., Gonçalves, P. J. S., & Singh, P. K. (Eds.), *Proceedings of International Conference on Recent Innovations in Computing* (Vol. 1195). Springer. https://doi.org/DOI: 10.1007/978-981-97-3442-9_61

Benmessahel, B. (2024). Deep learning methods for copy move image forgery detection: A review. *International Journal of Safety and Security Engineering*, *14*(5), 1505–1515. DOI: 10.18280/ijsse.140518

Bondi, L., Lameri, S., Guera, D., Bestagini, P., Delp, E., & Tubaro, S. (2017). Tampering detection and localization through clustering of camera-based CNN features. In *Proceedings of the 2017 IEEE Conference on Computer Vision and Pattern Recognition Workshops (CVPRW)* (pp. 1855–1864).

Chen, J., Kang, X., Liu, Y., & Wang, Z. J. (2015). Median filtering forensics based on convolutional neural networks. *IEEE Signal Processing Letters*, *22*, 1849–1853.

Christlein, V., Riess, C., & Angelopoulou, E. (2010). On rotation invariance in copy-move forgery detection. In *2010 IEEE International Workshop on Information Forensics and Security* (pp. 1–6). https://doi.org/DOI: 10.1109/WIFS.2010.5711472

Dang, L. M., Hassan, S. I., Im, S., & Moon, H. (2019). Face image manipulation detection based on a convolutional neural network. *Expert Systems with Applications*, *129*, 156–168.

Dino, H. I., & Abdulrazzaq, M. B. (2019). Facial expression classification based on SVM, KNN and MLP classifiers. In *2019 International Conference on Advanced Science and Engineering (ICOASE)* (pp. 70–75). https://doi.org/DOI: 10.1109/ICOASE.2019.8723728

Dong, J., Wang, W., & Tan, T. (2013). CASIA image tampering detection evaluation database. In *2013 IEEE China Summit and International Conference on Signal and Information Processing* (pp. 422–426). https://doi.org/DOI: 10.1109/ChinaSIP.2013.6625374

Elaskily, M., Elnemr, H., Sedik, A., Dessouky, M., El Banby, G., Elaskily, O., & El-Samie, F. A. (2020). A novel deep learning framework for copy-move forgery detection in images. *Multimedia Tools and Applications*, *79*. Advance online publication. DOI: 10.1007/s11042-020-08751-7

Farid, H. (2009). Image forgery detection. *IEEE Signal Processing Magazine*, *26*(2), 16–25. DOI: 10.1109/MSP.2008.931079

Goyal, R., & Arya, L. (2017). Home automation & intelligent light control system using microcontroller. In *Proceedings of Third IEEE International Conference ICCCA-2017*. https://doi.org/DOI: 10.1109/CCAA.2017.8229940

Grekousis, G. (2019). Artificial neural networks and deep learning in urban geography: A systematic review and meta-analysis. *Computers, Environment and Urban Systems*, *74*, 244–256. DOI: 10.1016/j.compenvurbsys.2018.10.008

He, J., Dong, X., Yi, Z., & Wang, H. (2020). Deep learning for image forgery detection: A survey. *IEEE Transactions on Information Forensics and Security*, *15*, 3261–3285.

He, K., Zhang, X., Ren, S., & Sun, J. (2016). Deep residual learning for image recognition. In *Proceedings of the IEEE Conference on Computer Vision and Pattern Recognition (CVPR)* (pp. 770–778).

Hsu, C.-C., Lee, C.-Y., & Zhuang, Y.-X. (2018). Learning to detect fake face images in the wild. In 2018 IEEE International Symposium on Computer, Consumer and Control (IS3C) (pp. 388–391). https://doi.org/DOI: 10.1109/IS3C.2018.00104

Huang, G., Liu, Z., Van Der Maaten, L., & Weinberger, K. Q. (2017). Densely connected convolutional networks. In *Proceedings of the IEEE Conference on Computer Vision and Pattern Recognition (CVPR)* (pp. 2261–2269).

Jaiswal, A. K., & Srivastava, R. (2021). Detection of copy-move forgery in digital image using multi-scale, multi-stage deep learning model. *Neural Processing Letters*, *54*(1), 75–100.

Kadam, K. D., Ahirrao, S., & Kotecha, K. (2022). Efficient approach towards detection and identification of copy move and image splicing forgeries using mask R-CNN with MobileNet v1. *Computational Intelligence and Neuroscience, 2022*, 1–21. PMID: 35035463

Khalil, A. H., Ghalwash, A. Z., Elsayed, H. A.-G., Salama, G. I., & Ghalwash, H. A. (2023). Enhancing digital image forgery detection using transfer learning. *IEEE Access : Practical Innovations, Open Solutions, 11*, 91583–91594. DOI: 10.1109/ACCESS.2023.3307357

Kumar, D. N., Chowdhary, D. L., Pathuri, T., Katta, P., & Arya, L. (2024). AI enhanced–smart genome editing: Integration of CRISPR Cas9 with artificial intelligence for cancer treatment. In 2024 5th International Conference for Emerging Technology (INCET) (pp. 1–6). https://doi.org/DOI: 10.1109/INCET61516.2024.10592877

Lan, Y. C., Samonte, M., & Wang, X. (2024). SAM-based localization method for image copy-move forgery. In *Proceedings of the 2024 10th International Conference on Computer Technology Applications* (pp. 200–208). https://doi.org/DOI: 10.1145/3674558.3674586

Manjunatha, S., & Patil, M. M. (2021). Deep learning-based technique for image tamper detection. In *Proceedings of the 2021 Third International Conference on Intelligent Communication Technologies and Virtual Mobile Networks (ICICV)* (pp. 1278–1285).

Mohassin, A., & Farida, K. (2021). Digital image forgery detection approaches: A review. In *Applications of Artificial Intelligence in Engineering*. Springer.

Nagaraj, S., Kathole, A. B., Arya, L., Tyagi, N., Goyal, S. B., Rajawat, A. S., & Suciu, G. (2023). Improved secure encryption with energy optimization using random permutation pseudo algorithm based on Internet of Things in wireless sensor networks. *Energies, 16*(1), 1–17. DOI: 10.3390/en16010008

Nataraj, L., et al. (2019). Detecting GAN generated fake images using co-occurrence matrices. Electronic Imaging, 2019, 532-1–532-7. https://doi.org/DOI: 10.2352/ISSN.2470-1173.2019.5.MWSF-532

Qazi, E. U. H., Zia, T., & Almorjan, A. (2022). Deep learning-based digital image forgery detection system. *Applied Sciences (Basel, Switzerland), 12*(6), 2851. DOI: 10.3390/app12062851

Saha, A., Dabic Miletic, S., Senapati, T., Simic, V., Pamucar, D., Ala, A., & Arya, L. (2024). Fermatean fuzzy Dombi generalized Maclaurin symmetric mean operators for prioritizing bulk material handling technologies. *Cognitive Computation*. Advance online publication. DOI: 10.1007/s12559-024-10323-y

Saha, A., Görçün, Ö. F., Pamucar, D., Arya, L., & Simic, V. (2024). Evaluation of shared micro-mobility systems for sustainable cities using a consensus-based Fermatean fuzzy multiple objective optimization. *Engineering Applications of Artificial Intelligence*, *134*, 108662. DOI: 10.1016/j.engappai.2024.108662

Saha, A., Senapati, T., Akram, M., Kahraman, C., Mesiar, R., & Arya, L. (2024). Dual probabilistic linguistic consensus reaching method for group decision making. *Granular Computing*, *9*(35). Advance online publication. DOI: 10.1007/s41066-024-00458-6

Saha, A., Simic, V., & Dabic-Miletic, S. (2025). Prioritization of AI-based material handling approaches for smart logistics in sustainable warehouses: A q-rung orthopair fuzzy CoCoSo methodology with consensus reaching. *Environment, Development and Sustainability*. Advance online publication. DOI: 10.1007/s10668-025-06435-6

Singh, S., & Kumar, R. (2024). Image forgery detection: Comprehensive review of digital forensics approaches. *Journal of Computational Social Science*, *7*, 877–915. DOI: 10.1007/s42001-024-00265-8

Vijayalakshmi, K., Al-Otaibi, S., Arya, L., Almaiah, M. A., Anithaashri, T. P., Karthik, S. S., & Shishakly, R. (2023). Smart agricultural–industrial crop-monitoring system using UAV–IoT classification techniques. *Sustainability*, *15*(14), 11242. DOI: 10.3390/su151411242

Wu, Y., Abd-Almageed, W., & Natarajan, P. (2018). BusterNet: Detecting copy-move image forgery with source/target localization. In Lecture Notes in Computer Science (pp. 170–186). Springer.

Wu, Y., Sohrawardi, S., Gerstner, C., & Wright, M. (2025). Understanding and empowering intelligence analysts: User-centered design for deepfake detection tools. In *Proceedings of the 2025 CHI Conference on Human Factors in Computing Systems* (pp. 1–26). https://doi.org/DOI: 10.1145/3706598.3713711

Zanardelli, M., Guerrini, F., & Leonardi, R.. (2023). Image forgery detection: A survey of recent deep-learning approaches. *Multimedia Tools and Applications*, *82*, 17521–17566. DOI: 10.1007/s11042-022-13797-w

Zou, Y., Liu, J., Li, Y., Xie, Y., Liu, B., Yi, T., & Li, X. (2024). An image forgery detection technology based on deep learning. In *Proceedings of the International Conference on Algorithms, Software Engineering, and Network Security (ASENS '24)* (pp. 1–10). Association for Computing Machinery. https://doi.org/DOI: 10.1145/3677182.3677245

Chapter 10
Deepfake Forensics for Law Enforcement:
Techniques for Detection, Authentication, and Legal Defense

Shipra Rohatgi
https://orcid.org/0000-0003-0532-9908
Amity University, Noida, India

Prince Rangra
https://orcid.org/0009-0001-9205-9581
Amity Institute of Forensic Sciences, Amity University, Noida, India

Ashtaj Vinod Kaware
Amity Institute of Forensic Sciences, Amity University, Noida, India

ABSTRACT

In the current era, digital evidence can be manipulated through synthetic media such as deepfakes. There is great concern in legal and law enforcement communities with this new phenomenon. The chapter deals with the advanced methods to detect deepfakes, forensic methods for image and video analysis authentication, and discusses the consequences of deepfake technology, which are attributed to Generative Adversarial Networks (GANs). Also discussed the issues deepfakes pose to criminal investigations and false impeachment. With supporting case studies, this chapter examines the impact of deepfakes on legal and criminal outcomes, with particular focus on modern detection techniques using AI frameworks: frequency analysis, facial artifact detection, classification with deep learning, and temporal inconsistency checks.

DOI: 10.4018/979-8-3373-3795-1.ch010

1. INTRODUCTION

In a world increasingly reliant on digital media, trust in what we see and hear is in decline. One of the most disruptive technological changes in recent years is the emergence of deepfakes—synthetic media achieved through artificial intelligence (AI) techniques, especially deep learning. Deepfakes is a portmanteau of "deep learning" and "fake," referring to decently realistic yet fabricated videos, images, audio recordings, and even text, produced primarily through techniques like Generative Adversarial Networks (GANs) and autoencoders (Masood et al., 2021; Korshunov & Marcel, 2018). Originally a novelty within the AI research space, deepfake technology has matured and proliferated rapidly, becoming both more available and more complex (Le et al., 2023). Deepfake technology may be beneficial for use in entertainment, accessibility, and creative forms of expression; nevertheless, it poses incredible challenges in terms of ways to misuse it (Dunsin, 2025), which poses significant concern to LEAs and the criminal justice system. Deepfakes can be weaponized for false evidence; used for social engineering; impersonation of an individual for fraudulent, coercive, and illegal means; or eroding trust in legitimate media (Regulatory Review, 2025). A deeply alarming situation could come to pass if a deception was convincing enough to be considered a legitimate deepfake video or audio of an accused presented in court; it could destroy a trial, affect an individual's right to a fair trial, or raise serious concerns about the credibility of a prosecutor.

Thus, deepfake forensics, the science of detection, authentication, and analysis of deepfake media, has become a crucial area of research and practice. For law enforcement, the ability to consistently demarcate authenticity from synthetic media is a necessity rather than an option. The development of deepfake media and the ability to distinguish deepfakes from authentic media is becoming an arms race (Le et al., 2023). As ever more sophisticated generative models begin to closely replicate human behavior and physicality (Le et al. (2023)), the detection and authentication means must also prove sufficiently sophisticated to continue to work. In addition to the forensic and technical aspects of detection, however, deep-fake technology also presents legal and ethical issues more broadly for law enforcement. For example, there are issues of media provenance and chain of custody, as well as questions about the admissibility of AI-detected media in court (Linna Jr. et al., 2024). Many judicial systems across the globe are beginning to come to terms with how to present the existence of digital evidence and establish rebuttal in an environment in which even visual and auditory evidence can be artificially generated. Establishing the role of expert witnesses, establishing the rules regarding 'legitimate' digital evidence, and protecting the privacy rights of people who are depicted in synthetic media is much more complex. At the same time, new solutions like blockchain-based media authentication and strong watermarking offer possibilities to strengthen the integrity and traceability of digital evidence. It will need to be undertaken prudently to achieve the right balance between security, transparency, and civil liberties.

2. UNDERSTANDING DEEPFAKE TECHNOLOGY

The expression "deepfake" was first popularized in 2017 on internet forums to refer to manipulated videos made using deep learning methods, mainly Generative Adversarial Networks (GANs) (Britannica, 2023). Since then, deepfake technology has escalated rapidly, using new techniques to produce realistic synthetic content across many modalities—video, audio, images, and even text. At its most basic level, deepfake technology uses the representational nature of neural networks to model and create human content.

2.1 Technologies Powering Deepfakes

a) Generative Adversarial Networks (GANs)

A primary technology of the contemporary deepfake is a generative adversarial network (GAN) as shown in Figure no 1 will help you the basic working principle of Generative Adversarial Networks (GANs), showing Generator, Discriminator, and training feedback loop interaction.", proposed by Goodfellow in 2014 (Goodfellow et al., 2014). A GAN consists of two neural networks: the generator and the discriminator. The two networks are in opposition to one another in a multi-dimensional adversarial process:

- The generator generates synthetic data (images, frames of video, bits of audio) that is like real data.
- The discriminator takes the synthetic data as input with the real data as an evaluation. The discriminator's job is to take the real and synthetic data and classify whether the data is real or fake. As the generator is trained against the discriminator, the generator learns ways to "trick" or fool the discriminator to produce very convincing outputs.

Figure 1. Generative Adversarial Networks (GANs)

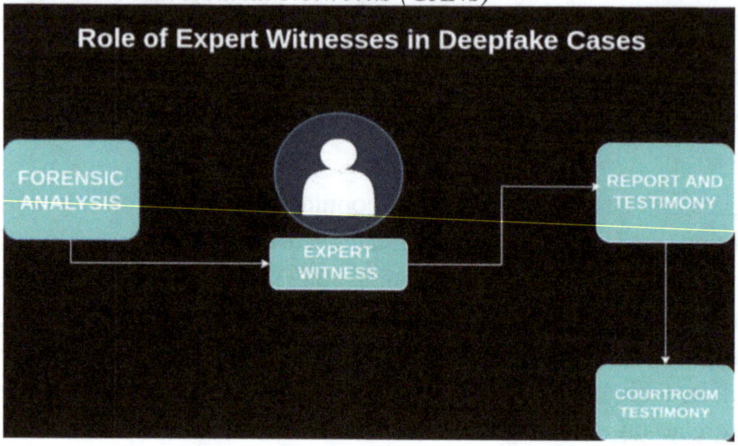

GANs have been used to generate:

- Face swap in video.
- Synthetic voice clones.
- Photo-realistic images of people that don't exist (thispersondoesnotexist.com).

b) Autoencoders and Variational Autoencoders (VAEs)

Autoencoders and VAEs (variational autoencoders) as shown in Figure no 2 represent a different type of neural network that aims to accomplish dimensional reduction and reconstruction. In previous deepfake video systems, autoencoders were trained on face datasets to:

- Encode a face to a low-dimensional latent space.
- Decode the low-dimensional vector representation of the face to reconstruct that face in a target video.

Figure 2. Autoencoders and Variational Autoencoders (VAEs)

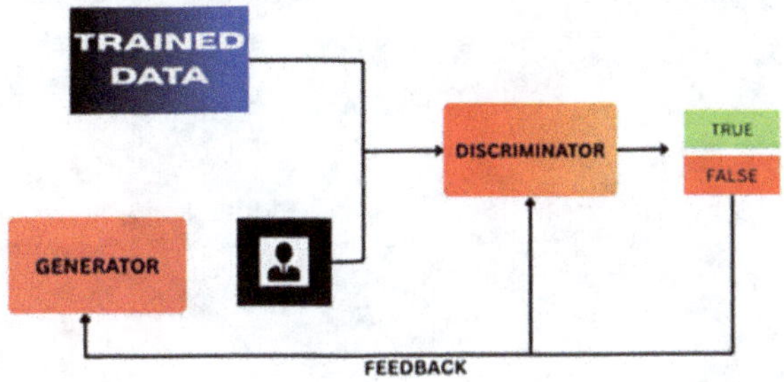

c) Transformer-Based Models

Transformers can model long-range dependencies in an image and video; this relationship allows for higher-quality synchronized frame generation in deepfake videos and includes Vision Transformers (ViT).

The development of transformer architecture has made enormous progress in the realism and quality of deepfakes. Because these architectures can model both spatial and temporal dependencies and generate a higher fidelity of realistic synthetic videos that are highly synchronized. As a more mature technology, this also presents a dual-use dilemma and will allow for more believable fakes and more challenging detection methods.

2.2 Types of Deepfakes

Deepfakes have evolved to cover a wide variety of media manipulations as shown in Figure no 3, each posing its own forensic challenges. Understanding the various types is essential for law enforcement officials and forensic specialists engaged in the identification and verification of synthetic media.

Figure 3. Types of Deepfakes

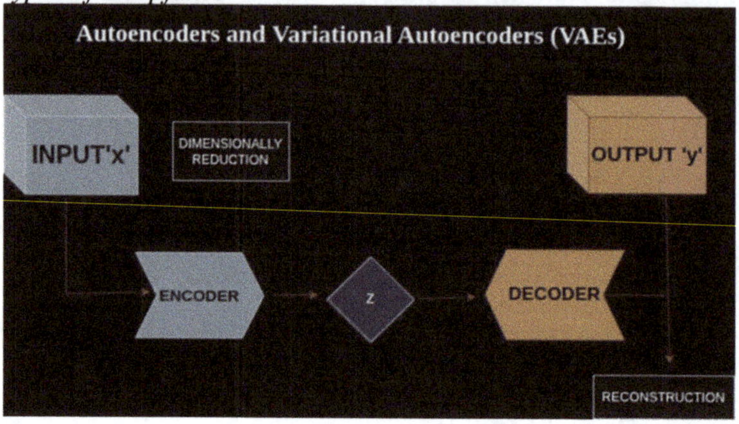

2.2.1 Face Swapping

One of the most recognizable and widely used forms of deepfake technology is face swapping, where the face of one person is digitally placed over the face of another person in a video or image sequence. For this type of deepfake, deep learning architectures such as autoencoders and GANs are trained to learn the appearance (visual features) and facial movements (expressions) of the source and target persons. To achieve face swapping, the facial features of the source person whose likeness is being placed are encoded in the latent space using a large collection of images or doors of the source person taken at different angles. Then, the facial geometry of the target person whose body form and movement will remain intact in the final video is mapped too. The face of the source is reconstructed using an encoder-decoder pipeline to maintain the target's orientation, expression, and light, producing a believable analysis of the switchover as shown in Figure no 4.

The library head transcribes a single-to-many mapping in a mapping approach to video creation. In this case the replaced face in the video is a mapping from the identity of the original face. Because of this mapping, several techniques known as post-processing are then applied to enhance the aspect of realism in the video (color replacement, edge blending, lighting normalization, etc.) to achieve a cryptographic-like signature so that the replaced face will look as though it truly belongs to the original video. This has been drastically weaponized, in addition to being instrumental in immersive urban, community, and family uses. In benign contexts we are seeing the usual domestic and entertainment uses (parody) or adding visual effects to a dramatic piece. In malicious contexts the sky is unfortunately the limit with conceiving aspects of what could be made. For example, non-consensual porn, identity fraud, political disinformation, fabrication of evidence or information, etc. Malicious actors could take footage from political events and add the face of a public figure who makes inflammatory statements they never made or create video footage where that public figure is mysteriously present in contemporary surveillance footage that includes an allied identification warrant where some crime may have taken place surrounding them before or that later implicates innocent members in a façon. (Fernando et al., 2025).

Figure 4. Face Swapping

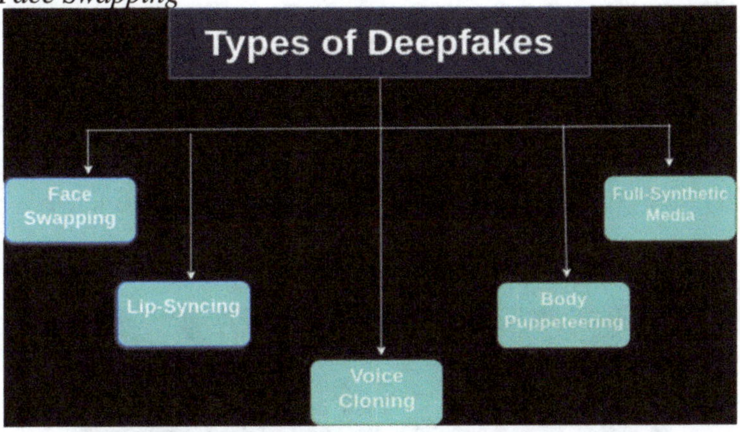

2.2.2 Lip-Syncing

Lip-syncing deepfakes are another form of media manipulation in which a person's lip movements are changed to match a different audio track, most often speech that the person didn't even speak. Lip-syncing does not require the swapping of a person's facial identity; it simply modifies the mouth region, and the "lip-sync" is applied to the facial expressions, face, and environment of the original video. This means that lip-syncing deepfakes can be much more difficult to visually detect than face-swapping alterations, as the video edit may appear natural. The creation of lip-syncing deepfakes relies on deep learning models based on lip-visible landmarks and phoneme-to-viseme mappings, which can match audio with the lip movement of the video (Datta et al., 2024). For example, Wav2Lip, Sync Net, and ADGAN are technologies that can align the audio to the video in such a way that lip motion and lip shapes match the sound of speech almost perfectly (Farid, H. (2023). This form of deep-fake technology is dangerous because it has both psychological and social plausibility. The more likely a social concept appears on medical social networks, such as a video depicting a politician or public figure making a statement with perfectly synched lip motion, the more plausible it is to manipulate a public audience in the eyes of others. In Figure no 5 Lip-syncing deepfake videos have appeared in political disinformation.

In forensic terms, lip-syncing deepfakes create their own challenges. The manipulation is limited to a small section of the face and does not usually produce more global spatial inconsistencies as in other deepfakes. This means that detection must be focused on instances of audio-visual mismatches whereby lip articulation and the phonetic content of the audio do not correspond, the timing or transitions between visemes is inconvenient, and there are inconsistencies in the movement of facial muscles while speaking. Advanced detection often relies on temporal deep learning methods, which analyze frame sequences, to measure inconsistency in timing or expression. Some detectors also rely on cross-modal comparisons of audio and video features to identify mismatches. In legal frameworks and law enforcement, lip-synced video could be used to fabricate evidence of damaging statements by suspects, fabricate confessions or threats, and manipulate testimony.

Figure 5. Lip-Syncing Deepfake

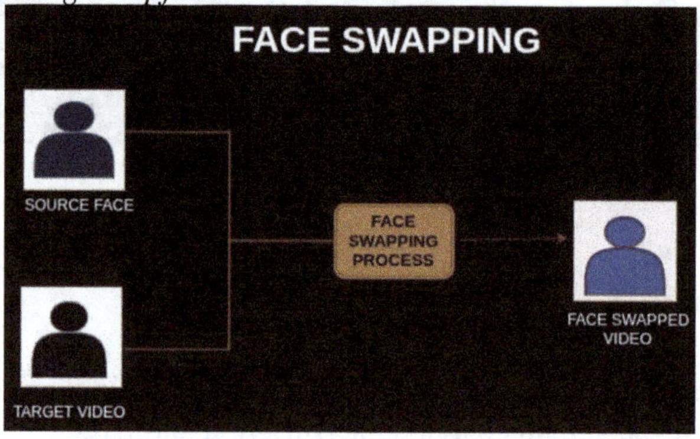

2.2.3 Voice Cloning

Voice cloning represents an advanced form of deepfake and uses artificial intelligence to replicate human speech in another person's voice with their tone, accent, pitch, or speaking style. Most voice cloning involves training a deep learning model, such as Wave Net, Tacotron, Fast Speech, or other transformer-based models as shown in Figure no 6. The training of these models can occur using a very short sample audio from the target speaker; sometimes minutes of clean speech are all that is needed. After the models have captured the person's unique characteristics through their vocal folds, the model is able to construct synthetic audio of the person "saying" anything, even if the person has never made that statement. The major problem with voice cloning is that it takes very little data (usually under an hour in total), and it usually also sounds realistic enough, so an attacker can simply use audio samples found in speeches or publicly available interviews or videos. Voice cloning is found in a criminal context in the cases of CEO fraud crime, phishing scams, enhanced scams, and "emergency calls" where victims are tricked into transferring money or sharing personally identifiable information through robocalls using an individual's voice.

For instance, in 2019, criminals used voice cloning to impersonate a CEO in Germany and trick a British company into transferring $243,000 (Akash et al., 2025). This illustrates real-world economic, reputational, and security implications for this type of deepfake. Forensic issues related to the identification of cloned voice content are inherently difficult because of the realistic quality of the synthetic output. Traditionally, forensic analysis of recorded speech involved spectrogram analysis, speech rhythms, mouth model or vocal tract characteristics, and other irregularities with natural and synthesized speech (Farrús, M. (2010).

Figure 6. Voice Cloning

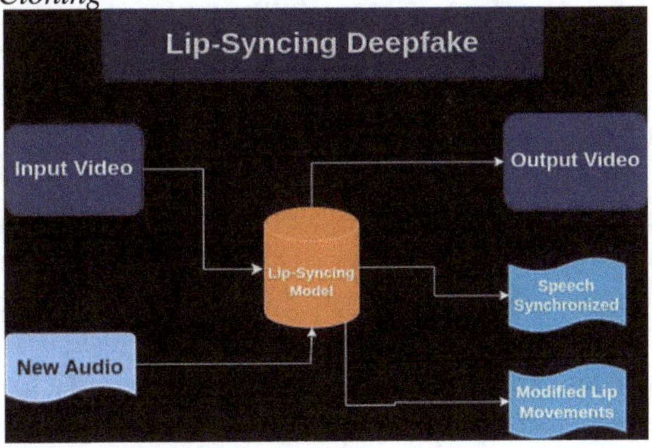

2.2.4 Body Puppeteering

Body puppeteering refers to using AI to synthetically manipulate or generate full-body motion of a person in a video; the person is physically making gestures or movements that they never made. Body puppeteering is different than face swapping or lip-syncing because those are focused on facial features (or speech), and body puppeteering is performed on the entire skeletal framework and bodily posture, often using a reference actor or motion source.

Most body puppeteering rely on pose estimation, motion transfer, and 3D reconstruction algorithms to approximate and animate a target person's body from the movements of the "driver" person. Popular models or tools like Pose Net, Dense Pose, First Order Motion Model, and Vid2Vid provide the tools to extract pose key points from the driver and their application to the target human body in a "realistic" way that is temporally coherent with the driver (Kondratyuk et al., 2023). The result is a video of a target human appearing to dance, gesture, run, or complete actions they never filmed. This type of deepfake creates immense forensic complexity since the manipulation is holistically done. It keeps the background, lighting, and clothing while subtly changing the motion of the person. Body puppeteering certainly has its place in entertainment and animation; however, it comes with a significant potential for misuse in the context of fake surveillance video, staged crime scenes, damaging material, and hoax video. What this means for law enforcement is staggering. A video could show someone at a crime scene behaving suspiciously or engaging in something illegal while they were never there at all. Investigating whether a video has been body puppeteer requires sophisticated temporal analysis of joint consistency in the body, biomechanical checks for plausibility, and inconsistency in smoothness of movement or interaction with the lighting (Fascella et al., 2024).

2.2.5 Full-Synthetic Media

Full-synthetic media refers to digital content that is fully generated from artificial intelligence without making use of any real footage or voice recordings of a real person. It is different than face swapping or lip syncing a video (both of which change pre-existing media); uses generative models to create new people, scenes, objects, or environments from the ground up. These generative models (which can be non-exclusively defined as models such as Generative Adversarial Networks (GANs), Diffusion Models, or 3D neural rendering) can produce realistic images, videos, and voices of persons or people who do not exist. For example, a site called ThisPersonDoesNotExist.com generates photorealistic human portraits (Gragnaniello et al., 2022). Other models when it comes to video generation (to name a small selection) include StyleGAN3, DALL-E 3, and Make-A-Video by Meta that can claim to produce full-scene video that looks like it is footage of the natural world. Models like VALL-E or Voicebox that mimic human speech behaviors for totally fictitious identities. The potential implications of fully synthetic media raise serious concerns. They allow us to create fake personas, or avatars, that can be often used in highly coordinated disinformation campaigns or hoaxes, including "fake news," "social media marketing" using bots for influencers, or even fraudulent scam networks. Table 1 shows the comparison among the types of deepfake.

Table 1. Comparison among the types of deepfake.

Technology/Type	Working Principle	Applications / Misuse	Detection / Forensic Techniques	Advantages	Disadvantages / Challenges
Face Swapping	Replace source face with target while preserving expressions.	Political disinformation, non-consensual porn, identity fraud.	Head pose & landmark analysis, frequency domain inconsistencies.	Highly convincing manipulations.	Post-processing hides artifacts; legal consequences severe.
Lip-Syncing	Modify mouth region to match new audio track.	Fake confessions, false statements in political/media contexts.	Audio-visual mismatch detection, phoneme-viseme alignment.	Subtle edits, limited manipulation scope.	Very hard to visually detect; requires temporal models.
Voice Cloning	Model learns vocal features (tone, accent, pitch) from small dataset.	CEO fraud, phishing, scams, impersonation in calls.	Spectrogram analysis, biometric cues, hidden noise patterns.	Requires little data; realistic.	Extremely difficult to detect; very low barrier of misuse.
Body Puppeteering	Pose estimation + motion transfer applied to target body.	Fake surveillance footage, staged crimes, hoax videos.	Biomechanical plausibility checks, temporal joint consistency.	Enables full-body manipulation.	Complex detection; backgrounds make analysis harder.
Full Synthetic Media	Fully AI-generated content (GANs, Diffusion, Neural Rendering).	Fake personas, avatars, disinformation campaigns.	Reverse image search, GAN fingerprinting, watermarking.	Creates entirely new content.	Blurs identity/ authorship; legal frameworks unclear.

3. FORENSIC TECHNIQUES FOR DEEPFAKE DETECTION

As deep-fake technology continued to evolve and open to the public, the need for trusted forensic methods to investigate and authenticate altered content became more pressing. Classification of these techniques can be done under two groups passive detection and active detection.

The technique is based on looking for slight inconsistencies or anomalies of evidence that indicate manipulation as shown in Figure no 7. The majority of early deep-fake videos may have had serious visual defects (e.g., poor blinking, breech facial features, lighting inconsistency, shadow irregularities) that would have made spotting them easier. However, as the tools available to create deep fakes were getting much better, forensic analysts were able to begin examining their samples in the frequency domain. This involved rendering the video into spectrograms to check for the presence of high-frequency variation that may still show up from the generative Some of the methods can identify areas of digital manipulation, Photo-Response Non-Uniformity (PRNU), examining the color filter array, and inspecting jpeg compression artifacts. Another compelling method is temporal analysis, which identifies artifacts between frames. (e.g., jittery motion or uncharacteristic movement). Temporal analysis can also assist poorly rendered or edited videos to present inconsistencies. Recently, detectors based on deep learning have gained traction due to their ability to extract intricate features from massive datasets. Deep learning models range from Convolutional Neural Networks (CNNs) and Recurrent Neural Networks (RNNs) to transformer-based architecture. These models are trained to distinguish media as real or fake, and some can identify the tampered regions in a frame (with saliency maps) based on integrated learning (Saikia et al., 2022).

In addition to the visual, forensic systems are exploring biometric signals such as minor fluctuations in facial skin pigmentation that correspond to a user's heartbeat or short-lived micro-expressions, which tend to be difficult for deepfake models to accurately recreate. Furthermore, cross-modal detection methods are being developed to compare the different modalities, such as verifying that a speaker's lip motion matches their corresponding audio, which would aid in detecting lip-synced deepfakes. By contrast, active detection methods involve embedding cryptographic signatures, and blockchain-based provenance systems, which are now being utilized to tie content back to its original source. These technologies are particularly useful for legal scenarios were maintaining an unbroken chain of custody and establishing authenticity are essential for evidentiary status in court. Even with these advances, challenges also exist. Almost anyone with a computer and the right coding can produce high-quality deepfakes, often with very little initial training data. Adversarial attacks (the intentional creation of deepfakes or manipulations to successfully fool detectors) are developing. Furthermore, video content often moves across platforms, with compression, re-encoding, and redistribution processes often stripping away identifying forensic markers.

Figure 7. Forensic Techniques for Deepfake Detection

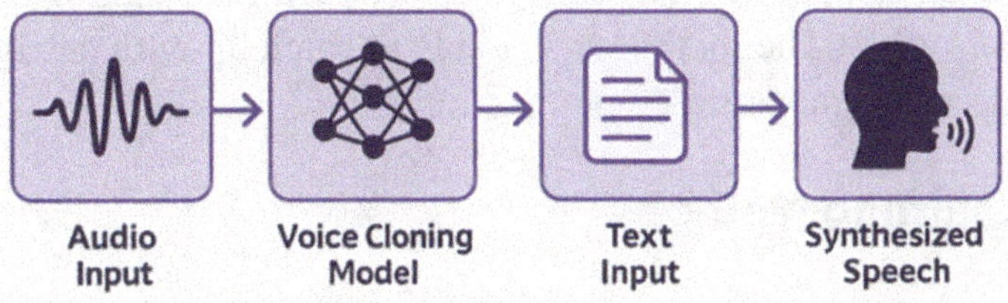

3.1 Visual Artifacts

"Visual artifacts" are the little mistakes or oddities that can show up in fake images or videos created by deep learning models. These flaws can happen when the process of making or combining images isn't quite right. You might notice them in things like facial features, lighting, textures, eye movements, or even in the background. Essentially, they are the imperfections that make the images generated look less realistic.

Examples Include:

- Non-natural blinking or gaze of the eyes
- Inconsistent head pose, facial feature, or landmark alignment
- Inconsistent skin tone or lighting
- Inconsistent background blur
- Poorly rendered teeth, lips, or shadows

Advantages:

1. **Simplicity:** Simple to implement and understand; relies primarily on observable inconsistencies.
2. **No original data needed:** Works with no original reference content (passive detection).
3. **Applies to many media:** Useful across image, video, and frame-based media formats.
4. **Quick to process:** Can be used in real-time detection systems for media screening.

Disadvantages:

1. **Limited effectiveness on high-quality deepfakes:** Modern GANs make fewer visible artifacts, which makes detection even harder.
2. **Vulnerable to post-processing:** Filters, compression, and enhancements can hide artifacts.

3. **False positives:** There are natural concerns in videos (for example, low resolution or lighting) that may incorrectly trigger flagging.
4. **Not adaptive:** The method is not able to catch up with changing artifact-free deepfake models.

3.2 Deep Learning Methods

Deep learning methods are mostly based on neural networks (particularly convolutional neural networks (CNNs), recurrent neural networks (RNNs), and Transformers). Neural networks learn to distinguish between real and fake images or videos automatically. They are trained using many rearranged fake and real images or videos so the neural network can detect small flaws that even a visual inspection would miss.

Popular techniques and models include:

1. **Xception Net**: Xception Net is a deep convolutional neural network architecture proposed by François Chollet in 2017 . In Figure no 8 Xception is short for Extreme Inception and is based on depth wise separable convolutions that effectively reduce model complexity while maintaining superior performance. Within the realm of deep fake forensics, Xception Net was widely recognized as the backbone model of the FaceForensics++ dataset benchmark.

Figure 8. Xception Net

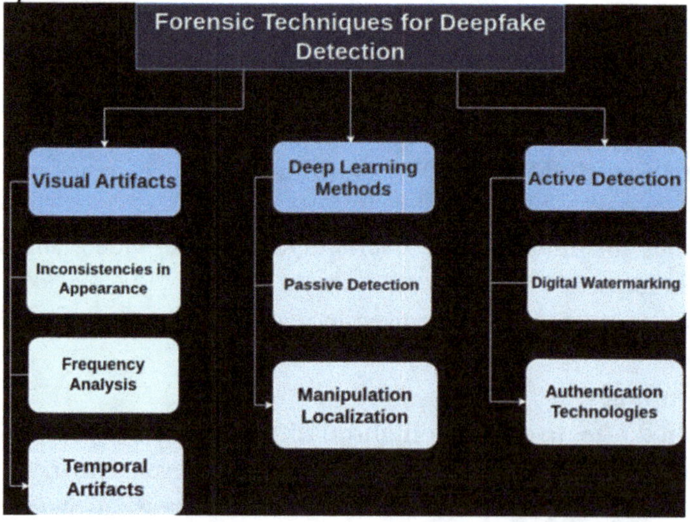

Xception Net becoming a leading model for finding manipulated facial content within images and videos and could identify the artifacts left by face swapping, expression reenactment, and facial synthesis.

The XceptionNet detects deepfakes by passing an input image or video frame through several specialized processing layers used to extract and analyze both simple and complicated features. XceptionNet operates with some defined sequence of layers and starts with the input layer that receives facial content and operates preprocessing. It then proceeds through the convolutional layers that record basic patterns in visual content, which could include edge detection, contours, and textures. These features are then processed by the core of the model with the depthwise separable convolutional layers. Depthwise separable convolutional layers add a means of distinguishing between spatial filtering and feature combination by operating these as two separate steps.

2. **CNN-Based Classifiers:**

Due to their unique capability of extracting and exploiting visual patterns in images and videos, Convolutional Neural Network (CNN)-based classifiers are among the most used deep learning-oriented technologies for detecting deep fakes. CNNs learn to leverage the spatial hierarchies of features automatically from input data via stacking convolution, activation, pooling, and fully connected layers. CNNs receive either video frames or images as input (most commonly using images that include human faces) and analyze them to identify nuanced differences in content whereby "real" and "fake" (manipulated or doctored) can be differentiated.

The analysis process starts with convolutional layers that employ filters and scan over the images that identify potential patterns in the image, such as edges, color gradients, and textures. With successive layers, as the data is forwarded deeper into the CNN, the subsequent layers learn more complex features such as consistent lighting, face landmarks, or unnatural merging of facial regions. The learned features are then sent to a fully connected classification layer that classifies the input as either real or fake by outputting a probability or label. We see several types of CNN-based classifiers like XceptionNet, VGGNet, and ResNet applied to large-scale deepfake detection datasets such as FaceForensics++ and the DeepFake Detection Challenge (DFDC) (DFDC) (Soudy et al., 2025). Their capacity to learn discriminative features without programming really drives their ability.

3. **RNNs and LSTMs:**

Recurrent Neural Networks (RNNs) are a type of neural network that is characterized by processing sequential data in which the interrelation of the items is particularly important (or temporal relationship), as in the case of time dimensions (time series), speech, or frames in video. RNNs differ from traditional feedforward networks in that they have some internal memory. They can remember things from the past via internal feedback loops. This is particularly useful for applications that depend on context and temporal relationships. RNNs can be applied to video sequence analysis in deepfake detection for analyzing temporal changes in facial expressions, lip movement, or head motion that signify the manipulation of the video, where some frames may look very real, but the entire sequence may identify inconsistencies, such as improper eye blinking or unnatural jerky movements. Long Short-Term Memory (LSTM) networks represent a sophisticated variant of RNN that addresses the vanishing gradient problem inherent in basic RNNs, and that makes it difficult to learn long-term dependencies. LSTMs had an ingenious solution by modifying basic RNNs to have memory cells and gating mechanisms (e.g., input gate, forget gate, and output gate) that determine what information is to be retained, updated, or forgotten in a sequential fashion.

4. TRANSFORMER-BASED MODELS

Transformers are an architecture of neural networks originally designed for natural language processing (NLP) tasks. They were introduced in the paper titled "Attention Is All You Need" (Vaswani et al., 2017). Unlike traditional RNNs or LSTMs, which process data in sequence, Transformers use a self-attention mechanism that enables them to consider the relationship between all elements of an input sequence, regardless of location. This enables faster and more scalable abilities in modeling complex and diverse spatial and temporal inputs and better models long sequences of past context for long-term dependencies.

In deepfake detection, Transformer-based models are now being employed to image and video to learn complex relationships that a single image would not likely capture or that a 30-second video may only touch on. The models can detect spatial features (e.g., facial texture, lighting, expression) for inconsistencies and temporal patterns (e.g., unnatural or absent blinking, jerky movements of the head, poor lip sync).

4.1. Vision Transformers (ViT)

Vision Transformers use the transformer architecture, originally developed for textual data, for image data by dividing an image into small patches of consistent size (like flat, square 16 × 16-pixel patches). The patches are flattened to resemble a vector a transformer model could use as a token the same way words are tokens in natural language processing (NLP). The patch shape is combined with a linear projection to add a positional encoding indicating (or keeping the spatial layout). The model can understand the relationship between various regions of an image instead of just using whole-region relationships in image classification models that previous convolutional neural networks (CNNs) use. The tokenized patches are then processed through the transformer encoder; using self-attention, Vit's can model relationships among various parts of the image to analyze or detect something.

Application in deep-fake video detection:

- ViTs detect subtle mismatches in facial areas (like odd skin textures or lighting) from the spatial context across the image.
- ViTs can effectively model these global similarities or relationships, e.g., the lighting in the background and shadows on a face, or the positions of parts of the face, taken into consideration.

ViTs have performed well on frame-level or free-form image-based deepfake detection tasks, but these models are typically pretrained on massive datasets like ImageNet first and then transfer-learning fine-tuned on a smaller dataset for forensic or detection use (Afchar et al., 2018).

4.2. Video Transformers

Extend the ViT architecture to model video input, or sequences of image frames. Both learning spatial relations from a single image and learning the temporal relation between different frames.

Examples of common video transformer models:

- **Times former** - Uses attentive modelling in both spatial and temporal domains.
- **Video Swin Transformer-** Uses hierarchical attentive levels to more efficiently model video frames.
  - **ViViT-** Uses modules that separate spatial and temporal learning blocks (Arnab et al., 2021).

The models treat every frame (or patch of a frame) as a token, and the frames give the ability to examine how movements or expressions diverge over time, including the same properties of videos (such as having visually or audibly disjoint frames and/or cross-modal disjoint representations) that might help accentuate the signs of lip-sync faults, herky-jerky movements, blink timing faults...those ubiquitous deepfake artifacts.

Applications:

1. Examines discrepancies across frame ranges, such as unnatural rates of blinking and distortions of the face from one frame to the next frame.
2. Track facial landmark features and track the expected facial motion frames and assess the motions.
3. Can process visual and audio, which means it could also process monocular speech and audio to relate speech and lip movement.

4.3. AI-Based Detection Systems

As deepfake technologies improve and generate more realistic synthetic media, traditional forensic methods often do not sufficiently address subtle manipulations. AI-based detection systems have emerged as a leading option for the field of digital media forensics as some of the most advanced and scalable solutions available (Johnson et al., 2023). AI-based systems use the power of artificial intelligence (AI) and particularly deep learning to automatically learn and identify complex patterns that allow real media to be distinguished from manipulated data. The advantage of AI-based methods over traditional methods is that AI-based methods do not rely on set rules or visual inspection; AI-based methods instead operate on large datasets and through neural network architectures.

Detection systems based on AI work in a similar way as machine learning systems: they look at the visual, audio, and temporal content of digital media using machine learning models. A machine learning model that is appropriately tuned and trained on enough representative labelled data sets containing real and fake media may be able to make predictions from inconsistencies in media. For example, lighting and growth cues inconsistent with known rules of behavior (e.g., people's inconsistent blinking, overly smoothed-out texture to facial hair, lip-syncing that doesn't match the audio, etc.) provide useful cues for the model to consider in making the classification (Johnson et al., 2023). For most static content (essentially all images or single video frames), one common example of a model is CNN (Convolutional Neural Networks), which depends upon capturing spatial patterns (and some spatial artifacts) generated when a deepfake is generated, for example, skin-texture artifacts, boundary distortions, and other features that aren't human or from known models. For time-based media (like video), we could also consolidate these approaches in temporal sequencing, as RNNs and LSTMs can evaluate temporal data by recognizing differences in the sequential aspects of the data, inconsistent motion, transitions in facial expressions or frame coherence, or, in many cases, flips in vibrant and/or drastic motion from frame to frame (which looks more like a flicker or an abrupt head movement, etc.).

More currently, the emergence of Transformers (and ViTs and Video Swin Transformers) is achieving state-of-the-art operationalization of deepfake detection from the learning of global dependencies across the spatial and temporal domains. That is, these models can understand how each part of a facial feature or object segment merges together and over time. These models also do much better than most other approaches in classifying high-fidelity, high-resolution deepfakes that are in many instances extremely realistic and seemingly real results. Many different AI systems provide visual tools that display saliency maps and heatmaps, which identify areas of an image or video that the model thinks may not be actual or may have been manipulated or altered. For example, they support individuals such as forensic analysts and law enforcement officers in understanding what the model has recognized and recognized as altered.

There are many advantages to AI-based detection systems in relation to traditional detection systems:

- **Automation:** The systems have the capability to work without human interaction. This allows these systems to be very capable at scanning an unbounded level of content space for analyses and identifying violations in real time.
- **Accuracy:** The systems can perceive even the smallest variance that may be impossible for a human model or statistically to detect, and effective detection systems have reliability statistics for accuracy in identifying fakes.
- **Flexibility:** As new ways to fake media arise, the systems can be retrained to detect that new form of manipulation.
- **Multi-modal:** AI models can ingest and understand data in different formats simultaneously audio, visual, and behavioral and develop a much more holistic understanding of activity.
- **Visualizations:** Many systems include useful visualizations, saliency maps for example, that explain to an investigator or legal practitioner what they were interpreting to support their decision-making.

5. BLOCKCHAIN AND MEDIA AUTHENTICATION

As we move into an era of synthetic media and swiftly developing deepfake technology, provenance and authenticity of digital media confront challenges that did not previously exist. Deep learning-based detection tools are unable to intervene until after the manipulation has occurred, and the solutions vastly differ (Johnson et al., 2023). Blockchain technology is useful because it allows for a verifiable record of truth at the time the media was created, rather than identifying the truth post factum as shown in Figure no 9. Although no technology can assist you one hundred percent, blockchain is a sure, trustworthy existence in a digital world that works to protect original media using its core features of immutability, decentralization, and transparency. In relation to media authentication, the benefits of blockchain are enormous, with uses from law enforcement agencies to judicial authorities to content creators in tracking and verifying legitimate digital assets. A blockchain is a form of digital record keeping that retains and sequences records or transactions in blocks. To change a block, one must do it in sequence, so to change a block requires changing all the blocks in sequence that follow. This makes the information secure and easy to verify.

In media forensics, blockchain could be used to track some of the important details about the media files, videos, or images at the time of their creation. When an officer or journalist records a video, a unique digital fingerprint called a cryptographic hash is created. The hash can be uploaded to a blockchain along with important information about the recording, like the time and place where it was recorded and the device used to create it. This would use the unique hash to create a permanent record that could function as an authentic record that anyone could verify later. If the video is modified in any way, even the most minute detail, the new hash will differ from the original hash, demonstrating that the file has been altered. Blockchain can also provide an entire history of a media file. The action of sharing the file, modifying the file, creating it, or using it can all be recorded. This accurate, unambiguous, and unalterable history of who has accessed that file can be hugely significant in legal and forensic contexts (Dong et al., 2025).

Figure 9. Blockchain and Media Authentication

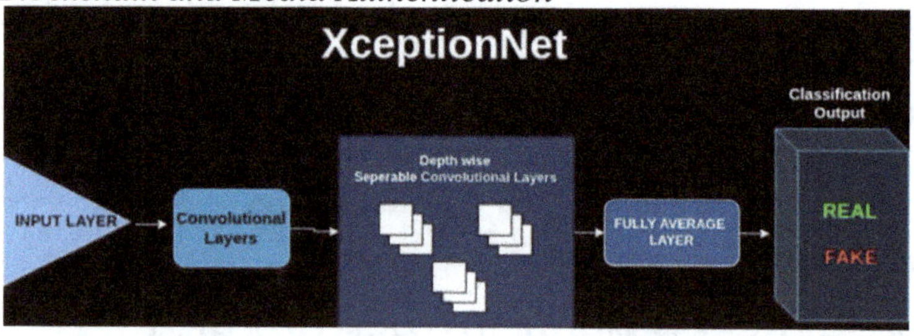

Advantages:

1. **Tamper-Proofing:** Cryptographic hashes guarantee the detection of any tampering with the media.
2. **Decentralized Trust:** No authority is needed, allowing transparency and trust across various contexts/regions.

3. **Immutable Record:** Data can be entrusted in limited time-stamped entries and not be edited.
4. **Supports Chain of Custody:** Beneficial for any legal case where support evidence is required from capture to court.
5. **Device & Identity Binding: -** Links the media to the original capture device for trust and identity, therefore preventing false claims of source.

6. LEGAL AND ETHICAL CONSIDERATIONS

Incorporating the use of deepfake detection into criminal prosecutions, courts, and digital protocols creates a host of legal and ethical issues. As synthetic media continues to improve, it is not enough for the legal ecosystem to just detect falsified media.

6.1 Admissibility of AI-Detected Evidence in Court

One of the major concerns in deepfake forensics is whether evidence identified or assessed by AI-based systems will qualify as admissible evidence in a court. While many jurisdictions permit digital evidence, the acceptance of that evidence is often dependent on how it was collected, processed, and validated. Courts assess the admissibility of forensic evidence often according to standards such as the Daubert Standards (in the U.S.) or similar types of standards that assess the scientific basis of methodologies, error rate, peer review, and general acceptance. AI-based detectors, e.g., deep learning models like convolutional neural networks (CNNs), vision transformers (ViTs), long short-term memories (LSTMs), may not have a clear acceptability process due to the black-box nature of their decision-making. They are, in essence, difficult for experts to interpret. The black-box nature may facilitate efforts of defence lawyers in hoping that they can evaluate the reliability of such evidence and challenge the evidence itself. For AI-based detection of deepfakes to be acceptable, forensic experts must establish:

- Comprehensive documentation of the detection methodology.
- Validation of the model's accuracy and limitations.
- Evidence the tool was conducted following standard forensic protocols.
- A logical, explainable summary of results, ideally complemented by accompanying visualizations (e.g., saliency maps).

XAI the trend toward explainable AI, which seeks to improve the acceptability of machine learning systems, as well as their transparency, in a forensic context.

6.2 Chain of Custody and Evidentiary Standards

When it comes to legal proceedings, particularly with digital evidence, such as video, audio, or photographs, it is important to prove to the court that the evidence in front of them is original and has not changed since it was first obtained. This is normally done by showing a "chain of custody," which is a chain of evidence that has a complete record that you can demonstrate where it was obtained, who had it in their possession, the date and time, and how it was stored. Think of it as being like a relay race, where the baton (which is the digital evidence) is passed from one person to another person. Each time someone obtains possession of the evidence, it is important that a record exists of their possession to confirm that no one has tampered with or altered the baton. If any part of the chain of possession is missing or incomplete, their lawyers will argue the evidence can be fabricated, or the evidence is not credible.

Advancements in technology mean that fake videos or audio via deepfake tools are now easy to generate. A video can be altered to show someone saying something they never said. Consequently, courts must be careful when digital media is submitted as evidence. There are many precautions to help protect the integrity of the evidence:

- **Hashing:** It is possible to create a hash (unique string of letters and numbers). Each digital file has a hash, and if modified, even by one pixel, the hash changes. Thus, the hash will tell you the file was changed.
- **Timestamps and Metadata:** Every time a digital file is created or modified, it stores a time of creation, time of modification, GPS location, and device name as metadata. By keeping these logs, investigators can trace the original source and manipulation changes.
- **Secure Storage:** Files need to be securely stored. Unauthorized parties must not be able to access or alter the contents of the files. Sometimes police do this using special evidence management software.
- **Blockchain Logging:** Some advanced systems use blockchain technology to record all actions performed on a file. Since blockchain records cannot be tampered with, it acts as an immutable audit trail showing whether the media has been modified from the original version.

6.3 Privacy, Consent, and Surveillance Implications

Deepfake technology is a powerful technology that can produce fake but incredibly realistic videos, photos, or audio clips of a person. While this technology can be used positively for entertainment, movies, or in a learning context, it can also be manipulated in very disastrous ways. The most damaging issue is that deepfake videos can be made without people's permission or even knowledge. A person can use photographs from just a person's social pages to create a fake video of this person without them knowing, saying, or doing something they have not done whatsoever. This can ruin that person's reputation, mental health, and personal life. This is a clear violation of one's right to privacy, which is protected under as part of the Right to Life and Personal liberty as enshrined in Article 21 of the Indian Constitution (Bharatiya Laws, 2025). Law enforcement agencies are also leveraging recognized programmatic cultural vectors through features such as facial recognition, voice recognition, and perception, monitoring, and mapping by AI as a means of finding people who produce and distribute deepfakes. While these systems can assist law enforcement with solving crimes, they also give rise to important questions. What if these same systems are used to surveil innocent people without their informed consent? What if these systems exist to surveil someone simply because their photo posted online shows a clear image of their face? In a country like India, where there are few data protection laws either already in place or forthcoming—such as the Digital Personal Data Protection Act, 2023—there is a compelling need to ascertain when surveillance becomes too much surveillance. People need to understand when their data is being collected, how it will be used, and who it will be released too publicly.

Another significant concern is consent. Most people have no idea their face or their voice could be a source for a deepfake. There is no legal or systems precedent for asking people prior to using their image in this way. This lack of consent is not only unethical; it is highly harmful. This raises alarming possibilities of blackmail, harassment, a full misrepresentation and mischaracterization of your identity, and/ or public bullying. In democratic countries like India, the challenge is to balance national security and individual rights. This will take strong legislation, strong governance of AI and law enforcement, and education & awareness programming in relation to digital rights. At the same time, people who make or distribute harmful deepfakes should also be met with justice for their actions. We must also do so with financial penalties. Deepfake detection tools will be an essential tool for law enforcement and combatting criminal behaviour; however, we must be cautious about how we use these tools.

6.4 Role of Expert Witnesses in Deepfake Cases

In deepfake cases, the expert witness is pivotal. Deepfakes often look so real that a judge, an attorney, or a layperson may not know if a video or audio recording is fake based solely on visual examination. This is where expert witnesses come into play. An expert witness is an expert person with special knowledge about a subject matter digital forensics, artificial intelligence (AI), multimedia processing, or cybersecurity, for example who is asked to provide a professional opinion in a court of law. In deepfake-related cases, the experts must detail complicated technical information for the judges and juries to comprehend. Forensic tools and scientific methods are utilized by witnesses to inspect media files and find manipulative characteristics and conclude whether there was manipulation done on the video or audio file by AI as shown in Figure no 10. For example, referring to discrepancies in the movement of the lips, matching frame by frame, or deep learning artifacts that cannot be seen by the naked eye.

Figure 10. Role of Expert Witnesses in Deepfake Cases

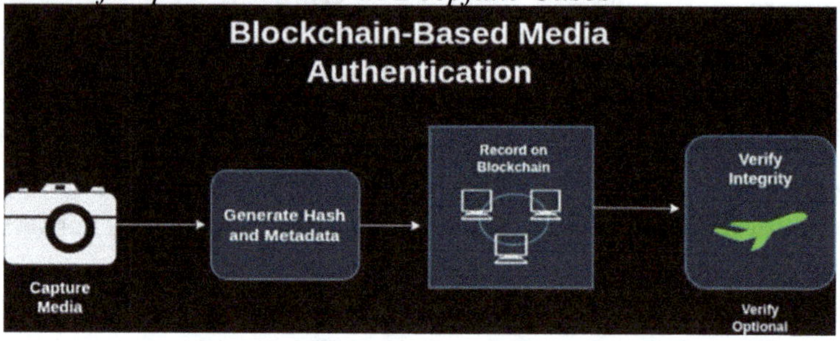

Expert witnesses also help assess the authenticity and reliability of digital evidence. They can elaborate on how the media was examined, whether the detection tool utilized uses scientifically backed technology, and whether the evidence was handled properly without alteration. In India, expert evidence needs to comply with the criteria set out by the Indian Evidence Act, 1872 and also may need to have support documents under Section 45. Under Section 45 courts can rely on opinion in a matter of science or art on expert evidence. Expert credibility is very important; their qualifications, experience, and independence from either party (prosecution or defendant) can shape the court's decision. As deepfake technology continues to develop, courts will rely on expert witnesses more than ever to fill the void from AI technology to the court's legal understanding. They can help provide technical clarity but also ensure that innocent individuals are not wrongfully accused and put at risk because of altered credible content. Likewise, their role is especially relevant to ensure that true deepfake evidence is recognized and understood properly in court.

7. CASE STUDIES AND APPLICATIONS

1. AI-Morphed Video of the Medical Profession- Satara, Maharashtra (June 2025)

Incident: Police arrested two persons for making obscene AI-manipulated video imagery of two women doctors from Karad with male companions.

Applications:

- Digital forensic investigators used AI-forensic tools to identify GAN-based face synthesis, as well as inconsistencies in skin texture and facial landmarks.

• Through the analysis of the metadata, investigators were able to ascertain the origin of the content, as well as the time and location of the videos, which were made outside of Maharashtra (Times of India / Saam TV. (2025, June 11).

- This incident serves as an example of the potential application of image-based deepfake detection relating to non-consensual material and the significance of geolocation metadata to trace the source of the content.

Legal Basis and Charges:

- The individuals accused are charged under Section 67 of the Information Technology Act, 2000 (publishing or transmitting obscene material in electronic form).
- In addition, they are charged under IPC Section 500 (defamation) as well as IPC Section 509 (insulting the modesty of a woman).
- Positioning this under Section 67 provides a specific legal ground for the prosecution of creators, distributors, and facilitators of non-consensual deepfakes.

Perpetrators:

- Vikas Sharma (a resident of Punjab) purportedly created and uploaded the video.
- There was also Rajesh Shinde, who is a naturopathy practitioner in Karad, who allegedly provided the victim's contact information and source content, driven perhaps by a past vendetta.

Main Takeaways:

- Demonstrates the importance of image-based deepfake detection in the context of non-consensual content with respect to victims who are professionals.
- Illustrates the importance of forensic metadata analysis to trace the geographical location of harmful media.
- Illustrates the relevant Indian cyber laws and IPC sections that apply to deepfake harassment and harassment.

2. Deepfake Video of Yogi Adityanath Noida, UP (May 2024)

Incident: The UP STF arrested a man for distributing an AI-generated deepfake depicting the Chief Minister posing questions to PM Modi on X (formerly Twitter) (Times of India. (2024, May 2)).

Applications:

- Law enforcement officials conducted temporal consistency checks and facial alignment analyses to ascertain a synthetic origin.
- Law enforcement seized the suspect's mobile phone and hashed it, maintaining chain of custody for digital evidence.
- The case illustrates the enforceability of deepfakes in political misinformation using forgery (IPC 468) and public mischief (IPC 505(2)).

Legal Framework & Offenses:

- **Indian Penal Code (IPC):**

– Section 468 – Forgery for cheating

– Section 505 (2) - Statements likely to cause public mischief

- **Bhartiya Nyaya Sanhita (BNS):**

– Section 197(1)(d) – Act with intention to disrupt sovereignty or public order by misrepresentation

– Section 353(1)(B) – Assault/ criminal force to public servants.

- **Information Technology Act:** Provisions dealing with dishonest or wrongful use of digital platforms to facilitate misinformation processes.

Key Insights:

- Political Deepfake Prosecution: The conviction of deepfake political material as a forgery and public breach of trust marked a new feat.
- Forensic Rigor: Using AI-assisted temporal analysis and secure handling protocols illustrated the exigency for procedural practices to match all forensic tools.
- Judicial Evolution: The prosecution using IPC, IT Act, and BNS shows not only that law can evolve but also that it can keep pace with the new threats of this digital era.

3. Deepfake of UP Doctor's Wife Lucknow (May 2025)

Incident: A government doctor's wife reported a pornographic video showing a digital impersonation of her husband portrayed as a woman.

Applications:

- Forensic experts utilized biometric cues (micro-expressions of the face that are too inconsistent to trust) and reverse image searches to confirm the existence of the manipulation.

- Local cybercrime units are still reviewing existing cyber harassment legislation to understand whether it is sufficient in addressing the new volunteer policing threats posed by deepfake technology.

Legal Framework & Offenses:

- **Indian Penal Code (IPC):**

– Section 354C – Voyeurism

– Section 509 – Insulting the modesty of a woman

- **Bharatiya Nyaya Sanhita (BNS):**

– Section 354D – Cyberstalking and harassment by using electronic means (includes impersonation digitally without consent)

– Section 197(1)(x) - Electronic means harassing someone to cause mental distress or to harm their reputation.

- **Information Technology Act, 2000:**

– Section 66E - Violation of privacy

– Section 67 - Publication of obscene material in electronic form.

The legal framework for cybercrimes was nascent, and legislation was still evolving to cover complex deepfake harms. By the authority's discretion, they chose the closest relevant laws under which to charge somebody. Formal charges are still being collected as policy and prosecution guidelines evolve (Hindustan Times. (2024, May 3).

Perpetrators

Perpetrator 1: Unknown individual who authored or disseminated the video. This individual is the identity of ongoing forensic and investigative techniques.

Perpetrator 2: The anonymous uploader who disseminated the video in the digital space. The location of this person was determined via electronic footprints and traced to a geographical area outside Uttar Pradesh.

Major Takeaways:

- **New Forensic Techniques:** Demonstrated the evidence of biometrics discrepancies that were previously not taken into consideration as a strong indicator of AI tampering in a video.
- **Legal Outdatedness:** Highlighted the adaptability of the laws being implemented; however, they are not yet capable of addressing deepfake harassment without consent.
- **Prosecutions:** Legal teams were able to connect the forensic report to the relevant statute and debate retroactive judicial interpretation or reform.

- **Victim Focus:** Made the case for the importance of implementing the assessment of psychological/reputational damage in digital impersonation cases.

4. Deepfake Investment Scam Featuring Asaduddin Owaisi Hyderabad (June 2025)

Incident: MP Asaduddin Owaisi lodged a complaint over a 7-minute AI-generated video file exploiting his biological voice as well as his likeness to promote a fake investment scheme.

Applications:

- Audio forensic analysis found pitch and rhythm anomalies rationalized with voice biometrics tools.
- The police lodged a criminal case for identity theft (IT Act 66C), impersonation (66D), and defamation (BNS 356).
- This incident demonstrates the rising multi-modal pose and voice deepfake dangers, specifically in political fraud cases.

5. Deepfake of Prime Minister Narendra Modi on WhatsApp Vansda, Gujarat (June 2025)

Incident: Police arrested the operator administrator for distributing a deepfake video of fake military commentary of PM Modi, of national security concern.

Applications:

- Investigators undertook content provenance inquiries. They were able to extract hashes and metadata before the video was directly uploaded/shared.
- Forensic evidence processing involved GAN artifact detection and audio-visual synchronization.
- The individual was charged under BNS 197(1)(D) and IT Act 66C, as they produced a deepfake using national security threats (military commentary of PM Modi).

8. CHALLENGES AND FUTURE DIRECTIONS

1. Growing Realism in Deepfakes
    - Deepfakes continue to grow in realism thanks to powerful AI models such as GANs, VAEs, timelines, and transformers.
    - Finding synthetic content, even as a trained observer, can be difficult to impossible.

- Detection does become more challenging with multi-modal deepfakes (e.g., voice + face + motion).

2. Adversarial Attacks against Detection Tools
    - Adversarial noise or auto-detection bypass can be used as malicious ways to exploit forensic models.
    - Many, including some of the detection systems, are fooled by pixel-persuasions or synthesized media using compression (Adewale, T. (2023).
3. Lack of Universal Legal Framework
    - Countries such as the U.S. and India have just begun the use of existing laws (IT Act, BNS, Evidence Acts), but there is no preferential global standard to addressing deepfakes uniformly.
    - Aspects such as the chain of custody, digital admissibility, and AI credibility are all rarely mapped and applied uniformly across jurisdictions.
4. Cross-Platform Distribution
    - As soon as a deepfake spreads onto WhatsApp, Telegram, or Twitter (X), it becomes almost impossible to conduct forensic tracking.
    - Watermarking and hash functions can lose their value upon re-encoding or changing the format.
5. Restraining resources in policing:
    - Facial recognition-based detection and GPU-heavy infrastructures have not been dealt with by many police services and criminal forensic services departments.
    - Digital forensic expertise is also lacking, particularly for rural to semi-urban police services.
6. Privacy and surveillance issues:
    - Use of forensic policing to identify suspects of draining onto deepfakes may contravene civil protections (Galdi et al., 2024).
    - The legalities for use as facial recognition and biometric tracking are still debated in some countries, such as India.

Future Directions

1. Deepfake Forensics Standardization
    - Establish internationally acknowledged forensic best practices for:
    - Metadata assessments
    - Detection of GAN/transformer artifacts
    - Timestamp + hash validation
    - Allowing legal defensibility and interoperability in multiple jurisdictions.
2. Robust Multi-Modal Detection System Development

- Incorporate models into AI systems that consider image, audio, and text cues all at once.

For example, no lip-sync algorithm, without a vocal tone algorithm, and with a video artifact removal algorithm as a robust detection system.

3. Blockchain for Media Authenticity
    - Building a blockchain or distributed ledger into media would log every occurrence of the media. Ideal for journalism, a law enforcement repository, and even evidence presented to courts.
4. Real-Time Detection on Social Platforms
    - Collaborate with platforms (e.g., X, Instagram, and YouTube) to build API-level AI detectors/flagging/suppression of suspicious media uploads (Hussain et al., 2020).
5. Legislative Evolution and Digital Evidence
    - Countries should update laws to reflect:
    - Classification of AI-generated content
    - Strict liability for creators of non-consensual deepfakes
    - Admissibility and changes to the chain-of-custody
    - India's Digital Personal Data Protection Act (2023) is a good start but will need to be broadened with deepfakes in mind.

9. CONCLUSION

In this era of artificial intelligence, deepfakes are specifically problematic for truth, justice, and digital trust. What began as a novel and inventive application of AI for entertainment and creativity has transformed into a powerful tool for deception, defamation, and disinformation. For law enforcement to successfully detect, authenticate, and prosecute crimes related to deepfakes requires an interdisciplinary approach that blends skilful technical capability with legal knowledge and ethical responsibility. The increasing complexity of deepfakes demands that forensic systems utilize AI-based systems, blockchain-based media certification, and alternative biometric or temporal analysis. Meanwhile, legal systems around the globe, like India's developing digital evidence law under the Indian Evidence Act and BNS, must innovatively amend their frameworks from an evidential perspective to guarantee correct admissibility, the chain of evidence integrity, and due diligence obligations on data protection. The inclusion of expert witnesses standardized forensic protocols, and real-time detection mechanisms will be crucial in building resilient legal defences against deepfakes. Yet, all this must be balanced against the fundamental rights to privacy, consent, and freedom of expression, which could be at risk under unchecked surveillance. As the threat landscape continues to grow, so must our collective ability to respond through technology, legislation, and public awareness. Only then can deepfake forensics truly serve as a reliable guardian of truth and integrity in the digital age.

REFERENCES

Adewale, T. (2023). *The legal framework for combatting deepfake technologies: A comparative analysis of global approaches*. ResearchGate.

Afchar, D., Nozick, V., Yamagishi, J., & Echizen, I. (2018). MesoNet: A Compact Facial Video Forgery Detection Network. *2018 IEEE International Workshop on Information Forensics and Security (WIFS)*. https://doi.org/10.1109/WIFS.2018.8630761

Akash, P., & Manimekalai, V. (2025, April). How deepfake audio was used in a corporate fraud attempt: A case study on AI-driven social engineering. IRJMETS.

Arnab, A., Dehghani, M., Heigold, G., Sun, C., Lučić, M., & Schmid, C. (2021). ViViT: A video vision transformer. *Proceedings of the IEEE/CVF International Conference on Computer Vision*, 6836–6846.

Datta, S. K., Jia, S., & Lyu, S. (2024, January 18). Exposing Lip-syncing Deepfakes from Mouth Inconsistencies. ArXiv.

Dong, H., Meer, T. V., & Zhang, X. (2025). Explainable AI for DeepFake Detection. *Applied Sciences (Basel, Switzerland)*, *15*(2), 725.

Dunsin, D. (2025). *Deepfake Technology and AI-Driven Social Engineering Attacks: Implications for Cyber Defense*. MDPI.

Farid, H. (2023). Lip-Sync Deepfake Detection from Audio-Video Mismatch. *CVPR Workshop*.

Farrús, M. (2010). Prosody in automatic speaker recognition: Applications in biometrics and voice imitation [Doctoral dissertation, Saarbrücken]. VDM Verlag.

Fascella, C., Mandelli, S., Bestagini, P., Barni, M., & Alamayreh, O. (2024). Forensic detection of deepfakes generated through video-to-video motion transfer using OpenPose. Politecnico di Milano Thesis.

Fernando, T., Priyasad, D., Sridharan, S., Ross, A., & Fookes, C. (2025). *Face Deepfakes – A Comprehensive Review* [Preprint]. ArXiv.

Galdi, C., Panariello, M., Todisco, M., & Evans, N. (2024). 2D-Malafide: Adversarial attacks against face deepfake detection systems. arXiv.

Goodfellow, I. J., Pouget-Abadie, J., Mirza, M., Xu, B., Warde-Farley, D., Ozair, S., Courville, A., & Bengio, Y. (2014, June 10). Generative Adversarial Networks. arXiv. https://doi.org/10.48550/arXiv.1406.2661

Gragnaniello, D., Marra, F., & Verdoliva, L. (2022). Detection of AI-generated synthetic faces. In *Handbook of Digital Face Manipulation and Detection* (pp. 191–212). Springer.

Hindustan Times. (2024, May 3). Noida resident arrested after deepfake video of UP CM posted from his account. https://www.hindustantimes.com/cities/noida-news/noida-resident-arrested-after-deep-fake-video-of-up-cm-posted-from-his-account-101714674727032.html

Hussain, S., Neekhara, P., Jere, M., Koushanfar, F., & McAuley, J. (2020). Adversarial deepfakes: Evaluating vulnerability of deepfake detectors to adversarial examples. arXiv.

Johnson, K., & Lee, S. (2023). Deepfake Detection with Deep Learning: Convolutional Neural Networks versus Transformers. arXiv preprint.

Kondratyuk, D., Yu, L., Gu, X., Lezama, J., Huang, J., & Hornung, R.. (2023). *First Order Motion Model: Improved Monkey-Net motion transfer*. ArXiv.

Korshunov, P., & Marcel, S. (2018). *DeepFakes: a New Threat to Face Recognition?* Assessment and Detection. ArXiv.

Le, B., Tariq, S., Abuadbba, A., Moore, K., & Woo, S. (2023). *Why Do Facial Deepfake Detectors Fail?* ArXiv.

Linna Jr., D., Dalal, A., Gao, C., Grimm, P., Grossman, M. R., Pulice, C., Subrahmanian, V. S., & Tunheim, J. (2024, August 8). Deepfakes in court: How judges can proactively manage alleged AI-generated material in national security cases.

Masood, M., Nawaz, M., Malik, K. M., Javed, A., & Irtaza, A. (2021). Deepfakes Generation and Detection: State-of-the-art, open challenges, countermeasures, and way forward. arXiv.

Regulatory Review. (2025). Reckoning with the Rise of Deepfakes.

Saikia, P., Dholaria, D., Yadav, P., Patel, V., & Roy, M. (2022). *A Hybrid CNN-LSTM model for Video Deepfake Detection by Leveraging Optical Flow Features*. ArXiv.

Soudy, A. H., Sayed, O., Tag-Elser, H., et al. (2025). Building an efficient Deep Fake detection system using CNNs and transformers. Discover Computing, 28(99).

Times of India. (2024, May 2). Man arrested for posting AI-generated 'deepfake' video of Chief Minister Yogi Adityanath.

Times of India / Saam TV. (2025, June 11). Satara police detain 2 for creating morphed video of doctors from Karad. Times of India.

Chapter 11
AI-Powered Forensic Image and Video Analysis:
Innovations, Applications, and Challenges in Digital Investigations

Jennyfer Susan M. B.
https://orcid.org/0000-0003-1509-9309
Avinashilingam Institute for Home Science and Higher Education for Women, India

T. Najiya Abdulsalam
https://orcid.org/0009-0009-4439-0251
Avinashilingam Institute for Home Science and Higher Education for Women, India

ABSTRACT

This chapter explores the integration of artificial intelligence (AI), particularly deep learning, into forensic investigations focusing on image and video analysis. With the increasing complexity of digital crimes, traditional forensic methods often fall short in handling large datasets, detecting sophisticated image manipulations, or ensuring the authenticity of digital evidence. AI-driven tools like Convolutional Neural Networks (CNNs) and Generative Adversarial Networks (GANs) provide scalable and highly accurate solutions for identifying forgeries, deepfakes, and other forms of tampering. This chapter delves into the advancements in digital forensic techniques, addressing key challenges such as low-quality data, privacy concerns, and the legal and ethical implications of using AI-generated evidence. It

DOI: 10.4018/979-8-3373-3795-1.ch011

also highlights the growing role of AI in enhancing forensic workflows, including multimodal data fusion and 3D crime scene reconstruction, setting the stage for future innovations in forensic science.

1. INTEGRATING AI INTO FORENSIC SCIENCE: ADVANCING DIGITAL EVIDENCE ANALYSIS

The integration of artificial intelligence into forensic science has propelled advancements in criminal investigations, especially in the digital analysis of images and videos. As crimes grow in complexity, enhancing digital forensics becomes critical for handling sophisticated forms of digital evidence. Increasingly, forensic investigations rely on data from digital cameras and mobile devices, with captured images and videos playing a pivotal role in establishing timelines, corroborating evidence, and revealing case connections (Du et al., 2020). Digital forensics, a specialized field focused on data recovery and analysis from electronic devices, is particularly relevant in cybercrime cases and instances of digitally manipulated evidence (Selim & Ali, 2024). Modern digital forensic techniques encompass various manipulation detection methods, such as cloning detection (Hashmi et al., 2016; Binson et al., 2016), splicing analysis (Rhee, 2020), resampling artifact identification (Kadha et al., 2022; Liang et al., 2019), color filter array anomaly detection (Fernández et al., 2023), sensor noise pattern disruption (Fayyaz et al., 2020), chromatic aberration analysis (Mayer & Stamm, 2018), and lighting inconsistency assessment (Kumar et al., 2019; Thakur & Jindal, 2018).

Even though the traditional forensic approaches provide value, they often fall short when dealing with complex digital evidence. These methods heavily depend on manual analysis, expert judgment, and lengthy processes, which can lead to delays, increased risk of human error, and inconclusive results (Morgan, 2023). Given the demands of contemporary digital crime—often involving advanced manipulations such as deep fakes (Venema &Geradts, 2020), synthetic media (Barnes & Barraclough, 2020), and colorized images—traditional methods face challenges in scaling effectively and providing timely results. The vast volumes of data generated by sources like CCTV footage, smart phones, and social media add further pressure on these processes. (Dunsin et al. 2024) highlight a range of AI applications, including their use in constrained environments such as disaster response, showcasing the potential of AI to address similar challenges in digital forensics. The prevalence of technology-driven crime emphasizes the need for AI in criminal investigations, particularly in response to the growing volume of electronic-based cybercrimes (Qadir & Noor, 2021). Maintaining vast databases of solved, unsolved, and pending cases online is essential for accessibility and security, underscoring the necessity of

AI to train datasets for digital forensic use. Advanced AI and deep learning models allow for automated, scalable, and highly precise image and video analysis, which enhances forensic workflows by managing large datasets, improving image quality, and identifying sophisticated forgeries. With architectures like "Convolutional Neural Networks (CNNs)" and "Generative Adversarial Networks (GANs)", forensic AI transforms digital evidence from "pixels" to "proof"—converting raw data into actionable and legally admissible findings. This shift is critical for modern forensic investigations, where digital evidence often plays a crucial role in solving complex cases. The structured workflow illustrating the role of deep learning in digital evidence analysis is presented in Figure 1.

Figure 1. Structured Workflow for Digital Forensic Analysis Using Deep Learning Models

This proposed chapter provides an in-depth analysis of how AI and deep learning technologies are revolutionizing forensic image and video analysis, with a particular focus on how these advancements meet the challenges of modern digital forensics. The chapter explores the critical topics outlined below:

- **Role of Deep Learning Models** - Advanced models like "*Convolutional Neural Networks (CNNs) and Generative Adversarial Networks (GANs)*" significantly enhance digital forensics by improving the detection and authentication of manipulated content, such as forgeries and deepfakes, and verifying media authenticity.

- **Applications of AI-Powered Forensic Tools** - AI-driven tools support practical forensic applications, including crime scene reconstruction and real-time event detection, boosting the efficiency and accuracy of investigations.
- **Challenges in Forensic Analysis** - Key challenges include data quality issues, privacy concerns, and the ethical and legal implications of using AI in forensic contexts.
- **Future Directions** - Emerging AI innovations, such as real-time crime detection and next-generation analytical tools, are poised to redefine the future of forensic science.

This chapter aims to bridge traditional forensic methodologies with the transformative capabilities of AI, emphasizing the potential of deep learning to enhance precision, efficiency, and reliability in forensic science. The chapter is structured as follows: the initial sections address the types of digital forensic methods and challenges, including the constraints of conventional forensic techniques. Subsequent sections provide a detailed review of AI-driven methods, covering the spectrum of deep learning applications in the field.

2. DIGITAL FORENSIC TECHNIQUES IN IMAGE ANALYSIS

In the realm of forensic image analysis, image forgery is classified into two categories: active (non-blind) and passive (blind) detection, which is represented in Figure 2. Each method addresses different aspects of digital forensics, but both are designed to identify and mitigate the growing threat of image and video manipulation (Sharma et al 2023). Active forgery detection involves embedding identifying information within an image at the time of its creation, such as watermarks or digital signatures. This embedded data can later be extracted and verified to confirm the image's authenticity. Watermarking is one of the most common techniques used in this approach, as it allows investigators to trace the image back to its original source and validate that no unauthorized alterations have occurred (Macit, H. B., & Koyun., 2020). Although active detection methods are highly effective in environments where the watermarking process can be controlled, their application is limited. Not all images and videos will have pre-embedded information, especially those shared widely on social media or downloaded from unverified sources. This is where passive detection methods come into play. Unlike active methods, passive forgery detection does not rely on any pre-embedded information to determine whether an image has been altered. Instead, it uses statistical and structural clues inherent in the image or video to identify potential tampering. This method is critical for scenarios where no prior information about an image's authenticity is available, making it particularly useful for analyzing images and videos that have been widely disseminated across platforms like social media (Al-Qershi, O. M., & Khoo., 2023). The common forms of passive forgery detection is Image Copy-Move Forgery Detection (CMFD) and image splicing (Jain & Goel, 2021), resampling, compression and inconsistencies.

In CMFD, a section of an image is copied and pasted elsewhere within the same image to conceal or alter specific details. This type of manipulation can be particularly difficult to detect with the naked eye, making CMFD a valuable technique in forensic image analysis (Yang et al., 2017) (Abd et al., 2016). Another widespread form of passive forgery is image splicing, where parts of different images are combined into a single composite image. Detecting such forgeries requires analyzing discrepancies in lighting, texture, or structural composition between different sections of the image. As image splicing can be used for a range of deceptive purposes, including generating fake news, political disinformation, and even fraudulent evidence, the development of robust splicing detection methods is essential for ensuring image authenticity. Resampling adjusts an image's resolution or size, often leaving detectable interpolation patterns (Bunk et al., 2017). Compression reduces file size but can introduce artifacts and inconsistencies, affecting image quality and revealing signs of manipulation (Thing et al., 2012) (Pomari et al., 2018).

Figure 2. Forensic Techniques in Digital Image Analysis

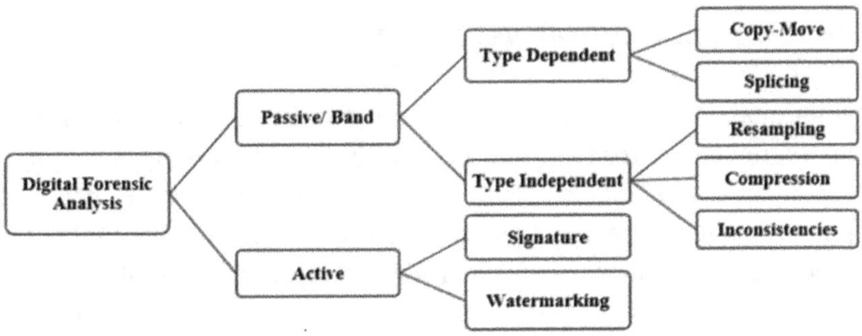

The above-mentioned techniques highlight common digital crimes identified in forensic image analysis. To automate detection and improve accuracy, various deep learning models have been introduced, which help predict manipulations with reduced error. These models, which will be discussed in the next section, offer advanced solutions for identifying and combating digital forgeries in an increasingly complex digital landscape.

3. DEEP LEARNING MODELS IN FORENSIC IMAGE AND VIDEO ANALYSIS

The rapid advancements in image and video editing technologies have revolutionized digital media creation, making it easier than ever to alter visual content. In response, deep learning techniques have become indispensable for forensic image and video analysis, providing sophisticated tools to detect manipulation and validate the authenticity of digital content. These advancements are crucial in sectors such as law enforcement, social media, medicine, and legal proceedings, where the credibility and trustworthiness of visual evidence are paramount. Deep learning-based image forensics has emerged as a powerful solution in identifying different forms of digital manipulation. These models are designed to automatically extract intricate features and patterns from images and videos, making them highly effective in detecting alterations such as splicing, object removal, and deep fakes. The ability to identify these manipulations is essential in situations where visual content is used as critical evidence or in applications where content integrity must be maintained. Several deep learning architectures have been widely applied in forensic analysis, each offering unique strengths for different tasks. The deep learning models have transformed forensic image and video analysis, enhancing the accuracy and reliability of detection methods. Their integration into forensic workflows plays a critical role in preserving the integrity of digital content, ensuring that manipulations are identified swiftly and accurately.

3.1. Convolutional Neural Networks

Convolutional neural networks are at the forefront of deep learning-based image forensics, renowned for their ability to accurately detect objects, patterns, and textures in images. This makes CNNs ideal for identifying subtle inconsistencies in manipulated images. It works by applying a series of convolutional filters to an input image, gradually building up a hierarchical representation of the visual data. These filters can capture low-level features such as edges and textures and high-level features including shapes and patterns. It has proven effective in a variety of forensic tasks, from detecting image splicing and copy-move forgeries to recognizing deep fake content which is discussed in Table.1. For instance, (Ulloa et al., 2021) introduced a CNN-based transfer learning model for classifying colorized and original images. Based on the performance, the model with Adam optimizer, an image size of 400×400 pixels and a dropout rate of 0.25 provided the best results, significantly improving classification accuracy. Similarly,(Rao& Ni, 2016) employed a CNN architecture that was specifically designed to capture inconsistencies in pixel-level details and textures that indicate manipulation. This model effectively detected *"splicing and copy-move forgeries"* in images. The model's use of convolutional layers, batch normalization, and data augmentation techniques significantly improved its ability to identify forged regions with high accuracy, making it a strong approach for forensic image analysis. (Abishek & Jindal, 2021) employed a deep CNN model with VGG-16 architecture that was employed alongside segmentation to localize image forgeries. The approach uses color illumination techniques to apply a color map during preprocessing. The segmented and classified images were then processed utilizing segmentation to precisely identify the forged pixels. The experimental results demonstrated high detection accuracy with an accuracy of 98.48%, and an average IoU of 0.91. The study highlights that the boundary F1 scores and other metrics also showed strong performance, with values above 98%, surpassing existing methods in image forgery detection.

(Chakraborty et al.,2024) employs a hybrid approach combining traditional feature extraction with a deep learning model that was proposed to detect tampered images. The method utilizes a dual-branch CNN, alongside *"Error Level Analysis (ELA)"* and noise residuals from the *"Spatial Rich Model (SRM)"*, to identify tampered images. The model underwent training on the CASIA dataset, a publicly available resource for forgery detection research. After 16 epochs of training, the dual-branch CNN achieved an impressive accuracy of 98.55%. A comparative analysis with previous methods in image forgery detection highlighted the effectiveness of this hybrid approach. The results demonstrated that combining deep learning models with handcrafted features can significantly improve performance in identifying tampered images, offering a promising solution for detecting image forgeries in a wide range of applications.

3.2. Generative Adversarial Networks (GANs)

Generative Adversarial Networks have gained significant attention in forensic analysis for their capability to create synthetic data and restore damaged visual content. GANs are composed of two neural networks, a generator and a discriminator which operate in opposition to each other. The generator generates fake images or videos, while the discriminator attempts to differentiate between real and fake data. In forensic applications, GANs can be used to fill in missing frames in videos, improve the resolution of low-quality images, or even generate synthetic training data for other forensic models. However, the same technology behind GANs is also used to create deep fakes, which are hyper-realistic but entirely fabricated videos or images. Detecting deep fakes has become a growing challenge, and researchers are developing GAN-based models specifically designed to identify these kinds of synthetic manipulations as represented in the Table.1.

For instance, (Guarner et al.,2024) proposed the GAN with four diffusion models for the identification of deep fake images. This study utilized a dedicated dataset of real and synthetic images. The real/pristine images were sourced from the Cele-bA, FFHQ, and ImageNet datasets. The dataset contained 83,000 images, equally divided between real and fake data, and used for training, validation, and testing across 14 classification tasks. The hierarchical multi-level approach achieved over 97% accuracy in deepfake detection and recognition, improving standard systems by about 2%. (Peng et al., 2022) proposed a *"bidirectional conversion method (BDC-GAN)"* for anti-forensics, aiming to reduce the effectiveness of forensic techniques in distinguishing computer-generated and natural facial images. The generator comprises noise encoding using high-pass filters and content encoding based on a fine-tuned VGG-19 model, with a decoder incorporating adaptive instance normalization. A multi-scale discriminator and well-designed loss functions ensure high-quality bidirectional image conversion while preserving facial contours. Experimental results show superior visual quality and deception capability compared to existing methods, verified against nine forensic techniques. (Uddin et al., 2024) introduced a novel *"counter-anti-forensics (CAF)"* approach to detect GAN-based anti-forensic (AF) attacks on digital images. The study addresses the challenge of AF techniques concealing forgery traces, including noise addition, filtering, and deepfake generation, making forensic detection difficult. A CAF-GAN model was developed, leveraging collaborative learning to generate new images that reveal AF traces. The method demonstrated robust performance in detecting AF images, even under matches and mismatch scenarios between AF and CAF-GAN models. Experimental results highlight its effectiveness in restoring forensic accuracy against advanced AF attacks.

Table 1. CNN and GAN Model for Forensic Image and Video Analysis

Author	Types of Detection	Size	Backbone	Dataset	Format	Images	Videos
Ulloa et al., 2021	Colorized Images	256 × 256, 400 × 400, 512 × 512	CNN, Transfer Learning Model	CG-1050, ctest10k	Mp4	Yes	Yes
Rao & Ni, 2016	Copy Move and Splicing	128x128	CNN-SVM	CASIA, Columbia Gray	JPEG	Yes	No
Abishek & Jindal, 2021	Copy-Move and Splicing Forgery Detection	128x128, 256x256	DCNN and VGG16 for Feature extraction	GRIP, DVMM, CMFD, and BSDS300	JPEG, PNG	Yes	Yes

continued on following page

Table 1. Continued

Author	Types of Detection	Size	Backbone	Dataset	Format	Images	Videos
Chakraborty et al., 2024	Image Tampering Detection	128 × 128	Dual Branch CNN	CASIA	JPEG	Yes	No
Guarner et al., 2024	Deep fake identification	-	GAN with four Diffusion Model	CelebA [30], FFHQ,1 and ImageNet	JPEG	Yes	No
Peng et al., 2022	GAN-based Anti-Forensic Detection	-	BDC-GAN		JPEG	Yes	No
Uddin et al., 2024	GAN-based Anti-Forensic Detection	-	CAF-GAN	Custom dataset	JPEG	Yes	NO

4. FORENSIC APPLICATIONS OF IMAGE AND VIDEO ANALYSIS

Image and video analysis have become crucial tools in forensic investigations, greatly benefiting from the advancements in deep learning technologies. These innovations enable law enforcement agencies to analyze and interpret visual data more efficiently, aiding in the identification of suspects, detection of fraudulent activities, and prevention of crimes. Deep learning models have significantly enhanced capabilities in areas such as facial recognition, forensic face manipulation detection, event detection, vehicle recognition, and fingerprint analysis. By leveraging these technologies, forensic experts can now examine vast amounts of visual data in real-time, offering higher accuracy, speed, and reliability in criminal investigations which is further discussed in the Table.2. For instance, (Elhoseny et al., 2021) introduced an IoT-enabled Face Sketch Synthesis model utilizing an optimal deep learning CNN optimized by the Elephant Herd Optimization (EHO) algorithm. This model generates suspect sketches based on surveillance footage captured by IoT devices. These AI-generated sketches are then compared with professional sketches drawn according to eyewitness descriptions. The model was rigorously tested through simulations, achieving impressive results, with an average Peak Signal-to-Noise Ratio (PSNR) of 20.11 dB, a Structural Similarity Index (SSIM) of 0.64, and an accuracy rate of 90.10%. (Do et al., 2018) The author employed a deep CNN model to detect forensic face manipulations, addressing challenges posed by GAN model, which can create fake images and videos leading to identity theft and privacy breaches. The authors utilized GANs to generate fake faces at various resolutions and sizes for data augmentation. A deep face recognition system was employed to transfer pre-trained weights for robust feature extraction, and the network was fine-tuned for real/fake image classification.

(Seibold et al., 2017) The authors employed the deep CNN for the identification of morphing attacks. A fully automated face image morphing pipeline with interchangeable components was developed to generate training and testing samples. The best performance was achieved by the pretrained VGG19 model, with a False Rejection Rate (FRR) of 3.5% and a False Acceptance Rate (FAR) of 0.8%. Similarly, another application is vehicle recognition, which is vital for tracking suspects using traffic cameras or identifying getaway vehicles. In forensic fingerprint and handprint matching, AI models can analyze partial prints left at crime scenes, helping link suspects to the scene. (Chen et al., 2020) developed a real-time automatic license plate recognition system using an AlexNetmodel. The model achieved a 98% success rate in localization and license plate recognition, proving effective for vehicle management in controlled environments and video monitoring. However, performance may decline in highly complex settings.(Kim, 2020) proposed a YOLO v2-based model for vehicle detection in tunnel environments, incorporating brightness smoothing and noise removal techniques. The system demonstrated an 87% detection rate and 94% accuracy, enabling real-time detection in low-light conditions. Challenges remain with environmental factors like pollution and visibility. Finally, event detection in crime scenes will be explored, with deep learning techniques helping to detect suspicious activities, such as fights or unauthorized entries, in real time. Gait and behavior analysis have also emerged as important tools in which AI systems analyze the unique walking patterns or behaviors of individuals caught on camera to identify potential suspects. (Majhi et al., 2020) proposed an enhanced E-CNN for detecting criminal activity in public spaces by analyzing video footage from surveillance cameras. The study emphasized the need for a highly accurate prediction system that minimizes false positives and negatives in pre-incident warning systems based on deep learning (DL). The experiment, analyzed using SPSS software, achieved impressive results: an average accuracy of 97.05%, precision of 96.74%, a false-positive rate of 2.96%, and a false-negative rate of 2.93%. These findings suggest that the enhanced security warning system can prevent potentially dangerous situations, ultimately improving the prediction and management of criminal activities.

Table 2. Forensic Application using Deep Learning Models

Author	Forensic Application	Tool/Technique Used	Key Outcome	Use Case	Limitation
Elhoseny et al., 2021	Face Sketch Synthesis	ODL-CNN (Optimal Deep Learning CNN) + EHO	High-quality suspect sketches; Average PSNR: 20.11 dB, SSIM: 0.64, Accuracy: 90.10%	Generating and comparing suspect sketches from IoT-captured surveillance footage with eyewitness descriptions for suspect identification	The performance is highly dependent on the quality of surveillance footage.
Do et al., 2018	Forensics Face Detection	DCNN and GAN	Successful detection of GAN-generated fake faces with fine-tuned CNN, with the accuracy of 80%.	Forensic image analysis, preventing identity theft and privacy breaches caused by GAN-generated fake faces in various applications.	The GAN-generated images differ significantly from real images, this may affect model performance in real-world scenarios.
Seibolde et al., 2017	Face Morphing Attack Detection	DCNN, Pretrained VGG19	Pretrained networks, especially VGG19, outperformed models trained from scratch with a FRR of 3.5% and FAR of 0.8%.	Detecting face morphing attacks in images using semantic artifact detection	Performance heavily relies on the choice of pretrained weights, which may not always be optimal for specific applications.
Chen et al., 2020	Real-time automatic license plate recognition	Alex net convolution neural network	98% success rate in localization and efficient license plate recognition system	Vehicle management in closed communities, video monitoring in natural environments	Performance and accuracy may be affected in highly complex environments or conditions
Kim, 2020	Vehicle Detection in Tunnel Road Environments	YOLO v2 model, Brightness Smoothing,	87% detection rate, 94% detection accuracy	Real-time vehicle detection in low-illumination environments like tunnels	Environmental factors such as pollution and low visibility may impact detection
Majhi et al., 2020	Crime Prediction in CCTV video	ECNN, Human Behavior Analysis, SPSS	97.05% accuracy, 96.74% precision, 2.96% false-positive rate, 2.93% false-negative rate	Crime behavior tracking and pre-incident warning in public surveillance systems using ML/DL techniques	False-positive and false-negative rates, though low, may still affect system reliability in critical scenarios

4.1. Detecting Fingerprint Alterations with Deep Learning Model: A Case Study

As a practical application, this case study focuses on fingerprint alteration detection. In forensic investigations, suspects may deliberately alter their fingerprints to avoid detection. Deep learning models can detect such alterations and match partial fingerprints left at crime scenes to known suspects or database records. This case study explores a deep learning approach using deep CNN to detect these alterations in fingerprints using the Coventry Fingerprints Dataset (Shehu et al., 2018).

4.1.1 Dataset Description

The CovFing Dataset consists of 6,110 real fingerprints collected from 611 individuals. These fingerprints were synthetically altered into three common types of modifications: central rotation, z-cut, and obliteration. The dataset is divided into three levels of alteration difficulty (easy, medium, and hard), producing a total of 55,249 images as represented in the Figure 3.The dataset includes additional attributes such as gender where 0 represents the female and 1 represents the male, the specific finger (0 - thumb, 1- index, 2 - middle, 3- ring, or little 4- finger), and whether the fingerprint belongs to the left hand i.e., 0 or right hand i.e., 1. This level of detail helps broaden the range of possible applications in forensic fingerprint analysis. The notation [100, 0, 0, 1] represents the specific attributes of an image systematically. Here, 100 represent the name of the image, while the first 0 indicates that the fingerprint belongs to a male individual. The second 0 signifies that the fingerprint is from the thumb finger, and the final 1 denotes that the fingerprint is from the right hand. This structured format helps categorize images efficiently, allowing quick reference to important characteristics in forensic analysis

Figure 3. Fingerprint altered image collected from the CovFing Dataset.

4.1.2 Methodology

The collected images were pre-processed by resizing them to 255×255 pixels and normalizing them, making them suitable for input to a deep C+0+3+3NN model. The model architecture consisted of five convolutional layers with increasing neuron counts of 20, 40, 60, and 80, using 3×3 filters. Each convolutional layer used a stride of 1×1 and padding of 2×2, ensuring feature extraction across the image while maintaining spatial dimensions. The final layer utilized the ReLU activation function which is used to incorporate non-linearity of the model. To train the model, the *"stochastic gradient descent (SGD)"* optimizer was employed, with batch normalization enabled for stability and faster convergence. A mini-batch size and a learning rate of 0.01 were used, along with a cross-entropy loss function and 100 epochs, to optimize the model parameters. The model was trained on real and altered fingerprint datasets, with labels indicating alteration types, aiming to classify these effectively.

4.1.3 Results and Conclusion

The deep CNN model classifies both real and altered fingerprints, achieving an average accuracy of 58% in detecting real fingerprints as represented in Figure 4. This drop in accuracy is due to training on a limited number of images. Training the model on a larger dataset would likely enhance its reliability, making it more suitable for real-time applications where accurately distinguishing between real and altered fingerprints is crucial.

Figure 4. Fingerprint altered Identified using deep CNN Model

5. VIDEO SUMMARIZATION AND CRIME SCENE RECONSTRUCTION

Given the vast amount of video data generated daily from surveillance cameras, drones, and personal devices, it is essential to effectively summarize videos for faster analysis. This section discusses advanced methods for video summarization, allowing forensic experts to focus on the most critical moments in lengthy footage. Techniques such as keyframe extraction and temporal segmentation are highlighted, along with the use of DL models to automate the process. For instance, (Ul et al., 2022) proposed a YOLOv3-based video summarization framework to detect Objects of Interest (OoI) and generate relevant video summaries. Extensive experiments were conducted on three datasets: VSUMM, TVSum, and a custom dataset. The framework achieved 99.6% accuracy and a time-saving of 82.8% on the VSUMM dataset, 99.9% accuracy and 78.8% summarization rate on the TVSum dataset, and 99.3% accuracy with 87.86% saved time on the custom dataset. The author (Wang et al., 2022) proposed AuDSN, a deep reinforcement model enhanced by auxiliary summarization loss in the decoder, designed to improve long-term dependency capture. By introducing a novel reward function with a dispersion reward and employing the Swish activation function, AuDSN generated more coherent, diverse and representative video summaries. Experiments on the SumMe and TVSum datasets showed improved performance. With a lightweight size of 2.7 MB, AuDSN can be deployed on edge devices. The author (Muhammad et al., 2020) proposed a lightweight CNN based video summarization method for resource-constrained surveillance systems. The Key frames are selected based on the highest memo ability and entropy scores. Experiments on two benchmark datasets demonstrated the method's adaptability for resource-constrained surveillance networks, achieving 18 fps processing. Future work includes improving the processing rate and extending the method to wireless sensor networks and IoT environments for smarter surveillance applications. The author (Song et al., 2016) proposed an event-based approach to summarize surveillance videos, offering key advantages over traditional keyframe-based methods. These include a higher summarization ratio, the ability to capture abnormal events, and the elimination of the need for shot boundary detection, which is challenging in surveillance footage. The approach involves object tracking-by-detection to obtain trajectories of pedestrians and vehicles, with abnormal events detected using trajectory features combined with a Random Forest classifier. A disjoint max-coverage algorithm is used to generate a concise summary by prioritizing blocked or hidden events. This method is automatic, fast, and robust, making it suitable for a range of scenarios from highways to crowded urban areas. Future work aims to combine keyframe-based and event-based techniques for enhanced summarization, and to apply the algorithm to a wider range of abnormal events or other types of videos.

The author (Zhang et al., 2016) introduced the *"Context-Aware Video Summarization (CAVS)"* framework, which focuses on identifying and summarizing the most informative portions of video sequences. Unlike traditional methods, CAVS captures local motion features and their spatiotemporal correlations through sparse coding and generalized sparse group lasso. This approach allows for an online update of video feature dictionaries, enhancing the summarization of new video segments. While the summarized outputs may contain some redundancy, strategies such as integration with lower-level summarization methods and threshold adjustments help manage this issue. Experimental results on multiple datasets demonstrate that CAVS effectively summarizes surveillance and user-generated videos, providing a more accurate representation of global events compared to existing frameworks. The advancements in video summarization techniques hold immense potential for forensic intelligence, enabling faster and more accurate analysis of large volumes of video data. Methods like key frame extraction, temporal segmentation, and deep learning-based models such as YOLOv3 and AuDSN offer forensic experts the ability to focus on critical moments, detect objects of interest, and analyze abnormal activities in surveillance footage. This is crucial for investigating crime scenes, where rapid identification of important events can accelerate the decision-making process. Techniques like the event-based approach by (Song et al., 2016) and the CAVS framework by (Zhang et al., 2016) are particularly beneficial for forensic intelligence, as they not only capture abnormal events but also highlight spatiotemporal correlations, providing a holistic view of the crime scene. By automating and enhancing the video summarization process, these methods help forensic analysts reduce processing time and focus on key evidence, significantly improving the efficiency and effectiveness of forensic investigations.

Table 3. Video Summarization and Crime Scene Reconstruction using DL Models

Author	Forensic Application	Tool/Technique Used	Key Outcome	Use Case	Limitation
Ul et al., 2022	Video surveillance analysis	YOLOv3	Achieved high accuracy in summarizing videos based on Object of Interest (OoI); 99.6% (VSUMM), 99.9% (TVSum), and 99.2% (own dataset)	Enhancing video surveillance systems by summarizing videos to monitor specific objects of interest (e.g., people, vehicles)	Requires high-speed computing hardware for processing large video datasets
Wang et al., 2022	Video surveillance analysis	Unsupervised deep reinforcement learning with LSTM and Swish activation function	Improved long-term dependency capture, with a 6.3% F-score increase on SumMe and 2.2% on TVSum datasets compared to DR-DSN model	Enhancing mobile video summarization systems to reduce server load while summarizing surveillance footage	May struggle with extremely long videos that require complex computations on mobile devices
Muhammad et al., 2020	Surveillance video analysis	CNN-based summarization with shot segmentation using deep features	Enhanced summarization through shot segmentation, image memorability, and entropy, showing promising results compared to state-of-the-art methods	Efficient indexing and retrieval of surveillance video data for resource-constrained devices	May face challenges with real-time processing in highly resource-constrained environments
Song et al.,2016	Large scale surveillance video summarization	Event detection, vehicle and pedestrian tracking, Random Forest classifier, trajectory features, disjoint max-coverage algorithm	Efficient event-centric summarization with high coverage and low redundancy	Surveillance for highways and crowded crossings	Potentially requires extensive computational resources for real-time performance on large datasets

continued on following page

Table 3. Continued

Author	Forensic Application	Tool/Technique Used	Key Outcome	Use Case	Limitation
Zhang et al., 2016	Video summarization in surveillance	Context-aware video summarization (CAVS) framework	Successfully identifies and summarizes the most informative video portions using local motion regions and their interactions; updates dictionaries online for new video segments	Enhancing video surveillance systems by providing concise summaries of important footage	Limited to the features captured by the learned dictionaries; effectiveness may vary with diverse video types
Bostanci, 2015	Crime Scene Reconstruction	3D Imaging, Laser Scanning Technology	Precise mapping of crime scenes with millimetre detail; enables analysis of bullet trajectories, bloodstains, and weapon comparisons	Reconstruction of crime scenes for investigators and jurors to explore, providing new insights not available through traditional methods	Acceptance in court requires standardization; best practice guidelines and oversight still developing
Zappalà et al(2024)	Crime Scene Reconstruction	Photogrammetric reconstruction, VR, Faster-RCNN	Accelerated and improved crime scene analysis through object recognition and measurement in VR environment	Analysis of hazardous or complex crime scenes with health and safety risks (e.g., fires, explosions)	Dependent on input quality; challenges with scene complexity and accuracy of object recognition algorithms

continued on following page

Table 3. Continued

Author	Forensic Application	Tool/Technique Used	Key Outcome	Use Case	Limitation
Vuyyuru et al., 2024	Automated Street Crime Detection using Drone	CNN, Embedding Bilateral Filter, Conv-ViT, ISSOA, MCS-GNet	High detection accuracy of street crime using drone-captured images with fusion models; achieved 0.783 and 0.974 accuracy on UCF-Crime and UCSD Ped2 datasets	Automated monitoring of security feeds to detect suspicious activities in real-time, reducing the manual burden of surveillance	Dependent on dataset quality, real-time application may require significant computational resources
Singh et al., 2018	Real-Time Drone Surveillance for Violent Individuals Detection	Feature Pyramid Network, ScatterNet Hybrid Deep Learning (SHDL)	Real-time detection of violent individuals using aerial images; efficient human pose estimation with fewer labeled examples	Monitoring public areas for violent individuals using drone surveillance, aiding law enforcement in real-time interventions	Dependent on cloud processing and the performance of pose estimation in varying conditions

Additionally, this chapter will explore 3D crime scene reconstruction, which involves creating a digital representation of the crime scene using multiple images or video feeds. These reconstructions are invaluable for understanding the sequence of events and gathering evidence that might otherwise have been missed. The use of drones for crime scene mapping will also be covered, showing how aerial imagery can provide a comprehensive view of crime scenes, especially in outdoor or large-scale environments. (Bostanci, 2015) presented an automated approach for reconstructing crime scenes in 3D to enhance visualization and facilitate investigations. By extracting keyframes from video footage of the crime scene, the method generates 3D point clouds that accurately represent different parts of the scene, ultimately merging them into a single cohesive model. The results demonstrate the effectiveness of sophisticated computer vision techniques in creating realistic reconstructions. Additionally, the paper addresses design considerations for a powerful interactive crime scene analysis tool. The study emphasizes the court acceptability of such automated reconstructions, asserting that evidence collected by law enforcement officers can support their validity. Future work will focus on creating a more interactive environment for using the 3D models in investigations. (Vuyyuru et al., 2024) introduced an automated drone-based street crime detection system that leverages advanced CNN models to analyze images captured by drones. It utilizes an *"Embedding Bilateral Filter (EBF)"* for image enhancement and integrates a fusion model with Inception-V3, ResNet-50, and a Vision Transformer (Conv-ViT) for effective feature extraction. The *"Improved Shark Smell Optimization Algorithm (ISSOA)"* optimizes feature selection, while the *"Multiscale Contextual Semantic Guidance Network (MCS-GNet)"* improves image classification. Evaluated on the UCF-Crime and UCSD Ped2 datasets, the system achieves impressive accuracy scores of 0.783 and 0.974, respectively. Future enhancements could include attention mechanisms, reinforcement learning, and real-time monitoring capabilities for law enforcement applications. The author (Singh et al., 2018) proposed a real-time *"Drone Surveillance System (DSS)"* for detecting violent individuals from aerial images. It employs a Feature Pyramid Network (FPN) for human detection and a *"ScatterNet Hybrid Deep Learning (SHDL)"* network for human pose estimation, followed by SVM for identifying violent behaviors. The system uses fewer labeled examples for pose estimation, making it efficient for large-scale surveillance. Additionally, the introduced Aerial Violent Individual (AVI) dataset enhances deep learning applications in aerial surveillance, with the DSS outperforming existing techniques on this dataset.

5.1 Case Study: Video Summarization of Hit and Run Detection Using Deep Learning

Hit-and-run incidents pose significant challenges to law enforcement, often requiring extensive reviews of surveillance footage to identify critical evidence. Manually analyzing hours of video is not only time-consuming but also prone to human oversight. This case study explores the application of deep learning-based video summarization techniques to streamline the process of detecting and analyzing hit-and-run incidents.

Figure 5. Frames Extracted from the input videos

5.1.1 Dataset Description

This dataset consists of multiple video clips from CCTV footage capturing various vehicles and crash incidents. It includes diverse environmental settings, such as day, night, and rainy conditions, to simulate real-world CCTV scenarios. The dataset is designed to support applications related to crash detection, vehicle behavior analysis, and environmental impact assessment (BenO et al., 2017).

5.1.2. Methodology

Initially, the input video was processed using OpenCV to extract individual frames, which were saved as image files for subsequent analysis. To balance computational efficiency with the retention of essential information, a total of 200 frames were selected. Features were then extracted from these frames using a pre-trained ResNet50 model, which generated high-dimensional embeddings representing the visual content of each frame. These embeddings were clustered using the K-Means algorithm, grouping the frames into five clusters based on visual similarity as represented in the Figure 5. From each cluster, a representative key frame was selected by identifying the frame closest to the cluster centroid. The chosen key frames were then processed using the BLIP (Bootstrapped Learning from Image Paragraphs) model, a state-of-the-art vision-language framework. BLIP generated descriptive captions for each key frame, capturing the visual and contextual details of the frames. Finally, the captions were aggregated and refined to form a coherent textual summary of the video, with additional sentences providing introductory and concluding context to enhance the summary's readability and completeness.

5.1.3. Results and Discussion

The video presented is summarized below, as illustrated in the accompanying Figure 6. It depicts a vehicle driving down the middle of a city street. This representation is derived from the input video. The summarization process achieves an accuracy of 62%.

Figure 6. Video summarization using the BLIP Model

```
a car is driving down the street in a city
a car is seen in the middle of a street
a car is seen in the middle of a street
a car is seen in the middle of a street
a car is seen in the middle of a street
a car is seen in this image from the video
a car is seen in the middle of a street
a car is seen in this image from the video
a car is seen in this image from the video
a car is seen in the middle of a street
```

6. FORENSIC IMAGE AND VIDEO ENHANCEMENT

This section focuses on enhancement techniques to overcome the quality issues inherent in forensic media. Image super-resolution is a technique in which deep-learning algorithms upscale low-resolution images to provide more detailed views of suspects or objects. Noise reduction and deblurring techniques are also discussed, as they are critical for improving the clarity of images captured under challenging conditions. In addition, this section covers video stabilization, which helps reduce motion-induced artifacts in surveillance footage, and frame interpolation, which can generate missing frames in videos for smoother analysis. Finally, artifact removal techniques, such as the use of bilateral filters or GAN-based restoration models, are presented, demonstrating their importance in forensic analysis for improving the usability of digital evidence. For instance, (Seibel et al.,2017) presented a super-resolution automatic license plate recognition to enhance low-quality surveillance videos, aiding forensic analysts in identifying license plates of suspects' vehicles. By combining tracking, alignment, SR enhancement, and OCR, the framework improves alphanumeric recognition, even in challenging conditions like motion blur and shadows. Experiments highlighted the PyrLK tracking and GSR super-resolution methods as effective, with customization options for different video conditions. Future enhancements include fully automated license plate detection for real-time application. (Liu et al., 2020) proposed an anti-forensics method leveraging GANs to challenge the effectiveness of sharpening detection in image forensics. While CNNs have largely solved the detection of sharpened images, the authors generated images that exhibit sharpening characteristics without traditional sharpening manipulations. Experimental results demonstrated that even state-of-the-art sharpening detectors based on CNNs were deceived by the GAN-generated images, highlighting the need for continued scrutiny in sharpening forensics despite advancements in detection techniques. (Shen et al., 2022) introduced a DL based image enhancement algorithm tailored for video surveillance scenes, aimed at improving image clarity for better recognition, tracking, and target analysis. By leveraging grayscale, color, texture, and shape information, the algorithm ensured consistent internal region characteristics while enhancing contrasts between regions to effectively distinguish the target from the background. Using MATLAB2016 for testing, the method demonstrated high segmentation accuracy and efficiency across diverse video surveillance scenarios, with an average enhancement time under 1.3 seconds. Comparative tests confirmed its ability to significantly increase image definition.

Table 5. Generative Adversarial network for Forensic Image and Video Analysis

Author	Forensic Application	Tool/Technique Used	Key Outcome	Use Case	Limitation
Seibel et al. (2017)	License Plate Recognition from Low-Quality Surveillance Videos	Super-Resolution (SR), Automatic License Plate Recognition (ALPR), Novel SR method with inpainting techniques	Enhanced detail in low-quality license plates; improved character recognition accuracy in challenging conditions	Identification of license plates in low-resolution traffic surveillance footage, aiding forensic analysts in crime scene investigations	Performance varies based on initial video quality, motion blur, and environmental conditions
Shen et al. (2020)	Anti-Forensics Method Using GAN to Investigate Sharpening Detection Limits	Generative Adversarial Network (GAN)-based anti-forensics technique	To examine the reliability of CNN-based sharpening detectors by creating images with sharpened features without traditional sharpening manipulations	Image forensics and detection of manipulated images	CNN-based detectors can be deceived by GAN-generated images, indicating that sharpening forensics may still face challenges from adversarial manipulations
Shen et al (2022)	Deep Learning-Based Image Enhancement Algorithm for Video Surveillance Scenes	Hybrid deep convolutional network for super-resolution, followed by a watershed morphology-based enhancement	To enhance target clarity and improve accuracy in video surveillance scenes	Video surveillance, target tracking, and behavior analysis	Performance may vary across different lighting conditions; requires substantial computational resources for real-time application

6.1 Case Study: License Plate Image Enhancement

In forensic investigations, the clarity and legibility of license plates captured in surveillance footage are often critical for identifying suspects or tracking vehicles involved in criminal activities. However, challenges such as poor lighting, adverse weather conditions, and suboptimal camera angles can significantly degrade image quality, complicating analysis and identification. To address these issues, advanced image enhancement techniques powered by deep learning have become invaluable tools in forensic workflows.

6.1.1 Dataset Description

The *"Chinese City Parking Dataset (CCPD)"* is ideal for a case study on license plate image enhancement due to its large-scale, diverse collection of 250,000 unique images. These images capture license plates under various conditions, including differing lighting, weather, and angles, making the dataset robust for testing image enhancement techniques (Xu et al., 2018).

6.1.2. Methodology

The RRDBNet model employs an advanced deep learning architecture designed for enhancing low-resolution images. Its core is the Residual in Residual Dense Block (RRDB), which consists of multiple dense blocks, each containing four convolutional layers that process concatenated outputs to effectively learn hierarchical features. The model begins with a convolutional layer to extract high-level features, followed by stacked RRDBs with residual connections for refined feature processing. Afterward, convolutional layers and depth-to-space operations (sub pixel convolutions) upsample the feature maps in stages, achieving an overall 8× resolution enhancement. The final convolutional layer restores the original number of channels, producing a high-resolution output. Throughout the architecture, Leaky ReLU activation is used to introduce non-linearity and prevent vanishing gradients. By leveraging residual learning and dense connections, RRDBNet ensures effective information flow, enabling the generation of high-quality super-resolved images. The model is trained with the learning rate of 1e-4, with the epoch of 100.

6.1.3 Results and Conclusion

The RRDBNet model effectively enhanced the resolution of the low-quality input image, as shown in Figure 7, producing a recovered image that closely matching the ground truth. With a PSNR value of 32.34 dB, the model demonstrated high accuracy in preserving details, such as the text "CALE408".

Figure 7. Enhanced Vehicle Plate using the DL Model

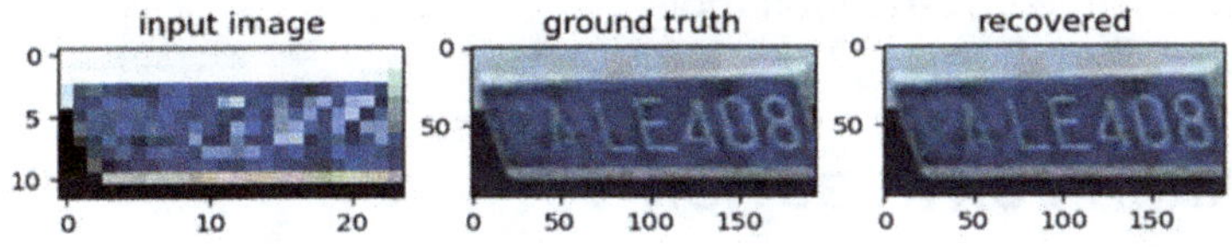

7. CHALLENGES AND FUTURE DIRECTIONS

This chapter delves into the critical challenges and future opportunities in applying image and video analysis technologies to forensic investigations. As artificial intelligence (AI) and deep learning methods continue to evolve, they offer promising solutions for crime detection and evidence analysis. However, integrating AI with modern tools such as Internet of Things (IoT) devices—like body cameras and smart city surveillance systems—introduces significant hurdles related to data management, security, and scalability. Additionally, the legal and ethical implications of deploying AI in courtrooms, particularly concerns around bias and explainability, remain pivotal issues. To address these challenges, the chapter discusses emerging trends such as leveraging edge computing for real-time forensic analysis and harnessing AI-driven tools to transform the landscape of crime investigations. The application of AI in digital forensics presents several pressing research challenges that demand scholarly attention. Data privacy and security are primary concerns, as improper management could lead to intrusions or breaches during forensic investigations. Furthermore, the quality and integrity of data collected during investigations may be compromised, resulting in inaccurate or unreliable outcomes. Data bias also poses a significant risk, as biased or incomplete training datasets can lead to discriminatory or unjust conclusions. Interpretability and explainability of machine learning models—often perceived as "black boxes"—present further challenges, especially in legal contexts where decisions must be transparent and evidence must be clearly justified.

Scalability and performance are additional concerns, with massive volumes of digital evidence necessitating optimized AI algorithms. Standardization of AI practices in digital forensics remains underdeveloped, creating uncertainty about the best techniques for specific investigations. The ability of models to generalize across diverse devices, file formats, and operating systems is another obstacle, as DL models often struggle to adapt to varying data inputs. Adversarial attacks, where inputs are designed to mislead deep learning models, further compound these challenges, underscoring the high stakes of achieving accuracy and reliability in forensic applications. Addressing these issues is vital to ensure the ethical, scalable, and secure integration of AI into forensic science, paving the way for more robust and actionable crime investigation tools.

8. RESEARCH CONTRIBUTION

The chapter significantly contributes to the field of forensic intelligence by showcasing how deep learning technologies provide innovative solutions to challenges in crime investigation. It highlights the use of advanced architectures such as Convolutional Neural Networks (CNNs) and Generative Adversarial Networks (GANs) for detecting image and video manipulations, authenticating digital evidence, and enhancing the accuracy of forensic workflows. Practical applications are demonstrated through real-world use cases like fingerprint alteration detection, license plate recognition, and video summarization for crime scene analysis, showcasing the relevance and utility of these technologies. Moreover, the chapter bridges the gap between traditional forensic methods and AI-driven solutions, emphasizing the pivotal role of deep learning in improving the efficiency and reliability of modern forensic investigations.

The chapter also addresses critical challenges such as scalability, computational efficiency, and the ethical implications of using AI in forensic science. It proposes solutions like leveraging edge computing for real-time analysis and employing explainable AI to enhance trust and transparency in forensic applications. By exploring future trends such as the integration of AI with IoT-enabled forensic tools and the development of more advanced crime investigation systems, the chapter underscores its alignment with the book's focus on forensic intelligence and deep learning solutions. Through these contributions, the chapter reinforces the transformative potential of AI in advancing crime investigation processes and delivering actionable insights to modern forensic workflows.

9. CONCLUSION

This chapter highlights the transformative role of AI and deep learning technologies in modern forensic investigations, particularly in the analysis of digital images and videos. By addressing the limitations of traditional methods, it emphasizes the importance of AI-powered tools in detecting and authenticating manipulations, enhancing digital evidence reliability, and streamlining forensic workflows. Advanced architectures like Convolutional Neural Networks (CNNs) and Generative Adversarial Networks (GANs) have been instrumental in improving accuracy and efficiency across various applications, including fingerprint alteration detection, license plate recognition, and video summarization. Despite these advancements, challenges such as data scalability, model interpretability, ethical concerns, and adversarial vulnerabilities remain critical. The chapter explores solutions like edge computing for real-time analysis and emphasizes the need for unbiased and standardized AI frameworks to ensure reliability in forensic applications. Looking forward, the integration of AI with IoT devices and the continued evolution of machine learning models hold immense potential for reshaping the landscape of crime investigation. By bridging the gap between traditional forensic practices and cutting-edge AI solutions, this chapter underscores the critical importance of embracing technological innovation to advance forensic intelligence and enhance the pursuit of justice.

REFERENCES

Barnes, C., & Barraclough, T. (2020). Deepfakes and synthetic media. In *Emerging technologies and international security* (pp. 206–220). Routledge.

Ben, O. jljones, Kumar H, Meg Risdal, MRao, Vadim Sherman, Vipul, Wendy Kan, & Yau Ben-Or. (2017). *Intel & MobileODT Cervical Cancer Screening* [Dataset]. Kaggle. https://kaggle.com/competitions/intel-mobileodt-cervical-cancer-screening

Binson, V. A., Thomas, N. M., Thoams, S., Augustine, A., & Sivakumar, K. S. (2016, October). An advance to cloning detection in digital forensics investigations. In *2016 International Conference on Emerging Technological Trends (ICETT)* (pp. 1-5). IEEE.

Bostanci, E. (2015). 3D reconstruction of crime scenes and design considerations for an interactive investigation tool. *International Journal of Information Security Science*, *4*(2), 50–58.

Bunk, J., Bappy, J. H., Mohammed, T. M., Nataraj, L., Flenner, A., Manjunath, B. S., . . . Peterson, L. (2017, July). Detection and localization of image forgeries using resampling features and deep learning. In *2017 IEEE conference on computer vision and pattern recognition workshops (CVPRW)* (pp. 1881-1889). IEEE.

Chakraborty, S., Chatterjee, K., & Dey, P. (2024). Detection of Image Tampering Using Deep Learning, Error Levels and Noise Residuals. *Neural Processing Letters*, *56*, 112. DOI: 10.1007/s11063-024-11448-9

Chen, Z., Yan, L., Yin, S., & Shi, Y. (2020). Vehicle license plate recognition system based on deep learning in natural scene. *Journal on Artificial Intelligence*, *2*(4), 167–175. DOI: 10.32604/jai.2020.012716

Do, N. T., Na, I. S., & Kim, S. H. (2018). Forensics face detection from GANs using convolutional neural network. *ISITC*, *2018*, 376–379.

Du, X., Hargreaves, C., Sheppard, J., Anda, F., Sayakkara, A., Le-Khac, N. A., & Scanlon, M. (2020, August). SoK: Exploring the state of the art and the future potential of artificial intelligence in digital forensic investigation. In *Proceedings of the 15th international conference on availability, reliability and security* (pp. 1-10).

Dunsin, D., Ghanem, M. C., Ouazzane, K., & Vassilev, V. (2024). A comprehensive analysis of the role of artificial intelligence and machine learning in modern digital forensics and incident response. *Forensic Science International Digital Investigation*, *48*, 301675.

Elhoseny, M., Selim, M. M., & Shankar, K. (2021). Optimal deep learning based convolution neural network for digital forensics face sketch synthesis in internet of things (IoT). *International Journal of Machine Learning and Cybernetics, 12*, 3249–3260.

Fayyaz, M. A., Anjum, A., Ziauddin, S., Khan, A., & Sarfaraz, A. (2020). An improved surveillance video forgery detection technique using sensor pattern noise and correlation of noise residues. *Multimedia Tools and Applications, 79*, 5767–5788.

Fernández, E. G., Orozco, A. L. S., & Villalba, L. J. G. (2023). A multi-channel approach for detecting tampering in colour filter images. *Expert Systems with Applications, 230*, 120498.

Hashmi, M. F., Keskar, A. G., & Yadav, V. (2016). Fuzzy based image forensic tool for detection and classification of image cloning. *International Journal of Computational Intelligence Systems, 9*(2), 351–375.

Jain, I., & Goel, N. (2021, January). Advancements in image splicing and copy-move forgery detection techniques: A survey. In *2021 11th international conference on cloud computing, Data Science & Engineering (confluence)* (pp. 470-475). IEEE.

Kadha, V., Vakamullu, V., Das, S. K., Mishra, M., & Bora, J. (2022, July). Image Resampling Forensics: A Review on Techniques for Image Authentication. In *International Conference on Computers, Management & Mathematical Sciences* (pp. 183-193). Cham: Springer International Publishing.

Kim, J. (2020). Vehicle detection using deep learning technique in tunnel road environments. *Symmetry, 12*(12), 2012.

Kumar, M., Rani, A., & Srivastava, S. (2019). Image forensics based on lighting estimation. *International Journal of Image and Graphics, 19*(03), 1950014.

Liang, Y., Fang, Y., Luo, S., & Chen, B. (2019, December). Image resampling detection based on convolutional neural network. In *2019 15th International Conference on Computational Intelligence and Security (CIS)* (pp. 257-261). IEEE.

Macit, H. B., & Koyun, A. (2020). Tamper detection and recovery on RGB images. In *Artificial Intelligence and Applied Mathematics in Engineering Problems: Proceedings of the International Conference on Artificial Intelligence and Applied Mathematics in Engineering (ICAIAME 2019)* (pp. 972-981). Springer International Publishing.https://doi.org//DOI: 10.1007/s11042-022-13808-w

Majhi, S., Dash, R., & Sa, P. K. (2020). Two-stream CNN architecture for anomalous event detection in real world scenarios. In *Computer Vision and Image Processing: 4th International Conference, CVIP 2019, Jaipur, India, September 27–29, 2019, Revised Selected Papers, Part II 4* (pp. 343-353). Springer Singapore.

Mayer, O., & Stamm, M. C. (2018). Accurate and efficient image forgery detection using lateral chromatic aberration. *IEEE Transactions on Information Forensics and Security*, *13*(7), 1762–1777.

Morgan, J. (2023). Wrongful convictions and claims of false or misleading forensic evidence. *Journal of Forensic Sciences*, *68*(3), 908–961. PMID: 36946413

Muhammad, K., Hussain, T., & Baik, S. W. (2020). Efficient CNN based summarization of surveillance videos for resource-constrained devices. *Pattern Recognition Letters*, *130*, 370–375.

Peng, F., Yin, L., & Long, M. (2022). BDC-GAN: Bidirectional conversion between computer-generated and natural facial images for anti-forensics. *IEEE Transactions on Circuits and Systems for Video Technology*, *32*(10), 6657–6670.

Pomari, T., Ruppert, G., Rezende, E., Rocha, A., & Carvalho, T. (2018, October). Image splicing detection through illumination inconsistencies and deep learning. In *2018 25th IEEE International conference on image processing (ICIP)* (pp. 3788-3792). IEEE.

Qadir, S., & Noor, B. (2021, May). Applications of machine learning in digital forensics. In *2021 International Conference on Digital Futures and Transformative Technologies (ICoDT2)* (pp. 1-8). IEEE.

Rao, Y., & Ni, J. (2016). A deep learning approach to detection of splicing and copy-move forgeries in images. *2016 IEEE International Workshop on Information Forensics and Security (WIFS)*. doi:DOI: 10.1109/wifs.2016.7823911

Rhee, K. H. (2020). Detection of spliced image forensics using texture analysis of median filter residual. *IEEE Access : Practical Innovations, Open Solutions*, *8*, 103374–103384.

Seibel, H., Goldenstein, S., & Rocha, A. (2017). Eyes on the target: Super-resolution and license-plate recognition in low-quality surveillance videos. *IEEE Access : Practical Innovations, Open Solutions*, *5*, 20020–20035.

Seibold, C., Samek, W., Hilsmann, A., & Eisert, P. (2017). Detection of face morphing attacks by deep learning. In *Digital Forensics and Watermarking: 16th International Workshop, IWDW 2017, Magdeburg, Germany, August 23-25, 2017, Proceedings 16* (pp. 107-120). Springer International Publishing. Selim, A., & Ali, İ. The Role of Digital Forensic Analysis in Modern Investigations. *Journal of Emerging Computer Technologies*, *4*(1), 1–5.

Sharma, P., Kumar, M., & Sharma, H. (2023). Comprehensive analyses of image forgery detection methods from traditional to deep learning approaches: An evaluation. *Multimedia Tools and Applications*, *82*(12), 18117–18150. PMID: 36213342

Shen, W. W., Chen, L., Liu, S., & Zhang, Y. D. (2022). An image enhancement algorithm of video surveillance scene based on deep learning. *IET Image Processing*, *16*(3), 681–690.

Shen, Z., Ding, F., & Shi, Y. (2020). Anti-forensics of image sharpening using generative adversarial network. In *Digital Forensics and Watermarking: 18th International Workshop, IWDW 2019, Chengdu, China, November 2–4, 2019, Revised Selected Papers 18* (pp. 150-157). Springer International Publishing.

Singh, A., Patil, D., & Omkar, S. N. (2018). Eye in the sky: Real-time drone surveillance system (dss) for violent individuals identification using scatternet hybrid deep learning network. In *Proceedings of the IEEE conference on computer vision and pattern recognition workshops* (pp. 1629-1637).

Song, X., Sun, L., Lei, J., Tao, D., Yuan, G., & Song, M. (2016). Event-based large scale surveillance video summarization. *Neurocomputing*, *187*, 66–74.

Thakur, A., & Jindal, N. (2018). Image forensics using color illumination, block and key point based approach. *Multimedia Tools and Applications*, *77*, 26033–26053.

Thing, V. L., Chen, Y., & Cheh, C. (2012, December). An improved double compression detection method for JPEG image forensics. In *2012 IEEE International Symposium on Multimedia* (pp. 290-297). IEEE.

Uddin, K., Jeong, T. H., & Oh, B. T. (2024). Counter-act against GAN-based attacks: A collaborative learning approach for anti-forensic detection. *Applied Soft Computing*, *153*, 111287.

Ulloa, C., Ballesteros, D. M., & Renza, D. (2021). Video forensics: Identifying colorized images using deep learning. *Applied Sciences (Basel, Switzerland)*, *11*(2), 476.

Venema, A. E., & Geradts, Z. J. (2020). Digital forensics, deepfakes, and the legal process. *The SciTech Lawyer*, *16*(4), 14–23.

Vuyyuru, L. R., Purimetla, N. R., Reddy, K. Y., Vellela, S. S., Basha, S. K., & Vatambeti, R. (2024). Advancing automated street crime detection: A drone-based system integrating CNN models and enhanced feature selection techniques. *International Journal of Machine Learning and Cybernetics*, •••, 1–23.

Wang, X., Li, Y., Wang, H., Huang, L., & Ding, S. (2022). A Video Summarization Model Based on Deep Reinforcement Learning with Long-Term Dependency. *Sensors (Basel)*, *22*(19), 7689. PMID: 36236789

Xu, Z., Yang, W., Meng, A., Lu, N., Huang, H., Ying, C., & Huang, L. (2018). Towards end-to-end license plate detection and recognition: A large dataset and baseline. In *Proceedings of the European conference on computer vision (ECCV)* (pp. 255-271).

Yang, F., Li, J., Lu, W., & Weng, J. (2017). Copy-move forgery detection based on hybrid features. *Engineering Applications of Artificial Intelligence*, *59*, 73–83.

Zappalà, A., Guarnera, L., Rinaldi, V., Livatino, S., & Battiato, S. (2024). Enhancing Crime Scene Investigations through Virtual Reality and Deep Learning Techniques. *arXiv preprint arXiv:2409.18458.*

Zhang, S., Zhu, Y., & Roy-Chowdhury, A. K. (2016). Context-aware surveillance video summarization. *IEEE Transactions on Image Processing*, *25*(11), 5469–5478. PMID: 27552758

Compilation of References

Abbasi, M., Váz, P., Silva, J., & Martins, P. (2025). Comprehensive Evaluation of Deepfake Detection Models: Accuracy, Generalization, and Resilience to Adversarial Attacks. *Applied Sciences (Basel, Switzerland)*, *15*(3), 1225. DOI: 10.3390/app15031225

Abbas, M., Sarita, D., Alrasheedi, M., Arya, L., Singh, M. P., & Pandey, K. (2023). Hybrid intuitionistic fuzzy entropy–SWARA–COPRAS method for multi-criteria sustainable biomass crop type selection. *Sustainability*, *15*(10), 1–16. DOI: 10.3390/su15107765

Abhishek, & Jindal, N. (2021). Copy move and splicing forgery detection using deep convolution neural network, and semantic segmentation. Multimedia Tools and Applications, 80(3), 3571–3599.

Acsintoae, A., Florescu, A., Georgescu, M.-I., Mare, T., Sumedrea, P., Ionescu, R. T., Khan, F. S., & Shah, M. (2022). UBnormal: New Benchmark for Supervised Open-Set Video Anomaly Detection. In *Proceedings of the IEEE/CVF Conference on Computer Vision and Pattern Recognition (CVPR)*. New Orleans, LA, USA.

Adewale, T. (2023). *The legal framework for combatting deepfake technologies: A comparative analysis of global approaches*. ResearchGate.

Afchar, D., Nozick, V., Yamagishi, J., & Echizen, I. (2018). MesoNet: A Compact Facial Video Forgery Detection Network. *2018 IEEE International Workshop on Information Forensics and Security (WIFS)*. https://doi.org/10.1109/WIFS.2018.8630761

Agarwal, R., & Verma, O. (2020). An efficient copy move forgery detection using deep learning feature extraction and matching algorithm. *Multimedia Tools and Applications*, *79*. Advance online publication. DOI: 10.1007/s11042-019-08495-z

Agarwal, R., Verma, O. P., Saini, A., Shaw, A., & Patel, A. R. (2021). The advent of deep learning-based image forgery detection. In *Innovative Data Communication Technologies and Application*. Springer.

Agrahari Baniya, A., Lee, T. K., Eklund, P., & Aryal, S. (2024). Frame selection using spatiotemporal dynamics and key features as input pre-processing for video super-resolution models. *SN Computer Science*, *5*(3), 323.

Ahmad, M. (2008). Human motion detection and segmentation from moving image sequences. In *Proceedings of the 2008 International Conference on Electrical and Computer Engineering*, Dhaka, Bangladesh.

Ahmed, S., Khan, M. F., Singh, B., Singh, N., & Sharma, B. (2025). Enhancing Crime Scene Analysis: The Impact of AI Technologies on Evidence Processing. In *Forensic Intelligence and Deep Learning Solutions in Crime Investigation* (pp. 63-84). IGI Global Scientific Publishing.

Ahmed, N. U. R., Badshah, A., Adeel, H., Tajammul, A., Duad, A., & Alsahfi, T. (2024). Visual Deepfake Detection: Review of Techniques, Tools, Limitations, and Future Prospects. *IEEE Access : Practical Innovations, Open Solutions*.

Akash, P., & Manimekalai, V. (2025, April). How deepfake audio was used in a corporate fraud attempt: A case study on AI-driven social engineering. IRJMETS.

Alaei, F., & Alaei, A. (2022). Handwriting Analysis: Applications in Person Identification and Forensic. *Breakthroughs in Digital Biometrics and Forensics*, 147–165. https://doi.org/DOI: 10.1007/978-3-031-10706-1_7

Albahar, M., & Almalki, J. (2019). Deepfakes: Threats and countermeasures systematic review. *Journal of Theoretical and Applied Information Technology*, *97*(22), 3242–3250.

Aleman, B. E., Diaz, M., & Ferrer, M. A. (2024). A short review on graphonometric evaluation tools in children. *Lecture Notes in Computer Science (Including Subseries Lecture Notes in Artificial Intelligence and Lecture Notes in Bioinformatics), 14285 LNCS*, 3–20. https://doi.org/DOI: 10.1007/978-3-031-45461-5_1

AlHalawani, S., Benjdira, B., Ammar, A., Koubaa, A., & Ali, A. M. (2024). Diff-Plate: A Diffusion Model for Super-Resolution of License Plate Images. *Electronics (Basel)*, *13*(13), 2670.

Ali, M. M. (2023). Real-time video anomaly detection for smart surveillance. *IET Image Processing*, *17*, 1375–1388.

Aliyev, E. (2024). Forensic Handwriting Analysis to Determine the Psychophysiological Traits. *International Journal of Religion*, *5*(6), 511–530. DOI: 10.61707/2R6B-MR11

Al-kfairy, M., Mustafa, D., Kshetri, N., Insiew, M., & Alfandi, O. (2024). Ethical Challenges and Solutions of Generative AI: An Interdisciplinary Perspective. *Informatics (MDPI)*, *11*(3), 58. DOI: 10.3390/informatics11030058

Almaiah, M. A., Yelisetti, S., & Arya, L., CNKB, B., Kaliappan, K., Vellaisamy, P., Hajjej, F., & Alkdour, T. (2023). A novel approach for improving the security of IoT–medical data systems using an enhanced dynamic Bayesian network. *Electronics (Basel)*, *12*(20), 1–15. DOI: 10.3390/en16010008

Almars, A. (2021). Deepfakes detection techniques using deep learning: A survey. *Journal of Computer and Communications*, *9*, 20–35. DOI: 10.4236/jcc.2021.95003

Alrashoud, M. (2025). Deepfake video detection methods, approaches, and challenges. *Alexandria Engineering Journal*, *125*, 265–277.

Alsubaei, F. S., Almazroi, A. A., & Ayub, N. (2024). Enhancing phishing detection: A novel hybrid deep learning framework for cybercrime forensics. *IEEE Access : Practical Innovations, Open Solutions*, *12*, 8373–8389.

Al-Taha, M., Wang, H., & Xu, C. (2024). Adaptive adversarial perturbations for steganography and watermarking. *Journal of Visual Communication and Image Representation*, *91*, 103819.

Altuncu, E., Franqueira, V. N., & Li, S. (2024). Deepfake: Definitions, performance metrics and standards, datasets, and a meta-review. *Frontiers in Big Data*, *7*, 1400024. PMID: 39296632

Amerini, I., Barni, M., Battiato, S., Bestagini, P., Boato, G., Bonaventura, T. S., Bruni, V., Caldelli, R., Natale, F. G. B. D., Nicola, R. D., Guarnera, L., Mandelli, S., Marcialis, G. L., Micheletto, M., Montibeller, A., Orrù, G., Ortis, A., Perazzo, P., Salvi, D., . . . Vitulano, D. (2024). Deepfake Media Forensics: State of the Art and Challenges Ahead. arXiv (Cornell University). https://doi.org//arxiv.2408 .00388DOI: 10.48550

Amerini, I., Barni, M., Battiato, S., Bestagini, P., Boato, G., Bruni, V., & Vitulano, D. (2025). Deepfake media forensics: Status and future challenges. *Journal of Imaging*, *11*(3), 73. PMID: 40137185

Amiri, Z., Heidari, A., Navimipour, N. J., Unal, M., & Mousavi, A. (2024). Adventures in data analysis: A systematic review of deep learning techniques for pattern recognition in cyber-physical- social systems. *Multimedia Tools and Applications*, *83*(8), 22909–22973.

Anderson, K.. (2024). Multimodal data integration for oncology in the era of deep neural networks: A review. *Frontiers in Artificial Intelligence*, *12*, 1408843. DOI: 10.3389/frai.2024.1408843

Andriluka, M., Pishchulin, L., Gehler, P., & Schiele, B. (2014). 2d human pose estimation: New benchmark and state of the art analysis. In *Proceedings of the IEEE Conference on computer Vision and Pattern Recognition.* Columbus, OH, USA.

Anusha, N., & Khushi, K. Madhumitha, Shet, M., and Alekhya, P. (2024). Deepfake detection using deep learning: A two-pronged approach with cnns and autoencoders. pages 24–29.

Arnab, A., Dehghani, M., Heigold, G., Sun, C., Lučić, M., & Schmid, C. (2021). ViViT: A video vision transformer. *Proceedings of the IEEE/CVF International Conference on Computer Vision*, 6836–6846.

Aroussi, M. E., Hassouni, M. E., Ghouzali, S., Rziza, M., & Aboutajdine, D. (2009). Block Based Curvelet Feature Extraction for Face Recognition, In *Proceedings of the 2009 International Conference on Multimedia Computing and Systems,* Ouarzazate, Morocco.

Arrieta, A. B., Díaz-Rodríguez, N., Del Ser, J., Bennetot, A., Tabik, S., Barbado, A., & Herrera, F. (2020). Explainable Artificial Intelligence (XAI): Concepts, taxonomies, opportunities and challenges toward responsible AI. *Information Fusion*, *58*, 82–115. DOI: 10.1016/j.inffus.2019.12.012

Arshad, H., Jantan, A. B., & Abiodun, O. I. (2018). Digital forensics: Review of issues in scientific validation of digital evidence. *Journal of Information Processing Systems*, *14*(2), 346–376.

Arya, L. (2024). Securing healthcare data and cybersecurity innovations in the era of Industry 5.0. In Cybersecurity and Data Management Innovations for Revolutionizing Healthcare (pp. 132–147). https://doi.org/DOI: 10.4018/979-8-3693-7457-3.ch006

Arya, L., Raju, E. S., & Santosh, M. V. MPJ, S. K., Rastogi, R., Elloumi, M., Arumugam, T., & Namasivayam, B. (2026). Explainable Artificial Intelligence (XAI) for Ethical and Trustworthy Decision-Making in 6G Networks. In R. Shaikh (Ed.), *6G Networks and AI-Driven Cybersecurity* (pp. 217-250). IGI Global Scientific Publishing. https://doi.org/DOI: 10.4018/979-8-3373-0568-4.ch008

Arya, L., Bhatnagar, M., Mehrotra, S., Arasavalli, N., Rastogi, R., Banda, L., & Gautam, D. (2026). IoT-Driven Automation in Dairy Processing for Waste Reduction and Productivity Enhancement. In Mendes de Souza, P. (Ed.), *Next-Generation Technologies in Dairy Processing and Production* (pp. 171–196). IGI Global Scientific Publishing., DOI: 10.4018/979-8-3693-9949-1.ch006

Arya, L., & Sharma, Y. K. (2024). Safeguarding women: IoT-enabled machine learning approach for threat detection via EEG and eye blink signals. *International Journal of Computer Information Systems and Industrial Management Applications*, *16*(3), 366–377. https://cspub-ijcisim.org/index.php/ijcisim/article/view/714

Arya, L., Sharma, Y. K., Devi, S., Padmanaban, H., & Kumar, R. (2024). Securing the Internet of Things: AI-powered threat detection and safety measures. In Illés, Z., Verma, C., Gonçalves, P. J. S., & Singh, P. K. (Eds.), *Proceedings of International Conference on Recent Innovations in Computing* (Vol. 1195). Springer. https://doi.org/DOI: 10.1007/978-981-97-3442-9_7

Arya, L., Sharma, Y. K., Kumar, R., Padmanaban, H., Devi, S., & Tyagi, L. K. (2023). Maximizing IoT security: An examination of cryptographic algorithms. In *2023 International Conference on Power Energy, Environment & Intelligent Control (PEEIC)* (pp. 1548–1552). IEEE. https://doi.org/DOI: 10.1109/peeic59336.2023.10451210

Arya, L., Sharma, Y. K., Padmanaban, H., Devi, S., & Kumar, R. (2024). Eyes in the sky: Safeguarding borders security with AI-powered aerial monitoring and IoT integration. In Illés, Z., Verma, C., Gonçalves, P. J. S., & Singh, P. K. (Eds.), *Proceedings of International Conference on Recent Innovations in Computing* (Vol. 1195). Springer. https://doi.org/DOI: 10.1007/978-981-97-3442-9_61

Asci, F., Scardapane, S., Zampogna, A., D'Onofrio, V., Testa, L., Patera, M., Falletti, M., Marsili, L., & Suppa, A. (2022). Handwriting Declines With Human Aging: A Machine Learning Study. *Frontiers in Aging Neuroscience*, *14*, 889930. DOI: 10.3389/FNAGI.2022.889930 PMID: 35601625

Awasthi, A., Rao, S. B., & Acharjya, K. (2024). *Efficient image feature extraction using convolutional neural networks.*

Baig, M. I., & Yadegaridehkordi, E. (2025). Factors influencing academic staff satisfaction and continuous usage of generative artificial intelligence (GenAI) in higher education. *International Journal of Educational Technology in Higher Education*, *22*(1). Advance online publication. DOI: 10.1186/s41239-025-00506-4

Bajpai, C., Gaur, M., Mori, G., & Keshwani, P. (2024). Deepmarknet for robust image and video watermarking embedding and detection. *ICTACT Journal on Image and Video Processing*, *15*, 3375–3378.

Banos, O., Garcia, R., & Saez, A. (2014). MHEALTH [Dataset]. *UCI Machine Learning Repository*. https://doi.org/DOI: 10.24432/C5TW22

Bao, Q., Wang, Y., Hua, H., Dong, K., & Lee, F. (2024). An anti-forensics video forgery detection method based on noise transfer matrix analysis. *Sensors (Basel)*, *24*(16), 5341. PMID: 39205036

Bappy, J. H., Roy-Chowdhury, A. K., Bunk, J., Nataraj, L., & Manjunath, B. S. (2017). Exploiting spatial structure for localizing manipulated image regions. In *Proceedings of the IEEE International Conference on Computer Vision* (pp. 4970–4979). https://doi.org/DOI: 10.1109/ICCV.2017.532

Barnes, C., & Barraclough, T. (2020). Deepfakes and synthetic media. In *Emerging technologies and international security* (pp. 206–220). Routledge.

Barocas, S., Hardt, M., & Narayanan, A. (2019). *Fairness and machine learning*. https://fairmlbook.org

Bas, P., Filler, T., & Pevný, T. (2011). "Break Our Steganographic System" – The ins and outs of organizing BOSS. In *Proceedings of the 13th International Conference on Information Hiding* (pp. 59–70).

Bau, D., Zhu, J.-Y., Wulff, J., Peebles, W., Zhou, B., Strobelt, H., & Torralba, A. (2019). Seeing What a GAN Cannot Generate. *2021 IEEE/CVF International Conference on Computer Vision (ICCV)*, 4501. https://doi.org/DOI: 10.1109/iccv.2019.00460

Bayar, B., & Stamm, M. C. (2016). A deep learning approach to universal image manipulation detection using a new convolutional layer. *Proceedings of the 4th ACM Workshop on Information Hiding and Multimedia Security*, 5–10. https://doi.org/ DOI: 10.1145/2909827.2930786

Beaugendre, A., Miyano, H., Ishidera, E., & Goto, S. (2010). Human tracking system for automatic video surveillance with particle filter. In *Proceedings of the 2010 IEEE Asia Pacific Conference on Circuits and Systems*, Kuala Lumpur.

Bell, A. E. (2013). Robust feature vector for efficient human detection. In *Proceedings of the 2013 IEEE Applied Imagery Pattern Recognition Workshop (AIPR)*. Washington, DC.

Ben Jabra, S., & Ben Farah, M. (2024). Deep learning-based watermarking techniques challenges: A review of current and future trends. *Circuits, Systems, and Signal Processing*, *43*, 4339–4368. DOI: 10.1007/s00034-024-02651-z

Ben, O. jljones, Kumar H, Meg Risdal, MRao, Vadim Sherman, Vipul, Wendy Kan, & Yau Ben-Or. (2017). *Intel & MobileODT Cervical Cancer Screening* [Dataset]. Kaggle. https://kaggle.com/competitions/intel-mobileodt-cervical-cancer-screening

Benmessahel, B. (2024). Deep learning methods for copy move image forgery detection: A review. *International Journal of Safety and Security Engineering*, *14*(5), 1505–1515. DOI: 10.18280/ijsse.140518

Bermejo Nievas, E., Deniz Suarez, O., Bueno García, G., & Sukthankar, R. (2011). Violence Detection in Video Using Computer Vision Techniques. In Real, P., Diaz-Pernil, D., Molina-Abril, H., Berciano, A., & Kropatsch, W. (Eds.), Lecture Notes in Computer Science: Vol. 6855. *Computer Analysis of Images and Patterns. CAIP 2011*. Springer.

Bertazzini, G., Baracchi, D., Shullani, D., Iuliani, M., & Piva, A. (2024). CoFFEE: A codec-based forensic feature extraction and evaluation software for H. 264 videos. *EURASIP Journal on Information Security*, *2024*(1), 34.

Bertolami, R., Uchida, S., Zimmermann, M., & Bunke, H. (2007). Non-uniform slant correction for handwritten text line recognition. *Proceedings of the International Conference on Document Analysis and Recognition, ICDAR, 1*, 18–22. https://doi .org/DOI: 10.1109/ICDAR.2007.4378668

Bhardwaj, M., & Srivastava, A. (2021). Psychological Assessment and Handwriting Analysis to Determine Personality Traits of a Convicted Criminal - A Case Study. [IJSR]. *International Journal of Scientific Research, 10*(10), 1000–1004. DOI: 10.21275/SR211019222113

Binns, R. (2018). *The ethics of artificial intelligence and robotics*. Stanford Encyclopedia of Philosophy. Retrieved from https://plato.stanford.edu/entries/ethics-ai/

Binson, V. A., Thomas, N. M., Thoams, S., Augustine, A., & Sivakumar, K. S. (2016, October). An advance to cloning detection in digital forensics investigations. In *2016 International Conference on Emerging Technological Trends (ICETT)* (pp. 1-5). IEEE.

Bird, C. L., & Yang, X. (2024). Forensic document examination: A global snapshot. *Forensic Sciences Research*, *9*(4). Advance online publication. DOI: 10.1093/FSR/OWAF001 PMID: 39911858

Bird, C., Found, B., & Rogers, D. (2010). Forensic document examiners' skill in distinguishing between natural and disguised handwriting behaviors. *Journal of Forensic Sciences*, *55*(5), 1291–1295. DOI: 10.1111/J.1556-4029.2010.01456.X PMID: 20533988

Blaskovic, A. K., Rusk, J.-D., Parker, V. C.Jr, & Payne, B. R. (2022). Cyber- crime and intellectual property theft: An analysis of modern digital forensics. In *Proceedings of the Future Technologies Conference*, pages 536–542. Springer.

Bochkovskiy, A., Wang, C. Y., & Liao, H. Y. M. (2020). Yolov4: Optimal speed and accuracy of object detection. *arXiv preprint arXiv:2004.10934*.

Bondi, L., Baroffio, L., Güera, D., Bestagini, P., Delp, E. J., & Tubaro, S. (2017). First steps toward camera model identification with convolutional neural networks. *IEEE Signal Processing Letters*, *24*(3), 259–263. DOI: 10.1109/LSP.2016.2633282

Bondi, L., Lameri, S., Guera, D., Bestagini, P., Delp, E., & Tubaro, S. (2017). Tampering detection and localization through clustering of camera-based CNN features. In *Proceedings of the 2017 IEEE Conference on Computer Vision and Pattern Recognition Workshops (CVPRW)* (pp. 1855–1864).

Borges, A., Zatt, B., Porto, M., & Correa, G. (2024). A systematic literature review on video transcoding acceleration: Challenges, solutions, and trends. *Multimedia Tools and Applications*, *83*(24), 64079–64108.

Boroumand, M., Chen, M., & Fridrich, J. (2019). Deep residual network for steganalysis of digital images. *IEEE Transactions on Information Forensics and Security*, *14*(5), 1181–1193. DOI: 10.1109/TIFS.2018.2871749

Bostanci, E. (2015). 3D reconstruction of crime scenes and design considerations for an interactive investigation tool. *International Journal of Information Security Science*, *4*(2), 50–58.

Bourouis, S., Alroobaea, R., Alharbi, A. M., Andejany, M., & Rubaiee, S. (2020). Recent advances in digital multimedia tampering detection for forensics analysis. *Symmetry*, *12*(11), 1811.

Braun, M., Krebs, S., Flohr, F., & Gavrila, D. M. (2018). The eurocity persons dataset: A novel benchmark for object detection. *arXiv preprint arXiv:1805.07193*.

Bregler, C., Covell, M., & Slaney, M. (1997) ''Video Rewrite: Driving visual speech with audio,'' *Proceedings of the 24th Annual Conference on Computer Graphics and Interactive Techniques, SIGGRAPH 1997*, pp 353–360, https://doi.org/DOI: 10.1145/258734.258880

Brennan-Marquez, E., & Henderson, S. E. (2019). From the database to the courtroom: Artificial intelligence and evidence. *Columbia Law Review*, *119*(7), 1911–1966.

Brenner, S. W. (2010). *Cybercrime: Criminal threats from cyberspace*. Praeger.

Bunk, J., Bappy, J. H., Mohammed, T. M., Nataraj, L., Flenner, A., Manjunath, B. S., . . . Peterson, L. (2017, July). Detection and localization of image forgeries using resampling features and deep learning. In *2017 IEEE conference on computer vision and pattern recognition workshops (CVPRW)* (pp. 1881-1889). IEEE.

Buolamwini, J., & Gebru, T. (2018). *Gender shades: Intersectional accuracy disparities in commercial gender classification. Proceedings of the 1st Conference on Fairness, Accountability and Transparency*, 77-91. https://doi.org/DOI: 10.1145/3287560.3287593

Cai, R., Zhang, H., Liu, W., Gao, S., & Hao, Z. (2021). Appearance-Motion Memory Consistency Network for Video Anomaly Detection. In *Proceedings of the AAAI-21/ IAAI-21/EAAI-21 Conference on Artificial Intelligence*, Virtual.

Camacho, I. C., & Wang, K. (2021). A Comprehensive Review of Deep-Learning-Based Methods for Image Forensics [Review of A Comprehensive Review of Deep-Learning-Based Methods for Image Forensics]. Journal of Imaging, 7(4), 69. Multidisciplinary Digital Publishing Institute. https://doi.org/DOI: 10.3390/jimaging7040069

Capasso, P., Cattaneo, G., & De Marsico, M. (2024). A comprehensive survey on meth- ods for image integrity. *ACM Transactions on Multimedia Computing Communications and Applications*, *20*(11), 1–34.

Cardenuto, J. P., Yang, J., Padilha, R., Wan, R., Moreira, D., Li, H., Wang, S., Andalo´, F., Marcel, S., & Rocha, A.. (2023). The age of synthetic realities: Challenges and opportunities. *APSIPA Transactions on Signal and Information Processing*, *12*(1).

Carletti, V., Foggia, P., Percannella, G., Saggese, A., & Vento, M. (2013). Recognition of Human Actions from RGB-D Videos Using a Reject Option. In Petrosino, A., Maddalena, L., & Pala, P. (Eds.), Lecture Notes in Computer Science: Vol. 8158. *New Trends in Image Analysis and Processing – ICIAP 2013. ICIAP 2013*. Springer.

Carreira, J., Noland, E., Hillier, C., & Zisserman, A. (2019). A short note on the kinetics-700 human action dataset. arXiv preprint arXiv:1907.06987.

Casey, E. (2011). *Digital evidence and computer crime: Forensic science, computers, and the internet* (3rd ed.). Academic Press.

Chakraborty, S., Chatterjee, K., & Dey, P. (2024). Detection of Image Tampering Using Deep Learning, Error Levels and Noise Residuals. *Neural Processing Letters*, *56*, 112. DOI: 10.1007/s11063-024-11448-9

Chan, C., Ginosar, S., Zhou, T., & Efros, A. (2018) "Everybody Dance Now," Proceedings of the IEEE International Conference on Computer Vision, vol. 2019-October, pp. 5932–5941,https://doi.org/DOI: 10.48550/arxiv.1808.07371

Chandanshiv, V., Ekhande, N., Dagade, R. V., and Lohar, R. (2025). A survey: Deep fake detection. *International Journal of Advanced Research in Science, Communication and Technol- ogy*, pages 106 – 109.

Chang, S. H., & Yu, N. Y. (2009). Computerized Handwriting Analysis in Children with/without Motor Incoordination. *IFMBE Proceedings, 23*, 402–405. DOI: 10.1007/978-3-540-92841-6_99

Chataut, R., & Upadhyay, A. (2025). Introduction to Deepfake Technology and Its Early Foundations. In Deepfakes and Their Impact on Business (pp. 1-18). IGI Global Scientific Publishing.

Chen, C., Jafari, R., & Kehtarnavaz, N. (2015). UTD-MHAD: A Multimodal Dataset for Human Action Recognition Utilizing a Depth Camera and a Wearable Inertial Sensor. In *Proceedings of the IEEE International Conference on Image Processing*. Canada, September.

Chen, B., Hong, Y., & Nie, Y. (2024). Deep video steganography using temporal-attention-based frame selection and spatial sparse adversarial attack. *Journal of Visual Communication and Image Representation*, •••, 104.

Cheng, M., Cai, K., & Li, M. (2021). RWF-2000: An Open Large Scale Video Database for Violence Detection. In *Proceedings of the 25th International Conference on Pattern Recognition (ICPR)*. Milan, Italy.

Cheng, Z., Qin, L., Ye, Y., Huang, Q., & Tian, Q. (2012). Human Daily Action Analysis with Multi-view and Color-Depth Data. In *Proceedings of the ECCV 2012 Workshop on Consumer Depth Cameras for Computer Vision*, Firenze, Italy.

Chen, J.-F., Ni, C.-C., Lin, P.-H., & Lin, R. (2024). Designing the Future: A Case Study on Human-AI Co-Innovation. *Creative Education, 15*(3), 474. DOI: 10.4236/ce.2024.153028

Chen, J., Kang, X., Liu, Y., & Wang, Z. J. (2015). Median filtering forensics based on convolutional neural networks. *IEEE Signal Processing Letters, 22*, 1849–1853.

Chennamma, H., & Madhushree, B. (2023). A comprehensive survey on image authentication for tamper detection with localization. *Multimedia Tools and Applications, 82*(2), 1873–1904.

Chen, Z., Yan, L., Yin, S., & Shi, Y. (2020). Vehicle license plate recognition system based on deep learning in natural scene. *Journal on Artificial Intelligence*, *2*(4), 167–175. DOI: 10.32604/jai.2020.012716

Chesney, R., & Citron, D. K. (2019). Deepfakes and the new disinformation war: The coming age of synthetic media. *Foreign Affairs*, *98*(1), 2–9.

Chesney, R., & Citron, D. K. (2019). Deepfakes: A looming challenge for privacy, democracy, and national security. *California Law Review*, *107*(6), 1753–1819. DOI: 10.15779/Z38S45D99X

Chiang, C. Y., Chua, H. N., Jasser, M. B., Wong, R. T., & Issa, B. (2025, February). Transformer-Based Ensemble Approach for Robust Deepfake Detection in Low-Resolution Short Videos. In *2025 21st IEEE International Colloquium on Signal Processing & Its Applications (CSPA)* (pp. 307-312). IEEE.

Choutas, V., Weinzaepfel, P., Revaud, J., & Schmid, C. (2018). PoTion: Pose MoTion Representation for Action Recognition. In *Proceedings of the 2018 IEEE/CVF Conference on Computer Vision and Pattern Recognition (CVPR)*, Salt Lake City, UT, USA.

Christlein, V., Riess, C., & Angelopoulou, E. (2010). On rotation invariance in copy-move forgery detection. In *2010 IEEE International Workshop on Information Forensics and Security* (pp. 1–6). https://doi.org/DOI: 10.1109/WIFS.2010.5711472

Ciliberto, M., Fortes, R. V., Calatroni, A., Lukowicz, P., & Roggen, D. (2021). Opportunity++: A Multimodal Dataset for Video- and Wearable, Object and Ambient Sensors-Based Human Activity Recognition. *Frontiers of Computer Science*, *•••*, 3.

Cordts, M., Omran, M., Ramos, S., Rehfeld, T., Enzweiler, M., Benenson, R., Franke, U., Roth, S., & Schiele, B. (2016). The cityscapes dataset for semantic urban scene understanding. In *Proceedings of the IEEE conference on computer vision and pattern recognition*. Honolulu, HI, USA

Corvi, R., Cozzolino, D., Prashnani, E., De Mello, S., Nagano, K., & Verdoliva, L. (2025). Seeing What Matters: Generalizable AI-generated Video Detection with Forensic-Oriented Augmentation. https://doi.org/DOI: 10.48550/ARXIV.2506.16802

Cox, I. J., Miller, M. L., Bloom, J. A., Fridrich, J., & Kalker, T. (2007). *Digital watermarking and steganography* (2nd ed.). Morgan Kaufmann.

Creswell, A., White, T., Dumoulin, V., Arulkumaran, K., Sengupta, B., & Bharath, A. A. (2018). Generative Adversarial Networks: An Overview. *IEEE Signal Processing Magazine*, *35*(1), 53. DOI: 10.1109/msp.2017.2765202

Dalal, N., & Triggs, B. (2005). Histograms of Oriented Gradients for human detection. In *Proceedings of the 2005 IEEE Computer Society Conference on Computer Vision and Pattern Recognition (CVPR'05).* San Diego, CA, USA.

Damen, D., Doughty, H., Farinella, G. M., Furnari, A., Kazakos, E., Ma, J., Moltisanti, D., Munro, J., Perrett, T., Price, W., & Wray, M. (2022). Rescaling egocentric vision: Collection, pipeline and challenges for epic-kitchens-100. *International Journal of Computer Vision*, ●●●, 1–23.

Dandekar, P., Aote, S. S., & Raipurkar, A. (2024). Low-resolution face recognition: Review, challenges and research directions. *Computers & Electrical Engineering, 120*, 109846.

Dang, L. M., Hassan, S. I., Im, S., & Moon, H. (2019). Face image manipulation detection based on a convolutional neural network. *Expert Systems with Applications, 129*, 156–168.

Das, A., & Balakrishnan, S. G., & Pramod. (2021). Network Intrusion Detection System based on Generative Adversarial Network for Attack Detection. *International Journal of Advanced Computer Science and Applications, 12*(11). Advance online publication. DOI: 10.14569/ijacsa.2021.0121186

Dastbaravardeh, E., Askarpour, S., Saberi Anari, M., & Rezaee, K. (2024). Channel Attention-Based Approach with Autoencoder Network for Human Action Recognition in Low-Resolution Frames. *International Journal of Intelligent Systems, 2024*(1), 1052344.

Datta, S. K., Jia, S., & Lyu, S. (2024, January 18). Exposing Lip-syncing Deepfakes from Mouth Inconsistencies. ArXiv.

Daubert v. Merrell Dow Pharmaceuticals, Inc., 509 U.S. 579 (1993).

Dave, I., Gupta, R., Rizve, M. N., & Shah, M. (2022). Tclr: Temporal contrastive learning for video representation. *Computer Vision and Image Understanding, 219*, 103406.

Deb, P., Deb, S., Das, A., & Kar, N. (2024). Image forgery detection techniques: Latest trends and key challenges. *IEEE Access : Practical Innovations, Open Solutions.*

Dehghani, A., & Saberi, H. (2025). Generating and Detecting Various Types of Fake Image and Audio Content: A Review of Modern Deep Learning Technologies and Tools. arXiv preprint arXiv:2501.06227.

Deng, S., Sun, Z., Zhuang, R., & Gong, J. (2023). Noise-to-Norm Reconstruction for Industrial Anomaly Detection and Localization. *Applied Sciences (Basel, Switzerland), 13*(22), 12436. DOI: 10.3390/app132212436

Deng, U., Luo, P., Loy, C. C., & Tang, X. (2014). Pedestrian attribute recognition at far distance. *ACM Multimedia, 2014*, 789–792.

Dhiman, C., & Vishwakarma, D. K. (2019). A Robust Framework for Abnormal Human Action Recognition Using R -Transform and Zernike Moments in Depth Videos. *IEEE Sensors Journal, 19*(13), 5195–5203.

Dino, H. I., & Abdulrazzaq, M. B. (2019). Facial expression classification based on SVM, KNN and MLP classifiers. In *2019 International Conference on Advanced Science and Engineering (ICOASE)* (pp. 70–75). https://doi.org/DOI: 10.1109/ICOASE.2019.8723728

Diwan, T., Anirudh, G., & Tembhurne, J. V. (2023). Object detection using YOLO: Challenges, architectural successors, datasets and applications. *Multimedia Tools and Applications, 82*, 9243–9275. DOI: 10.1007/s11042-022-13644-y PMID: 35968414

Dollar, P., Wojek, C., Schiele, B., & Perona, P. (2009). Pedestrian detection: A benchmark. In *Proceedings of the Computer Vision and Pattern Recognition*. Miami, FL, USA.

Do, N. T., Na, I. S., & Kim, S. H. (2018). Forensics face detection from GANs using convolutional neural network. *ISITC, 2018*, 376–379.

Dong, F., Zhang, Y., & Nie, X. (2020). Dual Discriminator Generative Adversarial Network for Video Anomaly Detection. *IEEE Access : Practical Innovations, Open Solutions, 8*, 88170–88176.

Dong, H., Meer, T. V., & Zhang, X. (2025). Explainable AI for DeepFake Detection. *Applied Sciences (Basel, Switzerland), 15*(2), 725.

Dong, J., Wang, W., & Tan, T. (2013). CASIA image tampering detection evaluation database. In *2013 IEEE China Summit and International Conference on Signal and Information Processing* (pp. 422–426). https://doi.org/DOI: 10.1109/ChinaSIP.2013.6625374

Doshi-Velez, F., & Kim, B. (2017). Towards a rigorous science of interpretable machine learning. *arXiv preprint arXiv:1702.08608.*

Dunsin, D. (2025). *Deepfake Technology and AI-Driven Social Engineering Attacks: Implications for Cyber Defense*. MDPI.

Dunsin, D., Ghanem, M. C., Ouazzane, K., & Vassilev, V. (2024). A comprehensive analysis of the role of artificial intelligence and machine learning in modern digital forensics and incident response. *Forensic Science International Digital Investigation, 48*, 301675. DOI: 10.1016/j.fsidi.2023.301675

Duong, H.-T., Le, V.-T., & Hoang, V. T. (2023). Deep Learning-Based Anomaly Detection in Video Surveillance: A Survey. *Sensors (Basel), 23*(11), 5024. PMID: 37299751

Durina, M. E. (2005). Disguised Signatures: Random or Repetitious? *Journal of the American Society of Questioned Document Examiners, 8*(1), 9–16. DOI: 10.69525/JASQDE.112

Dutta, M., & Saini, J.. (2024). A systematic literature review on image splicing detec- tion and localization using emerging technologies. *Multimedia Tools and Applications*, •••, 1–36.

Du, X., Hargreaves, C., Sheppard, J., Anda, F., Sayakkara, A., Le-Khac, N. A., & Scanlon, M. (2020, August). SoK: Exploring the state of the art and the future potential of artificial intelligence in digital forensic investigation. In *Proceedings of the 15th international conference on availability, reliability and security* (pp. 1-10).

Edupuganti, V., Mardani, M., Cheng, J. Y., Vasanawala, S., & Pauly, J. M. (2019). VAE-GANs for Probabilistic Compressive Image Recovery: Uncertainty Analysis. arXiv (Cornell University). https://arxiv.org/pdf/1901.11228.pdf

Ehsanpour, M., Reid, I., & Rezatofighi, H. (2024). Dataset: MuPoTS-3D. https://doi.org/ ro053DOI: 10.57702/im0

Elaskily, M., Elnemr, H., Sedik, A., Dessouky, M., El Banby, G., Elaskily, O., & El-Samie, F. A. (2020). A novel deep learning framework for copy-move forgery detection in images. *Multimedia Tools and Applications, 79*. Advance online publication. DOI: 10.1007/s11042-020-08751-7

Elhoseny, M., Selim, M. M., & Shankar, K. (2021). Optimal deep learning based convolution neural network for digital forensics face sketch synthesis in internet of things (IoT). *International Journal of Machine Learning and Cybernetics, 12*, 3249–3260.

El-Shafai, W., Fouda, M. A., El-Rabaie, E. S. M., & El-Salam, N. A. (2024). A comprehensive taxonomy on multimedia video forgery detection techniques: Challenges and novel trends. *Multimedia Tools and Applications, 83*(2), 4241–4307. PMID: 37362636

Engilberge, M., Grosche, F. W., & Fua, P. (2024). No Identity, no problem: Motion through detection for people tracking. *arXiv preprint arXiv:2411.16466.*

Engilberge, M., Liu, W., & Fua, P. (2023). Multi-view tracking using weakly supervised human motion prediction. In *Proceedings of the IEEE/CVF Winter Conference on Applications of Computer Vision* (pp. 1582-1592).

Epstein, Z., Hertzmann, A., Akten, M., Farid, H., Fjeld, J., Frank, M. R., Groh, M., Herman, L., Leach, N., Mahari, R., Pentland, A., Russakovsky, O., Schroeder, H., & Smith, A. (2023). Art and the science of generative AI. *Science, 380*(6650), 1110. DOI: 10.1126/science.adh4451 PMID: 37319193

Faigman, D. L., Kaye, D. H., Saks, M. J., & Sanders, J. (2014). *Modern scientific evidence: The law and science of expert testimony.* Thomson Reuters.

Farber, S. (2025). AI as a decision support tool in forensic image analysis: A pilot study on integrating large language models into crime scene investigation workflows. *Journal of Forensic Sciences.* Advance online publication. DOI: 10.1111/1556-4029.70035 PMID: 40186399

Farid, H. (2009). Image forgery detection. *IEEE Signal Processing Magazine, 26*(2), 16–25. DOI: 10.1109/MSP.2008.931079

Farid, H. (2023). Lip-Sync Deepfake Detection from Audio-Video Mismatch. *CVPR Workshop.*

Farrús, M. (2010). Prosody in automatic speaker recognition: Applications in biometrics and voice imitation [Doctoral dissertation, Saarbrücken]. VDM Verlag.

Fascella, C., Mandelli, S., Bestagini, P., Barni, M., & Alamayreh, O. (2024). Forensic detection of deepfakes generated through video-to-video motion transfer using OpenPose. Politecnico di Milano Thesis.

Faundez-Zanuy, M., Fierrez, J., Ferrer, M. A., Diaz, M., Tolosana, R., & Plamondon, R. (2020). Handwriting Biometrics: Applications and Future Trends in e-Security and e-Health. *Cognitive Computation, 12*(5), 940–953. DOI: 10.1007/S12559-020-09755-Z/TABLES/2

Fayyaz, M. A., Anjum, A., Ziauddin, S., Khan, A., & Sarfaraz, A. (2020). An improved surveillance video forgery detection technique using sensor pattern noise and correlation of noise residues. *Multimedia Tools and Applications, 79*, 5767–5788.

Fernández, E. G., Orozco, A. L. S., & Villalba, L. J. G. (2023). A multi-channel approach for detecting tampering in colour filter images. *Expert Systems with Applications, 230*, 120498.

Fernando, T., Priyasad, D., Sridharan, S., Ross, A., & Fookes, C. (2025). *Face Deepfakes – A Comprehensive Review* [Preprint]. ArXiv.

Fletcher, M. (2020). The role of expert testimony in digital forensics: Ensuring admissibility of AI-generated evidence. *Journal of Cybersecurity and Digital Forensics*, *15*(3), 38–47.

For. (2022). Forensic analysis of synthetically generated western blot images. *IEEE Access*, 10:59919 – 59932.

Francis, N. J., Jones, S., & Smith, D. P. (2025). Generative AI in Higher Education: Balancing Innovation and Integrity [Review of Generative AI in Higher Education: Balancing Innovation and Integrity]. British Journal of Biomedical Science, 81. Taylor & Francis. https://doi.org/DOI: 10.3389/bjbs.2024.14048

Freer, J. A., Beggs, B. J., Fernandez-Canque, H. L., Chevriert, F., & Goryashko, A. (1995). Automatic recognition of suspicious activity for camera-based security systems. In *Proceedings of the European Convention on Security and Detection*, Brighton, UK.

Fridrich, J. (2021). AI for digital media forensics: Hype and reality. *IEEE Signal Processing Magazine*, *38*(1), 82–90. DOI: 10.1109/MSP.2020.3036897

Friedman, A., Mikalef, P., & Kourouthanassis, P. (2022). Artificial Intelligence in Forensic Science: A Critical Analysis of Legal Implications. *Journal of Digital Forensics & Cybersecurity*, *18*(4), 215–230. DOI: 10.1002/jdfc.234

Frye v. United States, 293 F. 1013 (D.C. Cir. 1923).

Fu, Y., Hospedales, T. M., Xiang, T., & Gong, S. (2012). Attribute learning for understanding unstructured social activity. In *Proceedings of the 12th European conference on Computer Vision - Volume Part IV (ECCV'12).* Springer-Verlag, Berlin, Heidelberg.

Gaglio, S., Re, G. L., & Morana, M. (2015). Human Activity Recognition Process Using 3-D Posture Data. *IEEE Transactions on Human-Machine Systems*, *45*(5), 586–597.

Galdi, C., Panariello, M., Todisco, M., & Evans, N. (2024). 2D-Malafide: Adversarial attacks against face deepfake detection systems. arXiv.

Galekovic, J., Tkalac, Z., & Ledic, A. (2024). *Forensic Examination of Handwriting and Documents*. Selected ISABS Topics in Forensic Science and Molecular Anthropology. [Working Title], DOI: 10.5772/INTECHOPEN.115118

Gao, Y., Liu, J., & Wang, Q. (2021). Deep Learning in Digital Forensics: Opportunities and Challenges. *Journal of Computer Science and Technology, 36*(2), 341–355. DOI: 10.1007/s11390-021-1834-0

Garcia-Gonzalez, D., Rivero, D., Fernandez-Blanco, E., & Luaces, M. R. (2020). A Public Domain Dataset for Real-Life Human Activity Recognition Using Smartphone Sensors. *Sensors (Basel), 20*(8), 1–14. PMID: 32295028

Gawande, U., Hajari, K., & Golhar, Y. (2024). Novel person detection and suspicious activity recognition using enhanced YOLOv5 and motion feature map. *Artificial Intelligence Review, 57*, 16.

Geiger, A., Lenz, P., & Urtasun, R. (2012). Are we ready for autonomous driving? The KITTI vision benchmark suite. In *Proceedings of the 2012 IEEE Conference on Computer Vision and Pattern Recognition*, Providence, RI, USA.

Ghimire, A., Zhang, X., Werghi, N., Javed, S., & Dias, J. (2022). Deep learning framework for robot for person detection and tracking. *arXiv preprint*. arXiv:2205.04213.

Ghosh, P.. (2023). Activity Classification from First-Person Office Videos with Visual Privacy Protection. In Hossain, M. S., Majumder, S. P., Siddique, N., & Hossain, M. S. (Eds.), *The Fourth Industrial Revolution and Beyond. Lecture Notes in Electrical Engineering* (Vol. 980). Springer.

Gillespie, T. (2018). AI in legal contexts: The challenges of authenticity and accuracy in digital evidence. *Journal of Digital Evidence and Forensic Science, 25*(2), 103–112.

Goodfellow, I. J., Pouget-Abadie, J., Mirza, M., Xu, B., Warde-Farley, D., Ozair, S., Courville, A., & Bengio, Y. (2014, June 10). Generative Adversarial Networks. arXiv. https://doi.org/10.48550/arXiv.1406.2661

Goodfellow, I., Pouget-Abadie, J., Mirza, M., Xu, B., Warde-Farley, D., Ozair, S., & Bengio, Y. (2014). Generative adversarial nets. *Advances in Neural Information Processing Systems, 27*, 2672–2680.

Goodfellow, I., Pouget-Abadie, J., Mirza, M., Xu, B., Warde-Farley, D., Ozair, S., Courville, A., & Bengio, Y. (2017). GAN(Generative Adversarial Nets). *Journal of Japan Society for Fuzzy Theory and Intelligent Informatics, 29*(5), 177. DOI: 10.3156/jsoft.29.5_177_2

Goodfellow, I., Pouget-Abadie, J., Mirza, M., Xu, B., Warde-Farley, D., Ozair, S., Courville, A., & Bengio, Y. (2020). Generative adversarial networks. *Communications of the ACM, 63*(11), 139. DOI: 10.1145/3422622

Goodfellow, I., Shlens, J., & Szegedy, C. (2015). Explaining and harnessing adversarial examples. *International Conference on Learning Representations (ICLR).* https://arxiv.org/abs/1412.6572

Gorelick, L., Blank, M., Shechtman, E., Irani, M., & Basri, R. (2007). Actions as Space-Time Shapes. *IEEE Transactions on Pattern Analysis and Machine Intelligence, 29*(12), 2247–2253. PMID: 17934233

Goyal, S., Bahri, D., Dongre, Y. V., Kuppuraj, T., Arora, M., & Chitra, S. (2024, June). An Analysis of Transform Coding Techniques in Image and Video Compression. In *2024 15th International Conference on Computing Communication and Networking Technologies (ICCCNT)* (pp. 1-6). IEEE.

Goyal, R., & Arya, L. (2017). Home automation & intelligent light control system using microcontroller. In *Proceedings of Third IEEE International Conference ICCCA-2017.* https://doi.org/DOI: 10.1109/CCAA.2017.8229940

Goyal, R., Ebrahimi Kahou, S., Michalski, V., Materzynska, J., Westphal, S., Kim, H., Haenel, V., Fruend, I., Yianilos, P., Mueller-Freitag, M., Hoppe, F., Thurau, C., Bax, I., & Memisevic, R. (2017). The" something something" video database for learning and evaluating visual common sense. In *Proceedings of the IEEE international conference on computer vision (ICCV).* Venice, Italy.

Gozalo-Brizuela, R., & Merchan, E. E. G. (2024). A Survey of Generative AI Applications. *Journal of Computational Science, 20*(8), 801. DOI: 10.3844/jcssp.2024.801.818

Gragnaniello, D., Marra, F., & Verdoliva, L. (2022). Detection of AI-generated synthetic faces. In *Handbook of Digital Face Manipulation and Detection* (pp. 191–212). Springer.

Green, M.. (2024). Ethical considerations in adversarial embedding research: A multidisciplinary perspective. *AI and Ethics, 4*(3), 487–502.

Grekousis, G. (2019). Artificial neural networks and deep learning in urban geography: A systematic review and meta-analysis. *Computers, Environment and Urban Systems, 74,* 244–256. DOI: 10.1016/j.compenvurbsys.2018.10.008

Grm, K., Özata, B. K., Kantarcı, A., Štruc, V., & Ekenel, H. K. (2025). Degrade or super-resolve to recognize? Bridging the Domain Gap for Cross-Resolution Face Recognition. *IEEE Access : Practical Innovations, Open Solutions.*

Grossman, M., & Grimm, P. (2025). Judicial Approaches to Acknowledged and Unacknowledged AI-Generated Evidence. *Science and Technology Law Review, 26*(2).

Güler, R. A., Neverova, N., & Kokkinos, I. (2018). DensePose: Dense Human Pose Estimation in the Wild. In *Proceedings of the 2018 IEEE/CVF Conference on Computer Vision and Pattern Recognition.* Salt Lake City, UT, USA.

Gupta, S., Mohan, N., & Kaushal, P. (2022). Passive image forensics using universal techniques: A review. *Artificial Intelligence Review, 55*(3), 1629–1679.

Habib, S., Hussain, A., Albattah, W., Islam, M., Khan, S., Khan, R. U., & Khan, K. (2021). Abnormal Activity Recognition from Surveillance Videos Using Convolutional Neural Network. *Sensors (Basel), 21*(24), 8291–8306. PMID: 34960386

Hafner, M., Radovic, A., Langer, M., Findenig, S., & Uhl, A. (2024, June). Forensic Recognition of Codec-Specific Image Compression Artefacts. In *Proceedings of the 2024 ACM Workshop on Information Hiding and Multimedia Security* (pp. 131-136).

Hanlen, R. C., Manzolillo, P. A., Muehlberger, R. J., & Sperry, G. R. S. (1999). Survey of Handwriting Habit Areas Used by Forensic Document Examiners: Degree of Use and Discriminatory Power. *Journal of the American Society of Questioned Document Examiners, 2*(1), 45–50. DOI: 10.69525/JASQDE.27

Haoxuan, S., Yan, H., Jiahui, Z., Haoxing, C., Jun, L., Huijia, Z., Weiqiang, W., Liqing, Z., & Jianfu, Z. (2025). Robustness in AI-Generated Detection: Enhancing Resistance to Adversarial Attacks. https://doi.org/DOI: 10.48550/ARXIV.2505.03435

Harandi, M., Sanderson, C., Shen, C., & Lovell, B. (2013). Dictionary Learning and Sparse Coding on Grassmann Manifolds: An Extrinsic Solution. In *Proceedings of the 2013 IEEE International Conference on Computer Vision (ICCV '13).* IEEE Computer Society, USA.

Hashmi, M. F., Keskar, A. G., & Yadav, V. (2016). Fuzzy based image forensic tool for detection and classification of image cloning. *International Journal of Computational Intelligence Systems, 9*(2), 351–375.

Hassan, Y. A., & Rahma, A. M. S. (2023). *A comparative study between the fragile and robust watermarking techniques and proposing new fragile watermarking with embedded value technique.*

Hassner, T., Itcher, Y., & Kliper-Gross, O. (2012). Violent Flows: Real-Time Detection of Violent Crowd Behavior. In *Proceedings of the 3rd IEEE International Workshop on Socially Intelligent Surveillance and Monitoring (SISM) at the IEEE Conf. on Computer Vision and Pattern Recognition (CVPR),* Rhode Island.

Hayes, J., & Danezis, G. (2017). Generating steganographic images via adversarial training. In *Advances in Neural Information Processing Systems (NeurIPS), 30,* 1954–1963.

Heemskerk, J., Mioch, T., Maathuis, H., & Aldewereld, H. (2024). Long-Range Human Detection in Drone Camera Images. In *Proceedings of the 21st International ISCRAM Conference*. University of Münster, Germany. Embracing the Crisis Management Lifecycle.

Heilbron, F. C., Escorcia, V., Ghanem, B., & Niebles, J. C. (2015). ActivityNet: A large-scale video benchmark for human activity understanding. In *Proceedings of the 2015 IEEE Conference on Computer Vision and Pattern Recognition (CVPR)*, Boston, MA, USA.

He, J., Dong, X., Yi, Z., & Wang, H. (2020). Deep learning for image forgery detection: A survey. *IEEE Transactions on Information Forensics and Security, 15*, 3261–3285.

He, K., Zhang, X., Ren, S., & Sun, J. (2016). Deep Residual Learning for Image Recognition. In *Proceedings of the 2016 IEEE Conference on Computer Vision and Pattern Recognition (CVPR)*. Las Vegas, NV, USA.

He, K., Zhang, X., Ren, S., & Sun, J. (2016). Deep residual learning for image recognition. In *Proceedings of the IEEE Conference on Computer Vision and Pattern Recognition (CVPR)* (pp. 770–778).

Hemis, M., & Boudraa, B. (2023). Image watermarking technique using convolutional autoencoder. pages 1 – 6.

Hernandez-Orallo, E., Villagra, V. A., & Montañés, E. (2020). AI-based detection and prevention of child sexual abuse material. *IEEE Access : Practical Innovations, Open Solutions*, *8*, 124709–124719. DOI: 10.1109/ACCESS.2020.3007773

He, X. (2024). Enhancing image steganography through generative adversarial networks: Applications and innovations. *Applied and Computational Engineering*, *110*, 122–128.

Hindustan Times. (2024, May 3). Noida resident arrested after deepfake video of UP CM posted from his account. https://www.hindustantimes.com/cities/noida-news/noida-resident-arrested-after-deep-fake-video-of-up-cm-posted-from-his-account-101714674727032.html

Honarjoo, N., Abdari, A., & Mansouri, A. (2021). Violence detection using pre-trained models. In *Proceedings of the 5th International Conference on Pattern Recognition and Image Analysis (IPRIA)*. Kashan, Iran.

Hong, Y., Hwang, U., Yoo, J., & Yoon, S. (2019). How Generative Adversarial Networks and Their Variants Work [Review of How Generative Adversarial Networks and Their Variants Work]. ACM Computing Surveys, 52(1), 1. Association for Computing Machinery. https://doi.org/DOI: 10.1145/3301282

Hong, M., Li, S., Yang, Y., Zhu, F., Zhao, Q., & Lu, L. (2022). SSPNet: Scale Selection Pyramid Network for Tiny Person Detection from UAV Images. *IEEE Geoscience and Remote Sensing Letters*, *19*, 1–5.

Hou, X., Zhao, Y., Wang, S., & Wang, H. (2025). Model context protocol (mcp): Land- scape, security threats, and future research directions. *arXiv preprint arXiv:2503.23278.*

Hou, X., Shen, L., Ming, Z., & Qiu, G. (2023). Deep generative image priors for semantic face manipulation. *Pattern Recognition*, *139*, 109477. Advance online publication. DOI: 10.1016/j.patcog.2023.109477

Hou, Y., Zheng, L., & Gould, S. (2020). Multiview Detection with Feature Perspective Transformation. In Vedaldi, A., Bischof, H., Brox, T., & Frahm, J. M. (Eds.), Lecture Notes in Computer Science: Vol. 12352. *Computer Vision – ECCV 2020. ECCV 2020*. Springer.

Hsu, C., Lee, C., & Zhuang, Y.-X. (2018). Learning to Detect Fake Face Images in the Wild. https://doi.org/DOI: 10.1109/is3c.2018.00104

Hsu, C.-C., Lee, C.-Y., & Zhuang, Y.-X. (2018). Learning to detect fake face images in the wild. In 2018 IEEE International Symposium on Computer, Consumer and Control (IS3C) (pp. 388–391). https://doi.org/DOI: 10.1109/IS3C.2018.00104

Hu, C., Wu, F., Wu, W., Qiu, W., Lai, S. (2021). Normal Learning in Videos with Attention Prototype Network. *arXiv preprint.*

Huang, G., & Bors, A. G. (2022). Busy-Quiet Video Disentangling for Video Classification. In *Proceedings of the 2022 IEEE/CVF Winter Conference on Applications of Computer Vision (WACV)*, Waikoloa, HI, USA.

Huang, G., Liu, Z., Van Der Maaten, L., & Weinberger, K. Q. (2017). Densely connected convolutional networks. In *Proceedings of the IEEE Conference on Computer Vision and Pattern Recognition (CVPR)* (pp. 2261–2269).

Huang, H., Wang, B., Xiao, J., & Zhu, T. (2024). Improved small-object detection using YOLOv8: A comparative study. *Applied and Computational Engineering.*, *41*(1), 80–88.

Huang, H., Wu, Y., & Wang, Q. (2024). ROBIN: Robust and invisible watermarks for diffusion models with adversarial optimization. In *Proceedings of the 38th International Conference on Neural Information Processing Systems (NIPS '24), 37*, Article 129, 3937–3963.

Hu, J.-F., Zheng, W.-S., Pan, J., Lai, J., & Zhang, J. (2024). Dataset: SYSU 3D HOI Dataset. https://doi.org/DOI: 10.57702/1odneu7u

Hussain, S., Neekhara, P., Jere, M., Koushanfar, F., & McAuley, J. (2020). Adversarial deepfakes: Evaluating vulnerability of deepfake detectors to adversarial examples. arXiv.

Hussain, A., Muhammad, K., Ullah, H., Ullah, A., Imran, A. S., Lee, M. Y., Rho, S., & Sajjad, M. (2022). Anomaly based camera prioritization in large scale surveillance networks. *Computers, Materials & Continua, 70*(2), 2171–2190.

Hussein, O. A., Manap, N. A., Rahman, M. R. A., & Wahhab, B. M. A. (2022). Cyber blackmail on social media and its authenticity through criminal evidence. *NeuroQuantology : An Interdisciplinary Journal of Neuroscience and Quantum Physics*, *20*(6), 121–132.

Irshad, T., Asif, M., Hassan, A., Ahmad, U., Mahmood, T., Ashraf, R., & Faisal, C. M. (2023). A Deep Learning based Human Detection and Tracking for Security Surveillance Systems. *Applied and Computational Engineering*, *2*(1), 569–577.

Islam, U., Alsadhan, A. A., Alwageed, H. S., Al-Atawi, A. A., Mehmood, G., Ayadi, M., & Alsenan, S. (2024). Sentinelfusion based machine learning comprehensive approach for enhanced computer forensics. *PeerJ. Computer Science*, *10*, e2183.

ISO. (2015). Information technology – Security techniques – Guidelines for the analysis and interpretation of digital evidence. International Organization for Standardization., ISO/IEC 27042.

Jagadeesh, A., & Patil, C. M. (2019). Video Based Human Activity Detection, Recognition and Classification of actions using SVM. *Transactions on Machine Learning and Artificial Intelligence*, 6(6)

Jain, I., & Goel, N. (2021, January). Advancements in image splicing and copy-move forgery detection techniques: A survey. In *2021 11th international conference on cloud computing, Data Science & Engineering (confluence)* (pp. 470-475). IEEE.

Jaiswal, A. K., & Srivastava, R. (2021). Detection of copy-move forgery in digital image using multi-scale, multi-stage deep learning model. *Neural Processing Letters*, *54*(1), 75–100.

Janarthanan, S., Karthikeyan, S., & Saravanakumar, S. (2025). Human and Object Detection Deep Learning Model Using RCNN. *Journal of Information Systems Engineering & Management, 10*(30s), 748–756.

Jhuang, H., Gall, J., Zuffi, S., Schmid, C., & Black, M. J. (2013). Towards Understanding Action Recognition. In *Proceedings of the 2013 IEEE International Conference on Computer Vision.* Sydney, NSW, Australia.

Jia, D., Hermans, A., & Leibe, B. (2020). DR-SPAAM: A Spatial-Attention and Auto-regressive Model for Person Detection in 2D Range Data. In *Proceedings of the 2020 IEEE/RSJ International Conference on Intelligent Robots and Systems (IROS)*, Las Vegas, NV, USA.

Jia, X., Zhu, C., Li, M., Tang, W., & Zhou, W. (2021). Llvip: A visible-infrared paired dataset for low-light vision. In *Proceedings of the 2021 IEEE/CVF International Conference on Computer Vision Workshops (ICCVW)*, Montreal, BC, Canada.

Jia, Z. (2025). Research on image recognition and classification algorithms in cloud computing environment based on deep neural networks. *IEEE Access : Practical Innovations, Open Solutions.*

Ji, T., Liu, L., Zhu, W., Wei, J., & Wei, S. (2017). Fast and efficient integration of human upper-body detection and orientation estimation in RGB-D video. In *Proceedings of the 2017 IEEE 9th International Conference on communication Software and Networks (ICCSN).* Guangzhou, China.

Johnson, K., & Lee, S. (2023). Deepfake Detection with Deep Learning: Convolutional Neural Networks versus Transformers. arXiv preprint.

Kachouane, M., Sahki, S., Lakrouf, M., & Ouadah, N. (2012). HOG based fast human detection. In *Proceedings of the 2012 24th International Conference on Microelectronics (ICM).* Algiers.

Kadam, K. D., Ahirrao, S., & Kotecha, K. (2022). Efficient approach towards detection and identification of copy move and image splicing forgeries using mask R-CNN with MobileNet v1. *Computational Intelligence and Neuroscience, 2022,* 1–21. PMID: 35035463

Kader, T., Nasir, A. F. A., Toh, M. Z., Shapiee, M. N. A., Fakarullsroq, A., & Razak, A. (2025). Human Detection and Tracking with YOLO and SORT Tracking Algorithm. [IJACSA]. *International Journal of Advanced Computer Science and Applications, 16*(5), 133–143.

Kadha, V. K., Bakshi, S., & Das, S. K. (2025). Unravelling digital forgeries: A system- atic survey on image manipulation detection and localization. *ACM Computing Surveys.*

Kadha, V. K., Bakshi, S., & Das, S. K. (2025). Unravelling Digital Forgeries: A Systematic Survey on Image Manipulation Detection and Localization. *ACM Computing Surveys.*

Kadha, V., Vakamullu, V., Das, S. K., Mishra, M., & Bora, J. (2022, July). Image Resampling Forensics: A Review on Techniques for Image Authentication. In *International Conference on Computers, Management & Mathematical Sciences* (pp. 183-193). Cham: Springer International Publishing.

Kai, D., Zhang, Y., Wang, J., Xiao, Z., Xiong, Z., & Sun, X. (2025, April). Event-Enhanced Blurry Video Super-Resolution. *Proceedings of the AAAI Conference on Artificial Intelligence, 39*(4), 4175–4183.

Kaja, R. (2024). A comprehensive content verification system for ensuring digital integrity in the age of deep fakes.

Katz, D. M., & Bommarito, M. J. (2020). Legal analytics: The future of analytics in the legal profession. *Annual Review of Law and Social Science, 16*, 287–306. DOI: 10.1146/annurev-lawsocsci-112418-042533

Katzenbeisser, S., & Petitcolas, F. A. P. (2000). *Information hiding techniques for steganography and digital watermarking*. Artech House.

Kay, W., Carreira, J., Simonyan, K., Zhang, B., Hillier, C., Vijayanarasimhan, S., Viola, F., Green, T., Back, T., Natsev, P., Suleyman, M., & Zisserman, A. (2017). The kinetics human action video dataset. *arXiv preprint.*

Kenneally, E., & Brown, C. L. (2021). Explainable AI and admissibility: Navigating forensic epistemology. *Journal of Law and Artificial Intelligence, 1*(1), 14–39.

Kerr, O. S. (2005). Searches and seizures in a digital world. *Harvard Law Review, 119*(2), 531–585.

Khajuria, A., & Pillai, A. A. (2023). Forensic handwriting examination: An updated clinical review. *Santosh University Journal of Health Sciences, 9*(2), 223–228. DOI: 10.4103/SUJHS.SUJHS_47_23

Khalil, A. H., Ghalwash, A. Z., Elsayed, H. A.-G., Salama, G. I., & Ghalwash, H. A. (2023). Enhancing digital image forgery detection using transfer learning. *IEEE Access : Practical Innovations, Open Solutions, 11*, 91583–91594. DOI: 10.1109/ACCESS.2023.3307357

Kharabe, S. R., Hanwate, P. S., & Gaikwad, D. S. & kaliyamurthie, K. P. (2017). Human image segmentation. In *Proceedings of the 2017 International Conference on Algorithms, Methodology, Models and Applications in Emerging Technologies (ICAMMAET)*. Chennai, India.

Kim, J. (2020). Vehicle detection using deep learning technique in tunnel road environments. *Symmetry*, *12*(12), 2012.

Kingma, D. P., & Welling, M. (2019). An Introduction to Variational Autoencoders. Foundations and Trends® in Machine Learning, 12(4), 307. https://doi.org/DOI: 10.1561/2200000056

Kipouràs, P. (2022). The evolution of the simulated signature by the forger. *International Journal of Law in Changing World*, *1*(2), 60–72. DOI: 10.54934/IJLCW.V1I2.25

Kondratyuk, D., Yu, L., Gu, X., Lezama, J., Huang, J., & Hornung, R.. (2023). *First Order Motion Model: Improved Monkey-Net motion transfer*. ArXiv.

Konwar, L., Saikia, N., & Rajbongshi, S. C. (2024). Is the Activity Normal? If Not, What Type of Suspicious? *Journal of Systems Engineering and Electronics*, *34*(12), 695–708.

Konwar, L., Saikia, N., & Rajbongshi, S. C. (2025). *Revisiting human activity recognition using smaller DNN. CCF Trans*. Pervasive Comp. Interact.

Konwar, L., Talukdar, A. K., & Sarma, K. K. (2021). Robust Real Time Multiple Human Detection and Tracking for Automatic Visual Surveillance System. *WSEAS Transactions on Signal Processing.*, *17*, 93–98.

Konwar, L., Talukdar, A. K., Sarma, K. K., Saikia, N., & Rajbongshi, S. C. (2021). Segmentation and selective feature extraction for human detection to the direction of action recognition. *International Journal of Circuits. Systems and Signal Processing.*, *15*, 1371–1386.

Koppula, H. S., Gupta, R., & Saxena, A. (2024). Dataset: Northwestern-UCLA Multiview activity 3D Dataset. Resource: Original Metadata.

Kopuklu, O., Kose, N., Gunduz, A., & Rigoll, G. (2019). Resource efficient 3d convolutional neural networks. In *Proceedings of the 2019 IEEE/CVF International Conference on Computer Vision Workshop (ICCVW)*, Seoul, Korea (South).

Korkinof, D., Rijken, T., O'Neill, M., Yearsley, J., Harvey, H., & Glocker, B. (2018). High-Resolution Mammogram Synthesis using Progressive Generative Adversarial Networks. arXiv (Cornell University). https://arxiv.org/pdf/1807.03401

Korshunov, P., & Marcel, S. (2018). *DeepFakes: a New Threat to Face Recognition?* Assessment and Detection. ArXiv.

Korshunov, P., & Marcel, S. (2019, June). Vulnerability assessment and detection of deepfake videos. In *2019 International Conference on Biometrics (ICB)* (pp. 1-6). IEEE.

Krizhevsky, A., Sutskever, I., & Hinton, G. E. (2012). ImageNet classification with deep convolutional neural networks. *Advances in Neural Information Processing Systems*, *25*, 1097–1105.

Krubha, Y. S., Hou, A., Vester, B., Walker, W., Wang, X., Lin, L., & Hu, S. (2025). Robust AI-Generated Face Detection with Imbalanced Data. https://doi.org/DOI: 10.48550/ARXIV.2505.02182

Kuehlkamp, A., Boyd, A., Czajka, A., Bowyer, K., Flynn, P., & Chute, D., and Benjamin, E. (2022). Interpretable deep learning-based forensic iris segmentation and recognition. In *Proceedings of the IEEE/CVF Winter Conference on Applications of Computer Vision*, pages 359–368.

Kuehne, H., Jhuang, H., Garrote, E., Poggio, T., & Serre, T. (2011). HMDB: a large video database for human motion recognition, In *Proceedings of the International Conference on Computer Vision (ICCV)*. Barcelona, Spain.

Kumar, D. N., Chowdhary, D. L., Pathuri, T., Katta, P., & Arya, L. (2024). AI enhanced–smart genome editing: Integration of CRISPR Cas9 with artificial intelligence for cancer treatment. In 2024 5th International Conference for Emerging Technology (INCET) (pp. 1–6). https://doi.org/DOI: 10.1109/INCET61516.2024.10592877

Kumar, P., Deshmukh, A., Sharma, P., & Bhandari, Dr. D. (2024). Forensic examination of questioned documents. *Futuristic Trends in Social Sciences Volume 3 Book 19*, 284–316. https://doi.org/DOI: 10.58532/V3BJSO19P2CH13

Kumar, V., Sharma, U., & Louis, A. M. (2024, June). Improved GAN for Efficient Cyber Forensics. In *2024 15th International Conference on Computing Communication and Networking Technologies (ICCCNT)* (pp. 1-7). IEEE.

Kumar, A., Singh, D., Jain, R., Jain, D. K., Gan, C., & Zhao, X. (2025). Advances in DeepFake detection algorithms: Exploring fusion techniques in single and multimodal approach. *Information Fusion*, •••, 102993.

Kumari, R., & Garg, H. (2025). Image splicing forgery detection: A review. *Multimedia Tools and Applications*, *84*(8), 4163–4201.

Kumar, M., Rani, A., & Srivastava, S. (2019). Image forensics based on lighting estimation. *International Journal of Image and Graphics, 19*(03), 1950014.

Kumar, R., Mallick, P. K., & Tripathi, S. (2020). Blockchain-based forensic framework for digital image evidence. *Journal of Forensic Sciences, 65*(6), 1990–1999. DOI: 10.1111/1556-4029.14475

Kumar, S.. (2025). A deep learning-driven multi-layered steganographic approach for enhanced data security. *Scientific Reports, 15*, 89189. DOI: 10.1038/s41598-025-89189-5

Kushwaha, A. K. S., Sharma, C. M., Khare, M., Srivastava, R. K., & Khare, A. (2012). Automatic multiple human detection and tracking for visual surveillance system. In *Proceedings of the 2012 International Conference on Informatics, Electronics & Vision (ICIEV)*, Dhaka.

Kuznetsov, O., Frontoni, E., Romeo, L., & Rosati, R. (2024). Enhancing copy-move forgery detection through a novel cnn architecture and comprehensive dataset analysis. *Multimedia Tools and Applications, 83*(21), 59783–59817.

Kwak, N., Cho, S., & Yoon, C. (2025). Detection of Abnormal Human Behavior Using Unsupervised Learning in Video Surveillance Systems. arXiv *Preprints*.

Kwon, D. (2024). AI-generated images threaten science — Here's how researchers hope to spot them. *Nature, 635*(8038), 268. DOI: 10.1038/d41586-024-03542-8 PMID: 39501086

Kwon, M.-J., Nam, S.-H., Yu, I.-J., Lee, H.-K., & Kim, C. (2022). Learning jpeg com- pression artifacts for image manipulation detection and localization. *International Journal of Computer Vision, 130*(8), 1875–1895.

Kyrkou, C., & Theocharides, T. (2019). Deep-learning-based aerial image classification for emergency response applications using unmanned aerial vehicles. In *Proceedings of the 2019 IEEE/CVF Conference on Computer Vision and Pattern Recognition Workshops (CVPRW)*. Long Beach, CA, USA.

Lakshmi, N. D., Latha, Y. M., & Damodaram, A. (2013). Silhouette extraction of a human body based on fusion of HOG and graph-cut segmentation in dynamic background. In *Proceedings of the 3rd International Conference on Computational Intelligence and Information Technology (CIIT 2013)*, Mumbai, India.

Lamichhane, D. (2024). Advanced Detection of AI-Generated Images Through Vision Transformers. https://doi.org/DOI: 10.36227/techrxiv.172556912.28757771/v1

Lan, Y. C., Samonte, M., & Wang, X. (2024). SAM-based localization method for image copy-move forgery. In *Proceedings of the 2024 10th International Conference on Computer Technology Applications* (pp. 200–208). https://doi.org/DOI: 10.1145/3674558.3674586

Laptev, I., Marszalek, M., Schmid, C., & Rozenfeld, B. (2008). Learning realistic human actions from movies. In *Proceedings of the 2008 IEEE Conference on Computer Vision and Pattern Recognition*, Anchorage, AK, USA.

Le, B., Tariq, S., Abuadbba, A., Moore, K., & Woo, S. (2023). *Why Do Facial Deepfake Detectors Fail?* ArXiv.

Ledig, C., Theis, L., Huszár, F., Caballero, J., Cunningham, A., Acosta, A., Aitken, A. P., Tejani, A., Totz, J., Wang, Z., & Shi, W. (2017).. . *Photo-Realistic Single Image Super-Resolution Using a Generative Adversarial Network., 105*. Advance online publication. DOI: 10.1109/cvpr.2017.19

Lee, H.. (2024). Adversarial attacks and defenses in multimodal learning: A survey. *Pattern Recognition, 146*, 109987.

Lee, J., & Fridrich, J. (2023). Benchmarking deep learning-based steganalysis under adaptive attacks. In *Proceedings of the IEEE ISPA* (pp. 168–175).

Leyva, R., Sanchez, V., & Li, C.-T. (2017). The LV dataset: A realistic surveillance video dataset for abnormal event detection. In *Proceedings of the 2017 5th International Workshop on Biometrics and Forensics (IWBF)*. Coventry, UK.

Li, D., Zhang, Z., Chen, X., Ling, H., & Huang, K. (2016). A richly annotated dataset for pedestrian attribute recognition. *arXiv preprint arXiv:1603.07054*.

Li, J. (2024). Area under the roc curve has the most consistent evaluation for binary classification.

Li, X., Ren, J., Liu, C., & Jia, J. (2014). Deep Convolutional Neural Network for Image Deconvolution. Neural Information Processing Systems, 27, 1790. https://papers.nips.cc/paper/5485-deep-convolutional-neural-network-for-image-deconvolution.pdf

Li, Y., Yang, X., Sun, P., Qi, H., & Lyu, S. (2020). ''Celeb-DF: A Large-scale Challenging Dataset for DeepFake Forensics.'' [Online]. Available: https://deepfakedetectionchallenge.ai

Liang, Y., Fang, Y., Luo, S., & Chen, B. (2019, December). Image resampling detection based on convolutional neural network. In *2019 15th International Conference on Computational Intelligence and Security (CIS)* (pp. 257-261). IEEE.

Li, J., Li, B., & Lu, Y. (2024). Neural video compression with feature modulation. In *Proceedings of the IEEE/CVF Conference on Computer Vision and Pattern Recognition* (pp. 26099-26108).

Li, L., Fan, M., & Liu, D. (2021). AdvSGAN: Adversarial image steganography with adversarial networks. *Multimedia Tools and Applications, 80,* 25539–25555.

Liman, Z., Kayhan, U., & Yıldırım, M. Ş. (2025). Evaluation of Images Marked as Child Abuse by Digital Systems in Terms of Forensic Age Determination: A Retrospective Study. *Nigerian Journal of Clinical Practice*, *28*(1), 118–127. PMID: 40326945

Lin, L., Wang, M., Yang, J., Zhang, K., & Zhao, T. (2024). Toward Efficient Video Compression Artifact Detection and Removal: A Benchmark Dataset. *IEEE Transactions on Multimedia.*

Lin, M., Liu, L., Wang, F., Li, J., & Pan, J. (2021). License Plate Image Reconstruction Based on Generative Adversarial Networks. *Remote Sensing*, *13*(15), 3018. DOI: 10.3390/rs13153018

Linna Jr., D., Dalal, A., Gao, C., Grimm, P., Grossman, M. R., Pulice, C., Subrahmanian, V. S., & Tunheim, J. (2024, August 8). Deepfakes in court: How judges can proactively manage alleged AI-generated material in national security cases.

Lin, T.-Y., Goyal, P., Girshick, R., He, K., & Dollár, P. (2017). Focal Loss for Dense Object Detection. In *Proceedings of the 2017 IEEE International Conference on Computer Vision (ICCV)*. Venice, Italy.

Lin, T.-Y., Maire, M., Belongie, S., Hays, J., Perona, P., Ramanan, D., Doll'ar, P., & Zitnick, C. L. (2014). Microsoft coco: Common objects in context. [*th* *European Conference.* Zurich, Switzerland.]. *Proceedings of the Computer Vision–ECCV, 2014*, 13.

Liu, C., & Jia, K. (2024). Multi-Frame Quality Recovery Model for Compressed Video Enhancement. *IEEE Transactions on Consumer Electronics.*

Liu, J., Luo, J., & Shah, M. (2009). Recognizing Realistic Actions from Videos in the Wild. In *Proceedings of the IEEE International Conference on Computer Vision and Pattern Recognition (CVPR).* Miami, FL, USA.

Liu, M.. (2024). Advanced embedding techniques in multimodal retrieval augmented generation: A comprehensive study on cross modal AI applications. *Journal of Computing and Electronic Information Management*, *13*(3), 16–22. DOI: 10.54097/h8wf8vah

Liu, M., Luo, W., Zheng, P., & Huang, J. (2021). A new adversarial embedding method for enhancing image steganography. *IEEE Transactions on Information Forensics and Security*, *16*, 4621–4634.

Liu, M., Song, T., Luo, W., Zheng, P., & Huang, J. (2022). Adversarial steganography embedding via stego generation and selection. *IEEE Transactions on Dependable and Secure Computing*, *20*(3), 2375–2389.

Liu, Q., Che, X., & Bie, M. (2019). R-STAN: Residual Spatial-Temporal Attention Network for Action Recognition. *IEEE Access : Practical Innovations, Open Solutions*, *7*, 82246–82255.

Liu, Q., Zhou, P., & Zhang, L. (2021). ALASKA2: A challenge dataset for cover source mismatch steganalysis. In *Proceedings of the IEEE CVPR Workshops* (pp. 1134–1142).

Liu, X., Zhao, H., Tian, M., Sheng, L., Shao, J., Yi, S., Yan, J., & Wang, X. (2017). Hydraplus-net: Attentive deep features for pedestrian analysis. In *Proceedings of the 2017 IEEE International Conference on Computer Vision (ICCV)*. Venice, Italy.

Liu, Z., Lu, B., Wu, Y., & Gao, C. (2024). Multi-view daily action recognition based on Hooke balanced matrix and broad learning system. *Image and Vision Computing*, *143*, 104919.

Liu, Z., Mao, H., Wu, C.-Y., Feichtenhofer, C., Darrell, T., & Xie, S. (2022). A ConvNet for the 2020s. In *Proceedings of the 2022 IEEE/CVF Conference on Computer Vision and Pattern Recognition (CVPR)*. New Orleans, LA, USA.

Li, W., Zhang, Z., & Liu, Z. (2010). Action Recognition Based on A Bag of 3D Points. In *Proceedings of the IEEE International Workshop on CVPR for Human Communicative Behavior Analysis (in conjunction with CVPR2010)*, San Francisco.

Lopez, D. J. D., & Lien, C. C. (2020). CHU Surveillance Violence Detection Dataset. *IEEE Dataport*. September 4, 2020, doi:DOI: 10.21227/cd9g-xs15

Lovelace, K., Lytle, S. L., & Freeman, L. A. (2021). Technology-facilitated abuse: Gender-based violence and online harassment. *Journal of Interpersonal Violence*, *36*(13–14), 6603–6624.

Luber, M., Spinello, L., & Arras, K. O. (2011). People Tracking in RGB-D Data with On-line Boosted Target Models. In *Proceedings of the IEEE International Conference on Intelligent Robots and Systems (IROS)*. San Francisco, CA, USA

Lu, C., Shi, J., & Jia, J. (2013). Abnormal Event Detection at 150 FPS in MATLAB. In *Proceedings of the 2013 IEEE International Conference on Computer Vision.* Sydney, NSW, Australia.

Lu, M., Duan, Z., Zhu, F., & Ma, Z. (2024, March). Deep hierarchical video compression. *Proceedings of the AAAI Conference on Artificial Intelligence, 38*(8), 8859–8867.

Lung, F. B., Jaward, M. H., & Parkkinen, J. (2015). Spatio-temporal descriptor for abnormal human activity detection. In *Proceedings of the 14th IAPR International Conference on Machine Vision Application (MVA)*, Tokyo, Japan.

Lv, H., Zhou, C., Cui, Z., Xu, C., Li, Y., & Yang, J. (2021). Localizing Anomalies from Weakly-Labeled Videos. *IEEE Transactions on Image Processing, 30,* 4505–4515. PMID: 33872149

Ma, S., & Zhao, X. (2021). Generating JPEG steganographic adversarial example via segmented adversarial embedding. In X. Zhao et al. (Eds.), *Digital Forensics and Watermarking* (LNCS 12617, pp. 68–79). Springer.

Macit, H. B., & Koyun, A. (2020). Tamper detection and recovery on RGB images. In *Artificial Intelligence and Applied Mathematics in Engineering Problems: Proceedings of the International Conference on Artificial Intelligence and Applied Mathematics in Engineering (ICAIAME 2019)* (pp. 972-981). Springer International Publishing.https://doi.org//DOI: 10.1007/s11042-022-13808-w

Madry, A., Makelov, A., Schmidt, L., Tsipras, D., & Vladu, A. (2018). Towards deep learning models resistant to adversarial attacks. *International Conference on Learning Representations (ICLR).* https://arxiv.org/abs/1706.06083

Mahadevan, R., & Lee, Y. S. (2024). Energy-aware optimization for adversarial embedding in IoT scenarios. *IEEE Internet of Things Journal, 11*(2), 1992–2004.

Mahadevan, V., Li, W., Bhalodia, V., & Vasconcelos, N. (2010). Anomaly detection in crowded scenes. In *Proceedings of the IEEE Computer Society Conference on Computer Vision and Pattern Recognition*, San Francisco, CA, USA.

Mahanta, B., L., & Deka, A. (2013). A Study on Handwritten Signature. *International Journal of Computer Applications, 79*(2), 48–52. DOI: 10.5120/13717-1489

Mahara, A., & Rishe, N. (2025). Methods and Trends in Detecting Generated Images: A Comprehensive Review. https://doi.org/DOI: 10.48550/ARXIV.2502.15176

Mai, W. Y., Zhang, J., Fang, P., & Zhang, Z. (2024). Brain-Conditional Multimodal Synthesis: A Survey and Taxonomy. *IEEE Transactions on Artificial Intelligence*, *6*(5), 1080. DOI: 10.1109/tai.2024.3516698

Majhi, S., Dash, R., & Sa, P. K. (2020). Two-stream CNN architecture for anomalous event detection in real world scenarios. In *Computer Vision and Image Processing: 4th International Conference, CVIP 2019, Jaipur, India, September 27–29, 2019, Revised Selected Papers, Part II 4* (pp. 343-353). Springer Singapore.

Malik, A., Kuribayashi, M., Abdullahi, S. M., & Khan, A. N. (2022). DeepFake detection for human face images and videos: A survey. *IEEE Access : Practical Innovations, Open Solutions*, *10*, 18757–18775.

Mandayam, R. (2024).. . *The Impact of Artificial Intelligence on Digital Forensic.*, *3*(6), 1. DOI: 10.47363/jaicc/2024(3)414

Maneli, M. A., & Isafiade, O. (2022). 3D Forensic Crime Scene Reconstruction Involving Immersive Technology: A Systematic Literature Review. *IEEE Access : Practical Innovations, Open Solutions*, *10*, 88821. DOI: 10.1109/access.2022.3199437

Manjunatha, S., & Patil, M. M. (2021). Deep learning-based technique for image tamper detection. In *Proceedings of the 2021 Third International Conference on Intelligent Communication Technologies and Virtual Mobile Networks (ICICV)* (pp. 1278–1285).

Marakalala, M. C., & Matlala, M. M. (2024). Border management identi- fication: The biometric technology to detect criminals and terrorists often travel using falsified identity documents. *OIDA International Journal of Sustainable Development*, *17*(12), 57–70.

Marszaek, M., Laptev, I., & Schmid, C. (2009). Actions in context. In *Proceedings of the IEEE Conference on Computer Vision & Pattern Recognition CVPR*. Miami, FL, USA.

Masood, M., Nawaz, M., Malik, K. M., Javed, A., & Irtaza, A. (2021). Deepfakes Generation and Detection: State-of-the-art, open challenges, countermeasures, and way forward. arXiv.

Masood, M., Nawaz, M., Malik, K. M., Javed, A., Irtaza, A., & Malik, H. (2023). Deepfakes generation and detection: State-of-the-art, open challenges, countermeasures, and way forward. *Applied Intelligence*, *53*(4), 3974–4026.

Matern, F., He, R., & Kuo, S. (2020). AI-based detection of deepfake videos using temporal information. *Proceedings of the International Conference on Digital Forensics and Cyber Crime*. https://doi.org/DOI: 10.1007/978-3-030-39694-3_17

Maurin, B., Masoud, O., & Papanikolopoulos, N. (2002). Monitoring crowded traffic scenes. In *Proceedings of the IEEE 5th International Conference on Intelligent Transportation Systems*, Singapore.

Mayer, O., & Stamm, M. C. (2018). Accurate and efficient image forgery detection using lateral chromatic aberration. *IEEE Transactions on Information Forensics and Security*, *13*(7), 1762–1777.

Mazari, A. C., & Sahbi, H. (2019). MLGCN: Multi-Laplacian Graph Convolutional Networks for Human Action Recognition. *The British Machine Vision Conference (BMVC)*, Cardiff, United Kingdom.

McFarland, M., Nayak, A. R., Stockley, N., Twardowski, M., & Sullivan, J. (2020). Enhanced Light Absorption by Horizontally Oriented Diatom Colonies. *Frontiers in Marine Science*, *7*. Advance online publication. DOI: 10.3389/FMARS.2020.00494

Mehrabi, N., Morstatter, F., Saxena, N., Lerman, K., & Galstyan, A. (2021). A survey on bias and fairness in machine learning. *ACM Computing Surveys*, *54*(6), 1–35. DOI: 10.1145/3457607

Mehta, V., Gupta, P., Subramanian, R., & Dhall, A. 2021 ''FakeBuster: A DeepFakes Detection Tool for Video Conferencing Scenarios,'' *International Conference on Intelligent User Interfaces, Proceedings IUI*, pp. 61–63, https://doi.org/DOI: 10.48550/arxiv.2101.03321

Mengi, M., & Malhotra, D. (2021). SpSiSb: The Technique to Identify Forgery in Legal Handwritten Documents. *Advances in Intelligent Systems and Computing*, *1187*, 739–748. DOI: 10.1007/978-981-15-6014-9_89

Messing, R., Pal, C., & Kautz, H. (2009). Activity recognition using the velocity histories of tracked keypoints. In *Proceedings of the 2009 IEEE 12th International Conference on Computer Vision*. Kyoto, Japan.

Mirić, F., & Rodić Aranđelović, D. (2021). Forensic expertise of signatures and handwriting - multidisciplinary approach. *Facta Universitatis, Series. Law and Politics*, *207*. Advance online publication. DOI: 10.22190/FULP2003207M

Mirsky, Y., & Lee, W. (2020). The creation and detection of deep-fakes: A survey. *ACM Computing Surveys*. Advance online publication. DOI: 10.1145/3425780

Mohassin, A., & Farida, K. (2021). Digital image forgery detection approaches: A review. In *Applications of Artificial Intelligence in Engineering*. Springer.

Mondal, A., Roy, S., Bose, S., & Ghosh, P. (2024). Anomalous Action Detection Dataset [Data set]. Kaggle. https://doi.org/DOI: 10.34740/KAGGLE/DSV/8717699

Monfort, M., Andonian, A., Zhou, B., Ramakrishnan, K., Bargal, S. A., Yan, T., Brown, L., Fan, Q., Gutfreund, D., Vondrick, C., & Oliva, A. (2020). Moments in Time Dataset: One Million Videos for Event Understandin. *IEEE Transactions on Pattern Analysis and Machine Intelligence*, *42*(2), 502–508. PMID: 30802849

Montgomery, R. M. (2025). Augmenting Forensic Science Through AI: The Next Leap in Multidisciplinary Approaches. https://doi.org/DOI: 10.20944/preprints202501.1951.v1

Mookiah, B. (2023). Handwriting Analysis in Forensic Studies: Examining the Science behind It. *Journal of Forensic Toxicology & Pharmacology*, *2023*. Advance online publication. DOI: 10.4172/CICR.1000150

Morgan, J. (2023). Wrongful convictions and claims of false or misleading forensic evidence. *Journal of Forensic Sciences*, *68*(3), 908–961. PMID: 36946413

Muhammad, K., Hussain, T., & Baik, S. W. (2020). Efficient CNN based summarization of surveillance videos for resource-constrained devices. *Pattern Recognition Letters*, *130*, 370–375.

Mukta, M. S. H., Ahmad, J., Raiaan, M. A. K., Islam, S., Azam, S., Ali, M. E., & Jonkman, M. (2023). An investigation of the effectiveness of deepfake models and tools. Journal of sensor and actuator networks, 12(4), 61.

Müller, M., Röder, T., Clausen, M., Eberhardt, B., Krüger, B., & Weber, A. (2007). *Documentation mocap database HDM05. Computer Graphics Technical Reports*. Universität Bonn.

Nallasivan, G., Thatikonda, R., Geetha, M., Bhuvanesh, A., Ramraj, S., & Sreethu, S. (2024). Human Detection and Tracking using Machine Learning Algorithm. In *Proceedings of the 2024 International Conference on Advances in Computing Research on Science Engineering and Technology (ACROSET)*. Indore, India.

Nandhini, T. J., & Thinakaran, K. (2023). Optimizing forensic investiga- tion and security surveillance with deep reinforcement learning techniques. pages 1 – 5.

Narasimhan, M. G., & Kamath, S. S. (2018). Dynamic video anomaly detection and localization using sparse denoising autoencoders. *Multimedia Tools and Applications*, *77*, 13173–13195.

Nataraj, L., et al. (2019). Detecting GAN generated fake images using co-occurrence matrices. Electronic Imaging, 2019, 532-1–532-7. https://doi.org/DOI: 10.2352/ISSN.2470-1173.2019.5.MWSF-532

Navya, V., & Patil, K. A. (2022). *Identification of anomalies in images using cnn and autoencoders techniques.*

Ng, J. Y.-H., Choi, J., Neumann, J., & Davis, L. S. (2018). ActionFlowNet: Learning Motion Representation for Action Recognition. In *Proceedings of the 2018 IEEE Winter Conference on Applications of Computer Vision (WACV)*, Lake Tahoe, NV, USA.

Nguyen, T. T., Kawanishi, Y., John, V., Komamizu, T., & Ide, I. (2025). MultiSensor-Home: A Wide-area Multi-modal Multi-view Dataset for Action Recognition and Transformer-based Sensor Fusion. *arXiv preprint arXiv:2504.02287.*

Nguyen, V-T., & Chu, D-T., Study on Tracking Real-Time Target Human Using Deep Learning for High Accuracy, Journal of Robotics, 2023, 9446956, 11 pages, 2023.

Nguyen, M. D., & Nguyen, M. T. (2025). Artificial Intelligence for Human Detection, Identification and Tracking: Methods and Applications. Journal of Future Artificial Intelligence and Technologies. *Journal of Future Artificial Intelligence and Technologies.*, *2*(1), 79–94.

Ni, B., Wang, G., & Moulin, P. (2011). RGBD-HuDaAct: A color-depth video database for human daily activity recognition. In *Proceedings of the 2011 IEEE International Conference on Computer Vision Workshops (ICCV Workshops).* Barcelona.

Nievas, E. B., Suarez, O. D., Garcia, G. B., & Sukthankar, R. (2016). Hockey Fight Detection Dataset. 2016, hosted on bittorent.

Nihal, R. A., Yen, B., Itoyama, K., & Nakadai, K. (2025). UAV-Enhanced Combination to Application: Comprehensive Analysis and Benchmarking of a Human Detection Dataset for Disaster Scenarios. In Antonacopoulos, A., Chaudhuri, S., Chellappa, R., Liu, C. L., Bhattacharya, S., & Pal, U. (Eds.), Lecture Notes in Computer Science: Vol. 15314. *Pattern Recognition. ICPR 2024.* Springer.

NIST. (2020). *Digital Evidence: Standards and Best Practices.* National Institute of Standards and Technology. Retrieved from https://www.nist.gov/

Nitzan, Y.. (2022). *MyStyle: a personalized generative prior. ACM Trans Gr.* TOG., DOI: 10.1145/3550454.3555436

Niyishaka, P., & Bhagvati, C. (2021). Image splicing detection technique based on illumination-reflectance model and lbp. *Multimedia Tools and Applications*, *80*(2), 2161–2175.

OECD. (2021). *OECD Framework for the Classification of AI Systems*. OECD Publishing. https://www.oecd.org/innovation/oecd-framework-for-classification-of-ai-systems-2021.pdf

Office of Justice Programs. (n.d.). *History of questioned document examination in the United States* Retrieved April 6, 2025, from https://www.ojp.gov/ncjrs/virtual-library/abstracts/history-questioned-document-examination-united-states

Ofli, F., Chaudhry, R., Kurillo, G., Vidal, R., & Bajcsy, R. (2013). Berkeley MHAD: A comprehensive Multimodal Human Action Database. In *Proceedings of the 2013 IEEE Workshop on Applications of Computer Vision (WACV)*. Clearwater Beach, FL, USA.

Oguz, O., & Ikizler-Cinbis, N. (2024). Leveraging cross-resolution attention for effective extreme low-resolution video action recognition. *Signal, Image and Video Processing*, *18*(1), 399–406.

Okonji, O. R., Yunusov, K., & Gordon, B. (2024). Applications of Generative AI in Healthcare: algorithmic, ethical, legal and societal considerations. https://doi.org/ DOI: 10.36227/techrxiv.171527587.75649430/v1

Oreifej, O., & Liu, Z. (2013). HON4D: Histogram of Oriented 4D Normals for Activity Recognition from Depth Sequences. In *Proceedings of the 2013 IEEE Conference on Computer Vision and Pattern Recognition*. Portland, OR, USA.

Padilha, R., Salem, T., Workman, S., Andalo´, F. A., Rocha, A., & Jacobs, N. (2022). Content-aware detection of temporal metadata manipulation. *IEEE Transactions on Information Forensics and Security*, *17*, 1316–1327.

Pandey, N., Singh, B., & Singh, S. (2024). Review of handwriting examination on an unusual surface. *IP International Journal of Forensic Medicine and Toxicological Sciences*, *8*(4), 125–131. DOI: 10.18231/J.IJFMTS.2023.028

Pan, T., Song, Y., Yang, T., Jiang, W., & Liu, W. (2021). Videomoco: Contrastive video representation learning with temporally adversarial examples.In *Proceedings of the 2021 IEEE/CVF Conference on Computer Vision and Pattern Recognition (CVPR)*, Nashville, TN, USA.

Pappachan, P., Adi, N. S., and Firmansyah, G. (2024). Deep learning-based forensics. *Digital Forensics and Cyber Crime Investigation: Recent Advances and Future Directions*, page 211.

Pappachan, P., Adi, N. S., Firmansyah, G., & Rahaman, M. (2025). Deep learning-based forensics and anti-forensics. In *Digital Forensics and Cyber Crime Investigation* (pp. 211–240). CRC Press.

Pareek, P. K. S., B., and G, G. (2023). Deepfake video detection system using deep neural networks. pages 1 – 6.

Park, W. J., & Kim, D. H. Suryanto, Lyuh, C. G., Roh, T. M., & Ko, S. J. (2012). Fast human detection using selective block-based HOG-LBP. In *Proceedings of the 2012 19th IEEE International Conference on Image Processing*, Orlando, FL.

Parmar, P., & Morris, B. (2021). HalluciNeting spatiotemporal representations using a 2D-CNN. *Signals*, *2*(3), 604–618.

Parziale, A., Santoro, A., Marcelli, A., Rizzo, A. P., Molinari, C., Cappuzzo, A. G., & Fontana, F. (2014). An Interactive Tool for Forensic Handwriting Examination. *Proceedings of International Conference on Frontiers in Handwriting Recognition, ICFHR, 2014-December*, 440–445.

Patel, Y., Tanwar, S., Gupta, R., Bhattacharya, P., Davidson, I. E., Nyameko, R., & Vimal, V. (2023). Deepfake generation and detection: Case study and challenges. *IEEE Access : Practical Innovations, Open Solutions*, *11*, 143296–143323.

Peng, F., Yin, L., & Long, M. (2022). BDC-GAN: Bidirectional conversion between computer-generated and natural facial images for anti-forensics. *IEEE Transactions on Circuits and Systems for Video Technology*, *32*(10), 6657–6670.

Perez, M., Kot, A. C., & Rocha, A. (2019). Detection of real-world fights in surveillance videos. In *Proceedings of the ICASSP 2019 - 2019 IEEE International Conference on Acoustics, Speech and Signal Processing (ICASSP).* Brighton, UK.

Phong, N. H., & Ribeiro, B. (2023). Video action recognition collaborative learning with dynamics via PSO-ConvNet Transformer. *Scientific Reports*, *13*(1), 1–15. PMID: 36593249

Piva, A. (2013). An overview on image forensics. *ISRN Signal Processing*, *2013*, 1–22. DOI: 10.1155/2013/496701

Pomari, T., Ruppert, G., Rezende, E., Rocha, A., & Carvalho, T. (2018, October). Image splicing detection through illumination inconsistencies and deep learning. In *2018 25th IEEE International conference on image processing (ICIP)* (pp. 3788-3792). IEEE.

Poma, X., Salloum, R., Bappy, J., & Nataraj, L. (2020). Deep learning for image forensics. In Bhunia, S., Roy-Chowdhury, R., & Bhowmick, A. K. (Eds.), *Multimedia Forensics and Security* (pp. 71–96). Springer., DOI: 10.1007/978-3-030-37211-9_4

Powers, D. M. (2020). Evaluation: from precision, recall and f-measure to roc, informedness, markedness and correlation. *arXiv preprint arXiv:2010.16061*.

Pugliese, R., Badini, S., Frontoni, E., & Regondi, S. (2025). Generative Artificial Intelligence for Advancing Discovery and Design in Biomateriomics. *Intelligent Computing*. Advance online publication. DOI: 10.34133/icomputing.0117

Qadir, S., & Noor, B. (2021, May). Applications of machine learning in digital forensics. In *2021 International Conference on Digital Futures and Transformative Technologies (ICoDT2)* (pp. 1-8). IEEE.

Qawasmi, M., & Al-Kadi, O. (2025). Detecting face tampering in videos using deepfake forensics. *Multimedia Tools and Applications*, •••, 1–17.

Qazi, E. U. H., Zia, T., & Almorjan, A. (2022). Deep learning-based digital image forgery detection system. *Applied Sciences (Basel, Switzerland)*, *12*(6), 2851. DOI: 10.3390/app12062851

Qian, Y., Dong, J., Wang, W., & Tan, T. (2015). Deep learning for steganalysis via convolutional neural networks. In *Media Watermarking, Security, and Forensics 2015* (Vol. 9409, p. 94090J). International Society for Optics and Photonics. DOI: 10.1117/12.2081179

Qiao, T., Ma, Y., Zheng, N., Wu, H., Chen, Y., Xu, M., & Luo, X. (2023). A novel model watermarking for protecting generative adversarial network. *Computers & Security*, *127*, 103102.

Qin, C., Zhang, W., Dong, X., Zha, H., & Yu, N. (2021). Adversarial steganography based on sparse cover enhancement. *Journal of Visual Communication and Image Representation*, •••, 80.

Qiu, J., Han, W., Zhao, X., Long, S., Faloutsos, C., & Li, L. (2024). Evaluating durability: Benchmark insights into multimodal watermarking. *arXiv preprint arXiv:2406.03728*.

Qiu, Z., Yao, T., & Mei, T. (2017). Learning spatio-temporal representation with pseudo-3d residual network. In *Proceedings of the 2017 IEEE International Conference on Computer Vision (ICCV)*, Venice.

Qureshi, S. M., Saeed, A., Almotiri, S. H., Ahmad, F., & Ghamdi, M. A. A. (2024). Deepfake forensics: A survey of digital forensic methods for multimodal deepfake identification on social media. *PeerJ. Computer Science*, *10*. Advance online publication. DOI: 10.7717/peerj-cs.2037 PMID: 38855214

Rahmani, H., Mahmood, A., Huynh, D., & Mian, A. (2023). UWA 3D Multiview Activity II Dataset. *IEEE Dataport.* March 28, 2023.

Rajan, M., & Parameswaran, L. (2025). Key frame extraction algorithm for surveillance videos using an evolutionary approach. *Scientific Reports*, *15*(1), 536. PMID: 39748027

Raji, I. D., & Buolamwini, J. (2019). *Actionable auditing: Investigating the impact of public policy on AI ethics. Proceedings of the 2019 CHI Conference on Human Factors in Computing Systems*, 1-13. https://doi.org/DOI: 10.1145/3293663.3293678

Rajivkannan, A., Venkatesan, M., Sharmila, V., Mukesh, G., Sridhar, J., & Sujendran, J. (2025, May). A Comprehensive Framework for Forged Smartphone Video Detection with Dataset Development and Spatial Temporal Analysis. In *International Conference on Sustainability Innovation in Computing and Engineering (ICSICE 2024)* (pp. 1841-1856). Atlantis Press.

Raj, M., & Bakas, J. (2023). *Detection of object-based forgery in surveillance videos utilizing motion residual and deep learning.*

Ramachandra, B., & Jones, M. J. (2020). Street Scene: A new dataset and evaluation protocol for video anomaly detection. In *Proceedings of the 2020 IEEE Winter Conference on Applications of Computer Vision (WACV).* Snowmass, CO, USA.

Ramya, A., & Raviraj, P. (2014). Performance evaluation of detecting moving objects using graph cut segmentation. In *Proceedings of the 2014 International Conference on Green Computing Communication and Electrical Engineering (ICGCCEE).* Coimbatore, India.

Rana, M. S., Nobi, M. N., Murali, B., & Sung, A. H. (2022). Deepfake detection: A systematic literature review. *IEEE Access : Practical Innovations, Open Solutions*, *10*, 25494–25513. DOI: 10.1109/ACCESS.2022.3154404

Ranasinghe, K., Naseer, M., Khan, S., Khan, F. S., & Ryoo, M. S. (2022). Self-supervised Video Transformer. In *Proceedings of the 2022 IEEE/CVF Conference on Computer Vision and Pattern Recognition (CVPR)*, New Orleans, LA, USA.

Ranjan, R. & Singla, N. (2024). Image forgery detection.

Rao, Y., & Ni, J. (2016). A deep learning approach to detection of splicing and copy-move forgeries in images. *2016 IEEE International Workshop on Information Forensics and Security (WIFS).* doi:DOI: 10.1109/wifs.2016.7823911

Rastogi, K., & Tripathi, V. (2024, November). Video Compression by Spatial and Temporal Dimension Reduction using Seam Carving Algorithm. In *2024 3rd Edition of IEEE Delhi Section Flagship Conference (DELCON)* (pp. 1-4). IEEE.

Reddy, K. K., & Shah, M. (2012). Recognizing 50 Human Action Categories of Web Videos. Machine Vision and Applications. 24(2013), 971–981.

Regulation (EU) 2016/679 of the European Parliament and of the Council of 27 April 2016 on the protection of natural persons with regard to the processing of personal data. *Official Journal of the European Union.*

Regulatory Review. (2025). Reckoning with the Rise of Deepfakes.

Rehman, Y. A. U., Gao, Y., Shen, J., de Gusmão, P. P. B., & Lane, N. (2022). Federated Self-supervised Learning for Video Understanding. In Avidan, S., Brostow, G., Cisse, M., Farinella, G. M., & Hassner, T. (Eds.), Lecture Notes in Computer Science: Vol. 13691. *Computer Vision – ECCV 2022. ECCV 2022.* Springer.

Reilly, K. (2020). Chain of Custody in the Age of AI: Ensuring the Integrity of Digital Evidence. *International Journal of Cybersecurity Law, 22*(3), 129–143. DOI: 10.1177/2452096820907653

Remolina, N., & de la Osa, D. S. (2024). AI at the Bench: Legal and Ethical Challenges of Informing - or Misinforming - Judicial Decision-Making Through Generative AI. https://doi.org/DOI: 10.2139/ssrn.4860853

Renukadevi, P., John, S., & Shivani, N. (2024). Forensic science: Ai-powered image and audio analysis. In *2024 5th International Conference on Smart Electronics and Communication (ICOSEC)*, pages 1519–1525. IEEE.

Research Gate. (n.d.) *Forensic examination of digitally Fabricated signatures in printed documents (PDF).* Retrieved April 6, 2025, from https://www.researchgate.net/publication/335677718_Forensic_examination_oF_digitally_Fabricated_signatures_in_printed_documents

Research Gate. (n.d.). *A Perspective Analysis of Handwritten Signature Technology (PDF).* Retrieved April 6, 2025, from https://www.researchgate.net/publication/380820435_A_Perspective_Analysis_of_Handwritten_Signature_Technology

Research Gate. (n.d.). *A Study of Consistent Similarities Between Complete, Partial, And Initial Signatures of An Individual for Author Identification In Forensic investigation (PDF).* Retrieved April 6, 2025, from https://www.researchgate.net/publication/371125749_A_Study_of_Consistent_Similarities_Between_Complete_Partial_And_Initial_Signatures_of_An_Individual_for_Author_Identification_In_Forensic_investigation

Research Gate. (n.d.). *Analysis of Master Disguised Writing with the Aid of Specific Individual Writing Characteristics (PDF)*. Retrieved April 6, 2025, from https://www.researchgate.net/publication/344737641_Analysis_of_Master_Disguised_Writing_with_the_Aid_of_Specific_Individual_Writing_Characteristics

Research Gate. (n.d.). *Handwriting and gender: A statistical study (PDF)*. Retrieved April 6, 2025, from https://www.researchgate.net/publication/292848678_Handwriting_and_gender_A_statistical_study

Research Gate. (n.d.). *Handwriting and Visual Impairment: A Forensic Analysis of J. S. Bach's Signatures (PDF)*. Retrieved April 6, 2025, from https://www.researchgate.net/publication/281567269_Handwriting_and_Visual_Impairment_A_Forensic_Analysis_of_J_S_Bach%27s_Signatures

Research Gate. (n.d.). *Handwriting expertise: from paper to biometrics (PDF)*. Retrieved April 6, 2025, from https://www.researchgate.net/publication/280608896_Handwriting_expertise_from_paper_to_biometrics

Research Gate. (n.d.). *J Forensic Sci & Criminal Inves Artificial Aging of Paper (PDF)*. Retrieved April 6, 2025, from https://www.researchgate.net/publication/343054118_J_Forensic_Sci_Criminal_Inves_Artificial_Aging_of_Paper

Research Gate. (n.d.). *Raman spectroscopy for forensic analysis of inks in questioned documents | Request PDF*. Retrieved April 6, 2025, from https://www.researchgate.net/publication/256927581_Raman_spectroscopy_for_forensic_analysis_of_inks_in_questioned_documents

Research Gate. (n.d.). *The "handwriting brain": A meta-analysis of neuroimaging studies of motor versus orthographic processes | Request PDF*. Retrieved April 6, 2025, from https://www.researchgate.net/publication/247155789_The_handwriting_brain_A_meta-analysis_of_neuroimaging_studies_of_motor_versus_orthographic_processes

Rhee, K. H. (2020). Detection of spliced image forensics using texture analysis of median filter residual. *IEEE Access : Practical Innovations, Open Solutions*, *8*, 103374–103384.

Riadi, I., & Yudhana, A. (2023). Mobile forensic tools for digital crime inves- tigation: Comparison and evaluation. *International Journal of Safety and Security Engineering*, *13*, 11–19.

Ribeiro, M. T., Singh, S., & Guestrin, C. (2016). Why should I trust you? Explaining the predictions of any classifier. *Proceedings of the 22nd ACM SIGKDD International Conference on Knowledge Discovery and Data Mining*, 1135-1144. https://doi.org/DOI: 10.1145/2939672.2939778

Rob. (2023). Robust watermarking techniques for the authentication and copyright protection of digital images: A survey. *SLU Journal of Science and Technology*, pages 100 – 112.

Rodrigues, R., Bhargava, N., Velmurugan, R., & Chaudhuri, S. (2020). Multi-timescale Trajectory Prediction for Abnormal Human Activity Detection. In *Proceedings of the 2020 IEEE Winter Conference on Applications of Computer Vision (WACV)*. Snowmass, CO, USA.

Rogers, M., & Seigfried-Spellar, K. (2019). *Digital Forensics: An Interdisciplinary Approach*. Jones & Bartlett Learning.

Roshtkhari, M. J., & Levine, M. D. (2013). Online Dominant and Anomalous Behavior Detection in Videos. In *Proceedings of the IEEE Conference on Computer Vision and Pattern Recognition*, Portland

Rosinol, A., Gupta, A., Abate, M., Shi, J., & Carlone, L. (2020). 3D dynamic scene graphs: Actionable spatial perception with places, objects, and humans. *arXiv preprint*.

Rossler, A., Cozzolino, D., Verdoliva, L., Riess, C., Thies, J., & Nießner, M. (2019). FaceForensics++: Learning to detect manipulated facial images. *Proceedings of the IEEE/CVF International Conference on Computer Vision*, 1–11. https://doi.org/DOI: 10.1109/ICCV.2019.00009

S, M., D, S. M., S, R., Subramanian, A. K., V, V., and Swamy, M. (2024). Convolutional neural network-based image tamper detection with error level analysis. pages 1 – 7.

Saboune, J., & Laganiere, R. (2009). People detection and tracking using the explorative particle filtering. In *Proceedings of the 2009 IEEE 12th International Conference on Computer Vision Workshops, ICCV Workshops*, Kyoto.

Saha, A., Dabic Miletic, S., Senapati, T., Simic, V., Pamucar, D., Ala, A., & Arya, L. (2024). Fermatean fuzzy Dombi generalized Maclaurin symmetric mean operators for prioritizing bulk material handling technologies. *Cognitive Computation*. Advance online publication. DOI: 10.1007/s12559-024-10323-y

Saha, A., Görçün, Ö. F., Pamucar, D., Arya, L., & Simic, V. (2024). Evaluation of shared micro-mobility systems for sustainable cities using a consensus-based Fermatean fuzzy multiple objective optimization. *Engineering Applications of Artificial Intelligence, 134*, 108662. DOI: 10.1016/j.engappai.2024.108662

Saha, A., Senapati, T., Akram, M., Kahraman, C., Mesiar, R., & Arya, L. (2024). Dual probabilistic linguistic consensus reaching method for group decision making. *Granular Computing, 9*(35). Advance online publication. DOI: 10.1007/s41066-024-00458-6

Saha, A., Simic, V., & Dabic-Miletic, S. (2025). Prioritization of AI-based material handling approaches for smart logistics in sustainable warehouses: A q-rung orthopair fuzzy CoCoSo methodology with consensus reaching. *Environment, Development and Sustainability*. Advance online publication. DOI: 10.1007/s10668-025-06435-6

Saikia, P., Dholaria, D., Yadav, P., Patel, V., & Roy, M. (2022). *A Hybrid CNN-LSTM model for Video Deepfake Detection by Leveraging Optical Flow Features*. ArXiv.

Saini, K., Sharma, B., & Kaur, M. (2021). Forensic examination of the effects of rheumatoid arthritis on handwriting characteristics. *Egyptian Journal of Forensic Sciences, 11*(1). Advance online publication. DOI: 10.1186/S41935-021-00232-8

Sakthi, M., Kerofsky, L., Kumar, V. R., & Yogamani, S. (2024). Impact of video compression artifacts on fisheye camera visual perception tasks. In *Proceedings of the IEEE/CVF Conference on Computer Vision and Pattern Recognition* (pp. 1301-1310).

Sandhya, & Kashyap, A. (2024). A comprehensive analysis of digital video forensics techniques and challenges. *Iran Journal of Computer Science, 7*(2), 359-380.

Sandotra, N., & Arora, B. (2024). A comprehensive evaluation of feature-based AI techniques for deepfake detection. *Neural Computing & Applications, 36*(8), 3859–3887.

Sarker, M. I., Losada-Gutirrez, C., & Marrn-Romera, M., FuentesJimnez, D., & Luengo-Snchez, S. (2021). Semi-Supervised Anomaly Detection in Video-Surveillance Scenes in the Wild. *Sensors (Basel), 21*(12), 3993–4012. PMID: 34207883

Sato, F., Hachiuma, R., & Sekii, T. (2023). Prompt-Guided Zero-Shot Anomaly Action Recognition using Pretrained Deep Skeleton Features. In *Proceedings of the 2023 IEEE/CVF Conference on Computer Vision and Pattern Recognition (CVPR)*, Vancouver, BC, Canada.

Schonig, J. (2024). Rethinking# thedress: On the social aesthetics of viral ambiguity illusions. *new media & society*, 14614448241235192.

Schuldt, C., Laptev, I., & Caputo, B. (2004). Recognizing human actions: a local SVM approach. In *Proceedings of the 17th International Conference on Pattern Recognition.* Cambridge, UK.

Schwellnus, H., Cameron, D., & Carnahan, H. (2012). Which to Choose: Manuscript or Cursive Handwriting? A Review of the Literature. *Journal of Occupational Therapy, Schools & Early Intervention*, *5*(3–4), 248–258. DOI: 10.1080/19411243.2012.744651

Sedik, A., Kolivand, H., & Albeedan, M. (2024). An efficient image classification and segmentation method for crime investigation applications. *Multimedia Tools and Applications*, **•••**, 1–25.

Seemanthini, K., & Manjunath, S. S. (2018). Human Detection and Tracking using HOG for Action Recognition. *Procedia Computer Science*, *132*, 1317–1326.

Seibel, H., Goldenstein, S., & Rocha, A. (2017). Eyes on the target: Super-resolution and license-plate recognition in low-quality surveillance videos. *IEEE Access : Practical Innovations, Open Solutions*, *5*, 20020–20035.

Seibold, C., Samek, W., Hilsmann, A., & Eisert, P. (2017). Detection of face morphing attacks by deep learning. In *Digital Forensics and Watermarking: 16th International Workshop, IWDW 2017, Magdeburg, Germany, August 23-25, 2017, Proceedings 16* (pp. 107-120). Springer International Publishing. Selim, A., & Ali, İ. The Role of Digital Forensic Analysis in Modern Investigations. *Journal of Emerging Computer Technologies*, *4*(1), 1–5.

Seidenari, L., Varano, V., Berretti, S., Del Bimbo, A., & Pala, P. (2013). Recognizing actions from depth cameras as weakly aligned multi-part bag-of-poses. In *Proceedings of the 3rd International Workshop on Human Activity Understanding from 3D Data (HAU3D'13)*, Portland, Oregon, June 24, 2013.

Seow, J. W., Lim, M. K., Phan, R. C., & Liu, J. K. (2022). A comprehensive overview of Deepfake: Generation, detection, datasets, and opportunities. *Neurocomputing*, *513*, 351–371.

Sethi, M., Kumar, M., & Jindal, M. K. (2025). Forensic handwriting analysis: A hybrid classification framework for writer identification in Devanagari script. *Multimedia Tools and Applications*. Advance online publication. DOI: 10.1007/S11042-024-20574-4

Shahroudy, A., Liu, J., Ng, T.-T., & Wang, G. (2016). NTU RGB+D: A Large-Scale Dataset for 3D Human Activity Analysis. In *Proceedings of the IEEE Conference on Computer Vision and Pattern Recognition (CVPR).* Las Vegas, NV, USA.

Shalmani, S. M., Chiang, F., & Zheng, R. (2022). Efficient Action Recognition Using Confidence Distillation. In *Proceedings of the 2022 26th International Conference on Pattern Recognition (ICPR)*, Montreal, QC, Canada.

Shao, S., Zhao, Z., Li, B., Xiao, T., Yu, G., Zhang, X., & Sun, J. (2018). Crowdhuman: A benchmark for detecting human in a crowd. *arXiv preprint arXiv:1805.00123.*

Sharma, M., & Kaur, M. (2022) "A Review of deepfake technology: an emerging ai threat," Soft Computing for Security Applications, Proceedings of ICSCS, pp. 605–619, https://doi.org/DOI: 10.1007/978-981-16-5301-8_44

Sharma, D. K., Singh, B., Agarwal, S., Garg, L., Kim, C., & Jung, K.-H. (2023a). A survey of detection and mitigation for fake images on social media platforms. *Applied Sciences (Basel, Switzerland), 13*(19), 10980.

Sharma, P., Kumar, M., & Sharma, H. (2023b). Comprehensive analyses of image forgery detection methods from traditional to deep learning approaches: An evaluation. *Multimedia Tools and Applications, 82*(12), 18117–18150.

Sharma, S., Zou, J. J., Fang, G., Shukla, P., & Cai, W. (2024). A review of image watermarking for identity protection and verification. *Multimedia Tools and Applications, 83*(11), 31829–31891.

Shen, Z., Ding, F., & Shi, Y. (2020). Anti-forensics of image sharpening using generative adversarial network. In *Digital Forensics and Watermarking: 18th International Workshop, IWDW 2019, Chengdu, China, November 2–4, 2019, Revised Selected Papers 18* (pp. 150-157). Springer International Publishing.

Shen, W. W., Chen, L., Liu, S., & Zhang, Y. D. (2022). An image enhancement algorithm of video surveillance scene based on deep learning. *IET Image Processing, 16*(3), 681–690.

Shen, Y., & Foroosh, H. (2009). View Invariant Action Recognition from Point Triplets [PAMI]. *IEEE Transactions on Pattern Analysis and Machine Intelligence, 31*(10), 1898–1905. PMID: 19696457

Shi, C., Chen, L., Wang, C., Zhou, X., & Qin, Z. (2023). Review of Image Forensic Techniques Based on Deep Learning. *Mathematics, 11*(14), 3134. DOI: 10.3390/math11143134

Shor, P. W. (1997). Polynomial-time algorithms for prime factorization and discrete logarithms on a quantum computer. *SIAM Journal on Computing*, *26*(5), 1484–1509. DOI: 10.1137/S0097539791191289

Sigamani, A., & Selvaraj, P. (2024). Triplemask spatial linear filter and neutrosophic entropy for video denoising, face detection and recognition in forensic crime analysis using deep learning. *Neutrosophic Sets and Systems*, *67*, 21–56.

Singh, A., Patil, D., & Omkar, S. N. (2018). Eye in the sky: Real-time drone surveillance system (dss) for violent individuals identification using scatternet hybrid deep learning network. In *Proceedings of the IEEE conference on computer vision and pattern recognition workshops* (pp. 1629-1637).

Singh, S., & Kumar, R. (2024). Image forgery detection: Comprehensive review of digital forensics approaches. *Journal of Computational Social Science*, *7*, 877–915. DOI: 10.1007/s42001-024-00265-8

Singh, S., Velastin, S. A., & Ragheb, H. (2010). MuHAVi: A Multicamera Human Action Video Dataset for the Evaluation of Action Recognition Methods. In *Proceedings of the 2010 7th IEEE International Conference on Advanced Video and Signal Based Surveillance*, Boston, MA, USA.

Singla, A., & Khan, Z. (2025). Exploring Artificial Intelligence-Driven Gait Analysis for Suspect Identification in Forensic Video Footage. *International Journal of Sciences and Innovation Engineering*, *2*(1), 15–19.

Sita, J., Found, B., & Rogers, D. (2002). Forensic Handwriting Examiners' Expertise for Signature Comparison. *Journal of Forensic Sciences*, *47*(5), 1–8. DOI: 10.1520/JFS15521J PMID: 12353558

Sohail, S., Sajjad, S. M., Zafar, A., Iqbal, Z., Muhammad, Z., & Kazim, M. (2025). Deepfake image forensics for privacy protection and authenticity using deep learning. *Information (Basel)*, *16*(4), 270.

Solove, D. J. (2021). *Understanding privacy* (2nd ed.). Harvard University Press.

Song, X., Sun, L., Lei, J., Tao, D., Yuan, G., & Song, M. (2016). Event-based large scale surveillance video summarization. *Neurocomputing*, *187*, 66–74.

Soni, A., Kaur, K., & Sharma, C. (2025, March). A Review of Artificial Intelligence in Digital Watermarking Techniques. In *2025 International Conference on Automation and Computation (AUTOCOM)* (pp. 1601-1606). IEEE.

Soomro, K., Zamir, A. R., & Shah, M. (2012). Ucf101: A dataset of 101 human actions classes from videos in the wild, CRCV-TR-12-01, *arXiv preprint*.

Soudy, A. H., Sayed, O., Tag-Elser, H., et al. (2025). Building an efficient Deep Fake detection system using CNNs and transformers. Discover Computing, 28(99).

Spinello, L., & Arras, K. O. (2011). People Detection in RGB-D Data. In *Proceedings of the IEEE International Conference on Intelligent Robots and Systems (IROS).* San Francisco, CA, USA.

Srihari, S. N., Cha, S. H., Arora, H., & Lee, S. (2001). Individuality of handwriting: A validation study. *Proceedings of the International Conference on Document Analysis and Recognition, ICDAR, 2001-January,* 106–109. https://doi.org/DOI: 10.1109/ICDAR.2001.953764

Srihari, S. N., Cha, S. H., & Lee, S. (2001). Establishing Handwriting individuality using pattern recognition techniques. *Proceedings of the International Conference on Document Analysis and Recognition, ICDAR, 2001-January,* 1195–1204. https://doi.org/DOI: 10.1109/ICDAR.2001.953974

Srihari, S., Cha, S., Arora, H., & Lee, S. (2002). Individuality of Handwriting. *Journal of Forensic Sciences, 47*(4), 1–17. DOI: 10.1520/JFS15447J PMID: 12136998

Stefansson, T. (2003). Formative evaluation of handwriting quality. *Perceptual and Motor Skills, 97*(8), 1231. DOI: 10.2466/PMS.97.8.1231-1264 PMID: 15002869

Subash, S., Ezhilarasan, G. M., & Uma Maheswari, B. Anomaly Detection in Surveillance Videos Using Machine Learning. In Proceedings of the *2025 International Conference on Inventive Computation Technologies (ICICT).* Kirtipur, Nepal.

Sultani, W., Chen, C., & Shah, M. (2018). Real-world anomaly detection in surveillance videos. In *Proceedings of the 2018 IEEE/CVF Conference on Computer Vision and Pattern Recognition.* Salt Lake City, UT, USA.

Sun, C., & Mou, C. (2023). Survey on the research direction of EEG-based signal processing [Review of Survey on the research direction of EEG-based signal processing]. Frontiers in Neuroscience, 17. Frontiers Media. https://doi.org/DOI: 10.3389/fnins.2023.1203059

Sung, J., Ponce, C., Selman, B., & Saxena, A. (2011). *Human Activity Detection from RGBD Images. AAAI workshop on Pattern, Activity and Intent Recognition.* PAIR.

Sunil, R., Mer, P., Diwan, A., Mahadeva, R., & Sharma, A. (2025). Exploring autonomous methods for deepfake detection: A detailed survey on techniques and evaluation. *Heliyon, 11*(3). Advance online publication. DOI: 10.1016/j.heliyon.2025.e42273 PMID: 39968137

Sun, M. (2025). A method for solving the multiple degradation video quality enhancement problem: A processing framework for AI-based coding damage repair in concert with video super-resolution. *Multimedia Systems*, *31*(1), 52.

Sushir, R. D., & Bhutada, S. S. (2025). Harnessing Deep Learning for Advanced Video Forensics in Application Software Development. In *Essential Information Systems Service Management* (pp. 163–188). IGI Global.

Taddeo, M., & Floridi, L. (2018). The ethics of artificial intelligence. In *The Ethics of Cybersecurity* (pp. 137–158). Springer., DOI: 10.1007/978-3-030-03228-4_7

Tanenbaum, A. S., & van der Merwe, R. (2016). *Computer Networks* (5th ed.). Prentice Hall.

Tang, W., Zhang, H., Wang, L., & Yu, N. (2020). An adversarial example generation method based on gradient projection for deep steganography. *IEEE Access : Practical Innovations, Open Solutions*, *8*, 82599–82610. DOI: 10.1109/ACCESS.2020.2992013

Tang, W., Zhang, H., Yu, N., & Wu, H. (2021). Adversarial embedding: Evading steganalysis by modifying embedding distributions. *IEEE Transactions on Information Forensics and Security*, *16*, 1420–1434. DOI: 10.1109/TIFS.2020.3034110

Tan, M., Pang, R., & Le, Q. V. (2020). EfficientDet: Scalable and Efficient Object Detection. In *Proceedings of the 2020 IEEE/CVF Conference on Computer Vision and Pattern Recognition (CVPR)*. Seattle, WA, USA.

Tao, L., Wang, X., & Yamasaki, T. (2020). Pretext-contrastive learning: Toward good practices in self-supervised video representation leaning. *arXiv preprint.*

Tayebi, M., & Kafhali, S. E. (2025). Generative Modeling for Imbalanced Credit Card Fraud Transaction Detection. *Journal of Cybersecurity and Privacy*, *5*(1), 9. DOI: 10.3390/jcp5010009

Taylor, S.. (2024). A comprehensive review of adversarial machine learning in steganography and watermarking. *ACDI Computing Surveys*, *57*(2), 1–42.

Thakur, A., & Jindal, N. (2018). Image forensics using color illumination, block and key point based approach. *Multimedia Tools and Applications*, *77*, 26033–26053.

Thing, V. L., Chen, Y., & Cheh, C. (2012, December). An improved double compression detection method for JPEG image forensics. In *2012 IEEE International Symposium on Multimedia* (pp. 290-297). IEEE.

Thombre, D. V., Nirmal, J. H., & Das, L. (2009). Human detection and tracking using image segmentation and kalman filter. In *Proceedings of the 2009 International Conference on Intelligent Agent \& Multi-Agent Systems*. Chennai, India.

Thorat, N. N., Dhotre, P., Kulal, N., Pimpalkar, A. P., Patil, V. S., & Kolekar, S. M. (2024). Tamper-forgery image detection in security digital image: A review. In *2024 IEEE International Conference on Blockchain and Distributed Systems Security (ICBDS)*, pages 1–5. IEEE.

Thurau, C. (2007). Behavior histograms for action recognition and human detection. In *Proceedings of the 2nd conference on Human motion: understanding, modeling, capture and animation*. Springer-Verlag, Berlin, Heidelberg.

Thys, S., Ranst, W. V., & Goedemé, T. (2019). Fooling Automated Surveillance Cameras: Adversarial Patches to Attack Person Detection. In *Proceedings of the 2019 IEEE/CVF Conference on Computer Vision and Pattern Recognition Workshops (CVPRW)*, Long Beach, CA, USA.

Tian, Z., Shen, C., Chen, H., & He, T. (2019). FCOS: Fully Convolutional One-Stage Object Detection. In *Proceedings of the 2019 IEEE/CVF International Conference on Computer Vision (ICCV)*. Seoul, Korea (South).

Times of India / Saam TV. (2025, June 11). Satara police detain 2 for creating morphed video of doctors from Karad. Times of India.

Times of India. (2024, May 2). Man arrested for posting AI-generated ‘deepfake’ video of Chief Minister Yogi Adityanath.

Timothy, D. P., & Santra, A. K. (2024). Detecting digital image forgeries with copy-move and splicing image analysis using deep learning techniques. *International Journal of Advanced Computer Science and Applications*, *15*(5).

Tinkhede, N. N. (2024). *Advance image forgery detection.*

Tiwari, S., Dixit, A. K., & Pandey, A. K. (2024). Fake image detection using generative adversarial networks (gans) and deep learning models. pages 37 – 45.

Toering, M., Gatopoulos, I., Stol, M., & Hu, V. T. (2022). Self-supervised video representation learning with cross-stream prototypical contrasting. In *Proceedings of the 2022 IEEE/CVF Winter Conference on Applications of Computer Vision (WACV)*, Waikoloa, HI, USA.

Tolosana, R., Vera-Rodriguez, R., Fierrez, J., Morales, A., & Ortega-Garcia, J. (2020). Deepfakes and beyond: A survey of face manipulation and fake detection. *Information Fusion*, *64*, 131–148. DOI: 10.1016/j.inffus.2020.07.007

Tong, Z., Song, Y., Wang, J., & Wang, L. (2022). VideoMAE: Masked Autoencoders are Data-Efficient Learners for Self-Supervised Video Pre-Training. In *Proceedings of the 36th Conference on Neural Information Processing Systems (NeurIPS 2022)*, New Orleans, United States.

Tonpe, S., Reddy, J. S., Bhar, C., Pratap, A., & Nayak, J. (2024). Design of a super-resolution scheme for plenoptic images. *Journal of Optics*, ●●●, 1–6.

Tortora, L. (2024). Beyond Discrimination: Generative AI Applications and Ethical Challenges in Forensic Psychiatry. *Frontiers in Psychiatry*, *15*. Advance online publication. DOI: 10.3389/fpsyt.2024.1346059 PMID: 38525252

Tramèr, F., Kurakin, A., Papernot, N., Goodfellow, I., Boneh, D., & McDaniel, P. (2018). Ensemble adversarial training: Attacks and defenses. *International Conference on Learning Representations (ICLR)*. https://arxiv.org/abs/1705.07204

Tran, C. H., & Kong, S. G. (2023). An Iterative Learning Scheme with Binary Classifier for Improved Event Detection in Surveillance Video. *Electronics (Basel)*, *12*(15), 3275.

Tran, D., & Sorokin, A. (2008). Human activity recognition with metric learning. In *Proceedings of the European Conference on Computer Vision*, Marseille.

Tucciarelli, R., Vehar, N., Chandaria, S., & Tsakiris, M. (2022). On the realness of people who do not exist: The social processing of artificial faces. *iScience*, *25*(12), 105441. DOI: 10.1016/j.isci.2022.105441 PMID: 36590465

Tursunalieva, A., Alexander, D. L., Dunne, R., Li, J., Riera, L., & Zhao, Y. (2024). Making sense of machine learning: A review of interpretation techniques and their applications. *Applied Sciences (Basel, Switzerland)*, *14*(2), 496.

Tyagi, A. K., Kumari, S., and Richa (2024). Artificial intelligence-based cyber security and digital forensics: A review. *Artificial Intelligence-Enabled Digital Twin for Smart Manufacturing*, pages 391–419.

U.S. Department of Homeland Security. (2025). Increasing Threats of Deepfake Identities. https://www.dhs.gov/sites/default/files/publications/increasing_threats_of_deepfake_identities_0.pdf

Ubukata, T., Shibata, M., Terabayashi, K., Mora, A., Kawashita, T., Masuyama, G., & Umeda, K. (2014). Fast Human Detection Combining Range Image Segmentation and Local Feature Based Detection. In *Proceedings of the 2014 22nd International Conference on Pattern Recognition*. Stockholm, Sweden.

Uddin, K., Jeong, T. H., & Oh, B. T. (2024). Counter-act against GAN-based attacks: A collaborative learning approach for anti-forensic detection. *Applied Soft Computing*, *153*, 111287.

Ullah, W., Ullah, A., Hussain, T., Khan, Z. A., & Baik, S. W. (2021). An Efficient Anomaly Recognition Framework Using an Attention Residual LSTM in Surveillance Videos. *Sensors (Basel)*, *21*(8), 2811–2827. PMID: 33923712

Ulloa, C., Ballesteros, D. M., & Renza, D. (2021). Video forensics: Identifying colorized images using deep learning. *Applied Sciences (Basel, Switzerland)*, *11*(2), 476.

Umugwaneza, M. E. (2024). Legal analysis on the use of digital evidence under rwandan judicial system.

Upadhyay, S., Singh, J., Shukla, S. K., & Sareen, R. K. (2018). Natural variations in the signature on various surfaces. *Medico-Legal Update*, *18*(1), 183–188. DOI: 10.5958/0974-1283.2018.00038.5

Vaishnavi, K., Reddy, G. P., Reddy, T. B., Iyengar, N. C. S., & Shaik, S. (2023). Real-time Object Detection Using Deep Learning. *Journal of Advances in Mathematics and Computer Science*, *38*(8), 24–32.

Van den Goorbergh, R., van Smeden, M., Timmerman, D., & Van Calster, B. (2022). The harm of class imbalance corrections for risk prediction models: Illustration and simulation using logistic regression. *Journal of the American Medical Informatics Association : JAMIA*, *29*(9), 1525–1534.

van Erp, M., Vuurpijt, L., Franke, K., & Schomaker, L. (2018). The Wanda measurement tool for forensic document examination. *Journal of Forensic Document Examination*, *28*, 5–14. DOI: 10.31974/JFDE28-5-14

Venema, A. E., & Geradts, Z. J. (2020). Digital forensics, deepfakes, and the legal process. *The SciTech Lawyer*, *16*(4), 14–23.

Verdoliva, L. (2020). Media forensics and deepfakes: An overview. *IEEE Journal of Selected Topics in Signal Processing*, *14*(5), 910–932.

Vijayalakshmi, K., Al-Otaibi, S., Arya, L., Almaiah, M. A., Anithaashri, T. P., Karthik, S. S., & Shishakly, R. (2023). Smart agricultural–industrial crop-monitoring system using UAV–IoT classification techniques. *Sustainability*, *15*(14), 11242. DOI: 10.3390/su151411242

Villacres, M. C., Gonzalez, R., & Martinez, L. (2019). Chain of Custody and Digital Evidence: Legal Frameworks in the Age of AI. *Digital Evidence & Law Review*, *12*(2), 42–56. DOI: 10.1080/20365404.2019.1582784

Vinolin, V., & Sucharitha, M. (2021). Taylor-RNet: An approach for image forgery detection using Taylor-adaptive rag-bull rider-based deep convolutional neural network. *International Journal of Intelligent Systems*, *36*(11), 6503. DOI: 10.1002/int.22558

Volkhonskiy, D., Khodak, A., Pashkov, A., & Korzun, D. (2017). Steganographic generative adversarial networks. In *2017 International Conference on Intelligent Information Hiding and Multimedia Signal Processing (IIH-MSP)* (pp. 151–154). IEEE. DOI: 10.1109/IIH-MSP.2017.39

von Marcard, T., Henschel, R., Black, M. J., Rosenhahn, B., & Pons-Moll, G. (2018). Recovering Accurate 3D Human Pose in The Wild Using IMUs and a Moving Camera. In Ferrari, V., Hebert, M., Sminchisescu, C., & Weiss, Y. (Eds.), Lecture Notes in Computer Science: Vol. 11214. *Computer Vision – ECCV 2018. ECCV 2018*. Springer.

Vrskova, R., Hudec, R., Kamencay, P., & Sykora, P. (•••). (). Human Activity Classification Using the 3DCNN Architecture. *Applied Sciences (Basel, Switzerland)*, *12*(2), 931.

Vuyyuru, L. R., Purimetla, N. R., Reddy, K. Y., Vellela, S. S., Basha, S. K., & Vatambeti, R. (2024). Advancing automated street crime detection: A drone-based system integrating CNN models and enhanced feature selection techniques. *International Journal of Machine Learning and Cybernetics*, •••, 1–23.

Wan, B., Jiang, W., Fang, Y., Luo, Z., & Ding, G. (2021). Anomaly detection in video sequences: A benchmark and computational model. *IET Image Processing*, *15*(14), 3454–3465.

Wang, Z., She, Q., & Ward, T. E. (2019). Generative Adversarial Networks: A Survey and Taxonomy. arXiv (Cornell University). https://arxiv.org/abs/1906.01529v1

Wang, J., Liu, Z., Wu, Y., & Yuan, J. (2012). Mining actionlet ensemble for action recognition with depth cameras. In *Proceedings of the 2012 IEEE Conference on Computer Vision and Pattern Recognition*. Providence, RI, USA.

Wang, L.. (2024). Cross-modal retrieval based on multi-dimensional feature fusion hashing. *Frontiers in Physics*, *12*, 1379873. DOI: 10.3389/fphy.2024.1379873

Wang, R., Lin, J., & Wang, Y. (2021). Robust adversarial watermarking against unknown removal attacks. *ACM Transactions on Multimedia Computing Communications and Applications*, *17*(1), 1–24.

Wang, T., Miao, Z., Chen, Y., Zhou, Y., Shan, G., & Snoussi, H. (2019). AED-Net: An Abnormal Event Detection Network. *Engineering*, *5*(5), 930–939.

Wang, X., Li, Y., Wang, H., Huang, L., & Ding, S. (2022). A Video Summarization Model Based on Deep Reinforcement Learning with Long-Term Dependency. *Sensors (Basel), 22*(19), 7689. PMID: 36236789

Wankhade, T. D., Ingale, S. W., Mohite, P., & Bankar, N. (2022). *Artificial Intelligence in Forensic Medicine and Toxicology: The Future of Forensic Medicine* [Review of Artificial Intelligence in Forensic Medicine and Toxicology: The Future of Forensic Medicine]. Cureus. Cureus, Inc., DOI: 10.7759/cureus.28376

Weinland, D., Ronfard, R., & Boyer, E. (2006). Free Viewpoint Action Recognition using Motion History Volumes. [CVIU]. *Computer Vision and Image Understanding, 104*(2-3), 249–257.

Westerlund, M. (2019). The emergence of deepfake technology: A review. *Technology Innovation Management Review, 9*(11).

White, L.. (2025). Standardization challenges in adversarial embedding evaluation. *IEEE Security and Privacy, 23*(1), 45–54.

Wilson, P.. (2024). Multimodal fake news detection with contrastive learning and optimal transport. *Frontiers of Computer Science, 6*, 1473457. DOI: 10.3389/fcomp.2024.1473457

Wojek, C., Walk, S., & Schiele, B. (2009). Multi-Cue Onboard Pedestrian Detection. In *Proceedings of the IEEE Conference on Computer Vision and Pattern Recognition (CVPR)*. Miami, FL, USA

Wu, S., Z., & Ouyang, W. (2023). Revisiting Classifier: Transferring Vision-Language Models for Video Recognition. In *Proceedings of the AAAI Conference on Artificial Intelligence*. 37(3), 2847-2855.

Wu, Y., Abd-Almageed, W., & Natarajan, P. (2018). BusterNet: Detecting copy-move image forgery with source/target localization. In Lecture Notes in Computer Science (pp. 170–186). Springer.

Wu, B., & Nevatia, R. (2005). Detection of multiple, partially occluded humans in a single image by bayesian combination of edgelet part detectors. In *Proceedings of the Tenth IEEE International Conference on Computer Vision (ICCV'05)*. Beijing.

Wu, H., He, B., & Wang, W. (2019). Adversarial embedding networks for steganography. *IEEE Transactions on Information Forensics and Security, 15*, 838–852.

Wu, T., Zhao, Y., & Shi, Y. Q. (2022). Adversarial embedding with GAN regularization for robust image steganography. *IEEE Transactions on Information Forensics and Security, 17*, 3312–3324.

Wu, W., Wang, X., Luo, H., Wang, J., Yang, Y., & Ouyang, W. (2023). Bidirectional Cross-Modal Knowledge Exploration for Video Recognition with Pre-trained Vision-Language Models.In *Proceedings of the 2023 IEEE/CVF Conference on Computer Vision and Pattern Recognition (CVPR)*, Vancouver, BC, Canada.

Wu, Y., Sohrawardi, S., Gerstner, C., & Wright, M. (2025). Understanding and empowering intelligence analysts: User-centered design for deepfake detection tools. In *Proceedings of the 2025 CHI Conference on Human Factors in Computing Systems* (pp. 1–26). https://doi.org/DOI: 10.1145/3706598.3713711

Xia, L., Chen, C.-C., & Aggarwal, J. K. (2012). View invariant human action recognition using histograms of 3D joints. In *Proceedings of the 2012 IEEE Computer Society Conference on Computer Vision and Pattern Recognition Workshops.* Providence, RI, USA.

Xiang, A., Zhang, J., Yang, Q., Wang, L., & Cheng, Y. (2024). Research on splicing im- age detection algorithms based on natural image statistical characteristics. *arXiv preprint arXiv:2404.16296.*

Xin, Y., Walia, E., & Babyn, P. (2019). Generative adversarial network in medical imaging: A review [Review of Generative adversarial network in medical imaging: A review]. Medical Image Analysis, 58, 101552. Elsevier BV. https://doi.org/DOI: 10.1016/j.media.2019.101552

Xu, Z., Tang, X., Li, W., Zhao, Y., Gu, D., & Tian, Y. (2025). Human detection with smoke occlusion based on AI-generated images. *Journal of Safety Science and Resilience = An Quan Ke Xue Yu Ren Xing (Ying Wen), 2025*, 100235.

Xu, Z., Yang, W., Meng, A., Lu, N., Huang, H., Ying, C., & Huang, L. (2018). Towards end-to-end license plate detection and recognition: A large dataset and baseline. In *Proceedings of the European conference on computer vision (ECCV)* (pp. 255-271).

Yadav, B. (2025). Artificial Intelligence in Forensic Science: Navigating Ethical Frontiers and Transformative Applications. In *Generative AI Techniques for Sustainability in Healthcare Security* (pp. 175-194). IGI Global Scientific Publishing.

Yadav, A., & Vishwakarma, D. K. (2024). Datasets, clues and state-of-the- arts for multimedia forensics: An extensive review. *Expert Systems with Applications, 249*, 123756.

Yang, J., Yang, C., Zhai, Y., Wang, Q., Pan, X., & Wang, R. (2024, April). Improving Learned Video Compression by Exploring Spatial Redundancy. In *ICASSP 2024-2024 IEEE International Conference on Acoustics, Speech and Signal Processing (ICASSP)* (pp. 2860-2864). IEEE.

Yang, F., Li, J., Lu, W., & Weng, J. (2017). Copy-move forgery detection based on hybrid features. *Engineering Applications of Artificial Intelligence*, *59*, 73–83.

Yang, L.. (2025). JPEG image steganography with automatic embedding cost learning. *International Journal of Intelligent Systems*. Advance online publication. DOI: 10.1155/int/5309734

Yao, B., Jiang, X., Khosla, A., Lin, A. L., Guibas, L. J., & Fei-Fei, L. (2011). Human Action Recognition by Learning Bases of Action Attributes and Parts. In *Proceedings of the International Conference on Computer Vision (ICCV)*. Barcelona, Spain.

Ye, J., Ni, J., & Yi, Y. (2022). SRNet++: An enhanced deep network for image steganalysis. *IEEE Transactions on Circuits and Systems for Video Technology*, *32*(5), 2532–2545.

Yin, G., Liu, B., Zhu, H., Gong, T., & Yu, N. (2019). A large-scale urban surveillance video dataset for multiple-object tracking and behavior analysis. *arXiv preprint*.

Yin, K., Ding, Z., Dong, Z., Chen, D., Fu, J., Ji, X., Yin, G. & Wang, Z. (2023). NIPD: A Federated Learning Person Detection Benchmark Based on Real-World Non-IID Data. *arXiv preprint*.

Ying, Q., Liu, J., Li, S., Xu, H., Qian, Z., & Zhang, X. (2023). Retouchingffhq: A large-scale dataset for fine-grained face retouching detection. In *Proceedings of the 31st ACM International Conference on Multimedia*, pages 737–746.

Yoon, J. S., Yu, Z., Park, J., & Park, H. S. (2021). Humbi: A large multiview dataset of human body expressions and benchmark challenge. *IEEE Transactions on Pattern Analysis and Machine Intelligence*, *45*(1), 623–640. PMID: 34962862

Yousif, M. R., & Zhang, Y. (2020). Artificial intelligence in insurance fraud detection: A systematic literature review. *Applied Sciences (Basel, Switzerland)*, *10*(10), 3414. DOI: 10.3390/app10103414

Yu, L., Fei, J., Liu, X., Yao, Y., Zhao, J., Wang, G., & Li, X. (2025). MHAD: Multimodal Home Activity Dataset with Multi-Angle Videos and Synchronized Physiological Signals. In Proceedings of the ICASSP 2025-2025 IEEE International Conference on Acoustics, Speech and Signal Processing (ICASSP). Hyderabad, India.

Yuan, T., Zhang, X., Liu, K., Liu, B., Chen, C., Jin, J., & Jiao, Z. 2023. Towards Surveillance Video-and-Language Understanding: New Dataset, Baselines, and Challenges. arXiv Priprient.

Yu, I., Gong, Y., Jiang, N., Ye, Q., & Han, Z. (2020). Scale Match for Tiny Person Detection. In *Proceedings of the 2020 IEEE Winter Conference on Applications of Computer Vision (WACV).* Snowmass, CO, USA.

Yu, I.-J., Nam, S.-H., Ahn, W., Kwon, M.-J., & Lee, H.-K. (2020). Manipulation classifi- cation for jpeg images using multi-domain features. *IEEE Access : Practical Innovations, Open Solutions*, *8*, 210837–210854.

Yu, J., Xu, J., Chen, Y., Li, W., Wang, Q., Yoo, B., & Han, J.-J. (2021). Learning generalized intersection over union for dense pixelwise prediction. In *International Conference on Machine Learning*, pages 12198–12207. PMLR.

Yu, P., Xia, Z., Fei, J., & Lu, Y. (2021). A survey on deepfake video detection. *IET Biometrics*, *10*(6), 607–624. DOI: 10.1049/BME2.12031

Zaidi, M. M., Sampedro, G. A., Almadhor, A., Alsubai, S., Al Hejaili, A., & Gregus, M. (2024). Suspicious Human Activity Recognition From Surveillance Videos Using Deep Learning. *IEEE Access : Practical Innovations, Open Solutions*, *12*, 105497–105510.

Zanardelli, M., Guerrini, F., & Leonardi, R.. (2023). Image forgery detection: A survey of recent deep-learning approaches. *Multimedia Tools and Applications*, *82*, 17521–17566. DOI: 10.1007/s11042-022-13797-w

Zappalà, A., Guarnera, L., Rinaldi, V., Livatino, S., & Battiato, S. (2024). Enhancing Crime Scene Investigations through Virtual Reality and Deep Learning Techniques. *arXiv preprint arXiv:2409.18458.*

Zeng, Y., & Xue, D. (2022). An Overview of Generative Adversarial Networks. 2022 IEEE 2nd International Conference on Electronic Technology, Communication and Information (ICETCI). https://doi.org/DOI: 10.1109/icetci55101.2022.9832049

Zhang, A., Xing, L., Zou, J., & Wu, J. C. (2022). Shifting machine learning for healthcare from development to deployment and from models to data. *Nature Biomedical Engineering*, *6*(12), 1330–1345.

Zhang, H.. (2025). A transformer-based adversarial network framework for steganography. *Expert Systems with Applications*, *266*, 126391. DOI: 10.1016/j.eswa.2025.126391

Zhang, H., Fromont, E., Lefevre, S., & Avignon, B. (2020). Multispectral fusion for object detection with cyclic fuse-and-refine blocks. In *Proceedings of the 2020 IEEE International Conference on Image Processing (ICIP)*. Abu Dhabi, United Arab Emirates.

Zhang, J., Chen, D., Liao, J., Ma, Z., Fang, H., Zhang, W., Feng, H., Hua, G., & Yu, N. (2024). Robust model watermarking for image processing networks via structure consistency. *IEEE Transactions on Pattern Analysis and Machine Intelligence*, •••, 1–8.

Zhang, M., Chen, B., & Tan, S. (2023). A dual-path adversarial framework for covert communication and ownership verification. In *Proceedings of the ACM Workshop on Information Hiding and Multimedia Security* (pp. 21–30).

Zhang, R., & Wang, T. (2025). (in press). Diffusion-based adversarial watermarking for tamper-resistant authentication. *IEEE Transactions on Multimedia.*

Zhang, R., Zhang, J., Zhu, F., & Liu, Y. (2020). Invisible steganography via generative adversarial networks. *Multimedia Tools and Applications*, *79*(1), 667–691. DOI: 10.1007/s11042-019-08162-3

Zhang, S., Benenson, R., & Schiele, B. (2017). Citypersons: A diverse dataset for pedestrian detection. In *Proceedings of the IEEE conference on computer vision and pattern recognition.* Honolulu, HI, USA

Zhang, S., Zhu, Y., & Roy-Chowdhury, A. K. (2016). Context-aware surveillance video summarization. *IEEE Transactions on Image Processing*, *25*(11), 5469–5478. PMID: 27552758

Zhang, X., Guo, J., Zhao, S., Fu, M., Duan, L., Hu, J., Chng, Y. X., Wang, G.-H., Chen, Q.-G., Xu, Z., Luo, W., & Zhang, K. (2025). Unified Multimodal Understanding and Generation Models: Advances, Challenges, and Opportunities. https://doi.org/DOI: 10.48550/ARXIV.2505.02567

Zhang, Y., Zhou, D., Chen, S., Gao, S., & Ma, Y. (2016). Single-Image Crowd Counting via Multi-Column Convolutional Neural Network. In *Proceedings of the 2016 IEEE Conference on Computer Vision and Pattern Recognition (CVPR)*. Las Vegas, NV, USA.

Zhao, T., & Nevatia, R. (2004). Tracking multiple human in complex situations. *IEEE Transactions on Pattern Analysis and Machine Intelligence*, *26*(9), 1208–1221. PMID: 15742895

Zhao, Y., Hu, J., & Zhang, X. (2020).. . *Face Restoration Based on GANs and NST.*, *51*, 198. DOI: 10.1145/3395260.3395304

Zhao, Z., Wang, Y., Xu, K., Sun, T., & Jiang, X. (2024). HEVC Video Adversarial Samples Detection via Joint Features of Compression and Pixel Domains. *IEEE Transactions on Information Forensics and Security*.

Zheng, H., Zhao, Y., Zhang, B., Shang, G., Al-Shamri, M. Y. H., & Aldossary, H. (2024). A Low-Resolution Video Action Recognition Approach Based on Multi-Scale Reconstruction and Multi-Modal Fusion. *IEEE Transactions on Consumer Electronics*.

Zhong, X., Das, A., Alrasheedi, F., & Tanvir, A. (2023). A brief, in-depth survey of deep learning-based image watermarking. *Applied Sciences (Basel, Switzerland)*, *13*(21), 11852.

Zhou, P., Han, X., Morariu, V. I., & Davis, L. S. (2018). Learning rich features for image manipulation detection. In *Proceedings of the IEEE Conference on Computer Vision and Pattern Recognition* (pp. 1053–1061). https://doi.org/DOI: 10.1109/CVPR.2018.00116

Zhou, Q., Huang, H., Zheng, Z., & Bian, J. (2018). Solutions to scalability of blockchain: A survey. *IEEE Access : Practical Innovations, Open Solutions*, *8*, 16440–16455. DOI: 10.1109/ACCESS.2018.2894923

Zhu, J., Kaplan, R., Johnson, J., & Fei-Fei, L. (2018). HiDDeN: Hiding data with deep networks. In *Proceedings of the European Conference on Computer Vision (ECCV)* (pp. 682–697). DOI: 10.1007/978-3

Zhu, Q., Avidan, S., Yeh, M. C., & Cheng, K. T. (2006). Fast human detection using a cascade of Histograms of Oriented Gradients. In *Proceedings of the 2006 IEEE Computer Society Conf. Computer Vision and Pattern Recognition (CVPR'06)*, New York, NY, USA.

Zhu, Y., Long, Y., Guan, Y., Newsam, S., & Shao, L. (2018). Towards universal representation for unseen action recognition. In *Proceedings of the 2018 IEEE/CVF Conference on Computer Vision and Pattern Recognition*, Salt Lake City, UT, USA.

Zohar, A., Zohar, D., & Zohar, E. (2019). *Blockchain-based chain of custody for digital forensics*. Journal of Digital Forensics. *Security and Law*, *14*(1), 1–20.

Zou, Y., Liu, J., Li, Y., Xie, Y., Liu, B., Yi, T., & Li, X. (2024). An image forgery detection technology based on deep learning. In *Proceedings of the International Conference on Algorithms, Software Engineering, and Network Security (ASENS '24)* (pp. 1–10). Association for Computing Machinery. https://doi.org/DOI: 10.1145/3677182.3677245

Zubair, S., Zia, T., & Alsadoon, A. (2020). Ethical implications of adversarial AI: A review. *Procedia Computer Science*, *176*, 1736–1745.

Zuboff, S. (2019). *The age of surveillance capitalism: The fight for a human future at the new frontier of power*. PublicAffairs.

About the Contributors

Gunjan Gupta, (finalists for prestigious HERS SA Young achievers Award), received B.Tech (Electronics & Telecommunication) and M. Tech (VLSI) degrees from India in 2006 and 2011 respectively, DEng in Renewable Energy from Cape Peninsula University of Technology, Cape Town, in 2018. She started her career in 2006, an academic experience of more than 18 years and supervised more than 200 Undergraduate students. She worked as a Post Doctoral Researcher (Satellite Systems Design) at French South African Institute of Technology for three years (2020-2023). Currently, she is a Senior Lecturer in the Department of Electrical, Electronics and Computer Engineering, member of African Space Innovation Centre (ASIC), F'SATI at the Cape Peninsula University of Technology (CPUT), Bellville, South Africa. She has published numerous technical papers in accredited Journals, peer-reviewed conference proceedings and book chapters. Her research focusses on LoRa Networks (Reliability and accuracy), LPWAN Technologies, LoRa based Air quality IoT devices, LoRa WAN in satellite communication (CUBESATS), Satellite systems mission and design. Her current research activities include Integration of LoRaWAN and 5G for IoT, LoRa Direct-to-Satellites, IoT ground station. She lectured various subjects including Solid State Devices & Circuits, Digital Systems-(1 & 2), Communication Systems, Electronic Communication, Physics, Electromagnetic Field Theory, etc. She is a recipient of numerous awards which includes Teaching Excellence Award, Best adopting faculty, merit award for batch topper, Student activity council member, best paper awards in national and international conferences

Neha Goel, working as Professor in the Department of Electronics & Communication Engineering, RKGIT, Ghaziabad, India. She has Ph.D. degree from SRM University, Chennai, in 2019. She has 19 years of rich experience in teaching and research and development activities. Her area of interest is VLSI design, CMOS design, Internet of Things, and machine learning. She has more than 20 published papers in Scopus Indexed Journals/ Conferences and 4 other reputed journals along with more than 25 International/ National conferences papers presented. Also Published 3 Indian patent, 1 patent grant, 4 Books Published, 13 book Chapters. She has guided more than 42 B.Tech projects along with 4 M.Tech thesis projects. She has also attended various FDPs, workshops and seminars in various fields.

Mritunjay Rai is an accomplished researcher and Assistant Professor in the Department of Electrical and Electronics Engineering at Shri Ramswaroop Memorial University, Barabanki, India. With a specialization in digital image processing, machine learning, and thermal imaging, Dr. Rai's research addresses complex computational challenges in biomedical imaging, surveillance systems, and emotion recognition technologies. His doctoral research, completed in 2023 at the Indian Institute of Technology (ISM), Dhanbad, focused on algorithmic advancements for real-time thermal imaging applications. He holds a Master's degree in Instrumentation and Control from BIT Mesra, where his work centered on intelligent video surveillance systems. Dr. Rai has an extensive publication record in journals such as The Journal of Supercomputing and Multimedia Tools and Applications, where his studies contribute novel approaches to thermal imaging-based motion detection, deep learning frameworks for medical diagnostics, and automated systems for human emotion recognition via facial feature analysis. His research is underscored by a commitment to improving algorithmic accuracy and processing efficiency in real-time applications. Dr. Rai is also engaged in editing high-impact books with IGI Global, Wiley, and Elsevier, covering critical topics like AI-integrated surveillance and the use of computational intelligence in healthcare and disaster prediction. Among his significant projects is a government-funded initiative to develop a thermal imaging system for early detection of diabetic foot ulcers, leveraging advanced data processing and sensor fusion techniques. Dr. Rai's ongoing editorial work further spans areas like AI-driven agricultural quality assessment and predictive healthcare, alongside his primary focus on computational methodologies in next-generation surveillance systems. His research continues to bridge the gap between computational intelligence and practical applications in industrial, healthcare, and environmental contexts, marking him as a key innovator in the fields of machine learning and biomedical imaging.

R.K. Yadav, is a Professor and Head of Electronics and Communication Engineering at RGIT, Ghaziabad. He has more than 22 years of experience in teaching and research in the field of microwaves, EM waves and Image processing. He has 60 papers to his credit in international/national journals, conferences, and symposiums, and he has published a book on microwave engineering. Currently, his active research is in the field of microwave engineering, image processing, and integrated circuits. He is a member of IEEE.

Sandeep Bhatia, dedicated Associate Professor with more than 16 years of rich experience inteaching, research, and development activities. He is teaching undergraduate and post-graduate courses in the branch of CSE and ECE. He has one-year industry experience as ahardware engineer at C-DAC Mohali, Punjab. Presently, He is working as an AssistantProfessor in the Department of CSE, Galgotias University, Greater Noida. He also worked asScientific officer (TIFAC-CORE) and Assistant Professor at AKGEC Ghaziabad. He isPursuing Ph.D. from Jamia Millia Islamia, Central University, New Delhi in the field of IoTand Embedded System Design. He has completed his M.E from PEC University ofTechnology, Chandigarh in the field of Embedded System in the year 2010. He has completedhis B.Tech from PTU Jalandhar in the year 2008. He has more than 28 published papers in Scopus Indexed Journals/ Conferences and 4 other reputed journals along with more than 25 International/ National conferences papers presented. Also Published 7 patents, 1 Indiandesign patent grant, 2 Books Published, 5 book Chapters, attended various FDPs andcompleted various online courses including NPTEL. He has guided more than 42 B.Techprojects along with 6 M.Tech/ MCA thesis projects.

***

Najiya Abdulsalam T, A master student in Artificial Intelligence, Centre for Machine Learning and Intelligence at Avinashilingam Institute for Home Science and Higher Education for Women, Tamil Nadu, India. The Research area of interest includes Cyber Forensic, Forensic Intelligence and Image and video Processing.

Leena Arya is a Professor at the Department of Computer Science and Engineering at Koneru Lakshmaiah Education Foundation Deemed to be University, Vaddeswaram, a 22nd NIRF Ranking University in Guntur, AP, India. She completed her Ph.D. from IIT Roorkee in 2012. She has published over 70 research papers in Scopus and SCI-indexed international journals. She led a research project for the Department of Science and Technology (DST), New Delhi, as Principal Investigator under the Women Scientists Scheme (WOS-A). She has been granted a UK design and Australian Government Innovation patents. She has been a reviewer of many prestigious international journals and conferences. Her research area includes wireless communication, the Internet of Things (IoT), network security, and artificial intelligence.

Susnata Biswas is currently pursuing her Ph.D. in Computer Science at SVU Gajrola University. She holds an M.S. in Computer Science from Manipal University, Karnataka (2014) and a B.Tech. in Information Technology from North Eastern Hill University, Shillong (2010). She has over six years of professional experience in software development, specializing in C, C++, socket programming, and multithreading, with expertise in telecom and network management applications. She has contributed to multiple industry projects involving TCP/IP, Diameter, and real-time communication systems. Her research interests include computer networks, network security, and advanced communication technologies.

Kiranbhai Ramabhai Dodiya is an experienced Cyber Forensic Expert and Assistant Professor specializing in cyber security and digital forensics. He has taught at prestigious institutions and is currently pursuing a PhD in Biochemistry and Forensic Science. With a strong background in ethical hacking and malware analysis, Kiranbhai is passionate about educating students and contributing to the field of cyber forensics. His expertise includes malware forensic, computer forensics, and data recovery software. Kiranbhai's commitment to professional growth is evident through his participation in workshops, seminars, and research publications. He is dedicated to shaping the next generation of professionals in the field and combatting cybercrimes.

Rakshita Gautam is a forensic research scholar with a strong academic foundation and expertise across multiple sub-disciplines of forensic science. Her core areas of interest include postmortem interval (PMI) estimation, forensic toxicology, and, forensic chemistry with a dedicated focus on refining methodologies that enhance precision, consistency, and evidentiary reliability in forensic practice..

S. Ida Evangeline, presently working as an Assistant Professor in the Department of Electrical and Electronics Engineering at the Government College of Engineering, Tirunelveli, Tamilnadu, India. She obtained her Bachelor's in Electrical and Electronics Engineering from Manonmaniam Sundaranar University in 2003, and Master's in Power Systems Engineering from Anna University, Chennai, Tamilnadu, India in 2005. She completed her PhD degree in 2023 at Anna University, Chennai, Tamilnadu, India. She has published six research papers in international journals. Her current research interests include optimal power flow, renewable energy, soft computing, machine learning, and deep learning.

K. V. Rajani is an Associate Professor in CSE Department with 25+ years of work experience in teaching. Currently working at Keshav Memorial Institute of Technology, Narayanaguda, Hyderabad, Did M.C.A. from Andhra University, M.Tech from Acharya Nagarjuna University and Ph.D in Computer Science from

JJTU. Her current research interests are in Data Science, Cybersecurity and Artificial Intelligence Applications in Medical field. She has published more than 23 papers in these areas. She has guided more than 100 projects in UG.

Ashtaj Kaware is a dedicated final year B.Sc. Forensic Science student and an emerging research talent in the field. Focused on applying scientific techniques to criminal investigations, he combines theoretical knowledge with hands-on laboratory experience across key forensic disciplines such as biology, chemistry, and law. Throughout his academic journey, Mr. Ashtaj has demonstrated a passion for uncovering the truth through scientific rigor, and he is especially interested in pushing the boundaries of forensic research. As he approaches graduation, he continues to develop advanced analytical and investigative skills, preparing for a career aimed at supporting justice and advancing the forensic sciences.

Lakhyadeep Konwar has completed M. Sc. in Electronics and Communication Technology and M. Tech. in Electronics and communication Engineering with specialization in Signal processing and Communication from Gauhati University, Assam, India. Currently he is pursuing PhD in the field of Computer Vision at the same university. His research interest includes human detection and tracking, human action recognition, suspicious human activity classification, hand gesture recognition, automatic visual surveillance system design etc.

Anand Kumar is a forensic research scholar with a strong academic and research interest in diverse sub-disciplines of forensic science. His primary areas of focus include questioned document examination, forensic toxicology, and the integration of artificial intelligence in forensic investigations.

Kapil Kumar is the Coordinator of the Department of Biochemistry and Forensic Science, Gujarat University, Ahmedabad, Gujarat, India. He is a well-known expert in forensic science, with significant experience in academic leadership, teaching, and research. Dr. Kumar is actively involved in coordinating departmental academic and research activities and in advancing forensic science education and practice through scholarly contributions and professional engagement.

Sachil Kumar is an accomplished forensic scientist and academician with over a decade of experience in forensic chemistry, toxicology, and postmortem interval (PMI) estimation. He holds a Ph.D. in Forensic Chemistry and Forensic Medicine from King George's Medical University, where his pioneering research focused on the degradation of cardiac Troponin-T (cTnT) for PMI estimation. He has held academic positions at prestigious institutions in India and abroad, including Naif Arab University for Security Sciences, CHRIST University, and Amity University.

Dr. Kumar has a strong publication record in high-impact international journals and has been actively involved in editorial and peer-review work for several reputed scientific publications. He is skilled in analytical techniques such as GC-MS and SDS-PAGE and has supervised numerous postgraduate research projects. A recipient of multiple fellowships and international research travel support, Dr. Kumar is also a member of various professional forensic and toxicological societies, reflecting his deep commitment to advancing forensic science education and research.

Ritu Raj Lamsal is an accomplished academic and professional with a distinguished educational and research background. He earned his Bachelor of Engineering in Electronics and Communication Engineering from the Institution of Engineers, India, in 1999. In 2006, he completed his Master of Technology in VLSI Design at Bharat University, Chennai, where he graduated as the top rank holder. Dr. Lamsal pursued his doctoral studies at the University of Malaga, Spain, culminating in a PhD with a outstanding thesis centered on IoT-based agricultural innovations. With over two decades of university-level teaching experience, Dr. Lamsal has developed expertise in designing and implementing IoT-based hardware-software co-design solutions. He is a Fellow Member of the Institution of Engineers, India. Dr. Lamsal has an publication in SCIE and Scopus-indexed journals, focusing on IoT applications in agriculture and semiconductor technology. His research interests span the Internet of Things, Precision Agriculture, Machine Learning, VLSI Design, and Embedded Systems. He also serves as a peer reviewer for journals like IEEE Acess, Springer Nature.

D. Menaka is an Assistant Professor in the Department of Electronics and Communication Engineering at Sri Venkateswara College of Engineering (SVCE). Her research spans medical image processing, machine learning for biomedical applications, and secure information-hiding techniques such as steganography and watermarking.In addition to research and teaching, Dr. Menaka contributes to academic program development and event organization at SVCE, including conferences and student-engagement initiatives that promote industry–academia interaction and hands-on learning. Her work emphasizes practical solutions at the intersection of signal/image processing, secure data storage/transmission, and machine-learning methods for healthcare applications.

Ananya Pandey is a Research Scholar in School of Law at Christ University, Bangalore. She has her research interests in the field of Constitutional Law, Environment Law, Human Rights, Food Security, Intellectual Property Law and Jurisprudence.

Mohit Pandey, currently serving as Associate Professor and Additional Head of Department at PSIT Kanpur.I earned my Ph.D. from SMVDU Katra and completed my M.Tech from GJU Hisar. With over 10 years of teaching and research experience, I am deeply committed to academic excellence.My primary research area is medical image processing, where I explore advanced AI-driven healthcare solutions.

Karthikeyan Periyasami obtained his Bachelor of Engineering (B.E.) in Computer Science and Engineering from Anna University, Chennai, and Tamil Nadu, India in 2005 and received his Master of Engineering (M.E) in Computer Science and Engineering from Anna University Coimbatore, India in 2009. He completed his Ph.D. degree at Anna University, Chennai in 2018. He is working as an Associate Professor in the School of Computer Science and Engineering at RV University in India. He has worked as a post-doctorate research fellow at the Department of Computer Science and Information Engineering, National Chung Cheng University, Taiwan. He has contributed to the national projects on using Technology to promote Human Rights and sustainable development, supported by the National Science and Technology Council, Taiwan. He possesses a high proficiency in project development and research, specializing in the domains of Cloud computing and the practical application of deep learning. He is well-versed in programming languages, including Java, Python, R, and C. His research endeavours have led to the publication of more than 30 papers in esteemed international journals, many of which have garnered commend

Subhash Chandra Rajbongshi has completed M. Tech. and PhD from Gauhati University, Assam, India. Currently he is working as a Scientific Officer at Gauhati University. His research interest includes human detection, human action recognition, suspicious human activity classification, automatic visual surveillance system design etc

Prince Rangra is currently pursuing a Bachelor of Science in Forensic Science and is in his second year of study. With a keen interest in crime scene investigation, evidence analysis, and forensic technologies, he is dedicated to building a strong foundation in the scientific principles that support criminal justice. Prince actively participates in academic workshops, practical training sessions, and departmental events to enhance his skills and understanding of forensic methodologies. He aspires to contribute to the field through innovation, research, and integrity in forensic practice.

Ravi Rastogi received his Ph.D. in Computer Science and Engineering in December 2011 from Uttarakhand Technical University, Dehradun, Uttarakhand, India. MS in Computer Science degree in September 2005 from Fairleigh Dickinson

University, Teaneck, New Jersey, USA. He is working as a Professor in the Department of Computer Science and Engineering, JIMS Engineering Management Technical Campus, Greater Noida, India. He had worked at various Universities, Koneru Lakshmaiah Education Foundation Deemed to be a university, Andhra Pradesh, India and Bisha University, KSA and Galgotias University, Greater Noida, India and Sharda University, Greater Noida, India and Jaypee University of Information and Technology, Solan, India. He was a database developer for Microsoft, Seattle, USA, and ING, Philadelphia, USA. His research interests are interconnection networks, stable matching problems, data mining and intelligence in systems, the Internet of Things, and cloud computing. Refereed International Journal publications are 23 and Refereed International Conference Publications are 8.

Shipra Rohatgi is currently serving as an Assistant Professor-II at the Amity Institute of Forensic Sciences, Amity University, Noida, India. She is dedicated to shaping the minds of students at the Bachelors, Master, and PhD levels, imparting knowledge in various courses related to forensic sciences. She has earned her Ph.D. in the field of Questioned Documents. Her doctoral research showcases her commitment to advancing the field of forensic sciences. Prior to her current role, Dr. Shipra contributed significantly to the academic community as a Full-time Faculty Member at Amity University, Gurugram, Haryana, India, from 2014 to 2018. During this period, she demonstrated her expertise and passion for teaching.Dr. Rohatgi has a prolific research portfolio with numerous highly cited journal publications and conference articles. She has also garnered her recognition, including a Gold medal at the Masters level and the prestigious DST INSPIRE FELLOW (qualified candidate) . She is currently guiding two full-time research scholars under her, among which one is JRF. She has published more tha 25 papers, book chapters in Scopus indexed, web of science and highly reputed journals. Apart from her academic achievements, Dr. Rohatgi possesses hands-on experience in various advanced forensic techniques. She is proficient in the use of tools such as Docubox HD/Dragon, Projectina NIRVIS, Dynascope, and Advanced DNA fingerprinting techniques, showcasing her practical expertise in the field.In addition to her academic and research pursuits, Dr. Rohatgi is committed to continuous learning. She has completed several certification courses, including those from reputable institutions such as Cisco and Basis tech.

Navajit Saikia has completed M. Tech. and PhD from the Department of Electronics and Electrical Engineering, IIT Guwahati, Assam, India. Currently he is working as a Professor at the Department of Electronics and Telecommunication Engineering, Assam Engineering College, Guwahati, Assam, India. His research interest includes object detection, animal detection, human action recognition, pedestrian detection, suspicious human activity classification, hand gesture recognition, automatic visual surveillance system design etc.

Birendra Kr. Saraswat working as Associate Professor in the Department of Information Technology at GL Bajaj Institute of Technology & Management, Greater Noida. Dr. Saraswat has received M.Tech (CSE) Degree from Uttar Pradesh Technical University, Lucknow and Ph.D. (Computer Science & Engineering) from GLA University, Mathura. Worked as a Head of Department of Bachelors of Computer Application at HIET, Ghaziabad.

Mandalapu Sivaparvathi is working as an Assistant Professor in MAM Women's Engineering College, Kesanupalli Village, Narasaraopet, District Palnadu, Guntur, Andhra Pradesh, India

K S Subhashini is an academician and researcher with a strong background in Electronics and Communication Engineering, holding a B.E. in ECE and an M.E. in Communication Systems. With extensive teaching experience, she guides undergraduate and postgraduate students in areas such as IoT, wireless communication, embedded systems, and data science applications. Her research interests include Industrial IoT, healthcare monitoring systems, intelligent transportation, predictive and prescriptive analytics, and inclusive assistive technologies. Passionate about innovation, she actively mentors students in hackathons and project-based learning, focusing on converting student projects into research outcomes, Scopus-indexed publications, and patents.

Jennyfer Susan M B is an Assistant Professor in Centre for Machine Learning and Intelligence at Avinashilingam Institute for Home Science and Higher Education for Women, Tamil Nadu, and India. The author has published 4 journals, 1 national conference and 4 international conferences, 2 book chapter and 2 books publication. The research area of interest includes Vision AI, Medical Image Processing and Neural Networks

Index

Symbols

A

C

D

E

F

G

H

I

L

M

O

P

S

T

V

W

www.ingramcontent.com/pod-product-compliance
Lightning Source LLC
LaVergne TN
LVHW062328300926
849161LV00007B/1621
9798337337951